Utilizing AI and Smart Technology to Improve Sustainability in Entrepreneurship

Syed Far Abid Hossain
BRAC University, Bangladesh

A volume in the Advances in Business Information Systems and Analytics (ABISA) Book Series

IGI Global
PUBLISHER of TIMELY KNOWLEDGE

Published in the United States of America by
IGI Global
Business Science Reference (an imprint of IGI Global)
701 E. Chocolate Avenue
Hershey PA, USA 17033
Tel: 717-533-8845
Fax: 717-533-8661
E-mail: cust@igi-global.com
Web site: http://www.igi-global.com

Library of Congress Cataloging-in-Publication Data

Names: Hossain, Syed, 1982- editor.
Title: Utilizing AI and smart technology to improve sustainability in entrepreneurship / edited by: Syed Hossain.
Description: Hershey PA : Business Science Reference, [2024] | Includes bibliographical references. | Summary: "The key objective of the book is to discover the role of AI and smart technology in sustainable entrepreneurship development"-- Provided by publisher.
Identifiers: LCCN 2023056036 (print) | LCCN 2023056037 (ebook) | ISBN 9798369318423 (hardcover) | ISBN 9798369318430 (ebook)
Subjects: LCSH: Entrepreneurship--Technological innovations. | Business--Data processing. | Artificial intelligence--Industrial applications. | Sustainable development.
Classification: LCC HB615 .U834 2024 (print) | LCC HB615 (ebook) | DDC 658.4/21028563--dc23/eng/20240131
LC record available at https://lccn.loc.gov/2023056036
LC ebook record available at https://lccn.loc.gov/2023056037

This book is published in the IGI Global book series Advances in Business Information Systems and Analytics (ABISA) (ISSN: 2327-3275; eISSN: 2327-3283)

British Cataloguing in Publication Data
A Cataloguing in Publication record for this book is available from the British Library.

For electronic access to this publication, please contact: eresources@igi-global.com.

Advances in Business Information Systems and Analytics (ABISA) Book Series

Madjid Tavana
La Salle University, USA

ISSN:2327-3275
EISSN:2327-3283

Mission

The successful development and management of information systems and business analytics is crucial to the success of an organization. New technological developments and methods for data analysis have allowed organizations to not only improve their processes and allow for greater productivity, but have also provided businesses with a venue through which to cut costs, plan for the future, and maintain competitive advantage in the information age.

The **Advances in Business Information Systems and Analytics (ABISA) Book Series** aims to present diverse and timely research in the development, deployment, and management of business information systems and business analytics for continued organizational development and improved business value.

Coverage

- Business Decision Making
- Strategic Information Systems
- Information Logistics
- Decision Support Systems
- Business Information Security
- Business Intelligence
- Big Data
- Data Analytics
- Data Management
- Forecasting

IGI Global is currently accepting manuscripts for publication within this series. To submit a proposal for a volume in this series, please contact our Acquisition Editors at Acquisitions@igi-global.com or visit: http://www.igi-global.com/publish/.

The Advances in Business Information Systems and Analytics (ABISA) Book Series (ISSN 2327-3275) is published by IGI Global, 701 E. Chocolate Avenue, Hershey, PA 17033-1240, USA, www.igi-global.com. This series is composed of titles available for purchase individually; each title is edited to be contextually exclusive from any other title within the series. For pricing and ordering information please visit http://www.igi-global.com/book-series/advances-business-information-systems-analytics/37155. Postmaster: Send all address changes to above address.

Titles in this Series

For a list of additional titles in this series, please visit:
www.igi-global.com/book-series/advances-business-information-systems-analytics/37155

Strengthening Industrial Cybersecurity to Protect Business Intelligence
Saqib Saeed (Department of Computer Information Systems, College of Computer Science and Information Technology, Imam Abdulrahman Bin Faisal University, Saudi Arabia) Neda Azizi (Torrens University, Australia) Shahzaib Tahir (Department of Information Security, College of Signals, Pakistan & National University of Sciences and Technology, Islamabad, Pakistan) Munir Ahmad (School of Computer Science, National College of Business Administration and Economics, Lahore, Pakistan) and Abdullah M. Almuhaideb (Department of Networks and Communications, College of Computer Science and Information Technology, Imam Abdulrahman Bin Faisal University, Saudi Arabia)
Business Science Reference • © 2024 • 373pp • H/C (ISBN: 9798369308394) • US $275.00

AI and Data Analytics Applications in Organizational Management
Tereza Raquel Merlo (University of North Texas, USA & Merlo Management Consulting, USA)
Business Science Reference • © 2024 • 317pp • H/C (ISBN: 9798369310588) • US $300.00

Evolution of Cross-Sector Cyber Intelligent Markets
Eugene J. Lewis (Capitol Technology University, USA)
Business Science Reference • © 2024 • 469pp • H/C (ISBN: 9798369319703) • US $275.00

Leveraging ChatGPT and Artificial Intelligence for Effective Customer Engagement
Rohit Bansal (Department of Management Studies, Vaish College of Engineering, Rohtak, India) Abdul Hafaz Ngah (Faculty of Business Economics and Social DevelopmentUniversiti Malaysia Terenganu, Malaysia) Aziza Chakir (FSJES AC, Hassan II University, Casablanca, Morocco) and Nishita Pruthi (Maharshi Dayanand University, India)
Business Science Reference • © 2024 • 349pp • H/C (ISBN: 9798369308158) • US $265.00

Data Envelopment Analysis (DEA) Methods for Maximizing Efficiency
Adeyemi Abel Ajibesin (American University of Nigeria, Nigeria) and Narasimha Rao Vajjhala (University of New York Tirana, Albania)
Business Science Reference • © 2024 • 389pp • H/C (ISBN: 9798369302552) • US $250.00

IGI Global
PUBLISHER of TIMELY KNOWLEDGE

701 East Chocolate Avenue, Hershey, PA 17033, USA
Tel: 717-533-8845 x100 • Fax: 717-533-8661
E-Mail: cust@igi-global.com • www.igi-global.com

Editorial Advisory Board

Table of Contents

Detailed Table of Contents

This research examines the factors that shape consumers' attitudes towards chatbots, considering the unique cultural and contextual characteristics of the Malaysian market. The study employs a quantitative approach and utilises survey data gathered from a representative sample of Malaysian consumers. This study examines the independent variables (IV) of technology awareness, perceived usefulness, perceived simplicity of use, trust in chatbots, and prior experience with chatbots. The dependent variable (DV) is the likelihood of utilising chatbots. The research aims to offer valuable insights into the factors that drive Malaysian customers to embrace chatbots. The findings from this study can be utilised by businesses and organisations in Malaysia to enhance their customer service through the development of more effective chatbot strategies. This study holds significance not only for the academic community but also for businesses in Malaysia seeking to leverage chatbot technology for practical purposes.

AI has transformed leadership evaluation. According to "Leadership Competencies for the Age of Artificial Intelligence," leaders need particular attributes to handle AI's positives and downsides. After examining various studies, this study emphasizes the importance of adaptability, emotional intelligence, and creativity. The study focuses on leadership, practical applications, and regional skill gaps. Leaders must anticipate AI's effects, innovate, transition, and foster entrepreneurship. AI application requires organizational improvements. This demands digital skills and current HR. This chapter offers CEOs practical guidance for entering the growing AI environment. It focuses on merging technical and interpersonal skills for new leadership approaches. These broad and comprehensive results can assist leaders in solving contemporary problems. AI and interpersonal skills are vital for current leadership.

The digital era has brought significant changes to the business landscape, but it has also exacerbated inequality and posed challenges to achieving the Sustainable Development Goals (SDGs). This research employed exploratory sequential mixed methods to investigate how digitalization impacts rural entrepreneurship. Results highlight the diverse opportunities that digital transformation and technological advancements have created in rural entrepreneurship. These opportunities include the growth of family-run businesses, improved employment prospects, and enhanced regional economic development. By harnessing local humanist knowledge, a business model that promotes social solidarity and economic transformation has the potential to mitigate uncertainty and inequality. Consequently, this study provides empirical evidence and recommendations for institutional and social reforms, contributing to our understanding of the latest innovation theories associated with Kontratieff Schumpeter's wave in institutional and social entrepreneurship.

Redefining conventional business paradigms, the incorporation of artificial intelligence (AI) in small and medium-sized organizations (SMEs) has become a disruptive catalyst. This research explores the factors that motivate, hinder, and have repercussions for the adoption of AI in small and medium-sized enterprises (SMEs). This research aims to identify the critical elements influencing successful AI integration, the impact of AI on SME operations, and the potential for improving competitiveness and sustainability through a thorough analysis of industry case studies and a thorough review of the existing literature. This study provides important insights into the complex link between AI adoption and SME development by clarifying the way that technology is changing in the SME sector in terms of encouraging innovation and causing organizational transformation.

Artificial intelligence is essential for improving corporate operations and productivity optimization. Due to the Fourth Industrial Revolution's effects on digital competitiveness, businesses are becoming more interested in upgrading to a higher technical order. This is closely related to artificial intelligence-based "smart" automation, which removes human labor from various corporate processes. (Akter et al., 2020). This study aims to look into the role and advantages of artificial intelligence (AI) tools in small and medium-sized businesses, as well as how company management will change in the future as a result of their ability to gain a competitive edge via the use or advancement of technical features. This paradigm provides resources as standard utilities that users may rent and release over the Internet as needed. (Avram, 2014). To get a comprehensive grasp of the difficulties, advantages, and moral implications of AI-driven corporate initiatives, a qualitative methodology comprising focus groups and interviews will be employed.

The convergence of entrepreneurship and Artificial Intelligence is bringing a revolution in the business world. Recent technological advancements in the field of artificial intelligence are significantly impacting entrepreneurship and economic growth during the Fourth Industrial Revolution. This chapter investigates the combination of artificial intelligence and entrepreneurship offering the reader a perspective on the business landscape. The chapter aims to provide a framework to deploy actionable steps to stay ahead of competition and discuss about the application of AI in various industries like healthcare, finance and marketing. The chapter summaries many key strategies encouraging readers to embrace AI as a key element to their entrepreneurship strategy. AI will boost entrepreneurship by generating new knowledge, which will support economic growth. The aim is to serve as comprehensive guide for business leaders and innovators to explore full potential of AI in scaling up their future ventures.

Modern technologies are considered indispensable tools in companies' development. At this stage, with the emergence of artificial intelligence usage, several transformations have been experienced with the new strategic context which influences the business and the marketing of companies' activities. To do this, they take into consideration the need for the integration and the involvement with this technology to minimize the risks in their development. The importance of this work is to emphasize a literature review which specifies the role of AI in improving the business and marketing strategic to arrive at a relevant adoption solution.

Traditional conceptions of leadership have undergone a dramatic change with the introduction of robots into leadership positions (LP). AI and robots will continue to improve, and this will likely have an impact on leadership in enterprises in the future. The abstract explores the leadership capabilities of robots (LCR), highlighting their advantages in working automation. The model finishes by arguing that includes three queries about the uses of Al significantly affective on leadership in workplaces, leadership positions in the medical industry and needing ethical considerations to deal with patients' data to improve patient care. Moreover, this research has a quality assessment with five questionnaires based on the substantial impact on leadership in work systems, the study of potential futures for leadership, the standard of study's research model, following leadership ethics and matching a similar focus between our study and the papers that were collected from other researchers to watch the impact of future direction leadership activity in AI within the organization.

The integration of artificial intelligence (AI) into entrepreneurship has created a transformative landscape with immense opportunities and challenges for sustainability. This chapter explores the intersection of AI-driven entrepreneurship, social responsibility, and environmental sustainability. The first section delves into the social responsibility aspect, especially the ethical dilemmas that entrepreneurs face when developing and deploying AI systems. Shifting to environmental responsibility, the subsequent section explores how AI can reduce environmental footprints through various innovative efforts. The interplay between social and environmental responsibility is crucial, and the chapter advocates for a holistic approach. The chapter highlights the challenges and opportunities for entrepreneurs in balancing social and environmental responsibility in AI integration. In the end, the chapter presents a responsible business model for AI-driven enterprises to seamlessly incorporate advanced technology into their operations while upholding all aspects of sustainability.

SMEs play a vital role in global economies, contributing significantly to job creation and economic growth. The rapid evolution of smart technologies and AI presents both opportunities and challenges for SMEs. This chapter provides a comprehensive overview of the key opportunities, challenges, and enablers related to the adoption of smart technologies and AI in SMEs. It explores the landscape of SMEs in the context of adopting these technologies, covering opportunities and challenges. It concludes by discussing potential future prospects for SMEs in the realm of smart technology and AI integration, setting the stage for future research. This guide offers practical implications for SMEs, business leaders, researchers, and policymakers, facilitating their transformation into technology-driven organizations. The findings highlight the significance of addressing challenges proactively and leveraging enablers to harness the full potential of smart technologies and AI for sustainable growth and competitive advantage.

The fusion of AI and smart tech is revolutionizing entrepreneurship, reshaping strategies, and driving innovation. This abstract explores their collaborative potential for a successful entrepreneurial future. Entrepreneurs use AI for data-driven decisions, predicting market trends with unmatched accuracy. The symbiotic relationship between entrepreneurship and smart technologies is reshaping strategies, fostering innovation, and driving economic growth. Entrepreneurs leverage blockchain, AI, IoT, and social media for global reach, facing challenges such as ethical concerns and the need for strategic integration to thrive in the evolving digital era. Challenges include ethical considerations and data security. Entrepreneurs must navigate these issues for responsible AI use. This abstract envisions a future where AI and smart tech are crucial collaborators. Entrepreneurs adept at utilizing these technologies can reshape markets and disrupt established models. Embracing this revolution is imperative for companies aspiring to thrive in future landscapes.

This study explores ethical dimensions in AI adoption for digital entrepreneurship. Thematic analysis highlights transparency, fairness, and accountability. Findings recommend comprehensive ethical guidelines, inclusive decision-making, and robust accountability mechanisms. Practical implications extend to digital ventures, policymakers, and educators. Future research may delve into industry-specific nuances, cross-cultural analyses, and the longitudinal impact of ethical frameworks, contributing significantly to responsible AI adoption discourse in digital entrepreneurship.

The chapter examines the factors influencing the long-term use of smart wearables among users in Northern India. It integrates the Expectation-Confirmation Theory (ECT) and the Latent Variable Model to understand what drives users to continue using these devices. The study, involving 678 participants, employs Structural Equation Modeling (Smart PLS4) to analyze the effects of satisfaction, willingness to pay a premium, and accuracy of health information on the sustained use of smart wearables. The findings underscore that user satisfaction, precise health information, and the readiness to pay more significantly affect users' intentions to repurchase and keep using these devices. This research is particularly beneficial for smartwatch manufacturers and designers. By highlighting the importance of satisfaction, accurate health information, and price factors, it provides crucial insights for improving the design and marketing of smart wearables. These insights are key to fostering user loyalty and ensuring long-term engagement with these technologies.

Preface

Welcome to this edited reference book, *Utilizing AI and Smart Technology to Improve Sustainability in Entrepreneurship*, curated by Dr. Syed Far Abid Hossain, Asst. Professor, BRAC Business School, BRAC University. In an era defined by dynamic market landscapes and rapid technological evolution, the role of artificial intelligence (AI) and smart technologies in shaping entrepreneurial strategies cannot be overstated.

The 21st century has witnessed a profound transformation in business dynamics, compelling entrepreneurs to adapt and embrace advanced technologies to ensure their survival. This book delves into the pivotal role of AI and smart technologies in fostering sustainable entrepreneurship development. It explores how the integration of these technologies can not only streamline production processes but also enhance the overall value proposition for businesses and their customers.

The central aim of this book is to unravel the multifaceted impact of AI and smart technology on sustainable entrepreneurship. It serves as a valuable resource for the research community, offering insights that can guide entrepreneurs in executing effective strategies. Furthermore, it extends its impact beyond academia, influencing society by advocating for higher quality standards through the adoption of smart technologies and AI.

The target audience for this comprehensive volume primarily includes entrepreneurs across diverse industries. Within its pages, they will discover an expansive overview of smart technologies and AI utilization, along with theoretical and methodological frameworks for integrating these technologies into their entrepreneurial ventures. Additionally, the book caters to a broader audience, including policy makers, CEOs, investors, business analysts, and practicing experts.

The thematic chapters in this book address critical aspects of AI integration in entrepreneurship, ranging from blended entrepreneurship strategies and forming entrepreneurial systems to exploring the role of AI in digital entrepreneurship. The content spans various dimensions, from the challenges posed by AI in small businesses to its potential as a catalyst for business development.

As you embark on this insightful journey through the pages of *Utilizing AI and Smart Technology to Improve Sustainability in Entrepreneurship*, I trust that you will gain valuable perspectives on leveraging AI and smart technologies to navigate the complexities of modern entrepreneurial landscapes.

ORGANIZATION OF THE BOOK

Chapter 1: Modeling Factors Influencing Consumer Behavior: Intention to Use Chatbot Among Malaysian Public (Wang Xiya, Wong Chee Hoo, Mohd Abbas)

This chapter explores the intricate factors shaping Malaysian consumers' attitudes towards chatbots, considering unique cultural and contextual characteristics. Utilizing a quantitative approach and survey data, the study analyzes technology awareness, perceived usefulness, simplicity of use, trust in chatbots, and prior experience as variables influencing the likelihood of chatbot utilization. The findings offer valuable insights for businesses in Malaysia, aiding them in refining chatbot strategies for enhanced customer service. This research holds significance for both the academic community and businesses, providing a practical understanding of chatbot adoption within the Malaysian market.

Chapter 2: Leadership Competencies for the Age of Artificial Intelligence (Mayesha Tasnim)

Examining the transformative impact of AI on leadership, this chapter underscores the essential attributes leaders need to navigate AI's positives and negatives. Emphasizing adaptability, emotional intelligence, and creativity, the study offers practical applications and addresses regional skill gaps. It guides leaders in anticipating AI's effects, fostering innovation, and embracing new leadership approaches. With a focus on organizational improvements, the chapter provides CEOs practical guidance for thriving in the evolving AI environment, emphasizing the merging of technical and interpersonal skills for effective leadership in the age of artificial intelligence.

Chapter 3: Philosophical and Psychological Dimensions of AI Integration in Sustainable Business Development (Kaniz Kakon)

This chapter critically examines the convergence of Sustainable Business Development and AI, exploring their synergy, opportunities, and ethical challenges. Highlighting the parallel growth of Sustainable Business and AI's impact on consumer behavior, it emphasizes the need to adeptly manage AI's functions and ethics in corporate solutions. The chapter delves into diverse ethical frameworks, advocating for responsible AI integration to ensure sustainability and societal welfare. Drawing on Confucian ethics, organizational psychology, and leadership principles, it advocates for merging philosophy, psychology, and sustainable business practices to foster ethically sound and psychologically attuned AI systems for corporate use.

Chapter 4: From Clicks to Loyalty; Understanding the Dynamics of Consumer Brand Relationships in the Online Clothing Industry (Sarika Faisal)

This chapter offers an overview of the journey of a female entrepreneur in the clothing industry in Bangladesh. Using a Social Consumer Fashion Brand Engagement model, it delineates the dynamics of consumer brand relationships. Through qualitative data collection, the study concludes that effective marketing strategies, quality products, and alignment with contemporary trends are crucial for long-term success in the online clothing industry.

Chapter 5: Exploring Solopreneurs' Journey in the Digital Era (Pulkit Jain)

This study explores solopreneurship, focusing on managing digital enterprises aligned with personal interests. Analyzing the transformative impact of social media, task outsourcing, and collaborative ventures using Software as a Service (SaaS), the chapter highlights the substantial role of personal branding in audience growth. It delves into solopreneurs' motivations, challenges, and the role of social media in reshaping global business practices, emphasizing well-being aspects, identity management, and protective strategies in the digital era.

Chapter 6: Digital Transformation: Catalyzing Rural Entrepreneurship in the 21st Century (Sanjay Taneja, Kavita Dahiya)

Examining the impact of digitalization on rural entrepreneurship, this chapter utilizes exploratory sequential mixed methods to highlight the diverse opportunities created by digital transformation and technological advancements. It emphasizes the potential for social solidarity and economic transformation in rural areas, providing empirical evidence and recommendations for institutional and social reforms.

Chapter 7: Catalysts of Change: SMEs and Dynamics of AI Adoption (Rishi Shukla, Sanjay Taneja)

This chapter explores the disruptive impact of AI adoption in small and medium-sized enterprises (SMEs), identifying critical elements influencing successful integration. Through industry case studies and literature review analysis, the research aims to provide insights into the complex link between AI adoption and SME development, highlighting the role of technology in encouraging innovation and causing organizational transformation.

Chapter 8: The Role of Artificial Intelligence in Business Management: The Future of Small and Medium-sized Enterprise (Armana Hakim Nadi, Kazi Ayman Ahshan, Sadia Rahman, Mahbuba Sofin)

This chapter delves into the essential role of artificial intelligence (AI) tools in small and medium-sized businesses, focusing on their potential to bring about significant changes in corporate operations and productivity optimization. The study employs a qualitative methodology, including focus groups and interviews, to provide a comprehensive understanding of the challenges, advantages, and ethical implications of AI-driven corporate initiatives.

Chapter 9: The Future of Entrepreneurship Employing Artificial Intelligence (Venkat T, Goboori Harsh Vardhan, Kotamarti Sushanth)

This chapter investigates the convergence of entrepreneurship and artificial intelligence, offering a perspective on the evolving business landscape. It aims to provide a framework for deploying actionable steps to stay ahead of competition and discusses the application of AI in various industries like healthcare, finance, and marketing. The chapter serves as a comprehensive guide for business leaders and innovators to explore the full potential of AI in scaling up their future ventures.

Chapter 10: The Contribution of Artificial Intelligence to the Business and Marketing Strategy (Sahar Mesfar)

This chapter presents a literature review emphasizing the role of AI in improving business and marketing strategic activities. Modern technologies, particularly artificial intelligence, have transformed companies' development strategies. The chapter explores the integration and involvement with AI to minimize risks in business development, offering relevant adoption solutions for enhancing business strategy, marketing, and overall competitiveness.

Chapter 12: Social and Environmental Responsibility in AI-Driven Entrepreneurship (Md Abdus Salam, Rubaba Nawrin, Hasanuzzaman Tushar, Nanta Sooraksha)

This chapter explores the transformative landscape created by the integration of artificial intelligence (AI) into entrepreneurship, focusing on social and environmental responsibility. It addresses ethical dilemmas in AI systems' development and deployment, along with how AI can contribute to reducing environmental footprints. The chapter advocates for a holistic approach, providing a responsible business model for AI-driven enterprises to seamlessly incorporate advanced technology while upholding sustainability.

Chapter 13: Opportunities, Enablers, and Challenges of Smart Technologies and AI Adoption in SMEs (Hasanuzzaman Tushar, Nanta Sooraksa, Shaikh Sabbir Waliullah, Nayma Iftakhar)

This chapter offers a comprehensive overview of key opportunities, challenges, and enablers related to the adoption of smart technologies and AI in small and medium-sized enterprises (SMEs). It explores the landscape of SMEs in adopting these technologies, covering opportunities and challenges. The chapter discusses potential future prospects for SMEs in the realm of smart technology and AI integration, providing practical implications for their transformation into technology-driven organizations.

Chapter 14: Exploring AI and Smart Technologies in Entrepreneurship: The Future of Business Strategies (Armana Nadi, Krishna Paul, Kazi Ayman Ahshan, Sadia Rahman, Dipta Paul)

This abstract envisions the collaborative potential of AI and smart technologies for a successful entrepreneurial future. Entrepreneurs' use of AI for data-driven decisions and market trend predictions is emphasized, along with the challenges posed by ethical considerations and the need for strategic integration. The abstract positions AI and smart tech as crucial collaborators reshaping markets and disrupting established models for companies aspiring to thrive in future landscapes.

Chapter 15: Ethical Imperatives and Frameworks for Responsible AI Adoption in Digital Entrepreneurship: Unveiling the Ethical Landscape: Navigating Transparency, Fairness, and Accountability (Nipunika Shahid, Madan Singh, Sujata Chauhan)

This chapter explores ethical dimensions in AI adoption for digital entrepreneurship, highlighting transparency, fairness, and accountability. Thematic analysis recommends comprehensive ethical guidelines and inclusive decision-making, extending practical implications to digital ventures, policymakers, and educators. Future research avenues include industry-specific nuances, cross-cultural analyses, and longitudinal impact assessments, contributing significantly to responsible AI adoption discourse.

Chapter 16: Impact of Post-Use Satisfaction on Re-Purchase Intentions for AI-Driven Healthcare Smart Wearable (Munish Gupta, Pooja Chopra, Nitin Pathak)

This chapter examines the factors influencing the long-term use of AI-driven smart wearables in Northern India. Integrating the Expectation-Confirmation Theory and the Latent Variable Model, the study analyzes satisfaction, willingness to pay a premium, and accuracy of health information in driving users' intentions to repurchase and continue using these devices. The findings offer insights for smartwatch manufacturers and designers, emphasizing the importance of user satisfaction, precise health information, and pricing factors for fostering user loyalty.

Chapter 17: Enhanced Smart Irrigation Using Sensors: A Statistical Case Study (Ambika N)

This chapter presents a framework for enhanced smart irrigation using sensors, incorporating soil moisture sensors, passive infrared sensors (PIR), and water pumps controlled by an Arduino board. The statistical case study aims to maintain optimal water content in the ground, considering parameters like soil moisture and weather forecasts. The proposed design suggests a system to overcome water wastage and improve crop yield in smart irrigation practices.

Chapter 18: The Assessment of Artificial Intelligence for Business Performance in Bangladesh (Fm. Asikullah, Phonebuson Chakma, Md Nafis Hossain, Md Imam Mahdi)

This chapter explores the effects of artificial intelligence (AI) on the performance of small and medium business organizations in Bangladesh. Utilizing advanced statistical analysis, the study highlights the significant effects of AI on SME performance, emphasizing the role of Effective Business Management (EBM) as a partial mediator. The study provides theoretical and managerial implications for business owners, managers, stakeholders, and policymakers, aiding in the improvement of business performance through AI adoption.

IN CONCLUSION

In concluding this comprehensive edited reference book, *Utilizing AI and Smart Technology to Improve Sustainability in Entrepreneurship*, we reflect on the rich tapestry of insights woven by esteemed contributors from diverse fields. The collective expertise encapsulated in these chapters offers a panoramic view of the intricate relationship between artificial intelligence (AI), smart technologies, and the evolving landscape of entrepreneurship.

From examining the factors influencing consumer behavior in the context of chatbot adoption in Malaysia to unraveling the ethical imperatives of AI-driven entrepreneurship, each chapter contributes a unique perspective to the broader narrative. The exploration of leadership competencies, the transformative impact of solopreneurship in the digital era, and the catalyzing effect of AI on rural entrepreneurship paint a nuanced picture of the dynamic intersections between technology and entrepreneurship.

The chapters also delve into the critical role of AI in business management, the future of small and medium-sized enterprises, and the ethical considerations that accompany the integration of AI into corporate strategies. The book navigates through smart technologies in SMEs, the assessment of AI for business performance, and the potential impact of AI on the future of entrepreneurship across various industries.

The editor acknowledges the valuable contributions made by each author in addressing the complex challenges and opportunities presented by the integration of AI and smart technologies in entrepreneurship. From ethical considerations and consumer relationships to the transformative potential of technology in rural settings, the insights provided aim to guide both academics and practitioners in navigating this ever-evolving landscape.

As we move toward an AI-driven future, the chapters collectively paint a vivid canvas that calls for a holistic approach, emphasizing not only technological advancement but also social and environmental responsibility. The book underscores the need for thoughtful consideration of ethical frameworks, transparency, and fairness in the adoption of AI, ensuring that technological progress aligns with sustainable and responsible business practices.

I hope that this edited reference book serves as a valuable resource for entrepreneurs, researchers, policymakers, and business leaders seeking to harness the full potential of AI and smart technologies for sustainable and innovative entrepreneurship. The chapters presented here stand as beacons guiding us through the multifaceted terrain of technology-driven entrepreneurship, urging us to embrace the challenges and opportunities that lie ahead.

As editor, I extend my gratitude to the esteemed contributors for their scholarly endeavors, and I invite readers to delve into the pages of this book with enthusiasm, curiosity, and a commitment to shaping a future where technology and entrepreneurship coalesce for the betterment of society.

Syed Far Abid Hossain
BRAC University, Bangladesh

Acknowledgment

I extend my deepest gratitude to the Almighty Allah for granting me the strength, wisdom, and perseverance throughout the journey of editing this book. His guidance has been my constant source of inspiration.

I am indebted to BRAC University for providing me with a supportive academic environment. My sincere appreciation goes to the BRAC Business School (BBS) for their support and encouragement.

I would like to express my heartfelt thanks to the Dean (in charge) of BBS, Prof. Dr. Mohammad Mujibul Haque, BRAC University and the faculty members who played a pivotal role in shaping my academic journey.

Special appreciation is reserved for Professor Selina Nargis, Treasurer at IUBAT— International University of Business Agriculture and Technology and Prof. Dr. Sang H Lee, Ex-Dean, BBS, BRAC University, whose insightful feedback, motivation and guidance significantly contributed to the refinement of this work.

I am grateful to my family for their unwavering support. My deepest appreciation goes to my father, Syed Mobasser Ali, and my mother, Fatema Begum, for their love, encouragement, and sacrifices. A special acknowledgment is extended to my beloved wife, Jabun Nesa, whose support and understanding have been the cornerstone of my success.

Last but not least, I express my sincere gratitude to my grandparents, Late Syed Altal Ali & Sabera Begum, for laying the foundation of my academic pursuits.

This edited book stands as a testament to the collaborative efforts and support of these remarkable individuals and institutions.

Syed Far Abid Hossain
BRAC Business School, BRAC University, Bangladesh

Chapter 1
Modeling Factors Influencing Consumer Behavior:
Intention to Use Chatbot Among Malaysian Public

Wang Xiya
Inti International University, Malaysia

Wong Chee Hoo
https://orcid.org/0000-0003-0691-4463
Inti International University, Malaysia

Mohd Saleh Abbas
Inti International University, Malaysia

ABSTRACT

This research examines the factors that shape consumers' attitudes towards chatbots, considering the unique cultural and contextual characteristics of the Malaysian market. The study employs a quantitative approach and utilises survey data gathered from a representative sample of Malaysian consumers. This study examines the independent variables (IV) of technology awareness, perceived usefulness, perceived simplicity of use, trust in chatbots, and prior experience with chatbots. The dependent variable (DV) is the likelihood of utilising chatbots. The research aims to offer valuable insights into the factors that drive Malaysian customers to embrace chatbots. The findings from this study can be utilised by businesses and organisations in Malaysia to enhance their customer service through the development of more effective chatbot strategies. This study holds significance not only for the academic community but also for businesses in Malaysia seeking to leverage chatbot technology for practical purposes.

DOI: 10.4018/979-8-3693-1842-3.ch001

INTRODUCTION

The increasing popularity of chatbots in recent years has significantly transformed the communication methods employed by companies when interacting with their clients. Chatbots, which are powered by AI, have the capability to facilitate automated and personalised conversational interactions. This technology enables businesses to enhance their customer service, streamline transaction processing, and efficiently distribute information. According to Ikumoro and Jawad (2019), the adoption of chatbots is increasing in Malaysia, a country known for its advanced technology and thriving digital economy. In order to effectively utilise chatbot technology, businesses and organisations need to comprehend the factors that impact consumers' inclination to use chatbots within a particular cultural and contextual setting.

The level of consumers' willingness to adopt technology serves as a crucial indicator for determining their actual usage of it. Several studies have been conducted to examine the factors that drive individuals to embrace novel forms of technology, including smartphones, online stores, and social media (Casale et al., 2021). The factors that drive Malaysian consumers' interest in engaging with chatbots remain largely unknown. The adoption of chatbot technology by consumers is influenced by various factors. These factors include the consumers' familiarity with the technology, their perception of its usefulness and convenience, their level of trust in chatbots, and their prior experience with chatbots.

The level of consumers' tech savvy can be seen as an indicator of their understanding and comfort with chatbots. As individuals gain knowledge about chatbots, their inclination to adopt and utilise them increases. Perceived usefulness refers to the ways in which customers perceive chatbots as beneficial and the expectations they have regarding their assistance. According to Mogaji et al. (2021), consumers are more likely to embrace chatbots when they perceive them as valuable tools that enhance the quality of their interactions and transactions. This metric is based on customers' perceptions of the ease with which they can achieve their goals when interacting with chatbots. The likelihood of customers showing interest in using chatbots is higher when they perceive them as easy to use.

The extent to which consumers trust chatbots plays a significant role in their decision to utilise them. The user's text highlights the importance of confidence in chatbots, specifically in terms of their dependability, safety, and ability to protect users' privacy. According to Beattie et al. (2020), the likelihood of customers engaging with chatbots is higher when they hold a favourable perception of them. Additionally, it is important to note that consumers' attitudes and intentions towards the use of chatbots are greatly impacted by their previous encounters with these automated systems. Poor interactions with chatbots can lead to a lack of trust or hesitation in using them again in the future.

The purpose of this study is to fill a gap in knowledge by examining the factors that influence Malaysian consumers' decision to interact with chatbots. The success of chatbot implementation in Malaysian enterprises and organisations will depend on their ability to consider the mentioned aspects. The research findings will contribute to our comprehension of consumer behaviour regarding the adoption of chatbots. Additionally, it will provide insights into the unique circumstances surrounding Malaysia.

This study explores the factors that influence consumers' inclination to use chatbot technology, specifically focusing on its implications for businesses and organisations in Malaysia. According to Jo et al. (2023), the utilisation of this tool can assist individuals in developing and implementing chatbot services that effectively cater to the needs and preferences of their specific target audience.

The upcoming sections of the study will provide a detailed explanation of the methodology used, present the findings and analysis of the study, and examine the potential consequences of the study. The report will provide recommendations to businesses and organisations in Malaysia on how they can effectively utilise chatbots to enhance their communication and support for their customers.

Problem Statement

The utilisation of chatbot technology is becoming more prevalent among businesses and organisations in Malaysia as a means to enhance customer engagement and satisfaction. The current popularity of chatbots is on the rise, but there is limited knowledge regarding the specific factors that influence Malaysian consumers' willingness to use them. According to Sidaoui et al. (2020), firms need to identify certain elements in order to effectively utilise chatbot services and maximise their potential benefits. It is crucial to analyse the cultural and contextual characteristics of the Malaysian market when studying the factors that impact consumers' intention to use chatbots in the country.

This study aims to address a gap in the existing literature by analysing the key characteristics that significantly influence the adoption of chatbots among Malaysian customers. The study's findings have the potential to offer valuable guidance to companies and organisations in Malaysia. By incorporating chatbot tactics, these entities can enhance customer experiences.

Research Objectives (RO)

To determine the influence of Technology Adoption Attitude,Perceived Ease of Use, Consumer Trust and Perceived Usefulness on Intention to Use Chatbots in Malaysia.

Research Questions (RQ)

RQ1: Would service quality has an influence on Intention to Use Chatbots in Malaysia?
RQ2: Will Perceived Ease of Use has an influence on Intention to Use Chatbots in Malaysia?
RQ3: Will Consumer Trust has an influence on Intention to Use Chatbots in Malaysia?
RQ4: Will Perceived Usefulness has an influence on Intention to Use Chatbots in Malaysia?

Significance of Study

Significance to Academia

There are important academic ramifications of this work. First, it adds to the literature on consumer behaviour and technology adoption by exploring what makes Malaysian customers interested in interacting with chatbots. This study's results will add to our knowledge of chatbot adoption and the role that factors like these play in various markets. This study will spark new academic conversations and research into the impact of new technology on consumer behaviour.

Furthermore, the study contributes cross-cultural insights to the study of technology adoption by focusing on Malaysia. It provides academics with a basis for comparisons of consumer attitudes towards chatbots and sheds light on the role that cultural and contextual factors play in shaping those attitudes.

Significance to Industry

This research has important ramifications for businesses and organisations in Malaysia who want to make the most of chatbot technology from an operational standpoint. Organisations may better meet the demands of their customers and meet their expectations for chatbot use if they can determine the variables that have the most impact on consumers' decisions to adopt them. With this knowledge in hand, businesses can create chatbot interfaces that not only provide customers with useful features, but also earn their confidence.

The results of this research will be useful to businesses as they consider how best to introduce and market chatbot services inside their operations. Organisations can save time and money by using chatbots to improve their customers' experiences, which in turn leads to happier clients. In addition, businesses may use this research as a springboard for creating chatbot marketing and communication plans that resonate with their specific demographic.

This research might help businesses use their resources wisely by highlighting the most important elements that influence consumers' intent to use chatbots. By giving these considerations top billing, businesses can get the most out of their chatbot investments and improve their methods of client interaction.

This research is significant since it adds to the literature on consumer behaviour and the spread of new technologies. It also has real-world ramifications for businesses in Malaysia, illuminating how they might boost customer happiness and productivity through smarter chatbot strategies and more engaging interactions.

Literature Review

Underlying Theory

The Technology Acceptance Model (TAM) is widely used in research to examine individuals' responses and behaviours towards emerging technologies. According to the Technology Acceptance Model (TAM), the user's perception of a technology's utility and ease of use are key factors in determining their decision to adopt and use it. Both factors have an impact on the user's level of comfort with technology. According to a study conducted by Ashfaq et al. (2020), individuals who have a preference for chatbots based on their perceived helpfulness and ease of use are more likely to utilise them.

According to trust theory, the extent to which individuals are willing to adopt and experiment with new technology is heavily influenced by their level of confidence in its effectiveness. The utilisation of chatbots is contingent upon the level of trust that consumers have in their reliability, security, and confidentiality, as highlighted by Ng et al. (2020). According to trust theory, there is a positive correlation between customer trust in chatbots and their affinity towards them.

The Innovation Diffusion Theory is utilised to analyse the adoption of chatbots as a means to spread innovative technology. According to Kernecker et al. (2021), the acceptance of innovation is influenced by factors such as perceived complexity, observability, and proportional advantage. This theory has the potential to provide valuable insights into the impact of these elements on the aspirations of Malaysian clients regarding chatbot adoption.

Review of Variables

Technology Adoption Attitude

Mohd Rahim, Iahad, Yusof, and Al-Sharafi (2022) present an AI-based chatbot adoption paradigm. Colleges and universities serve as a convenient sample for this study. To further understand what factors are driving chatbot adoption in the academy, researchers conducted an online survey.

A approach for using AI-enabled chatbots in the classroom is proposed by Rahim, Iahad, Yusof, and Al-Sharafi (2022). This study is similar to its predecessor in that they both use an online survey to collect data from their target population of college and university students. Both probes, albeit likely conducted independently, may share common goals. The attitudes of millennials in Malaysia towards the adoption of banking chatbots are investigated by Toh and Tay (2022). The method of sampling is not explained. This study aims to investigate how young people in Malaysia view and interact with banking chatbots. A questionnaire has been designed to collect data and explore the factors that encourage millennials to use banking chatbots.

The studies include a wide range of issues, such as millennials' attitudes towards banking in Malaysia, online shopping, higher education, and SMEs. Convenience sampling and online surveys/questionnaires are common methods of data collection today (Stratton, 2021). The primary objective of these studies is to reveal the factors that influence users' receptivity to and tendency to embrace these intelligent gadgets. More information about the study's procedures and findings may be found in the accompanying graphic.

Perceived Ease of Use

The study by Tan and Lim (2023) examines the factors that affect the satisfaction of Generation Z shoppers using e-commerce chatbots. Convenience and snowball sampling are used to acquire information from the population under study. Researchers found out how satisfied people were with e-commerce chatbots and what made them happy with a survey questionnaire.

Mai's (2022) study looks into the reaction of university students in Malaysia to AI chatbots. Online surveys and interviews with participants selected via convenience sampling are used to compile data. The study investigates how students in Malaysia perceive and interact with artificial intelligence chatbots designed for instructional purposes.

It is expected by Chan et al. (2022) that people in Malaysia will use their mobile devices to shop during the COVID-19 lockdown. Malaysian mobile shoppers make up the population of interest, and they are selected via random sampling. Before, during, and after the shutdown, web users are polled online about their intentions and experiences with mobile purchases.The study's goals are twofold: to ascertain how customers' tendency to adopt mobile shopping was impacted by the COVID-19 blackout, and to identify the factors that influence consumers' inclination to adopt mobile shopping.

Consumer attitudes towards and future use of smart retail technologies in Malaysia are investigated by Perumal et al. (2022). Selected at random, respondents fill out an online survey regarding their thoughts and intentions with respect to "smart retail" technologies. The purpose of this study was to better educate the adoption of smart retail technologies in Malaysia by shedding light on the factors that influence buyers' attitudes and preferences.

Overall, the results of these studies provide new insight into the complex factors that influence Malaysian consumers' openness to smart retail technologies like chatbots (Lim et al., 2021). The surveys cover a wide range of market participants, from Generation Z buyers to Malaysian students to mobile shoppers to regular Malaysian consumers. The findings of these studies can inform the design of new chatbot systems and the installation of smart retail technology in Malaysia, both of which will enhance user experiences and better meet the preferences of the target groups there.

Consumer Trust

Tan and Liew (2022) conducted research to find out how m-commerce chatbot interfaces influence customers' faith in the brand, their willingness to make a purchase, and the credibility of the information they receive. Similar to the last study, convenience sampling was used. The table, however, does not reveal its target demographic. The study's online poll likely asked participants about their trust in the chatbot, how much they relied on it, the legitimacy of its social media presence, and whether or not they were likely to make a purchase after interacting with it.

Suresh et al. (2023) investigated the opinions of millennial and Gen Z consumers on the topic of AI in e-commerce. Generation Z is the target audience, however the table gives no indication of how the data was collected. Researchers likely used online questionnaires to gauge Generation Z members' attitudes towards the application of AI to online retail.

Through interviews with customers and business owners, Selamat and Windasari (2021) explore how small and medium-sized enterprises (SMEs) may make the most of chatbots. Convenience sampling was utilised to collect data from SME clients and business owners. The study's authors conducted in-depth interviews, focus groups, and an online survey with customers and business owners to get their feedback on chatbot integration for SMEs.

These studies employ a wide variety of research methods, from convenience sampling and online surveys to in-person interviews and focus groups. These studies recruit a diverse sample of people, including healthcare consumers, millennials, and business owners and managers. Research aims to perform things like study e-commerce success strategies, identify the elements that affect technology adoption, investigate the effects of chatbot interfaces, and evaluate consumers' openness to artificial intelligence.

Perceived Usefulness

The goal of the study by Al-Sharafi et al. (2022) was to determine how knowledge management factors affect the sustainability of AI-based chatbots in the classroom. The article does not describe the sample process or the participants. In order to fully comprehend the data, the group fused structural equation modelling (SEM) with artificial neural networks (ANN). In order to ensure the long-term viability of AI chatbots in educational contexts, this study aimed to investigate the connections between knowledge management factors (such as information acquisition, knowledge storage, and knowledge transfer). The study findings provide insight into the factors that influence the successful and sustained adoption of chatbot technology in educational settings.

The "The MERLIN Project" was conducted by researchers Mai (2022) and Mai (2022) to learn more about the attitudes of Malaysian students towards the use of an artificial intelligence chatbot in the classroom. Convenience sampling and snowball sampling were used to collect data from students in Malaysia. The majority of the information was gathered using online questionnaire questionnaires. Children's reactions to the use of a chatbot programmed with artificial intelligence were investigated.

The study aimed to discover how students perceived the AI chatbot and how it affected their education. The study's results expand our understanding of how AI chatbots can be put to good use in classrooms.

Chan et al. (2022) studied consumers' likelihood to use and uptake of mobile shopping in Malaysia during the COVID-19 lockout. Consumers in Malaysia were polled via an online, self-administered survey. The study's overarching goal was to investigate the factors that influence consumers' interest in and adoption of mobile shopping during the COVID-19 quarantine. The survey included questions regarding consumers' confidence in, fear about, and overall contentment with mobile purchase. By illuminating the factors that influence customers' behaviour in the context of mobile purchase, the study's findings can assist businesses and policymakers in developing more efficient ways to promote mobile commerce.

Intention to Use Chat Bots in Malaysia

The study conducted by Toh and Ta(2022) aims to determine whether or not young people in Malaysia are amenable to interacting with banking chatbots. Due to a lack of information, such as the sampling strategy and data collection procedures, evaluating their study methodology is challenging. Young adults in Malaysia are the primary responders, and their opinions and preferences about banking chatbots will be investigated.

Ameen, Cheah, and Kumar (2022) examine the impact of augmented reality, chatbots, & social media on the body image & self-esteem of Gen Z women. The study's data on Gen Z women shoppers was collected using a convenience sample. Online questionnaires and in-person interviews were used to compile the data. The findings provide insight into how the digital media consumption habits of millennials have an effect on their self-perception.

Rahim et al. (2022) provide a framework for the implementation of AI-powered chatbots in the classroom. A survey was conducted online at several educational institutions using a convenience sample technique. The study's overarching goal is to create a model that specifies the variables that contribute to the widespread use of chatbots powered by artificial intelligence in academic settings.

Gaps in Literature

Other studies have looked at the characteristics that impact customers' intention to use other technological advancements, such as mobile apps and e-commerce platforms, but there is a dearth of research on chatbot adoption in the Malaysian context. Existing research provides scant insight into what motivates customers to use chatbots, especially in the cultural and social setting of Malaysia. Because of this information gap, researchers in Malaysia need to investigate the factors that shape people's views on chatbots. Meanwhile, the current literature is mostly geared towards the Western market, completely omitting consideration for the unique cultural characteristics and shopper preferences of Malaysians. The diverse population of Malaysia has drastically varying consumer habits, attitudes, and aspirations. For this reason, research into the Malaysian market is essential for understanding the factors that motivate consumers to interact with chatbots in that country. This research sets out to address a gap in the existing literature by investigating the factors that significantly influence Malaysian consumers' propensity to embrace chatbots. The results of this study will help businesses and organisations in Malaysia better their interactions with customers by employing chatbot strategies.

Figure 1. Conceptual framework

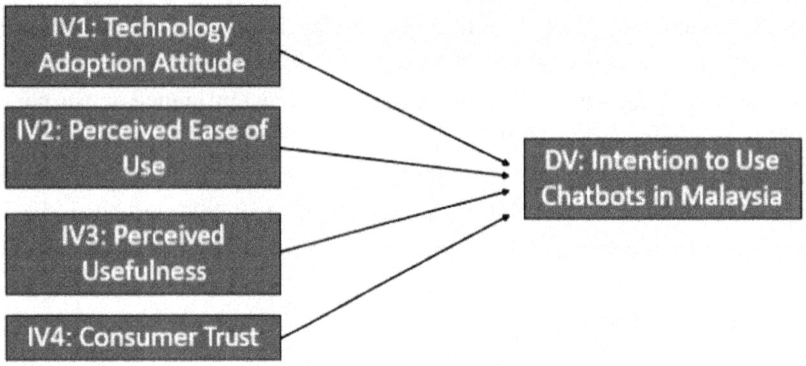

METHODOLOGY

Research Design

The cross-sectional study approach collects data in one time period. A systematic questionnaire with open-ended and Likert-scale items will be designed based on the literature analysis. Malaysian consumers' chatbot expectations will be assessed with a standardised questionnaire. The prepared response options in closed-ended questions will speed up data collection and processing. Likert scale questions will test respondents' agreement or disagreement with comments about chatbot variables that affect their propensity to use them.

The literature has found several factors that influence customers' chatbot use, which will be included in the questionnaire. Privacy and security concerns and chatbot technology performance may potentially be factors. The questionnaire will be created after reviewing research and theoretical frameworks. It will try to understand the different factors that affect Malaysian customers' chatbot adoption. The questionnaire will be pilot-tested for readability, validity, and accuracy.

A statistically valid sample of Malaysian shoppers will be surveyed. Stratified random sampling will be used to select the sample, which will represent the population. Statistical concerns like analytical power and precision will determine sample size. Depending on sample size and accessibility, we will collect data via online surveys, in-person interviews, or telephone interviews. Prioritising response rates and minimising non-response bias will be done.

Malaysian chatbot users are the focus of this study. The best applicants have used chatbots for customer service, e-commerce, and knowledge base enquiries. The study participants will vary in age, gender, education, and profession. Focusing on this subset of Malaysians may help us understand what factors influence consumers' chatbot use. This study employed a convenient sample technique for this investigation. It's called "convenience sampling." Malaysian chatbot users will be approached for this study. Convenience sampling reduces data collection time and cost. Convenience sampling may limit generalizability and sample bias, but this should not be ignored. As this is a preliminary study on Malaysian consumer views towards chatbots, convenience sampling is permissible.

The 385-person survey captures a wide spectrum of Malaysian chatbot users' thoughts and experiences. This cross-sectional study can yield a large data collection with this sample size. Whether data can be acquired in time and resources will determine sample size.

The questionnaire is this study's main data collection method. For data collection from respondents, a questionnaire will be employed. This strategy collects data relevant to the study's goals and ensures participant homogeneity.

The survey is deliberately designed to gather Malaysian customers' chatbot attitudes. It will include concerns like privacy, security, and chatbot confidence, among others. The questions will invite responders to share their ideas, opinions, and experiences on the themes.

The form has open-ended and closed-ended questions. Closed-ended questions standardised data collecting by giving respondents a limited number of predetermined responses. However, Likert-scale respondents can assess each statement's agreement or disagreement using a single, standardised scale. This design allows quantitative analysis and cross-participant comparison.

Descriptive analysis will summarise and describe data. For each variable, we will calculate central tendency (mean, median, and mode) and dispersion (standard deviation and range) measurements. Descriptive statistics summarise participant characteristics and response distribution. We can learn about the respondents and how much they agree or disagree with the questions by studying their Likert-scale responses.

PLS analysis uses measurement and structural models. Perceived utility, simplicity of use, trust, privacy, and security concerns will be utilised to evaluate the measurement model's latent components. This analysis will help determine construct reliability and measurement scale validity.

The structural model will examine latent construct interrelationships to determine direct and indirect implications on consumers' chatbot use. The analysis will reveal how each factor affected customers' choices. PLS analysis can also be used to see if other factors moderate or mediate the study's aims and literature.

The PLS analysis will reveal how several factors affect Malaysian clients' chatbot utilisation. This inquiry can help explain the mechanisms and main determinants of consumer intentions.

FINDINGS

Demographic Information

The provided table presents a gender-based breakdown of the study participants. A total of 385 individuals participated in the survey. The data shows that 62.9% of the sample identified themselves as female, while 37.1% identified as male. Based on the gender breakdown of the study, it can be observed that there is a slightly higher representation of female participants compared to male participants. In order to ensure a comprehensive analysis of the results, researchers should be mindful of the potential implications and insights related to gender imbalance.

The provided table displays the distribution of participants' ages in the study. The participants were categorised into four groups according to their age: individuals aged 51 and above, individuals aged 20-30, individuals aged 31-40, and individuals aged 41-50. The data shows that around 57.7% of the participants fell within the age range of 31 to 40. The age groups of twenty-and-thirty, forty-one to fifty, and fifty-one-plus comprised 25.2%, 15.3%, and 1.8% of the sample, respectively. The distribution of age groups in the study's participants offers insights into the demographic composition and helps in understanding the dynamics of how individuals from different age groups engage with chatbots in Malaysia.

The table provides information on the marital status of the respondents. The study revealed a significant prevalence of committed relationships, with 59.5% of participants reported being married. Simultaneously, it is worth noting that a significant portion of the population, specifically 33.5%, remains unattached. The percentage of the population consisting of individuals who are single and have never been married is 7.0%. The study's findings emphasise the diverse marital situations of the participants, which could be important for understanding potential variations in attitudes towards technology adoption, perceived ease of use, consumer trust, and perceived utility among different marital groups who plan to use chatbots.

The provided table presents a detailed breakdown of the educational background of the respondents involved in the study. According to the findings, it is evident that 37.4 percent of the participants hold a Bachelor's degree, making it the highest educational attainment level among them. Following closely behind is the category of Diploma/A level/STPM, which accounts for 31.2 percent of the participants. The percentage of individuals who have earned a Master's degree is significantly lower at 11.4 percent. Similarly, the percentage of individuals who hold O level/SPM certification is also relatively low at 10.4 percent. According to the data, 4.2% of the population falls under the category of "Others," while 5.5% of individuals have obtained degrees in Professional Studies. The data indicates that the respondents have diverse educational backgrounds, which may contribute to a broader range of perspectives and information for the study. It is important to consider the potential impact of educational diversity on research outcomes in order to draw accurate conclusions.

The user's text provides a breakdown of the companies that responded, categorised by their respective categories. According to the data, joint ventures make up the largest proportion (33.5%) of all enterprises, surpassing both privately held businesses and those with 100% foreign ownership. According to the dataset, joint-stock companies account for 14.5% of all companies, while nationalised businesses make up 4.9% and the remaining 3.1% are classified as other types of companies. The findings emphasise the importance of joint ventures in the business world because of their collaborative nature and the potential advantages they offer for international relationships. The study's findings shed light on the varying impacts of different types of businesses on study outcomes and decision-making within the relevant economic or industrial setting.

The provided table displays the various occupations held by the participants involved in the study. The sample exhibits a diverse range of professions. Approximately 30.4% of the population is comprised of individuals employed in the service and sales sectors. The inclusion of a diverse range of professions in the sample enhances the study's ability to draw general conclusions about the factors that influence chatbot adoption.

The provided table displays the income of each participant in the study. The data set includes individuals from various economic backgrounds in Malaysia. The income range of RM2001 to RM3000 had the highest percentage of total respondents, accounting for 33% of the participants. The proportion of participants with incomes below RM2000 (13%) and those with incomes between RM3001 and RM4000 (35.3%) are particularly significant. Furthermore, it is worth noting that 11.4% of the individuals surveyed reported earnings falling within the range of RM4001 to RM5000. Additionally, 7.3% of respondents indicated that their incomes exceeded RM5000. The economic diversity of the sample may impact the study's findings and conclusions regarding chatbot adoption in Malaysia, as indicated by the distribution.

Pilot Test

Independent variables (IV1: Technology Adoption Attitude; IV2: Perceived Ease of Use; IV3: Consumer Trust; IV4: Perceived Usefulness) and their respective item-total statistics are displayed in the table that can be found directly above it (DV: Intention to Use Chatbots in Malaysia). These statistical measures shed light on the correlations that exist between the various variables and the overarching scale or concept that the variables represent.

The mean of the scale is displayed in the first column of the table if the data item (question or statement) associated with each variable is removed. The mean represents the average response to the item provided by all of the people who participated in the study. The second column presents the scale variance without the item, informing us of the degree to which the responses were separated from one another.

The adjusted item-total correlation, which is shown in the third column, reflects the strength of the association between each item and the overall scale as well as the direction in which that association points (i.e., the combined scores of all items within the respective variable). When it comes to the measurement of a certain construct, an item is considered to be highly relevant if it has a high correlation with the construct that it claims to be measuring.

The amount of total scale variance that can be attributed to each individual item is presented in the form of a squared multiple correlation in the fourth column. The r-value gives an indication of the percentage of the construct's variability that can be attributed to the particular item being measured. It is an indication that an item is a reliable measure of its corresponding construct if the squared multiple correlation between that item and the construct is high.

In the event that the item being selected is removed, the Cronbach's alpha will be displayed in the final column. The reliability coefficient known as Cronbach's alpha is an indicator of how effectively individual items on a scale measure the same underlying construct. Cronbach's alpha can be found in many statistical packages. If an item's Cronbach's alpha is high, it indicates that the item is more likely to be an accurate measure of the construct that it purports to capture.

Cronbach's alpha values are high for all variables (IV1, IV2, IV3, IV4, and DV) if the corresponding item is removed from the study. This is based on the item-total statistics. Due to the fact that there is a high level of internal consistency within each variable, this suggests that the items are measuring the concepts that they are intended to be measuring in an accurate manner. In addition to this, the item-total correlations that have been corrected are all higher than 0.7, which indicates that they are fairly robust. This indicates that each item has a strong relationship with the construct that it is measuring, and as a result, each item makes a sizeable contribution to the evaluation of the variables.

All of the survey items that were used to measure technology adoption attitude (IV1), perceived ease of use (IV2), consumer trust (IV3), perceived usefulness (IV4), and intention to use chatbots in Malaysia (DV) had high Cronbach's alpha, corrected item-total correlation, and squared multiple correlation values, all of which indicate that the survey items are reliable and valid.

Multiple Regression

The estimated value of the intercept, denoted by the constant term (B), is 3.989. This indicates that the DV is predicted to be around 3.989 when all other variables are held constant at zero. When other factors are held constant, the coefficients of the individual IVs reveal how much of an effect they have on the DV. The coefficient for IV1 is 0.308, so we can estimate a 0.308-unit boost to DV for every 1-unit increase in IV1. The low p-value of 0.000 indicates that this coefficient is statistically significant, while the high t-value of 6.023 indicates that it is highly significant. A coefficient of 0.259 has also been assigned to IV2, indicating that an increase of one unit in IV2 is correlated with a predicted increase of about 0.259 units in DV. The t-value for this coefficient is 4.802, and the p-value for its significance is 0.000.

Table 1. Multiple regression

ANOVA[a]						
Model		Sum of Squares	df	Mean Square	F	Sig.
1	Regression	2442.203	4	610.551	126.890	.000[b]
	Residual	1828.431	380	4.812		
	Total	4270.634	384			

a. Dependent Variable: DV
b. Predictors: (Constant), IV4, IV1, IV3, IV2

An increase of one unit in IV3 is expected to result in a predicted increase of about 0.102 units in DV, as indicated by the coefficient of 0.102 for IV3. This coefficient, however, has weaker statistical significance than the preceding variables. With a p-value of 0.051, the level of evidence for a significant correlation between IV3 and the DV is slightly above the more typical 0.05 threshold. Similarly, IV4 has a coefficient of 0.126, which means that a predicted increase in DV of roughly 0.126 units is associated with a one-unit increase in IV4. The p-value of 0.027 indicates statistical significance for this coefficient. Again, when we look at the standardised coefficients (Beta), we see that IV1 is the most significant. This indicates that IV1 has the greatest effect on the DV in terms of standard deviations, relative to the other IVs. The significance of these connections is further supported by the t-values. All t-values for the IVs are significantly greater than zero, providing strong evidence against the null hypothesis. Confidence intervals for the true population coefficients are provided as intervals with a 95 percent level of certainty. Indicative of a statistically significant effect on the DV, all IVs have confidence intervals that do not contain zero.

Table 2. Confidence of variables

Coefficients[a]								
Model		Unstandardized Coefficients		Standardized Coefficients	t	Sig.	95.0% Confidence Interval for B	
		B	Std. Error	Beta			Lower Bound	Upper Bound
1	(Constant)	3.989	.644		6.190	.000	2.722	5.256
	IV1	.308	.051	.327	6.023	.000	.208	.409
	IV2	.259	.054	.275	4.802	.000	.153	.365
	IV3	.102	.052	.109	1.954	.051	-.001	.206
	IV4	.126	.057	.133	2.213	.027	.014	.238

a. Dependent Variable: DV

Therefore, we can conclude that:

H1: Technology Adoption Attitude has a significant positive influence on Intention to Use Chatbots in Malaysia.
H2: Perceived Ease of Use has a significant positive influence on Intention to Use Chatbots in Malaysia.
H3: Consumer Trust has a significant positive influence on Intention to Use Chatbots in Malaysia.
H4: Perceived Usefulness has a significant positive influence on Intention to Use Chatbots in Malaysia.

This research looked into what influences Malaysian customers' willingness to interact with chatbots. The results illuminate the significance of Consumer Trust, Perceived Usefulness, Perceived Ease of Use, and Technology Adoption Attitude in determining whether or not consumers intend to embrace and use chatbots. All four IVs were found to have a positive and statistically significant relationship with customers' intent to employ chatbots (DV).

One of the most important factors found to affect consumers' propensity to use chatbots is their attitude toward adopting new technologies. Customers that have a positive outlook on adopting new technologies are more likely to welcome chatbots into their interactions with businesses and service providers, as there is a strong association between attitude and intention about technology adoption. Customers' willingness to employ chatbots was significantly impacted by their impressions of their usability. Consumers are more likely to embrace and incorporate chatbots into their daily contacts when they consider them to be easy to use and communicate with, the study found, whether for customer service, information retrieval, or other objectives.

There was a significant correlation between consumers' trust in chatbots and their intent to employ them. Users are more inclined to embrace and make use of chatbots for a variety of tasks and services if they believe chatbots will give them with accurate and reliable information and support. One of the most important factors found to influence consumers' intent to utilise a chatbot was its perceived usefulness. Users are more likely to accept and integrate chatbots into their interactions if they believe that these technologies can successfully meet their demands and provide valuable support.

The results of the study stress the significance of encouraging widespread use and acceptance of chatbots in Malaysia by promoting favourable attitudes, building trust, assuring ease of use, and displaying their value. These findings will help businesses and policymakers create more effective plans to increase the use of chatbots and improve the quality of interactions with customers.

This study has some drawbacks despite the helpful contributions. The information was gathered through surveys, which could introduce biases due to respondents' need to appear honest and successful. Furthermore, the survey only included consumers in Malaysia, therefore the results can only be applied locally. To better understand the dynamics and changes in customers' intention to use chatbots over time, future research could explore additional variables and undertake longitudinal studies.

This research sheds light on what influences consumers' decisions to engage with chatbots in Malaysia. The relevance of aspects like Technology Adoption Attitude, Perceived Ease of Use, Consumer Trust, and Perceived Usefulness in determining chatbot adoption and usage is highlighted by the positive and strong correlations between these variables and customers' intentions to use chatbots. Understanding and addressing these factors can pave the way for effective implementation and utilisation of chatbot technology, ultimately leading to improved customer service and satisfaction in the Malaysian context, as chatbot technology continues to evolve and become an integral part of various industries.

Conclusion

This study examined what determines Malaysian customers' chatbot interaction. The results show that Consumer Trust, Perceived Usefulness, Perceived Ease of Use, and Technology Adoption Attitude influence chatbot adoption. Customers' intent to use chatbots was positively and statistically significant for all four IVs.

DISCUSSION, CONCLUSION, AND IMPLICATIONS

Discussion of Findings

The study focuses on the factors that Malaysian customers consider when deciding whether to engage with chatbots. The study's findings indicate a significant correlation between customers' perceptions of the technology's ease of use, trustworthiness, usefulness, and their intent to use a chatbot. The findings provide insights into consumer attitudes towards chatbots, potentially aiding businesses and policymakers in promoting chatbot adoption and enhancing user experiences. The publication of these findings took place in the Journal of Consumer Research.

A notable discovery suggests a connection between individuals' inclination towards embracing new technologies and their inclination towards interacting with chatbots. This area requires additional investigation. The finding highlights the significant influence of consumers' attitudes towards new technology on their acceptance of chatbots as a communication medium. Customers who exhibit a higher level of openness towards adopting new technologies tend to have a better understanding of the benefits associated with using chatbots. As a result, they are more inclined to actually utilise chatbots in their interactions. This suggests that businesses should prioritise creating a culture that embraces new technologies like chatbots in order to provide satisfying digital experiences for their customers.

The second realisation is that there is a direct relationship between how easy customers perceive chatbots to be and their likelihood of using them. The ease of user interaction with chatbots is expected to lead to an increased adoption of chatbots in routine communications. The study emphasises the significance of prioritising user-friendliness and simplicity in the creation of chatbots. It also underscores the benefits of intuitive design and smooth interactions during the development process. The adoption of a chatbot by a company is influenced significantly by two key factors: the usability of the chatbot and its ease of use.

The level of trust that customers place in chatbots is a crucial factor that influences their decision-making process when it comes to utilising these tools. The correlation between trust and intent highlights the importance of credibility in influencing customers' perceptions of chatbots. It is crucial for customers to have confidence in the reliability of chatbots as trustworthy sources of information. Chatbots should be capable of addressing customer inquiries thoroughly and maintaining confidentiality. In order to establish trust with customers, it is crucial for your business to prioritise several key factors. These include maintaining transparent and accessible communication channels, implementing robust data protection protocols, and ensuring the consistent and reliable transmission of accurate information through chatbots.

The fourth finding suggests a relationship between customers' perceptions of chatbots' usefulness and their intentions to use these tools in the future. The perception of chatbots as useful tools that provide assistance and solutions to users' inquiries and issues positively impacts the adoption of chatbots by businesses in their customer interactions. The research emphasises the importance of showcasing the practical advantages of using chatbots, such as their ability to offer timely customer support, efficiently solve issues, and offer tailored recommendations. In order to enhance customer perception of chatbot usefulness, it is advisable for companies to highlight the practical applications and benefits associated with utilising chatbots in real-life scenarios.

The findings emphasise the importance of prioritising user experience, building credibility, and showcasing the practical advantages of chatbots to boost their adoption and usage in Malaysia. Companies and governments should consider the following concerns when it comes to the development, implementation, and promotion of chatbot services. One effective strategy for maximising the potential for widespread adoption and use of chatbots is to actively listen to and address user feedback regarding their experiences.

However, it is important to note that this study does have some notable limitations. The data was collected through surveys, which may introduce bias and raise concerns about the representativeness of the results in capturing all aspects of consumers' interactions with chatbots. The survey respondents were limited to residents of Malaysia, which means that the findings can only be applied within the region. Future research has the potential to expand the range of data collection methods employed. For instance, incorporating interviews with users or observing their interactions with chatbots could yield valuable insights into the actual usage patterns of individuals. The evolution of consumers' attitudes and behaviour towards chatbots will be an intriguing observation as their familiarity with the technology grows.

Implications of Study

The technological literacy of the general population in Malaysia should be increased, and Malaysian businesses should back efforts to do so. By raising people's consciousness about the numerous advantages offered by emerging technologies like chatbots, businesses can make their environments more receptive to the introduction of such innovations. In addition, businesses may use chatbots in innovative ways, such as providing individualised recommendations or streamlining customer service, in order to draw attention to the numerous advantageous aspects of the technology and encourage positive mentalities among customers.

Conclusion

This study provides insights into the key factors that influence Malaysian consumers' decision-making process regarding their engagement with chatbots. The findings highlight the significance of consumers' attitudes towards adopting new technologies, their perception of how easy it is to use, their trust in the technology, and their perception of its usefulness in determining their willingness to use chatbot technology. The independent variables mentioned are important factors that contribute to the adoption and usage of chatbots in Malaysia. They are associated with customers' intention to use chatbots, making them significant in driving chatbot adoption in the Malaysian context.

The study's findings emphasise the significance of cultivating a tech-savvy culture and promoting customer adoption and growth within that context. The enhancement of consumers' perceptions of chatbots and the increase in adoption rates can be achieved by emphasising the practicality of chatbots and showcasing the valuable benefits they offer. In order to gain the trust of consumers in chatbot technology, it is essential to prioritise the development of user-friendly interfaces and implement transparent data procedures.

From a business perspective, these findings have the potential to enhance the implementation of chatbot initiatives, leading to improved effectiveness. Implementing chatbots that are both efficient and user-friendly can have a positive impact on various business metrics such as customer service, productivity, and pricing. Respecting customers' privacy and accurately meeting their information requirements are crucial factors for a company to establish trust and loyalty among its customers.

Policymakers can utilise enabling rules and regulations to promote the ethical use of chatbots, as demonstrated by the information provided. Ensuring the successful integration of chatbots across industries requires a careful balance between innovation and consumer protection. Ensuring the success of the integration is crucial.

This research establishes a basis for future investigations into the ever-changing landscape of chatbot adoption. It serves as a fundamental starting point for further studies in this field. A comprehensive understanding of chatbots can be achieved by exploring additional factors, conducting longitudinal studies, and analysing the cultural impacts of chatbots.

However, it is crucial to consider the study's limitations, including its reliance on survey data and its narrow cultural scope. It is important to approach the findings with caution when applying them to populations or countries other than Malaysia. This research expands on the current understanding of how chatbots have impacted businesses, policymakers, and academics in Malaysia. The presence of positive correlations among technology adoption attitude, perceived ease of use, consumer trust, and consumers' intentions to use chatbots underscores the importance of prioritising user-centric design, trust-building, and value proposition when encouraging chatbot adoption. By incorporating these valuable insights and effectively addressing the limitations of the study, Malaysia can enhance customer experiences, expedite digital transformation, and uphold its status as a frontrunner in technological innovation.

REFERENCES

Al-Emran, M., AlQudah, A. A., Abbasi, G. A., Al-Sharafi, M. A., & Iranmanesh, M. (2023). Determinants of using AI-based Chatbots for knowledge sharing: Evidence from PLS-SEM and fuzzy sets (fsQCA). *IEEE Transactions on Engineering Management*.

Al-Sharafi, M. A., Al-Emran, M., Iranmanesh, M., Al-Qaysi, N., Iahad, N. A., & Arpaci, I. (2022). Understanding the impact of knowledge management factors on the sustainable use of AI-based chatbots for educational purposes using a hybrid SEM-ANN approach. *Interactive Learning Environments*, 1–20.

Ameen, N., Cheah, J. H., & Kumar, S. (2022). It's all part of the customer journey: The impact of augmented reality, chatbots, and social media on the body image and self-esteem of Generation Z female consumers. *Psychology and Marketing*, *39*(11), 2110–2129. doi:10.1002/mar.21715

Ashfaq, M., Yun, J., Yu, S., & Loureiro, S. M. C. (2020). I, Chatbot: Modeling the determinants of users' satisfaction and continuance intention of AI-powered service agents. *Telematics and Informatics*, *54*, 101473. doi:10.1016/j.tele.2020.101473

Beattie, A., Edwards, A. P., & Edwards, C. (2020). A bot and a smile: Interpersonal impressions of chatbots and humans using emoji in computer-mediated communication. *Communication Studies*, *71*(3), 409–427. doi:10.1080/10510974.2020.1725082

Casale, S., Musicò, A., & Spada, M. M. (2021). A systematic review of metacognitions in Internet Gaming Disorder and problematic Internet, smartphone and social networking sites use. *Clinical Psychology & Psychotherapy*, *28*(6), 1494–1508. doi:10.1002/cpp.2588 PMID:33783920

Chan, X. Y., Rahman, M. K., Mamun, A. A., Salameh, A., Wan, A., Hussain, W. M. H., & Alam, S. S. (2022). Predicting the intention and adoption of mobile shopping during the COVID-19 lockdown in Malaysia. *SAGE Open*, *12*(2), 21582440221095012. doi:10.1177/21582440221095012

Ikumoro, A. O., & Jawad, M. S. (2019). Intention to use intelligent conversational agents in e-commerce among Malaysian SMEs: An integrated conceptual framework based on tri-theories including unified theory of acceptance, use of technology (UTAUT), and TOE. *International Journal of Academic Research in Business & Social Sciences*, *9*(11), 205–235. doi:10.6007/IJARBSS/v9-i11/6544

Jalbert, C. L. (2019). *Archaeology in Canada: an analysis of demographics and working conditions in the discipline*. Memorial University of Newfoundland.

Jenneboer, L., Herrando, C., & Constantinides, E. (2022). The impact of chatbots on customer loyalty: A systematic literature review. *Journal of Theoretical and Applied Electronic Commerce Research*, *17*(1), 212–229. doi:10.3390/jtaer17010011

Jo, E., Epstein, D. A., Jung, H., & Kim, Y.-H. (2023). Understanding the benefits and challenges of deploying conversational AI leveraging large language models for public health intervention. Proceedings of the 2023 CHI Conference on Human Factors in Computing Systems. IEEE.

Kernecker, M., Seufert, V., & Chapman, M. (2021). Farmer-centered ecological intensification: Using innovation characteristics to identify barriers and opportunities for a transition of agroecosystems towards sustainability. *Agricultural Systems*, *191*, 103142. doi:10.1016/j.agsy.2021.103142

Lim, X.-J., Cheah, J.-H., Ng, S. I., Basha, N. K., & Liu, Y. (2021). Are men from Mars, women from Venus? Examining gender differences towards continuous use intention of branded apps. *Journal of Retailing and Consumer Services*, *60*, 102422. doi:10.1016/j.jretconser.2020.102422

Liu, Y., Chin, W. L., Nechita, F., & Candrea, A. N. (2020). Framing film-induced tourism into a sustainable perspective from Romania, Indonesia and Malaysia. *Sustainability (Basel)*, *12*(23), 9910. doi:10.3390/su12239910

Madan, S., Pérez-Morón, J., Chua, X. N., Kee, D. M. H., Chua, J., Chua, K. Z., Chuah, Y. W., & Vidal, L. D. S. (2022). Analysis of the Shopee's Strategies to Succeed in the Global E-commerce Market: Malaysia Case. [IJTHAP]. *International Journal of Tourism and Hospitality in Asia Pasific*, *5*(1), 34–48. doi:10.32535/ijthap.v5i1.1400

Mai, N. (2022). THE MERLIN PROJECT: MALAYSIAN STUDENTS'ACCEPTANCE OF AN AI CHATBOT IN THEIR LEARNING PROCESS. *Turkish Online Journal of Distance Education*, *23*(3), 31–48. doi:10.17718/tojde.1137122

Mogaji, E., Balakrishnan, J., Nwoba, A. C., & Nguyen, N. P. (2021). Emerging-market consumers' interactions with banking chatbots. *Telematics and Informatics*, *65*, 101711. doi:10.1016/j.tele.2021.101711

Mondal, S., Das, S., & Vrana, V. G. (2023). How to bell the cat? A theoretical review of generative artificial intelligence towards digital disruption in all walks of life. *Technologies, 11*(2), 44. doi:10.3390/technologies11020044

Nasharuddin, N. A., Sharef, N. M., Mansor, E. I., Samian, N., Murad, M. A. A., Omar, M. K., Arshad, N. I., Shahbodin, F., & Marhaban, M. H. (2021). Designing an Educational Chatbot: A Case Study of CikguAIBot. *2021 Fifth International Conference on Information Retrieval and Knowledge Management (CAMP).*

Ng, M., Coopamootoo, K. P., Toreini, E., Aitken, M., Elliot, K., & van Moorsel, A. (2020). Simulating the effects of social presence on trust, privacy concerns & usage intentions in automated bots for finance. *2020 IEEE European Symposium on Security and Privacy Workshops* (EuroS&PW). IEEE.

Perumal, S., Qing, Y., & Jaganathan, M. (2022). Factors influencing attitudes and intentions towards smart retail technology. *International Journal of Data and Network Science, 6*(2), 595–602.

Rahim, N. I. M., Iahad, N. A., Yusof, A. F., & Al-Sharafi, M. A. (2022). AI-Based chatbots adoption model for higher-education institutions: A hybrid PLS-SEM-Neural network modelling approach. *Sustainability, 14*(19), 12726. doi:10.3390/su141912726

Salam, M. T., Muhamad, N., & Leong, V. S. (2019). Measuring religiosity among Muslim consumers: Observations and recommendations. *Journal of Islamic Marketing, 10*(2), 633–652. doi:10.1108/JIMA-02-2018-0038

Selamat, M. A., & Windasari, N. A. (2021). Chatbot for SMEs: Integrating customer and business owner perspectives. *Technology in Society, 66*, 101685. doi:10.1016/j.techsoc.2021.101685

Sidaoui, K., Jaakkola, M., & Burton, J. (2020). AI feel you: Customer experience assessment via chatbot interviews. *Journal of Service Management, 31*(4), 745–766. doi:10.1108/JOSM-11-2019-0341

Sitthipon, T., Siripipatthanakul, S., Phayaphrom, B., Siripipattanakul, S., & Limna, P. (2022). Determinants of Customers' Intention to Use Healthcare Chatbots and Apps in Bangkok, Thailand. *International Journal of Behavioral Analytics, 2*(2), 1–15.

Stratton, S. J. (2021). Population research: Convenience sampling strategies. *Prehospital and Disaster Medicine, 36*(4), 373–374. doi:10.1017/S1049023X21000649 PMID:34284835

Suresh, T. P., Yong, P. L., Chyi, Y. S., & Musa, R. (2023). Connecting with Generation Z: Consumer Acceptance of the Use of Artificial Intelligence in Online Shopping. [JEB]. *Journal of Entrepreneurship and Business, 11*(1), 56–68. doi:10.17687/jeb.v11i1.921

Tan, P. K., & Lim, C. M. (2023). Factors That Affect User Satisfaction of Using E-Commerce Chatbot: A Study on Generation Z. *International Journal of Business and Technology Management, 5*(1), 292–303.

Tan, S.-M., & Liew, T. W. (2022). Multi-chatbot or single-chatbot? The effects of m-commerce chatbot interface on source credibility, social presence, trust, and purchase intention. *Human Behavior and Emerging Technologies, 2022*, 2022. doi:10.1155/2022/2501538

Toh, T. J., & Tay, L. Y. (2022). Banking Chatbots: A Study on Technology Acceptance among Millennials in Malaysia. *Journal of Logistics. Informatics and Service Science*, *9*(3), 1–15.

Zhang, Q., Husnain, M., Usman, M., Akhtar, M. W., Ali, S., Khan, M. A., Abbas, Q., Ismail, R., Rehman, T., & Akram, M. (2022). Interplay of eco-friendly factors and islamic religiosity towards recycled package products: A cross-cultural study. *Frontiers in Psychology*, *13*, 13. doi:10.3389/fpsyg.2022.840711 PMID:36248529

Chapter 2
Leadership Competencies for the Age of Artificial Intelligence

Mayesha Tasnim
Ateneo de Manila University, Philippines

ABSTRACT

AI has transformed leadership evaluation. According to "Leadership Competencies for the Age of Artificial Intelligence," leaders need particular attributes to handle AI's positives and downsides. After examining various studies, this study emphasizes the importance of adaptability, emotional intelligence, and creativity. The study focuses on leadership, practical applications, and regional skill gaps. Leaders must anticipate AI's effects, innovate, transition, and foster entrepreneurship. AI application requires organizational improvements. This demands digital skills and current HR. This chapter offers CEOs practical guidance for entering the growing AI environment. It focuses on merging technical and interpersonal skills for new leadership approaches. These broad and comprehensive results can assist leaders in solving contemporary problems. AI and interpersonal skills are vital for current leadership.

INTRODUCTION

The advent of artificial intelligence (AI) has brought about a noticeable transformation in human cognitive processes, prompting a reassessment of the essential abilities required for effective leadership. Artificial intelligence (AI) is a primary catalyst for the rapid progress of the globe in the twenty-first century. The demand for an increasing number of leaders to navigate the challenges and opportunities presented by the ongoing technological revolution is escalating. These leaders must possess a broad spectrum of skills. Businesses grappling with this predicament recognize the crucial significance of integrating artificial intelligence (AI) into their internal operations. The present study, titled "Leadership Competencies for the Age of Artificial Intelligence," investigates the fundamental attributes that effective team managers must possess in order to thrive in the future dominated by AI.

DOI: 10.4018/979-8-3693-1842-3.ch002

Watson et al. (2021) assert that individuals aspiring to lead the artificial intelligence business must possess a fundamental set of talents. This skill set should possess enough adaptability to meet the distinct demands of the firm. The study emphasizes the significance of leadership abilities in forecasting future patterns and strategically utilizing artificial intelligence (AI) to foster innovation, enhance consumer satisfaction, and establish lasting competitive advantages. In this phase, individuals with the potential to fill artificial intelligence (AI) positions are identified and evaluated based on their compatibility with the organization's overarching objectives. CEOs should prioritize staff training and skill development, and actively implement initiatives to attract and retain individuals with specialized expertise. Achieving this objective necessitates deliberate and strategic endeavors to attract and retain workers possessing specialist expertise. Based on the research conducted by Santana and Dáz-Fernández (2023), the effectiveness of leaders depends on their ability to promote an entrepreneurial culture and adeptly navigate the significant transformations occurring in the labor and technology industries. Santana and Dáz-Fernández argue that a leader's ability to cultivate an intrapreneurial culture is crucial for their achievement. In addition to technology, artificial intelligence has the capacity to profoundly transform an organization's culture and system of principles. An effective leader in the contemporary day must possess the ability to adjust, recover quickly, and manage opposition to conventional modifications. Within the realm of artificial intelligence, this assertion holds particular significance. Baki et al. (2023) argue that for an organization to fully exploit the potential benefits of artificial intelligence, it must exhibit a specific range of capabilities. These encompass the proficiency to effectively utilize digital skills and the capacity to modify HRM protocols to address the issues presented by AI. These talents also encompass the capacity to adjust and modify.

Yadav (2019) highlights the significance of specific skills that are necessary in different regions, especially Southeast Asia. Adapting effectively to change is a crucial ability that integrates technology, social dynamics, cognitive abilities, emotional intelligence, and technology. Eddy (2012) argues that the successful utilization of artificial intelligence (AI) necessitates a significant transformation in the conventional responsibilities and attributes linked to capable leadership. To expedite this process of transformation, it is crucial to cultivate key abilities such as emotional intelligence, humility, foresight, flexibility, and drive. The consensus among contemporary individuals is that effective leadership requires a blend of technical expertise and interpersonal abilities, with particular focus on adaptability to different situations. This phenomenon is attributed to the extensive implementation of artificial intelligence in contemporary culture.

This research paper offers leaders a comprehensive manual that equips them with the precise information and skills required to effectively handle the opportunities and challenges arising from the artificial intelligence (AI) era. Individuals that actively cultivate and refine these talents will possess a strategic edge in efficiently managing forthcoming challenges and prospective prospects, particularly as artificial intelligence increasingly impacts career prospects. In order to thrive as a leader in the contemporary era of artificial intelligence, it is imperative to effectively merge proficient technical abilities with remarkable interpersonal aptitude. Individuals capable of performing this task will possess a significant edge over their competitors.

Research Objective

The main objective of this study is to conduct a comprehensive assessment and analysis of the essential leadership abilities required in the era of artificial intelligence. The primary goal is to comprehend how CEOs can derive advantages from the integration of AI into the workplace and adeptly traverse the associated hurdles. This research investigates the effective strategies that leaders can employ to navigate the challenges and advantages associated with integrating artificial intelligence (AI) into organizational operations, with the aim of accomplishing the study's objectives. The primary objectives of this study are twofold: firstly, to enumerate and rank the essential skills and attributes discussed in the article; secondly, to examine the tangible outcomes that these skills and attributes can yield, such as fostering innovation, enhancing customer satisfaction, and attaining sustained competitive advantages. The objective of this study is to examine the extent to which leaders are engaged in the task of selecting and assessing qualified candidates for jobs related to artificial intelligence (AI). Furthermore, it aims to develop strategic initiatives for the recruitment and retention of highly skilled individuals, while also prioritizing the retraining of the existing workforce. This study will also analyze the implementation of an intrapreneurial culture in response to significant technical breakthroughs. The primary focal points of this study will encompass adaptation, resilience, and proficient management of resistance to change. Furthermore, the main aim of this research is to conduct a comprehensive examination of leadership competences, including regional differences and encompassing both interpersonal and technical abilities. The primary objective is to furnish CEOs with practical guidance on how to acquire a competitive advantage in the swiftly evolving business landscape of the twenty-first century. In contemporary times, it is widely recognized that successful leadership necessitates the fusion of technological expertise with interpersonal agility, particularly in view of the increasing allure of artificial intelligence. In order to effectively tackle the problems posed by artificial intelligence (AI) systems, CEOs need to prioritize the utilization of data and develop a comprehensive understanding of digital skills (Tang et al., 2023). Moreover, it is imperative for persons in positions of power to have a mindset that places great importance on continuous learning and personal growth, enabling them to swiftly adapt to evolving situations (Watson et al., 2021). Developing close, personal relationships with those who foster and endorse one's ambitions is essential. Workplaces that heavily depend on technology-based interactions may provide difficulties in attaining this objective (Vasudevan, 2022). To address these issues, leaders should prioritize setting up regular in-person meetings and researching different strategies for influencing people on a personal level (Pendleton, 2021). The advice offered will give leaders looking to establish a strong position in the rapidly shifting landscape of the twenty-first century useful guidance.

Research Question

- What potential changes in leadership capacities might be anticipated as a direct consequence of the implementation of artificial intelligence (AI) in corporate operations?
- To effectively handle the difficulties and opportunities presented by the technological revolution in the twenty-first century, leaders must prioritize the cultivation of crucial abilities and qualities.
- In what ways may the cultivation of a foundational skill set, precise prediction, and the tactical utilization of artificial intelligence (AI) facilitate the emergence of inventive concepts, the enhancement of customer experiences, and the attainment of enduring competitive benefits within the marketplace?

- To what extent does the establishment of an intrapreneurial culture, characterized by a focus on adaptability, resilience, and the strategic handling of resistance to change in the context of substantial technical advancements, enhance the effectiveness of leadership? The objective of this investigation is to examine the ramifications of artificial intelligence beyond the realm of technology.
- What is the impact of regional conditions, specifically in Southeast Asia, on the requisite skill set that is unique to this particular region? The competencies encompassed in this framework encompass technology, cognitive, social and emotional well-being, and change management.

Based on the research paper's findings, it is imperative to redefine the framework of proficient leadership in the era of artificial intelligence, incorporating a comprehensive assessment of technical expertise alongside the capacity to engage in productive interpersonal interactions. To thrive in the ever-changing digital landscape, individuals must demonstrate adaptability and embrace emerging digital technologies, protocols, and viewpoints, including artificial intelligence (Milton & Al-Busaidi, 2023).

SYSTEMATIC REVIEW

This study looks into the tactics used by executives to get beyond challenges and seize opportunities pertaining to artificial intelligence (AI) integration into enterprises. Finding the essential leadership abilities needed in the age of artificial intelligence is the goal. The test measures core competencies, appraises how well they are used in the real world, and looks at the roles that leadership reskilling and AI candidate selection play in the workforce. The paper offers a thorough examination of the theories and research on AI leadership that have been done. To provide a thorough and comprehensive review, this work integrates the findings of Watson et al. (2021), Santana and Dáz-Fernández (2023), and Baki et al. (2023). The competency in regional governance—which encompasses both interpersonal and technical skills—is examined in this study. Beyond the confines of technology, this essay investigates how artificial intelligence affects organizational ideals and practices. The test evaluates leaders' duties in recruiting and retaining staff in a planned manner and managing resistance during revolutionary processes. The study underscores the need for leaders to possess a constant mindset of learning and flexibility to promptly adapt to evolving AI technologies and circumstances. According to the report, in order for leaders to thrive in the ever-changing environment, they must blend their technical and interpersonal skills. To support the identified leadership attributes, the study suggests undertaking comprehensive case studies and obtaining further empirical data. In summary, the thorough analysis presented in the paper incorporates references from the body of existing literature with theoretical frameworks. This inquiry looks at what makes a great leader, differences seen in various places, and artificial intelligence's effects on businesses. It could be easier to support it if additional empirical data or case studies were included.

Applying theory to research enhances its quality by providing a methodical framework for analyzing and assessing the findings. In order to assess how AI will affect leadership, the article "Leadership Competencies for the Age of Artificial Intelligence" looks at how transformational leadership theories might be applied. Scholars can investigate the impact of AI integration on leadership paradigms through the application of established theories. The cultivation of resilience, adaptability, and proficiency in both technical and interpersonal skills are necessary for this analysis. This theoretical framework guides academic study and advancement in the field of digital leadership by offering crucial insights into the shifting landscape of leadership.

Transformation of Leadership Abilities in Light of Artificial Intelligence Integration

Artificial intelligence (AI) integration into a business's everyday operations invariably necessitates a significant restructuring of the fundamental leadership competencies needed. Known for emphasizing strategic planning, decision-making, and strong interpersonal skills, modern leadership techniques increasingly demand a deep comprehension of artificial intelligence (AI) technology and its associated ramifications. To successfully negotiate the challenges of integrating artificial intelligence (AI), assess its strategic implications, and make informed decisions about its integration into business workflows, leaders need to possess significant technical skills. According to Pearce (2018), in order for leaders to effectively handle the intricate parts of using artificial intelligence (AI), they need to possess a high degree of technical understanding. This entails assessing the technology's strategic ramifications and choosing wisely how to integrate it into the business's operational procedures. Flexibility and a deep comprehension of digital literacy are prerequisites for effective leadership. It emphasizes how important it is for executives to stay current with technology and actively use artificial intelligence (AI) to boost productivity and encourage creativity in their companies. To succeed in today's professional environment, one must acquire and master digital skills such as digital literacy and the capacity to comprehend complex challenges (Tomašević, 2023). Furthermore, cultivating a culture that promotes ongoing education and aids in the development of AI-related skills is seen as a crucial leadership quality, ensuring that businesses are prepared for the ever-evolving artificial intelligence landscape. Senior executives need to put improving workforce capacities and successfully attracting and retaining highly skilled individuals at the top of their priority list, according to Watson et al. (2021). In addition, they must create an environment that encourages creativity within the organization and effectively adapt to the significant changes brought about by advancements in technology and changing labor practices. Any particular company's success depends on having the aforementioned capability. According to this theory, competent leaders are able to skillfully blend traditional leadership traits with a technologically advanced strategy. These locations offer favorable conditions for businesses to thrive in the artificial intelligence (AI) era.

To effectively handle the opportunities and challenges brought about by the 21st-century digital revolution, leaders need to be endowed with a diverse variety of skills and abilities. Possessing a strong technical competency is essential to properly assess changes and fully benefit from them. To effectively carry out this duty, one must have a solid understanding of emerging technology, particularly artificial intelligence. Pierog (2023) contends that in order for leaders to skillfully traverse the quickly changing digital ecosystem with resilience and understanding, they must exhibit critical qualities like agility and flexibility. Effective communication is essential for elucidating difficult scientific ideas and turning them into workable solutions. It also promotes cooperation across various organizations. According to Maini (2022), having these qualities enables leaders to make complex judgements and negotiate challenging circumstances with skill. Furthermore, it is imperative to recognize that critical leadership competencies encompass imaginative problem-solving, tactical planning, inspiring and guiding others towards a shared technical objective, and anticipating future prospects (Mumford, 2017). In an era of rapid technology advancement, it is imperative to cultivate a culture of continuous learning and encourage digital competency across the board for the organization to remain relevant. Leaders that are equipped to navigate the challenges of the digital revolution and reap its potential rewards are those who have a blend of technical know-how, flexibility, effective communication abilities, strategic vision, and a commitment to lifelong learning.

Fundamental Abilities Required for Leadership in AI

To effectively maneuver through the complexities of today's technology environment, one must develop a core set of competencies intended to address the unique demands of artificial intelligence (AI) leadership. Given the speed at which artificial intelligence (AI) is developing and being incorporated into organizational structures, executives need to be fully aware of the implications of these technologies as well as the strategic opportunities they offer. In order to effectively provide well-informed assessments, implement AI applications in an efficient manner, and accurately estimate the significant effects of AI on organizational operations, it is imperative to cultivate a robust proficiency in AI leadership. This entails having the ability to identify, assess, and align possible artificial intelligence candidates with the organization's overarching objectives. Furthermore, developing a labor force with the capacity to pursue advanced training in artificial intelligence is increasingly crucial. According to Morandini et al. (2023), in order for employees to effectively adapt to the changes brought about by artificial intelligence (AI), it is imperative that they enhance their skill sets through upskilling and reskilling efforts. This emphasizes the necessity of having a broad range of skills and provides strategies that can be used to support and mentor individuals inside a company. In addition to technical proficiency, employees need to be able to effectively leverage the potential of artificial intelligence in order to provide creative solutions, improve customer experiences, and create sustainable competitive advantages. As artificial intelligence (AI) becomes more and more important for organizational success, leaders with the necessary skills are in a good position to take advantage of AI's potential, foster innovation, and guarantee long-term strategic sustainability in a changing environment. Artificial intelligence (AI) plays a critical role in decision-making, which leads to improved individual productivity, organizational performance, and the formation of corporate culture (Singh et al., 2023).

The capacity of a leader to accurately predict and effectively apply artificial intelligence (AI) is essential for driving innovation, enhancing customer experiences, and building long-term competitive advantages. Leaders in AI strategically take advantage of technological advancements to gain a competitive edge through automated tasks, intelligent suggestion generation, and predictive analysis (Wager, 2020). Accurate forecasting necessitates considering the possible influence of artificial intelligence (AI) on future advancements in consumer behavior, industrial trends, and technology advancements. By integrating AI technologies strategically, leaders can use artificial intelligence (AI) to foster innovation within their organizations. Artificial intelligence (AI) can be integrated by organizations into their innovation management processes, leading to improved commercial value outcomes (Füller et al., 2022). This can help leaders encourage the development of novel goods, services, and approaches. Through customized interactions, anticipatory client preferences, and pleasure enhancement, artificial intelligence (AI) may optimize customer experiences. Furthermore, well-executed execution plans guarantee the seamless integration of artificial intelligence (AI) into organizational processes, enhancing productivity and operational performance. Strategic leaders must be able to take use of technology, comprehend the financial effects of artificial intelligence, and effectively lead organizational change in order to create corporate and business plans that integrate artificial intelligence (AI) (Wagner, 2020). As such, this event makes it possible to achieve sustainable competitive advantages through maintaining a leading position in market trends, offering enhanced value to customers, and establishing the company as a pioneer in the era of artificial intelligence. Thus, the ability to drive and anticipate the application of AI is crucial for attaining organizational success in terms of innovation, customer experiences, and sustained competitiveness.

Effectiveness of Leadership and the Culture of the Entrepreneurial Organization

Developing an intrapreneurial culture that encourages innovation, flexibility, and proactive problem-solving can significantly increase a company's leadership effectiveness. By fostering better communication, inspiring others, and improving the work environment, effective leadership raises team and group performance (Lindsey, 2016). Intrapreneurial leadership is motivating people to think like entrepreneurs so they can actively look for novel ideas, weigh the pros and cons of taking calculated risks, and take the lead on projects that will help the company succeed. This approach not only promotes a consistent environment for growth, but it also enhances the organization's ability to adapt to changing conditions and capitalize on emerging opportunities. Leaders that use an intrapreneurial approach cultivate a work culture that prioritizes flexibility and determination by promoting the practice of gaining insights from failures and actively participating in experimenting. They establish a professional environment that promotes a positive perception of a conducive learning atmosphere, recognition of the significance of learning, and a helpful learning setting (Van Mourik et al., 2023). Leaders possess the ability to inspire people to question and disrupt existing norms, fostering an environment of creativity within a company, by promoting an intrapreneurial mindset. Leadership that is effective plays a crucial role in enhancing staff innovation by encouraging employee creativity and motivating innovative behavior (Kozioł-Nadolna, 2020). The organization's strategic positioning allows it to achieve long-term success in dynamic and competitive business environments.

Leaders play a vital role in successfully managing major changes in the nature of work and the underlying technologies by taking on the responsibilities of being visionaries, agents of change, and culture shapers. The presence of effective leadership plays a crucial role in effectively managing the various changes that arise in relation to individuals and operational procedures, thereby ensuring success in a fiercely competitive international economy (Basu, 2015). The individuals are assigned with the responsibility of comprehending the consequences that technology advancements will entail, providing guidance to their organizations during periods of change, and ensuring that teams can proficiently employ novel tools and methodologies. The scope of this leadership position extends beyond technological domains, encompassing the capacity to exert influence over essential aspects of the organization's culture and values. Leaders bear the responsibility of setting the discourse surrounding technical advancements and fostering a culture that highly values innovation, continuous learning, and adaptability. The individuals in question bear the duty of augmenting the acquisition of knowledge and fostering creativity among employees through the provision of assistance and the display of technical proficiency (Minh et al., 2017). Leaders play a crucial role in establishing a conducive climate that fosters individuals' empowerment to embrace change and actively contribute to the organization's achievements. This is achieved by aligning cultural elements with the ever-evolving nature of work. Ultimately, leaders play a crucial role in designing a complete and adaptable organizational culture that not only accepts technological advancements but also maintains the core values that shape the character of the company amidst ongoing transformations. The presence of effective leadership is crucial in the management of organizational change and the attainment of long-term success (Haruna, 2022). This particular cultural framework not only accommodates advancements in technology but also supports the core principles that define the organizational identity.

Variations in the Capabilities Needed to Lead Depending on Location

The impact of regional circumstances, particularly in Southeast Asia, significantly shapes the distinct proficiencies that leaders must possess. The region exhibits diverse leadership patterns that are not influenced by overarching institutional and structural issues. This suggests that leaders have a significant impact on transitional processes (Sulague et al., 2022).These proficiencies encompass technological, cognitive, social and emotional, and change management capabilities. The aforementioned influence is evident through the inclusion of change management as a core competency. Within the context of Southeast Asia's diverse and dynamic commercial environment, organizational executives face the challenging responsibility of effectively maneuvering through unique barriers that are influenced by cultural intricacies, varying levels of technological infrastructure, and specific market requirements. Corporate governance methods, such as reduced managerial ownership and more board independence, have a favorable effect on cash holdings and contribute to the alignment of interests inside organizations (Akhtar et al., 2020). In order to cultivate technological competencies, it is imperative to not only remain abreast of contemporary digital advancements, but also adapt them to suit specific geographical contexts. Technological competence encompasses the aptitude to acquire knowledge and skills in emerging technologies, as well as the capacity to adjust to technological advancements. This proficiency is crucial for mitigating inequality and sustaining competitiveness within the labor market (Puckett, 2022). In order to effectively understand and handle the intricacies of diverse marketplaces and customer behaviors, cognitive abilities play a crucial role. The establishment of meaningful connections and efficient cross-cultural communication necessitates a solid grounding in social and emotional competencies. Moreover, there is evidence to suggest that social-emotional competences exhibit variations among persons hailing from diverse cultural and national backgrounds (Kaur et al., 2022). In a geographical area characterized by swift economic growth and a diverse cultural landscape, the acquisition of change management competencies assumes paramount importance. Effective leadership necessitates adeptly guiding teams through periods of change, while also acknowledging and addressing the social and emotional aspects inherent in the process of change. The ability to adapt to rapid change and transition is of paramount importance for the success of companies (Janovac & Đoković, 2022). The utilization of the leadership grid model facilitates the identification of leaders' and managers' behavioral orientation, while the representation of the compromise management style may be achieved (Lei, 2022). In summary, it may be argued that leaders in Southeast Asia need a comprehensive range of talents that extend beyond mere technical expertise. The necessary skill set should encompass a deep understanding of the intricacies of the region, coupled with the ability to effectively lead via cultural acumen and flexibility.

Integration of Technical Abilities and Social Competences

Amidst the prevalent use of artificial intelligence, there is a significant reevaluation taking place regarding the conventional notion of effective leadership in the present era. The reappraisal is prompted by the recognition of the crucial requirement to integrate technology proficiency with interpersonal adaptability. Acquiring proficiency in comprehending the intricacies of artificial intelligence and making educated decisions necessitates a considerable degree of technical proficiency. Furthermore, the utilization of artificial intelligence (AI) in decision-making holds the capacity to diminish inequality and foster worldwide sustainable development. The assessment of fairness in AI decision-making might differ among persons, influenced by both the attributes of the AI system and the personal qualities of each individual (Loughlin & Copeland, 2021). Nevertheless, the capacity to effectively oversee various teams and establish an environment that fosters collaboration necessitates an equivalent degree of interpersonal aptitude. Indeed, CEOs possessing technological proficiency have the ability to foster innovation and effectively implement artificial intelligence (AI) technology in a strategic manner. Artificial intelligence (AI) has the capacity to profoundly transform goods, markets, and paradigms. Leaders that possess technical skills have the ability to successfully utilize this capability in order to promote innovation and strategic behavior inside their organizations (El Namaki, 2019). Nevertheless, it is their aptitude for effectively conveying information, motivating teams, and successfully managing the complexities of human reactions to change that ultimately enhances their effectiveness as leaders. In the modern age of artificial intelligence, exceptional leaders are recognized for their ability to combine technical proficiency with other qualities such as emotional intelligence, adaptability, and effective communication abilities. Leaders that exhibit high emotional intelligence are considered to be effective because they can effectively utilize their own and others' natural human skills. The importance of emotional intelligence in defining good leadership is well acknowledged (Drigas et al., 2023).This integration facilitates the efficient utilization of AI technology, while concurrently fostering a favorable corporate culture that prioritizes technological advancement and the human element. Consequently, it has the potential to completely transform conventional notions of effective leadership. This fusion successfully integrates both objectives.

Implications for Leaders in Their Daily Lives

Acknowledging leadership aptitude has significant implications for the real-world aspects of business, especially when it comes to fostering innovation, raising customer satisfaction, and gaining sustainable competitive advantages in the artificial intelligence (AI) space. Executives with a highly developed and specialised skill set specifically designed to meet the requirements of artificial intelligence are best positioned to strategically use AI technology to promote innovation inside their companies. Furthermore, it is imperative that businesses place a high value on the development of new talents in their workforce in addition to recruiting and retaining people with exceptional skill sets. Moreover, it is imperative to foster an intrapreneurial culture within the company and effectively manage the significant advancements in technology and shifts in labour dynamics (Watson et al., 2021). It also calls for the ability to plan ahead and carry out creative artificial intelligence (AI) projects, all the while fostering a culture that welcomes continuous innovation and development. Leaders that are proficient in utilising artificial intelligence (AI) to personalise experiences, do predictive analysis, and improve communication are better suited to satisfy the constantly evolving needs of their clientele. Consequently, this makes it possible to enhance user experiences. Maintaining sustainable competitive advantages also requires creating a staff with specialised understanding in artificial intelligence, implementing focused recruitment and retention strategies, and successfully executing change management procedures. The executives demonstrate sophisticated abilities that surpass fundamental technical proficiencies, as they place a high value on the deliberate integration of artificial intelligence into business processes and are able to align AI projects with more expansive corporate goals. In the end, this puts their businesses at the forefront of innovation, customer pleasure, and sustained competitiveness.

In order to strategically position themselves in a favourable way when faced with opportunities and challenges arising from artificial intelligence (AI), leaders must be able to consciously acquire and develop the essential talents. One of the main duties of people in leadership positions is to make continual learning a priority and to emphasise the need of keeping abreast of the most recent developments in artificial intelligence (AI). Furthermore, it is imperative that they engage in relevant training initiatives that are designed to advance their technical proficiency. Effective leaders possess the ability to adopt an adaptable and transparent viewpoint, which enables them to adeptly mentor their groups through the always evolving field of artificial intelligence (AI). Developing a "innovation culture" within the company makes it possible to test theories and find possible uses for artificial intelligence (AI). Additionally, CEOs possess the ability to actively engage in strategic workforce development initiatives, prioritising the improvement of employees' proficiency in AI-related skills. Strong communication skills are essential for effectively communicating the benefits of artificial intelligence to a diverse group of stakeholders and gaining their support. To cultivate a perception of being forward-thinking, flexible, and skilled in navigating the age of artificial intelligence, leaders might present themselves as actively supporting a seamless fusion of technical expertise and interpersonal abilities. This situates them in a favorable position to leverage the capabilities of artificial intelligence in order to achieve success inside their respective enterprises.

IMPLICATIONS FOR THE THEORY

The idea of transformational leadership prioritizes the promotion of motivation and inspiration among followers, with the aim of fostering optimal performance and surpassing individual goals. This particular leadership approach places a significant emphasis on fostering robust interpersonal connections, cultivating trust, and promoting intellectual advancement within the team (Alamri, 2023). Transformational leadership is characterized by several key attributes, including the capacity to adeptly adapt to change, cultivate creativity and innovation, and develop a compelling vision for the future of the organization.

Transformational leadership refers to an individual's capacity to inspire and empower their followers, enabling them to exceed their expected performance and achieve exceptional results (Maini, 2022). The leadership style under consideration goes beyond the mere management of daily operations. The process entails developing an inspiring vision that drives and energizes employees, fostering a shared sense of purpose, and fostering innovation and creativity inside the firm (Gloria et al., 2023). The ability to articulate a compelling vision, foster passion and commitment among team members, and motivate individuals to realise their full potential are characteristics of a transformational leader. The notion that transformational leadership has a positive and notable influence on a number of variables, such as employee performance, intrinsic motivation, organisational citizenship behaviour (OCB), and innovative behaviour, has been empirically supported by previous research (Farheen et al., 2023). The fundamental characteristics that define a transformational leader are as follows. These employees often exhibit qualities like charm, intellectual curiosity, individualised care, and a strong commitment to fostering a great workplace atmosphere. Transformational leaders have the ability to inspire and enable their followers to put the benefit of the group ahead of their own interests, while also encouraging originality and innovation in their followers (Farheen et al., 2023). Individuals possess the capacity to establish robust connections with their teammates, foster a foundation of confidence, and inspire them to attain optimal output (Wardana & Anisah, 2023). This method makes it possible for firms to convert and guarantees their long-term success going forward.

Thinking With a Vision and Having Strategic Foresight

This essay highlights the need for leaders in the artificial intelligence era to have a thorough understanding of AI technology and the possible consequences associated with its implementation. Forward-thinking and creative thinking are skills that transformational leaders possess, and they are excellent at persuading others with a compelling future vision. They are able to predict how artificial intelligence (AI) may affect current market trends, consumer behavior, and the development of new technologies. The purposeful application of artificial intelligence (AI) stimulates innovation and propels the development of new goods, services, and protocols. Artificial intelligence (AI) can improve consumer experiences, streamline supply chain operations, enable data-driven decision-making, and automate a variety of tasks (Goto, 2023). In the present era of artificial intelligence (AI), transformational leaders are motivated to create a compelling vision for their organizations. Socio-technical work systems have been significantly impacted by the broad adoption and deployment of artificial intelligence (AI), underscoring the critical role that leaders and leadership play in effectively integrating and using AI technology (Peifer et al., 2022). They want to empower their teams to not only embrace technological advancements but also perceive them as avenues for progress, rather than perceiving them as potential threats. This objective can be achieved by effectively communicating a persuasive vision for their organizations. Effective communication of an organization's vision by leaders is crucial in fostering commitment and inspiring individuals to comprehend, retain, and disseminate said vision (Cartwright & Baldwin, 2007).

Capacity for Adaptation and Resilience

It is imperative for leaders to possess the qualities of adaptability and resilience in order to flourish among the perpetual flux and adversities (Pierog, 2023). Transformational leaders thrive in dynamic workplaces characterized by frequent changes, effectively motivating their subordinates to embrace emerging technologies and adjust to evolving circumstances. This article underscores the necessity for leaders to effectively navigate the challenges associated with the utilization of artificial intelligence (AI), with transformational leaders exhibiting a strong aptitude for managing these intricate issues. The paper additionally emphasizes the necessity for leaders to effectively handle the hurdles associated with the use of artificial intelligence. Transformational leaders demonstrate resilience through adapting their leadership styles to incorporate artificial intelligence, fostering a culture of ongoing learning, and promoting flexibility among team members. Transformational leaders have the capacity to proficiently handle resistance to change through skillfully communicating the advantages of change, developing a culture that fosters innovation, and addressing concerns in a compassionate manner. Employees who exhibit higher levels of job engagement and task performance are more likely to be influenced by leaders who possess transformational leadership qualities (Chao, 2023).

Culture Inside the Intrapreneurial Space

Santana and Dáz-Fernández (2023) assert that leaders bear the obligation of fostering an intrapreneurial culture. The cultivation of an innovative culture inside a company is facilitated by the presence of transformational leaders (Sueb & Sopiah, 2023). Employees are granted the autonomy to explore innovative concepts, undertake suitable risks, and spearhead activities that foster the expansion of the organization. This approach aligns with the notion of "intrapreneurial leaders," as expounded upon in the aforementioned article. Transformational leaders play a crucial role in fostering the intrapreneurial attitude among individuals within an organization. They actively encourage employees to engage in calculated risk-taking, explore the potential of artificial intelligence solutions, and make entrepreneurial contributions that add to the overall success of the firm.

Bringing Together Your Technical and Interpersonal Abilities

Eddy (2012) posits that successful leadership in the age of artificial intelligence necessitates a fusion of technical expertise and interpersonal skills. Transformational leaders possess an abundance of both of these characteristics. Furthermore, individuals possessing the requisite technical proficiency to comprehend artificial intelligence (AI) technology also exhibit exceptional interpersonal abilities, facilitating effective communication, motivation, and adept negotiation of the human dimensions associated with transformative change. These individuals possess the ability to engage in critical evaluation of digital technologies, demonstrate strong collaboration skills, and effectively employ artificial intelligence as a tool in many contexts (Weiss et al., 2022). Transformational leaders have exceptional proficiency in integrating technological expertise with emotional intelligence, so guaranteeing effective dissemination of advancements in artificial intelligence and prioritizing human considerations during the implementation phase.

Learning New Things Constantly and Making Progress

This essay highlights two practical consequences for company executives, namely the importance of fostering a culture of innovation and the need for continual education. Leaders who possess the capability to effectuate organizational transformation are those who consistently engage in self-education throughout their professional journeys and encourage their subordinates to do the same. These leaders prioritize the enhancement of organizational learning and the cultivation of creativity, skills, innovation, and capacities among their organizational members (Mohamed & Otman, 2021). The organization cultivates a cultural milieu that highly esteems the pursuit of ongoing enhancement and experimentation, in accordance with the ever-evolving attributes of artificial intelligence. The influence of transformational leaders in the modern digital environment is noteworthy, especially considering the incorporation of Artificial Intelligence (AI) (Munir et al., 2023). Transformational leaders have a profound dedication to their personal and professional growth, continually pursuing avenues to augment their understanding and proficiency in the realm of artificial intelligence (AI). Furthermore, they deliberately foster a culture that prioritizes ongoing learning among their teams, placing significant emphasis on the importance of lifelong education. According to Wardana and Anisah (2023), the firm cultivates a cultural environment that encourages employee initiative, stimulates innovative thinking, and embraces risk-taking as means to achieve corporate goals. The continuous development of knowledge and skills is a basic characteristic of transformative leadership. Transformational leaders are those who demonstrate a profound dedication to their personal and professional growth, actively pursuing fresh insights and alternative perspectives. Leaders who possess the ability to effect organizational change demonstrate a significant degree of proficiency in fostering an environment that encourages innovation among their staff. The leaders consistently communicate forward-thinking visions in order to invigorate the group and demonstrate a strong sense of determination and eagerness in their convictions. According to Bush (2018), this phenomenon has the potential to stimulate the followers to adopt the leader's vision and participate in activities that surpass their designated responsibilities. The organization fosters an environment that promotes creative thinking, a propensity for experimentation, and a dedication to ongoing development, all of which are important for effectively responding to evolving conditions. Transformational leaders not only prioritize their own education but also motivate and inspire team members to engage in ongoing education and personal development. A vital attribute exhibited by transformational leaders is their unwavering commitment to their personal and professional development. The organization prioritizes personal growth and fosters a similar level of commitment among its team members.

Variations by Region and the Importance of Contextual Leadership

This paper acknowledges the influence of regional circumstances on an individual's capacity to exert leadership. Transformational leaders acknowledge the significance of contextual knowledge and possess the ability to adapt their leadership style to accommodate diverse geographical settings. The individuals possess an understanding of the importance of engaging in negotiations within diverse marketplaces, developing the requisite social and emotional aptitudes for effective cross-cultural collaboration, and adjusting their technological proficiencies to suit the unique contexts of different locations. The attribute of flexibility holds significant importance for transformational leaders as it empowers them to modify their methods in accordance with the distinct challenges and prospects presented by diverse regional settings. Additionally, there is empirical data supporting the notion that transformational leadership has a positive influence on employees' inclination to participate in innovative work behavior. The aforementioned effect is impacted to some degree by psychological capital attributes, specifically hope and self-efficacy (Madi Odeh et al., 2023). Transformational leaders demonstrate a significant level of proficiency in promoting collaboration among heterogeneous groups. This is accomplished by leveraging their social and emotional aptitudes to cultivate interpersonal relationships and surpass cultural obstacles. Transformational leaders exhibit remarkable proficiency in adapting their technical expertise to effectively meet the distinct technology frameworks and demands of their specific circumstances. Gaining insight into the distinct attributes inherent to each setting is an essential element of contextual intelligence. Transformational leaders exhibit their aptitude for effectively adapting to various situations by recognizing the significance of contextual factors and showcasing their remarkable skills. Transformational leaders are incredibly flexible, which enables them to adjust their strategies to suit the different opportunities and difficulties that arise from different local circumstances. The individuals skillfully apply their abilities to cultivate a collaborative and inclusive work environment by building rapport with colleagues and overcoming cultural differences. Within the scope of transformative leadership, cooperation is crucial. This type of leadership is characterized by a leader's active encouragement of cooperation and creation of an atmosphere that facilitates productive teamwork among members. One of the most important traits for leaders who drive major change is the ability to quickly adapt to changing technical settings. The organization makes certain that its technological expertise is customized to meet the unique needs of various industries.

Integration of AI in a Strategic Manner

Baki et al.'s (2023) research on organizations highlights the necessity of exhibiting fundamental AI abilities. It is the responsibility of transformational leaders to link AI initiatives with the organization's overarching objectives. It is critical to evaluate the attitudes and degree of involvement that managers demonstrate during the implementation phase because, according to research, line managers are less likely than senior executives in the organization to be receptive to artificial intelligence (AI) (Kolbjørnsrud et al., 2017). The organization ensures the intentional integration of artificial intelligence (AI) into its processes, fortifying its enduring competitive edge. It is often known that strategic thinking is an essential quality of transformative leadership. Leaders that employ this methodology demonstrate proficiency in formulating and implementing tactics that result in enduring accomplishments. In order to successfully integrate artificial intelligence, one must have a thorough understanding of its implications, forecast its impact on the market in advance, and use it skillfully to gain a competitive advantage. It is crucial to have a deep comprehension of the elements that improve artificial intelligence's (AI) effectiveness in a business's strategy (Niet et al., 2023). The above qualities are necessary to achieve effective strategic integration and are intrinsically linked to transformational leadership. Leaders that possess the capacity to bring about significant changes within organizations are acknowledged for their proficiency in inspiring and guiding others towards a common objective. It is essential to have a leader who can successfully articulate a compelling vision and ensure that technological advancements directly support the strategic goals of the company in order to ensure that AI efforts are in line with organizational objectives. To further promote employee openness to the adoption of technology, the leader must demonstrate a strategic leadership mentality, skillful communication, and tenacity (Vlok et al., 2019). Organizational transformation leaders prioritize the organization's long-term survival and prosperity in addition to its immediate accomplishments. The individuals in question have exhibited their commitment to ensuring the enduring prosperity of the organization by strategically leveraging artificial intelligence as a means to attain a competitive edge. One of the distinguishing attributes of transformational leaders is their ability to inspire and guide individuals towards achieving shared goals. The aforementioned leaders are capable of attaining this outcome by the exhibition of attributes such as idealized influence, inspirational motivation, intellectual stimulation, and individualized consideration (Ahmed & Amiri, 2022). In the context of artificial intelligence (AI), it is imperative to motivate teams to comprehend the strategic significance of AI initiatives and establish a connection between their endeavors and the broader objectives of the organization. Transformational leaders possess a notable proficiency in effectively leading change. The individuals demonstrate a cognizance of the significance of organizational change and exhibit proficient leadership skills in guiding their teams through the various stages of the change process. Within the realm of artificial intelligence, this involves the alteration of preexisting methodologies and the fostering of an environment that embraces novel technological advancements.

In summary, the essay's emphasis on leadership attributes within a period characterized by artificial intelligence holds significance within the context of the Transformational Leadership theory, as expounded upon in the aforementioned article. The theory's emphasis on visionary thinking, adaptability, fostering creativity, and integrating technical and interpersonal skills is very congruent with the challenges and possibilities arising from the incorporation of artificial intelligence (AI) into organizational workflows.

LIMITATIONS, THE CONCLUSION, AND THE PATH FORWARD FOR FUTURE RESEARCH

This study has the potential to generalize leadership abilities to a wide range of organizational settings and economic sectors. Factors including the size and nature of the company as well as the challenges it faces might affect how effective a leader is. A more focused analysis inside a particular sector may contribute to a more comprehensive understanding of the situation. The research study lacks comprehensive empirical evidence or case studies that directly substantiate the claimed leadership traits. In order to enhance the credibility of the required abilities, it would be beneficial to take a more empirical approach and include real-world examples, in addition to referring other authors and studies. The research findings suggest that rapid technological advancements, particularly in the field of artificial intelligence (AI), may render emphasized talents obsolete within a little timeframe. The study would greatly benefit from conducting a comprehensive review of how cultural factors impact the efficacy of leadership techniques in the realm of artificial intelligence. Studying the notable differences in leadership styles and skills among other cultures could improve our understanding. The main objective of this research is to highlight the beneficial qualities of leadership skills in the realm of artificial intelligence (AI). Conducting an examination of any negative outcomes or difficulties linked to the proposed skills would be advantageous. Several instances of these could encompass ethical considerations, concerns regarding privacy, or inadvertent consequences arising from the integration of artificial intelligence. The skills that have been suggested prioritize a considerable emphasis on an individual's technical proficiencies. While possessing technical proficiency is undeniably essential, effective leadership also necessitates the possession of softer skills, like the capacity to make ethical judgments, demonstrate empathy towards others, and communicate proficiently. Enhancing the comprehensiveness of the competences could potentially be achieved through the implementation of a plan that assigns equal importance to both technical and interpersonal proficiencies. One aspect of the study focuses on Southeast Asia, while the entire geographical scope is fairly limited. In addition to Southeast Asia, variations in geography can exert influence on an individual's leadership capabilities. A more comprehensive understanding of leadership in diverse global contexts can be achieved through the implementation of a more extensive study.

Future study should prioritize the implementation of longitudinal studies in order to observe the progression of leadership competencies over an extended period, specifically in the context of ongoing integration of artificial intelligence. This particular study methodology may track the evolution of organizational cultures, decision-making procedures, and leadership styles in tandem with the advancement of AI technology. This study aims to shed light on the resilience and adaptability of leadership qualities in the face of continuous technological advancements. Future research should use an approach that looks into how cultural variations affect how effective leadership abilities are when utilizing AI. It is imperative to prioritize a complete analysis of leadership techniques in various nations, taking into consideration the nuances of cultural norms, in order to fully appreciate the global acknowledgment of artificial intelligence (AI)-based leadership talents. Future scholarly research has a lot of opportunity to examine how artificial intelligence affects organizational hierarchies and structures. In a particular field of study, our research attempts to investigate the emergence of new leadership roles, the potential reduction of hierarchical structures, and modifications to reporting techniques. To increase productivity and foster innovation, CEOs ought to think about reorganizing their companies to take use of artificial intelligence's (AI) inherent advantages. The purpose of this study is to examine the moral ramifications of leadership in artificial intelligence-enabled businesses. The purpose of this study is to examine the strategies leaders have employed to address ethical conundrums brought about by the widespread usage of artificial intelligence (AI), including algorithmic prejudice, privacy concerns, and responsible AI use. Developing customized ethical leadership frameworks for artificial intelligence (AI) can enhance companies' sustainable and ethical business operations. Future research endeavors may find these phenomena to be fascinating topics for investigation. Examining how AI integration affects workers' psychological health and job satisfaction is another important subject. The purpose of this research is to examine how leadership qualities affect the development of productive workplaces in the rapidly developing field of artificial intelligence. In AI-driven companies, developing effective leadership requires addressing job displacement concerns, putting knowledge-leveling tactics into practice, and placing a high priority on maintaining a healthy work-life balance.

"Leadership Competencies for the Age of Artificial Intelligence," a research paper, offers a thorough and perceptive examination of the changing responsibilities and roles of leaders in the current era, which is marked by the incorporation of artificial intelligence (AI) into organizational structures. The study emphasizes how crucial it is for leaders to have a broad variety of competencies, including both a thorough understanding of AI technology and conventional leadership traits. Because of the significant influence of the current technological revolution, acquiring this expertise is imperative.

The findings highlight how important it is for leaders to have essential abilities that can be flexible enough to fulfil the unique requirements of AI leadership. To effectively integrate artificial intelligence, one needs to possess the requisite technical capabilities and be able to align AI initiatives with business objectives. In order to improve customer experiences and sustain competitive advantages, the paper emphasizes the critical role that leaders play in proactively predicting the effects of artificial intelligence (AI), strategically implementing it into operational processes, and fostering innovation.

The adoption of an intrapreneurial culture adds a new perspective to the field of effective leadership by highlighting the influence of artificial intelligence (AI) on the core characteristics of companies. In addition to being accountable for adjusting to new technology, leadership is essential for stimulating creativity, skillfully handling opposition to change, and aggressively encouraging experimentation inside the framework of the company.

The research highlights how important it is to implement structural changes at the organizational level. In order for businesses to effectively benefit from artificial intelligence (AI), they need to have certain core competencies, such as digital proficiency and modern HR practices. The results of the study show that employing artificial intelligence effectively calls for more than simply human leadership abilities. It calls for a comprehensive reorganization of the whole company.

The scientific research emphasizes how crucial it is for leaders to adapt their skills to different business, technological, and cultural contexts. The study acknowledges the existence of regional disparities, especially in Southeast Asia, and emphasizes how critical it is to modify leadership techniques to fit these unique situations. Possessing a broad range of skills that extend beyond fundamental technical knowledge is essential, since the effectiveness of leadership relies on the specific circumstances and environment in which it is used.

Artificial intelligence (AI) is developing at a rapid pace, and the combination of technology and interpersonal skills as a redesigned foundation for effective leadership corresponds with this. Prominent figures in leadership are questioning the conventional wisdom of leadership, which primarily emphasizes technical proficiency. These leaders skillfully blend emotional intelligence, flexibility, good communication, creative thinking, and technical proficiency.

This research delves into the concrete results of artificial intelligence in the modern day, offering CEOs targeted tactics to foster creativity, enhance consumer satisfaction, and secure sustainable competitive advantages. People who are highly skilled at using artificial intelligence (AI) to propel their organizations' success are viewed as leaders. They accomplish this by placing a high value on lifelong learning, adaptability, and the promotion of a creative culture. For CEOs facing the opportunities and difficulties of the artificial intelligence era, this study report is an invaluable resource.

In order to thrive in the quickly changing 21st-century landscape, leaders can fortify their position by actively fostering and strengthening the attributes associated with successful leadership. People will be able to seize new chances as a result. This study provides a wide range of insights and suggestions that improve our knowledge of leadership in the age of artificial intelligence. The conclusions and suggestions given above highlight the complex interplay between technical expertise and social graces.

REFERENCES

Ahmed, G., & Amiri, N. A.Nabeel Al Amiri. (2022). The transformational leadership of the founding leaders of the united arab emirates: Sheikh zayed bin sultan al nahyan and sheikh rashid bin saeed al maktoum. *International Journal of Technology* [IJTIM]. *Innovation and Management*, *2*(1). doi:10.54489/ijtim.v2i1.58

Akhtar, T., Tareq, M. A., & Rashid, K. (2020). Chief Executive Officers' monitoring, board effectiveness, managerial ownership, and cash holdings: Evidence from ASEAN. *Review of Managerial Science*. doi:10.1007/s11846-020-00421-0

Alamri, M. (2023). Transformational leadership and work engagement in public organizations: Promotion focus and public service motivation, how and when the effect occurs. *Leadership and Organization Development Journal*, *44*(1), 137–155. 137-155.doi.org/10.1108/LODJ-12-2021-0544. doi:10.1108/LODJ-12-2021-0544

Basu, K. K. (2015). The Leader's Role in Managing Change: Five Cases of Technology-Enabled Business Transformation. *Global Business and Organizational Excellence*, *34*(3), 28–42. doi:10.1002/joe.21602

Bush, T. (2018). Transformational leadership. *Educational Management Administration & Leadership*, *46*(6), 883–887. doi:10.1177/1741143218795731

Cartwright, T., & Baldwin, D. (2007). Seeing your way: Why leaders must communicate their visions. *Leadership in Action*, *27*(3), 15–24. doi:10.1002/lia.1208

Chao, W. (2023). A Study of Transformational Leadership Behavior and Employee Performance in Chinese Futures Firms. *International Journal of Science and Business*, *23*(1), 22–37. doi:10.58970/IJSB.2132

Drigas, A., Papoutsi, C., & Skianis, C. (2023). Being an Emotionally Intelligent Leader through the Nine-Layer Model of Emotional Intelligence—The Supporting Role of New Technologies. *Sustainability (Basel)*, *15*(10), 8103. doi:10.3390/su15108103

El Namaki, M. S. S. (2019). Will Artificial Intelligence Change Strategic Top Management Competencies. *SCHOLEDGE International Journal of Management & Development*, *6*(4), 34. 34-doi.org/10.19085/journal.sijmd060401. doi:10.19085/journal.sijmd060401

Farheen, N., Rabie, O., Hussain, T., & Rehmani, M. (2023). Transformational Leadership, Knowledge Sharing and Innovative Behavior of Employees in Information Technology Industry of Pakistan. *Review of Applied Management and Social Sciences*, *6*(1), 29–43. doi:10.47067/ramss.v6i1.287

Füller, J., Hutter, K., Wahl, J., Bilgram, V., & Tekic, Z. (2022). How AI revolutionizes innovation management–Perceptions and implementation preferences of AI-based innovators. *Technological Forecasting and Social Change*, *178*, 121598. doi:10.1016/j.techfore.2022.121598

Gloria, T. J., Michael, M., & Joyce, K. (2023). The Moderating Effect of Transformational Leadership on the Relationship Between Entrepreneurial Orientation and Performance of Manufacturing Firms in Nairobi County. *International Journal of Entrepreneurship and Business Innovation.*, *6*(1), 68–86. doi:10.52589/IJEBI-8DKOT4CX

Goto, M. (2023). Anticipatory innovation of professional services: The case of auditing and artificial intelligence. *Research Policy*, *52*(8), 104828. doi:10.1016/j.respol.2023.104828

Haruna, J. B. (2022). The Role of Leadership on Organizational Change. [IJRASET]. *International Journal for Research in Applied Science and Engineering Technology*, *10*(10), 249–254. doi:10.22214/ijraset.2022.46978

Janovac, T. D., & Đoković, G. (2022). The application of the "leadership grid" model: Case study of human resources sector in the ministry of internal affairs of serbia. *KULTURA POLISA*, *19*(4), 27–45. doi:10.51738/Kpolisa2022.19.4r.27jdj

Kaur, S., Ayana, T., & Kaur, H. (2022). Assessing Social and Emotional Competencies of Undergraduates: A Cross-Cultural Study. *Issues and Ideas in Education*, *9*(2), 75–83. doi:10.15415/iie.2021.92007

Kolbjørnsrud, V., Amico, R., & Thomas, R. J. (2017). Partnering with AI: How organizations can win over skeptical managers. *Strategy and Leadership*, *45*(1), 37–43. doi:10.1108/SL-12-2016-0085

Kozioł-Nadolna, K. (2020). The role of a leader in stimulating innovation in an organization. *Administrative Sciences*, *10*(3), 59. doi:10.3390/admsci10030059

Lei, J. (2022). On the effective representation of teachers' leadership role from the change of children's emotional behavior in language learning. *The International Journal of Neuropsychopharmacology*, *25*(Supplement_1), A59–A60. doi:10.1093/ijnp/pyac032.082

Lindsey, J. L. (2016). How Can Leaders Cultivate an Organizational Culture of Creativity and Innovation, Particularly in the Academy? *Journal of Leadership Studies*, *10*(1), 76–77. doi:10.1002/jls.21454

Loughlin, M., & Copeland, S. M. (2021). Humans, machines and decisions: Clinical reasoning in the age of artificial intelligence, evidence-based medicine and Covid-19. *Journal of Evaluation in Clinical Practice*, *27*(3), 475–477. doi:10.1111/jep.13572 PMID:33890703

Madi Odeh, R. B. S., Obeidat, B. Y., Jaradat, M. O., Masa'deh, R., & Alshurideh, M. T. (2023). The transformational leadership role in achieving organizational resilience through adaptive cultures: The case of Dubai service sector. *International Journal of Productivity and Performance Management*, *72*(2), 440–468. doi:10.1108/IJPPM-02-2021-0093

Maini, S. (2022). Leadership Transformation in Changing Times. *International Journal for Global Academic & Scientific Research, 1*(4), 48–59. doi:10.55938/ijgasr.v1i4.29

Milton, J., & Al-Busaidi, A. (2023). New Role of Leadership in AI Era: Educational Sector. In *SHS Web of Conferences* (*Vol. 156*, p. 09005). EDP Sciences. 10.1051/shsconf/202315609005

Minh, N. V., Badir, Y. F., Quang, N. N., & Afsar, B. (2017). The impact of leaders' technical competence on employees' innovation and learning. *Journal of Engineering and Technology Management*, *44*, 44–57. doi:10.1016/j.jengtecman.2017.03.003

Mohamed, I. A., & Otman, N. M. M. (2021). Exploring the link between organizational learning and transformational leadership: A review. *OAlib*, *8*(5), 1–19. doi:10.4236/oalib.1107242

Morandini, S., Fedrico, F., De Angelis, M., Puzzo, G., Giusino, D., & Pietrantoni, L. (2023). The impact of artificial intelligence on workers' skills: Upskilling and reskilling in organisations. *Informing Science*, *26*, 39–68. doi:10.28945/5078

Mumford, M. D., Todd, E. M., Higgs, C., & McIntosh, T. (2017). Cognitive skills and leadership performance: The nine critical skills. *The Leadership Quarterly*, *28*(1), 24–39. doi:10.1016/j.leaqua.2016.10.012

Munir, S., Shakeel, M., & Waheed, K. Z. (2023). The Importance of Emotional Intelligence for Transformational Leaders: A Critical Analysis. *Pakistan Journal of Humanities and Social Sciences*, *11*(1), 332–339. doi:10.52131/pjhss.2023.1101.0353

Niet, I., Van den Berghe, L., & van Est, R. (2023). Societal impacts of AI integration in the EU electricity market: The Dutch case. *Technological Forecasting and Social Change*, *192*, 122554. doi:10.1016/j.techfore.2023.122554

Pearce, J. M. (2018). Ensuring technical competency for management of research-focused organizations. *The Journal of High Technology Management Research*, *29*(2), 172–180. doi:10.1016/j.hitech.2018.09.002

Peifer, Y., Jeske, T., & Hille, S. (2022). Artificial intelligence and its impact on leaders and leadership. *Procedia Computer Science*, *200*, 1024–1030. doi:10.1016/j.procs.2022.01.301

Pendleton, D., Derbyshire, P., & Hodgkinson, C. (2021). Leadership in the Fourth Industrial Age. In *Work-Life Matters* (pp. 125–141). Palgrave Macmillan., doi:10.1007/978-3-030-77768-5_9

Pierog, A. (2023). Instead of competencies, leadership qualities are a new direction in leadership development. *GiLE Journal of Skills Development*, *3*(1), 3–6. doi:10.52398/gjsd.2023.v3.i1.pp3-6

Puckett, C. (2022). Digital Adaptability: A new measure for digital inequality research. *Social Science Computer Review*, *40*(3), 641–662. doi:10.1177/0894439320926087

Singh, S., Thakur, P., & Singh, S. (2023). How Does the Use of AI in HRM Contribute to Improved Business Performance?: A Systematic Review. In N. Sharma & K. Shalender (Eds.), *Managing Technology Integration for Human Resources in Industry 5.0* (pp. 131–139). IGI Global. doi:10.4018/978-1-6684-6745-9.ch008

Sueb, S., & Sopiah, S. (2023). Exploring the Relationship between Transformational Leadership and Innovative Work Behavior: A Systematic Literature Review. *Jurnal Visi Manajemen*, *9*(2), 62–83. doi:10.56910/jvm.v9i2.287

Sulague, R. M., Lim, X., Baticulon, R. E., & Kpodonu, J. (2022). Southeast Asia must invest in strengthening surgical systems. *Journal of Global Health*, *12*, 03090. doi:10.7189/jogh.12.03090 PMID:36579398

Tang, O. Y., Ali, R., Connolly, I. D., Fridley, J. S., Sullivan, P. L. Z., Cielo, D., & Asaad, W. F. (2023). The Urgency of Neurosurgical Leadership in the Era of Artificial Intelligence. *Neurosurgery*, *93*(3), 69–70. doi:10.1227/neu.0000000000002576 PMID:37319400

Tomašević, A. N. (2023). Reshaping the future of work: Navigating the impacts of lifelong learning and digital competences in the era of 5.0 industry. *Social Informatics Journal*, *2*(1), 1–6. doi:10.58898/sij.v2i1.01-06

Van Mourik, O., Grohnert, T., & Gold, A. (2023). Mitigating work conditions that can inhibit learning from errors: Benefits of error management climate perceptions. *Frontiers in Psychology*, *14*, 1033470. doi:10.3389/fpsyg.2023.1033470 PMID:36743251

Vasudevan, H (2022). Management and Leadership in the Klang Valley IT Sector: Conceptual Approach. *Marketing and management of innovation, 3*, 56-65. doi:10.21272/mmi.2022.3-05

Vlok, A., Ungerer, M., & Malan, J. (2019). Integrative leadership for technology innovation. *International Journal of Technology Management*, *79*(3/4), 247. doi:10.1504/IJTM.2019.099608

Wagner, D. N. (2020). Strategically managing the artificially intelligent firm. *Strategy and Leadership*, *48*(3), 19–25. doi:10.1108/SL-08-2019-0119

Wardana, A. P., & Anisah, H. U. (2023). The Influence of Transformational Leadership on Employee Performance Through Intrinsic Motivation and Organizational Citizenship Behavior as Intervening Variables: Study at the High Religious Court of Jakarta Indonesia. *Open Access Indonesia Journal of Social Sciences*, *6*(5), 1129–1141. doi:10.37275/oaijss.v6i5.182

Watson, G. J., Desouza, K. C., Ribiere, V. M., & Lindič, J. (2021). Will AI ever sit at the C-suite table? The future of senior leadership. *Business Horizons*, *64*(4), 465–474. doi:10.1016/j.bushor.2021.02.011

Weiss, D., Liu, S. X., Mieczkowski, H., & Hancock, J. T. (2022). Effects of using artificial intelligence on interpersonal perceptions of job applicants. *Cyberpsychology, Behavior, and Social Networking*, *25*(3), 163–168. doi:10.1089/cyber.2020.0863 PMID:35021895

Chapter 3
Philosophical and Psychological Dimensions of AI Integration in Sustainable Business Development

Kaniz Kakon
https://orcid.org/0000-0001-7147-9424
University of South-Eastern Norway, Norway

ABSTRACT

This chapter critically explores how sustainable business development and artificial intelligence (AI) converge, examining their synergy, opportunities, and ethical challenges. It highlights the parallel growth of sustainable business and AI's impact on consumer behavior, emphasizing the crucial need to adeptly manage AI's functions and ethics in corporate solutions. It delves into diverse ethical frameworks and explores their guidance for integrating AI responsibly, aiming for sustainability and broader societal welfare. Additionally, it delves into Confucian ethics, organizational psychology, and leadership principles, uncovering human potential in the AI era. It advocates merging philosophy, psychology, and sustainable business practices to foster ethically sound and psychologically attuned AI systems for corporate use.

INTRODUCTION

The 21st-century landscape witnesses the ascendancy of Sustainable Business Development as a cornerstone embraced by multinational corporations on a global scale. This paradigm, intricately woven into operational frameworks, catalyzes innovation while aligning seamlessly with contemporary business imperatives. Rooted in the legacy of the United Nations' Rio Earth Summit of 1992, Sustainable Business Development pivots on the imperative of curbing environmental degradation and meticulously oversees the entirety of the value chain, instilling a resolute commitment to sustainability (Rainey, 2009). In contrast, the contemporary technological milieu, featuring Artificial Intelligence (AI), machine learning, the

DOI: 10.4018/979-8-3693-1842-3.ch003

Internet of Things (IoT), and blockchain, presents a transformative narrative in understanding consumer behavior and amplifying marketing impact across diverse sectors such as retail, luxury markets, and media. The assimilation of AI hinges upon cultural, skill-based, and linguistic parameters, fundamentally reshaping the landscape of business-consumer dynamics into a competitive sphere founded upon trust in technological innovations. Despite persistent challenges, particularly surrounding consumer trust in AI-driven chatbots, empirical studies underscore the positive impact of AI on social media and conversion rates (Sadiku et al., 2021). The optimization of outcomes emerges from the fusion of human ingenuity and AI's logical prowess, with AI excelling in logic-driven content, while the indispensable human touch retains its significance in crafting emotionally resonant content (Maican et al., 2023).

Mastery over stakeholder aspirations, nuanced understanding of AI functionalities, and cultural intricacies become imperative in devising efficacious AI-powered business solutions, notably within the realm of social media marketing. By accounting for socio-cultural variables, advancements in AI hold the potential to significantly augment marketing strategies, elevate customer experiences, and redefine client engagement paradigms (Ameen et al., 2022). The meteoric rise of AI not only forecasts economic prosperity but also provokes profound ethical and policy inquiries. A fundamental prerequisite for the conscientious development of AI lies in the establishment of robust ethical standards, tethering its progression to justifiable frameworks. As AI permeates diverse sectors, addressing ethical dilemmas gains precedence, necessitating grounding in human rights and legal considerations. While AI's evolution reshapes human-machine interactions and decision-making capabilities, it invokes profound philosophical and psychological contemplations (Hossain et al., 2022; Marvin et al., 2023; Asikullah et al., 2024; Nadi et al., 2023; Ushie et al., 2023; Faisal et al., 2023; Hossain et al., 2021; Hossain et al., 2022a). The rapid trajectory of AI underscores the imperative of harnessing its potential for societal advancement, underscoring the importance of stakeholders' acumen regarding the latest AI advancements. This chapter embarks on a comprehensive analysis of the philosophical and psychological underpinnings inherent in integrating AI within the framework of sustainable business development.

PHILOSOPHICAL PRACTICALITIES OF AI INTEGRATION

The integration of Artificial Intelligence (AI) stands as an indispensable facet within contemporary business operations, offering unparalleled potential for efficiency and innovation. However, the pervasive adoption of this technology underscores the pressing need for a comprehensive framework aligning AI applications with sustained corporate growth. Businesses face an imperative not only to harness AI's capabilities but to do so in a manner that aligns with ethical and societal responsibilities. Philosophical frameworks serve as fundamental tools for examining, interrogating, and formulating the ethical principles and societal commitments that shape human interactions and communal well-being. Consequently, the nexus between business ethics and philosophy emerges as the former relies on philosophical precepts to ascertain ethical behaviors, steering decision-making processes within corporate environments. A profound comprehension of the legal and ethical dimensions accompanying AI utilization emerges as a pivotal stride toward this objective. By navigating these considerations, enterprises not only ensure compliance with regulatory standards but also exhibit a steadfast commitment to responsible AI implementation, thereby bolstering the broader tenets of sustainable business development. Such an approach not only cultivates trust among stakeholders but also positions the company as a vanguard in the integration of cutting-edge technology, while concurrently upholding ethical values and long-term sustainability.

The assessment and guidance of AI integration behaviors benefit immensely from structured ethical frameworks. Within the context of AI integration, several established ethical frameworks, each espousing unique perspectives on moral rightness or wrongness, come to the fore, guiding and evaluating the ethical dimensions of AI adoption and implementation.

BRIDGING ETHICAL ORIENTATIONS WITH UTILITARIAN AND DEONTOLOGICAL FRAMEWORKS

In philosophical discussions, deontology offers a systematic framework that emphasizes moral obligations, universal principles, and ethical decision-making that are grounded in inherent rightness rather than just results. It is, associated with philosophers like Immanuel Kant, who emphasizes duty and adherence to rules or principles. It asserts that actions are morally obligatory, permissible, or forbidden based on whether they comply with a set of universal rules (Bednar & Spiekermann, 2022). And when applied to AI integration, deontology would focus on establishing a set of ethical principles that AI systems must adhere to. This could involve creating specific rules for AI behavior, such as respecting user privacy, avoiding discrimination, and ensuring transparency. The philosophical theory of utilitarianism emphasizes assessing the total ethical consequences of acts. This notion echoes the fundamental tenet of artificial intelligence—pursuing the greater good for society—and is consistent with how the technology operates, employing massive user data as a technological tool. Utilitarianism is a common ethical framework used in decision-making, particularly when large populations are involved. It helps us weigh the relative benefits and drawbacks of our choices (Feldman, 1997).

Generative AI tools like ChatGPT, though remarkable in their ability to replicate human language, can sometimes produce inaccurate information, a phenomenon referred to as AI hallucinations (Alkaissi & McFarlane, 2023). This issue has raised concerns about their reliability and applicability in various domains. It is critical to think about the possible effects of such errors in the context of sustainable business development. In sectors like healthcare, law, and finance, where precision is of paramount importance, the risk posed by unverified generative AI is particularly pronounced. This underscores the need for a cautious approach in adopting and implementing this technology in businesses, ensuring that it aligns with the principles of sustainability and responsible business practices. It's important to think of businesses as moral agents, implying that if they have moral agency, they have moral duties and responsibilities just like people have (Shaw, 2017). By carefully evaluating and mitigating the risks associated with AI-generated inaccuracies, businesses can pave the way for more robust and sustainable integration of these tools into their operations.

To furnish a specific exemplification, Bartneck et al. (2021) demonstrated that Facebook's ad-centric business model, as underscored during Mark Zuckerberg's 2018 Senate hearing, emphasizes the pivotal function of advertising-driven revenue in upholding the continued provision of complimentary services. This reliance on advertising revenue raises important considerations for sustainable business development. By optimizing the use of user data for targeted marketing, Facebook not only enhances its value proposition for advertisers but also exemplifies the potential for responsible data-driven practices in the digital landscape. This focus on constructively leveraging user data extends beyond advertising and into the realm of artificial intelligence. The rich tapestry of user data on Facebook serves as a valuable resource for developing AI systems. These systems, when applied in various domains such as companion robots and smart homes, enable personalized interactions and drive operational efficiency. This signifies a broader application of technology beyond advertising, with the potential to significantly impact sustainability efforts. As AI systems become more adaptive and tailored to individual needs, they can revolutionize how businesses operate, fostering a more efficient and personalized customer experience.

The most extensive analysis of AI ethics guidelines to date, presented by Jobin et al. in 2019, outlines a comprehensive set of ethical principles. Openness, equity, impartiality, accountability, confidentiality, kindness, independence, self-governance, sustainability, respect, and unity are all included in this. These concepts all consist of discrete elements. Transparency, for instance, is a concept that includes related ideas like communication, disclosure, understandability, rationality, and explicability. These ideas usually have ill-defined relationships between them, and these connections could reflect different ethical viewpoints.

In essence, the responsible use of user data not only supports Facebook's advertising-driven business model but also catalyzes sustainable business development. By recognizing the broader applications of improved user data, businesses can contribute to the advancement of technology while simultaneously prioritizing ethical and sustainable practices in their operations. This dual focus on profitability and ethics exemplifies a forward-thinking approach that aligns with the principles of sustainable business development in the digital age (Bartneck et al., 2021).

It is imperative to acknowledge that while deontology and utilitarianism offer valuable frameworks for assessing ethical implications in the realm of AI and technology, they are by no means the exclusive paradigms available for consideration. Stahl B. C. (2021) thinks that beyond these, there exists a diverse array of ethical theories, including virtue ethics, which warrants deeper exploration. Moreover, strong ethical viewpoints that are pertinent to the moral assessment of AI applications include feminist ethics of care (Gilligan, 1990) and ethical tenets derived from several religious traditions. As further evidenced by the fields of computer ethics (Bynum & Rogerson, 2003; Bynum, 2008; van den Hoven, 2010), information ethics (Capurro, 2006; Floridi, 2006), and technology ethics (Brey, 2011), he (Stahl, 2021) notes that the subtle incorporation of ethical theories within particular domains has produced rich dialogues.

EMERGENT LEARNING WITH RULE-BASED FOUNDATIONS

Dr. Kim, (2018) explores two main approaches to applying ethics to artificial intelligence (AI). The first is "Top-down Rule-based Ethics," akin to following clear, predefined rules such as the 10 Commandments, the Golden Rule in Christianity, or the Four Laws of Robotics by Asimov. While this approach is relatively straightforward, it can be challenging to implement effectively. It provides a structured framework for AI, like giving it specific instructions to follow. The second approach, "Bottom-up Emergent Ethics," involves learning from experience and adapting over time. This mirrors how humans develop their ethical compass as they grow, or how species evolve ethically. Here, ethical values arise naturally through interactions with the environment, akin to learning without explicit instructions. This method works with both humans and robots, highlighting the significance of unsupervised learning and the grouping of concepts and categories to create a morally sound procedure.

The integration of these two moral frameworks into AI-assisted sustainable company development provides unique approaches to directing ethical AI use in the business sector. The "Top-down Rule-based Ethics" approach provides a structured foundation for AI-driven decisions in business processes. One way of doing this is for a company to develop specific ethical principles, similar to a code of conduct, that will be used to monitor whether AI applications comply with sustainable practices, ethical sourcing, and responsible natural resources governance. This method helps to keep all AI actions within a specific set of rules, thus minimizing unethical and unsustainable ones.

However, this "Bottom-up Emergent Ethics" philosophy fosters flexibility and gaining experience through actual practice. In a sustainable business sense, it would mean allowing AI systems to learn about what is ethically acceptable and what is not continuously by engaging with customers, suppliers, and the environment. As an example, an AI-driven supply chain management would be able to figure out eco-friendly suppliers and energy-efficient logistic routes with time. Such an approach promotes AI towards more sensitive responses, thus integrating green supply chain initiatives that are consistent with sustainability standards.

This is what makes sustainable businesses make use of AI while practicing ethical and responsible behavior. "Top-down Rule-based Ethics" outlines the definite parameters and standards that should be followed, while "Bottom-up Emergent Ethics" is flexible and sensitive to develop along with the sustainability guidelines. This fosters ethical and eco-conscious AI business practices.

ETHICAL DELIBERATIONS IN THE INTEGRATION OF ARTIFICIAL INTELLIGENCE FOR SUSTAINABLE BUSINESS DEVELOPMENT

Ethical frameworks form the basis of integrating AI for sustainable business growth. They provide indispensable guidance for the ethical development, application, and regulation of big data and AI technologies. These innovations should benefit society and minimize any harmful effects. They should be in line with the principles of sustainability practice in business. It involves an in-depth analysis of diverse ethical theories grounded on philosophical reasoning that provide essential directions toward understanding the complex ethical terrain associated with AI incorporation in sustainable practice. These structures allow businesses, legislators, and developers to measure the moral consequences of their decisions, guiding AI toward ethical and human-centered outcomes that support sustainable business growth goals. Leading theories of ethics in this context include Utilitarianism, which places the greatest good for the greatest number first; Deontology, which emphasizes moral obligation and adherence to principles; Virtue Ethics, which promotes the development of ethical virtues; Rawlsian Justice, which emphasizes justice and equality; Rights-Based Ethics, which protects fundamental human rights; Care Ethics, which values care and relationships; and Consequentialism, which assesses actions according to their results (Nassar & Kamal, 2021). Nevertheless, the integration of AI into sustainable business development requires a specific application of such frameworks due to their inherent complexities and indeterminacies that characterize such domains. Since various frameworks are used in organizations, some organizations incorporate many of them to engage stakeholders and ethicists in ethical deliberations to understand the ethical dilemmas that are context-specific. Ethical standards should be a moving target, changing with the times and advances in technology. This is why governments and others must develop specific moral standards and laws for these issues concerning the use of AI in a sustainable economy.

Here are some case-based examples, illustrating the pivotal role of ethical frameworks in the integration of AI into sustainable business development:

The utilitarian ethical framework dominates in sustainable supply chain management. A case in point is a multinational retail entity that uses AI-driven analytics in efforts to optimize various aspects of its supply chain including reducing transportation emissions, waste generation, and ensuring equal working conditions among various departments. The commercial viability is also ensured in this approach because it is in tandem with the utilitarian axiom, which seeks to maximize societal welfare.

The ethical framework, based on duty and principle (deontology), is fundamental to protecting customer data privacy. For example, it could be noted in a fintech business using AI algorithms to customize financial advice. However, this is done carefully observing principles concerning informed consent and anonymity, thus ensuring that all clients' privacy rights are respected and protected.

In the case of a technology start-up venture, Virtue Ethics should take priority in protecting employee wellness. This organization creates a virtuous culture supported by virtue ethics, which allows for monitoring employee workload using AI tools resulting in an equilibrium and general welfare environment. Such ethos leads to a responsible and compassionate workplace and finally to the sustainable growth of the venture.

In the pursuit of guaranteeing fair access to healthcare services enabled by artificial intelligence, the Rawlsian Justice doctrine holds significant importance. To address existing healthcare disparities, a healthcare provider, for example, operationalizes AI-based diagnostic tools and deploys them wisely in underserved and marginalized communities. This approach aligns with Rawlsian justice, which emphasizes the importance of equity and parity in the provision of healthcare business.

One essential component in the creation of customized marketing strategies is rights-based ethics. An e-commerce site, for example, uses AI algorithms to precisely protect users' privacy rights while simultaneously customizing product recommendations. This is accomplished by putting strong consent procedures in place and enacting clear data usage policies.

A fundamental principle in the context of AI-assisted senior care is care ethics. For example, a healthcare facility incorporates AI-driven monitoring systems to prioritize the mental and social health of senior citizens, guaranteeing that they receive individualized attention and care. This method, which has its roots in care ethics, emphasizes the value of compassionate concern and relationships.

Consequentialism's ethical paradigm emphasizes efforts to reduce carbon emissions. An energy company, for example, uses AI algorithms to optimize energy resource production and distribution, resulting in a noticeable decrease in carbon emissions. This is an example of a consequentialist strategy, in which the positive environmental effect outweighs any potential negative effects, promoting social welfare and environmentally friendly business practices.

These concrete examples support the need for ethical frameworks to influence practical AI applications in sustainable company development. All of the scenarios show how ethical considerations have a discernible impact on decision-making processes, which in turn leads to positive consequences for society and the environment.

RETHINKING HUMAN-MACHINE INTERACTION: INTEGRATING AI WITH CONFUCIAN ETHICS

A thorough understanding of the moral principles underlying this technological advancement is necessary for integrating AI into sustainable economic development. A useful foundation for approaching this confluence of AI and sustainability is provided by the discourse summarized in "Blame-Laden Moral Rebukes and the Morally Competent Robot: A Confucian Ethical Perspective" (Zhu et al., 2020). This perspective emphasizes the urgent need to create an environment that is ethically flourishing and extends beyond human-human interactions to encompass human-machine dynamics. At its core is the concept of a moral ecosystem in human-robot interactions. This means carefully analyzing how AI systems are integrated into company operations, as well as their functions and potential effects on the moral fabric of the business environment. Additionally, the focus on rhetorical agency and communication is consistent with the need for AI systems in sustainable business operations to be open and morally sound. Making sure AI technologies are used wisely and morally becomes increasingly important as they become more and more like communicative beings in corporate operations. This entails explaining algorithmic decision-making in detail, outlining AI's function precisely, and taking proactive measures to mitigate any biases or unforeseen effects. A useful conceptual foundation for negotiating the complex ethical terrain of AI integration in sustainable company development is provided by the Confucian idea of role-based ethics. Businesses can approach AI adoption with a heightened understanding of the specific roles and duties that AI systems undertake by emphasizing the contextual and relational nature of moral considerations. This viewpoint promotes evaluating AI's broader ethical ramifications when applied in certain corporate contexts, in addition to its technical capabilities. However, care must be taken to prevent the reductionist confusion of Confucian ethics with more general ethical systems. Rather, it ought to be viewed as an additional viewpoint that enhances the conversation around AI ethics in the context of sustainable corporate development. This involves acknowledging the distinctive contributions of Confucian ethics, especially its focus on the psychological aspects of morality, and using it to inspire responsible AI integration techniques by combining it with other ethical perspectives. Businesses may manage the complex ethical issues inherent to this technology transformation while promoting sustainable and socially responsible behaviors by including moral ecology, communication, and role-based ethics in the AI deployment process. The objective is to maximize AI's usefulness so that it better satisfies human needs and ideals rather than anthropomorphizing it. The goal of incorporating philosophical concepts into the realm of artificial intelligence research is to make sure that these systems accurately reflect not just our scientific prowess but also our moral principles and societal ideals.

THE PSYCHOLOGICAL BASIS FOR THE SMOOTH INTEGRATION AND COOPERATION IN AI-POWERED SUSTAINABILITY PROJECTS

From organizational psychology, adaptability, leadership, and positive psychology perspectives, the seamless integration and interoperability of AI technologies, labor force, policies, and political will of decision-makers within the context of sustainability align with several psychological principles. The goal of this integration is to establish a productive workplace that supports worker well-being and a common commitment to environmentally friendly business practices.

First of all, it is consistent with the theory of organizational psychology, which highlights the need to establish a harmonious and efficient work environment. A seamless blend of AI technology with the current workforce and operational guidelines is what is meant by "smooth integration." This might lessen possible sources of resistance or conflict inside the organization by fostering a sense of coherence and unity.

In this sense, interoperability is synonymous with the psychological notions of flexibility and adaptation. It implies that human labor and AI technology ought to coexist peacefully, with the latter being able to adjust to new situations and obstacles as they emerge. Employees must be psychologically adaptable and eager to adopt new tools and methods of operation to achieve this.

Leadership psychology is further introduced by the political intent and involvement of company decision-makers. Effective leaders have a crucial duty to establish the direction and tone of their organizations (Kraus et al., 2020). Their support of environmentally friendly initiatives, coupled with a clear objective and honest communication, can have an impact on the workplace culture. Employee dedication, motivation, and a sense of purpose may all rise as a result.

The primary goal of this integration aligns with positive psychology ideas within the context of sustainability. The objective is to establish a workplace that fosters employee fulfillment and well-being in addition to optimal performance. Higher levels of job satisfaction and general psychological well-being can result from people believing that their labor is serving a greater, lasting purpose.

AUTOMATING COGNITIVE PROCESSES AND ENCOURAGING DECISIONS

The phrase "cognitive automation" has become widely used in the context of the evolution of the digital industry. This is a revolutionary approach that requires a deep integration of artificial intelligence (AI), business process monitoring (BPM), and robotic process automation (RPA) to be operationalized and effective. Today's business environment values originality beyond all other skills. It is the engine that propels creative problem-solving, providing businesses with a competitive advantage and increasing overall output. Businesses still need creative minds to bring new ideas to the table and maximize the possibilities of technology, even in the age of automation and artificial intelligence. Finding answers is only one aspect of creative thinking; other aspects include seeing opportunities and addressing problems from many angles. Combining passion, creativity, and teamwork can be difficult, but the results are great ideas that can solve any difficult challenge that arises in the corporate world. AI collaboration upends accepted conventions and questions the conventional role of human creativity in business. Similar to how it challenges human creativity in art, the advent of AI technologies undermines the idea that humans are the only ones capable of making decisions and solving problems in the business world (Stocker et al., 2021).

Similar to how prior scientific discoveries like Copernicus' heliocentric model and Darwin's theory of evolution altered our perceptions of the world, artificial intelligence (AI) upends the conventional perspective of business processes. It's like a paradigm change, bringing to light the notion that other factors outside human intellect can be used to predict trends or optimize company strategy. The diverse responses to artificial intelligence (AI) in sustainable company development, which span from fascination to trepidation, are indicative of the wider societal influence of technology on our activities and customs. AI is a reflection of the ways we currently conduct business; therefore, we must evaluate and adjust to its significant differences, which is similar to recognizing and valuing the diversity of human cultures.

Just as Gerfried Stocker (2021) questioned if AI's basic distinctions should be accepted, accepting and implementing different viewpoints into corporate plans also presents difficulties. Similar to recognizing and appreciating diversity in a corporate setting, accepting and utilizing AI's distinctive qualities in sustainable business development calls for a certain amount of flexibility and openness.

REVEALING HUMAN POTENTIAL IN THE AI AGE: INVESTIGATING JUNGIAN PSYCHOLOGY

Artificial intelligence (AI) is a profoundly transformative technology that marks a turning point in human history in terms of purpose, behavior, and adaptability. As it becomes more and more integrated into daily life, it profoundly changes the dynamics of work, social relationships, and overall viewpoints. This has led to discussions about how to interpret it using psychologist Carl Jung's ideas (Jacoby, 1991; Jung, 1969). Jung's significant insights into the human psyche and personal development pathways are utilized to further explore how human purpose may evolve inside the AI-infused paradigm. The integration of artificial intelligence (AI) into routine tasks has the potential to reveal hidden abilities (Individuation), encourage people to identify with universal symbols in their roles (Archetypes), reveal hidden aspects of personalities (Shadow Work), and enable gender-related characteristics to emerge in a changing environment (Anima and Animus). The mutually beneficial relationship between humans and AI has the potential to mold a shared story and hence impact how purpose develops within this unique context (Collective Unconscious and Cultural Evolution). In the end, the AI revolution goes beyond its technical breakthroughs, changing how people approach life and search for meaning in a constantly changing environment. This calls for an investigation of how Jung's insights shed light on this transforming process.

Now consider a sustainable business that wants to use AI to support its operations and environmental goals.

Imagine a company that is committed to reducing its environmental impact and that uses AI integration to optimize its supply chain. AI systems are freeing workers from boring jobs as they take over regular responsibilities like logistics and inventory management. This increased independence enables them to explore hidden abilities and talents that were previously neglected in their professions. An employee in charge of inventory management, for instance, might discover they have a knack for data analysis when working with AI systems to forecast demand trends.

This situation is consistent with Jung's theory of "Individuation," which holds that people discover their innate talents and potential. Within this framework, AI integration not only simplifies procedures but also enables members of the organization to grow and contribute in unexpected and innovative ways.

Additionally, think about how integrating AI could reveal aspects of "Shadow Work" in the workplace culture. AI systems may uncover inefficiencies or ignored problems in the supply chain as they gather and evaluate data, bringing to light previously unknown or thought to be unduly difficult regions. This discovery may lead to a more thorough understanding and recognition of these fundamental problems, which would then require the company to deal with them to improve things all around.

AI's influence on decision-making procedures may also be reflected in Jung's idea of "Archetypes." When AI algorithms direct and suggest the best courses of action based on gathered data, people in the company might find themselves drawn to particular symbolic roles or patterns of behavior that align with widely accepted models for efficient supply chain management or environmentally friendly business practices.

In the combined field of human-AI cooperation in the creation of sustainable business, Jung's theories offer a framework for understanding how people change, adapt, and engage in this dynamic environment. AI goes beyond its purely technical function to act as a catalyst for organizational and human development, influencing how people view their positions, deal with obstacles, and support the long-term goals of the business.

AI-INFUSED SUSTAINABLE BUSINESS: UNITING ADLER'S SOCIAL INTEREST THEORY

Alfred Adler, a pioneering figure in individual psychology, advocated a holistic perspective of individuals rather than a reduction to fragmented elements (Williams, 2004). Central to his framework was the concept of social interest, encapsulating a communal orientation counter to egocentric preoccupations. Adler posited that possessing social interest facilitated a fulfilling societal existence, whereas its absence led to self-centered and unproductive lives. Ferguson's (2007) exploration of Adler's principles applied in workplace contexts contends that the integration of social-interest methods augments interrelationships among colleagues and between managerial tiers. This approach not only assists individuals in discerning and pursuing collective objectives but also ameliorates organizational dynamics, nurturing a sense of belonging and contributing significantly to overall welfare. These investigations underscore the pragmatic significance of Adler's theory of social interest across diverse settings, emphasizing its potential to augment interpersonal dynamics and engender constructive impacts on both individual and organizational realms of well-being.

Alfred Adler's social interest theory can be supported by several real-world applications that show how AI can be integrated into sustainable corporate development. AI-powered collaborative decision-making platforms in the workplace are one example of this; they promote group problem-solving by appreciating varied viewpoints and stimulating a variety of inputs. Furthermore, Adler's focus on community and shared well-being is aligned with AI-driven programs that enhance worker engagement and well-being via tailored experiences. The use of AI algorithms in sustainable supply chain management to give social responsibility and environmental effect top priority is an example of how social interest concepts are applied in company operations. Adler's emphasis on societal welfare over self-centered actions is further supported by the adoption of AI-supported ethical decision frameworks and customer-centric practices that take into account broader societal concerns while satisfying individual preferences. These actions demonstrate a commitment to holistic and sustainable business practices.

By Adler's social interest theory, let's examine a case study of a hypothetical company called EcoTech Innovations that uses AI to advance sustainable business development.

CASE STUDY: ECOTECH INNOVATIONS

1. Background: EcoTech Innovations is an expert in environmentally sustainable practices and renewable energy solutions. They choose to use AI technologies in several facets of their business operations to further their dedication to societal welfare and holistic business practices.
2. Practical Applications: Collaborative Decision-Making Driven by AI: EcoTech uses an AI-powered platform to plan projects and make decisions. This platform synthesizes feedback from several teams while taking community needs, environmental effects, and engineering into account. Through its analysis of this collective input, the AI system suggests the best renewable energy projects that balance social welfare with economics, encouraging a group approach to problem-solving.
3. Worker Well-Being with AI-Powered Personalization: An AI-powered employee wellness initiative has been launched by the corporation. This tool makes use of AI algorithms to customize professional development opportunities and wellness programs according to stress levels, work patterns, and individual preferences. EcoTech's focus on individual well-being and the development of a sense of community support is consistent with Adler's emphasis on the welfare of the group at work.

4. AI-Enhanced Sustainable Supply Chain: EcoTech prioritizes sustainability by incorporating AI into its supply chain management. The AI system minimizes waste, lowers carbon footprint, and improves logistics by acquiring supplies from providers who practice environmental responsibility. This strategy takes into account broader societal and environmental implications in addition to ensuring profitability and adhering to social interest ideals.
5. Making Ethical Decisions AI-backed: EcoTech integrates ethical frameworks that are powered by AI into decision-making procedures. In response to moral quandaries, the AI system considers the possible effects on different stakeholders and offers recommendations for actions that respect environmental responsibility and societal values. This reflects Adler's emphasis on the welfare of society over personal benefit.
6. Consumer-Centric AI Practices: The business uses AI algorithms to examine consumer input and preferences, adjusting its renewable energy offerings to satisfy both personal and societal needs. This customer-focused strategy prioritizes social well-being by coordinating corporate aims with societal sustainability objectives.
7. Outcome: By emphasizing group welfare, encouraging collaboration, and taking into account broader societal impacts beyond individual gains, EcoTech's integration of AI in sustainable business development not only spurs innovation but also exemplifies Adler's social interest principles, solidifying its reputation as a socially conscious and sustainable enterprise.

THE INTERSECTION OF PHILOSOPHY AND PSYCHOLOGY IN AI INTEGRATION FOR LONG-TERM SUSTAINABLE BUSINESS GROWTH

AI is growing exponentially, which emphasizes the need for a multidisciplinary approach that goes beyond technical expertise. Working together with experts in philosophy, psychology, and sustainable business growth is essential to integrating ethical principles and human values into the creation of AI. Their combined wisdom is essential for dispelling long-held beliefs and balancing the goals of society with the pace of technological development. The revolutionary potential of AI goes beyond technological innovation; it catalyzes a resurgence of philosophical inquiry, a psychological prism through which to see relationships between humans and machines, and a force behind the integration of sustainable business practices. Adopting this comprehensive viewpoint guarantees that AI systems give precedence to moral concerns, psychological welfare, and concrete socio-economic advantages, thereby promoting not just a revolutionary advancement in technology but also a fair and sustainable development in AI's future environment.

In the framework of artificial intelligence, let us look at a real-world example that combines psychology, philosophy, and sustainable business development:

Consider a tech business creating an online retail recommendation system driven by AI. Ethicists and philosophers are included in the system development process to make sure it adheres to moral standards. They question the presumptions regarding the kinds of goods that are suggested, taking into account both the items' possible social effects and ethical implications.

Figure 1. Balancing human values and AI Integration for sustainable business growth
(Source: The author)

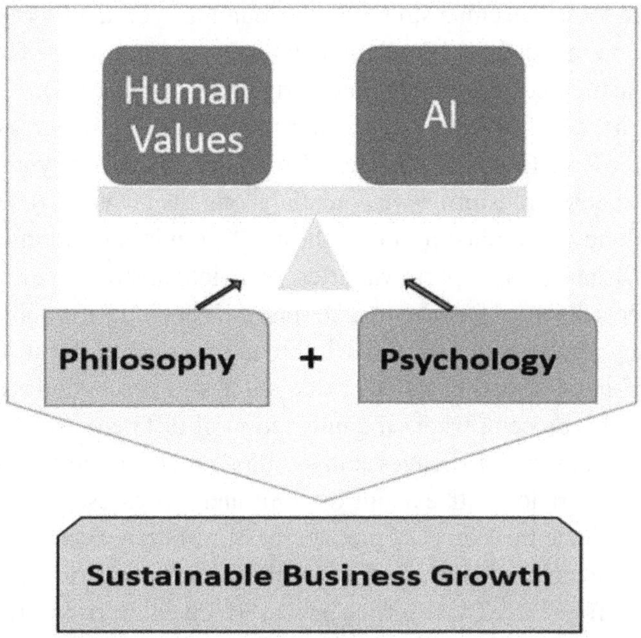

Psychologists work together to have a deeper understanding of user behavior and preferences. They prevent cognitive biases and improve the user experience by designing the system with the concepts of cognitive psychology in mind. For example, taking into account the psychological effects of trust and transparency on user engagement, they might include components of user consent and transparency in suggestions.

In addition, specialists in sustainable company growth contribute by analyzing the products' supply chain and environmental effects. They support the company's commitment to sustainability by endorsing goods from suppliers who follow fair labor standards or who take environmental responsibility seriously.

The AI recommendation system becomes more morally sound, takes into account the psychological aspects of user interaction, and supports sustainable business practices by combining various disciplines. By taking a comprehensive approach, the AI system is guaranteed to give ethical considerations, user well-being, and sustainable commerce top priority, which reflects a more responsible and comprehensive technical innovation. Moreover, it can convert obstacles into opportunities for long-term, significant impact.

CONCLUSION

The evolution of human consciousness mirrors the philosophical concept of Heraclitus's doctrine: "Everything flows" or Change is inherent (Barnes, 1982), weaving through the human condition and prompting us to adapt and evolve continually. In psychology, this resonates with the concept of cognitive adaptation, where individuals adjust their perceptions and behaviors in response to changing circumstances. Yet, our tendency to idealize the past while scrutinizing the present and future creates a dichotomy, blinding us to the unique opportunities within each phase of evolution. Although intelligent systems are frequently thought of as gradually taking the place of human roles, their primary promise is to enhance human skills rather than replace them. Machine strengths are found in accuracy, speed, and scalability, while human strengths are found in creativity, flexibility, and interpersonal skills. The whole potential of AI and humans is shown via their collaboration (Daugherty and Wilson, 2018).

When viewed through the lens of sustainable business development, integrating artificial intelligence (AI) becomes a reflection of the Hegelian dialectic (Van Tuinen, 2020) —a synthesis of conflicting ideas and technologies. AI embodies transformative potential along the business value chain, akin to Hegel's notion of thesis and antithesis culminating in synthesis. It promises to optimize operations, handling tasks through virtual assistants, yet its portrayal often veers into abstraction, reminiscent of how Hegel criticized abstract concepts divorced from reality. Despite AI's potential to enhance enterprise efficiency and elevate processes, it grapples with a state akin to Freud's concept of the unconscious mind—largely unexplored and in its infancy (Stocker et al., 2021). Its application necessitates aligning strategic goals, akin to Jung's individuation process, where the integration of different aspects leads to a harmonious whole. However, organizations face challenges akin to Adler's social interest (Williams, 2004) —balancing the readiness for AI integration with existing systems and processes.

Businesses need to evaluate their level of preparedness, resource capacities, and the extent of AI's impact, much like in existential philosophy, which emphasizes the individual's freedom and responsibility to negotiate life's difficulties. These intricacies, in which enterprises struggle with the weight of decisions about AI adoption and integration, are reminiscent of Sartre's existential suffering (Gosetti-Ferencei, 2020). In sustainable business development, transferring successful AI models to other companies resembles Kuhn's (2012) paradigm shifts in scientific revolutions—requiring recognition of the nuanced intricacies within organizational contexts for effective implementation. Understanding these philosophical and psychological parallels is essential for businesses navigating the integration of AI, ensuring sustainable and effective deployment. Ethical alignment and psychological preparedness are prerequisites for integrating AI into a sustainable company. It is imperative for entrepreneurs to foster a culture that values human-AI collaboration and to carefully use AI solutions that align with sustainability goals. Stakeholder participation, openness, and ongoing assessment all can help to enable the ethical and adaptable integration of AI into sustainable business processes.

REFERENCES

Alkaissi, H., & McFarlane, S. I. (2023). Artificial Hallucinations in ChatGPT: Implications in Scientific Writing. *Cureus, 15*(2), e35179. doi:10.7759/cureus.35179 PMID:36811129

Ameen, N., Sharma, G. D., Tarba, S., Rao, A., & Chopra, R. (2022). Toward advancing theory on creativity in marketing and artificial intelligence. *Psychology and Marketing*, *39*(9), 1802–1825. doi:10.1002/mar.21699

Asikullah, F., Chakma, P., Hossain, S. F. A., & Hussain, K. (2024). Evaluating Employee Motivation and Productivity in Bangladesh During the Post-pandemic Era. *Management and Labour Studies*, 0258042X231220489.

Barnes, J. (1982). The natural philosophy of Heraclitus. In J. Barnes (Ed.), *The Presocratic Philosophers* (pp. 43–62). Routledge Taylor & Francis Group.

Bartneck, C., Lütge, C., Wagner, A., & Welsh, S. (2021). Privacy Issues of AI. In An Introduction to Ethics in Robotics and AI. Springer. doi:10.1007/978-3-030-51110-4_8

Bednar, K., & Spiekermann, S. (2022). Eliciting Values for Technology Design with Moral Philosophy: An Empirical Exploration of Effects and Shortcomings. *Science, Technology & Human Values*, *0*(0). doi:10.1177/01622439221122595

Brey, P. (2011). Anticipatory Technology Ethics for Emerging IT. In J. Mauger (Ed.), *CEPE 2011: Crossing Boundaries* (pp. 13–26). INSEIT.

Bynum, T. W. (2008). Norbert Wiener and the Rise of Information Ethics. In J. van den Hoven & J. Weckert (Eds.), *Information Technology and Moral Philosophy* (pp. 8–25). Cambridge University Press. doi:10.1017/CBO9780511498725.002

Bynum, T. W., & Rogerson, S. (2003). *Computer Ethics and Professional Responsibility: Introductory Text and Readings*. Blackwell Publishers.

Capurro, R. (2006). Towards an Ontological Foundation of Information Ethics. *Ethics and Information Technology*, *8*(4), 175–186. doi:10.1007/s10676-006-9108-0

Daugherty, P. R., & Wilson, H. J. (2018). *Human + Machine: Reimagining Work in the Age of AI*. Harvard Business Review Press.

Faisal, S., Hossain, S. F. A., Fahmida, S., & Rayhana, R. (2023). Leveraging Business Intelligence to Enhance Cyber Security Innovation. In Cyber Security and Business Intelligence (pp. 1-14). Routledge. doi:10.4324/9781003285854-1

Feldman, F. (1997). Utilitarianism. In Utilitarianism, Hedonism, and Desert: Essays in Moral Philosophy (Cambridge Studies in Philosophy, pp. 15-16). Cambridge: Cambridge University Press.

Ferguson, E. D. (2007). Business and organizations. *Journal of Individual Psychology*, *63*(1), 110–117.

Floridi, L. (2006). Information Ethics, Its Nature and Scope. *Computers & Society*, *36*(3), 21–36. doi:10.1145/1195716.1195719

Gilligan, C. (1990). *In a Different Voice: Psychological Theory and Women's Development (Reissue)*. Harvard University Press.

Gosetti-Ferencei, J. A. (2020). Existential Suffering, Happiness, and Hope. In *On Being and Becoming: An Existentialist Approach to Life (Guides to the Good Life Series). New York*. Academic. doi:10.1093/oso/9780190913656.003.0020

Hossain, S. F. A., Khan, R. A., Sohan, M. A. I., Karmoker, T., Asikullah, F., Chakma, P., & Chisty, K. K. S. (2022). Investigating the Role of Social Media on Student Engagement and Authentic Learning during Post COVID-19. In *Virtual Technologies and E-Collaboration for the Future of Global Business* (pp. 68–81). IGI Global. doi:10.4018/978-1-6684-5027-7.ch004

Hossain, S. F. A., Nurunnabi, M., Nadi, A. H., & Ahsan, F. T. (2021). Exploring the Role of AI in K12: Are Robot Teachers Taking Over? In Emerging Realities and the Future of Technology in the Classroom (pp. 120-135). IGI Global.

Hossain, S. F. A., Sofyan, Y., Ushie, A. M., & Srimuang, K. (2022). Exploring the Relationship Between Student Engagement and Authentic Learning During COVID-19: Moderating Role of Lack of Attention via WeChat. *International Journal of e-Collaboration (IJeC), 18*(1), 1-20.

Jacoby, M. (1991). *Individuation and Narcissism: The Psychology of Self in Jung and Kohut* (1st ed.). Routledge. doi:10.4324/9780203753897

Jobin, A., Ienca, M., & Vayena, E. (2019). The global landscape of AI ethics guidelines. *Nature Machine Intelligence*, *1*(9), 389–399. doi:10.1038/s42256-019-0088-2

Jung, C. G. (1969). *Collected Works of C.G. Jung, Volume 9 (Part 1): Archetypes and the Collective Unconscious* (G. Adler & R. F. C. Hull, Eds.). Princeton University Press. https://www.jstor.org/stable/j.ctt5hhrnk

Kim, D. (2018, May 31). Human Ethics for Artificial Intelligent Beings. *AI Strategy & Policy Blog*. https://aistrategyblog.com/category/utilitarianism/

Kraus, M., Feuerriegel, S., & Oztekin, A. (2020). Deep learning in business analytics and operations research: Models, applications and managerial implications. *European Journal of Operational Research*, *281*(3), 628–641. doi:10.1016/j.ejor.2019.09.018

Kuhn, T. S. (2012). *The structure of scientific revolutions* (50th ed.). University of Chicago Press. doi:10.7208/chicago/9780226458144.001.0001

Maican, C. I., Sumedrea, S., Tecau, A., Nichifor, E., Chitu, I. B., Lixandroiu, R., & Brătucu, G. (2023). Factors Influencing the Behavioural Intention to Use AI-Generated Images in Business: A UTAUT2 Perspective with Moderators. *Journal of Organizational and End User Computing*, *35*(1), 1–32. doi:10.4018/JOEUC.330019

Marvin, G., Tamale, M., Kanagwa, B., & Jjingo, D. (2023). Philosophical Review of Artificial Intelligence for Society 5.0. In *Proceedings of International Conference on Paradigms of Communication, Computing and Data Analytics*. DOI: 10.1007/978-981-99-4626-6_1

Nadi, A. H., Hossain, S. F. A., Hasan, A. M., Sofin, M. R., Shabab, S., Sohan, M. A. I., & Yuan, C. (2023). Discovering the Role of M-Learning Among Finance Students: The Future of Online Education. In *Novel Financial Applications of Machine Learning and Deep Learning: Algorithms, Product Modeling, and Applications* (pp. 183–196). Springer International Publishing. doi:10.1007/978-3-031-18552-6_11

Nassar, A., & Kamal, M. (2021). Ethical Dilemmas in AI-Powered Decision-Making: A Deep Dive into Big Data-Driven Ethical Considerations. *International Journal of Responsible Artificial Intelligence*, *11*(8), 1–11. https://neuralslate.com/index.php/Journal-of-Responsible-AI/article/view/43

Rainey, D. (2009). *Sustainable business development. inventing the future through strategy, innovation, and leadership*. Cambridge University Press. doi:10.1017/CBO9780511617607

Sadiku, M. N. O., Ashaolu, T. J., Ajayi-Majebi, A., & Musa, S. M. (2021). Artificial intelligence in social media. *International Journal of Scientific Advances*, *2*(1), 15–20.

Shaw, W. H. (2017). *Business ethics* (9th ed.). Cengage Learning.

Stahl B. C. (2021). Concepts of Ethics and Their Application to AI. *Artificial Intelligence for a Better Future: An Ecosystem Perspective on the Ethics of AI and Emerging Digital Technologies*, 19–33. doi:10.1007/978-3-030-69978-9_3

Stocker, G., Jandl, M., & Hirsch, A. J. (Eds.). (2021). *The Practice of Art and AI.* Hantje Cantz Verlag., https://ars.electronica.art/newdigitaldeal/files/2021/08/artandai.pdf

Ushie, A. M., Samson, T. K., Hossain, S. F. A., & Ojie, M. P. (2023). Competitive intensity, managerial commitment, and corporate performance: The moderating role of innovation input in post-COVID-19. *International Journal of Work Organisation and Emotion*, *14*(3), 282–302. doi:10.1504/IJWOE.2023.132868

van den Hoven, J. (2010). The Use of Normative Theories in Computer Ethics. In L. Floridi (Ed.), *The Cambridge Handbook of Information and Computer Ethics* (pp. 59–76). Cambridge University Press. doi:10.1017/CBO9780511845239.005

Van Tuinen, S. (2020). Philosophy in the light of AI. *Angelaki*, *25*(4), 97–109. doi:10.1080/0969725X.2020.1790838

Williams, T. (2004). The Theory and Practice of Adlerian Psychology. *Self and Society*, *32*(2), 5–9. doi:10.1080/03060497.2004.11083774

Zhu, Q., Williams, T., Jackson, B., & Wen, R. (2020). Blame-Laden Moral Rebukes and the Morally Competent Robot: A Confucian Ethical Perspective. *Science and Engineering Ethics*, *26*(5), 2511–2526. doi:10.1007/s11948-020-00246-w PMID:32632786

Chapter 4
From Clicks to Loyalty:
Understanding the Dynamics of Consumer Brand Relationships in the Online Clothing Industry

Sarika Faisal
BRAC University, Bangladesh

ABSTRACT

The core purpose of this chapter is to highlight the journey of a female entrepreneur and to give an overview of clothing industry in Bangladesh. However, with the help of Social consumer fashion brand engagement model it was viable to delineate a synopsis of consumer brand relationship. Moreover, qualitative data collection has been used to conduct the research. The findings of the study conclude that effective marketing strategies along with quality products and flawless synchronisation with contemporary trends can ensure long term success.

INTRODUCTION

Autumn sky, mild wind and with a heavy heart Sarika thought about all the years she has spent for Clothes Over Bae's. She was supposed to be happy today but instead of that she's just immersed in her thoughts; taking a small sip of coffee and giving a small glance at the annual report. A report which is basically a manuscript of all the obstacles, challenges, hard work and sleepless nights. Although she had something very similar in her mind yet the consistent sale rate just left her in utter dismal. However, she understands that now she has come to a point where she has to take certain risks, grasp new opportunities and go beyond her limits to push the sales. And to do that she first has to learn about her consumers, how the consumers resonate themselves with different brands and what triggers them most.

DOI: 10.4018/979-8-3693-1842-3.ch004

To enjoy rapid growth at first the problem has to be identified for which the sale is not thriving like it should. One of her friends suggested that it's alway better to start from the family by which she meant to her loyal customers. So Sarika hired a team of few reputed consultants to ascertain various viewpoints regarding the brand; the concrete reason behind choosing this brand and also what more they seek from this brand. After getting done the qualitative research Sarika realized that she needs to increase the product category with emerging marketing strategy.

HOW IT ALL STARTED

Life as a teenager is indeed filled with curiosity. At this age, everything has a predetermined standard, including what to pursue, how to feel, and even what to achieve. Anyone who dares to perform better than that or worse than that instantly becomes the center of attention. But then along comes Ms. Sarika, a strong, tenacious, and independent person. She was more focused on pursuing her own passion than trying to live up to the expectations of others.

When her academics should have been her main priority as an 18-year-old girl, she devoted her days and nights to making a name and a legacy for herself. An apparently unimportant incident—a closed eatery that she had driven by innumerable times over the previous 5 to 8 years—sparked this journey. Because of how much this incident affected her, she understood that if she didn't do something unusual or unconventional, people would forget about her just like they had that old restaurant.

The journey of "Clothes over baes" started in 2017 in this manner. She initially debuted a collection with just six pieces to test consumer interest. To her astonishment, the designs were adored by working women and teenagers, and the merchandise ran out in less than a week. They began moving to "Clothes over baes" because of its fashionable designs from popular foreign brands including Zara, H&M, and Forever 21. The company swiftly rose to the position of an industry pioneer.

They captured 40% of the online clothes market the next year as a result of their incredible selection and quality, which helped them steadily build brand loyalty. They didn't need to spend any money on marketing, particularly influencer marketing, because the brand became so well-known among teenagers. Additionally, they began with just one machine but now run four due to the tremendous demand. Moreover, she always kept up with the market and customers while managing routine orders. Every week, she performed research on new brands, examining their marketing strategies and target market demographics. She was able to connect and learn because of this.

However, they observed that growth had been consistent for a number of years in a succession, and they sought to address this problem. They carefully examined annual reports and gleaned as much data as they could about their customers from the records, including demographics, purchasing habits, psychographics, and customer lifetime value. The brand was able to launch and design products that were specifically catered to their clients' interests thanks to their in-depth understanding of their target market, further cementing their relationship with them.

ONLINE CLOTHING INDUSTRY OF BANGLADESH

The online industry in Bangladesh has undergone a remarkable metamorphosis in recent years. The sector has witnessed an unprecedented surge, propelled by the burgeoning popularity of e-commerce platforms and Bangladesh's robust presence in the global garment manufacturing arena.

The online clothing industry in Bangladesh is growing rapidly, with a predicted market size of US$1,975.8 million for fashion eCommerce and US$1,279.1 million for apparel eCommerce by 2023.

The projected growth rate of the apparel market in Bangladesh is 15.12% between 2023-2027, resulting in a market volume of US$2246.00m in 2027. This presents an opportunity for online clothing stores to tap into this growth and increase their market share. Additionally, online clothing stores can improve the quality of their products to attract more customers and enhance the user experience of their websites to make it easier for customers to shop online, saving them time and money.

Overall, the online clothing industry of Bangladesh presents significant opportunities for growth and innovation, and is expected to continue to grow in the coming years.

CONSUMER RESEARCH

For this segment, 15 female consumers from a variety of backgrounds were interviewed. The selection procedures made sure that responses were fully representative by accounting for differences in educational background, age, demography, and other factors. As a result, the report offers insightful information about customers' purchasing habits and brand perception. Therefore, Sarika committed herself to reading all fifteen interviews, each of which lasted at least 30 minutes, as she understood the value of having a thorough grasp of her target audience. Hence, highlights from the five interviews, which show the various consumer viewpoints are stated below:

CONSUMER INTERVIEW

Archita Kundu

A working woman, animal lover, and self-described shopaholic, Archita Kundu offered her viewpoint on fashion in the interview. She highlighted the value of comfort when asked what fashion meant to her. Meanwhile, she expressed disappointment with the few plus-size selections offered in the majority of Dhaka establishments which also made her think certain clothes wouldn't look good on her.

Archita's dissatisfaction with the limited choices offered by Baes for ready-to-wear apparel highlights the importance of catering to diverse consumer preferences. This aspect resonates with the findings of the study conducted by Hossain et al. (2020), which investigated how mobile buying behavior on smartphones is enabling women entrepreneurs in emerging Asia. By understanding and responding to the varied preferences of consumers like Archita, entrepreneurs can leverage mobile technology to innovate and provide a wider range of choices, ultimately enhancing the overall shopping experience and empowering women in the entrepreneurial landscape.

Tasnia Haque

Tasnia Haque, a third-year student, is equally passionate about her education and her love of fashion. She is adamant that maintaining a decent appearance is essential to her overall performance and wellbeing. She places great attention on each dress, and choosing the perfect one is similar to practicing meditation, which reduces tension and gives her more energy to work harder. She listed Clothes over Baes as one of her favorite retailers.

Tasnia's comments on Clothes over Baes emphasize how crucial it is to have strong marketing plans in place to make sure that customers can easily find and enjoy a brand's goods. Her insistence on businesses keeping abreast of fashion trends is consistent with the idea of utilizing social media entrepreneurship, as discussed by Cousté et al. (2022). According to the research, social media can give disadvantaged female students in developing countries a platform to present their work and connect with a larger audience. Businesses like Clothes over Baes may profit from the natural exposure provided by social media by coordinating marketing initiatives with consumers' natural browsing behaviors. This will ultimately increase the visibility of their brand and increase customer interaction.

Roksana Begum

Roksana Begum, a dedicated homemaker and mother of two girls, takes comfort in dressing up on special occasions. She uses social media to pass the time and relieve tension after a long, exhausting day. She now always practices this form of self-care. She has also established a custom for her family to dress alike on major occasions to represent their closeness and togetherness. Finding stores that sell dresses that may be tailored to a customer's desired designs has proven to be fairly difficult.

In the middle of these annoyances, Roksana came across Clothes Over Baes in 2020 during the COVID-19 pandemic, and ever since, she has remained a devoted client. She expressed her appreciation for the company's dependable and helpful assistance and her satisfaction with their service. She did, however, also express a hint of sadness because she frequently has trouble finding things from their usual assortment that suit her unique style and age. Many of the brand's offerings don't quite fit her preferences or sense of style because they are too trendy.

Roksana is a devoted customer, but she yearns for a greater selection of solutions that satisfy her unique requirements and fashion tastes. In order to ensure that customers like Roksana can continue to find clothes that reflect their own sense of style and benefit from the brand's excellent service, it would be advantageous for the company to think about extending their range to include styles that appeal to a wider age group.

Adiba Karim

Adiba Karim is a modest follower who appreciates content creation in addition to being a part-time baker. However, slowly she turned her hobby into a business and has considered content creation as a part time job. Being a content creator, she always does various experimental looks for her audience for which she has to be updated with the current brands. Thus she acknowledged that she has been a fan of Clothes Over bae's for many years when question raised how loyal she considers herself to be.She does, however, favor modest clothing, thus the brand's product selection hasn't always been easy for her. But she can't help but buy outfits from them because of their unique pieces which are a treat to the eyes.

Adiba has recently been pleased that Clothes Over Bae's has begun developing a small collection dedicated only to their modest consumers. Moreover, now she no longer has to go to the extra trouble of styling the garments to meet her modest preferences, this development has made her extremely happy. By launching product lines specifically for that market, she believes the company will continue to serve niches like modest fashion. She also says that in order to appeal to a wider spectrum of clients, the business should concentrate on staying current with modern trends.

Shanika Rahman

Being Gen Z, Shanika contains a very discerning nature regarding her lifestyle choices. She has just completed her A Levels and now she's exploring various facets of life. Her lifestyle or even fashion choices mostly comes from the realm of kpop or trendy drama that's been streaming since she spends a substantial amount of time on the internet; browning different things. That's pretty much how she caters to her various needs and desires. While discussing fashion with her, it's quite fascinating to highlight the fact that how inspirations vary from generation to generation and also take a sudden paradigm shift. According to Aboulilah, H. M. A. E., Hossain, S. F. A., Vuong, B. N., & Jebril, T. (2022), behavioral intention plays a critical role in determining whether or not users would adopt technology, including applications.

However, she prefers a more minimal color plate, nothing too fleshy can be added to her cart that was her specification. Moreover, clothes which let her to breathe, baggy fits with neutral plates. She added that Clothes Over Baes being her number 1 fashion brand not only because they have trendy designs but because of their amazing size chart which includes chest 28 which is very hard to find. As she's very skinny it's her everyday hassle to find the perfect size. Furthermore she added a modest collection if the brand launched a separate for the Gen z catering to their style it will be amazing since they are one the highest online consumers nowadays.

WHAT TO DO

In 2021, Mohsin, A. K., Hongzhen, L., and Hossain, S. F. A. examined how the COVID-19 pandemic affected the consumer economy and suggested solutions. The essay explores the ways in which the macroeconomy and consumer economy are being impacted by COVID-19 and how they may be in the future. It also talks about how the epidemic is expected to accelerate the retail business model and looks into the prospect of a surge in the "home economy." The paper sheds light on the macroeconomic climate impacted by the recent coronavirus outbreak by drawing comparisons with the 2003 severe acute respiratory syndrome (SARS) outbreak. E-commerce clothing stores in Bangladesh can employ various strategies to attract more customers and increase their market size. These strategies include social media marketing, email marketing, offering high-quality products, excellent customer service, and having a strong online presence. By expanding their target market through offering a wider range of products, providing promotions and discounts, and using effective marketing strategies, online clothing stores can reach a larger customer base and contribute to the growth of the industry.

Strategies for online clothing brands to increase their product line and build strong relationships with consumers. Firstly, is to segment the target audience based on demographic, psychographic, and behavioral factors and incorporate social proof into marketing efforts. Secondly, is to conduct market research to identify trends, demands, and preferences related to clothing products and develop a pricing strategy that aligns with the target audience's perceived value.

Consistent brand messaging and communication encourages the use of user-generated content and social proof to build trust and credibility. Online clothing brands are also advised to tailor their product line expansion efforts to cater to the unique requirements of each consumer segment and adapt based on changing market dynamics. Gathering feedback from existing customers is also recommended to better understand their needs and preferences.

Overall, the success of online clothing stores in Bangladesh relies on employing effective marketing strategies, offering high-quality products, providing excellent customer service, and staying up to date with industry trends and growth opportunities. By using these strategies, online clothing stores can increase their market share and contribute to the growth of the industry in Bangladesh.

TEACHING NOTES

Synopsis

1. Study explores factors that influence social consumer fashion engagement and buying decisions.
2. Strong brand passion and engagement can create intent to pay high price, strong word of mouth, brand engagement, and buying intentions.
3. Consumers' love for a brand enhances level of attachment, positive evaluations, and sharing of love for a brand.
4. Social media posts inspire people to purchase fashion items.
5. User-generated content on fashion brands on social media can create emotional and social engagement.
6. Over a billion social media users made a significant contribution toward changes related to brand engagement and lifestyle of consumers.
7. There is evidence that celebrities and brand-sponsored advertisements have little impact on purchase decisions.
8. There is a strong connection between social media and fashion.
9. Social ties and trust, credibility, homophily, and discounts are the drivers of purchasing decisions for fashion brands.
10. Almost half of BD online fashion shoppers made their most recent purchase based on social media inspiration.
11. Social passion, social tendency, individual warmth, and social liking enhance social fashion brand engagement.
12. Qualitative surveys in different studies involved an average of 30 participants.
13. This study culminates in a theoretical framework based on social impact theory and the triangulation theory of love to understand SCFBE in the context of SMPs.
14. People accept recommendations and influence from socially credible and relevant sources.
15. User-generated content on SMPs is a source of social factors that enhance word of mouth and customer brand engagement.
16. Capability of SMPs to offer opportunities to create socially generated brand passion between customers and fashion brands is limited.

An Imaginary Class Design

Topic: social consumer fashion engagement and buying decisions. Duration: 80 minutes
Learning Objectives: End of the session students will be able to:

i. Use suitable case study solution
ii. Know the case study in depth

Number of students: 30–40
Learning Activity (LA) Activity type

Part 1

(25 + 5)

LA1. Download sample case study from renowned source Q1. What is case study?
Q2. Why should you learn and use case study?
Lecture
Group work consists of 6 students in each group
minutes)
LA2. Introduction referencing style. Independent, referred and practical learning
Study Topic: Learning case solution procedure – step by step Duration: 1 hour Part 2 LA3. Download 4-5 cases
Q1. Know about the key pointsCollective work: Group activity

(15 +15 minutes)

Q2. Introduce a solution
Q3. Brainstorming consists of 6 members in each group
Part 3
(15 minutes)
LA4. Study in groups of 6 people to analyze the cases 1. Group 1: Discuss the objectives of the cases:

1. Group 2: Discuss the background
2. Group 3: Analyze the key information
3. Group 4: Identify possible solution

LA5. Compile all the tasks from each group

1. A group member from every group will make a presentation for 2 minutes
2. Clarification for other group members if they are not clear about the presentation.

Collective work: Group activity consists of 6 members in each group
Collective work: Group activity consists of 6 members in each group
Part 4
(10 minutes)
LA6. Exercise time Independent ability to assess the students
LA7. Complete the exercise and provide feedback
Post class
(5 minutes)

Students' feedback assessment
Need for a review class
Miscellaneous
Intuitive activity

REFERENCES

Aboulilah, H. M. A. E., Hossain, S. F. A., Vuong, B. N., & Jebril, T. (2022). Exploring the Relationship between WeChat Usage and E-purchase Intention During the COVID-19 Pandemic Among University Students in China. *SAGE Open, 12*(4). doi:10.1177/21582440221139447

Cousté, P. E., Qin, S., Hossain, S. F. A., & Hussain, K. (2022). Factors influencing social-media-based entrepreneurship prospects among female students in China. *Heliyon, 8*(12), e12041. doi:10.1016/j.heliyon.2022.e12041 PMID:36483305

ECRA | Electronic Commerce Research and Applications | Consumer Brand Relationships in Online Communities and E-commerce Channels | ScienceDirect.com by Elsevier. (n.d.). Retrieved from https://www.sciencedirect.com/journal/electronic-commerce-research-and-applications/special-is sue/10NKZRJHBP8

Fetscherin, M., & Heinrich, D. (2014). Consumer brand relationships: A research landscape. *Journal of Brand Management, 21*(5), 366–371. doi:10.1057/bm.2014.22

Hossain, S. F. A., Nurunnabi, M., Hussain, K., & Shan, X. (2020). Smartphone-based m-shopping behavior and innovative entrepreneurial tendency among women in emerging Asia. *International Journal of Gender and Entrepreneurship, 12*(2), 173–189. doi:10.1108/IJGE-03-2019-0054

Mohsin, A. K., Hongzhen, L., & Hossain, S. F. A. (2021). Impact of COVID-19 pandemic on consumer economy: Countermeasures analysis. Journal Name. Advance online publication. doi:10.1177/21582440211008875

Naeem, M., & Ozuem, W. (2021). Understanding the social consumer fashion brand engagement journey: Insights about reputed fashion brands. *Journal of Brand Management, 28*(5), 510–525. doi:10.1057/s41262-021-00239-5

Vuong, B. N., Tushar, H., & Hossain, S. F. A. (2022). The effect of social support on job performance through organizational commitment and innovative work behavior: Does innovative climate matter? [DOI number]. *Asia-Pacific Journal of Business Administration, 14*(2), 156–172. https://doi.org/

APPENDIX

Exhibit 1

Figure 1. Fashion Brand Relevance
Source: According to Fetscherin and Heinrich (2014), their research on consumer brand relationships offered valuable insights (p. 367).

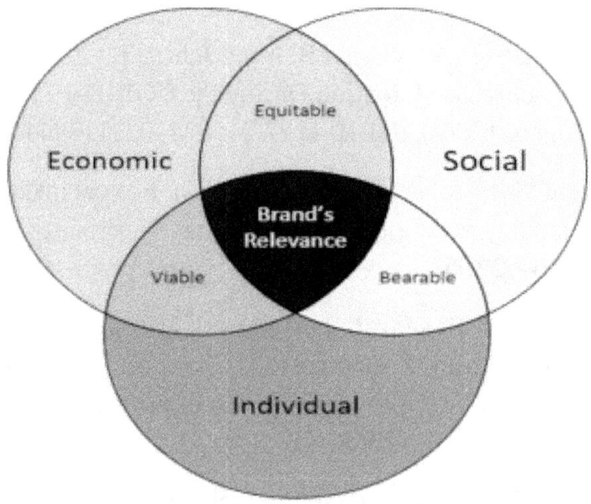

Exhibit 2

Figure 2. Social Consumer Fashion Brand Engagement Model
Source: According to Naeem and Ozuem (2021), in their study on reputed fashion brands, they gained insights into the social consumer fashion brand engagement journey (p. 513).

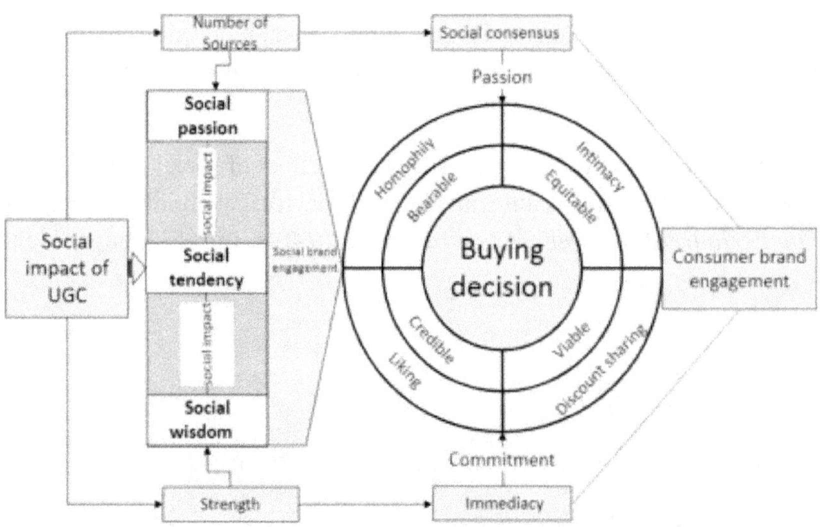

Exhibit 3

Bangladesh, a dynamic nation in South Asia, has seen a notable change in its internet buying habits. A digital revolution has swept the country, changing how people purchase as a result of the rapid growth of technology and rising internet usage. Online shopping has crossed geographic barriers, linking customers to a world of limitless possibilities, from the busy streets of Dhaka to the peaceful villages of rural Bangladesh. The ease of use, accessibility, and wide variety of items provided by e-commerce platforms have caught the interest of the country, enabling people to browse, contrast, and buy goods and services at the touch of a button.

This change in customer behavior not only demonstrates an increase in consumer confidence in online services, but it also represents a fundamental shift in how Bangladeshis view and embrace the digital age. Online shopping has evolved into a representation of development, empowerment, and boundless potential as the nation sets off on this exciting adventure, catapulting Bangladesh to the front of the digital era.

Exhibit 4

Figure 3. Sales Growth over the Years
Source: Collected from the annual reports of clothes over bae's, 2022.

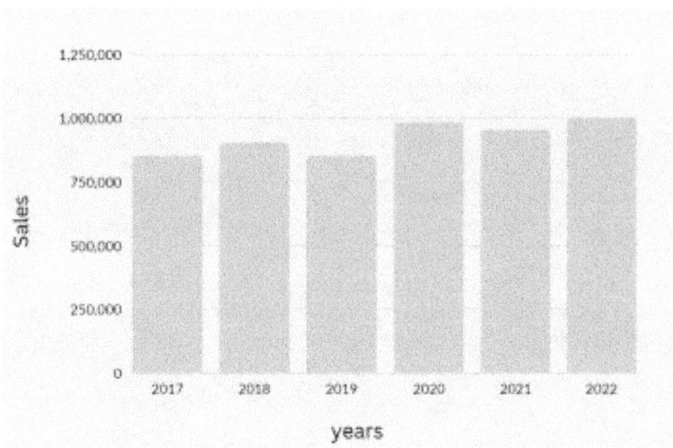

Exhibit 5

Table 1. Consumer Quotes

Archita kundu	"There shouldn't not be anything like a standard size that doesn't consider a plus size body. Fashion should be for everyone, I suppose."
Tasnia Haque	"Inner peace is always connected to the outer look. How you are feeling now is direct to the result of how you are looking now. Hence, a nice top always boosts your inner and outer energy."
Roksana Begum	"Age is just a number. If my daughters can adorn themselves in floral prints, so can I. Only accessibility is needed to change the mindset."
Adiba karim	" Modest fashion is not niche anymore; it never was. We only need acknowledgement by good brands and designers to hop on trends."
Shanika Rahman	" Like flexibility in life ; we too prefer flexibility in fashion. It should be easy, fun, minimal and a term that everyone can own by their own way. "

Source: Primary data collection by the authors

Chapter 5
Exploring Solopreneurs' Journey in the Digital Era

Pulkit Jain
https://orcid.org/0000-0003-2385-5645
School of Liberal Studies, University of Petroleum and Energy Studies, Dehradun, India

ABSTRACT

This study explores solopreneurship, an autonomous entrepreneurial model centered on managing digital enterprises aligned with personal interests. It analyzes the transformative impact of social media, investigating strategies like task outsourcing and collaborative ventures using Software as a Service (SaaS). Emphasizing platforms such as YouTube, X, and LinkedIn, the study highlights personal branding's substantial role in audience growth. Amid broader societal shifts, globalization, and economic growth, it delves into solopreneurs' motivations and challenges, stressing social media's indispensable role in reshaping global business practices. The research also probes well-being aspects, identity management, and protective strategies in the digital era. Identifying supportive ecosystems as pivotal, it emphasizes the critical examination of megatrends for a comprehensive understanding of solopreneur dynamics in digital entrepreneurship.

1. INTRODUCTION

In the dynamic realm of entrepreneurship, the term "entrepreneur" is formally defined as an individual organizing, managing, and assuming business risks (Merriam-Webster, 2018). However, this definition requires nuanced consideration for a comprehensive understanding of entrepreneurship, as noted by Tobak (2015). Tobak posits that genuine entrepreneurship entails a strategic equation integrating entrepreneurship, capital, products, customers, and business establishment.

The contemporary entrepreneurial landscape experiences a paradigm shift with the emergence of solopreneurship, where individuals independently conceive, create, and manage businesses, aiming to build scalable digital enterprises. Solopreneurs contribute significantly to economic growth, diversification, and content creation, emphasizing adept use of digital marketing and personal branding on platforms such as LinkedIn, X, YouTube, and Instagram.

DOI: 10.4018/979-8-3693-1842-3.ch005

Table 1. Analysis of Branding of Social Media Platforms

Social Network	Visual Identity	Brand Persona	Positioning
Facebook	Lowercase blue "f" in a square, blue color scheme	Connectivity, community, content sharing	User-friendly platform fostering interpersonal relationships and content dissemination
X	Bold 'X' design with intersecting lines.	Conveys innovation, convergence of ideas, and global interconnectedness.	The 'X' symbolizes twitter's transformative journey, signaling a commitment to adapt and evolve. Potential interpretations align with X's role as a platform for diverse ideas and connectivity.
LinkedIn	Custom-font "LinkedIn" with blue "in" icon, blue	Professional networking, career development, business-oriented community	Essential tool for individuals and businesses aiming to establish and expand professional networks
Instagram	Stylized camera icon on a gradient background	Creativity, visual expression, storytelling through images	Platform for sharing visually compelling content, fostering a community driven by artistic expression
YouTube	Red play button icon next to the name, red and white	Video content, creativity, entertainment	Leading platform for diverse video content, offering an immersive and engaging visual experience for online video consumption

Analyzing the branding of major social media platforms in table 1, reveals diverse strategies in presenting unique user experiences. Facebook's iconic blue "f" emphasizes connection and community, fostering a sense of security. X employs a bold 'X' design symbolizing innovation and global interconnectedness. Instagram uses a stylized camera icon, vibrant colors, promoting visual story-sharing and creativity. YouTube's red play button signifies a hub for diverse video content, evoking energy. LinkedIn, with a custom "LinkedIn" font and professional blue, caters to career development and professionalism. (Al-Zyoud, 2018; Lund, Cohen, & Scarles, 2018). Solopreneurs strategically leverage these platforms for digital marketing, aligning with evolving entrepreneurial definitions. Each platform's distinct features support solopreneurs in managing businesses and crafting personal brands.

Solopreneurs, navigating challenges, leverage social media for marketing and customer care (Tobak, 2015). In a changing societal landscape, social media enables effective digital marketing and customer care for entrepreneurs, with many relying exclusively on these platforms (Baccarella et al., 2018; Kaplan & Haenlein, 2010). The solo self-employed, despite ubiquity, operate inconspicuously and face multifaceted challenges (Bögenhold & Klinglmair, 2016).

Digital business, particularly digital entrepreneurship, is reshaping global business practices at an unprecedented pace. According to The Economist Intelligence Unit (EIU), nearly 80% of companies acknowledge significant modifications in customer interactions with goods and services (EIU, 2013). Furthermore, over 51% of these companies are adapting pricing and delivery models to align with evolving consumer behavior (EIU, 2013). Siwicki predicts a substantial increase in consumer spending via mobile, projecting a surge from US$ 204 billion in 2014 to US$ 626 billion in 2018, with almost half of all e-commerce sales attributed to mobile commerce (Siwicki, 2014).

Statista reports a noteworthy ascent in e-retail sales, accounting for 7.4% of total retail sales globally in 2015. This figure is anticipated to escalate to 13% by 2019. The European landscape exemplifies the rapid integration of e-commerce, with e-sales climbing from 13% of total sales in 2008 to 20% in 2015 (Statista, 2017; Eurostaat, 2016).

Digital entrepreneurship is diversifying the entrepreneurial population and altering its demographic profile, possibly indicating a socio-significant factor influencing this trend (Amorós & Bosma, 2013). The digital market's inherent international character, coupled with low initial investment requirements for highly digitized enterprises, makes it a fertile ground for business venturing (Ziyae et al., 2014). A variety of business frameworks, such as the "peer-to-peer economy" and "sharing economy," and working concepts like "digital solopreneurs," are emerging, blurring traditional boundaries and giving rise to new entrepreneurial practices (Eurostaat, 2017).

As digital entrepreneurship continues to rise, it necessitates supportive ecosystems, as highlighted by Al Omoush et al., playing a crucial role in defining economic dynamism and warrant in-depth analysis (Nambisan, 2016). The intertwining of social/human and digital agencies in the entrepreneurial context underscores the importance of studying megatrends to understand evolving entrepreneurial practices.

This study aims to redress biases against solo self-employment and social media, exclusively exploring their nexus among solopreneurs (Bögenhold & Klinglmair, 2016). Focusing on their unique business structure and the interplay between private and entrepreneurial identities, the research delves into the impact of well-being aspects on social media use, emphasizing identity management and protective strategies. Additionally, the study considers negative consequences for both solopreneurs and their businesses. Contextualizing solopreneurship in the digital realm (Martín-Rojas et al., 2020), a quantitative analysis outlines characteristics of solopreneurs, with social media's importance underscored.

This study aims to comprehensively explore solopreneurship, covering its definition, differentiation from traditional models, the role of social media, scaling strategies, personal branding, economic impact, challenges, and future prospects. In the context of the multifaceted impacts of digitalization on entrepreneurship, this research contributes valuable insights into the evolving nature of solopreneurs, emphasizing their social media dynamics and entrepreneurial strategies in the digital era. The study's findings shed light on the personal self's role in solopreneurs' businesses, bridging a knowledge gap and offering a detailed empirical understanding of their social media behavior and self-presentation as an identity management tool. The insights provided encompass both positive and negative consequences of social media use, enriching the ongoing discourse on entrepreneurship in the digital era.

1.1 Research Statement

This study delves into solopreneurship, an entrepreneurial model marked by independent digital enterprise management. Focused on the transformative role of social media, particularly in task outsourcing and SaaS collaborations, the study highlights personal branding's pivotal role on platforms like YouTube, X and LinkedIn for audience expansion. Examining motivations and challenges amid societal shifts, globalization, and solo self-employment, it underscores social media's paradigmatic impact on global business practices and economic growth. Providing nuanced insights into solopreneurs' social media use and the interplay between personal and professional identities online, the research addresses acknowledged challenges and explores mitigation strategies. While recognizing social media's role in audience connection, it calls for an investigation into its long-term sustainability. Cultural and regional variations, consequences of social media collaborations, and a holistic understanding of solopreneurial ecosystems are identified as understudied aspects. The study advocates for research into the intersectionality of solopreneurship, considering gender and ethnicity, and emphasizes addressing gaps in understanding emerging technologies' impact on strategies.

2. REVIEW OF LITERATURE

The contemporary business landscape has undergone a noteworthy transformation with the emergence of solopreneurship, signifying a burgeoning sector within the entrepreneurial community. This literature review seeks to comprehensively delve into the journey of solopreneurs in the digital age, with a particular emphasis on the role of social media. By drawing upon a varied array of literature, this review aims to furnish a nuanced understanding of the challenges, opportunities, and dynamics encountered by solopreneurs in the swiftly evolving digital business milieu.

Digital technologies, particularly social media, have become integral components influencing the solopreneurial experience and its sustainability (Adkins, 2016; Morgan, 2013; Rosário & Dias, 2023). Social media platforms, such as Instagram, Facebook, and X, play a crucial role in connecting solopreneurs with their target audiences, facilitating marketing efforts, and creating growth opportunities (Rosário & Dias, 2023). The accessibility of digital platforms has leveled the competitive field for solopreneurs, allowing them to effectively compete with larger entities in the digital marketplace.

Social media serves a central role in the solopreneurial journey as a cost-effective marketing tool. Platforms like Instagram, Facebook, and X provide solopreneurs with avenues for brand promotion and the ability to reach a global audience through targeted campaigns, enhancing visibility and business potential (Rosário & Dias, 2023). Additionally, these platforms facilitate the creation and cultivation of networks, a crucial aspect of solopreneurship. Platforms like LinkedIn offer opportunities for solopreneurs to connect with other professionals, potential clients, and collaborators (Zhao et al., 2023), allowing the establishment of meaningful relationships in the digital space, crucial for creating a supportive ecosystem.

Furthermore, social media acts as a catalyst for opportunity creation in the solopreneurial context. Exposure on social platforms can lead to collaborations, partnerships, and unexpected business opportunities. The viral nature of content on social media amplifies the reach of solopreneurs, opening doors to new ventures and collaborations. However, it is important to acknowledge the challenges associated with social media use by solopreneurs, including information overload, privacy concerns, and algorithmic uncertainties (Brown & Jones, 2017).

Insights from Ernst & Young's Megatrends report (2012) and global reports like the Global Entrepreneurship Monitor (Amorós & Bosma, 2013) provide a broader perspective on the global trends shaping the entrepreneurial landscape. The report by Frey and Osborne (2013) on the future of employment and its susceptibility to computerization adds depth to the understanding of the evolving nature of work and entrepreneurship.

The evolution of e-commerce is a crucial aspect of the solopreneurial journey. Eurostat's data on e-sales and turnover (2016, 2017) and insights from Siwicki (2014) on the increasing role of mobile commerce contribute to understanding the dynamics of the digital entrepreneurship era.Olanrewaju et al. (2020) provide a comprehensive literature review on the intersection of social media and entrepreneurship, offering insights into how solopreneurs navigate and leverage social media in their ventures.

Hobsbawm's (2023) article challenges conventional career narratives, advocating continuous reinvention amid contemporary job insecurity. Introducing "solopreneurship" as a concept marked by flexible schedules and diverse career paths, the article observes a global upswing in LinkedIn members diversifying skills. Highlighting Herminia Ibarra's strategies for career reinvention, including network activation and experimenting with alternative professional identities, the narrative unexpectedly shifts to the entrepreneurial journey of music journalist Pete Paphides. Paphides' story serves as a compelling case study, illustrating the adaptability and versatility in solopreneurship as he ventures into manufacturing and food retail. The article concludes by underscoring the rising trend of solopreneurs and the intrinsic value of career diversity for heightened job satisfaction, contributing nuanced insights to the literature on solopreneurship.

In the exploration of solopreneurship, sociological insights from "Extending Mixed Embeddedness" (Berwing, 2019) gain significance, shifting away from individualistic paradigms in entrepreneurship research. This aligns with the broader investigation into solopreneurship, including migrant entrepreneurship and critiquing ethnic reductionism, providing a nuanced contextual background. The review's call for historical analyses and comprehensive datasets resonates with the solopreneurship study, addressing data constraints through robust research methodologies. Integration of Norbert Elias' figurational analysis aligns with the solopreneurship study's aim to explore solopreneurs' strategies, like process automation and strategic collaborations, in the digital era.

Insights from sociology and entrepreneurship form a theoretical foundation, emphasizing solopreneurship's collective facets. Kathryn White's examination of freelancing motivations (White, 2015) adds practical depth, underscoring autonomy, networking, and conducive work environments. Her recommendations on online presence, marketing, and legal considerations contribute to the discourse on solopreneurship, extending to effective workload management, negotiations, automation, delegation, and continuous development.

Large-scale workfare programs, like Argentina's Jefes initiative, shield the vulnerable during crises but face sustainability challenges (Besley & Coate, 1992; Ravallion, 1999). In response, Argentina introduced the Microemprendimientos Productivos (MEP) program, targeting Jefes beneficiaries' transition to self-employment (Almeida & Galasso, 2010). The MEP program, providing financial aid and technical support, addresses credit constraints and inadequate business training hindering entrepreneurial pursuits. The study examines 'poverty trap' and 'entrepreneurial' perspectives, exploring non-convex production technologies and credit constraints' impact on self-employment. While a uniform income increase is absent, certain subgroups, like younger and more educated beneficiaries, experience positive outcomes. Results align with the 'entrepreneurial' view, emphasizing motivation and initial human capital's impact on jumpstarting self-employment (Beckerman, Olivas, & Dar, 2004; McKenzie & Woodruff, 2006).

By 2025, millennials are projected to constitute over 75% of the workforce, signaling a paradigm shift (Frey, 2013). Limited engagement with Fortune 500 companies steers millennials toward an entrepreneurial approach, navigating an involuntary path into entrepreneurship. The trend toward project-based work aligns with diminishing physical office significance, an enhanced freelancer toolbox, and a surge in niche job markets. Companies, driven by cost minimization imperatives, favor project-oriented hiring, leveraging freelancers' flexibility and diverse skill sets. Despite the absence of conventional benefits, freelancers enjoy control and influence over their careers. Millennials adopt a sampler approach, exploring projects to identify optimal career paths.

The evolving landscape witnesses the emergence of business colonies, facilitated by coworking spaces and specialized talent pools, challenging traditional hiring practices. This transformative era sees skill credentials associated with colonies gaining prominence, signaling a departure from conventional business models toward a freelancing-dominated future.

Thickstun's (2019) study, "Every Lesson Every Day," explores the entrepreneurial traits of young music professionals. The research focuses on those assuming diverse roles, such as studio owners, bloggers, and entrepreneurs, reflecting their multifaceted nature. Notably, independent music teachers redefine traditional roles, with examples like Joy Morin's innovative "teacher retreat" and Christopher Oill's fusion of technology and composition. The study emphasizes the entrepreneurial spirit, advocating for small, strategic steps with available resources. Drawing on scholars like Saras D. Saravathy and Adam Grant, the article suggests that success comes from being different or better, not necessarily the first. It concludes by urging music teachers to embrace entrepreneurial thinking, promoting innovation in teaching practices through small, deliberate steps.

The chapter "What It Means to Freelance (or Jumping in with Your Eyes Wide Open)", authored by Reed, C. (2018), meticulously examines the intricacies of freelancing and entrepreneurship, delving into the evolving definitions of these terms (Freelance, 2018). It emphasizes the current trend toward freelance work, citing influences such as the fragmentation of traditional jobs, stagnant wages, and the rise of platforms like Airbnb and Upwork (Wang, 2018; Fox, 2017). Autonomy, flexible schedules, and the ability to choose projects are portrayed as key benefits of freelancing. The chapter explores diverse motivations for individuals embracing freelancing, from pursuing varied interests to supplementing income (Freelancing in America, 2017; Fox, 2017). It underscores the entrepreneurial mindset necessary for successful freelancing, acknowledging challenges such as the need for diverse business skills and potential social isolation. Additionally, the chapter provides valuable insights into discovering freelance opportunities, emphasizing the significance of online platforms and industry-specific spaces. Conclusively, it positions freelancing as a dynamic career choice within the contemporary gig economy.

The article titled "Lenders need to understand that self-employment is the new employment" by Pilkerton and Gandhi (2023) highlights the crucial necessity for lenders to comprehend the emerging trend of self-employment as a predominant form of work. The authors stress the importance of financial institutions adapting their strategies to accommodate the unique financial requirements of self-employed individuals. The article advocates for a shift in the perception of employment by lenders, recognizing the increasing significance of self-employment in the contemporary job landscape. Overall, Pilkerton and Gandhi urge lenders to align their services with the evolving nature of employment, acknowledging self-employment as a substantial and influential aspect of the present-day workforce.

Solopreneurship has gained increasing prominence in recent years, indicating a shift wherein individuals opt to independently operate small businesses. This shift is intricately tied to the digital age, where technological progress has empowered solopreneurs to establish and manage businesses with unprecedented ease. The digital landscape provides a distinctive context for comprehending the trajectory of solopreneurs, and their experiences are molded by various factors, including technological trends, market dynamics, and social influences.

2.1 Theoretical Framework

The concept of self-employment encompasses various terms such as own account worker, self-employed, freelancer, solo self-employed, and solopreneur (Gartner, 1985; van Stel et al., 2012; Kitching and Smallbone, 2012). The U.S. Census Bureau refers to businesses without paid employees as nonemployers (U.S. Census Bureau, 2013). This study adopts the term "solopreneur" to characterize entrepreneurs who work independently, without co-entrepreneurs or personnel, aligning with the definition by Andersson and Wadensjö (2007) and the Urban Dictionary (2015). Solopreneurs, akin to other entrepreneurs, impact their surroundings and can influence their own roles in entrepreneurship (Andersson and Wadensjö, 2007). Motivations for solopreneurs vary, ranging from economic success to the pursuit of autonomy and challenge in contrast to employment by large organizations (Bradley and Roberts, 2004; Vivarelli,

1991). Autonomy is a significant factor favoring self-employment (Kolvereid, 1996). Despite the potential for satisfaction, self-employment is not without challenges, as evidenced by job-related stress, insomnia, and conflicts reported by self-employed individuals (Blanchflower, 2004; Eden, 1976; Katz, 1993; Blanchflower and Oswald, 1998; Blanchflower et al., 2001; Hundley, 2001).

2.2 Digital Entrepreneurship

Digital entrepreneurship has gained prominence in contemporary business dynamics, with Zaheer, Breyer, and Dumay (2019) delineating its essential components as Digital Business Models, Technological Adaptation, and Online Market Strategies. This conceptual framework lays the groundwork for an in-depth exploration of the intricate dynamics of solopreneurship in the digital age. Solopreneurs grapple with the complexities of shaping their digital business models, adapting to evolving technologies, and strategically positioning themselves within online markets.

In the realm of entrepreneurship, a clear dichotomy exists between traditional entrepreneurship and digital business models. Traditional entrepreneurship involves the establishment and management of physical businesses, relying on conventional marketing strategies, face-to-face customer interactions, and adherence to established industry practices (Richter et al., 2017). In contrast, digital business models heavily depend on digital technologies, the internet, and online platforms, enabling virtual operations and global audience engagement (Ruggieri et al., 2018). This dichotomy underscores the integration of technology, data-driven decision-making processes, and a global outreach that distinguishes digital business models from their traditional counterparts, emblematic of the evolving entrepreneurial landscape in the digital era (Scuotto et al., 2019).

Aligned with Alvesson and Deetz's (2000) three objectives of critical management research—insight, critique, and transformative redefinition—a structured literature review approach is adopted. This approach addresses three interconnected research questions aimed at unraveling the development, focus, and future of digital entrepreneurship research (Massaro et al., 2016). Through the utilization of systematic literature review technology, the study integrates insight, critique, and transformative redefinition, contributing to the generation of new knowledge in the field.

Despite a comprehensive, multi-disciplinary literature search, the review identifies critical gaps in the dynamic digital entrepreneurship landscape. The field's development appears fragmented, lacking consensus on key terms and exhibiting limited exploration of entrepreneurial themes. Integrative frameworks are notably absent, and entrepreneurship education remains underexplored. Consequently, the study calls for a new research phase to address these gaps and enhance relevance to practice, anticipating a shift beyond explanatory research. Digital entrepreneurship, though a fraction of the broader digital business research landscape, offers scholars opportunities to delve into the intricacies of entrepreneurship in the digital era, aligning with the dynamic observations made by Finkelstein (2001) in the internet era.

In their book "Digital Entrepreneurship: Research and Practice" (Zhao & Collier, 2016), the authors propose a comprehensive model for studying digital entrepreneurship. They posit that digital entrepreneurship deviates from traditional entrepreneurship and present a model comprising five crucial components: Digital knowledge base and ICT market, Digital business environment, Access to finance, Digital skills and e-leadership, and Entrepreneurial Culture.

Figure 1. Source - "Digital Entrepreneurship: Research and Practice" (Zhao & Collier, 2016)

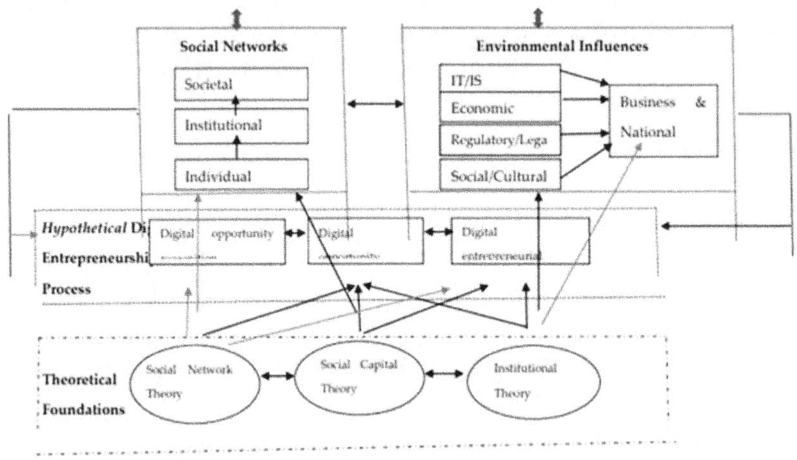

This proposed model in Figure 1 facilitates an investigation into the role and intensity of social networks and social capital in the development and outcomes of digital entrepreneurship. It seeks to answer two pivotal research questions: 1) The role of social networks in digital opportunity identification and exploration at individual, institutional, and societal levels, and 2) How social networks become a significant source of social capital in digital entrepreneurial development and performance. These inquiries aim to scrutinize whether digital entrepreneurs follow the same entrepreneurial process as their traditional counterparts, encompassing opportunity recognition, exploration, and entrepreneurial outcomes. The model also explores environmental influences, particularly the enduring systems or institutions shaping digital entrepreneurship. Here, the model draws on institutional theory, emphasizing that institutional forces, whether formal (laws, regulations) or informal (social norms, values), play a novel role in digital entrepreneurship research, influencing the survival and legitimacy of organizations (DiMaggio and Powell, 1983).

Satalkina and Steiner's (2020) research endeavors to systematize core performance indicators of digital entrepreneurship, providing insights into the impact of digital trends on business frameworks and their connection to innovation system resilience. Drawing from a systematic literature review in digital entrepreneurship, the study identifies 10 determinants within three dimensions—Entrepreneur, Entrepreneurial process, and Ecosystem as shown in figure 2. The analysis explores current trends in digital entrepreneurship across various countries, examining the interrelatedness of indicators with these determinants through correlation analysis.

The findings underscore the significance of a systematic approach in comprehending the digital transformation of socioeconomic systems. The research not only offers an overview of digital entrepreneurship indicators, emphasizing their strengths, focuses, and potential implications but also serves as a valuable resource for diverse readers, including policymakers, business agents, entrepreneurs, and researchers.

The study advocates for an extended exploration of societal transitions triggered by digital transformation. It emphasizes the importance of applying a systems science approach to understand the interplay between entrepreneurial processes and socioeconomic system dimensions, particularly amid global societal transitions. This approach can shed light on the resilience and sustainability of socioeconomic systems, considering the impact of disturbances and vulnerability factors. Additionally, it defines the role of digital entrepreneurs in bolstering innovation system resilience and overall socioeconomic sustainability.

Figure 2. Digital Transformation of Socioeconomic Systems, Source - Satalkina and Steiner's (2020)

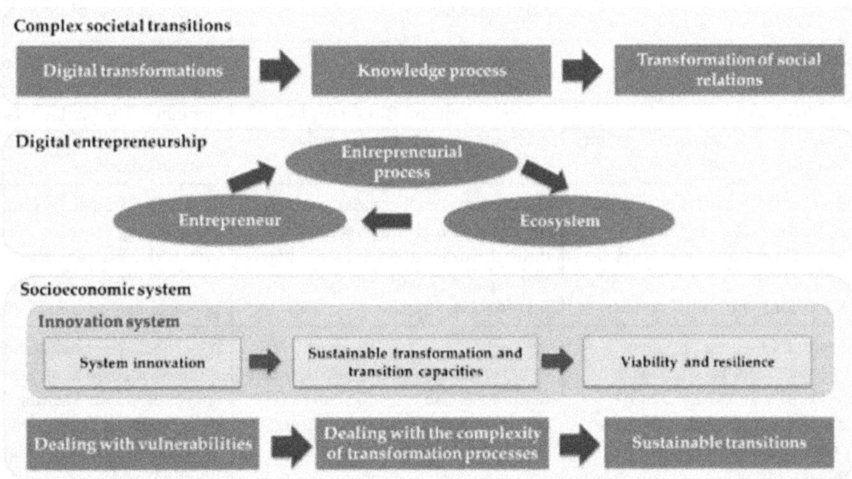

2.3 Social Media and Personal Branding

Understanding the scope of personal branding on social media, Urbanová and Slind (2016) conducted a study that delves into successful personal branding, specifically focusing on YouTubers. Employing content analysis on 72 videos from four YouTubers, the researchers identified patterns related to the creation and development of personal brands. The study proposes a conceptual framework based on three key success factors: maintaining a clear brand profile, ensuring constant visibility on multiple social media platforms, and interacting with the audience. Successful YouTubers exhibit consistency in content, enhancing their authenticity. They actively promote themselves on various social media sites, thereby increasing visibility and popularity. Interaction with the audience, including addressing viewers and encouraging content co-creation, plays a crucial role in building strong connections.

Examining personal branding across social media platforms reveals diverse strategies (Table 2). Facebook fosters an informal environment for users to share updates and engage with friends, reflecting multidimensional identity expression. X distinguishes itself with concise real-time interactions due to character limits, shaping brief communication. Instagram prioritizes visual and creative expression, enabling users to curate appealing profiles with stories and reels. YouTube focuses on video-centric content creation, allowing users to shape personal brands through thumbnails and titles. LinkedIn maintains a professional and career-oriented atmosphere, emphasizing achievements and skills for networking in the professional sphere (Nanayakkara & Dissanayake, 2020; Lo & Peng, 2022). These varied approaches underscore the multidimensional nature of personal branding on social media, with visual elements playing a crucial role.

Table 2. Key Features of Personal Branding on Social Media Platforms

Social Network	Approach to Personal Branding	Key Features	Analysis
Facebook	Embraces an informal and personal approach, allowing users to share personal updates, photos, and engage with friends and family.	Users often include personal photos, fostering genuine interaction. Encourages a multidimensional personal expression.	Facebook cultivates an informal and personal environment, supporting authentic interaction and allowing users to express various aspects of their personalities.
X	Fosters concise and real-time interactions, requiring brevity due to character limits. Users engage in dynamic conversations and craft concise profile bios.	The character limit shapes succinct communication, promoting real-time engagement. Bio serves as a brief introduction to personal or professional identity.	X's character limit encourages dynamic engagement, shaping succinct personal branding. The platform facilitates real-time interactions, emphasizing immediate and concise communication.
Instagram	Emphasizes visual and creative expression, allowing users to curate visually appealing profiles. Incorporates Stories and Reels for more casual updates.	Focuses on visual content, aesthetic themes, and real-time updates through Stories and Reels. Enables creative and visually engaging personal branding.	Instagram prioritizes visual content, encouraging users to express their identity creatively. The platform allows for curated, visually cohesive profiles with a blend of personal and aspirational elements.
YouTube	Centrally focused on video content creation, where users tell stories and share creative content. Thumbnails and titles contribute to a distinctive personal brand.	Users create and share videos, using thumbnails and titles to shape a unique personal brand. Emphasizes storytelling and content quality.	YouTube's personal branding revolves around video content, allowing for extended self-expression. The importance of thumbnails and titles underscores the role of storytelling and content quality in shaping a unique brand.
LinkedIn	Maintains a professional and career-oriented environment, emphasizing achievements and connections within the professional sphere.	Profiles highlight professional achievements, detailed work experience, and skills. Facilitates networking and connections within the professional realm.	LinkedIn's formal and career-oriented approach emphasizes professional accomplishments and networking. Users leverage the platform to build a reputable personal brand within their professional sphere.

The research posits that personal branding on social media is an ongoing process involving a combination of these key factors. Beyond contributing to theories of personal branding, the study extends insights to the broader field of branding. Ethical implications are highlighted, emphasizing the need for both YouTubers and viewers to be aware of the virtual nature of online relationships and potential influences. The study also provides managerial recommendations for marketing professionals, underscoring the influential power of YouTubers and the importance of monitoring their impact on brand perception. The authors call for future research to explore personal branding on other social media platforms, consider audience perceptions, and further enhance the proposed framework by incorporating insights from the audience's perspective.

Chen, Rui, and Whinston (2021) contribute to the academic literature by exploring the impact of social media personal branding on executive job market outcomes. Motivated by the increasing popularity of personal branding on platforms like X, the study proposes a conceptual framework based on product advertising theory, suggesting positive effects on career outcomes through awareness and persuasive mechanisms. The authors delve into the concept of personal branding, originally popularized by Tom Peters in 1997, emphasizing its relevance in the social media era. Personal branding involves actively shaping public perception to establish authority, enhance credibility, and stand out professionally.

While acknowledging the powerful tool that social media platforms, particularly X, offer for personal branding, the study underscores the need for a dedicated, full-time commitment to this endeavor. Building on parallels with product advertising, the authors hypothesize that social media personal branding positively influences executive career outcomes, drawing on Goffman's dramaturgical analysis and impression management in sociology. The study employs an empirical approach, measuring personal branding through an executive's tweets and investigating its effects on compensation and job acquisition. Using a two-sided matching model, the research considers the mutual and exclusive aspects of executive hiring, ultimately finding evidence that personal branding enhances job market performance for executives.

In practical terms, the research suggests potential benefits for job seekers, especially executives, through social media personal branding. The study hints at a prospective business model for personal branding platforms, emphasizing the current provision of such functionality by X for free. While acknowledging limitations, focusing solely on executive labor markets and omitting consideration of potential heterogeneous effects, the study encourages future research with refined data and improved identification strategies to deepen insights into the impact of social media personal branding on career outcomes.

2.4 Research Objectives

- Understand how solopreneurs use platforms YouTube, X and LinkedIn to grow their businesses and connect with people.
- Examine the impact of personal branding and different strategies like task outsourcing.
- Identify the challenges solopreneurs encounter on social media, such as information overload or concerns about privacy. Also, assess the long-term effectiveness of their social media usage.
- Explore the ways social media supports collaboration, examining both the positive and negative aspects of partnerships, and gain insights into how solopreneurs operate in both online and offline settings.

2.5 Research Questions

1. How do solopreneurs run their own businesses, using platforms YouTube, X and LinkedIn to discover opportunities for themselves and the community? Also, how do these social networks impact the opportunities that solopreneurs can access?
2. How important is it for solopreneurs to create a personal brand on social media platforms to succeed in their online businesses?
3. In what ways do various strategies, such as seeking assistance from others for specific tasks, contribute to the success of solopreneurs in their digital businesses?

3. RESEARCH METHODOLOGY

The researcher used in-depth interviews and case studies to learn from solo entrepreneurs (solopreneurs) who used platforms like YouTube, X and LinkedIn. These methods helped the researcher understand how solopreneurs discovered opportunities and tackled challenges in the digital world. The researcher looked closely at their experiences, motivations, and strategies.

In-depth interviews allowed the researcher to dive deep into the stories of solopreneurs. By talking to those who actively used platforms like YouTube, X and LinkedIn, the researcher aimed to uncover the different ways they found opportunities and navigate their online business journeys. The interviews gave the researcher a detailed understanding of their perspectives.

The researcher examined real-life cases to explore strategies and outcomes in the world of solopreneurs. Each case represented a unique scenario, helping the researcher see the varied aspects of digital entrepreneurship. Through these studies, the researcher identified patterns, challenges, and unique details that might be missed with a broader approach.

After collecting all this information, the researcher used thematic analysis to make sense of it. Thematic analysis was a way of carefully looking at the data to find recurring themes and patterns. It helped the researcher organize the information and discover key insights. This method aligned with the goal of exploring and understanding the experiences of solopreneurs.

To make sure the findings were strong and reliable, the researcher used cross-validation. This meant comparing the results from different methods, like interviews and case studies. By doing this, the researcher aimed to ensure that the conclusions were consistent and not biased. Cross-validation helped the researcher have a more complete understanding of the solopreneurship world.

3.1 Sampling Approach

The research employs a sample size determined through a dual approach of purposive and convenience sampling. The study involves in-depth interviews with 5 solopreneurs and case studies featuring 5 solopreneurs, constituting a total sample of 10 solopreneurs. The selection process targets individuals from India, Europe, and the US, identified through a Google search to pinpoint the top 10 solopreneurs in each region. The final sample size is contingent on the availability and time constraints specified by solopreneurs for interviews. The sample size is further refined through a meticulous process, ensuring inclusion of solopreneurs providing complete and relevant answers to the interview questions. The names of solopreneurs are kept confidential to address identification concerns.

3.2 Findings and Discussions

3.2.1 Case Study Analysis

The solopreneurs in Table 3 have all sorts of reasons for doing what they do. Some are really into supporting causes, others want to be their own bosses, some are after financial freedom, and many just love the industries they work in. Each solopreneur faces their own set of challenges, like dealing with industry rules, competing with others, and figuring out how to grow their businesses. What's interesting is how flexible they are with using technology. They're into creating content, offering online courses, selling stuff online, and being active on digital platforms.

Another big part of their success is how they connect with people. They've got strong social networks, building communities and relationships in their industries. They also understand the power of personal branding – shaping how people see them on platforms like YouTube, X, and LinkedIn. This helps them stand out and make meaningful connections. The impact of this intentional personal branding is huge – it leads to partnerships, business success, writing bestselling books, and landing influential roles in their fields.

Table 3. Case Study Analysis of 5 Solopreneurs Under Study

Variable	Solopreneur A	Solopreneur B	Solopreneur C	Solopreneur D	Solopreneur E
Youtube Presence	High	Moderate	High	Low	Moderate
LinikedIn Presence	High	Moderate	High	High	Low
X Presence	Moderate	High	Low	High	Moderate
Motivations for Solopreneurship	Pursuit of Autonomy, Advocacy for Inclusivity	Passion for Coaching, Entrepreneurial Spirit	Desire for Financial Independence	Passion for Writing and Storytelling	Vision to Empower Entrepreneurs
Challenges in Solopreneurship	Navigating Beauty Industry Standards, Content Diversity	Balancing Multiple Ventures, Time Management	Supply Chain Management, Competition	Building Author Platform, Literary Industry Challenges	Scaling Operations, Media Industry Dynamics
Digital Business Models and Technological Adaptation	Beauty and Lifestyle Content Creation, Affiliate Marketing	Online Courses and Coaching Programs	E-commerce Business with Technological Integration	Digital Publishing, Online Presence	Digital Media Platform, Online Content Delivery
Social Networks and Social Capital	Extensive YouTube Community, Brand Collaborations	Online Courses Community, B-School Network	Industry Networks, Customer Base	Professional Connections, Author Network	Media Industry Collaborations, Entrepreneurial Network
Personal Branding on Social Media	Authentic Beauty Advocate, Makeup Tutorial Expert	Multi-Passionate Entrepreneur, Life Coach	E-commerce Expert, Transparent Business Owner	Bestselling Author, Thought Leader	Founder and CEO, Inspirational Leader
Impact of Social Media Personal Branding on Career Outcomes	Brand Collaborations, Makeup Line, Entrepreneurial Ventures	B-School Success, Bestselling Author	Successful E-commerce Business, Industry Recognition	Bestselling Novelist, Speaking Engagements	Media Influence, Platform Growth

So, when we look at all of this, it shows us that being a solopreneur is not just about doing your own thing. It's about what drives you, being adaptable with technology, building strong social networks, and shaping your image online. This study gives us a closer look at how these factors come together and influence the success of solopreneurs in today's digital world.

3.2.2 In Depth Interviews Analysis

As shown in Table 4, Solopreneurs are driven by various motivations, ranging from wanting financial independence to having a deep passion for specific industries. In the realm of solopreneurship, challenges are diverse, including dealing with competition, managing workloads, building audiences, and shaping how industries perceive them. Solopreneurs stand out for their ability to adapt, using different digital business models like consulting, affiliate marketing, content creation, and online courses to navigate the ever-changing technological landscape. Social networks play a crucial role in their success, with each solopreneur creating unique communities within their industries. Actively building a personal brand on social media is another key aspect contributing to their success, helping them carve a distinct identity in their respective fields. The positive influence of personal branding is evident in various achievements, such as successful consulting, product sales, gaining fame, and becoming influential figures in their industries. This thorough analysis highlights how motivations, challenges, digital strategies, social networks, and personal branding collectively shape the careers of solopreneurs.

Table 4. In-depth Interview Analysis of 5 Solopreneurs Under Study

Variable	Solopreneur F	Solopreneur G	Solopreneur H	Solopreneur I	Solopreneur J
X Presence	Moderate	High	Low	High	Moderate
YouTube Presence	High	Moderate	High	Low	Moderate
LinkedIn Presence	High	Moderate	High	High	Low
Motivations for Solopreneurship	Challenge and Autonomy in Sales Consulting	Financial Independence, Passion for Digital Marketing	Creativity, Content Creation, Entrepreneurial Spirit	Comedy, Entertaining People, Building Personal Brand	Financial Education Advocacy, Empowering Women in Finance
Challenges in Solopreneurship	Balancing Client Expectations, Competition	Adapting to Marketing Trends, Managing Workload	Content Consistency, Online Presence	Building and Retaining Audience, Industry Saturation	Industry Perception, Breaking Financial Taboos
Digital Business Models and Technological Adaptation	Sales Consulting, Online Courses	Affiliate Marketing, Digital Product Creation	YouTube Channel, Merchandise Sales	Digital Content Creation, Brand Collaborations	Authorship, Podcast, Online Courses
Social Networks and Social Capital	LinkedIn Community, Professional Networks	Affiliate Marketing Networks, Digital Marketing Communities	YouTube Community, Fan Base	Instagram Following, Industry Collaborations	Financial Industry Networks, Media Connections
Personal Branding on social media	Sales Expert, Thought Leader	Digital Marketing Guru, Productivity Expert	YouTube Star, Comedy Influencer	Lifestyle and Fashion Guru, Entertainer	Financial Expert, Author, Women Empowerment Advocate
Impact of social media Personal Branding on Career Outcomes	Consulting Success, Course Sales	Successful Digital Products, Industry Recognition	YouTube Fame, Merchandise Sales	Brand Collaborations, Media Features	Authorship Success, Podcast Influence

The study utilizes a qualitative data triangulation method, merging insights from a case study and in-depth interviews with solopreneurs. This approach aligns with the research objectives, allowing for a comprehensive analysis. By comparing findings from diverse sources, the study reveals commonalities and unique conclusions regarding intrinsic motivations, shared challenges, digital adaptation, the role of social networks, and the transformative impact of personal branding on solopreneurial success. This triangulation enhances the study's reliability, validity, and overall understanding of solopreneurial experiences.

3.2.3 Common Findings

Motivations for Solopreneurship: Solopreneurs are motivated by diverse factors, including a passion for their industries, financial independence, and a desire for autonomy. These intrinsic motivations drive them to leverage platforms like YouTube, X, and LinkedIn to connect with their audience, showcase their expertise, and foster meaningful professional relationships.

Challenges in Solopreneurship: Challenges identified among solopreneurs include competition, workload management, and industry-specific issues. These challenges, especially on social media, include information overload and privacy concerns. By examining these challenges, the study aims to assess how solopreneurs navigate and overcome obstacles in the dynamic landscape of social media, providing insights into the long-term effectiveness of their strategies.

Digital Business Models and Technological Adaptation: Solopreneurs in both tables demonstrate adaptability to digital business models by utilizing technology for consulting, online courses, digital products, and content creation. This aligns with the objective of understanding how they leverage platforms like YouTube, X, and LinkedIn to grow their businesses, emphasizing the importance of embracing digital strategies for solopreneurial success.

Social Networks and Social Capital: Solopreneurs actively build and leverage social networks within their industries, emphasizing the crucial role of networking and social capital. The study aims to explore how social media facilitates collaboration, examining both positive and negative aspects of partnerships. Additionally, insights into how solopreneurs operate in both online and offline settings will provide a comprehensive understanding of their networking strategies.

Personal Branding on Social Media: Solopreneurs actively shape their public image through personal branding on social media platforms, contributing to their success. This aligns with the objective of examining the impact of personal branding. Additionally, understanding the diverse challenges they face, such as workload management and competition, provides insights into different strategies, including task outsourcing, adopted to enhance their personal brand and overall business success.

Impact of Social Media Personal Branding on Career Outcomes: The consistent impact of personal branding on career outcomes is observed, with solopreneurs experiencing success in collaborations, sales, fame, and industry influence. This aligns with the objective of examining the impact of personal branding on their overall career trajectories and business outcomes.

3.2.4 Unique Findings

Motivations Beyond Financial Independence: Understanding how solopreneurs use platforms like YouTube, X, and LinkedIn is crucial. The motivations highlighted in interviews, such as autonomy in sales consulting and passion for empowering women in finance, provide insights into their strategic use of these platforms to connect with audiences.

Innovative Strategies in Digital Business Models: Examining the impact of personal branding and different strategies like task outsourcing is key. Innovative approaches in digital business models, emphasizing productivity expertise, reflect the varied strategies solopreneurs employ to enhance their brand and optimize operations.

Diverse Challenges in Solopreneurship: Identifying challenges solopreneurs encounter on social media, including information overload and privacy concerns, aligns with the objectives. The case study and interviews reveal nuanced difficulties, such as facing industry saturation on YouTube and navigating audience challenges. This sheds light on the challenges solopreneurs face in the online landscape.

Varied Approaches to Social Networks: Exploring how solopreneurs use platforms like LinkedIn aligns with this point. Emphasis on professional networks on LinkedIn and focus on fan communities on YouTube and Instagram showcase diverse engagement strategies on different platforms.

Strategic Evolution of Personal Branding: Examining the impact of personal branding aligns with this point. Strategic evolution beyond the initial brand establishment illustrates the long-term effectiveness of personal branding. It provides insights into how solopreneurs strategically shape and evolve their brands over time.

3.3 Discussions

The study significantly contributes to existing knowledge on solopreneurship in the digital age, emphasizing the transformative impact of social media platforms like Instagram, Facebook, and X (Adkins, 2016; Morgan, 2013; Rosário & Dias, 2023). These platforms play a crucial role in connecting individuals with their target audiences, facilitating effective marketing, and creating growth opportunities, thereby enhancing competitiveness in the digital marketplace (Rosário & Dias, 2023). Despite the benefits, challenges such as information overload, privacy concerns, and algorithmic uncertainties on social media platforms are notable (Brown & Jones, 2017).

Insights from global reports and studies on e-sales contribute to a comprehensive understanding of the evolving nature of work and entrepreneurship, highlighting the emergence of e-commerce as a crucial aspect of the entrepreneurial journey (Amorós & Bosma, 2013; Siwicki, 2014). Sociological perspectives, emphasizing collective facets of entrepreneurship, and studies on freelancing motivations provide practical depth, shedding light on how individuals leverage digital platforms (Berwing, 2019; White, 2015; Olanrewaju et al., 2020).

The paradigm shift towards freelancing, particularly among millennials, challenges traditional hiring practices, leading to the emergence of business colonies and evolving skill credentials associated with freelancing (Frey, 2013). Studies emphasizing entrepreneurial thinking among professionals and comprehensive examinations of freelancing underscore the need for strategic approaches and small, deliberate steps within the contemporary gig economy (Thickstun, 2019; Reed, 2018).

Recognition of the shift towards self-employment urges financial institutions to adapt their strategies to accommodate the unique financial requirements of individuals, emphasizing the need for lenders to recognize self-employment as a predominant form of work (Pilkerton & Gandhi, 2023).

The study's nuanced understanding of challenges and opportunities in entrepreneurship is further enriched by unique findings from in-depth interviews. Individuals showcase motivations beyond financial independence, emphasizing autonomy in sales consulting and a passion for empowering others in finance, respectively. One case demonstrates innovative strategies in digital business models, adding depth beyond traditional approaches. Diverse challenges in entrepreneurship, such as industry saturation and audience building, are revealed through cases.

Furthermore, varied approaches to social networks, as seen in formal use of LinkedIn compared to a focus on fan communities, highlight diverse engagement strategies. The strategic evolution of personal branding over time adds a layer of sophistication beyond the initial establishment of a personal brand.

4. CONCLUSION

The study reveals that solopreneurs actively engage with platforms like YouTube, X, and LinkedIn, leveraging them not just for personal gain but as tools to connect with communities and create opportunities. LinkedIn and YouTube, in particular, play pivotal roles in expanding opportunities for solopreneurs, showcasing the integral use of social media for business operations and community engagement.Personal branding emerges as a critical factor in solopreneurs' online success, with active shaping of public image on social media platforms significantly contributing to their achievements. The consistent impact of personal branding on collaborations, sales, fame, and industry influence underscores its importance in shaping solopreneurs' career trajectories and overall business outcomes.

The research uncovers diverse strategies employed by solopreneurs in enhancing their success in digital businesses. While not explicitly seeking assistance from others, solopreneurs adapt various strategies, including the evolution of personal branding, innovative digital business models, and varied approaches to social networks. These multifaceted strategies collectively contribute to their success in digital ventures. Insights drawn from the research emphasize the significance of digital platforms, personal branding, and adaptive strategies in shaping solopreneurs' success in the online business landscape. The study offers a comprehensive understanding of how solopreneurs navigate challenges and leverage opportunities in the dynamic world of digital entrepreneurship.

In the future, solo entrepreneurs will likely gain advantages from new technologies, digital tools, and smart computer systems. These advancements will help them organize their work better and make their tasks more efficient (Dvouletý et al., 2021). The acceptance of remote work empowers solo entrepreneurs to tap into a global talent pool, fostering a diverse workforce. However, challenges such as cybersecurity, data privacy, and the need for continuous adaptation to emerging technologies persist. Shifting societal attitudes towards work-life balance and the pursuit of purpose-driven careers may influence the future of solo entrepreneurship, emphasizing holistic well-being and social responsibility (Van Stel et al., 2014). The evolving landscape of solo entrepreneurship is expected to be shaped by technological advancements, changing work paradigms, and the pursuit of meaningful and sustainable business practices.

4.1 Limitations

- The solopreneurs chosen for analysis may not reflect the experiences of all solopreneurs, leading to a narrow understanding. Additionally, the made-up nature of the case study may not mirror real-world scenarios.
- Interviews can be influenced by the solopreneurs' personal biases, and they might not share all challenges. Interviewers' own biases and interpretations can impact the results, possibly giving an incomplete picture.
- Findings may not apply to all solopreneurs. The patterns identified may not work for everyone due to variations in industries, locations, and business sizes, limiting the broad applicability of the conclusions.
- The reliability and accuracy of data depend on the truthfulness of the information provided. Mistakes, misunderstandings, or inconsistencies could affect the quality of the findings.
- Unlike quantitative research, qualitative approaches lack statistical robustness. This means it's harder to measure relationships, establish cause-and-effect, or precisely quantify variables, reducing the precision of the study.

REFERENCES

Al-Zyoud, M. F. (2018). Social media marketing, functional branding strategy and intentional branding. *Problems and Perspectives in Management, 16*(16, Iss. 3), 102–116. doi:10.21511/ppm.16(3).2018.09

Almeida, R. K., & Galasso, E. (2010). Jump-starting self-employment? Evidence for welfare participants in Argentina. *World Development, 38*(5), 742–755. doi:10.1016/j.worlddev.2009.11.018

Andersson, P., & Wadensjö, E. (2007). Do the unemployed become successful entrepreneurs? *International Journal of Manpower, 28*(7), 604–626. doi:10.1108/01437720710830070

Baccarella, C. V., Wagner, T. F., Kietzmann, J. H., & McCarthy, I. P. (2018). Social media? It's serious! Understanding the dark side of social media. *European Management Journal, 36*(4), 431–438. doi:10.1016/j.emj.2018.07.002

Belt, P., Paloniemi, K., & Sinisammal, J. (2015). One-Person Enterprises and Business Growth. *Journal of Enterprising Culture, 23*(3), 381–404. doi:10.1142/S0218495815500132

. Berwing, S. (2019). Extending Mixed Embeddedness. Historical Social Research/Historische Sozialforschung, 44(4 (170), 162-185.

Blanchflower, D. (2004). Self-employment: More may not be better. Working paper No. 10286, National Bureau of Economic Research, available at: http://www.nber.org/ papers/w10286

Blanchflower, D., & Oswald, A. (1998). What makes an entrepreneur? *Journal of Labor Economics, 16*(1), 26–60. doi:10.1086/209881

Blanchflower, D., Oswald, A., & Stutzer, A. (2001). Latent entrepreneurship across nations. *European Economic Review, 45*(4), 680–691. doi:10.1016/S0014-2921(01)00137-4

Bögenhold, D., & Klinglmair, A. (2016). Independent work, modern organizations and entrepreneurial labor: Diversity and hybridity of freelancers and self-employment. [Cambridge Core.]. *Journal of Management & Organization, 22*(6), 843–858. doi:10.1017/jmo.2016.29

Bradley, D., & Roberts, J. (2004). Self-Employment and job satisfaction: Investigating the role of Self-Efficacy, depression, and seniority. *Journal of Small Business Management, 42*(1), 37–58. doi:10.1111/j.1540-627X.2004.00096.x

Chen, Y., Rui, H., & Whinston, A. (2021). Tweet to the Top? Social Media Personal Branding and Career Outcomes. *Management Information Systems Quarterly, 45*(2), 499–534. doi:10.25300/MISQ/2021/14617

DictionaryU. (2015). http://www.urbandictionary.com/define.php?term1/4solopreneur

Dvouletý, O., Procházka, D. A., & Starnawska, M. (2021). Who earns more: Job creators, solo-entrepreneurs or employees? Empirical evidence from Visegrad countries. *International Journal of Entrepreneurship and Small Business, 43*(4), 517–530. doi:10.1504/IJESB.2021.117345

Eden, B. (1976). On the specification of the demand for money: The real rate of return versus the rate of inflation. *Journal of Political Economy, 84*(6), 1353–1359. doi:10.1086/260520

Frey, T. (2013). The great freelancer movement: Eight reasons why your next job will be a project. *Journal of Environmental Health, 76*(5), 46. PMID:24437051

Gartner, W. (1985). A conceptual framework for describing the phenomenon of new venture creation. *Academy of Management Review, 10*(4), 696–706. doi:10.2307/258039

Hobsbawm, J. (2023). *The Rise of the Solopreneur: Reinvention Is the Key to Career Longevity. Bloomberg.Com, N.* PAG.

. Huđek, I., Tominc, P., & Širec, K. (2020). Entrepreneurship vs. Freelancing: What's the Difference? Our Economy / Nase Gospodarstvo, 66(3), 56–62.

Hundley, G. (2001). Why and when are the self-employed more satisfied with their work? *Industrial Relations, 40*(2), 293–316. doi:10.1111/0019-8676.00209

Kaplan, A. M., & Haenlein, M. (2010). Users of the world, unite! The challenges and opportunities of Social Media. *Business Horizons, 53*(1), 59–68. doi:10.1016/j.bushor.2009.09.003

Katz, J. (1993). How satisfied are the self-employed: A secondary analysis approach. *Entrepreneurship Theory and Practice, 17*(3), 35–35. doi:10.1177/104225879301700303

Kitching, J., & Smallbone, D. (2012). Are freelancers a neglected form of small business? *Journal of Small Business and Enterprise Development, 19*(1), 74–91. doi:10.1108/14626001211196415

Kolvereid, L. (1996). Organizational employment versus self-employment: Reasons for career choice intentions. *Entrepreneurship Theory and Practice, 20*(3), 23–32. doi:10.1177/104225879602000302

Lam, H. K. S., Yeung, A. C. L., & Cheng, T. C. E. (2016). The impact of firms' social media initiatives on operational efficiency and innovativeness. *Journal of Operations Management, 47–48*(1), 28–43. doi:10.1016/j.jom.2016.06.001

Li, L., Du, K., Zhang, W., & Mao, J.-Y. (2023). Empowering digital transformation: The roles of platforms. *Journal of Information Technology, 0*(0), 02683962231219520. Advance online publication. doi:10.1177/02683962231219520

Lo, F. Y., & Peng, J. X. (2022). Strategies for successful personal branding of celebrities on social media platforms: Involvement or information sharing? *Psychology and Marketing, 39*(2), 320–330. doi:10.1002/mar.21597

Lund, N. F., Cohen, S. A., & Scarles, C. (2018). The power of social media storytelling in destination branding. *Journal of Destination Marketing & Management, 8*, 271–280. doi:10.1016/j.jdmm.2017.05.003

Mababu, R., & Merino-Hijosa, A. (2015). Solo-entrepreneurs and Motivation of Business Development in Technology Industry. *International Journal of Business and Management, 3*, 202–2010.

Martín-Rojas, R., Garrido-Moreno, A., & García-Morales, V. J. (2020). Fostering Corporate Entrepreneurship with the use of social media tools. *Journal of Business Research, 112*, 396–412. doi:10.1016/j.jbusres.2019.11.072

Mizrahi, O. (2018). Succeeding as a Solopreneur. (cover story). *Home Business Magazine: The Home-Based Entrepreneur's Magazine, 25*(3), 24–26.

Nambisan, S. (2017). Digital Entrepreneurship: Toward a Digital Technology Perspective of Entrepreneurship. *Entrepreneurship Theory and Practice*, *41*(6), 1029–1055. doi:10.1111/etap.12254

Nanayakkara, N. W. O. K. D. S. P., & Dissanayake, D. M. R. (2020). Application of social media for personal branding: A conceptual review. *International Journal of Business and Management*.

Olanrewaju, A. S. T., Hossain, M. A., Whiteside, N., & Mercieca, P. (2020). Social media and entrepreneurship research: A literature review. *International Journal of Information Management*, *50*, 90–110. doi:10.1016/j.ijinfomgt.2019.05.011

Pilkerton, C., & Gandhi, S. (2023). *Lenders need to understand that self-employment is the new employment. American Banker, N.* PAG.

. Reed, C. What It Means to Freelance (or Jumping in with Your Eyes Wide Open).

Richter, C., Kraus, S., Brem, A., Durst, S., & Giselbrecht, C. (2017). Digital entrepreneurship: Innovative business models for the sharing economy. *Creativity and Innovation Management*, *26*(3), 300–310. doi:10.1111/caim.12227

Rosário, A., & Dias, J. (2023). Marketing Strategies on Social Media Platforms. *International Journal of E-Business Research*, *19*(1), 1–25. doi:10.4018/IJEBR.316969

Ruggieri, R., Savastano, M., Scalingi, A., Bala, D., & D'Ascenzo, F. (2018). The impact of Digital Platforms on Business Models: An empirical investigation on innovative start-ups. Management & Marketing. *Challenges for the Knowledge Society*, *13*(4), 1210–1225. doi:10.2478/mmcks-2018-0032

Satalkina, L., & Steiner, G. (2020). Digital entrepreneurship: A theory-based systematization of core performance indicators. *Sustainability (Basel)*, *12*(10), 4018. doi:10.3390/su12104018

Scuotto, V., Serravalle, F., Murray, A., & Viassone, M. (2019). The shift towards a digital business model: A strategic decision for the female entrepreneur. In *Women entrepreneurs and strategic decision making in the global economy* (pp. 120–143). IGI Global. doi:10.4018/978-1-5225-7479-8.ch007

Skrzek-Lubasińska, M., & Szaban, J. M. (2019). Nomenclature and harmonised criteria for the self-employment categorisation. An approach pursuant to a systematic review of the literature. *European Management Journal*, *37*(3), 376–386. doi:10.1016/j.emj.2018.11.001

Thickstun, K. (2019). Every Lesson Every Day. *American Music Teacher*, *68*(5), 10–13.

Urbanová, M., & Slind, T. (2016). *Successful Personal Branding on Social Media*. Lund University, School of Economics and Management.

Van Stel, A., Wennekers, S., & Scholman, G. (2014). Solo self-employed versus employer entrepreneurs: Determinants and macro-economic effects in OECD countries. *Eurasian Business Review*, *4*(1), 107–136. doi:10.1007/s40821-014-0003-z

Vivarelli, M. (1991). The birth of new enterprises. *Small Business Economics*, *3*(3), 215–223. doi:10.1007/BF00400026

White, K. (2015). Freelancing–Are you ready to go solo? *Medical Writing*, *24*(3), 140–144. doi:10.1179/2047480615Z.000000000309

Zaheer, H., Breyer, Y., & Dumay, J. (2019). Digital entrepreneurship: An interdisciplinary structured literature review and research agenda. *Technological Forecasting and Social Change*, *148*, 119735. doi:10.1016/j.techfore.2019.119735

Zhao, F., Barratt-Pugh, L., Suseno, Y., Standen, P., & Redmond, J. (2023). A framework for exploring digital entrepreneurship development from a social interaction perspective. *Journal of General Management*, *48*(2), 115–126. doi:10.1177/03063070211044578

. Zhao, F., & Collier, A. (2016). Digital entrepreneurship: Research and practice.

Chapter 6
Digital Transformation: Catalyzing Rural Entrepreneurship in the 21st Century

Sanjay Taneja
https://orcid.org/0000-0002-3632-4053
Graphic Era University (Deemed), India

Kavita Dahiya
Manipal University, Jaipur, India

ABSTRACT

The digital era has brought significant changes to the business landscape, but it has also exacerbated inequality and posed challenges to achieving the Sustainable Development Goals (SDGs). This research employed exploratory sequential mixed methods to investigate how digitalization impacts rural entrepreneurship. Results highlight the diverse opportunities that digital transformation and technological advancements have created in rural entrepreneurship. These opportunities include the growth of family-run businesses, improved employment prospects, and enhanced regional economic development. By harnessing local humanist knowledge, a business model that promotes social solidarity and economic transformation has the potential to mitigate uncertainty and inequality. Consequently, this study provides empirical evidence and recommendations for institutional and social reforms, contributing to our understanding of the latest innovation theories associated with Kontratieff Schumpeter's wave in institutional and social entrepreneurship.

INTRODUCTION

The digitization of rural entrepreneurship is rapidly gaining significance, and it has garnered attention in policies aimed at both regional and global development (World Bank, 2022). This transformation introduces a range of fresh possibilities and challenges, all of which are rooted in the local knowledge potential inherent in the paradigm of rural Social Solidarity Economy (SSE) transformation. Additionally, digitization holds the potential to significantly impact economic advancement and promote regional

DOI: 10.4018/979-8-3693-1842-3.ch006

growth (Baranauskas & Raisiene, 2022). However, it is important to note that previous discussions have primarily focused on the challenges, with limited attention given to the potential benefits.

Digital technology may clearly provide economic value, but in order to fully realise its potential for creating value, it's also critical to identify and take advantage of the opportunities it presents (Kreuzer et al., 2022). Therefore, our study's main goal was to find out how, in the particular context of India, technological digitalization is affecting rural entrepreneurship.

The Sustainable Development Goals (SDGs) are both challenging and advanced by the digitalization and technological transformation of entrepreneurship. Scholars and organisations have given this dual impact a great deal of attention (Qureshi & Woo, 2022; World Bank, 2022).

On the one hand, through encouraging innovation, improving access to resources and information, and generating new economic opportunities, digitalization has the potential to greatly accelerate progress towards the SDGs. But it's important to understand that the same digital revolution might also make economic inequality worse, which can make it difficult to accomplish these same objectives i.e. SDGs. Digitalization can exacerbate economic inequality by creating a digital divide. When some populations have limited access to digital technologies, skills, or resources, they may miss out on the economic opportunities and benefits that digitalization can offer. This inequality can make it challenging to achieve the goal of reducing inequality within and among countries (SDG 10-Reduced Inequality).

Issues related to data privacy, cybersecurity, and digital surveillance can undermine trust in digital systems and infringe on personal freedoms. This erosion of trust can hinder progress toward building strong and inclusive institutions (SDG 16-Peace, Justice, and Strong Institutions) that ensure equal access to justice and protection of human rights. The digital revolution, while offering efficiency gains, can also contribute to increased energy consumption and electronic waste, which may contradict efforts to combat climate change (SDG 13-Climate Action). Managing the environmental impact of digitalization is essential for aligning it with the goal of environmental sustainability. In summary, the difficulties in accomplishing the SDGs arise from the negative consequences associated with digitalization, such as economic inequality, privacy concerns, and environmental impact. To overcome these challenges, it is crucial to implement policies and practices that address these issues while harnessing the positive aspects of digitalization to accelerate progress toward the SDGs.

Concerns about the possible effects of digitalization, such as the possibility of rising unemployment and income inequality, are becoming more prevalent in industrialised nations like the US (Yusuf, 2021). Furthermore, despite their tremendous advancements in technology, developing nations like China and India are seeing a concurrent rise in inequality (Qureshi, 2019). The digital divide is widened by these discrepancies being further compounded by unequal access to high-speed internet, especially among low-income households (Chiou & Tucker, 2020).

In addition, the digital revolution has brought about a technical revolution that has made economic inequality worse and made it more difficult for low-income households to support the growth of youth and human capital (World Bank, 2022). This has resulted in a growing economic disparity between employers and employees, which emphasises the need to carefully weigh the benefits and drawbacks of the technological revolution brought about by digitalization (Aboulilah et al., 2022).

It is noteworthy that studies and real-world observations suggest that modern digital technology has sparked worries about possible detrimental psychological impacts that could be difficult to identify or completely comprehend in addition to being unpleasant (Rijswijk et al., 2021). These consequences highlight how crucial it is to thoroughly investigate the ramifications of digitalization outside of its economic context. Understanding the causes behind digital transformation in entrepreneurship and its potential impact on economic growth necessitates a thorough analysis of institutional elements in addition to the economic and psychological dimensions (Zhang et al., 2022). These institutional studies provide valuable insights into the broader context in which digitalization operates, shedding light on the regulatory, policy, and governance frameworks that shape its outcomes. By delving into these aspects, we can gain a more holistic understanding of the multifaceted nature of digitalization's influence on entrepreneurship and its implications for society as a whole (Hossain et al., 2020).

The rapid advancement of sustainable digitalization technology stands out as a significant driver of the ongoing industrial revolution, as highlighted by various scholars (Qin et al., 2022). This remarkable transformation is intricately tied to Schumpeter's innovation theory, which offers insights into how entrepreneurship evolves in response to technological advancements (Langroodi, 2021).

Schumpeter's theory posits that innovation is the process of amalgamating new knowledge to create entirely original products, services, businesses, and systems. It emphasizes that technological innovation is the primary driving force behind entrepreneurship and the industrial revolution (Hilbert, 2020). In this context, the application of digital technology to reshape rural entrepreneurship into a knowledge-based manufacturing process can be seen as an innovative approach. Consequently, Schumpeter's theory of innovation remains pertinent and continues to fuel long-term exponential growth. Schumpeter's socio-economic innovation theory is supported and complemented by the new concept of Social Solidarity Economy (SSE) transformation social innovation, which is presented in groundbreaking study. The study contributes to our understanding of how entrepreneurial and socio-economic dynamics are changing in response to the digitalization era by highlighting these components of SSE transformation social innovation. The interplay between Schumpeter's theory and the novel concepts put forth in this research highlights the significance of adopting fresh perspectives in order to successfully navigate the dynamic terrain of economic advancement and entrepreneurship.

Digital platforms, infrastructure, and technology have driven a fundamental revolution in the landscape of entrepreneurial innovation. This paradigm change influences the direction of upcoming research projects in addition to producing new employment prospects (Nambisan, 2022; Qin et al., 2022). According to Nambisan and colleagues (2019), further research is necessary to fully understand the effects of these developments, especially when it comes to rural areas, where good governance and the environmental benefits of digitalization technologies are crucial.

But it's important to acknowledge that there could be negative aspects to the digital revolution as well, such as issues with welfare and social inequality (Ferrari et al., 2022). Numerous studies have highlighted how digitalization-related technologies contribute to economic growth and the creation of new job opportunities (Korchagina et al., 2019). As explored in the works of Qureshi (2019), Yusuf (2021), and Bourguignon (2022), these improvements have also prompted concerns about how they may affect inequality and the labour market.

There is still hope that it is feasible to optimise the advantages of digitalization while minimising its drawbacks, notwithstanding the ongoing global digital divide (Ho & Tseng, 2006; Ferrari et al., 2022). In order to reduce the digital gap in rural areas, research aimed at minimising the negative effects can produce important insights and policy recommendations (Nambisan, 2022; Navarro et al., 2020). Through tackling these obstacles, scholars and decision-makers can collaborate to guarantee that the advantages of digitization are fairly dispersed, promoting inclusive economic development and societal advancement.

Exploring the Intersection of Digitalization, Entrepreneurship, and Social Innovation

Recent research underscores that the integration of digital technology into entrepreneurship has served as a catalyst for innovation, inspiring many family businesses to explore novel business models (King et al., 2022). However, while this progress is promising, it has also brought to the forefront a range of global digital divides and inequalities, spanning areas such as disability, gender, age, ethnicity, and disparities between rural and urban regions (Kasimov et al., 2021).

These shifts in entrepreneurial behavior, spurred by the potential of digitalization technologies in rural entrepreneurship, have unveiled intriguing possibilities. Nevertheless, it is essential to acknowledge that the current understanding of this concept may have limitations (Steininger et al., 2022). Steininger and colleagues (2022) argue that a critical gap exists in terms of microeconomic evidence regarding the effects of governmental interventions aimed at promoting the emergence and expansion of digital entrepreneurship. Consequently, there is a pressing need for further research that delves into the core microeconomic data highlighted in this work. Such research endeavors can play a pivotal role in bridging this knowledge gap and shedding light on the intricacies of fostering digital entrepreneurship, ultimately contributing to a more comprehensive understanding of its impacts and potential solutions.

While opportunities for leveraging digital technology in rural contexts still abound, empirical research highlights the transformative effects of rural digitalization on a spectrum of attitudes, behaviors, and skills (Dewi et al., 2022). This shift has profound implications, particularly for the vast population of small-scale farmers worldwide, as the digitization of rural entrepreneurship holds the potential to alleviate severe poverty and food insecurity (Sathya, 2019).

Recent studies have underscored that technology designed for digitalization in rural areas can serve as a bridge in institutional theories, fostering the growth of micro-enterprises and entrepreneurship, particularly in countries like India (Soluk et al., 2021). However, it is vital to acknowledge that the sustainability of this technology is not assured in many developing nations, primarily due to the disparities between large-scale and small-scale farmers (Mushi et al., 2022). These disparities pose a significant challenge in ensuring equitable access and benefits from digitalization efforts, highlighting the need for tailored solutions to address the unique circumstances of different regions and agricultural sectors.

As a result, the importance of digital entrepreneurship continues to gain prominence, sparking increasing interest in future research endeavors (Kollmann et al., 2022). This evolving field offers rich opportunities for exploration, innovation, and the development of strategies to harness the potential of digital technology in advancing entrepreneurial initiatives and socioeconomic progress.

Digital technology has played a pivotal role in advancing empirical research within the realms of innovation and entrepreneurial strategy. Its impact extends beyond the private sphere, potentially enhancing the value of public goods and fostering collective economic activity (George et al., 2021;). However, research underscores the need for a more comprehensive understanding of digital technology to keep pace with the socio-economic transformations affecting individuals, businesses, ecosystems, and society as a whole. This nuanced comprehension should encompass cross-level analyses, incorporating insights, ideas, and concepts from diverse fields (Nambisan, 2022).

The development of digital technology has not only been a catalyst for technical innovation but has also been perceived as a vital resource for life and a strategic tool for survival in a competitive and sustainable business environment (Lokuge, 2021). Moreover, the economic revolution driven by digital technology stands as the primary driving force behind Micro, Small, and Medium-sized Enterprises (MSMEs) and entrepreneurship, significantly contributing to both national and local economic growth (Turuk, 2019). This symbiotic relationship between digital technology and business underscores the critical role that technology plays in shaping the contemporary economic landscape.

Digital technology has introduced a multitude of uncertainties and transformed the operational landscape, reshaping the inherent uncertainty within the entrepreneurial manufacturing process (Nambisan, 2017, 2022). Furthermore, this transition presents significant potential for developing applications and enduring solutions to address issues such as unemployment and poverty (Rosario et al., 2022). To tackle the existing digital inequality, this technology promotes multifaceted policy approaches and encourages sustainable circular economic-social transformation (Rosario et al., 2022). However, it's important to note that there has been relatively limited research conducted on the challenges associated with the adoption of digitalization technologies, particularly in rural regions. This underscores a notable gap in the utilization of digitalization technology in developing nations like Indonesia, as well as in the realms of sustainable social entrepreneurship and innovative institutional theory. Addressing these gaps represents an opportunity for future research and policy development, highlighting the need for a more holistic understanding of the implications and potential drawbacks of digitalization in diverse socio-economic contexts.

In rural India, the absence of innovative institutional and entrepreneurial concepts has partially been addressed by the support provided by family and community businesses (Soluk et al., 2021). Rural business owners are increasingly embracing digital technology for business development, driven by social considerations and the supportive family environment. However, the successful execution of Small and Medium-sized Enterprise (SME) digitization strategies in rural areas has often been impeded by inadequate planning (Dewi et al., 2022). The realization of technology's potential depends on a multitude of factors, encompassing the political, social, cultural, and digital infrastructure landscape. These factors not only influence the effectiveness of specific technologies but also shape the level of interest rural populations have in adopting new technology (Vanlauwe et al., 2019). This suggests that lower-income countries should consider the implementation of digital technologies; however, it's important to note that prior research has yet to provide conclusive evidence regarding the impacts of utilizing digital technology (Nambisan, 2017, 2022). Addressing these complexities is crucial for making informed decisions and formulating effective strategies for digitalization in rural areas.

The increasing ease with which digital technology enables novel forms of communication and information exchange has paved the way for the formation of new and improved economic networks (Niu, 2022). The framework of the information society evolution hypothesis provides a valuable foundation for this research and is further bolstered in the context of the digital economy. Consequently, social innovation becomes a lens through which to evaluate the success of digitalization technology from the perspective of social network information theory. In accordance with this notion, business owners can leverage social networks to access additional resources, thereby enhancing their competitiveness, efficiency, and overall effectiveness. In essence, these efforts contribute to the advancement of digital success in sustainable entrepreneurship (Soltanifar et al., 2021).

Under this perspective, business owners have the potential to leverage social networks to access supplementary resources that enhance their competitiveness, efficiency, and overall effectiveness. In essence, this approach serves to bolster the digital success of sustainable entrepreneurship (Soltanifar et al., 2021). This viewpoint underscores the transformative power of social networks in shaping the entrepreneurial landscape within the digital era, ultimately fostering sustainable and thriving economic endeavors.

Prior research, supporting the hypothesis, has indicated that entrepreneurs can access significant resources through networks (Zhao & Aram, 1995). Watson (2007) has highlighted a notable correlation between the survival and growth of businesses and their participation in such networks. In a previous investigation centered on network theory, digital technology was introduced as a moderating variable. The primary objective was to illustrate that, in the rapidly evolving entrepreneurial landscape of today, the adoption of digital technology plays a pivotal role in achieving success (Ma & Chen, 2020).

This study stands out for its unique approach, as it delves into the less explored aspects of novel and innovative business model concepts within the realm of local social entrepreneurship. These concepts come with their distinct set of guidelines, limitations, and advantages, making this research distinctive in its exploration of their potential drawbacks and challenges.

According to social capital theory, the key to achieving distinct and advantageous entrepreneurial competitiveness that fosters economic growth lies in the "tuna satak bathi sanak" main model (Prasetyo et al., 2020). Notably, there exists a significantly positive correlation between economic growth, entrepreneurial competitiveness, and social capital (Prasetyo & Kistanti, 2020;). New ventures, entrepreneurship, and technological innovation all play pivotal roles in influencing Schumpeter's model of economic growth. Interestingly, in line with this theory, it is suggested that there is no causal relationship between technology and innovation (Callegari & Nybakk, 2022).

In this dynamic landscape, traditional business models are supplanted by innovative technologies, and thriving entrepreneurial endeavors emerge. The advent of digitization leads to the creation of new industries while rendering old ones reliant on conventional technologies obsolete. This signifies that an entrepreneur's objectives may not always align entirely with a capitalist system. Consequently, a crucial element of success in digital technology initiatives lies in fostering trust between social innovators and communities that operate on qualitative differences from monetary transactions (Steininger et al., 2022). Building and maintaining this trust is essential for the success of digital technology initiatives, especially in contexts where the goals extend beyond traditional economic paradigms. In this analysis, the concept of Social Solidarity Economy (SSE) transformation is introduced as a form of social innovation that aligns with the theories of capitalist socio-economic innovation proposed by Schumpeter and Karl Marx. This notion suggests that the realization of SSE's potential can be achieved through human effort, where intra-entrepreneurship plays a role in promoting social innovation (Cavallaro, 2020). While Schumpeter and Marx's theories of the capitalist socio-economic system lean toward materialism, they are dynamic economic models with a social orientation. In contrast, the SSE approach is not solely materialistic but also embraces a more humanist perspective. Within the SSE framework, social innovation is geared towards mobilizing communities to address emerging societal needs. This approach offers a fresh perspective on effectively and efficiently tackling social issues while advancing the attainment of Sustainable Development Goals (SDGs) (Joel & Nel, 2021; Qureshi, 2021). By emphasizing community engagement and a human-centered approach, SSE introduces a valuable dimension to the discourse on socio-economic innovation, offering a potential path towards more inclusive and sustainable solutions.

The dimension of digital social innovation (DSI) appears to lack both technological and social innovation elements (Qureshi, 2021). This suggests that the potential for social innovation remains susceptible to varying levels of influence from digital transformation. Digital initiatives, increasingly recognized for their transformative social potential, are evolving into social technologies that facilitate the establishment of diverse knowledge connections among various actor coalitions (Certoma & Corsini, 2021).

To address this, the utilization of indices such as the Social Innovation Index (SII) and the Digital Economy and Society Index (DESI) becomes pertinent (Nagy & Somosi, 2022). These indices offer a means to gauge the impact of economic and social digital transformation on social innovation capacity. The index values indicate a substantial and positive correlation between social innovation capacity and the ongoing economic and social digital transformations. Furthermore, these findings provide valuable insights into potential policy directions and implications stemming from the convergence of digital and social dynamics (Nagy & Somosi, 2022).

A comprehensive understanding of the impact of digitalization technology on sustainable rural entrepreneurship and inequality can be achieved by delving into the theoretical underpinnings of Schumpeter's theory of digital economic growth. Digital entrepreneurship, in the context of Schumpeter's theory, differs from its non-digital counterpart, particularly in terms of creative entrepreneurship. While the fundamental characteristics and motivations remain consistent, the path to disruption through social innovation may have evolved (Steininger et al., 2022).

Recognizing the limitations of institutional performance in addressing societal challenges, social innovation emerges as a pivotal element within the realm of social entrepreneurship (Joel & Nel, 2021). This perspective adds a fascinating dimension to the analysis, shedding light on the optimistic bias inherent in the Neo-Schumpeter viewpoint regarding the intricate interplay of technology, economics, and society.

Moreover, Schumpeter's entrepreneurial philosophy underscores the technology's potential to drive robust economic growth and enhance social well-being (Weiss et al., 2021). These advantages hold the potential to reshape the post-crisis landscape, influencing the trajectory of institutionalization and the establishment of a new normal. They may also play a crucial role in either reinforcing or diminishing the public's response to the challenges posed by crises (Callegari & Nybakk, 2022).

Methodological Approach and Research Framework for Assessing the Impact of Digitalization on Sustainable Entrepreneurship

The principal factor influencing conventional environmental sustainability assessment models is uncertainty, as pointed out by Cavallaro (2020). In response, a case study was meticulously designed, employing exploratory sequential mixed methods. The central objective of this study revolved around defining specific objectives for the examination and assessment of the dual impacts of digitalization technologies on sustainable entrepreneurship and rural poverty. The overarching aim was to identify strategies for mitigating adverse effects.

Furthermore, this hybrid approach encompassed two key stages: generalization and the validation of context through measurement. In the initial phase, the exploratory design method was employed to analyze qualitative data. Subsequently, during the second phase, an explanatory design was adopted to elucidate the quantitative data. This comprehensive methodology facilitated a robust exploration of the intricate dynamics at play within the context of digitalization technologies, sustainable enterprise, and rural poverty.

The study employed the experimental theoretical Policy Acceptance Model (PAM) technique to measure and analyze the awareness and behavioral adjustments of policy institutions and entrepreneurial business actors. This method served to reduce the potential for misinterpreting hidden, standardized, and non-generalizable behavioral patterns. In the initial phase of this study, the primary drivers of digitalization technology's impact on rural entrepreneurship were thoroughly investigated (Creswell & Creswell, 2018).

The subsequent qualitative phase of the sequential approach delved into the entrepreneurial behaviors within rural areas, using digitalization technology as a focal point. By synthesizing and merging data from various sources, this exploratory sequential mixed methods approach facilitated the exploration of the core issue and the absorption of digital technology in dynamic and complex rural settings (Poth & Munce, 2020). This comprehensive methodology enabled a more holistic examination of the intricate dynamics at play in the realm of rural entrepreneurship and digital technology adoption.

The collection of primary data involved the use of semi-structured interviews, questionnaires, and ethnographic observations conducted with rural business owners. The methodology employed was semi-structured, as per Bell et al. (2019). To further augment the primary quantitative data, purposive and snowball sampling techniques were utilized in accordance with the exploratory approach. However, the transition of digitalization as a variable impacting entrepreneurship posed challenges for the subsequent phase of the qualitative study. This necessitated the adoption of an experimental design approach in the following stage.

This study builds upon the foundation laid in the initial qualitative stage, leveraging the insights gained from the first stage's data. To gather quantitative data from the same set of respondents, a straightforward random sampling method was employed. Although it was still in the experimental model stage, this approach had scientific utility. To rectify any potential errors, enhance the analysis, and bolster the validity and reliability of the data, a comprehensive literature review was conducted (Weiss et al., 2020; Negri et al., 2021). These measures were taken to ensure a robust and well-informed research process.

The overall framework of this investigation is depicted in Figure 1. One of the central research topics addressed in this study is "What is the context of digitalization technology for rural entrepreneurship?" This question needs to be explored before delving into the pressing need for further investigation into mitigating negative effects. Focusing on the virtual utilization of digitalization technology in rural entrepreneurship, the objective of this research, employing a semi-structured interview and ethnographic research approach, is to identify and analyze the behavioral patterns within the socio-cultural context of entrepreneurial practices in specific sample areas.

The validity and reliability of the research instrument have been established based on the outcomes of testing the tool with numerous respondents who completed the questionnaire before this re-evaluation. It has been ascertained that the trial results of the instrument are credible, trustworthy, and suitable for gathering pertinent and representative primary data. Nevertheless, due to the inherent limitations of this research approach as a case study, it cannot be universally applied to all contemporary challenges. What adds intrigue to this research is the examination of how real-world behavioral patterns, which are inherently complex to generalize, respond to technological advancements.

Leveraging digitalization technologies in rural regions presents a promising avenue for advancing environmental sustainability. The objective of this study was to precisely outline the specific variables related to new business models within the framework of sustainable social entrepreneurship. These variables warranted investigation in order to address the pertinent concerns (Davies & Chambers, 2018).

The adoption of a qualitative research design was recommended as a means to develop a more nuanced theoretical framework for examining institutional logic (Reay & Jones, 2016). This approach aimed to provide a deeper understanding of the intricate dynamics at play within the context of digitalization technologies and their implications for sustainable social entrepreneurship.

Moreover, the systematic use of the exploratory method facilitates engagement with the theoretical framework (Corley, 2015). Subsequently, the study adopted a more responsible approach to innovation in the wake of the foundational investigation, necessitating a deeper comprehension and anticipation of unforeseen consequences (Shim et al., 2021).

Figure 1. The process of digitalization technology circular economy research framework

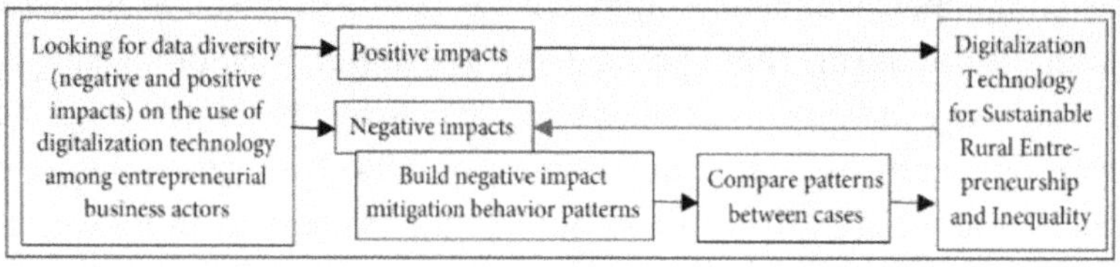

The fundamental phases within this research framework contribute to a clearer understanding of the challenges associated with the digital transition. These phases draw upon extensive research in the realms of social theory of entrepreneurship and new institutional economics. A strategy for distinguishing between positive and negative impacts was employed to underpin this knowledge (Rijswijk et al., 2021).

Data sources encompassing economic inequality and global policy institutions aligned with the promotion of the Sustainable Development Goals (SDGs) were integrated into the research (E. Massah & Mohieldin, 2020). Consequently, it is anticipated that this research approach will serve to reduce uncertainty and further narrow the existing gap (Bathelt & Li, 2020)

Digital Transformation and Sustainable Entrepreneurship in Rural Communities: Challenges and Prospects

The progress of digital technology has played a pivotal role in the development of the rural villages under examination. This shift to digital technology has brought about significant changes in economic behavior, even in rural settings. Consumption, production, and sustainable business practices have transitioned from analog to digital technology within the economy. However, it is crucial to acknowledge that the uneven and inequitable development of digital technology has also resulted in increased inequality. While digital technology may have contributed to a reduction in inequality between rural and urban areas in the context of rural development, it's important to note that this study didn't primarily focus on the disparities between rural and urban inequality.

Digital technology plays a pivotal role in driving economic development in rural areas, fostering the emergence of new business opportunities, and mitigating poverty and unemployment. However, instead of reducing inequality, the digital revolution has widened economic disparities. The alleviation of poverty, reduction of income inequality, and curbing unemployment are all intimately linked with achieving sustainable and high-quality economic growth.

Economist Dudley Seers (1969) posited that a nation could be deemed developed when it achieves freedom from unemployment, inequality, and poverty. It's worth noting that even if per capita income rises, a development cannot be considered successful if any of these three aspects deteriorates. This underscores the presence of economic inequality stemming from the adoption of digital technologies in rural areas. Consequently, development efforts may prove ineffective and potentially hinder the attainment of the Sustainable Development Goals (SDGs). Dudley Seers' emphasis on the significance of socio-economic development within development theory highlights that true development transcends mere economic growth (Naylin, 2020).

There are indications that the advancement of digital technology in rural areas may encroach upon human rights. This development primarily leverages material wealth and its monetary aspects to drive sustained economic growth and inclusion. However, this emphasis on economic outcomes often neglects the social capital and the importance of social inclusion in rural areas, exacerbating the loss of a compassionate social environment.

This suggests that Indonesia's development vision and mission do not sufficiently prioritize the ethical use of digital technologies in rural settings. The broader Indonesian society and its social fabric have not been fully considered in the current digital transformation. Moreover, this development paradigm aligns with the viewpoints of economists Edgar Owens (1987) and Dudley Seers (1969).

Edgar Owens (1987) posited that human development should take precedence over material development. In this perspective, human development signifies the essence of development itself, emphasizing a people-centered approach that resonates with Indonesia's development mission. Consequently, success is seen as failure when development overlooks human rights and lacks compassion. This underscores the lingering concerns surrounding the sustainable development of digital technology in rural areas. To address these issues and formulate equitable policies, it requires the capability and commitment of appropriate institutions.

The economic theory's historical perspective highlights the central concerns of inequality and digital technology, as outlined by Freeman and Perez. They argued that the core social tension during each long economic wave arises from inequality and becomes evident during the installation or discomfort phase. This phase is characterized by a decline when production capital supersedes finance capital, and stagnation, as noted by Knell (2021), often serves as a turning point marked by speculation.

The strategies pursued by Presidents SBY and Jokowi during their administrations, such as the triple and four-track approaches, are closely intertwined with the outcomes (Prasetyo & Kistanti, 2020; Prasetyo et al., 2021). The Indonesian government has recognized that addressing rural poverty, inequality, and unemployment hinges on economic development. To expedite progress in rural areas, especially given their large populations, the government has implemented Village-Owned Enterprises (BUMDes) programs. These programs not only empower the community but also involve building essential infrastructure, software, and internet network access across the region. However, for this transition to be successful, all relevant stakeholders must actively engage as institutional actors, facilitating, safeguarding, and empowering the process. The program's shortcomings reveal gaps and unintended consequences within the framework of new institutional theory.

The local administration and the community have made efforts to mitigate the negative impacts by installing internet network equipment in the village. However, this initiative falls short because the introduction of a 5G network system exacerbates inequality. To address this issue, the study explored an alternative approach using a humanist Social Solidarity Economy (SSE) model. The SSE model promotes symbiotic mutualism, aiming for shared prosperity and fostering social capital cohesion within a diverse society. This social innovation model offers a potential solution to mitigate the adverse effects of rural digitalization technology.

To foster more humane digital and social technology innovations, there is a pressing need for new business models in the context of SSE transformation. These models encompass areas like green technology, human capital and the green economy, as well as social and green entrepreneurship (Prasetyo et al., 2022, 2020; Prasetyo & Kistanti, 2020; Esteves et al., 2021; Makarovič, 2022; Pangarso et al., 2022).

The development of sustainable digital technology for rural communities necessitates innovative business strategies capable of effectively addressing societal challenges. These transformations should promote the establishment of a human-economic, cultural, and ecological work ethic system that is more productive and efficient. While it's impossible to halt the progress of digital technology in rural areas, mitigating its adverse effects is essential. Leveraging the potential of local community knowledge, the SSE (Social and Solidarity Economy) business model emerges as one of the institutional frameworks that can help alleviate these negative consequences.

A significant aspect of harnessing the potential of recent technological advancements for sustainable rural development is the adoption of the SSE (Social and Solidarity Economy) business model. Over time, its implementation has the potential to enhance the attainment of SDG (Sustainable Development Goals) targets by creating profitable, innovative, and socially responsible business opportunities that reduce poverty, unemployment, and inequality. Furthermore, it is anticipated that the SSE model will improve upon the traditional capitalist socio-economic system model proposed by Max Weber, Karl Marx, and Schumpeter. This aligns with previous research suggesting that the expertise and effectiveness of local capacity in SSE transformation can enhance the implementation of the SDGs (Esteves et al., 2021).

Esteves et al. (2021) define SSE as a method for creating and utilizing products, services, and information to more effectively address the economic, social, and environmental challenges of the modern world. The SSE approach emphasizes the utilization of local wisdom, recognizing that expanding the digital economy solely through platforms focused on financial inclusion as a new paradigm for delivering goods and services may lead to less compassionate outcomes, fostering social unrest and inequality. This dimension poses challenges to the quality and capacity of public policy institutions at both national and international levels, as it dynamically expands and becomes increasingly complex. The advent of new 5G networks, which can operate faster than what public institutions can manage, is converging information technology. Therefore, in the absence of adequate human capital understanding and capacity, the introduction of a new 5G network can exacerbate inequality in rural areas.

To address these challenges effectively, several key measures need to be taken. Firstly, there is a need for regulation, policy development, and the coordination and integration of all relevant components. Additionally, increased funding is essential for the development of the necessary infrastructure for connected digital technologies. Another critical requirement is the establishment of a new, more focused institutional structure that can work diligently and strategically in rural areas. This aligns with prior research, which has emphasized the importance of enhancing the quality of institutional structures and their performance, as well as promoting the integration and collaboration of various related elements (Negri et al., 2021).

However, the current institutional framework tends to favor outdated and unsustainable business models and systems over modern technologies. As a result, digital entrepreneurs may need to initiate unofficial institutional reforms to bring about the necessary changes (Rosario et al., 2022). To effectively incorporate the essential functions of digital technology that are most relevant to the circular economy agenda, sound policy implications and a robust framework are indispensable (Liu et al., 2022).

The framework plays a vital role in advancing the achievement of several Sustainable Development Goals (SDGs) within a circular economy context:

- **Enhancing Digital Connectivity:** The framework promotes digital transformation, providing rural entrepreneurs engaged in home-based businesses with high-quality digitalization connectivity. This contributes to SDGs related to technological advancement and connectivity.
- **Boosting Entrepreneurial Productivity:** It has a positive impact on the overall productivity of entrepreneurs, particularly in rural communities. Factors such as regulation, infrastructure invest-

ment, institutional quality, and capacity-building contribute to positive externalities, leading to more humane income growth. This aligns with SDGs aimed at reducing poverty and promoting economic growth.

- **Fostering Cultural and Local Economic Sectors:** The framework influences the growth of new economic sectors that are rooted in cultural values and local knowledge. This helps raise productivity levels within the community, aligning with SDGs related to sustainable communities and economic development.

In rural areas, the full utilization of digital technology for enhancing overall corporate productivity remains uncommon. In fact, the early adoption of this technology has often resulted in inconveniences and exacerbated inequalities among rural family business groups and individuals. Despite its potential to stimulate regional economic growth and create quality jobs, its presence has not led to a reduction in income disparity. Therefore, it becomes evident that digitalization technology alone cannot effectively address issues such as unemployment, poverty, or inequality in rural areas; it primarily contributes to a form of pseudo-rural economic growth. This outcome aligns with prior research findings that indicate a negative correlation between regional economic growth rates and inequality in neighboring areas, with growth being contingent on existing inequalities (Panzera & Postiglione, 2022). This perspective echoes the sentiment expressed by Calligiari and Nybakk (2022) regarding the optimistic bias associated with the impacts of digitalization technologies in rural regions. Consequently, it underscores the close interconnection between the twin challenges of multiple digital disparities and the phenomenon of optimistic bias (Kasimov et al., 2021).

With the emergence of new employment opportunities driven by digital technology, there arises an increasingly intriguing phenomenon known as optimistic bias. In rural areas, the rapid introduction of digital technology initially leads to creative destruction, resulting in a surplus of new unemployment compared to the creation of fresh job prospects. This unemployment stems from the community's delayed adoption of the new technology, a consequence of the cumulative disruptive impact of digital technology. As such, Schumpeter's theory regarding the growth of human capital capacity remains relevant in the present day (Prasetyo, 2020; Prasetyo & Kistanti, 2020).

The widening gap becomes more apparent when the existing institutional performance capacity struggles to adapt promptly to the digital technology development revolution. Consequently, certain institutional actors may exhibit reluctance to change, particularly when they are accustomed to the current institutional frameworks (Rosario et al., 2022; Prasetyo et al., 2022; Prasetyo & Dzaki, 2020)

Furthermore, this study has identified several factors that contribute to inequality, including one's proficiency in using digital platforms, the availability of infrastructure, and access to technology. Despite the government's efforts to develop software, internet network infrastructure, and promote digital literacy communities, their impact has been limited, especially during the COVID-19 pandemic. In line with prior research, contemporary understanding of digital inequality is less associated with internet access infrastructure and more linked to individuals' capacity to effectively utilize technology to improve their lives (Inna & Elena, 2021). When individuals possess the ability to harness their technological skills, they become the primary agents of transformation (Govindharaj, 2021; Prasetyo, 2020).

Even though the software and internet infrastructure remain unchanged, their effective and efficient functioning is not guaranteed. This is due to the increasing self-awareness of digital literacy communities, which exacerbates the disparities in rural communities' capacity to adopt digital technology. While there may be an uptick in digital literacy, the implementation of the new business model related to SSE transformation may not go as planned. Understanding and implementing SSE's new business model will require time, effort, collaboration, and heightened awareness. In most cases, the increase in digital literacy and technology use is evident through social media and online gaming. However, few rural communities are harnessing this technology effectively and purposefully for their new business needs, and the majority of usage is for consumer-driven online shopping rather than manufacturing activities. Consequently, there is no significant improvement in overall productivity. Meanwhile, a small number of rural residents who have mastered digital technologies are progressing rapidly, further widening existing inequalities. Family businesses find it challenging to compete in the current era of digitization against those who can effectively utilize the new system.

Enhancing human and institutional resources through the incorporation of digital literacy awareness into digitalization-focused social entrepreneurship education and training is essential. In this context, adopting a future business strategy that utilizes digital-based training and education proves advantageous (Fodranova & Antalova, 2021; Hansen, 2022). The high unemployment rates result from the workforce's lack of education and skills, particularly when compared to the essentials of the digital economy (Fodranova & Antalova, 2021). This underscores the importance of digitally-based social entrepreneurship education and training to enhance overall efficiency, productivity, and reduce unemployment (Padilla-Vento, 2021). Consequently, rural economic fundamentals (FE) have the potential to foster the development of more productive regions (Reynolds et al., 2022). An institutional policy grounded in ethnographic research that carries socioeconomic implications for developing regions can be effectively implemented through this model (Reynolds et al., 2022).

The endorsement of the optimistic bias statement occurs when digitalization technology merely stimulates pseudo-rural economic growth without mitigating inequality, poverty, or unemployment in rural areas (Callegari & Nybakk, 2022). Consequently, there arises a need for a new entrepreneurial economic strategy that leverages the potential of local community wisdom and adopts the SSE model of social innovation transformation system. In sustainable villages, this new approach could work in conjunction with digital technology to alleviate poverty, reduce unemployment, and lessen inequality while enhancing production. The SSE model of social innovation, characterized by its humanistic nature and differentiation from the traditional materialistic capitalist socio-economic model, has the potential to bridge the gap in social entrepreneurship theory. Therefore, social innovation in rural regions does not entail overthrowing an established order; rather, it pertains to how multiple social innovations can coexist in a pluralistic environment that benefits the community (Slee & Polman, 2021).

CONCLUSION

The transition to digital technology has resulted in a multitude of both good and bad effects, creating a dynamic and complex environment that requires a comprehensive global assessment to accurately ascertain its impact on sustainable development.

Without a question, the creation of well-paying jobs and new business opportunities brought about by technology's digitalization has boosted economic growth in rural areas. It is true that there is benefit to the early uptick in economic activity. However, there is a major catch: families' and individuals' financial disparities have widened as a result of technology, which has a detrimental effect on people's general wellbeing. Another concerning pattern is that, when technology is still developing, it has a tendency to create jobs less fast than it can create new ones, which is a big problem.

Analysing the long-term sustainability of digitalization's positive effects reveals that these advantages are intertwined with the rural areas' growing economic disparity. However, there is cause for hope with the concept of the SSE (Social and Solidarity Economy) transformation system. This tactic could reduce this gap by utilising the skills and natural knowledge of the local humanist community. A key component of the SSE transformation system concept is raising opportunities for high-quality jobs while reducing inequality.

It is important to realise that the classic models—such as those developed by Schumpeter and Karl Marx—and the SSE transformation system model are based on slightly different socio-economic ideas. The goals and fundamental principles of a family social entrepreneur working inside the SSE model could not exactly match the constraints of the existing capitalist socioeconomic structure. This discrepancy demonstrates how the consequences of digitization are dynamic and include both advantages and disadvantages.

The trajectory of digitalization technology should continue to progress towards a digital economy in the future with a conscious attempt to mitigate its disadvantages. It is essential to address these barriers in order to attain more equitable outcomes. Finding a balance between the benefits and drawbacks of digitization remains challenging, necessitating careful consideration and the development of new laws.

In their attempts to reduce inequality, traditional capitalist socio-economic theories—which frequently incorporate financial components like the corporate social responsibility model—have not been able to yield a truly humanistic and egalitarian outcome. Reducing inequality can be achieved in this way by implementing digitalization technologies within the scope of the Social and Solidarity Economy (SSE) transition. This approach overcomes disparities by utilising social entrepreneurship and local expertise more effectively.

Nonetheless, it's critical to recognise that the concept of SSE has many sides and that many civilizations may interpret and apply it differently. As a result, determining its overall influence can be challenging and contingent upon several factors. One key factor to take into account is the extent to which local knowledge is acknowledged and maximised. Moreover, the degree of social diversity observed within communities significantly influences the outcomes of SSE-based initiatives.

Furthermore, there is growing interest in examining the intricate relationship that emerges between the development of cultural variety and inventiveness in productive entrepreneurship and institutional fortification inside family businesses. This area of research has a great deal to teach us about how businesses may foster an environment that is innovative and welcoming of various forms of entrepreneurship.

In order to effectively address the primary concerns surrounding digital entrepreneurship, public digital security regulations must be prioritised in their creation and implementation. These regulations are critical for risk reduction and for ensuring a safe and secure digital environment for businesses and entrepreneurs. In conclusion, this study aims to contribute to the body of knowledge on socio-cultural entrepreneurship and new institutional theory by exploring the potential for SSE transformation, shedding light on the challenges associated with reducing inequality, and highlighting the role of institutions in encouraging creativity and diversity in entrepreneurship. This study is expected to help close the existing information gaps regarding these significant subjects.

REFERENCES

Abeysinghe, D. U., & Malik, M. (2021). The Role of Digital Technology in Rural Entre- preneurship and Innovations. In S. Lokuge & D. Sedera (Eds.), *Rural Entrepreneurship and Innovation in the Digital Era* (pp. 20–38). IGI Global. doi:10.4018/978-1-7998-4942-1.ch002

Aboulilah, H. M. A. E., Hossain, S. F. A., Vuong, B. N., & Jebril, T. (2022). Exploring the Relationship between WeChat Usage and E-purchase Intention During the COVID-19 Pandemic Among University Students in China. *SAGE Open*, *12*(4). Advance online publication. doi:10.1177/21582440221139447 PMID:36466966

Baranauskas, G., & Raišienė, A. G. (2022). Transition to digital entrepreneurship with a quest of sustainability: Development of a new conceptual framework. *Sustainability (Basel)*, *14*(3), 1104. doi:10.3390/su14031104

Bathelt, H., & Li, P. (2020). Building Better Methods in Economic Geography. *Zeitschrift für Wirtschaftsgeographie*, *64*(3), 103–108. doi:10.1515/zfw-2020-0014

Bell, E., Bryman, A., & Harley, B. (2022). *Business research methods*. Oxford university press. doi:10.1093/hebz/9780198869443.001.0001

Callegari, B., & Nybakk, E. (2022). Schumpeterian theory and research on forestry innovation and entrepreneurship: The state of the art, issues and an agenda. *Forest Policy and Economics*, *138*, 102720. doi:10.1016/j.forpol.2022.102720

• Cavallaro, F. (2020). Development of a Index for Sustainable Energy Technologies Based on an Intelligent Fuzzy Expert System. Economic and Policy Implications of Artificial Intelligence, 137-143.

Certomà, C., & Corsini, F. (2021). Digitally-enabled social innovation. Mapping discourses on an emergent social technology. *Innovation (Abingdon)*, *34*(4), 560–584. doi:10.1080/13511610.2021.1937069

Chiou, L., & Tucker, C. (2020). *Social distancing, internet access and inequality (No. w26982)*. National Bureau of Economic Research., doi:10.3386/w26982

Corley, K. G. (2015). A commentary on "what grounded theory is..." engaging a phenomenon from the perspective of those living it. *Organizational Research Methods*, *18*(4), 600–605. doi:10.1177/1094428115574747

Creswell, J. W., & Creswell, J. D. (2017). *Research design: Qualitative, quantitative, and mixed methods approaches*. Sage publications.

Davies, I. A., & Chambers, L. (2018). Integrating hybridity and business model theory in sustainable entrepreneurship. *Journal of Cleaner Production*, *177*, 378–386. doi:10.1016/j.jclepro.2017.12.196

Dawadi, S., Shrestha, S., & Giri, R. A. (2021). Mixed-Methods Research: A Discussion on its Types, Challenges, and Criticisms. *Journal of Practical Studies in Education*, *2*(2), 25–36. doi:10.46809/jpse.v2i2.20

Dewi, M. P., Havidz, I. L. H., & Atmaja, D. R. (2022). Digital Marketing for SMEs Cido- kom Village Plant Cultivation Group. *Majalah Ilmiah Bijak*, *19*(1), 47–55. doi:10.31334/bijak.v19i1.2199

ElMassah, S., & Mohieldin, M. (2020). Digital Transformation and Localizing the Sus- tainable Development Goals (SDGs). *Ecological Economics*, *169*, 106490. Advance online publication. doi:10.1016/j.ecolecon.2019.106490

Esteves, A. M., Genus, A., Henfrey, T., Penha-Lopes, G., & East, M. (2021). Sustainable Entrepreneurship and the Sustainable Development Goals: Community-Led Initiatives, the Social Solidarity Economy and Commons Ecologies. *Business Strategy and the Environment*, *30*(3), 1423–1435. doi:10.1002/bse.2706

Ferrari, A., Bacco, M., Gaber, K., Jedlitschka, A., Hess, S., Kaipainen, J., Koltsida, P., Toli, E., & Brunori, G. (2022). Drivers, Barriers and Impacts of Digitalisation in Rural Areas from the Viewpoint of Experts. *Information and Software Technology*, *145*, 106816. Advance online publication. doi:10.1016/j.infsof.2021.106816

Fodranová, I., & Antalová, M. (2021). How Can Digital Sharing Economy Reduce Unem- ployment? *Journal ofTechnology Management & Innovation*, *16*(1), 51–57. doi:10.4067/S0718-27242021000100051

Gavrila, S. G., & Ancillo, A. L. (2021). Spanish SMEs' Digitalization Enablers: E-Receipt Applications to the Offline Retail Market. *Technological Forecasting and Social Change*, *162*, 120381. Advance online publication. doi:10.1016/j.techfore.2020.120381 PMID:33082601

• Hossain, S.F.A., Nurunnabi, M., Hussain, K. and Shan, X. (2020), "Smartphone-based m-shopping behavior and innovative entrepreneurial tendency among women in emerging Asia", International Journal of Gender and Entrepreneurship, Vol. 12 No. 2, pp. 173-189. https://doi.org/ doi:10.1108/IJGE-03-2019-0054

Prasetyo, P. E., & Setyadharma, A. (2022). Digitalization Technology for Sustainable Rural Entrepreneurship and Inequality. *Journal of Human Resource and Sustainability Studies*, *10*(3), 464–484. doi:10.4236/jhrss.2022.103028

Chapter 7
Catalysts of Change:
SMEs and Dynamics of AI Adoption

Rishi Prakash Shukla
https://orcid.org/0000-0003-0854-7302
Chandigarh University, India

Sanjay Taneja
https://orcid.org/0000-0002-3632-4053
Graphic Era University (Deemed), India

ABSTRACT

Redefining conventional business paradigms, the incorporation of artificial intelligence (AI) in small and medium-sized organizations (SMEs) has become a disruptive catalyst. This research explores the factors that motivate, hinder, and have repercussions for the adoption of AI in small and medium-sized enterprises (SMEs). This research aims to identify the critical elements influencing successful AI integration, the impact of AI on SME operations, and the potential for improving competitiveness and sustainability through a thorough analysis of industry case studies and a thorough review of the existing literature. This study provides important insights into the complex link between AI adoption and SME development by clarifying the way that technology is changing in the SME sector in terms of encouraging innovation and causing organizational transformation.

INTRODUCTION

- **Background and Significance of AI Adoption in SMEs:** The explosive growth of artificial intelligence (AI) in recent years has given small and medium-sized businesses (SMEs) a game-changing chance to modernize their operational procedures, boost productivity, and maintain their competitiveness in the ever-changing business environment. The emergence of AI technology has caused a transformation in traditional business models, leading small and medium-sized enterprises to view the integration of AI as an essential strategic endeavor (Riaz *et al.*, 2022).

DOI: 10.4018/979-8-3693-1842-3.ch007

Explore the entrepreneurship opportunities for young female students in emerging nations. Adopting the technology acceptance model paradigm, the authors attempt to understand the moderating effects of perceived usefulness on social media behavior. The authors conduct a person-administered survey on 241 female students with entrepreneurship intentions. The survey is analyzed using structural equation modeling (Amos). According to the findings, the variables such as social influence, perceived ease of use, perceived enjoyment, perceived usefulness, attitude toward social media and social-media behaviors have a significant relationship, indicating tremendous entrepreneurial opportunities, especially social-media-based, for young women in emerging nations. Results also show that social media attracts women entrepreneurs positively in emerging countries. Since the data was collected only in a single Asian nation, the results may not be generalizable. The study have a significant impact on social media and entrepreneurial development.(Emmanuel et al. 2022). The ubiquitous role of the smartphone in expanding entrepreneurial opportunity among women in emerging Asia. This study attempted to explore the hidden issues behind increased innovative entrepreneurial tendency. Results show a significant relationship among the independent and dependent variables of the study which indicates a significant entrepreneurship opportunity for women in emerging Asia.(Hossain et al. 2020). The study reviews the literature on social media, social networking, mobile usage, and media entrepreneurship. This research identifies the immense popularity of social networking, online shopping, and digital media entrepreneurship due to available and affordable usage of mobile phones. To do so, the research investigates related literature from the last five years (2013 and 2018). The findings indicate that even though media entrepreneurship gained increased popularity, it has not been implemented or initiated properly. This research also indicates a new path towards ease of online shopping, building trust, ease of decision making in online purchase, as well as reduction of unemployment problem in emerging and developing nations. Despite some limitations discussed in the study such as inconsistent research papers, limited studies in the specific field, and limited empirical evidence, it still offers implications and contributions for online shoppers, marketers, policymakers, and entrepreneurs. Finally, the research acknowledges the emerging role of social networking in media entrepreneurship development in the context of mobile phone usage in online shopping. (Hossain et al. 2019).

- **Problem Statement and Research Questions**: Notwithstanding the potential advantages, SMEs have had difficulty implementing AI due to a number of issues, including as limited resources, sophisticated technology, and a lack of thorough knowledge about the effects of integrating AI(Vijayakumar, 2021). In order to shed light on the methods necessary to support a smooth and successful integration process, this study aims to address the fundamental challenge of identifying the major catalysts and obstacles driving AI adoption in SMEs(Taherizadeh and Beaudry, 2023). This raises a number of important research questions, including what factors lead to the effective adoption of AI, how AI affects the performance of SMEs, and what steps need to be taken to get over barriers to AI implementation in SMEs(Hanelt *et al.*, 2021).
- **Purpose and Objectives of the Study:** This study's main goal is to offer a thorough examination of the dynamics and consequences of AI adoption in the SME market. The goal of this project is to provide important insights into the efficient application of AI technologies to support development, innovation, and sustainability inside SMEs by investigating the underlying variables driving AI integration and the difficulties related to this process(Yathiraju, 2022). The report also aims to pinpoint useful tactics and suggestions for small and medium-sized enterprises (SMEs) looking to integrate AI efficiently into their operational frameworks(Riaz *et al.*, 2022).

- **Structure of the Book Chapter**: This chapter gives a synopsis of the book's later chapters, detailing their orderly structure and the main ideas of the study(Hanelt *et al.*, 2021). A thorough literature review, the study's methodology, the theoretical framework that directed the investigation, and a model framework for comprehending AI adoption in the context of SMEs are all covered in detail in the parts that follow. The chapter then delves into case studies and analysis before offering some suggestions and outlining possible paths for AI adoption in SMEs.

LITERATURE REVIEW

- **Understanding AI Adoption Trends in SMEs**

The body of research on the trends in AI adoption in small and medium-sized businesses (SMEs) emphasizes how important AI technologies are becoming for revolutionizing conventional business procedures(Yathiraju, 2022). The adoption of AI by SMEs is examined in this section, along with the trends, patterns, and adoption rates that are most common in different industries and geographical areas. It also looks at what influences the different levels of AI integration in SMEs and how these trends affect the expansion and sustainability of the business(Taherizadeh and Beaudry, 2023).

- **Key Drivers and Barriers to AI Integration in SMEs**

To fully grasp the difficulties businesses encounter in implementing AI technologies, it is essential to understand the key factors and obstacles that influence the effective integration of AI in SMEs. The main factors encouraging SMEs to use AI are thoroughly examined in this part, including cost savings, improved decision-making skills, and increased operational effectiveness. It also outlines the main obstacles to AI integration at the same time, including a lack of funding, a lack of appropriate skills, worries about data protection, and an aversion to technological change(Hanelt *et al.*, 2021).

- **The Impact of AI on Business Operations and Competitiveness**

This section looks at the various ways AI is affecting SME operations and competition in general. It explores the ways in which AI technologies support data-driven decision-making, process automation, and resource allocation optimization in small and medium-sized enterprises. Additionally, it investigates how adopting AI might improve market positioning, customer engagement, and product/service innovation. All of these aspects contribute to a thorough knowledge of how AI strengthens SMEs' competitive advantage in the modern marketplace(Yathiraju, 2022).

- **Case Studies of Successful AI Implementation in SMEs**

Case studies that show how AI has been successfully used in SMEs are included to give readers practical insights into actual situations where AI has drastically changed business operations and sparked organizational expansion. In order to demonstrate how SMEs have used AI technology to enhance decision-making, streamline operations, and take advantage of new market possibilities, this section examines a few case studies from several business verticals. These case studies demonstrate best practices, obstacles faced, and the quantifiable effects of AI on SMEs' overall performance and long-term viability(Taherizadeh and Beaudry, 2023).

- **Critique of Existing Research and Knowledge Gaps**

This section assesses the corpus of research on AI adoption in SMEs critically, pointing out any shortcomings, biases, and gaps in the present body of knowledge(Yathiraju, 2022) The study seeks to highlight the need for more empirical research and theoretical advancements in particular domains pertaining to AI integration in the context of small and medium-sized enterprises (SMEs) by tackling these deficiencies. It also highlights how important it is to bridge these knowledge gaps in order to promote a more thorough and nuanced understanding of the dynamics of AI adoption and its consequences for SMEs.

THEORETICAL FRAMEWORK

- **Overview of SMEs' Operational Dynamics**

This section offers a thorough summary of the operational dynamics unique to small and medium-sized businesses (SMEs), highlighting the traits, organizational configurations, and operational difficulties that set the SME sector apart. This framework seeks to provide a contextual knowledge of the operational environment that surrounds AI adoption by clarifying the particular subtleties of SME operations. This will help create the foundation for understanding the consequences of AI integration for SMEs.

- **The Role of Innovation in SME Growth**

As a driver of competitive advantage, product/service diversity, and market differentiation, innovation is essential to the expansion and sustainability of SMEs. This section delves into the complex role that innovation plays in the growth of small and medium-sized enterprises (SMEs), emphasizing the importance that technology, process, and business model innovation play in assisting SMEs in achieving long-term success and sustainable development. In addition to highlighting the revolutionary potential of AI as a tool for driving innovation within the SME ecosystem, it highlights the relationship between innovation and AI adoption.

- **Theoretical Perspectives on Technology Adoption in Small Businesses**

This section explores the conceptual frameworks and models that clarify the decision-making procedures and behavioral patterns that support the adoption of technological innovations in the context of small and medium-sized enterprises (SMEs), drawing on well-established theoretical perspectives on technology adoption in small businesses. This framework aims to identify the cognitive and behavioral aspects impacting AI adoption in SMEs by analyzing theories like the Unified Theory of Acceptance and Use of Technology (UTAUT), the Diffusion of Innovations theory, and the Technology Acceptance Model (TAM).

- **Linking AI Adoption with Business Performance and Sustainability**

This section creates a theoretical connection between the adoption of AI and how it affects the sustainability and performance of SME businesses. It looks at the theoretical foundations that highlight how AI technologies might improve decision-making, increase operational efficiency, and promote long-term growth in SMEs. It also looks at the theoretical implications of integrating AI for enhancing the quality of products and services, making the most use of available resources, and strengthening SMEs' competitive positions in their individual marketplaces.

Figure 1. Opportunities Enabled by AI

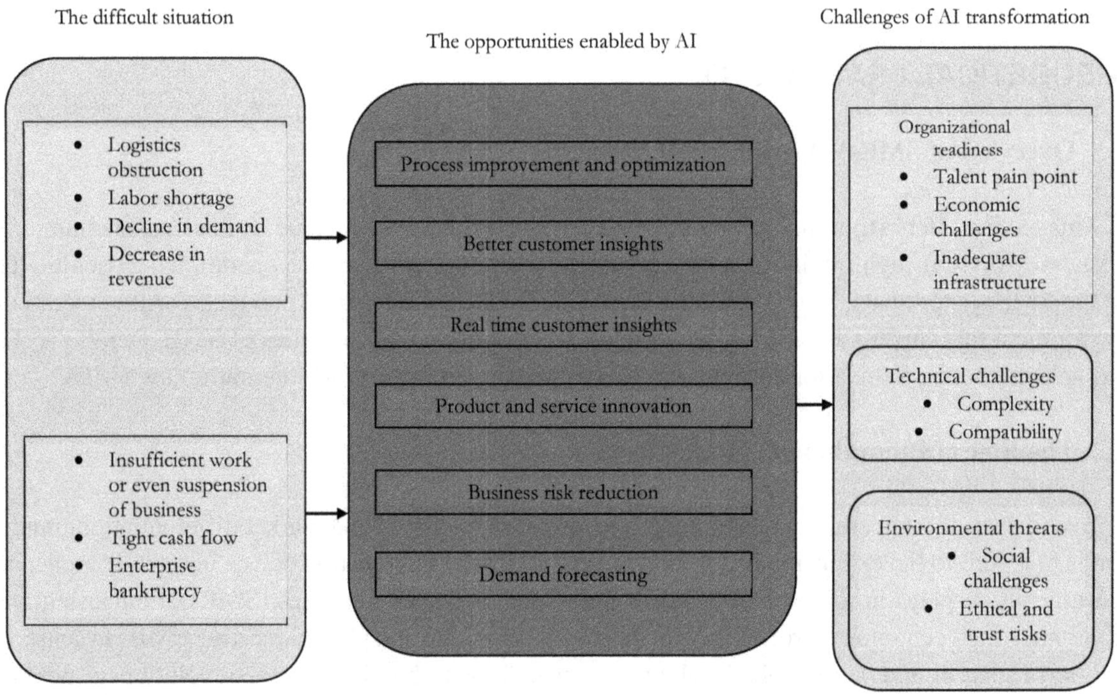

METHODOLOGY

- **Research Design: Exploratory Case Studies**

This section describes the research design that was used for the study, with a focus on the major research approach, which is the utilization of exploratory case studies. It goes into further detail about the reasoning for choosing this strategy, emphasizing how well-suited it is for examining intricate phenomena and gathering detailed information about the dynamics of AI adoption inside SMEs. This section also outlines the criteria used to find representative SMEs in various industries for the research, as well as the process of selecting cases.

- **Data Collection Methods: Surveys and Interviews**

The study utilized a combination of surveys and interviews as data collecting methods to get both qualitative and quantitative information from small and medium-sized enterprises. A summary of the survey's design is given in this part, along with information on how structured questions were created to provide precise insights into the motivations for, difficulties with, and effects of AI adoption in SMEs. It also outlines the interview process for carrying out in-depth interviews with industry experts, SME owners, and important stakeholders in order to obtain nuanced viewpoints on the nuances of AI integration inside the SME ecosystem.

- **Sampling Techniques for SMEs in Various Industries**

Considering that SMEs operate in a variety of industries, this section explains the sampling strategies used to provide a representative and varied sample of SMEs for the research. It describes the stratified random sample procedure, highlighting the selection standards according to industry size, geography, and AI adoption preparedness. The objective of this study is to improve the generalizability and application of the research findings by capturing a wide range of SME viewpoints on AI adoption through the use of a systematic sampling technique.

- **Data Analysis Techniques: Qualitative and Quantitative Approaches**

The present study employs a combination of qualitative and quantitative data analysis methodologies in order to provide complete insights from the acquired data. The technique of thematic analysis for qualitative data is described in this part, with an emphasis on finding recurrent themes, patterns, and trends about the dynamics and consequences of AI adoption inside SMEs. It also describes how statistical analysis and data visualization methods are applied to the quantitative data in order to derive significant relationships and correlations between SME performance indicators and AI adoption characteristics.

- **Ethical Considerations in AI Adoption Research**

This section highlights the ethical issues that are present in the research process and stresses how crucial it is to protect data privacy, confidentiality, and informed consent when collecting and analyzing data. It tackles the moral issues raised by AI adoption research, such as data security, data usage transparency, and intellectual property rights protection. It also emphasizes the protocols and ethical standards that are followed to guarantee the validity and reliability of the study findings and suggestions.

MODEL FRAMEWORK

- **Building an Adaptive AI Adoption Framework for SMEs**

An adaptable model framework designed to make it easier for SMEs to successfully integrate AI is presented in this section. It describes the framework's elements, such as organizational capacity building, change management techniques, and assessments of AI readiness. In order to facilitate a smooth and iterative AI adoption process that is in line with the particular requirements and goals of SMEs across a variety of industries, the framework places a strong emphasis on the necessity of flexibility and adaptability in order to accommodate the distinctive operational dynamics and resource constraints inherent to SMEs.

- **Factors Influencing Successful AI Integration in SMEs**

This section outlines the critical elements that have a major impact on SMEs' ability to successfully integrate AI. It analyzes and groups these elements into environmental, organizational, and technological categories, emphasizing how each influences how AI is adopted by SMEs. The framework endeavors to furnish SMEs with practical insights and suggestions for maneuvering through the intricacies of adopting AI and cultivating a favorable atmosphere for the sustained integration and usage of AI by clarifying the interactions among these aspects.

- **Developing a Scalable and Sustainable AI Implementation Strategy**

The creation of a sustainable and scalable AI deployment plan that is adapted to the particular needs and limitations of SMEs is the main goal of this section. It highlights how crucial it is to match AI implementation methods with the long-term goals and expansion ambitions of SMEs in order to guarantee the smooth integration and long-term application of AI technology. The framework places a strong emphasis on the implementation strategy's iterative and adaptive nature, highlighting the need of ongoing monitoring, assessment, and modification to support SMEs' innovation and technological resilience.

- **Identifying Key Performance Indicators (KPIs) for AI-Driven SMEs**

An essential part of the model architecture is identifying the key performance indicators (KPIs) unique to AI-driven SMEs. The process of creating and selecting a set of quantifiable KPIs that are in accordance with the strategic goals and results of AI adoption inside SMEs is described in this section. It highlights how important it is to create KPIs that encompass both financial and non-financial performance metrics. This will help small and medium-sized businesses (SMEs) monitor and assess the concrete and intangible effects of integrating AI on operational effectiveness, competitive positioning, and overall business performance.

ANALYSIS OF AI ADOPTION DYNAMICS IN SELECTED SMES

- **Case Study 1: Successful AI Integration in Manufacturing Sector**

This case study explores a thorough examination of an effective AI integration project in a small and medium-sized enterprise's manufacturing division. It looks at the particular AI applications used, the operational issues resolved, and the quantifiable effects on supply chain management, quality assurance, and production efficiency. In addition to highlighting the transformative potential of AI technologies in streamlining operations, reducing costs, and enhancing overall productivity within the manufacturing domain, the analysis highlights the key strategies and best practices used in the successful integration of AI within the manufacturing workflow.

- **Case Study 2: AI Implementation Challenges in Service Industry**

This case study is centered on a thorough examination of the difficulties and roadblocks that a small and medium-sized enterprise (SME) had when using artificial intelligence (AI) technology. It clarifies the organizational opposition, talent shortages, and operational complexity that hampered the smooth adoption and application of AI-driven solutions. The analysis highlights the need for customized strategies and capacity-building initiatives to overcome these obstacles and realize the full potential of AI in improving service quality and customer experiences. It also sheds light on the unique challenges faced by service-based SMEs in integrating AI technologies into their service delivery models.

- **Case Study 3: The Role of AI in Enhancing SMEs' Global Competitiveness**

This case study looks at how important AI is to SMEs working in a highly competitive and dynamic market landscape in terms of improving their global competitiveness. It showcases the calculated risks and AI-powered interventions made by a chosen cohort of SMEs in order to increase their market penetration, cultivate cross-border partnerships, and seize new global market possibilities. The research highlights how AI can revolutionize SMEs' capacity for adaptation, agility in the market, and competitive positioning in the international arena. This makes integrating AI a critical strategic requirement for SMEs hoping to grow internationally and maintain long-term growth.

FINDINGS AND DISCUSSION

- **Analysis of Data from SME Case Studies**

A thorough analysis of the information gleaned from the SME case studies is provided in this part, providing a nuanced knowledge of the many experiences, difficulties, and results connected to AI adoption inside SMEs. The research highlights the similarities and differences in the dynamics of AI adoption across various industry sectors and operational environments by synthesizing the major conclusions and trends found in the case studies. This part offers a comprehensive view of the various effects of AI adoption on SMEs' operational effectiveness, capacity for innovation, and competitiveness in the market by analyzing the empirical data and the qualitative insights obtained from the case studies.

- **Identification of Critical Success Factors for AI Adoption**

This section outlines the essential success elements that support the efficient and long-term adoption of AI inside SMEs, based on practical evidence and theoretical ideas. It highlights how important it is to have an organizational preparation strategy, build human capital, have a technology infrastructure, and plan strategically in order to successfully integrate AI. The conversation also emphasizes how crucial it is for SMEs to establish a culture of technological innovation and resilience, as well as to create an environment that is favorable to AI adoption. These factors include effective change management, stakeholder involvement, and ongoing learning.

- **Discussion on the Implications of AI Integration for SMEs**

This talk section explores the more general effects of AI integration for small and medium-sized enterprises (SMEs), explaining how it may revolutionize business models, operational procedures, and market positioning. It looks at how SMEs may use AI to improve customer engagement, product/service innovation, operational efficiency, and overall business performance. The strategic implications of integrating AI for SMEs' long-term sustainability, resilience, and adaptability are also covered in the discussion. This highlights the necessity of proactive adaptation, strategic agility, and strategic foresight in order to fully utilize AI's potential for SMEs' competitive advantage and sustainable growth.

- **Addressing Challenges and Risks Associated with AI Implementation**

This section offers a thorough examination of the dangers and difficulties involved with implementing AI technology within SMEs, along with strategic suggestions and insights for dealing with these issues head-on. It looks at the operational, financial, and cultural difficulties that come with adopting AI, highlighting the need for strong risk management plans, capacity-building programs, and frameworks for engaging stakeholders in order to reduce potential risks and create an atmosphere that is favorable for long-term AI integration within SMEs. In order to address the ethical and societal difficulties connected with the adoption of AI, the debate also emphasizes the significance of regulatory compliance, data security, and ethical concerns. This promotes trust, transparency, and responsible AI governance within the SME ecosystem.

RECOMMENDATIONS AND FUTURE DIRECTIONS

- **Policy Implications for Encouraging AI Adoption in SMEs**

In order to promote an ecosystem that will facilitate the adoption of AI in SMEs, this section provides policymakers, industry players, and government organizations with strategic suggestions and implications for policy. It outlines the necessity of specialized legislative actions, financial incentives, and regulatory frameworks to advance AI literacy, encourage the development of technological infrastructure, and make it easier for SMEs to use AI-driven resources and support systems. The suggestions place a strong emphasis on the value of cooperative alliances, knowledge-sharing forums, and capacity-building programs to improve the SME sector's preparedness and adoption of AI technology.

- **Strategies for Overcoming AI Implementation Barriers in SMEs**

This section offers a collection of doable tactics and best practices for successfully getting over the implementation hurdles of AI in SMEs, building on the risks and obstacles that have been highlighted. To close the gap in AI adoption among SMEs, it highlights the need of creating an innovative culture, raising technological awareness, and funding worker training and skill development programs. The recommendations stress the need of developing strategic alliances, utilizing outside knowledge, and adopting a cooperative mindset when implementing new technologies. By doing so, SMEs will be better equipped to negotiate the challenges and ambiguities of integrating AI and take advantage of its revolutionary potential for resilient and sustainable business growth.

- **Suggestions for Future Research and Long-Term Industry Development**

The main recommendations for upcoming studies and long-term industrial development programs that are meant to push the boundaries of knowledge and promote technical innovation in the SME sector are outlined in this part. In order to fully understand the changing dynamics of AI adoption and its consequences for the sustainable growth and global competitiveness of SMEs, it emphasizes the necessity of multidisciplinary research collaborations, cross-sectoral information exchange, and longitudinal studies. The recommendations stress the need of investigating cutting-edge AI trends, disruptive technologies, and creative business models in order to foresee changes in the industry and proactively position SMEs for long-term success and resilience in a global marketplace that is becoming more and more connected and driven by technology.

- **Conclusion: Envisioning a Technology-Driven Future for SMEs**

This section, which wraps up the study, provides a thorough summary of the research findings and suggestions, capturing the revolutionary potential of AI adoption in determining the future course of SMEs. It highlights how crucial it is for SMEs to adopt a technology-driven attitude, cultivate a culture of ongoing innovation, and maintain a supporting ecosystem in order to integrate AI. The conclusion highlights how AI can revolutionize the SME sector by improving market competitiveness, boosting operational efficiency, and promoting sustainable growth. This helps to envision a future in which AI is a keystone that unlocks the full potential of SMEs and steers them in the direction of long-term prosperity, resilience, and global relevance in the digital age.

CONCLUSION

- **Summary of Key Findings and Contributions**

This section offers a succinct overview of the study's major conclusions and contributions, emphasizing the important lessons, patterns, and ramifications for SMEs' adoption of AI. It highlights the critical role of AI in transforming SME operations, promoting innovation, and boosting market competitiveness by synthesizing the empirical data, theoretical viewpoints, and industrial case studies. This summary provides SMEs with practical guidelines for navigating the complexities of technological adoption and innovation. It also contributes to the existing body of knowledge by summarizing the challenges, success factors, and strategic recommendations identified for creating a supportive environment for sustainable AI integration within SMEs.

- **Reflection on the Importance of AI Integration for SMEs**

This section highlights the importance of AI integration as a transformational enabler for SMEs, supporting operational efficiency, market resilience, and sustainable growth in an increasingly digitized and linked global economy. It does this by reflecting on the study's findings and theoretical ideas. The statement highlights the crucial function of artificial intelligence (AI) in enabling small and medium-sized enterprises (SMEs) to leverage data-driven insights, make well-informed decisions, and take advantage of emerging market opportunities. This, in turn, improves SMEs' adaptability and establishes them as important agents of technological innovation and economic growth. The study highlights the importance of AI as a strategic necessity for SMEs looking to grow and prosper in the digital era, underscoring its transformational impact in developing an innovative, agile, and competitive culture within the SME sector.

- **Final Remarks on the Role of Technology in Driving SME Growth and Innovation**

This part, which wraps up the study, provides closing thoughts on the larger role that technology plays in propelling SME growth and developing an innovative and resilient culture within the SME sector. It highlights how technology innovations, particularly artificial intelligence (AI), have the power to revolutionize SMEs by allowing them to break through conventional operating barriers, reach a wider audience, and promote sustainable growth and global competitiveness. In order to fully realize the potential of SMEs as important drivers of economic growth, job creation, and societal prosperity, it is critical to adopt a technology-driven attitude, promote ongoing learning and adaptation, and take proactive use of emerging technologies. The section ends with a request for cooperation from industry leaders, legislators, and stakeholders in creating a technology-enabled, inclusive ecosystem for SMEs. This will ensure their ongoing prosperity and significance in a world economy that is becoming more competitive and dynamic.

REFERENCES

Aggarwal, M., Zubair, M., Unal, D., Al-Ali, A., Reimann, T., & Alinier, G. (2021). Fuzzy Identification-Based Encryption for healthcare user face authentication. Journal of Emergency Medicine. *Trauma & Acute Care*, *2022*(1), 72.

Bellavista, P., Bosi, F., Corradi, A., Foschini, L., Monti, S., Patera, L., . . . Solimando, M. (2019, June). Design guidelines for big data gathering in industry 4.0 environments. In 2019 IEEE 20th International Symposium on" A World of Wireless, Mobile and Multimedia Networks"(WoWMoM) (pp. 1-6). IEEE.

Emmanuel, C. P., Qin, S., Hossain, S. F. A., & Hussain, K. (2022). Factors influencing social-media-based entrepreneurship prospect among female students in China. *Heliyon*, *8*(12), e12041. doi:10.1016/j.heliyon.2022.e12041 PMID:36483305

Fan, Z., Yang, W., Wu, F., Cao, J., & Shi, W. (2021). Serving at the edge: An edge computing service architecture based on icn. *ACM Transactions on Internet Technology*, *22*(1), 1–27. doi:10.1145/3464428

Ferraz, O., Menezes, P., Silva, V., & Falcao, G. (2021, November). Benchmarking Vulkan vs OpenGL Rendering on Low-Power Edge GPUs. In *2021 International Conference on Graphics and Interaction (ICGI)* (pp. 1-8). IEEE. 10.1109/ICGI54032.2021.9655285

Gorospe, J., Mulero, R., Arbelaitz, O., Muguerza, J., & Antón, M. Á. (2021). A generalization performance study using deep learning networks in embedded systems. *Sensors (Basel)*, *21*(4), 1031. doi:10.3390/s21041031 PMID:33546252

Hanelt, A., Bohnsack, R., Marz, D., & Antunes Marante, C. (2021). A systematic review of the literature on digital transformation: Insights and implications for strategy and organizational change. *Journal of Management Studies*, *58*(5), 1159–1197. doi:10.1111/joms.12639

Hansen, E. B., Iftikhar, N., & Bøgh, S. (2020). Concept of easy-to-use versatile artificial intelligence in industrial small & medium-sized enterprises. *Procedia Manufacturing*, *51*, 1146–1152. doi:10.1016/j.promfg.2020.10.161

Hossain, S. F. A. (2019). Social networking and its role in media entrepreneurship: Evaluating the use of mobile phones in the context of online shopping–A review. [JMME]. *Journal of Media Management and Entrepreneurship*, *1*(1), 73–86. doi:10.4018/JMME.2019010105

Hossain, S. F. A., Nurunnabi, M., Hussain, K., & Shan, X. (2020). Smartphone-based m-shopping behavior and innovative entrepreneurial tendency among women in emerging Asia. *International Journal of Gender and Entrepreneurship*, *12*(2), 173–189. doi:10.1108/IJGE-03-2019-0054

Janbi, N., Katib, I., Albeshri, A., & Mehmood, R. (2020). Distributed artificial intelligence-as-a-service (DAIaaS) for smarter IoE and 6G environments. *Sensors (Basel)*, *20*(20), 5796. doi:10.3390/s20205796 PMID:33066295

Jian, M. S., & Pan, C. J. (2022). Blockchained industry information handoff based on internet of things devices with intelligent customized object recognition. *Sensors (Basel)*, *22*(6), 2312. doi:10.3390/s22062312 PMID:35336483

Li, J., Ma, R., Mailthody, V. S., Samplawski, C., Marlin, B., Chen, S., . . . Abdelzaher, T. (2021, November). Towards an accurate latency model for convolutional neural network layers on gpus. In MILCOM 2021-2021 IEEE Military Communications Conference (MILCOM) (pp. 904-909). IEEE. doi:10.1109/MILCOM52596.2021.9652907

Martikkala, A., David, J., Lobov, A., Lanz, M., & Ituarte, I. F. (2021). Trends for low-cost and open-source iot solutions development for Industry 4.0. *Procedia Manufacturing*, *55*, 298–305. doi:10.1016/j.promfg.2021.10.042

Mitrica, I., Pic, X., San Antonio, E. G., Dimopoulou, M., & Antonini, M. (2022, June). Efficient classification of DNA reads for robust decoding of data stored in synthetic DNA. In Munich Workshop on Coding and Cryptography 2022,1-5.

Riaz, H., Baig, U., Meidute-Kavaliauskiene, I., & Ahmed, H. (2021). Factors effecting omnichannel customer experience: Evidence from fashion retail. *Information (Basel)*, *13*(1), 12–22. doi:10.3390/info13010012

Taherizadeh, A., & Beaudry, C. (2023). An emergent grounded theory of AI-driven digital transformation: Canadian SMEs' perspectives. *Industry and Innovation, 30*(9), 1244–1273. doi:10.1080/13662716.2023.2242285

Vijayakumar, H. (2021). Impact of AI-Blockchain Adoption on Annual Revenue Growth: An Empirical Analysis of Small and Medium-sized Enterprises in the United States. *International Journal of Business Intelligence and Big Data Analytics, 4*(1), 12–21.

Yathiraju, N. (2022). Investigating the use of an Artificial Intelligence Model in an ERP Cloud-Based System. International Journal of Electrical. *Electronics and Computers, 7*(2), 1–26. doi:10.22161/eec.72.1

Zhang, X., Hu, M., Xia, J., Wei, T., Chen, M., & Hu, S. (2020). Efficient federated learning for cloud-based AIoT applications. *IEEE Transactions on Computer-Aided Design of Integrated Circuits and Systems, 40*(11), 2211–2223. doi:10.1109/TCAD.2020.3046665

Chapter 8
The Role of Artificial Intelligence in Business Management:
The Future of Small and Medium-Sized Enterprise

Armana Hakim Nadi
https://orcid.org/0000-0003-3238-8217
Bangladesh University of Professionals, Bangladesh

Kazi Ayman Ahshan
https://orcid.org/0009-0008-6099-7865
University of Adelaide, Australia

Sadia Rahman
Bangladesh University of Professionals, Bangladesh

Mahbuba Rahman Sofin
International University of Business Agriculture and Technology, Bangladesh

ABSTRACT

Artificial intelligence is essential for improving corporate operations and productivity optimization. Due to the Fourth Industrial Revolution's effects on digital competitiveness, businesses are becoming more interested in upgrading to a higher technical order. This is closely related to artificial intelligence-based "smart" automation, which removes human labor from various corporate processes. (Akter et al., 2020). This study aims to look into the role and advantages of artificial intelligence (AI) tools in small and medium-sized businesses, as well as how company management will change in the future as a result of their ability to gain a competitive edge via the use or advancement of technical features. This paradigm provides resources as standard utilities that users may rent and release over the Internet as needed. (Avram, 2014). To get a comprehensive grasp of the difficulties, advantages, and moral implications of AI-driven corporate initiatives, a qualitative methodology comprising focus groups and interviews will be employed.

DOI: 10.4018/979-8-3693-1842-3.ch008

INTRODUCTION

The potential of artificial intelligence (AI) to revolutionize business and improve adoption opportunities for small and medium-sized firms (SMEs) through reduced costs and more research is contributing to AI being exponentially more prominent (Govori & Sejdija, 2023). Small and medium-sized businesses (SMEs) are essential to the economic foundation of many nations. The European Commission defines SMEs as those with less than 250 people and less than €50 million in turnover or income as they want to encourage entrepreneurship and enhance the business environment of SMEs. Additionally, 99% of EU workers are employed by SMEs. SMEs contribute to two-thirds of the new employment opportunities, according to the US government (Hansen & Bøgh, 2021). Artificial Intelligence (AI) provides SMEs with growth opportunities in the business world. AI has the potential to change the way businesses function completely. SMEs may significantly reduce their operating expenses by utilizing AI, which opens the door to greater productivity and market competitiveness. The exponential growth of AI is further fueled by ongoing research and development, which gives SMEs access to advanced technologies to improve their goods and services. Consequently, AI is emerging as a key driver of innovation and leading SMEs into a new era of sustained growth and prosperity. Adopting AI can be a wise strategic move for SMEs hoping to prosper in a changing, technologically-driven business climate. The adoption of digital technologies by small and medium-sized businesses (SMEs) has been particularly slow (Bettoni, Matteri, Montini, Gładysz, & Carpanzano, 2021). SMEs face challenges while implementing AI-based innovations, frequently as a result of limited resources and a lack of awareness of social and technological advancements, which hampers their capacity to apply AI to decision-making processes in an efficient manner (Bettoni, Matteri, Montini, Gładysz, & Carpanzano, 2021). For example, bookkeeping is essential for managing financial transactions and recording business activities as bookkeeping management evolved from manual to electronic, tasks became more streamlined and efficient. Although machine learning, auto journal record entries, document recognition, optical character recognition (OCR), and other automated bookkeeping systems have become more effective due to artificial intelligence, small and medium-sized businesses are still hesitant to adopt these systems (Azman, Mohamed, & Jamil, 2021). These innovative technologies can automate and simplify bookkeeping procedures for small and medium-sized firms, which will enhance accuracy, minimize human error, and save an immense amount of time, and will increase efficiency enabling businesses to handle their finances and resource allocation effectively, concentrate on their primary operations, and eventually increase their overall production.

Through the analysis of patterns in unstructured data, artificial intelligence (AI) is transforming business and enabling small and medium-sized enterprises (SMEs) to become more efficient and operate more successfully, particularly in the areas of finance, human resources, supply chain management, marketing, and production (Ingalagi, Mutkekar, & Kulkarni, 2021). Artificial intelligence aims to gain strategic advantages in various sectors, including E-business, human capital, operations, market research, customer relationships, accounting, finance, sales, and marketing. It improves operational efficiency, increases sales volume, minimizes costs, automates customer management, and collects advanced data. AI-based applications are suitable for large organizations and SMEs, enabling functional marketing and healthcare applications. AI solutions can help SMEs identify prospective customers, communicate relevant information, and align products and services with consumer buying behavior, providing a competitive advantage (Bhalerao, Kumar, Kumar, & Pujari, 2022).

In SMEs, artificial intelligence (AI) is crucial because it can analyze vast amounts of data, identify potential threats, improve productivity and inventory, enhance financial stability, assist in talent acquisition and employee engagement, and improve collaboration, and customer relationships. With resource optimization and intelligent energy management, AI also assists SMEs in monitoring and reducing their negative environmental impact. Further demonstrating the revolutionary potential of AI across a range of business disciplines, chatbots and virtual assistants powered by AI also improve customer service by offering real-time assistance and increasing customer satisfaction. While AI can be used as an accelerator for digitization, many businesses contend that they must initially learn digital transformation before using AI, and operations such as digitizing analog data and creating digital systems can be accelerated through AI. Due to the high expense, risk, and complexity of creating their own applications, SMEs are frequently unwilling to implement AI as their manufacturing, distribution, and customer service are instead handled by cloud-based and AI-as-a-service systems. Due to the value of interpersonal abilities and the limited number of applications for positions available, AI has become less widespread in HR (Szedlak, Poetters, & Leyendecker, 2020). Furthermore, a majority of individuals understand the significance of AI in marketing and R&D, rendering it neutral in these areas (Szedlak, Poetters, & Leyendecker, 2020). To improve the market value and their competitive advantage, nowadays, SMEs are using artificial intelligence (AI) applications in their goods and services, customer support, and communication as these applications monitor consumer behavior and provide recommendations for influencing customer purchasing intentions and QR code technology is another recent innovation that is used for inventory management, data recording, and demand prediction (Govori & Sejdija, 2023).

This study explores the role of artificial intelligence in business management, focusing on its potential for small and medium-sized enterprises (SMEs). It explores how artificial intelligence (AI) improves competitiveness, operational effectiveness, and strategic decision-making. It also provides observations on the advantages and challenges associated with implementing AI successfully in SMEs business management. The study aims to identify the best procedure for successful AI adoption, enhancing understanding of AI's potential for SMEs' future business direction.

LITERATURE REVIEW ON AI IN ENTREPRENEURSHIP

Industry 4.0, a new phase of the industrial revolution, develops automated systems with technological advancement and digitalized production procedures by integrating technical innovations and prospective models (Muhuri, Shukla, & Abraham, 2019). With artificial intelligence at this sophisticated stage, entrepreneurs are now able to operate innovatively and efficiently (Pamungkas, Asyivadibrata, Susilawati, & Huda, 2023). According to the author, The way entrepreneurs operate and manage businesses could be significantly changed by the capacity of artificial intelligence to transform entrepreneurship theory development and research, receiving substantial interest from the academic community (Lévesque, Obschonka, & Nambisan, 2020). Entrepreneurship requires systematizing information, dynamic observation, and automated decision-making algorithms to reduce costs in a competitive environment with incomplete information (Bogachov, Kwilinski, Miethlich, Bartosova, & Gurnak, 2020). Artificial Intelligence (AI) has transformed entrepreneurship by providing innovative approaches for a range of organizational requirements. AI has already been used by entrepreneurs for consumer interaction, market research, and optimized marketing strategies. Solutions based on artificial intelligence improve decision-making, accelerate operations, and improve overall business effectiveness, providing entrepreneurs an opportunity to respond to changing marketplace dynamics and a competitive advantage in the rapidly evolving business environment. AI may enhance and transform entrepreneurship in the future, but it may also change certain aspects of the real-world phenomena that entrepreneurs often analyze to better understand the causes and consequences of the entrepreneurial process (Obschonka & Audretsch, 2020). Digital technologies are automating procedures that require human input, therefore modifying the realm of entrepreneurship (Chalmers, MacKenzie, & Carter, 2020). In addition, the Author stated that large unstructured data sets may now be processed by machines using advanced algorithms because of artificial intelligence (AI) and these developments have generated arguments over the innovation of AI and raised the possibility that it could offer advantages in terms of productivity and cost as well as essential tools for creativity (Chalmers, MacKenzie, & Carter, 2020). Businesses are evolving quickly due to advanced technology including blockchain, AI, robotics, and IoT. Using AI for activities such as cost prediction and route mapping helps entrepreneurs become more innovative and intelligent. Organizations can use AI to establish new strategies and generate new revenue streams due to this rapid development. AI has also had an impact on robotics, retail, insurance, healthcare, and finance and it has made it possible for entrepreneurs to create and implement feasible plans, and corporate strategies, and acquire funding to support economic expansion where entrepreneurs constantly search for ways to improve and bring about revolutions while AI advances (Sharma, 2020).

According to Rawashdeh, Bakhit, & Abaalkhail, (2022), the global Artificial Intelligence in the Accounting market is expected to reach USD 16069.8 million by 2028, driven by the need to automate accounting processes due to the COVID-19 pandemic, enhancing operational and strategic performance (Rawashdeh, Bakhit, & Abaalkhail, 2022). According to Vaio, Palladino, Hassan, & Escobar, (2020) AI has significantly impacted business practices, influencing trade and management practices in sectors offering competitive and sustainable products or services but the interaction between AI and human intelligence relies on algorithms to help managers make informed decisions and another context, Knowledge Management Systems (KMS) promote intelligent work by bringing together human, organizational, and technological factors that foster a corporate culture and uses AI for operational process improvement and business models, connecting innovation and sustainability (Vaio, Palladino, Hassan, & Escobar, 2020). AI and entrepreneurship are tools with the potential for both productive and destructive outcomes where misuse can lead to destructive consequences when users lack knowledge about their usage, function, and full implications, and combining AI with entrepreneurial processes could enhance outcomes. For example, Amazon recruitment algorithm led to discriminatory practices, highlighting the need for a widespread understanding of AI and entrepreneurship to promote productive outcomes and prepare entrepreneurs for unintended consequences (Shepherd & Majchrzak, 2022). AI might have an impact on an organization's competitiveness and productivity, which could raise inequality and unemployment but the primary challenge lies in maintaining a balance between the potential benefits of AI technologies and the differences in wealth and job shortages where AI technology is widely used by entrepreneurs, and academic discussions about AI produce a "green field" (Giuggioli & Pellegrini, 2022). According to the author, AI startup business models are categorized into core AI value and continuous learning where core AI value refers to the value created by AI solutions, such as analyzing data, creating cognitive insights, monitoring, and automating tasks and continuous learning refers to how AI solutions learn from new data over time, improving accuracy (Weber, Beutter, Weking, Böhm, & Krcmar, 2021). AI and entrepreneurship in developing new products and enhancing economic growth generate awareness of the administrative component, create an environment of entrepreneurship, lead to creative projects, and advance economic growth where entrepreneurship and artificial intelligence are two of the advancement pillars that aim in the traditional yet progressive business world (Hassan, Hassan, & Moaraj, 2022).

AVAILABLE TECHNOLOGIES FOR SMALL AND MEDIUM SIZE ENTERPRISE

In today's rapidly evolving business landscape, technology plays a pivotal role in the success and sustainability of enterprises, regardless of their size. Small and medium-sized enterprises (SMEs), often characterized by limited resources and manpower, can particularly benefit from adopting suitable technologies to streamline operations, enhance productivity, and stay competitive in the market. In this article, we delve into some of the key technologies readily accessible to SMEs. Cloud computing is the distribution of computer services such as servers, storage, databases, networking, software, analytics, and intelligence via the Internet ("the cloud") in order to provide faster innovation, more flexible resources, and economies of scale. Cloud computing has transformed how businesses store, manage, and access data and applications. According to Gupta and Raj (2013), SMEs are rapidly adopting cloud computing solutions. Their research dives into the numerous aspects that influence SMEs' adoption of cloud technology, giving light on the benefits and problems they face. By adopting cloud-based services such as software as a service (SaaS), SMEs can save significant upfront IT infrastructure costs while obtaining access to enterprise-grade tools and resources.

Enterprise resource planning (ERP) is a form of software that firms use to manage day-to-day business operations. ERP systems can help streamline a variety of organizational activities, including finance, human resources, and supply chain management. Carvalho and Johansson (2010) emphasized its significance, providing significant insights on the development and use of these technologies in the context of smaller firms. However, the study emphasizes the significance of tailoring implementation tactics to meet the specific needs and restrictions of SMEs. Customer relationship management is a process in which a business or other organization administers its interactions with customers, typically using data analysis to study large amounts of information. Effective customer relationship management is essential for SMEs aiming to nurture long-term customer loyalty and drive growth. CRM has significant impact when incorporated by SMEs and technological implementations behind it provides competitive advantage (Mozaheb, 2015).

Ecommerce is the trading of goods and services on the internet. With the proliferation of online shopping, SMEs can expand their reach and tap into new markets through e-commerce platforms. Scholars like Chen (2020) highlight the transformative impact of e-commerce on SMEs, enabling them to overcome geographical limitations and connect with global consumers. By embracing e-commerce solutions, SMEs can diversify revenue streams, enhance brand visibility, and adapt to evolving consumer preferences. Cyber security is the practice of defending computers, servers, mobile devices, electronic systems, networks, and data from malicious attacks. As cyber threats continue to proliferate, safeguarding sensitive data and digital assets is paramount for SMEs. Most SMEs do not implement cyber security measures due to lack of awareness, due to which awareness programs must be introduced (Bada & Nurse, 2019). However, it possible to implement an Information Security Assurance Cyber Control (ISACC) for SMEs against common threats at a cost-effective measure (Sangani *et al,* 2012).

THE IMPACT OF BUSINESS MANAGEMENT DUE TO AI

Artificial Intelligence (AI) has notably reshaped the business management landscape. AI encompasses a broad range of technologies, such as chatbots, machine translation, and self-learning algorithms, which can all be simulated by human intelligence processes; besides, its greatest potential is when it can detect, anticipate, and interact with humans, in addition to streamlining current procedures and enhancing automation, information, and transformation impacts (Wamba-Taguimdje, Fosso Wamba, Kala Kamdjoug, & Tchatchouang Wanko, 2020). However, AI is rapidly advancing to become a vital tool for businesses in a wide range of industries. In the last few years, with an abundance of data and an immense increase in computing resources, businesses have been looking for ways to turn to technology such as artificial intelligence (AI) to provide economic value (Enholm, Papagiannidis, Mikalef, & Krogstie, 2021). Although AI systems can quickly evaluate large datasets using advanced machine learning techniques, traditional approaches fail to uncover significant insights. Also, advanced machine technology gives businesses the ability to make data-driven, well-informed decisions that give them a competitive edge in a market that is becoming more and more dynamic. Apart from that, the algorithm's impacts extend to a range of management and business processes, including project management, decision-supporting, supply chain management, human resources, finance and operations, and health and safety.

Since the beginning of the industrial era, technological progress has been transforming manual tasks, and currently, AI holds the potential to replace or enhance human operations in a variety of industrial, intellectual, and social domains (Dwivedi et al., 2021). Nowadays, businesses are finding it difficult to integrate and use AI in their everyday operations. Throughout a study, several ethical concerns related to AI are emphasized, such as biases, ethical design, consumer privacy, cybersecurity, individual autonomy, wellbeing, and unemployment (Du & Xie, 2021). In the era of AI, business leaders are increasingly raising questions regarding privacy and data security. The possibility of giving consumers or businesses misleading information is a serious problem since it could result in enormous losses for businesses. Ensuring responsible AI use in businesses requires more than just ethical AI principles; it necessitates strong, legally mandated governance controls, which, equipped with technologies for process management and audit trail creation, can reduce the risks related to artificial intelligence by putting in place solid governance structures that are supervised by an ethical board and reinforced by appropriate training (Eitel-Porter, 2020). The tools of AI and algorithms continually reshape customer behavior, marketing plans, and strategy in industrial markets, yet the effectiveness of such tool's performance is frequently hampered by biases in the data, models, and marketplaces (Akter et al., 2023). While AI systems learn from historical data, which contains historical biases, they might not be able to eliminate every undesired bias, even with careful examination of the algorithms and data sets (Roselli, Matthews, & Talagala, 2019).

The primary objective of business management is to develop dependable, standard methods for product quality control and to explore novel approaches for customer outreach and low-cost customer service. With the blessing of technology, business operations remain easier with the use of machine learning and deep learning, which are most often used AI applications (Pallathadka et al., 2023). Although strategic business management requires unbiased decision-making based on cost and revenue and other processes, businesses can resolve business problems more effectively and make smarter decisions in their operations with the use of machine learning applications. The use of virtual assistants and chatbots driven by AI. There are several prospects in business intelligence brought about by AI and machine learning. These technologies enable businesses to streamline processes, reduce expenses, and find new revenue sources. Examples of these technologies include demand forecasting, dynamic pricing, automated data analysis, and the identification of errors (Bharadiya, 2023). To make informed decisions in business management, it is crucial to conduct predictive analysis using existing data. AI applications simplify this procedure and provide businesses with valuable information and insights to inform their strategic decisions. Furthermore, predictive analysis using AI improves efficacy and accuracy, helping managers make more informed and data-driven decisions (Henrys, 2021). There are some tools widely available that can be used in business decision-making processes, including deep learning and machine learning-based open-source analytics tools like those found in Microsoft Power BI, Google Analytics, SETLBI, and the accessible GitHub repositories models (Chen, Li, & Wang, 2022).

The impact of artificial intelligence development on the labor force's employment skill structure, with a focus on ways to encourage the coordinated growth of AI and job skill structure regarding the background of innovation-driven development (Ma, Gao, Li, & Zhang, 2022). Whenever a new technology emerges, there is a fear that the workforce could decline. The world has also seen, though, that historically, the loss of employment due to automation has been balanced by the development of novel professions. However, technology innovation has led to the creation of new jobs, which has greatly increased employment and new opportunity. Therefore, considering the impact of AI on business operations, job seekers should adopt AI and upgrade skills based on organizational desires because higher computer skills are linked with higher employment opportunities. The promise of artificial intelligence (AI) to generate value for customers, employees, and organizations has led to its rising adoption in the field of human resource management (HRM). Organizations have not yet seen the anticipated advantages of adopting AI, despite investing time, energy, and resources in the process (Chowdhury et al., 2023). They are still waiting to see the benefits of their artificial intelligence investment that they had hoped for. Ultimately, artificial intelligence (AI) has a widespread influence on company management that spans across industries, encouraging innovation and changing organizational dynamics to meet the demands of a constantly changing global corporate environment.

HOW BUSINESS MANAGEMENT EVOLVED DUE TO TECHNOLOGY

In today's dynamic landscape, technology has completely revolutionized how businesses manage and utilize data. In the past, businesses used to have to keep track of and save data manually using spreadsheets and paper records. There are a variety of databases and software solutions available today, which makes data management simpler than it has ever been. Besides, Technology has been playing a vital role in every aspect of contemporary life, and the business management sector does not constitute an exception. Businesses of all sizes, from small to large, use technology to change the way they do business and engage with their customers. The emergence of internet-based technology has resulted in a notable transformation of conventional operations and management. For this reason, giving up traditional business management models and structures in favor of innovation and advancement is necessary to adopt a digital mindset (Yiwen, 2023). In particular, new business models that have the potential to quickly and successfully replace established company models have been made possible by technological breakthroughs like the Internet of Things, big data, the sharing economy, and crowdsourcing (Niemimaa, Järveläinen, Heikkilä, & Heikkilä, 2019). In contrast, traditional business management techniques commonly involve rigid procedures, centralized decision-making, and hierarchical structures. Although these methods place a high value on predictability and stability, they might not be as flexible in quickly evolving contexts. In the cutting-edge era, information and communication technologies (ICT) are contributing to billions of requests for searches, emails, audio and video streaming, social media posts, and the sharing of graphical information, which is driving up the cost of energy (Shahzad et al., 2020).

In modern times, every transaction, product view, service review, shopping cart, canceled order—all of these things are data due to technology generating new business models and marketplaces. The combination of modern technologies, such as big data, cloud computing, and the Internet of Things

(IoT), provides structural support for the development of innovative service systems (Sharma, Chang, Tim, Wong, & Gadia, 2019). In the case of Cloud-Based Services, CBBS, have been a popular technology trend over the past decade that businesses are using to improve the deployment of information and communication technology services and gain a competitive edge (Al-Sharafi, Arshah, Abu-Shanab, & Alajmi, 2019). The benefits of cloud computing technology include inexpensive initial costs, excellent dependability, adaptable scalability, and on-demand services. This increases the return on an organization's information technology investment by making it simpler for businesses to implement financial information systems (Chen & Metawa, 2020). The adaptability of cloud services enables businesses to more successfully adjust to changing requirements at various phases. Hence, Cloud-based services and applications have made it possible for large data centers to maximize the use of the benefits that virtualization technologies enable in order to improve automation, self-service provisioning, continuity, predictability, efficiency, manageability, quality of service, scalability, and flexibility (Hagos, 2019).

Furthermore, modern workplaces are experiencing growth in the use of virtual teams and collaboration in corporate management, due to technological improvements. The first virtual work teams were established in software development companies in the 1990s as a result of the widespread use of the Internet and communications technologies, as companies already possess some of the critical elements essential to virtual work, including cultural diversity, defined tasks, geographically distributed workforces, communication, task interdependence, leadership, cohesion, empowerment, confidence, and virtuality (Garro-Abarca, Palos-Sanchez, & Aguayo-Camacho, 2021). Virtual teams engage in a range of collaborative activities, including formal and casual meetings through the use of technology, file transfers, application sharing, and video conferencing (e.g., Zoom and Skype) as well as text conferencing (e.g., Slack and Microsoft Teams) (Morrison-Smith & Ruiz, 2020). Nonetheless, leading remote teams presents a unique set of difficulties. In addition, time zone and cultural variations can make communication difficult. It takes deliberate work to create a strong team culture and to make members feel connected even though they may never meet in person.

Digital technology and artificial intelligence are two examples of sales digitalization methods that have the potential to have a greater and wider impact than earlier sales technology (Singh et al., 2019). Hence, marketers have access to a wide range of ever-evolving tools in the era of technology to manage customer connections throughout e-commerce, social media, online communities, mobile, big data, artificial intelligence, and augmented reality, among other contexts (Steinhoff, Arli, Weaven, & Kozlenkova, 2019). With the emergence of platform-based multisided marketplaces like Amazon, Alibaba, eBay, JD.com, and Rakuten, retail is going through substantial transformations, as the traditional business environment, which was dominated by retail chains, shopping malls, and brick-and-mortar businesses in the 1900s, is currently evolving to become increasingly digital (Hänninen, Mitronen, & Kwan, 2019). Multi-sided marketplaces are bringing in a new era in retail by combining online and physical components and providing customers with more individualized and sophisticated experiences.

Leveraging technological developments, businesses are utilizing social media platforms extensively for marketing. Social media integration has grown to be a potent and effective marketing tactic that enables businesses to engage with their target market globally. Among the most widely used social media networks are Instagram, Facebook, Twitter, and TikTok; now almost every business owner uses social media to promote their goods and services without hesitation (Bintaro, Sokibi, Amsyar, & Ayu Sanjaya, 2022). Businesses use social media platforms to create content and run targeted ads, among other things, to increase their visibility, connect with more potential customers, and maintain their competitiveness in the rapidly changing field of digital marketing.

The innovative solutions that technology brings to the business sector and management operations also raise an unfamiliar concern, like cyber threats. In an era where cyberattacks are becoming more frequent, it is critical to remember that a security breach may damage reputations and drive away clients, even if it does result in a substantial loss of user data. Moreover, security is essential for Internet of Things (IoT) systems to safeguard infrastructure and sensitive data, but safety issues have become more expensive, especially in Industrial Internet of Things (IoT) domains (Raimundo & Rosário, 2022). However, addressing those security concerns in IoT domains presents multiple important obstacles including applications that work in dispersed contexts, like blockchains, where a variety of smart devices are used and limited machine resources are available for sensors. But it is possible to prevent cyberattacks with regular updates to the technology systems that are used for managing confidential information and good practices to check the security controls on a regular basis. Though every facet of business management is evolving as a result of sophisticated technology, it is essential to keep up to date with new technological issues and advantages.

DEVELOPMENT IN BUSINESS MANAGEMENT DUE TO ARTIFICIAL INTELLIGENCE

An era of development is taking place in the fast-paced world of modern business with the integration of artificial intelligence (AI). AI has become a key component in the advancement of corporate management, from optimizing processes to changing customer experiences. The applications of AI in business management develop the way people used to handle routine queries and identify complex errors. AI offers a unique opportunity to handle the managerial issues associated with sustainability, in addition to having an essential effect on attaining sustainability in corporate management development (Sulich, Sołoducho-Pelc, & Grzesiak, 2023). Sustainability can appear to be promoted through smart energy management that is fueled by AI algorithms.

The development of business management is expected to follow a dynamic, flexible, and intrinsically connected path as firms continue to use AI technologies. Thus, business development is the glue that holds all other departments and activities of an organization together when it comes to organizational growth. It helps a firm grow and enhance its sales, revenues, product offerings, talent, customer service, and brand awareness.

The authors advised implementing Industry 4.0 into manufacturing processes in order to accomplish long-term business objectives (Tang, Chau, Fatima, & Waqas, 2022). However, it's crucial to comprehend the way conventional businesses in the telecom, healthcare, and retail sectors allocate their funds to AI projects. In terms of machine learning, artificial intelligence is supposed to open up the next frontier of digitalization (Sharma, Singh, Vats, & Jain, 2022). Consequently, companies need to be ready for this kind of advancement as it gives the corporate sector a practical advantage due to the forthcoming digital transformations. The analytical capabilities of AI help companies with strategic planning. Hence, businesses can create data-driven plans by studying market trends, competitive environments, and future prospects. AI insights support long-term planning, guaranteeing flexibility in a business environment that is changing rapidly.

While implementing AI poses obstacles for traditional production models, businesses that adopt the technology see a revolutionary shift in corporate management (Burström, Parida, Lahti, & Wincent, 2021). Moreover, AI in traditional manufacturing not only addresses difficulties but also moves enterprises into an era of greater productivity, cost-effectiveness, and competitiveness in the global market. AI and manufacturing working together to reshape industry standards for innovation and efficiency marks a new era in business management. The incorporation of AI not only improves workflows but also opens up opportunities for organizations to rethink how they work and flourish in the digital era. The development emphasizes how crucial artificial intelligence is to redefining business paradigms and building industrial landscape resilience.

As an analytical methodology, natural language processing (NLP) uses algorithmic methods to interpret and extract meaning from human conversation (Kang, Cai, Tan, Huang, & Liu, 2020). Large amounts of text data are handled using NLP automatic processing. It can be used in a variety of sectors, including customer service, finance, and healthcare. In addition, the use of NLP to analyze customer reviews and feedback to understand sentiment helps in improving products and services. Furthermore, utilizing AI can focus on the development of personalized product services in the business management system and provide excellent customer experience. But. many businesses tend to oversimplify their marketing tactics by concentrating on building short-term relationships with their clients rather than figuring out how to draw in new business and cultivate long-term relationships. Customization and personalization of marketing is necessary to be tailored to each and every potential client (Anshari, Almunawar, Lim, & Al-Mudimigh, 2019). The area of business management is changing at a rapid pace due to the growing use of AI by companies for a variety of functions, from customer service to supply chain optimization. It represents a paradigm shift in how firms function and survive in the digital age.

LIMITATIONS OF IMPLEMENTING AI IN SME

Artificial intelligence (AI) has a significant impact on society and organizations where applications of AI can be found in numerous areas, such as environmental sustainability, air traffic control, medical diagnostics, autonomous vehicles, and transportation management (Ali, Hamdan, & Alareeni, 2021). Artificial intelligence is rapidly gaining in several business areas, providing small and medium-sized businesses with both potential advantages and disadvantages that enable them a competitive advantage through effective data analysis and rapid decision-making (Jabłońska & Pólkowski, 2017). AI can enhance consumer experiences by providing personalized recommendations. For example, an e-commerce SME using AI algorithms may evaluate customer preferences and generate suggestions for products based on individual preferences. Although SMEs may find it financially difficult to adopt AI, affordable AI-as-a-service options may be able to assist. AI reduces inventory costs by forecasting demand and optimizing the supply chain but integration, however, might be challenging and require enhancement of employees. Strategic planning is necessary for successful AI implementation.

Compared to larger organizations, small and medium-sized enterprises (SMEs) experience significant challenges when using AI-based technology such as a lack of support, severe ROI constraints, a lack of expertise, digital standards, data security, insufficient funds, and a lack of tools and technology, etc and the primary obstacles to AI adoption include insufficient funds, a shortage of skilled labor, and organizational readiness (Iftikhar & Nordbjerg, 2021). When implementing AI in SMEs, there are several challenges to be faced, including high implementation costs, a lack of internal system management expertise, concerns about data security and privacy, difficulties integrating AI with existing systems, as well as potential employee resistance to change. Because of these limitations, small and medium-sized businesses may find it more difficult to embrace AI technologies smoothly. As a result, successful implementation will require extensive research and strategic planning. Despite their ability to adapt, SMEs face difficulties obtaining funding and resources for global expansion. These businesses have been affected by the economic crisis, but their adaptability helps them deal with larger-scale challenges. There are limited AI applications and experts in SMEs, and its advantages must be evaluated. AI service providers must provide insight into the efficiency benefits that drive the adoption of new technologies, including AI.

AI has significantly improved the performance of Small and Medium-sized Enterprises (SMEs) and AI applications, such as process automation, analytics, and prediction, can enhance revenue, efficiency, agility, productivity, reliability, decision-making, and customer experience but SMEs have limitations in adopting AI because of factors like vulnerability, incomprehensibility, and problems with acceptance and transparency and another major obstacle for SMEs is financial limitations, such as restricted access to financing where large organizations have greater financial resources to invest in technological advancements and take on greater challenges and risks (Baabdullah, Alalwan, Slade, Raman, & Khatatneh, 2021). Small and medium-sized enterprises worldwide struggle with funding, staffing difficulties, high costs, and high competition where many are old and traditional that they have a reputation in the market, but outdated devices that often break down, due to low profit, productivity, and production, they cannot afford new, fully automated machines (Ingaldi & Ulewicz, 2019). Small, and Medium-Sized Enterprises (SMEs) in the manufacturing industry have not yet completely acknowledged the potential of AI implementation, particularly in terms of employee expertise and data quality by utilizing AI, SMEs can stay competitive by enhancing their core processes and developing new products (Simone, Pasquale, & Miranda, 2023). AI in organizations faces challenges in securing sufficient human talent, especially for non-technological firms. Data scientists and AI engineers are scarce, and companies cannot afford high compensation or be technology-based companies as they should hire new AI-skilled employees and retrain existing ones (Benbya, Davenport, & Pachidi, 2020). In particular in non-technological sectors, SMEs face an expertise shortage when intending to adopt AI. They may not be able to fully capitalize on the revolutionary potential of AI due to financial limitations that make it more difficult to obtain excellent results from AI professionals. Complexity is increased by the requirement to acquire or retrain employees, causing the need for infrastructure and resources that smaller businesses cannot afford. AI technology integration becomes more difficult due to this talent shortage. AI-driven systems are changing the ethical, social, and legal landscape at a rapid pace with challenges with interpretation and application including model building, individual rights, and logical reasoning because they have fewer resources in terms of finances, employees, and expertise, small and medium-sized businesses find this particularly difficult (Crockett, Colyer, Gerber, & Latham, 2021). The rapid development of AI presents significant challenges for small and medium-sized enterprises (SMEs), including financial constraints, legal issues, and ethical considerations. Limited resources and a lack of logical reasoning proficiency may create challenges to their ability to interpret and integrate AI effectively.

CONCLUSION

In conclusion, it is indisputable that the mutually beneficial interaction between enterprises and AI is redefining company strategy, encouraging innovation, and accelerating economic growth. Smart technologies have a profoundly transformational effect on entrepreneurship, with major inventions leading this entrepreneurial revolution including blockchain, artificial intelligence (AI), and the Internet of Things (IoT). Businesses are embracing and using IoT, blockchain, and AI to monitor performance, improve security, and innovate as the worldwide use of smart technology rises. Social media has developed into an indispensable instrument for fundraising and networking, helping start-up companies access a worldwide audience. The Internet is a vital tool for enterprise as the wave of digitization makes it easier and requires less capital to begin a firm. But adopting technology is not without its difficulties; for example, entrepreneurs' intents are influenced by openness and performance expectations. By providing scalable IT resources, improving flexibility and efficiency, and enabling businesses to analyse data trends, make wise judgements, and streamline operations, cloud computing, artificial intelligence, and machine learning are essential components in the revolution of business operations. Despite AI's many possibilities, there are still issues and restrictions with it, such as its high implementation costs, manipulation susceptibility, and incapacity to fully replace human intuition. Careful consideration must be given to ethical issues like bias and transparency in AI decision-making. Concerns over the possible loss of human relationships and the necessity of a balanced approach are brought up by the merging of marketing and AI. Digital technologies have caused a shift in the company environment that has triggered strategic changes. Digital transformation involves integrating digital tools, processes, and cultural changes to promote efficiency and creativity. Blockchain, AI, and big data analytics have transformed inventory, logistics, and supply chain management by streamlining processes and generating cost savings.

Emerging AI will have a direct impact on small and medium-sized businesses in the future. Virtual reality, augmented reality, and the environment are all going to be important. By enhancing user interaction, creating new income streams, and linking physical items to the internet, AI, IoT, and digital servitization will continue to upend businesses. Businesses need to take the initiative in order to manage this constantly evolving technology world. Success requires the strategic combination of strong cybersecurity measures, AI, machine learning, and cloud computing. How companies prosper in the digital age will depend on the confluence of technology advancements, entrepreneurship, and prudent application. Companies that successfully integrate technology, handle moral dilemmas, and overcome obstacles will be well-positioned to prosper over the long term in the ever-changing business environment. The capacity to strategically use AI will be essential to corporate success and resilience as the digital revolution progresses.

REFERENCES

Akter, S., Sultana, S., Mariani, M., Wamba, S. F., Spanaki, K., & Dwivedi, Y. K. (2023). Advancing algorithmic bias management capabilities in AI-driven marketing analytics research. *Industrial Marketing Management, 114*, 243–261. doi:10.1016/j.indmarman.2023.08.013

Al-Sharafi, M. A., Arshah, R. A., Abu-Shanab, E. A., & Alajmi, Q. (2019). The effect of sustained use of cloud-based business services on organizations' performance: Evidence from SMEs in Malaysia. 2019 5th International Conference on Information Management (ICIM), 285-291. 10.1109/INFOMAN.2019.8714699

Ali, M. H., Hamdan, A., & Alareeni, B. (2021). The Implementation of Artificial Intelligence in Organizations' Systems: Opportunities and Challenges. Retrieved from https://link.springer.com/chapter/10.1007/978-3-030-69221-6_12

Anshari, M., Almunawar, M. N., Lim, S. A., & Al-Mudimigh, A. (2019). Customer relationship management and big data enabled: Personalization & customization of services. *Applied Computing and Informatics*, *15*(2), 94–101. doi:10.1016/j.aci.2018.05.004

Azman, N. A., Mohamed, A., & Jamil, A. M. (2021). Artificial Intelligence in Automated Bookkeeping: A Value-added Function for Small and Medium Enterprises. Retrieved from doi:10.30630/joiv.5.3.669

Baabdullah, A. M., Alalwan, A. A., Slade, E. L., Raman, R., & Khatatneh, K. F. (2021). SMEs and artificial intelligence (AI): Antecedents and consequences of AI-based B2B practices. Retrieved from doi:10.1016/j.indmarman.2021.09.003

Bada, M., & Nurse, J. R. (2019). Developing cybersecurity education and awareness programmes for small-and medium-sized enterprises (SMEs). *Information and Computer Security*, *27*(3), 393–410. doi:10.1108/ICS-07-2018-0080

BenbyaH.DavenportT. H.PachidiS. (2020). Artificial Intelligence in Organizations: Current State and Future Opportunities. Retrieved from doi:10.2139/ssrn.3741983

Bettoni, A., Matteri, D., Montini, E., Gładysz, B., & Carpanzano, E. (2021). An AI adoption model for SMEs: a conceptual framework. Retrieved from doi:10.1016/j.ifacol.2021.08.082

Bhalerao, K., Kumar, A., Kumar, A., & Pujari, P. (2022). A study barriers and benefits of artificial intelligence adoption in small and medium enterprise. Retrieved from https://www.researchgate.net/publication/360912025_a_study_of_barriers_and_benefits_of_artificial_intelligence_adoption_in_small_and_medium_enterprise

Bharadiya, J. P. (2023). Machine Learning and AI in Business Intelligence: Trendsand Opportunities. [IJC]. *International Journal of Computer*, *48*(1), 123–134.

Bintaro, B. K., Sokibi, P., Amsyar, I., & Ayu Sanjaya, Y. P. (2022). Utilizing digital marketing as a business strategy. [SABDA Journal]. *Startupreneur Business Digital*, *1*(1), 63–71. doi:10.33050/sabda.v1i1.79

Bogachov, S., Kwilinski, A., Miethlich, B., Bartosova, V., & Gurnak, A. (2020). Artificial intelligence components and fuzzy regulators in entrepreneurship development. Retrieved from doi:10.9770/jesi.2020.8.2(29)

Burström, T., Parida, V., Lahti, T., & Wincent, J. (2021). AI-enabled business-model innovation and transformation in industrial ecosystems: A framework, model and outline for further research. *Journal of Business Research*, *127*, 85–95. doi:10.1016/j.jbusres.2021.01.016

Chalmers, D., MacKenzie, N. G., & Carter, S. (2020). Artificial Intelligence and Entrepreneurship: Implications for Venture Creation in the Fourth Industrial Revolution. Retrieved from doi:10.1177/1042258720934581

Chen, W. H., Lin, Y. C., Bag, A., & Chen, C. L. (2023). Influence Factors of Small and Medium-Sized Enterprises and Micro-Enterprises in the Cross-Border E-Commerce Platforms. *Journal of Theoretical and Applied Electronic Commerce Research*, *18*(1), 416–440. doi:10.3390/jtaer18010022

Chen, X., & Metawa, N. (2020). Enterprise financial management information system based on cloud computing in big data environment. *Journal of Intelligent & Fuzzy Systems*, *39*(4), 5223–5232. doi:10.3233/JIFS-189007

Chen, Y., Li, C., & Wang, H. (2022). Big data and predictive analytics for business intelligence: A bibliographic study (2000–2021). *Forecasting*, *4*(4), 767–786. doi:10.3390/forecast4040042

Chowdhury, S., Dey, P., Joel-Edgar, S., Bhattacharya, S., Rodriguez-Espindola, O., Abadie, A., & Truong, L. (2023). Unlocking the value of artificial intelligence in human resource management through AI capability framework. *Human Resource Management Review*, *33*(1), 100899. doi:10.1016/j.hrmr.2022.100899

Crockett, K., Colyer, E., Gerber, L., & Latham, A. (2021). Building Trustworthy AI Solutions: A Case for Practical Solutions for Small Businesses. Retrieved from https://ieeexplore.ieee.org/abstract/document/9658213

de Carvalho, R. A., & Johansson, B. (2010). Enterprise resource planning systems for small and medium-sized enterprises. In Information Resources Management: Concepts, Methodologies, Tools and Applications (pp. 365-373). IGI Global.

Du, S., & Xie, C. (2021). Paradoxes of artificial intelligence in consumer markets: Ethical challenges and opportunities. *Journal of Business Research*, *129*, 961–974. doi:10.1016/j.jbusres.2020.08.024

Dwivedi, Y. K., Hughes, L., Ismagilova, E., Aarts, G., Coombs, C., Crick, T., ... Duan, Y. (2021). Artificial Intelligence (AI): Multidisciplinary perspectives on emerging challenges, opportunities, and agenda for research, practice and policy. *International Journal of Information Management*, *57*, 101–994. doi:10.1016/j.ijinfomgt.2019.08.002

Eitel-Porter, R. (2020). Beyond the Promise: Implementing Ethical AI. *AI and Ethics*, *1*(1), 73–80. doi:10.1007/s43681-020-00011-6

Enholm, I. M., Papagiannidis, E., Mikalef, P., & Krogstie, J. (2021). Artificial Intelligence and Business Value: A Literature Review. *Information Systems Frontiers*, *24*(5), 1709–1734. doi:10.1007/s10796-021-10186-w

Garro-Abarca, V., Palos-Sanchez, P., & Aguayo-Camacho, M. (2021). Virtual teams in times of pandemic: Factors that influence performance. *Frontiers in Psychology*, *12*, 624637. Advance online publication. doi:10.3389/fpsyg.2021.624637 PMID:33679543

Giuggioli, G., & Pellegrini, M. M. (2022). Artificial intelligence as an enabler for entrepreneurs: a systematic literature review and an agenda for future research. Retrieved from https://www.emerald.com/insight/content/doi/10.1108/IJEBR-05-2021-0426/full/html

Govori, A., & Sejdija, Q. (2023). *Future prospects and challenges of integrating artificial intelligence within the business practices of small and medium enterprises*. Governance & Regulation., doi:10.22495/jgrv12i2art16

Gupta, P., Seetharaman, A., & Raj, J. R. (2013). The usage and adoption of cloud computing by small and medium businesses. *International Journal of Information Management*, *33*(5), 861–874. doi:10.1016/j.ijinfomgt.2013.07.001

Hagos, D. H. (2019). Software-defined networking for scalable cloud-based services to improve system performance of hadoop-based big data applications. Web Services: Concepts, Methodologies, Tools, and Applications, 1460-1484. doi:10.4018/978-1-5225-7501-6.ch076

Hänninen, M., Mitronen, L., & Kwan, S. K. (2019). Multi-sided marketplaces and the transformation of retail: A service systems perspective. *Journal of Retailing and Consumer Services*, *49*, 380–388. doi:10.1016/j.jretconser.2019.04.015

Hansen, E. B., & Bøgh, S. (2021). Artificial intelligence and Internet of things in small and medium-sized enterprises. *Journal of Manufacturing Systems*, *58*, 362–372. Advance online publication. doi:10.1016/j.jmsy.2020.08.009

Hassan, A., Hassan, A. M., & Moaraj, A. A. (2022). The Role of Artificial Intelligence in Entrepreneurship. Retrieved from https://link.springer.com/chapter/10.1007/978-3-030-93464-4_52

Henrys, K. (2021). Role of predictive analytics in business. SSRN Electronic Journal. doi:10.2139/ssrn.3829621

Iftikhar, N., & Nordbjerg, F. E. (2021). *Adopting Artificial Intelligence in Danish SMEs: Barriers to Become a Data Driven Company*. Its Solutions and Benefits., doi:10.5220/0010691800003062

Ingalagi, S. S., Mutkekar, R. R., & Kulkarni, P. M. (2021). Artificial Intelligence (AI) adaptation: Analysis of determinants among Small to Medium-sized Enterprises (SME's). doi:10.1088/1757-899X/1049/1/012017

Ingaldi, M., & Ulewicz, R. (2019). Problems with the Implementation of Industry 4.0 in Enterprises from the SME Sector. Retrieved from doi:10.3390/su12010217

Jabłońska, M. R., & Półkowski, Z. (2017). Artificial Intelligence-based processes in SMEs. Retrieved from https://openurl.ebsco.com/EPDB%3Agcd%3A10%3A21868650/detailv2?sid=ebsco%3Aplink%3Ascholar&id=ebsco%3Agcd%3A129396054&crl=c

Kang, Y., Cai, Z., Tan, C., Huang, Q., & Liu, H. (2020). Natural language processing (NLP) in management research: A literature review. *Journal of Management Analytics*, *7*(2), 139–172. doi:10.1080/23270012.2020.1756939

Lemos, S. I., Ferreira, F. A., Zopounidis, C., Galariotis, E., & Ferreira, N. (2022). Artificial intelligence and change management in small and medium-sized enterprises: an analysis of dynamics within adaptation initiatives. Retrieved from https://link.springer.com/article/10.1007/s10479-022-05159-4

Lévesque, M., Obschonka, M., & Nambisan, S. (2020). Pursuing Impactful Entrepreneurship Research Using. *Artificial Intelligence*. Advance online publication. doi:10.1177/1042258720927369

Ma, H., Gao, Q., Li, X., & Zhang, Y. (2022). AI development and employment skill structure: A case study of China. *Economic Analysis and Policy*, *73*, 242–254. doi:10.1016/j.eap.2021.11.007

Morrison-Smith, S., & Ruiz, J. (2020). Challenges and barriers in virtual teams: A literature review. *SN Applied Sciences*, *2*(6), 1–33. doi:10.1007/s42452-020-2801-5

Mozaheb, A., Alamolhodaei, S. M. A., & Ardakani, M. F. (2015). Effect of customer relationship management (CRM) on performance of small-medium sized enterprises (SMEs) using structural equations model (SEM). International Journal of Academic Research in Accounting. *Finance and Management Sciences*, *5*(2), 42–52.

Muhuri, P. K., Shukla, A. K., & Abraham, A. (2019). Industry 4.0: A bibliometric analysis and detailed overview. Retrieved from doi:10.1016/j.engappai.2018.11.007

Niemimaa, M., Järveläinen, J., Heikkilä, M., & Heikkilä, J. (2019). Business continuity of business models: Evaluating the resilience of business models for contingencies. *International Journal of Information Management*, *49*, 208–216. doi:10.1016/j.ijinfomgt.2019.04.010

Obschonka, M., & Audretsch, D. B. (2020). Artificial intelligence and big data in entrepreneurship: a new era has begun. Retrieved from doi:10.1007/s11187-019-00202-4

Pallathadka, H., Ramirez-Asis, E. H., Loli-Poma, T. P., Kaliyaperumal, K., Ventayen, R. J., & Naved, M. (2023). Applications of artificial intelligence in business management, e-Commerce and finance. *Materials Today: Proceedings*, *80*, 2610–2613. doi:10.1016/j.matpr.2021.06.419

Pamungkas, M. R., Asyivadibrata, A., Susilawati, T., & Huda, M. N. (2023). Unleashing the Potentials of Artificial Intelligence for Micro, Small, and Medium Enterprises: A Systematic Literature Review. Retrieved from doi:10.47233/jteksis.v5i3.860

Raimundo, R. J., & Rosário, A. T. (2022). Cybersecurity in the Internet of things in industrial management. *Applied Sciences (Basel, Switzerland)*, *12*(3), 1598. doi:10.3390/app12031598

Rawashdeh, A., Bakhit, M., & Abaalkhail, L. (2022). Determinants of artificial intelligence adoption in SMEs: The mediating role of accounting automation. Retrieved from doi:10.5267/j.ijdns.2022.12.010

Roselli, D., Matthews, J., & Talagala, N. (2019). Managing bias in AI. Companion Proceedings of The 2019 World Wide Web Conference, 539–544. 10.1145/3308560.3317590

Sangani, N. K., & Vijayakumar, B. (2012). Cyber security scenarios and control for small and medium enterprises. *Informações Econômicas*, *16*(2), 58.

Shahzad, Y., Javed, H., Farman, H., Ahmad, J., Jan, B., & Zubair, M. (2020). Internet of energy: Opportunities, applications, architectures and challenges in smart industries. *Computers & Electrical Engineering*, *86*, 106739. doi:10.1016/j.compeleceng.2020.106739

Sharma, A. (2020). Entrepreneurship and Role of AI. Retrieved from doi:10.1145/3372806.3374910

Sharma, A. K., Singh, P., Vats, P., & Jain, D. (2022). Deep learning and machine intelligence for operational management of strategic planning. *Proceedings of Third International Conference on Computing, Communications, and Cyber-Security*, 475-485. 10.1007/978-981-19-1142-2_38

Sharma, S., Chang, V., Tim, U. S., Wong, J., & Gadia, S. (2019). Cloud and IoT-based emerging services systems. *Cluster Computing*, *22*(1), 71–91. doi:10.1007/s10586-018-2821-8

Shepherd, D. A., & Majchrzak, A. (2022). Machines augmenting entrepreneurs: Opportunities (and threats) at the Nexus of artificial intelligence and entrepreneurship. Retrieved from doi:10.1016/j.jbusvent.2022.106227

Simone, V. D., Pasquale, V. D., & Miranda, S. (2023). An overview on the use of AI/ML in Manufacturing MSMEs: solved issues, limits, and challenges. Retrieved from doi:10.1016/j.procs.2022.12.382

Singh, J., Flaherty, K., Sohi, R. S., Deeter-Schmelz, D., Habel, J., Le Meunier-FitzHugh, K., Malshe, A., Mullins, R., & Onyemah, V. (2019). Sales profession and professionals in the age of digitization and artificial intelligence technologies: Concepts, priorities, and questions. *Journal of Personal Selling & Sales Management*, *39*(1), 2–22. doi:10.1080/08853134.2018.1557525

Steinhoff, L., Arli, D., Weaven, S., & Kozlenkova, I. V. (2019). Online relationship marketing. *Journal of the Academy of Marketing Science*, *47*(3), 369–393. https://link.springer.com/article/10.1007/s11747-018-0621-6. doi:10.1007/s11747-018-0621-6

Sulich, A., Sołoducho-Pelc, L., & Grzesiak, S. (2023). Artificial intelligence and sustainable development in business management context – Bibliometric review. *Procedia Computer Science*, *225*, 3727–3735. doi:10.1016/j.procs.2023.10.368

Szedlak, C., Poetters, P., & Leyendecker, B. (2020). Application of Artificial Intelligence In Small and Medium-Sized Enterprises.

Tang, Y. M., Chau, K. Y., Fatima, A., & Waqas, M. (2022). Industry 4.0 technology and circular economy practices: Business management strategies for environmental sustainability. *Environmental Science and Pollution Research International*, *29*(33), 49752–49769. doi:10.1007/s11356-022-19081-6 PMID:35218493

Vaio, A. D., Palladino, R., Hassan, R., & Escobar, O. (2020). Artificial intelligence and business models in the sustainable development goals perspective: A systematic literature review. Retrieved from doi:10.1016/j.jbusres.2020.08.019

Wamba-Taguimdje, S., Fosso Wamba, S., Kala Kamdjoug, J. R., & Tchatchouang Wanko, C. E. (2020). Influence of artificial intelligence (AI) on firm performance: The business value of AI-based transformation projects. *Business Process Management Journal*, *26*(7), 1893–1924. doi:10.1108/BPMJ-10-2019-0411

Weber, M., Beutter, M., Weking, J., Böhm, M., & Krcmar, H. (2021). AI Startup Business Models. Retrieved from https://link.springer.com/article/10.1007/s12599-021-00732-w

Yiwen, C. (2023). An exploration to the innovation path of traditional business management based on internet background. *Academic Journal of Business & Management*, *5*(21), 60–66. doi:10.25236/AJBM.2023.052109

Chapter 9
The Future of Entrepreneurship: Employing Artificial Intelligence

Venkat Narayana Rao T.
Sreenidhi Institute of Science and Technology, India

Goboori Harsh Vardhan
Sreenidhi Institute of Science and Technology, India

Kotamarti Sushanth
Sreenidhi Institute of Science and Technology, India

ABSTRACT

The convergence of entrepreneurship and Artificial Intelligence is bringing a revolution in the business world. Recent technological advancements in the field of artificial intelligence are significantly impacting entrepreneurship and economic growth during the Fourth Industrial Revolution. This chapter investigates the combination of artificial intelligence and entrepreneurship offering the reader a perspective on the business landscape. The chapter aims to provide a framework to deploy actionable steps to stay ahead of competition and discuss about the application of AI in various industries like healthcare, finance and marketing. The chapter summaries many key strategies encouraging readers to embrace AI as a key element to their entrepreneurship strategy. AI will boost entrepreneurship by generating new knowledge, which will support economic growth. The aim is to serve as comprehensive guide for business leaders and innovators to explore full potential of AI in scaling up their future ventures.

INTRODUCTION

Convergence of Artificial Intelligence and Entrepreneurship

In the rapidly evolving world of business and technology, two major forces are converging to bring about a revolution in the industry. On one side, we have entrepreneurship, the constant pursuit of identifying opportunities, producing value, and analyzing the uncertainties of the market. Entrepreneurship is often

DOI: 10.4018/979-8-3693-1842-3.ch009

characterized by a strong sense of risk-taking and a desire to achieve growth and success (Hasan et al., 2021). On the other side, there is Artificial Intelligence (AI), a field of computer science that uses algorithms and data to try to imitate human intelligence, judgments, analysis, and problem-solving. In the research and development of AI, software and hardware systems are created to perform activities that would typically require human intellect, such as comprehending natural language, identifying patterns, making judgment, and picking up knowledge via experience(Aghion et al., 2017). The combination of these two forces are paving the way for a future where innovation and business acumen know no bounds as shown in figure 1.

The Synergy of AI and Entrepreneurship

One of the key contributions of AI to entrepreneurship is the ability to make data-driven decisions. AI systems can process huge amounts of data, identify and track patterns, and extract valuable insights, enabling entrepreneurs to make more informed and strategic choices (Berger et al., 2022). Startups and established businesses alike are increasingly relying on AI-powered analytics to improve everything from product development, marketing, logistics management. AI helps in automation of monotonous processes and minimalizing operational costs. This helps in increasing focus and time on more creative and strategic endeavors. As a result, more capable start-up survive in a dynamic market.

Hence, this synergy is characterized by a strong interaction between artificial intelligence and human creativity, which amplifies entrepreneurial potential and causes a revolution in how a business is operated (Saini et al., 2022).

Figure 1. AI integration with conventional industries

Significance of AI in Business

AI is revolutionizing and transforming industries. Most businesses are realizing that the key is to use evolving AI technologies to improve their outcome. AI has created an abundance of new opportunities for businesses to manage their workflow and complicated processes.

In the long run, sectors such as education, finance, marketing, entertainment, and retail are considering using AI to strengthen their workforce, enhance efficiency, and take development to new heights (Kshetri et al., 2020).

Here are some statistics that highlight the importance of AI in business as shown in Figure 2 and 3:

1. AI-powered business applications are exponentially increasing. According to one report, the worldwide AI business would be worth more than $1811.75 billion by 2030.
2. The rise of AI will eliminate 85 million jobs and create 97 million new ones by 2025
3. .AI continues to impact numerous industries, with Grand View Research predicting a 37.3% annual growth rate between 2023 and 2030. This fast expansion highlights the growing importance of AI technology in the next years (Taeihagh et al., 2021).
4. Self-Driving Cars: It is expected that 10% of vehicles will be driverless in 2030.
5. Voice Search: Voice search is on the rise, with 27% of the global population mobile users using it daily.
6. AI's Impact on GDP: AI is expected to contribute a significant 21% net increase to the United States GDP by 2030.
7. ChatGPThad 1 million users within the first five days of being available.
8. 64% of businesses expect AI to increase productivity.
9. 47% of business leaders will consider using AI to carry out tasks over hiring new staff. According to Forbes Advisor, a staggering 97% of business owners believe that ChatGPT will benefit their businesses (Gao et al., 2022). One in three businesses plan to use ChatGPT to create website content, while 44% aim to generate content inmultiple languages.

The following case studies show how AI affects entrepreneurship:

1. **Bata**: To enhance in-store sales, operations, and customer satisfaction, the footwear retailer Bata implemented an AI-based video analytics system. The solution implemented data harvesting and insight generation on smart conversion and audience segmentation by leveraging the store's existing video infrastructure.
2. **Blackberrys**: Through omni-channel engagement, the menswear fashion chain Blackberrys increased revenue via artificial intelligence. Using its in-house AI platform, Zero AI, Capillary Technologies developed the Engage+ platform for Blackberry devices. The best Blackberry campaigns were produced by implementing machine learning and artificial intelligence algorithms.
3. **Tata Cliq**: The eCommerce division of the Tata group, Tata Cliq, has implemented Vue.ai's Personalization Suite to facilitate product discovery for users on its website. The solution enabled the marketing, product, and cataloguing teams to obtain actionable insights by extracting catalogue data using image recognition and data science and analyzing it with user behavior.

These case studies demonstrate how artificial intelligence (AI) can help entrepreneurs by improving opportunities, performance, decision-making, and research and education.

AI is already adept at speeding and enhancing common commercial tasks like copywriting, social media post planning, image production and editing, and even cash flow predictions

Figure 2. Start up using AI as developing platform

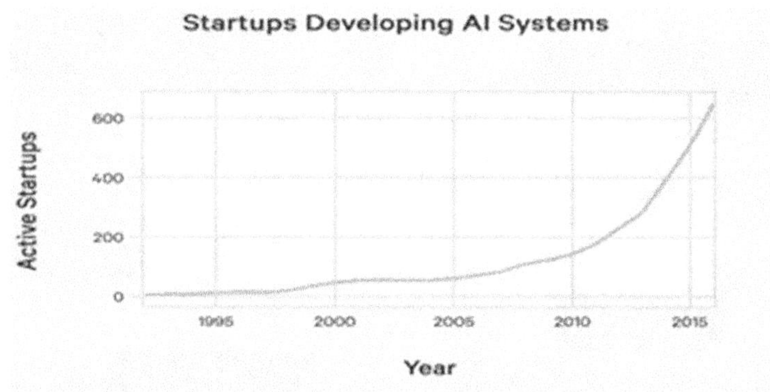

Figure 3. Corporate investment in AI

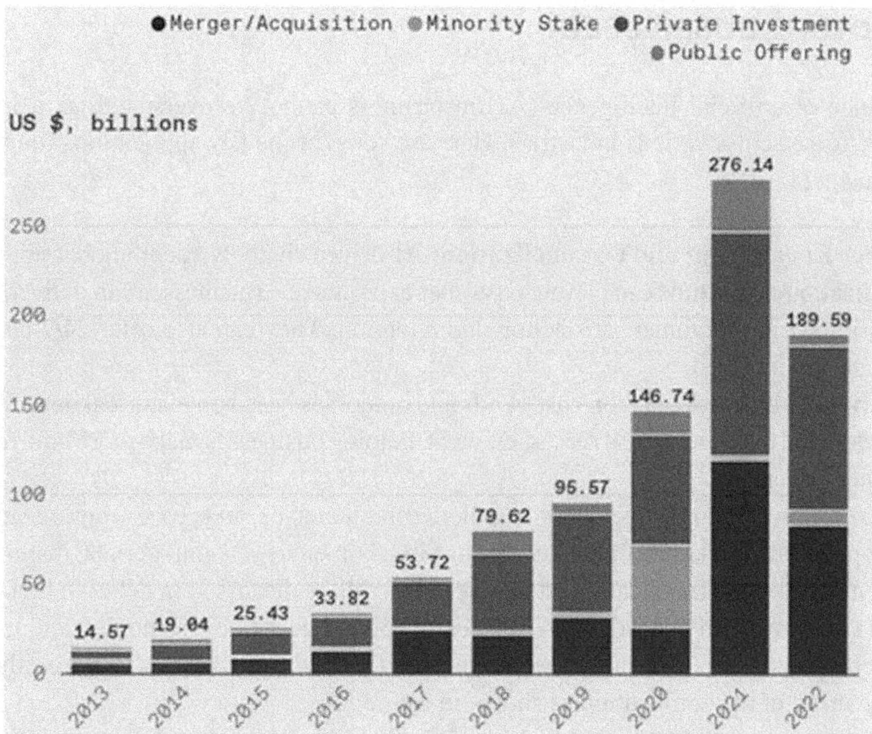

Within the next **20 years**, the AI revolution is expected to reach its full potential. It will have an bigger impact than the combined effects of the Industrial and Digital revolutions. The AI revolution's rapid technological advancements will create enormous prospects for growth and profitability as shown in Figure 4.

Figure 4. Potential of AI in business

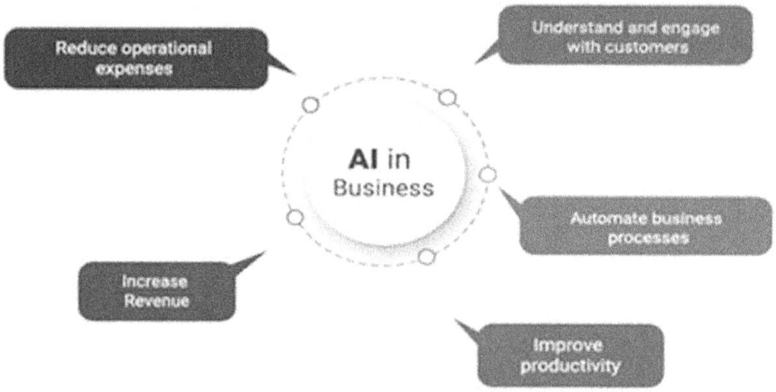

PRACTICAL APPLICATIONS AND OPPORTUNITIES OF AI IN FUTURE BUSINESSES

The significance of artificial intelligence (AI) in business cannot be overstated, as it has become a transformative force across various industries. Here are some of the key applications future companies can use (Strong et al., 2016):

1. **Customer Engagement and Personalization:** AI-driven chatbots, recommendation engines, and personalization algorithms can elevate customer experiences. Businesses can deliver personalized content, improving customer satisfaction and retention. They can also offer 24/7 chat support as no humans are involved.
2. **Predictive Analytics:** AI can forecast trends and outcomes based on historical data. This is invaluable for demand forecasting, and risk assessment, helping businesses make more informed decisions and reduce mistakes.
3. **Cost Reduction:** Through automation, predictive maintenance, and process optimization, AI helps reduce operational costs. This includes savings in labor, energy, and materials, making businesses more competitive and financially sustainable. This will be discussed in detail in this chapter later.
4. **Market and Competitive Analysis**: AI-powered tools can continuously monitor and analyze market trends, competitor activities, and consumer mindset, allowing businesses to devise their strategies and stay ahead of the competition as shown in figure 5.
5. **Security and Fraud Detection**: AI can enhance cybersecurity by identifying and mitigating threats in real-time. It's also used in fraud detection, protecting businesses and customers from financial losses.
6. **Global Reach**: Online businesses can leverage AI-driven language translation and localization to reach a global audience, transcending language barriers.
7. **Calendar Management:** AI can help in finding free slots in a schedule for an entrepreneur. It can also help in auto-scheduling of appointment (Tripathi et al., 2018).

Figure 5. AI applications

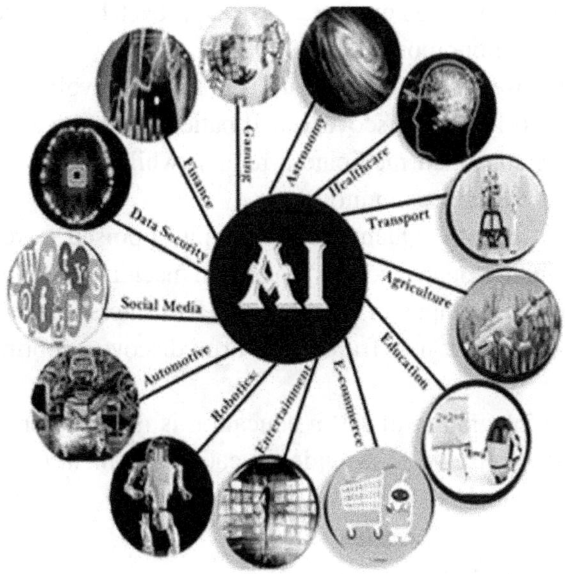

Exploration of Current AI Trends

Artificial intelligence (AI) has emerged as a transformational force in technology and industry. Its rapid development marked a new era in which machines can learn, reason, and make decisions, affecting the way we work, live, and interact. We will go deeper into the interesting world of AI tools and trends that are driving innovation and influencing our future (Obschonka et al., 2020).

1. **Machine Learning**: A branch of artificial intelligence, machine learning has led the way in many recent developments. This field involves creating algorithms that enable computers to learn from and make predictions or decisions based on huge amounts of data.
2. **Deep learning**: A branch of machine learning, has had a profound impact on areas like image and speech recognition, natural language processing (NLP), and autonomous vehicles. The development of neural networks and convolutional neural networks (**CNNs**) has led the way for breakthroughs, making them essential tools in AI development.
3. **Natural Language Processing (NLP)**: Natural Language Processing is a branch of AI that focuses on enabling machines to understand, interpret, and generate human language. NLP tools like **GPT-3** have been crucial in developing AI tools like Chat-Bots. This technology has wider application for industries like customer service, content creation, and e-commerce, where effective communication is paramount (Chalmers et al., 2021).
4. **Computer Vision**: Computer vision refers to a computer's ability to perceive and comprehend the visual world. AI-powered computer vision applications are used in facial recognition, autonomous vehicles, medical image analysis, and more. Tools like **OpenCV**, **Tensor Flow**, and **PyTorch** have democratized the development of computer vision applications, allowing businesses and researchers to leverage this technology for a wide range of purposes.

5. **Reinforcement Learning:** Reinforcement learning is an AI approach that focuses on training models through interactions with environment. This approach has gained recognition in fields such as robotics, gaming, and autonomous systems.
6. **AI in Healthcare**: The use of AI in healthcare is constantly evolving. Machine learning models can aid in disease diagnosis, drug discovery, and patient outcome assessment.AI tools like **IBM Watson** are making personalized medicine a reality, while wearable devices and telemedicine platforms are using AI to enhance monitoring.
7. **Quantum Computing and AI**: Quantum computing is poised to revolutionize AI by solving complex problems at unprecedented speeds. Quantum machine learning is a field that aims to harness the power of quantum computers for AI tasks. This intersection of quantum computing and AI holds the potential to unlock new frontiers in drug discovery, optimization, and cryptography (Wilson et al., 2022).
8. **AI in Education**: The integration of AI in education is making personalized learning a reality. Adaptive learning systems use AI to provide educational content to individual students, helping them reach their full potential.

Exploration of CurrentAI Tools

Artificial intelligence (AI) is a dynamic field of invention that is constantly reshaping the way we live and work. As we continue on this path of discovering AI technologies, it is critical to remember that the AI environment is always changing. At an alarming rate, new tools and technologies emerge, influencing sectors and redefining possibilities. Therefore, as you dive into the world of AI tools, keep in mind that what is considered groundbreaking today may soon become commonplace, and what is unknown could rapidly become indispensable. We need to be stay updated with AI and its tools which will enhance our potential (Tkachenko et al., 2019).

1. **Tara:** Tara stands out as a highly favoured AI application for businesses. It empowers small businesses by offering services like project management, team collaboration, technical specification writing, and task allocation. Additionally, (Cavallo et al., 2019). Tara aids in marketing automation and facilitates the monitoring of overall business performance.
2. **Jasper:** Jasper serves as an AI writing tool designed to enhance digital marketing strategies. Its machine-learning algorithm can generate personalized content, such as emails and blog posts, at a rate up to 10 times faster than human capability.
3. **Growbots:** Growbots excels at enhancing sales by optimizing lead generation. It offers business owners and marketing teams access to tailored lists of potential customers aligned with their specific business objectives. Moreover, it provides access to a database of over 100 million potential clients, facilitates personalized email communication, supports marketing campaign scheduling, and issues follow-up notifications (Popkova et al., 2020).
4. **Sapling:** Sapling stands out as a top-notch method for incorporating AI into business customer service. This virtual messaging assistant is a valuable tool for swift and efficient communication, ultimately enhancing the brand's reputation. Among its standout features is the provision of automated suggestions for both company and consumer interactions, significantly streamlining the communication process (Fossen et al., 2021). Furthermore, it offers valuable suggestions to customer service teams for enhancing the grammar and overall quality of their written responses.

How can you find AI tools for your business? First, you need to identify your needs. What tasks do you need to automate? What areas of your business could be under improvement? Only after you get answers to these questions, start researching AI tools (Gupta et al., 2023).

A COMPREHENSIVE GUIDE FOR FUTURE ENTREPRENEURS

Integrating AI in business operation requires just more than starting to use AI tools. Many factors must be considered, like any other step of the business journey. Given below are few guidelines that are very much helpful to understand the basics of integrating AI with business:

Step 1: Learn about Artificial Intelligence

Without a solid understanding of how AI functions, it becomes challenging to leverage it effectively for business growth. With the abundance of AI tools and technologies available, making informed choices is virtually impossible without a foundational knowledge (Pfau et al., 2021).

It is highly advisable to invest considerable time in acquiring insights into various business AI software by exploring diverse courses and resources. For instance, small business owners can educate themselves about technologies like Machine Learning (ML), predictive analytics, and other popular AI solutions to determine their suitability for their specific needs.

Step 2: Identify the Issues at Hand

Relying solely on AI to solve problems is not advisable, even though it can be a valuable tool. It's crucial to pinpoint the issues affecting business growth and operations, such as HR challenges, delayed payments, or cyber threats. Once the areas in which technology can benefit are identified, it's essential to explore relevant AI tools and solutions. For instance, if concerns arise regarding cybersecurity, one can proactively seek out AI solutions for small business security to mitigate potential disasters. Additionally, reviewing case studies to understand how larger businesses and competitors have effectively employed AI to overcome diverse challenges is strongly recommended.

Step 3: Prioritise the Issues

Not all problems demand immediate attention, so it's prudent to begin by addressing the most pressing issues. But how do we determine the order of priority?

A highly effective method is to compile a list of the current business challenges and assess the corresponding financial impact. It doesn't necessarily require precise figures; estimates or percentages will suffice. Subsequently, arrange the issues in descending order, starting with those causing the most substantial losses, and seek out AI solutions to address them.

Step 4: Bring Experts On Board

Individuals with the right expertise in AI technologies, particularly for small businesses, play a pivotal role in bridging the gap between one's capabilities and business objectives. This "lag" often manifests in the context of resources and the execution of short-term, time-bound business goals. When it comes to incorporating AI into business operations, a similar situation arises. This is where AI experts and consultants can step in to provide valuable insights and address crucial questions, such as:

- Is the organization adequately prepared for AI integration?
- What is the expected timeline for training and implementation?
- How will project management and overall operations be affected?
- Is the investment in AI justified and likely to yield positive returns?
  Step 5: Conduct Sample Projects

Incorporating AI into daily business operations represents a significant leap, and it's not an overnight process. Even if one's confident in outfitting their organization with the necessary infrastructure and equipping staff with AI knowledge, running sample projects is essential to gain a practical sense of the progress.

A practical approach is to begin by integrating AI tools for smaller tasks. Additionally, when dealing with data collection and analysis, it's a critical juncture to determine your storage requirements and select appropriate storage solutions.

METHODS FOR COST REDUCTION AND CUSTOMER EXPERIENCE ENHANCEMENT

Artificial intelligence will be used by future companies in a wide range of industries to improve customer experiences, increase productivity, and make data-driven choices. Here are some common business processes and examples of how AI can be used:

Cost Reduction

1. **Process Automation:** Utilising robotic process automation (**RPA**) driven by AI to automate routine, rule-based operations, thereby minimising human error and the requirement for manual labour.
2. **Predictive Maintenance:** Artificial intelligence (AI) has the potential to improve maintenance schedules and prevent costly equipment breakdowns by doing predictive maintenance on machinery and other equipment.
3. **Supply Chain Optimisation:** With the help of AI, supply chain logistics, inventory management, and predicting demand may all be improved, resulting in lower inventory costs and more effective transportation.
4. **Efficiency in Energy:** Artificial intelligence (AI)-driven systems are capable of analysing patterns of energy use and making instantaneous adjustments to save energy expenditures.
5. **Data Analytics:** AI can be used for advanced data analytics to identify cost drivers and assist businesses in making data-driven decisions to save unnecessary expenditures.

Customer Experience Enhancement

1. **Personalisation:** To improve the overall customer experience, AI may use consumer data to analyse and generate personalised product suggestions, content, and marketing communications.
2. **Chatbots and Virtual Assistants:** Using chatbots and virtual assistants that are powered by AI to respond to client enquiries right away and to give round-the-clock service (Levesque et al., 2022).
3. **Voice and Speech Recognition:** To enhance customer interactions over the phone and with voice-activated devices, voice recognition and speech-to-text technology can be integrated.
4. **Sentiment Analysis:** To understand consumer opinions and address issues quickly, AI can be used to analyse social media, customer reviews, and feedback.
5. **Customer Journey Mapping:** With the help of AI, customer journeys can be mapped and analysed to find areas of concern and opportunities for customer experience enhancement.
6. **Visual Recognition:** Use AI-driven image recognition to improve product searches and suggestions so that customers can find what they're looking for more easily.
7. **Natural Language Processing (NLP):** NLP can be used to analyse customer comments and inquiries, assisting organisations in learning more about the preferences and issues that customers have.
8. **Virtual Reality (VR) and Augmented Reality(AR):** In particular in sectors like retail and real estate, using AI in combination with VR and AR technology to create immersive and engaging customer experiences.

THE FUTURE GOVERNMENT'S ROLE IN AI REGULATION

For AI to achieve its potential, it is essential to recognise and manage the risks it creates. Many socio-economic benefits of AI that can support smart and sustainable development include improved safety in healthcare, transportation, and emergency response, as well as increased efficiency and quality in the delivery of goods and services. Therefore, as AI systems advance and become more complex, their risks and connectivity to other intelligent devices and systems will also grow. As a result, both specialised governance frameworks for AI, such as those for autonomous weapons, transportation, and healthcare, as well as a more general global governance framework for AI, will be required (Chung et al., 2011).

The intricacies and unpredictable nature of the AI environment pose significant challenges for governments in establishing effective AI governance regulations. The inherent unpredictability of AI makes it difficult for governments to set clear policy goals. Additionally, limited understanding of the technology and regulatory lag exacerbate the challenges in addressing societal issues related to AI. Major tech companies such as Google, Facebook, Microsoft, and Apple have a substantial informational and resource advantage over governments in regulating AI, creating an information gap that hinders the effective application of laws to AI.

To address these challenges, there is a growing call for innovative governance strategies, including adaptive governance and hybrid or "de-centered" governance. These approaches acknowledge the government's limited influence in resource allocation and propose combining state and non-state actors to create a blend of industry norms and public regulatory oversight. Drawing lessons from previous technologies and adapting governance frameworks is essential to effectively control AI, considering its unique characteristics and rapid advancements (Ciresan et al., 2015).

AI AND INTELLECTUAL PROPERTY IN THE FUTURE

In today's evolving, technologically advanced society, AI systems have been gaining momentum all around. With advanced technology implemented, it is only a matter of time before these systems begin to create wonderful inventionsin the future without any form of human involvement as shown in figure 4. This raises important issues with **intellectual property rights (IPR)**, as it calls into question not only established ideas about things like patents and copyrights, but also creates concerns with the laws governing of such technologies, among other things (Soni et al., 2018).

The Legal and Intellectual Property considerations for future entrepreneurial ventures are:

1. Patenting AI Innovations:
    - Find out if a patent is innovative and eligible.
    - Avoid public disclosure and be clear about ownership.
    - Take global defence as an example.
2. Protecting AI-Generated Content:
    - Understand copyright and fair use.
    - Use licensing agreements to protect data rights.
3. Trade Secrets:

Sometimes, entrepreneurs prefer to protect their AI innovations and models as trade secrets rather than disclosing them through the patent system (Lu et al.,2022). Keep in mind that trade secret protection relies on maintaining confidentiality, and any breach can have significant legal consequences.

4. Ethical and Privacy Considerations:
    - When creating and implementing AI systems, adhere to ethical standards and privacy rights as shown in figure 6.
    - Adhere to data protection regulations such as **GDPR (General Data Protection Regulation)** and respect ethical AI guidelines (Murray, 2018).

To ensure legal compliance, safeguard intellectual property, and maintain a positive reputation in the future ventures, these factors are essential.

CHALLENGES FACED WITH AI INTEGRATION

Although integration AI with entrepreneurship can have many advantages, it also brings numerous difficulties that future entrepreneurs must overcome (Sousa M J et al., 2019). The main difficulties which can be faced by future entrepreneurs are listed below:

- **High Initial Costs**: It can be expensive to develop and implement AI systems. Hiring AI specialists, obtaining data, and creating or purchasing AI software and hardware can all come at a high upfront cost for entrepreneurs.

Figure 6. AI and legal framework

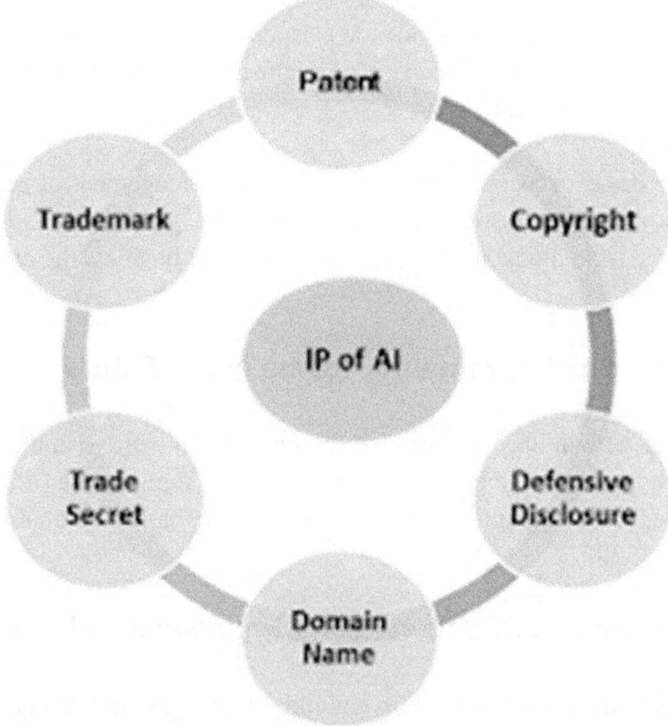

- **Lack of AI Expertise:** It's possible that many entrepreneurs lack knowledge of AI and machine learning. People with the appropriate skills might be difficult to find and expensive to train.
- **Data Privacy and Security:** Although handling a lot of data is necessary for AI, it also raises questions regarding data security and privacy. Entrepreneurs must make sure they follow by applicable regulations (like the **GDPR**) and safeguard private customer data.
- **Ethical Concerns:** AI algorithms may unintentionally reinforce prejudice and discrimination. Entrepreneurs must keep a close eye on their AI systems to make sure they are just and moral. Addressing data bias, algorithmic judgements, and potential social and moral consequences are all included in this.
- **Integrating with Existing Systems:** It might be challenging to integrate AI into current business systems and processes. During this process, problems with compatibility and employee resistance could appear.
- **Customer Trust:** Customers may be sceptical about AI-powered products or services. Building trust in AI and ensuring transparency in how AI is used can be a significant challenge.
- **Scalability:** AI programs may need to scale as a company expands in order to deal with increasingly complex jobs and larger amounts of data. Securing the scalability of AI systems can be difficult.
- **Competition:** The market is experiencing an increase in rivalry as AI becomes more widespread. Entrepreneurs must constantly innovate with AI and identify new applications in order to stay ahead of the competition.

- **User Experience:** It must be ensured that AI enhances the experience of the users. Poorly implemented AI can frustrate customers and drive them away.
- **Intellectual Property:** Working with outside partners or vendors makes it more difficult to protect intellectual property connected to AI. Copyrights, trade secrets, and patenting are important considerations for business owners.

Careful planning, strategic decision-making, and constant management of these obstacles are necessary for successfully incorporating AI into entrepreneurship. Additionally, it requires a thorough understanding of both the technology and the particular sector of business the entrepreneur operates in (Soni N et al., 2018).

Building AI-Enhanced Entrepreneurial Teams in the Future

Utilizing the potential of AI will become essential for staying competitive in the future. It is crucial to form teams with diverse skill sets, including AI expertise. The significance of building such teams is presented in this section, along with guidance on how to find, develop AI professionals inside the organization (Rajagopal et al., 2022).

The Importance of Diverse Skill Sets in Future Entrepreneurial Teams

- **Problem Solving:** Startups often deal with complex challenges, and AI can be a game-changer in tackling these issues. A diverse team includes people with unique problem-solving approaches, boosting the possibility of discovering new AI-enabled solutions.
- **Innovation:** Entrepreneurship focuses on innovation. A team should provide fresh perspectives and solutions, which can be critical in discovering creative applications of AI.
- **Risk Reduction: Startups** are risky ventures. A team should reduce risks by offering a range of skills and experiences, making it easier to adapt to unexpected obstacles (Syed Far Abid Hossain et al., 2021).
- **Market Insights:** A team should offer a broader understanding of various markets, cultures, and consumer psychology.

Recruitment of Future AI Professionals

- **Recruit qualified personnel:** Define the AI-related positions and talents that the startup will require (Kollmann et al., 2022). Data scientists, machine learning engineers, and AI researchers may be included.
- **Test Real-world Problem Solving:** During interviews, present candidates with problems your startup faces and ask how they would approach them using AI. This can reveal problem-solving skills and creativity (Mnih V et al., 2015).
- **Cultural Fit:** Candidates should be tested not just for their technical talents, but also for their aptitude to operate in a startup environment. Team members at startups should be flexible, collaborative, and self-driven.

Training Future AI Professionals

- **Continuous Learning:** Encourage AI experts to stay updated with the latest AI trends and technologies through courses, workshops, and conferences. Create an environment in which team members share their knowledge and experiences (Syed Far Abid Hossain et al., 2019).
- **Cross-disciplinary Knowledge:** AI experts should understand the broader business context, and non-AI team members should have a basic understanding of AI concepts. This enhances communication and collaboration.
- **Project-Based Learning:** Assign projects that align with startup's goals, which can accelerate learning and create practical, relevant experience.

A successful AI-enhanced team relies on effective management. Ensure that your startup efficiently integrates AI into its fundamental strategy, promote collaboration, embrace flexible strategies, and communicate freely. As a result, your team will be able to capitalize on AI's capabilities and push your start-up to greater success.

ENTREPRENEURSHIP POSSIBILITIES AND SUSTAINABILITY

Entrepreneurship and sustainability are complimentary forces driving economic progress and societal well-being. The intersection of environmental awareness, technological innovation, and shifting consumer values will give a plethora of exciting opportunities for future entrepreneurs.Here are some of the ways entrepreneurship and sustainability work together (Soni N et al., 2018).

1. **Green Technology Startups**: As the world's focus on mitigating climate change increases, green technology start-ups continue to thrive. Entrepreneurs will have the opportunity to capitalize on innovations in renewable energy, energy-efficient appliances, sustainable transportation, and waste reduction technologies. These ventures will not only address pressing environmental issues but also present lucrative investment prospects. The future of green technology start-ups promises a more sustainable and economically viable world.
2. **Circular Economy Ventures:** In the future, the concept of a circular economy, which promotes recycling, reusing, and reducing waste, willl gain even more momentum. Entrepreneurs will have the opportunity to explore new avenues in up-cycling, re-manufacturing, and sustainable product design(Loureiro et al., 2021). These businesses will not only contribute to resource conservation but can also lead to substantial cost savings. The future of entrepreneurship promises a more sustainable and resource-efficient world.
3. **Sustainable Agriculture:** Agriculture will continue to be a major business in the future, but it will face considerable modifications. Organic farming, precision agriculture, vertical farming, and sustainable food production technologies will be prioritized by entrepreneurs. These businesses will not only help the environment, but will also give customers with better food alternatives. The future of agriculture promises a greener and healthier world (Murray S, 2018).
4. **E-commerce with a Purpose:** In the future, the growth of e-commerce will likely continue, and sustainable practices will become a key differentiator for businesses. Entrepreneurs will have the opportunity to create eco-friendly e-commerce platforms, curate sustainable products, or implement

carbon offset programs (Chatzopoulos et al., 2020). These initiatives will appeal to environmentally conscious consumers, driving a new wave of sustainable e-commerce (Syed Far Abid Hossain, 2019).

5. **Social entrepreneurship**: Social entrepreneurship will continue to play a pivotal role in addressing societal challenges. In the future, social entrepreneurs will likely devise innovative solutions to combat issues like poverty, education, and healthcare disparities. These solutions will not only have a positive societal impact but also attract investors who are interested in contributing to sustainable development. The future of social entrepreneurship promises a more equitable and sustainable world.

CONCLUSION

Artificial intelligence (AI) and entrepreneurship will both play major roles in the future, presenting both enormous opportunities and significant challenges. Entrepreneurs are at the forefront of innovation as AI technologies continue to advance and impact a variety of industries. This essay examines how entrepreneurship and artificial intelligence are interacting, emphasising the transformative potential and important factors to take into account for success in this quickly evolving environment.

In the AI era, entrepreneurship is defined by the capacity to use AI technology to break through conventional business frameworks, generate novel solutions, and stimulate economic growth. Because AI can process enormous volumes of data, find patterns, and make predictions, it has the potential to revolutionise the business world by empowering entrepreneurs to make data-driven decisions and provide individualised goods and services. AI is being used by start-ups in a variety of industries, including finance, e-commerce, healthcare, and logistics, in order to increase productivity and competitiveness.

Entrepreneurship powered by AI has a lot of potential. For instance, by offering affordable automation, boosting operational effectiveness, and enhancing customer experiences, it can reduce entry barriers for entrepreneurs. AI may also provide small businesses with access to high-end capabilities that were previously only available to the largest tech companies, such chatbots, recommendation engines, and data analytics. The democratisation of AI enables business owners to participate on an even playing field.

New sectors are emerging as a result of AI innovation. Autonomous vehicles, AI-powered healthcare diagnostics, and smart cities are just a few industries where entrepreneurship is having a big influence. These inventions could raise living standards, lessen their negative effects on the environment, and promote economic expansion.

But there are difficulties ahead for entrepreneurs in the AI era. AI-related ethical issues include algorithmic prejudice, privacy, and the possibility of employment displacement need to be addressed. To secure trust and longevity in their companies, entrepreneurs must prioritise ethical AI development and go through difficult regulatory regimes. In addition, the digital divide is widening, with people who don't have access to AI technologies falling behind. Entrepreneurs need to think about ways to increase the accessibility and inclusivity of AI-driven goods and services.

Future of work concerns are also brought up by AI's role in entrepreneurship. AI has the potential to improve human capabilities and automate repetitive tasks, but it can also result in job displacement in some sectors of the economy. In order for workers to adjust to these changes, entrepreneurs need to think about retraining and upskilling them. Government regulations and public-private collaborations will be essential to guaranteeing a fair transition for labourers impacted by automation driven by AI.

A further difficulty is the quick speed at which AI is developing. Entrepreneurs that want to stay competitive need to keep up with the most recent developments in AI and constantly modify their approaches. Entrepreneurs can gain access to state-of-the-art AI technologies and expertise through collaboration between research institutions, startups, and established corporations.

In conclusion, there is a lot of potential and complexity in the future of AI and entrepreneurship. Businesses have never-before-seen chances to innovate, upend markets, and generate revenue thanks to artificial intelligence. To fully utilise AI's potential, entrepreneurs must, however, address moral issues, advance inclusivity, and get ready for the way that work is evolving. In this ever-changing environment, success requires constant learning and adaptability. The way businesses and society develop in the AI era will be greatly influenced by the decisions made by entrepreneurs. Those who embrace AI as a tool for positive change will be at the forefront of innovation and progress in this extremely promising and challenging future.

REFERENCES

Aghion, P., Jones, B. F., & Jones, C. I. (2017). Artificial intelligence and economic growth (No. w23928). National Bureau of Economic Research. 3

Berger, T., Lévesque, M., Rojas, E., Tuomi, I., & Townsend, D. (2022). Artificial intelligence and entrepreneurial ecosystems: Understanding the implications for policy and practice. Journal of Entrepreneurship. *Emerging Economies and Technology, 10*(3), 1–19.

Cavallo, A., Ghezzi, A., & Balocco, R. (2019). Entrepreneurial ecosystem research: Present debates and future directions. *The International Entrepreneurship and Management Journal, 15*(4), 1291–1321. doi:10.1007/s11365-018-0526-3

Chalmers, D., MacKenzie, N. G., & Carter, S. (2021). Artificial intelligence and entrepreneurship: Implications for venture creation in the fourth industrial revolution. *Entrepreneurship Theory and Practice, 45*(5), 1028–1053. doi:10.1177/1042258720934581

Chatzopoulos, C. G., & Weber, M. (2020). Digitization and artificial intelligence for lean customer experience management. *Transformation, 22*, 24.

Chung, J., Gulcehre, C., Cho, K., & Bengio, Y. (2011). Empirical evaluation of gated recurrent neural networks on sequence modeling. *NIPS 2014 Workshop on Deep Learning*. IEEE.

Fossen, F. M., & Sorgner, A. (2021). Digitalization of work and entry into entrepreneurship. *Journal of Business Research, 125*, 548–563. doi:10.1016/j.jbusres.2019.09.019

Gao, Y., Liang, X., & Zhang, X. (2022). The impact of artificial intelligence on entrepreneurship: A bibliometric analysis from 2000 to 2020. *Journal of Business Research, 141*, 1–13.

Gupta, B. B., Gaurav, A., Panigrahi, P. K., & Arya, V. (2023). Analysis of artificial intelligence-based technologies and approaches on sustainable entrepreneurship. Technological Forecasting and Social Change, 186, 122152. doi:10.1016/j.techfore.2022.122152

Hossain, S. F. (2019). Social networking and its role in media entrepreneurship. *Journal of Media Management and Entrepreneurship, 1*(1), 73–86. doi:10.4018/JMME.2019010105

Hossain, S. F., Nurunnabi, M., Hussain, K., & Saha, S. K. (2019). Effects of variety-seeking intention by mobile phone usage on university students' academic performance. *Cogent Education*, *6*(1), 1574692. doi:10.1080/2331186X.2019.1574692

Hossain, S. F., Shan, X., Nurunnabi, M., Tushar, H., Mohsin, A. K., & Ahsan, F. T. (2021). Opportunities and challenges of M-learning during the COVID-19 pandemic. *Advances in Social Networking and Online Communities*, 210–227. doi:10.4018/978-1-7998-7764-6.ch007

Kollmann, T., Kleine-Stegemann, L., de Cruppe, K., & Then-Bergh, C. (2022). Eras of digital entrepreneurship: Connecting the past, present, and future. *Business & Information Systems Engineering*, *64*(1), 1–17. doi:10.1007/s12599-021-00728-6

Kshetri, N., & Voas, J. (2020). Blockchain-enabled sharing economy and prospects for its adoption in industries beyond finance. *IEEE Transactions on Engineering Management*, *67*(4), 1165–1178.

Lévesque, M., Obschonka, M., & Nambisan, S. (2022). Pursuing impactful entrepreneurship research using artificial intelligence. *Entrepreneurship Theory and Practice*, *46*(4), 803–832. doi:10.1177/1042258720927369

Loureiro, S. M. C., Guerreiro, J., & Tussyadiah, I. (2021). Artificial intelligence in business: State of the art and future research agenda. *Journal of Business Research*, *129*, 911–926. doi:10.1016/j.jbusres.2020.11.001

Lu, X., Wijayaratna, K., Huang, Y., & Qiu, A. (2022). AI-enabled opportunities and transformation challenges for SMEs in the post-pandemic era: A review and research agenda. *Frontiers in Public Health*, *10*, 885067. doi:10.3389/fpubh.2022.885067 PMID:35570947

Mnih, V., Kavukcuoglu, K., Silver, D., Rusu, A. A., Veness, J., Bellemare, M. G., Graves, A., Riedmiller, M., Fidjeland, A. K., Ostrovski, G., Petersen, S., Beattie, C., Sadik, A., Antonoglou, I., King, H., Kumaran, D., Wierstra, D., Legg, S., & Hassabis, D. (2015). Human-level control through deep reinforcement learning. *Nature*, *518*(7540), 529–533. doi:10.1038/nature14236 PMID:25719670

Murray, S. (2018). *As Global Leader in Digital Transformation Market Research, IDC Reveals Worldwide Digital Transformation Predictions. International Data Corporation.* IDC.

Obschonka, M., & Audretsch, D. B. (2020). Artificial intelligence and big data in entrepreneurship: A new era has begun. *Small Business Economics*, *55*(3), 529–539. doi:10.1007/s11187-019-00202-4

Pfau, W., &Rimpp, P. (2021). AI-enhanced business models for digital entrepreneurship. *Digital Entrepreneurship: Impact on Business and Society*, 121-140.

Popkova, E. G., & Sergi, B. S. (2020). Human capital and AI in industry 4.0.Convergence and divergence in social entrepreneurship in Russia. *Journal of Intellectual Capital*, *21*(4), 565–581. doi:10.1108/JIC-09-2019-0224

Rajagopal, N. K., Qureshi, N. I., Durga, S., Ramirez Asis, E. H., Huerta Soto, R. M., Gupta, S. K., & Deepak, S. (2022). Future of business culture: An artificial intelligence-driven digital framework for organization decision-making process. *Complexity*, *2022*, 1–14. doi:10.1155/2022/7796507

Saini, R., & Singh, S. (2022). Artificial Intelligence and Entrepreneurship: A Review of Literature and Future Research Directions. *Journal of Entrepreneurship Education*, *25*(1), 1–12.

Soni, N., Sharma, E. K., Singh, N., & Kapoor, A. (2018). Impact of Artificial Intelligence on Business. *Digital Innovations, Transformation, and Society Conference 2018 (Digits 2018)*. IEEE.

Soni, N., Singh, N., Kapoor, A., & Sharma, E. K. (2018). *Low-Resolution Image Recognition UsingCloud Hopfield Neural Network*. Progress in Advanced Computing and Intelligent.

Sousa, M. J., & Rocha, A. (2019). Skills for disruptive digital business. *Journal of Business Research*, *94*, 257–263. doi:10.1016/j.jbusres.2017.12.051

Strong, A. I. (2016). Applications of artificial intelligence & associated technologies. *Science [ETEBMS-2016]*, *5*(6).

Taeihagh, A. (2021). Governance of artificial intelligence. *Policy and Society*, *40*(2), 137–157. doi:10.1080/14494035.2021.1928377

Tkachenko, V., Kuzior, A., & Kwilinski, A. (2019). Introduction of artificial intelligence tools into the training methods of entrepreneurship activities. *Journal of Entrepreneurship Education*, *22*(6), 1–10.

Tripathi, S., & Ghatak, C. (2018). Artificial intelligence and intellectual property law. *Christ ULJ*, *7*, 83.

Wilson, M., Paschen, J., & Pitt, L. (2022). The circular economy meets artificial intelligence (AI): Understanding the opportunities of AI for reverse logistics. *Management of Environmental Quality*, *33*(1), 9–25. doi:10.1108/MEQ-10-2020-0222

Chapter 10
The Contribution of Artificial Intelligence to the Business and Marketing Strategy

Sahar Mesfar
https://orcid.org/0000-0001-8869-6644
University of Sfax, Tunisia & University of Monastir, Tunisia

ABSTRACT

Modern technologies are considered indispensable tools in companies' development. At this stage, with the emergence of artificial intelligence usage, several transformations have been experienced with the new strategic context which influences the business and the marketing of companies' activities. To do this, they take into consideration the need for the integration and the involvement with this technology to minimize the risks in their development. The importance of this work is to emphasize a literature review which specifies the role of AI in improving the business and marketing strategic to arrive at a relevant adoption solution.

INTRODUCTION

Modern technologies like artificial intelligence are considered one of the innovative tools for business development. At this stage, the business and marketing of services of companies have been affected by several transformations which have appeared in a new strategic context. For this, the need for integration and involvement with this technology is considered essential to ensure business success.

The scope of AI in business is likely to cover all strategic and functional dimensions of the company (El Namaki, 2018).

Today, AI is increasingly deployed in operational marketing, for example contact center response management, risk identification as well as in marketing, including customer targeting and analysis, selection and design of advertising texts tailored to target customers, pricing to maximize returns from individual customers (Marinchak et al., 2018; cited by Stone, et al. 2020). According to Stone et al, (2020) who

DOI: 10.4018/979-8-3693-1842-3.ch010

indicated that tomorrow they will expect AI to be used in strategic decision making. However, the use of AI in marketing strategy has not been discussed much in the public domain (Stone et al, 2020). For this objective, the need of a new process is indispensable.

The objective of this work is to present a review of the literature toward Artificial Intelligence to the business and marketing strategy. And to achieve a better understanding of this proposed problematic, the principal research questions are presented as follows:

1. What is the role of the integration of Artificial Intelligence on marketing strategy?
2. What is the contribution of AI on business strategy?

And to arrive at a better understanding to these questions, this review study was conducted on the basis of recent articles, the selection of these articles insist on the role of Artificial Intelligence business and marketing strategy, while specifying the contribution of this study to the marketing and business literature in referring to the importance of this study for the practitioners of marketing and business. For these reasons, our chapter includes a presentation about the methods, then the conceptual framework about AI, business and marketing strategies and the contribution of AI to both of those strategies. And finally, our chapter focuses on the discussion part, the theoretical and managerial contributions, and the limitations of our study and the future research.

METHODOLOGY

To answer our basic problematic, the selection of articles is based through the "Google Scholar" database by referring to the following keywords in the first step, we used the following words: "Artificial Intelligence" Or "AI " "business strategy" and in the second step, we used these keywords "Artificial Intelligence" Or "AI" "marketing strategy".

The Effect of AI on Marketing Strategy

The marketing strategy is developed to support a specific objectives (Dean and Sharfman, 1996; Varadarajan et al., 2010), for example gain and retain customers and ensure that the portfolio of clients of the company generates income (Simkin and Dibb 2012). The strategic decision concerns, for example, the products, markets, resource allocation and appropriate marketing activities (Mintzberg, 1978; Nutt and Wilson, 2010). The marketing strategy plays a key role in the communication with clients, the creation and product delivery, and ultimately the creation of value for clients (Varadarajan et al., 2010). The experts discuss the growing importance of AI for strategy formulation (Martınez-Lopez and Casillas, 2013). They discussed how they view the role of AI in the strategy-making process, now and in the future. The responses highlighted the ability to use AI for data collection and analysis, to systematically and efficiently identify underlying patterns and signals that humans might miss. These patterns and signals are an important element that the strategic marketer must consider when making decisions. Furthermore, the experts also discussed how these could be used directly by AI acting as an independent agent, capable of making strategic decisions without human support. The responses explained that perceived value creation from AI ranges from the lower analytical maturity stage of GAAM, descriptive analytics, to the mature stage of predictive analytics. The value is directly attributable to the ability to manage the abundance of data. Some respondents talked about reducing the complexity of consumer behavior analysis. Furthermore, the importance of AI was linked to its use to overcome the shortage of human resources, for example in small businesses.

The Effect of AI on Business Strategy

Companies concerned about the legal, ethical, and social issues created by AI applications must consider these forces to understand the effect of AI on the well-being of workers and consumers at the bottom of the economic pyramid (Xie et al., 2017). For example, all companies, especially multinationals, should be interested in the economic inequalities and negative externalities of the return of jobs from emerging markets to mature markets due to AI-driven productivity gains. We believe companies should consider whether opaque applications of AI will harm human self-determination (Zhou et al., 2012; Cited by Zhou et al, 2022). Regarding institutional influence on AI-based business strategy, the three institutional pillars posed by Scott (2008); Quoted by Zhou et al, 2022– regulatory, normative and cultural-cognitive – provide a useful framework. Regulatory institutions are the laws and regulations established by governments. Central and local governments play a critical role in defining the legal foundations, establishing industrial policies, providing capital and creating a roadmap to exploit AI-related business opportunities in emerging markets. Normative institutions establish industry association norms and standards for data access, data privacy, security, and public trust. Cultural cognitive institutions refer to AI-related business behavior; for example, business people and consumers may be wary of AI-related technologies and decisions made by AI.

CONCLUSION

Our study contributes to the marketing and management literature by specifying. The contribution of Artificial Intelligence to the business and marketing strategy. Despite the contribution of this study is based on an narrative literature study which was conducted only on a limited number of articles and for a limited publication period, referring to a single database such as "google scholar", future research can integrate a quantitative research in order to develop a recent research model that consists of variables such as AI and marketing strategy on the one hand, and to test the effect of AI on marketing strategy and management strategy on the other hand, so it is important to test empirically the proposed variables of the model with the linear regression test, to explore the significant value of the variables. Future research can integrate a qualitative study to explore the challenges raised when companies adopt this innovation.

REFERENCES

El Namak, M. S. S. (2018). How Companies are Applying AI to the Business Strategy Formulation. *Scholedge International Journal of Business Policy & Governance, 5*(8), 77-82.

Eriksson, T., Bigi, A., & Bonera, M. (2020). Think with me, or think for me? On the future role of artificial intelligence in marketing strategy formulation. *The TQM Journal*, *32*(4), 795–814. doi:10.1108/TQM-12-2019-0303

Stone, M., Aravopoulou, E., Ekinci, Y., Evans, G., Hobbs, M., Labib, A., Laughlin, P., Machtynger, J., & Machtynger, L. (2020). Artificial intelligence (AI) in strategic marketing decision-making: A research agenda. *The Bottom Line (New York, N.Y.)*, *33*(2), 183–200. doi:10.1108/BL-03-2020-0022

Zhou, X., Yang, Z., Hyman, M. R., Li, G., & Munim, Z. H. (2022). Guest editorial: Impact of artificial intelligence on business strategy in emerging markets: a conceptual framework and future research directions. *International Journal of Emerging Markets*, *17*(4), 917–929. doi:10.1108/IJOEM-04-2022-995

Chapter 11
Artificial Intelligence (AI) and Future Directions of Leadership From Robots (LFR) in Organizations

Abdullah Al Farabe
BRAC University, Bangladesh

Ahmad Saleheen
BRAC University, Bangladesh

Samin Yaser Noman
BRAC University, Bangladesh

S. M. Farhan Atique
BRAC University, Bangladesh

ABSTRACT

Traditional conceptions of leadership have undergone a dramatic change with the introduction of robots into leadership positions (LP). AI and robots will continue to improve, and this will likely have an impact on leadership in enterprises in the future. The abstract explores the leadership capabilities of robots (LCR), highlighting their advantages in working automation. The model finishes by arguing that includes three queries about the uses of Al significantly affective on leadership in workplaces, leadership positions in the medical industry and needing ethical considerations to deal with patients' data to improve patient care. Moreover, this research has a quality assessment with five questionnaires based on the substantial impact on leadership in work systems, the study of potential futures for leadership, the standard of study's research model, following leadership ethics and matching a similar focus between our study and the papers that were collected from other researchers to watch the impact of future direction leadership activity in AI within the organization.

DOI: 10.4018/979-8-3693-1842-3.ch011

INTRODUCTION

Artificial intelligence (AI) has brought to us in this new era a new scientific method that is going to change our whole life criteria. Once upon a time, people used to work by themselves but now science has developed so much that computer science is dominating the whole world. In films or fiction, we have seen that AI would take the world in one hand easily replacing humans which is now almost transforming into a reality. In the business sector, medical sector and institutes, AI is used to ease their workload. Digital is taking full advantage everywhere as AI automation and as a result, humans are being replaced by digital systems which have become a competitive advantage in industries (Lee, 2019). In this era of advanced technology, the fourth industrial revolution (4IR) period is fully under the new scientific tools or gadgets. Innovations are motivated to bring new tech so that old models can be replaced (Lee, 2019). As in the business sector, AI is also performing for the medical sector as well. All over the world, AI is being used to improve patient analysis. AI would help secure which treatment and which tests would be beneficial for a dangerous particular disease. For example, COVID-19 had become the top disease to defend and when all the tests were failing then AI helped the researchers to develop new treatments by going through all the tests by AI. A range of academics, physicians, technologists, and programmers, as well as consumers, are interested in AI because it has the potential to make revolutionary improvements to recover public health and also develop the treatment of the patient (Mohsin et al., 2021).

Technology based on artificial intelligence (AI) is no longer only for futurologists; it is already an essential aspect in many IT firms, business industries, and medical sectors which have been planned for many years worldwide by each country's governments. AI is transforming day by day and has drawn serious attention in academics. Current studies concentrate on the ramifications and immediate situations of the technology rather than watching or focusing on the bad impacts/performance of AI, which appears to have been the primary study issue for many years. Daugherty and Wilson (2018) demonstrates that the creativity and innovation of AI have become so demandable that AI has surpassed so many innovative sectors made by humans with their own hands. It could be finance, marketing, HRM or others. The effectiveness of medical resources and the standard of treatment given have recently been improved by the widespread deployment of AI-supported technology in healthcare facilities (Yoon & Lee, 2019). IT is the only AI that has innovations to the next level and upgrading the tech through machine learning, deep learning IOT, image processing, NLP, and others. Once more, Safavi and Kalis claim that by 2026, "AI applications could result in up to $150 billion in annual savings for U.S. healthcare". Numerous startups and well-known manufacturers of image devices presented at the Radiological Society of North America (RSNA, 2018) conference in Chicago declared that it is possible to get new results in medical treatment based on the help of AI by researching datasets of patients continuously.

Figure 1 that we have made to give a clear vision of the whole procedure and model of our workflow. In our model, we have focused on robotics which has AI intelligence and has the potential to become a future leader in the future. We have found three research questions related to our main topic. Each question has a different topic to discuss as our first question is based on the historical significance of technology on principles of leadership, AI, and leaders in socio-technical workplaces. The increasing application and use of Al significantly affect leadership in socio-technical workplaces. Our second question is about the current state of AI in healthcare, and the challenges and opportunities of AI in the medical section. The successful robots would assume leadership positions in the medical industry with the help of artificial intelligence (AI) integration. Finally, the last question provides the importance of ethical considerations of AI, how AI is used in patient care, and ethical threats due to lack of knowledge of AI. The reasons behind the ethical considerations needed to deal with patients' data and the process to educate professionals to use artificial intelligence effectively to improve patient care.

Figure 1. Model workflow chart

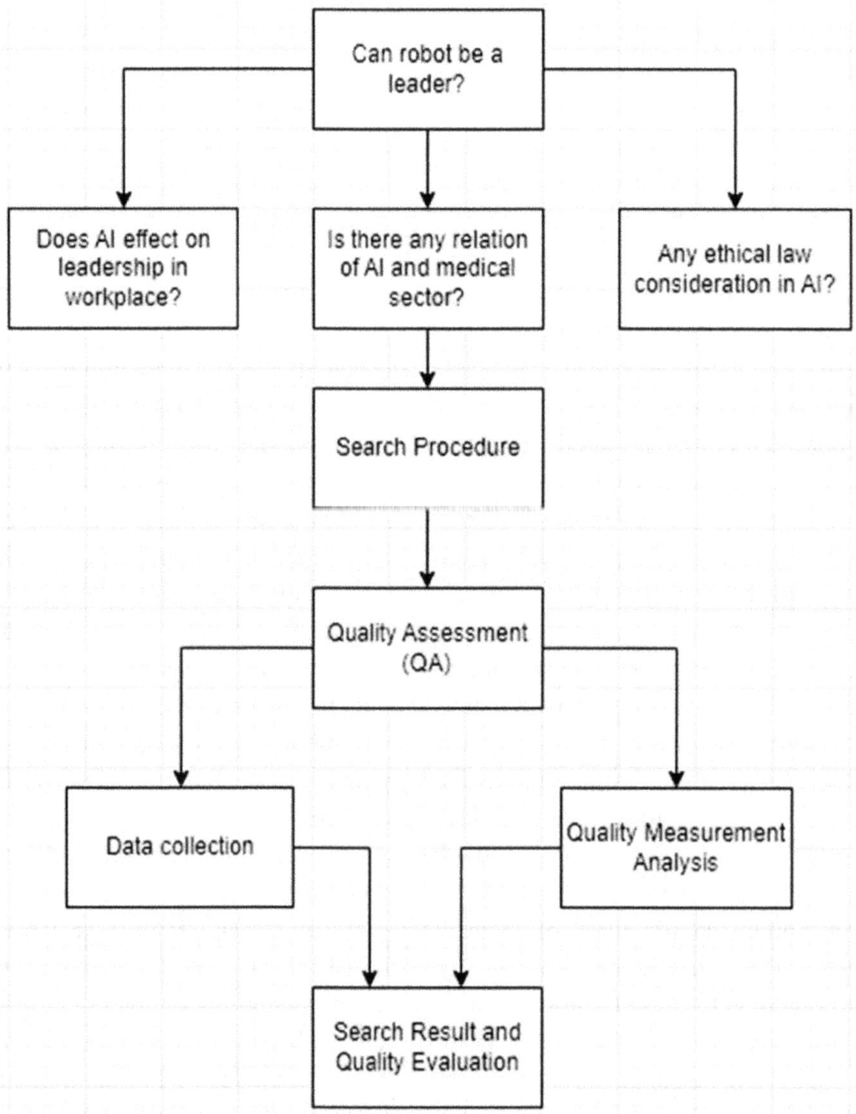

Next, we have a quality assessment check where we have searched a few books and scholars from different recognized websites. We figured a total of five questions that asked about whether AI has a substantial impact on leadership in appropriately designed socio-technical work systems, whether the study piece adequately describes and analyzes the potential futures for leadership inside an organization, whether the study's research model conforms to standards, whether the essay uses AI to examine or follow leadership ethics, whether the papers that were collected from this study have a similar focus with our model. A total of 20 works of literature/journals have been taken in Table 2 and compared with the five questions in Table 3 in the quality assessment section which have been discussed later on.

MOTIVATION

Our whole proposal model provides the future directions of leadership from robots (LFR) in organizations that lead the future and the whole world is researching the wonder of schine what would be beneficial for us. This paper presents three questions that answer about the historical significance of technology on principles of leadership, AI and leadership at the socio-technical workplaces, challenges and opportunities of AI in Healthcare, the importance of ethical considerations of AI and lastly quality measurement of the papers that we have been through to find out best papers highly indexed journals which indicate our research quality. This research also provides a proper AI leadership study by finding out the best highly recommended indexed journals.

LITERATURE REVIEW

Peifer et al. (2022) conducted a study on the existing literature on the process of use of cyber-physical systems in industrial settings and greater IT system networking is increasing the quantity of data that is now accessible. Artificial intelligence (AI) is being used by businesses more and more to examine by taking huge datasets in any field. That is why the main member of the team which we recommend as a leader is crucial for effectively adopting and exploiting AI. In light of all of these aspects as well as the dynamic evolution of AI, more research into the impact of AI on leaders and leadership is required to offer organizations practical advice and recommendations. These have been constructed after a careful investigation of the existing literature, and this analysis will form the basis for future work. The process of strategic transformation, credentials and skills, culture, and human-AI interaction were the four main clusters into which the findings of the literature study were divided. The results are thoroughly discussed, and a forecast for the remaining research and development phases is given.

Another study by Lee and Yoon (2021) has examined that the stage of AI-based innovation technology of today would be beneficial for the medical sector if it is used in a good way. In this study, they viewed some real examples of using AI automation in healthcare. Based on their study, a few famous hospitals have completely enabled to use of AI in medical treatment in diagnosis to treat patients without any harm. Although AI is welcomed by healthcare professionals, the procedure provides both dystopian (challenges to overcome) and utopian (new opportunities) viewpoints. They have examined on few particular opportunities to evaluate fairly and fight those challenges in healthcare. There is no doubt that in health care AI and used technology will make an enormous impact for better treatment. However, advantage of AI would be helpful for doctors but also has to be ethical in every sector that automation is not working on. On one side it is demandable but on the other hand, it would also be risky if AI is not researched fairly and highly sourced.

Dwivedi et al. (2021) state in another research paper that since the start of the Industrial Revolution for years. AI has big potential and will be successful in replacing humans one day in economics and academics. The velocity of change in this new era of artificial intelligence technology is stunning, opening up new opportunities for continuous innovation. Upgrading algorithms based on ML and deep learning is helping to make decisions early in a short time and would be also successful. This research provides pertinent insight into AI technology and its implications for future business and society while acknowledging the influence of industry and society on the speed of AI.

We have found another existing literature written by Capelli et al. (2023) works on the Artificial Intelligence Surgery (AIS) task force on Artificial Intelligence (AI) Ethics and the AIS Editorial Board Study Group on Ethics came to a consensus in this white paper regarding the moral issues and current reliability of artificial intelligence and autonomous actions in surgery. The Task Force established 6 areas of ethics, which were grouped into categories: Use of comprehensive and representative (i.e., impartial) data; Respect for privacy and sensitive data; Reliability of robotic and AI systems; AI transparency and uncertainty and equalizer role of technology in surgical education.

After reading all this literature have come up with an idea that we are going to work with robots and AI to be a leader in future directions of leadership in organization. AI is needed for the business sector, medical sector, and others. Nowadays AI has become an essential part of health care checking to observe how a particular harmful disease is responding based on the time. For example, COVID-19 has become a big threat to the whole world in AI is helping to observe its behavior. That is why our paper's focus is on the relationship between AI and health care. In the previous literature, they have discussed the result of increased IT system networking (Hossain et al., 2020) and the utilization of cyber-physical systems in industrial environments, necessitating excellent planning and strategies to revolutionize the overall care service and implications for future business and society, the moral issues and current reliability of artificial intelligence and autonomous actions in surgery. We have also searched many other works of literature and gathered them to analyze quality assurance if these famous researchers have focused and are concerned with the relationship between AI and medical healthcare which will lead us to become a leader generation.

RESEARCH METHOD

This article looks at the future of leadership in organizations with artificial AI. The study provided a few research questions (RQ) to help SLR accomplish its goal.

Leadership and Descriptions

RQ1: Will the increasing application and use of Al significantly affect leadership in socio-technical Work Systems/Workplaces?

The concept of leadership is a complex idea that has no universal definition. Although for research, the definition can be designed in various ways. Responsibilities, leadership, and followers are all interconnected. Leaders are responsible for the tasks they assign to their followers, ensuring their well-being, and communicating with them in different matters. It means there are countless variations of effective leadership. Previously, certain traits, abilities, and styles were seen as necessary components for excellent leadership. The responsibility of a leader also differs in different management positions in a company. A leader directs, develops, controls, and Produces goals and ways to achieve them through necessary communications. As a result, employees feel safe and supported in terms of achieving their organizational goals (Ueberschaer, 2014). This situational approach is applied to many cases in different organizations but theoretically makes the concept of leadership very broad.

On the other hand, there is a behavioral approach to leadership. This approach emphasizes the behavior of the leader, and how they take action and react in different situations. Several studies across the world were developed to understand the behavior of leaders in organizations. The Ohio State University published a study in the late 1940s. The University of Michigan also started studying how leaders acted in small groups. Blake and Mouton designed a managerial (leadership) grid to better understand how managers blend task and relationship behavior for their employees (Northouse, 2021). These three studies concluded that leaders could act in two ways: task-oriented and employee-oriented. Successful leadership always requires both components such as employee and orientation (Hettl, 2013). Specific leadership behavior is diTask-oriented leaders give priority to task organization, time management, and giving structure for setting duties to their employees. while on the other hand, employee-oriented leaders develop a friendly relationship environment, building trust, respect, and liking between staff members. The aim is to influence the lead employees by positive leadership behaviors.

The Historical Significance of Technology on Principles of Leadership

Technology has always shaped the history of leadership in workplaces. Significant technological innovations and social media have influenced authors of the creation tendency of the theories of leadership to think and reconsider (Hossain et al., 2023). In this paper to understand we highlight important technical advancements and how they have influenced leadership throughout history and into the present to lay the groundwork for potential future scenarios regarding how AI may change the nature of the leadership job. It also moderates the effect of creative climate and the mediating roles of organizational commitment, innovative work behavior, and social support on job performance (Vuong et al., 2023). The Industrial Revolution, often known as the First Machine Age, took place in the 18th century. It arrived together with the concepts of mass manufacturing, operating factories, and innovative work management techniques. The early industrial age paved the path for management as a discipline since factories' infrastructure required organization and supervision. Even though no formal theories of leadership have yet developed. However, a popular belief known as the "Great Man Theory" emerged in the 19th century, which held that great leaders were born with their abilities and that it is impossible to teach excellent leadership.

The earliest recognized leadership theory, known as trait theory, appeared in the 1920s. The idea behind trait theory was to determine the distinctive traits that all successful leaders held and to argue that these traits were innate. Trait theory was replaced with ideas on various leadership styles and behaviors, concentrating on what leaders do rather than their innate traits after multiple attempts to identify common leadership characteristics failed. And then came the situational and behavioral approach of leadership in the late 1960s as discussed in the earlier part of the paper. Currently, "McAfee and Brynjolfsson" (2016) refer to the tech as the "second machine age," which is centered on the computer and the advancements it provides to technology. The internet and computers facilitate communication and make it simpler to connect individuals, knowledge, and talents. Brand brand-upgraded technologies, organizations are working at a faster pace and accelerating their innovation processes. Additionally, efficiency makes it possible to focus more on employee satisfaction.

Artificial Intelligence and Leaders at Socio-Technical Workplace

Now in the 21st century, the technology of Artificial Intelligence has added a new dimension to the process of leadership. As we discussed leadership is a complex term Artificial intelligence on the other hand is a complex technology. AI is a combination of several computer systems that emulate or illustrate a certain human-like intelligence or intelligent behavior and characteristic, such as learning, thinking, and problem-solving. It is an arrangement of several technologies with a variety of intelligent actions and behaviors produced by algorithms and computational models. Using real datasets and analyzing them in medical or business industries would be challenging with the help of AI (Emmanuel et al., 2022). The role of the leader is shifting change, among other things, as a result of AI. This is particularly evident in the process of interactions being evaluated and now new leaders are to direct how their employees will interact with AI. In this situation, leaders must prepare themselves as strong and make effective use of each actor's unique skills. The objective should be to use AI to increase industrial competitiveness and productivity.

Relationship and Impact of AI in Medical Industries

RQ2: How successfully can robots assume leadership positions in the medical industry with the help of artificial intelligence (AI) integration?

Rapid developments in AI and robotics have changed the face of healthcare, improving patient care, treatment planning, and diagnostic accuracy. The notion of robots taking on leadership roles inside healthcare organizations is gaining popularity as technology progresses. This study examines the viability of such a scenario while taking into account the challenges of leadership, the potential of AI, and the particular requirements of the healthcare industry.

The Current State of AI in Healthcare

Applications like medication development, surgical aid, and medical imaging analysis shows how AI and robots are being integrated into healthcare. AI's capacity for processing enormous volumes of data and identifying patterns has produced better results and simpler procedures. Robotic systems have the potential to increase the capabilities of healthcare practitioners, from telemedicine robots to surgical assistance.

Challenges and Opportunities of AI in Healthcare

i. Decision-Making complexity: Complex decision-making including emotional intelligence, ethics, and interpersonal interaction is required for leadership responsibilities. AI is excellent at analyzing facts, but it has difficulty comprehending emotions and the complexities of human behavior.
ii. Human-Centered Leadership: Empathy, emotional intelligence, and the capacity to recognize and respond to the needs of both patients and employees are frequently necessary for effective healthcare leadership. Robots are devoid of these human characteristics and may perform poorly in circumstances demanding complex interpersonal relations.
iii. Ethical and Legal Considerations: Robot decisions could lack the moral justification necessary to resolve ethical quandaries. Putting robots in charge raises moral concerns regarding accountability,

responsibility, and the capacity for moral judgment. Robotic judgments might not always reflect human values or moral principles.

iv. Unpredictable Situations: Because healthcare environments are unpredictable, leaders must be flexible. AI systems may struggle to handle unusual or unique situations.

v. Bias and Fairness: As researchers work on a particular dataset the AI would be biased on the particular data and give wrong information even if the dataset is not up to the mark. This could exacerbate already existing differences by resulting in biased decision-making in leadership positions.

vi. Adaptability and Creativity: Leadership in the healthcare industry frequently calls for innovative problem-solving and flexibility in the face of constant change. Robots can find it difficult to manage unforeseen circumstances or come up with creative solutions.Due to the widespread and reasonably priced availability of mobile phones, social networking, online shopping, and digital media entrepreneurship has become incredibly popular. In light of mobile phone usage for online purchasing, the research recognizes the growing significance that social networking is playing in the growth of media entrepreneurship (Hossain, 2019).

Potential Success Factors

i. **Data Processing and Analysis:** Robots using artificial intelligence (AI) can swiftly evaluate enormous volumes of data, allowing them to offer data-driven insights that might guide decision-making. When making operational choices based on real-time data, this might be especially helpful. Robots with AI capabilities can swiftly collect and analyze enormous volumes of data to produce insights that can guide decision-making. Concerning COVID-19, for example, Epidemiological Analysis Robots might identify trends in the spread of diseases by analyzing real-time data from different sources, including patient health records, test results, and geographic data. Leaders in the healthcare industry may find this knowledge useful when deciding how to allocate resources, implement quarantine policies, and design focused therapies. Many people have introduced new platforms of e-purchasing apps which have introduced a new business leadership in the new era (Aboulilah et al., 2022).

ii. **Efficiency and Precision:** In some administrative or operational leadership jobs where repetitive activities are required, robots can accomplish duties with a high degree of precision and consistency. Resource Management: AI-powered robots can aid with resource allocation, enhancing workflows, and better managing inventory, which may result in cost savings. Robots are noted for their accuracy and consistency, which may be very useful in situations where efficiency and accuracy are required. Example: Sterilization and disinfection Robots using UV-C light technology were employed to precisely clean hospital rooms and other areas during the COVID-19 epidemic. These autonomous robots might provide comprehensive and reliable cleaning, lowering the risk of infection for patients and healthcare professionals.

iii. **Task Automation:** Routine duties can be automated by robots, freeing up human leaders to concentrate on more complicated and strategic elements of leadership. Robots can take over monotonous and mundane jobs, allowing human leaders to concentrate on more difficult and strategic duties. Example: Delivery of supplies and medications robots were used to transport food, supplies, and medications to patients' rooms at healthcare institutions that were overflowing with COVID-19 patients. Healthcare workers were able to emphasize direct patient care and important decision-making thanks to the automation of delivery activities (Hossain et al., 2021).

Future Suggestions and Directions

A multidisciplinary strategy encompassing AI research, ethics, psychology, and management is necessary for the effective integration of robots into leadership roles. It is a must to create AI systems that can comprehend emotions, ethical subtlety, and flexibility. Companies must concentrate on fostering an innovative culture while retaining the personal touch that customers and staff value.

The idea of AI-integrated robots taking over leadership roles in healthcare organizations is exciting but fraught with difficulties. While artificial intelligence and robots have shown their utility in the healthcare industry, effective leadership entails complex human attributes that are difficult to imitate. A successful transition requires a careful strategy that involves cooperation between AI and human leaders, combined with ongoing review and modification. The potential for robot leaders in healthcare is still being investigated as technology develops further. Healthcare firms can create a future where human and machine leadership coexist for the benefit of patient care and organizational success by tackling the difficulties head-on and utilizing the possibilities that AI and robots bring.

Maintaining Ethics in AI Automation Research

RQ3: Why are ethical considerations needed to deal with patients' data and how to educate professionals to use artificial intelligence effectively to improve patient care?

Importance of Ethical Considerations of AI

Patient's medical data are very sensitive and contain personal information about diseases, diagnoses, test reports, etc. This is why proper ethical practices are valuable to protect data privacy and prevent the misuse of patients' data. However, ethical consideration becomes increasingly significant and essential when it comes to the use of artificial intelligence (AI) in the healthcare industry. Because, technology (AI) plays an important part in tracking patients' records, and tests and making further diagonal decisions.

How AI Is Used in Patient Care

Nearly all innovations in this age of artificial intelligence (AI) are created by non-medical persons. Because doctors are not experts in computer programming. So ultimately, the clinical sector also has to rely on programmers and data science experts. BDSM tries to analyze more and more similar kinds of medical cases that match the patient. It helps to generate more accurate outcomes. So it is difficult for medical professionals to update regularly with the latest medical cases, which can lead the database to become inaccurate, and wrong records or wrong use of AI can lead to wrong outcomes.

Ethical Threats Due to Lack of Know-How of AI

Capelli et al. (2023) focused on 2 types of ethical threats of AI while dealing with the patient's data. One of them is Extra technical support. All the surgical departments need extra technical experts in their teams to generate and use AI data for each medical case. Also, due to the continuous innovation and upgradation of technology, maintenance costs get higher for hospitals to use AI and hire AI experts. This problem results in 2 ways. Firstly, due to extra maintenance costs, hospitals cannot update the database frequently. And secondly, not every hospital employs technological specialists to collaborate with physicians. So when medical experts work with artificial intelligence without the help of technical experts, there is a high risk of getting wrong outcomes.

Use of AI During COVID-19

In recent years we have seen the use of AI in covid 19 tests. It has been used in many steps including automatic test analysis, prediction modeling, potential contact tracking, discovering potential vaccines and drugs, patients' health monitoring, massive data analysis including case numbers and results, and allocating the right resources to the right place. However, artificial intelligence frequently failed to provide satisfactory outcomes. because the quality and validity of the provided data are what determine its correctness and efficacy. However, AI is one of the many tools that has been used to fight against COVID-19.

According to a report by K. W. U. (2021), one private laboratory in England published around 43,000 results with faulty test outcomes in just 4 days. And up until it was shut down, the lab had examined about 4,000 cases. A similar case was reported by BBC News (2021), in Australia, during Christmas time, 500 people were informed of the negative but later on 486 people found it positive. These mistakes are big in numbers to change the further AI analysis when these results are used in the AI database (BBC News, 2021).

Ethical Threats Due to Economic Condition

Capelli et al. (2023) also focused on economic inequalities among countries, due to technology misuse, the potential for AI to benefit healthcare must be moderated. Although AI can generate clean and accurate results if the database is accurate. If economically undeveloped countries use artificial intelligence, then their medication cost will be higher than regular. Many people could not afford these treatments. Also, the risk of intentional manipulation of data is unavoidable.

Cousins (2020) showed Bangladeshi hospitals charged from 2.12 to 37.23 USD per covid test. So, many people could not afford to do covid tests. Not only that but the actual death rate was 4 times higher than the official records. The same situation had been raised in Zimbabwe. Cheng and Mutsaka (2022) highlighted how difficult covid test was for locals where the test cost 15 USD each. At the end of January 2022, WHO claimed the COVID cases had been recorded 1,25,000 and the death rate was 1,600 although it was undercount due to a lack of COVID testing (PBS NewsHour, 2022).

Search Procedure

The goal of this study is to look for research publications that look into artificial intelligence (AI) and potential roles for leaders in the future. The data was taken from an electronic database throughout the search process, which took place between 2016 and 2023. As shown in Table 1, six renowned databases were used in the study for the search operation.

Table 1. Research database

Source	Online Access
Researchget.net	"https://www.researchgate.net/"
Google Scholar	"https://scholar.google.com/"
Scopus	"https://www.scopus.com/"
Springer	"https://link.springer.com/"

Quality Assessment (QA)

QA1: Does AI have a substantial impact on leadership in appropriately designed socio-technical work systems?
QA2: Does the study piece adequately describe and analyze the potential futures for leadership inside an organization?
QA3: Does the study's research model conform to standards?
QA4: Does the essay use AI to examine or follow leadership ethics?
QA5: Do the papers that were collected from this study have a similar focus?

For QA1, QA2, QA3, QA4, and QA5, Y (yes) indicates the literature is focused and describes well of our QA questions. N (no) means this literature is not well described; and if the answer is both yes or no we can indicate them as P (partially) According to Kitchenham et al. (2009), the following rating or scoring method is utilized for articles: Y = 1, P = 0.5, and N = 0. This rating system was used to assess the caliber of the papers used in this investigation. Table 3 shows that the publications were excluded from the study if they received a score on the QA questions of less than 2.

RESULTS

The study's next part presents the results of the systemic literature review. The authors initially provide a brief description of the search results presented in Table 2. The main sources that were selected also underwent a quality evaluation, with results shown in Table 3.

Search Result

We eventually decided to choose 20 scholarly papers for further consideration after conducting a comprehensive search. Information about the selected articles is shown in the Table 2. We used the same procedure to extract all the articles in the same way search method. For each and every item that was chosen, Table 2 included information on the author(s), the publication year, the study's purpose and goals, its methodology, and its main conclusions. The majority of the selected publications were released within the previous seven years in reputable, highly indexed journals.

Table 2. Data collection

Author (s) ID	Year	Objective	Method	Relevant Finding(s)
Peifer et al. (2022)	2022	IT and cyber-physical systems are becoming more and more networked in the industrial setting	analysis of existing literature-books, journals	Four clusters: Culture, Human-AI Interaction, Qualification and Competencies, and Strategic Transformation Process
Lee and Yoon (2021)	2021	focused on providing both the utopian viewpoint and the dismal vision, influencing the healthcare industry	analyzed examples which are related to AI applications in healthcare	Discussion of presenting both a utopian and a dystopian viewpoint Opportunities and difficulties
Dwivedi et al. (2021)	2021	while acknowledging that societal and industrial influences have an effect on the society and firms	workshop entitled "Artificial Intelligence (AI): Emerging Challenges, Opportunities, and Agenda for Research and Practice" held at the School of Management, Swansea University, UK	Industries including finance, healthcare, retail, supply chain, and utilities might all be impacted by the development of AI technology.
Capelli et al. (2023)	2023	Ethics regarding the moral implications, present reliability of AI, and the use of autonomous acts in surgery	24-item electronic questionnaire (reported in the Supplementary Materials)	reliability of robotic and AI systems, data privacy, and sensitive information Fairness, healthcare access inequities, technology as an equalizer in surgical education, the utilization of unbiased data, and the unpredictability of AI
Davenport smf Kalakota (2019)	2019	Exploring AI in healthcare	Case studies, journals	AI will play a significant role in future healthcare options.
Shuaib et al. (2020)	2020	Inventing AI in Healthcare	Case studies, journals	AI in healthcare and medicine is a fast-expanding subject with great promise.
Shaheen (2021)	2021	To explore the applications of AI replacing people in healthcare	Books, journals, cases	Before AI in healthcare replaces people for a variety of medical vocations, a lengthy period will pass
Rajpurkar et al. (2022)	2022	To discover how AI can necessarily reduce human effort in healthcare	Journals, books, cases,	AI could significantly reduce inefficiency in healthcare
JASON (2017)	2017	How AI can assist in improving health and healthcare	Books, journals, cases	AI finds new innovation based on new supporting data unless it gives permission to use
Nuffielld Council on Bioethics (2018)	2018	Indicating health issues that might be constrained by the caliber of accessible health data and with the help of AI and human traits	Books, journals, and cases	Numerous ethical concerns are highlighted by the use of AI and also concern the more using data and healthcare technology continuously
Chen and Decary (2020)	2019	to comprehend the principles of artificial intelligence (AI) technology and help medical doctors by creating AI plans	Books, journals, cases	Numerous AI apps have been invented to face those odds created in AI medical tech
Chandra and Saxena (2021)	2018	focusing on how AI mimics human cognitive functions and Healthcare data Taking a survey of the current situation/ status of AI applications in health care	journal	A successful AI system must possess two important categories - ML and NLP for handling structured data and for mining unstructured texts. This algorithm needs to be trained through Healthcare data.
Björkman and Johansson (2017)	2017	Future transformation leadership position with a stronger focus	Future transformation leadership position with a stronger focus	Leadership, Leadership Role, Technology
Hasija and Esper (2022)	2022	bridging the disparities between the potential SCM advantages of AI and the role of organizational variables	vendors' theme analysis methods and CEOs of organizations' interviews	the usage of AI for managing Social chain management and the role of AI trustworthiness
Jagatheesaperumal et al. (2021)	2021	a thorough review of the various uses of AI and big data in the industry	Books, journals	how the Industry 4.0 combination of AI and big data is assisting in several applications
Arslan et al. (2022)	2022	highlight the difficulties that modern organizations' departments and directors of human resource management	multiple streams of literature	illustrate how a variety of organizations and sectors have seen human workers and robots interacting and working together.
Gladden et al. (2022)	2022	describe the evolution of technology's organizational role over time.	Literature, cases	discussion of the several issues that mankind will face as a result of the use of powerful posthuman agents in the workplace
Ding et al. (2020)	2020	Making decisions on classification, taxonomy, issues, and future directions from the perspective of AI and applications	Literature, books, journals	Behaviour managementSubgroup clustering
Nguyen et al. (2020)	2020	AI against COVID-19	COVID-19 related data sources	Helping with image processing and data analysis based on AI
Titareva (2021)	2021	Leadership in AI	Journal, books	main perspectives of the scholarly and practitioner research directions

Table 3. Quality measurement analysis

PaperID	Q1	Q2	Q3	Q4	Q5	Total Score
P1	Y	Y	Y	Y	P	4.5
P2	Y	N	Y	N	P	2.5
P3	Y	Y	Y	N	Y	4
P4	N	N	Y	Y	Y	3
P5	N	P	Y	P	Y	3
P6	P	N	Y	P	P	2.5
P7	N	P	P	Y	Y	3
P8	P	P	Y	P	P	3
P9	N	P	Y	P	Y	3
P10	N	P	Y	Y	P	3
P11	P	P	P	Y	Y	3.5
P12	P	P	N	Y	P	2.5
P13	Y	Y	Y	P	Y	4.5
P14	N	P	N	Y	Y	2.5
P15	Y	N	Y	N	Y	3
P16	Y	Y	Y	N	P	3.5
P17	Y	Y	Y	Y	P	4.5
P18	P	P	Y	N	P	2.5
P19	Y	N	Y	N	Y	3
P20	Y	Y	Y	N	Y	4

Quality Evaluation of the Papers

Table 3 from the study's evaluation of a scoring system for quality evaluation analysis. The basis for the quality assessment was five quality assessment questions, which are provided in Table 2. As mentioned, the study excluded the publications that failed the quality evaluation test. Table 3 provides further information about the articles that were picked and shows that they at least got a 2.5 out of 5. The majority of the time, however, the papers appear to have a better grade, between 3.5 and 4.0.

CONCLUSION, LIMITATIONS, AND FURTHER RESEARCH DIRECTIONS

The study of whether robots can hold leadership positions and the application of artificial intelligence (AI) to executive positions inside enterprises have shed light on a landscape full of opportunities and difficulties. By using instances like the use of AI-powered robots during the COVID-19 epidemic, it has become clear that data-driven decision-making, operational efficiency, and job automation are possible advantages of AI-driven leadership. These developments do, however, have inherent drawbacks that highlight the necessity of human traits for efficient leadership.

However, while AI is excellent at automating and processing data, it is currently unable to handle the complexity of leadership, which involves a variety of viewpoints, moral quandaries, and dynamic human relationships. Another ethical issue that needs careful analysis and mitigation is the potential for AI to reinforce biases found in training data. As we have found only 20 journals but we should select more journals for better accuracy. We could also take a survey of people to make this model stronger and make a serious debate about how most people think about leadership from robots. Finding the best-indexed quality journals and surveys of people could lead the model to a higher supervision project where researchers could get help to find and link their findings about the leadership of robots in AI.

The development of AI-assisted leadership is still in its infancy, necessitating more study to negotiate the complex interactions between technology and human-centric leadership. Working on ethical frameworks, human-AI collaboration, bias mitigation, leadership skillset, human-centered AI design, and long-term impacts would be impactful in the modern era.

REFERENCES

Aboulilah, H. M. A. E., Hossain, S. F. A., Vuong, B. N., & Jebril, T. (2022). Exploring the Relationship between WeChat Usage and E-purchase Intention During the COVID-19 Pandemic Among University Students in China. *SAGE Open*, *12*(4). doi:10.1177/21582440221139447 PMID:36466966

Arslan, A., Cooper, C., Khan, Z., Golgeci, I., & Ali, I. (2022). Artificial intelligence and human workers interaction at team level: A conceptual assessment of the challenges and potential HRM strategies. *International Journal of Manpower*, *43*(1), 75–88. doi:10.1108/IJM-01-2021-0052

BBC News. (2021, December 28). Australia: Hundreds given false Covid results in Sydney lab error. *BBC News*. https://www.bbc.com/news/world-australia-59752091

Björkman, I., & Johansson, S. (2017). *What impact will Artificial Intelligence have on the future leadership role*. Research Gate.

Capelli, G., Verdi, D., Frigerio, I., Rashidian, N., Ficorilli, A., Grasso, V., Majidi, D., Gumbs, A. A., & Spolverato, G. (2023). White paper: Ethics and trustworthiness of artificial intelligence in clinical surgery. *Artificial Intelligence Surgery*, *3*(2), 111–122. doi:10.20517/ais.2023.04

Chen, M., & Decary, M. (2020, January). Artificial intelligence in healthcare: An essential guide for health leaders. *Healthcare Management Forum*, *33*(1), 10–18. doi:10.1177/0840470419873123 PMID:31550922

Cousins, S. (2020). Bangladesh's COVID-19 testing criticised. *Lancet*, *396*(10251), 591. Retrieved August 27, 2023, from. doi:10.1016/S0140-6736(20)31819-5 PMID:32861296

Daugherty, P. R., & Wilson, H. J. (2018). *Human+Machine: Reimagining work in the age of AI*. Harvard Business Press.

Davenport, T., & Kalakota, R. (2019). The potential for artificial intelligence in healthcare. *Future Healthcare Journal*, *6*(2), 94–98. doi:10.7861/futurehosp.6-2-94 PMID:31363513

Ding, R. X., Palomares, I., Wang, X., Yang, G. R., Liu, B., Dong, Y., Herrera-Viedma, E., & Herrera, F. (2020). Large-Scale decision-making: Characterization, taxonomy, challenges and future directions from an Artificial Intelligence and applications perspective. *Information Fusion*, *59*, 84–102. doi:10.1016/j.inffus.2020.01.006

Dwivedi, Y. K., Hughes, L., Ismagilova, E., Aarts, G., Coombs, C., Crick, T., Duan, Y., Dwivedi, R., Edwards, J., Eirug, A., Galanos, V., Ilavarasan, P. V., Janssen, M., Jones, P., Kar, A. K., Kizgin, H., Kronemann, B., Lal, B., Lucini, B., & Williams, M. D. (2021). Artificial Intelligence (AI): Multidisciplinary perspectives on emerging challenges, opportunities, and agenda for research, practice and policy. *International Journal of Information Management*, *57*, 101994. doi:10.1016/j.ijinfomgt.2019.08.002

Emmanuel, C. P., Qin, S., Hossain, S. F. A., & Hussain, K. (2022). Factors influencing social-media-based entrepreneurship prospect among female students in China. *Heliyon*, *8*(12), e12041. doi:10.1016/j.heliyon.2022.e12041 PMID:36483305

Gladden, M., Fortuna, P., & Modliński, A. (2022). The empowerment of artificial intelligence in post-digital organizations: Exploring human interactions with supervisory AI. *Human Technology*, *18*(2), 98–121. doi:10.14254/1795-6889.2022.18-2.2

Hasija, A., & Esper, T. L. (2022). In artificial intelligence (AI) we trust: A qualitative investigation of AI technology acceptance. *Journal of Business Logistics*, *43*(3), 388–412. doi:10.1111/jbl.12301

Hettl, M. (2013). *Mitarbeiterführung mit dem LEAD-Navigator® - Erfolgreich und wirksam führen.* Springer Fachmedien Wiesbaden. doi:10.1007/978-3-658-00100-1

Hossain, S. F. A. (2019). Social networking and its role in media entrepreneurship: Evaluating the use of mobile phones in the context of online shopping–A review. *Journal of Media Management and Entrepreneurship*, *1*(1), 73–86. doi:10.4018/JMME.2019010105

Hossain, S. F. A., Shan, X., Musa, M., & Rahman, P. (2023). Social media and increased venture creation tendency with innovative ideas: the case of female students in Asia. In *Research Anthology on Applying Social Networking Strategies to Classrooms and Libraries* (pp. 1716–1731). IGI Global.

Hossain, S. F. A., Shan, X., Nurunnabi, M., Tushar, H., Mohsin, A. K. M., & Ahsan, F. T. (2021). Opportunities and challenges of m-learning during the COVID-19 pandemic: A mixed methodology approach. *E-Collaboration Technologies and Strategies for Competitive Advantage Amid Challenging Times*, 210-227.

Hossain, S. F. A., Xi, Z., Nurunnabi, M., & Hussain, K. (2020). Ubiquitous role of social networking in driving M-Commerce: Evaluating the use of mobile phones for online shopping and payment in the context of trust. *SAGE Open*, *10*(3). doi:10.1177/2158244020939536

Jagatheesaperumal, S. K., Rahouti, M., Ahmad, K., Al-Fuqaha, A., & Guizani, M. (2021). The duo of artificial intelligence and big data for industry 4.0: Applications, techniques, challenges, and future research directions. *IEEE Internet of Things Journal*, *9*(15), 12861–12885. doi:10.1109/JIOT.2021.3139827

JASON. (2017). *Artificial intelligence for health and health care.* Research Gate.

K. W. U. (2021, October 18). 43,000 people in England could have received wrong COVID-19 test results. *USA Today*. https://www.usatoday.com/story/news/world/2021/10/15/england-wrong-covid-19-test-results-thousands-people/8465832002/

Kitchenham, B., Brereton, O. P., Budgen, D., Turner, M., Bailey, J., & Linkman, S. (2009). Systematic literature reviews in software engineering–a systematic literature review. *Information and Software Technology*, *51*(1), 7–15. doi:10.1016/j.infsof.2008.09.009

Lee, D. (2019). Effects of Key Value Co-creation Elements in the Healthcare System: Focusing on Technology Applications. *Service Business*, *13*(2), 389–417. doi:10.1007/s11628-018-00388-9

Lee, D., & Yoon, S. N. (2021). Application of Artificial Intelligence-Based Technologies in the Healthcare Industry: Opportunities and Challenges. *International Journal of Environmental Research and Public Health*, *18*(1), 271. doi:10.3390/ijerph18010271 PMID:33401373

Mohsin, A. K. M., Hongzhen, L., & Hossain, S. F. A. (2021). Impact of COVID-19 pandemic on consumer economy: Countermeasures analysis. *SAGE Open*, *11*(2). doi:10.1177/21582440211008875

Nguyen, T. T., Nguyen, Q. V. H., Nguyen, D. T., Yang, S., Eklund, P. W., Huynh-The, T., & Hsu, E. B. (2020). Artificial intelligence in the battle against coronavirus (COVID-19): a survey and future research directions. *arXiv preprint arXiv:2008.07343*.

Northouse, P. G. (2021). *Leadership: Theory and practice*. Sage Publications.

Nuffielld Council on Bioethics. (2018). *Artificial intelligence (AI) in healthcare and research.* Nuffield Council on Bioethics.

PBS NewsHour. (2022, February 3). *In Africa at-home COVID tests are scarce and expensive, help may not come until next year*. https://www.pbs.org/newshour/world/in-africa-at-home-covid-tests-are-scarce-and-expensive-help-may-not-come-until-next-year

Peifer, Y., Jeske, T., & Hille, S. (2022). Artificial intelligence and its impact on leaders and leadership. *Procedia Computer Science*, *200*, 1024–1030. doi:10.1016/j.procs.2022.01.301

R. S. N. A. (2018). *RSNA 2018 Newsroom Schedule.* RSNA. Available online: https://press.rsna.org/timssnet/media/rsna/newsroom2018.cfm

Rajpurkar, P., Chen, E., Banerjee, O., & Topol, E. J. (2022). AI in health and medicine. *Nature Medicine*, *28*(1), 31–38. doi:10.1038/s41591-021-01614-0 PMID:35058619

Saxena, A. (2021). *Artificial intelligence and machine learning in healthcare* (S. Chandra, Ed.). Springer. doi:10.1007/978-981-16-0811-7

ShaheenM. Y. (2021). Applications of Artificial Intelligence (AI) in healthcare: A review. *ScienceOpen* Preprints.

Shuaib, A., Arian, H., & Shuaib, A. (2020). The Increasing Role of Artificial Intelligence in Health Care: Will Robots Replace Doctors in the Future? *International Journal of General Medicine*, *13*, 891–896. doi:10.2147/IJGM.S268093 PMID:33116781

Titareva, T. (2021). *Leadership in an Artificial Intelligence Era.* Research Gate.

Ueberschaer, N. (2014). *Führung - Kompaktes Wissen - Konkrete Umsetzung - Praktische Arbeitshilfen*. Carl Hanser Verlag GmbH & Company KG.

Vuong, B. N., Tushar, H., & Hossain, S. F. A. (2023). The effect of social support on job performance through organizational commitment and innovative work behavior: Does innovative climate matter? *Asia-Pacific Journal of Business Administration*, *15*(5), 832–854. doi:10.1108/APJBA-06-2021-0256

Yoon, S., & Lee, D. (2019). Artificial Intelligence and Robots in Healthcare: What are the Success Factors for Technology-based Service Encounters? *International Journal of Healthcare Management*, *12*(3), 218–225. doi:10.1080/20479700.2018.1498220

Chapter 12
Social and Environmental Responsibility in AI-Driven Entrepreneurship

Md. Abdus Salam
St. Theresa International College, Thailand

Rubaba Nawrin
St. Theresa International College, Thailand

Hasanuzzaman Tushar
https://orcid.org/0000-0002-4829-5843
International University of Business Agriculture and Technology, Bangladesh

Nanta Sooraksha
National Institute of Development Administration, Thailand

ABSTRACT

The integration of artificial intelligence (AI) into entrepreneurship has created a transformative landscape with immense opportunities and challenges for sustainability. This chapter explores the intersection of AI-driven entrepreneurship, social responsibility, and environmental sustainability. The first section delves into the social responsibility aspect, especially the ethical dilemmas that entrepreneurs face when developing and deploying AI systems. Shifting to environmental responsibility, the subsequent section explores how AI can reduce environmental footprints through various innovative efforts. The interplay between social and environmental responsibility is crucial, and the chapter advocates for a holistic approach. The chapter highlights the challenges and opportunities for entrepreneurs in balancing social and environmental responsibility in AI integration. In the end, the chapter presents a responsible business model for AI-driven enterprises to seamlessly incorporate advanced technology into their operations while upholding all aspects of sustainability.

DOI: 10.4018/979-8-3693-1842-3.ch012

INTRODUCTION

The revolutionary technology of artificial intelligence (AI), along with its recent advancements in several domains such as machine learning, has resulted in significant advancements in industries and marketplaces. Artificial intelligence possesses the capacity to not only assist in corporate operations but also to modify business frameworks. Hence, in addition to producing applications to aid enterprises, the development of novel AI-powered business models has become as crucial. The emergence of new business models is fundamentally transforming the organizational structure, business processes, and commercial relationships (Giuggioli & Pellegrini, 2023; Pfau & Rimpp, 2021). Despite being in its early stages, the extensive implementation of AI in business holds immense potential, although uncertainties persist regarding the speed of advancement and the attainment of "general intelligence." According to research conducted by the McKinsey Global Institute, it is projected that by 2030, artificial intelligence (AI) might provide an additional $13 trillion to the global economy annually (Bughin, Seong, Manyika, Chui & Joshi, 2018).

An AI-driven business organization is a company that extensively utilizes artificial intelligence (AI) technologies and solutions throughout its operations to improve efficiency, decision-making, and innovation (AlZayani, Hamdan & Shoaib, 2023). These organizations incorporate artificial intelligence (AI) into many aspects of their business in order to enhance their competitive advantage and streamline their operations (John, Olsson, & Bosch, 2023). Companies that place a high importance on AI-driven initiatives typically allocate resources to acquire skilled individuals with knowledge in AI, formulate comprehensive plans for AI implementation, and implement AI applications across different departments in order to accomplish their business goals. These organizations seek to enhance efficiency, drive innovation, maintain competitiveness, and meet the changing market demands and customer expectations by efficiently utilizing AI technologies. The field of AI-driven entrepreneurship is characterized by its dynamic nature, since continuous breakthroughs in AI technology continually create fresh prospects for innovation (Hahn, Traunecker, Niever, & Basedow, 2020). Entrepreneurs who remain updated on AI trends and possess a strategic understanding of how to effectively utilize these technologies might attain a competitive edge across many industries.

Successfully implementing AI-driven plans necessitates the simultaneous adoption of technology, effective management of data, and a deliberate approach to integration. It is vital for firms to comprehend their distinct requirements, establish unambiguous goals, and consistently assess the influence of AI on their operations. In addition, it is crucial to examine ethical factors, protect data privacy, and provide transparency when implementing AI-driven decision-making in business in order to be responsible. Thorough deliberation of social, ethical, and environmental obligations is essential for the effective execution of this business strategy. Therefore, this chapter examines the social and environmental implications of AI-powered businesses and proposes strategies to tackle these concerns.

Companies that engage in multi-platform internet presence can acquire data from a plethora of sources. Certain pieces of information, such as contact details or purchase records, are directly supplied by users. Additional data is gathered by methods such as the utilization of cookies and other tracking technologies, which operate discreetly. AI's ability to learn and predict customer trends, such as navigation habits, grouping interests, purchase behaviors, and more, improves when it gets access to a greater number of data sources for analysis (Hossain et al., 2021). By delving deeper into extensive data analysis, AI can also have an impact on customer management and marketing. AI systems exhibit a continual learning process and enhance their intelligence as they study larger data sets and accumulate more data. They have the potential to enhance automation in areas such as customer relationship management and strategic marketing analysis.

CORPORATE SOCIAL AND ENVIRONMENTAL RESPONSIBILITY

Corporate social responsibility (CSR) or corporate sustainability refers to the social and environmental responsibilities of an enterprise. It encompasses the actions taken by a business to create a positive impact on society and the environment, in addition to its main objective of generating profit (Tushar, 2017). Furthermore, it is posited that CSR is not merely a voluntary reaction to societal demands, but rather a means of compensating the society/environment for the contributions made to enterprises (Ararat, Colpan, & Matten, 2018). Since its inception in the 1960s by Davis (1960), the literature on Corporate Social Responsibility (CSR) has been enhanced by a multitude of writings from many perspectives. Despite being a novel and growing business model, there is a dearth of study on the corporate social responsibility of AI-driven enterprises. Thus, this chapter delineates the societal and ecological obligations associated with this novel form of enterprises.

SOCIAL RESPONSIBILITIES OF AI DRIVEN ENTERPRISES

The social responsibility of an AI-driven firm comprises several crucial aspects that pertain to the ethical, moral, and societal consequences of their technology. An AI-driven firm should carefully evaluate several crucial elements related their social responsibility:

Ethical Business Practices

Ethical business practice entails operating business in accordance with ethical principles, encompassing fair labor procedures, anti-corruption measures, and honest marketing in corporate operations. Hodges (2015) asserts that corporate organizations should be capable of providing consistent and compelling evidence of their dedication to ethical and equitable practices, which is entrusted by many stakeholders such as regulators, employees, suppliers, customers, and others. The fundamental components of ethical business practices are as follows:

Ethical AI development: Ethical AI development should be the foremost priority for any commercial company that utilizes AI technology. Ethical AI pertains to the utilization of artificial intelligence with benevolent motives, ensuring equitable effects on customers and society, while also empowering employees and other internal stakeholders (Eitel-Porter, 2021). Ethical AI development encompasses the principles of justice, transparency, and accountability across the stages of design, deployment, and decision-making. It also involves elucidating the decision-making process of AI algorithms and assuming responsibility for their behaviors (Kar, 2016). Although responsible AI concepts serve as a solid foundation, organizations require the implementation of governance mechanisms that facilitate the progression of AI applications from proof of concept to widespread deployment in order to ensure success.

AI systems that adhere to ethical principles will actively reduce unintended and undesirable consequences, such as damage to one's reputation. The growing incorporation of AI into both public and private sector organizations highlights the importance of risk management (Di Bona, Cesarotti, Arcese & Gallo, 2021). This involves developing ethical and technological structures that software can effectively communicate. In order to ensure the ethical integrity and operational efficiency of the system over its lifespan, it is imperative that these frameworks undergo a thorough and periodic testing and evaluation procedure. The plan will mitigate organizations' exposure to risk and cultivate customer confidence in their products or services. Acquiring this trust is of utmost importance since AI is increasingly anticipated to make consequential judgments, including but not limited to granting mortgages or determining appropriate medical treatments (Accenture, 2022).

In order to ensure ethical AI practices, organizations need to establish accountability frameworks for their AI systems. This encompasses clear and explicit regulations for ensuring responsibility, supervision, and examination of AI algorithms and their outcomes (Mughal, 2018). The transparency of AI decision-making processes facilitates the identification of errors, biases, or unethical conduct, enabling prompt corrective measures to be taken.

Data protection, privacy and security: Businesses employ artificial intelligence (AI) for several purposes, including data analysis, predicting customer behavior, emulating human decision-making, and categorizing vast and highly intricate datasets (Enholm, Papagiannidis, Mikalef & Krogstie, 2021). This utilization of AI raises concerns regarding data protection, privacy, and security. While artificial intelligence (AI) has great promise as a valuable tool, its advancement may pose hazards to data security and privacy, as well as legal and regulatory challenges. How can firms effectively balance the utilization of AI to improve business operations while prioritizing user privacy and data protection?

Ensuring the security of data and respecting user privacy are essential. AI-driven organizations must give priority to data protection and enforce strong security measures to ensure the safety of user information (Jayashree, Reza, Malarvizhi & Mohiuddin, 2021). The vast quantity of unstructured data being acquired from many sources such as the internet, social media, mobile devices, sensors, and the Internet of Things poses challenges in effectively processing, categorizing, connecting, and utilizing the data. This may inadvertently lead to the exploitation or disclosure of private information that was concealed within anonymized data. An emerging concern is the potential for criminals to exploit seemingly harmless financial, health, and marketing data collected by enterprises to fuel AI systems. If security measures are insufficient, these threads can be stitched together to create counterfeit identities (Cheatham, Javanmardian, & Samandari, 2019).

Data privacy has emerged as a significant risk when employing AI in various sectors of business. Inaccurate comprehension of AI systems can lead to chaos by facilitating the disclosure of data. An example of such an occurrence involved the National Health Service (NHS) sharing the data of 1.6 million patients with Google's DeapMind app (Gerke, Minssen, & Cohen, 2020). A substantial volume of data, frequently encompassing confidential and delicate information, is necessary for AI. The ethical issues underscore the importance of upholding user privacy and complying with data protection rules. In order to safeguard user information, enterprises must implement robust security measures, as well as employ data anonymization tactics and adhere to secure data handling processes.

The European Union and the United States have implemented stringent data protection regulations, including the General Data Protection Regulation (GDPR) and California's Consumer Privacy Act (CCPA). The objective of such legislation is to safeguard the privacy and data of citizens. Ensuring the proper utilization of personal information in AI necessitates the implementation of dedicated legislation in addition to standard data protection laws. The European Union introduced a legislation in 2021 called the "Artificial Intelligence Act". The act is currently undergoing parliamentary negotiations and is expected to shortly be enacted into law.

Companies should have a robust privacy policy and operational playbook that places a high priority on safeguarding privacy when utilizing AI. In addition, organizations should adhere to particular best practices as the rules and their scope evolve alongside technological advancements. Additionally, it is advisable to stay updated on any alterations in the government's plans to regulate artificial intelligence. Additionally, businesses should have knowledge of the legislation in jurisdictions where they lack a physical presence, as privacy regulations often pertain to the location of data subjects and/or processing.

Organizations that utilize third parties to process AI data must adhere to the same regulations and guidelines that are applicable to any other instances of third-party data access or processing (Giuggioli & Pellegrini, 2023). Prior to, during, and after processing, organizations must ensure data security and compliance. As previously said, this can encompass a range of measures such as robust anonymization, secure algorithms, and thorough deletion of unnecessary data. Organizations must conduct a privacy assessment to identify and classify risks, not just for privacy or general data-related operations, but also for the specific context of AI. Specifically, consent management must consider the responsibilities and outcomes associated with AI. Furthermore, when the utilization of AI advances and expands, it is imperative to upgrade and sustain these systems.

In addition, enterprises must exert effort to ensure transparency on the objectives and techniques employed in the data processing conducted by AI. This is essential for effectively communicating with users or customers and for optimizing their procedures and operations. A corporation has a greater risk of noncompliance in data usage and communication if its personnel lack a comprehensive understanding of the objectives and operations of artificial intelligence (AI) and machine learning. The level of complexity of operations necessitates that those in charge exhibit increasingly advanced competence and experience.

Mitigating bias and discrimination: Addressing bias in AI systems is crucial for mitigating bias and discrimination. Corporations must to strive to uncover and eradicate biases present in data and algorithms in order to guarantee equitable and impartial decision-making. AI models trained on biased data can lead to unjust outcomes as they have the potential to strengthen and amplify existing biases. In order to ensure fairness and avoid discrimination based on protected characteristics such as age, gender, or race, organizations must acknowledge and rectify biases present in AI algorithms. This necessitates careful data curation, preprocessing of the AI model, and continuous monitoring of the model (Mungoli, 2023).

Biases and biases may emerge from the data utilized to train AI models, the algorithms employed, or the design and implementation procedures. AI systems acquire knowledge from past data, which may encompass societal biases. Should the training data exhibit bias, the AI model has the potential to perpetuate and maybe magnify such biases (Buolamwini & Gebru 2018). The current AI data sets are obtained from restricted geographical areas, and the majority of them lack the required information to assess the performance of models within specific subgroups. Variations in data collection and processing might lead to instances when models rely on unrelated characteristics, which are considered as "shortcuts". Inadequate efficacy in the process of picking impartial data may result in the incorporation of biased data during the training of the AI system. In addition, the presence of flawed or negligent algorithm design and hiring procedures can lead to biased decision-making in artificial intelligence systems (Obermeyer, Powers, Vogeli, & Mullainathan, 2019).

Implementing a lifecycle approach can help pinpoint specific points in time where well-established guidance, assurance, and governance processes can aid business units and data and social scientists in jointly integrating processes to minimize bias without causing unnecessary obstacles or hindering progress (Schwartz, et. al., 2022). To tackle bias and discrimination in AI business, a comprehensive strategy is necessary, integrating researchers, policymakers, and industry practitioners to guarantee fairness, transparency, and accountability in AI systems. To eliminate prejudice in AI systems, one might utilize tactics such as fairness-aware machine learning and the utilization of varied and representative datasets. Efforts should be focused on enhancing the processes of model training, evaluation, and explainability. In addition, it is essential for both recruiters and algorithm developers to exercise caution and exhibit an understanding of the prevailing biases in society and the system (Mitchell, et. al., 2019). Bias can arise intentionally or unintentionally, or it might manifest when the AI system is utilized, affecting society as a whole by propagating and magnifying biased and discriminatory results. Embracing a socio-technical viewpoint introduces additional criteria, many of which are context-dependent, to the many stages that make up the AI lifecycle. Gaining comprehension of the interplay between computational and statistical elements and systemic and human biases is crucial.

Empowering the Workforce

Employees who are given authority and autonomy are more inclined to have a sense of ownership and commitment towards their work, resulting in a range of favorable business consequences. When employees see that their activities, decisions, and efforts have significance, they are more likely to have higher levels of job satisfaction and consequently, exhibit greater loyalty to the organization. According to a Gallup survey, engaged employees had a reduced likelihood of seeking other jobs by up to 43% (Gallup, 2022). Enhanced employee retention enables employees to focus on their specialized tasks rather than investing time in training new colleagues. The entire organization can prioritize enhancing the caliber of services it offers, hence potentially boosting customer happiness.

Employee empowerment can be defined in two main ways: the top-down approach, which focuses on relationships and mechanics, and the bottom-up approach, which focuses on psychological factors. The top-down approach prioritizes the corporation's capacity to guide employees, assign responsibilities, and engage in collaborative efforts by sharing information with them (Randolph, 1995; Spreitzer, 1997). In contrast, the bottom-up approach refers to an organizational strategy that focuses on empowering people by fostering a sense of empowerment from their psychological standpoint, with the aim of achieving an empowerment objective (Quinn & Spreitzer, 1997; Spreitzer, 1997).

Amidst a rapidly changing work environment, AI is emerging as the driving force behind a transformative period in HR, revolutionizing the methods by which firms attract, recruit, oversee, and keep their workforce (Enholm et al., 2021). By using data analytics, machine learning, and automation, AI is optimizing HR activities, allowing for more efficient use of time and improving the overall quality of results. As artificial intelligence progresses from basic automation to advanced augmentation, firms are investigating how AI tools may improve the HR experience for both employees and job seekers (Tekic et al., 2019). This revolution transcends mere time efficiency; it equips HR professionals with up-to-the-minute data, invaluable insights, and well-informed suggestions, ushering in a future where AI serves as an essential partner in HR's endeavor to support and engage talent.

AI-powered entrepreneurship can facilitate employee empowerment and improve employee well-being through several strategic approaches. One such endeavor involves liberating employees from mundane and repetitive tasks. An important benefit of AI for businesses is its capacity to automate monotonous and time-consuming jobs (Enholm et al., 2021). AI-powered bots and systems may effectively manage routine tasks including as data entry, invoice processing, and customer assistance. By eliminating mundane responsibilities, firms enable their staff to concentrate on innovative, tactical, and high-value endeavors.

In addition, artificial intelligence-powered analytics solutions are furnishing firms with important insights obtained from extensive volumes of data. These insights are extremely important for making well-informed decisions. Employees can utilize AI-driven dashboards and reports to retrieve up-to-the-minute data, facilitating expedited and precise decision-making (Alam & Mohanty, 2022). This enables employees to assume ownership of their duties and make valuable contributions to the organization's achievements. AI-driven predictive maintenance is a revolutionary development for sectors that depend on machinery and equipment. Through the analysis of sensor data and previous records, AI systems have the capability to anticipate the occurrence of equipment failure, enabling firms to proactively plan and schedule maintenance activities. This not only reduces the amount of time that operations are halted but also enables maintenance crews to operate with more efficiency, prioritizing essential jobs rather than merely responding to urgent situations (Dubey et al., 2021).

Furthermore, learning platforms powered by artificial intelligence can offer staff customized training and development programs. These platforms evaluate individual talents and identify areas of knowledge that need improvement, customizing training materials and courses accordingly (Sucharita & Seethalakshmi, 2022). This strategy facilitates the development of employees' skills and ensures their relevance in a dynamic labor market, fostering ongoing progress and empowerment (Pathak & Solanki, 2021). AI can assist firms in scaling their operations and empowering their people by automating tedious processes, offering important insights, personalizing consumer experiences, and promoting a culture of continuous learning. Businesses that can effectively leverage the power of AI will experience sustained success, benefiting from a workforce that is more adaptable, knowledgeable, and involved.

Community Engagement and Social Initiatives

AI development entails the creation of systems that have the potential to impact the lives, rights, and values of many groups of individuals. Hence, it is crucial to incorporate communities in the process of AI development, in order to guarantee the inclusion and acknowledgment of their viewpoints, requirements, and concerns. Incorporating communities into AI development entails actively including individuals who are currently or will potentially be impacted by AI systems, whether as users, beneficiaries, or stakeholders (Borsatto, Marcolin, Abdalla & Amaral, 2023). By incorporating communities, individuals might acquire profound understanding of their surroundings, inclinations, anticipations, and apprehensions. Corporations have the ability to identify any risks, harms, or biases that the AI systems may pose or perpetuate. Furthermore, businesses have the potential to cultivate trust, openness, and responsibility between AI developers and communities, enabling people to participate in the process of designing, implementing, and assessing AI systems (Zerilli, 2021). All of these factors are essential for achieving success in business. Demonstrating a commitment to social responsibility involves contributing to society through social projects and community involvement programs. Examples of such activities encompass pro bono work, bolstering local communities, or employing AI for the betterment of society.

Community engagement can be achieved through several approaches, including surveys, interviews, focus groups, workshops, co-creation sessions, feedback channels, or advisory boards. The selection of methodologies is contingent upon the objectives, assets, and limitations of your AI endeavor, as well as the attributes, inclinations, and accessibility of the communities involved (Musikanski et al., 2020). The fundamental tenets for involving communities are: honoring their independence, self-worth, and traditions; conveying information in a transparent, truthful, and courteous manner; actively, empathetically, and analytically listening; and responding in a responsible, cooperative, and morally upright manner.

Community participation is a perpetual and iterative process, rather than a singular or linear event. Sustained dedication, exertion, and allocation of resources are necessary from both the AI developers and the community. In order to foster community involvement, businesses must uphold and enhance their relationships, trust, and communication with the communities. Enterprises must diligently observe and adjust to the alterations, requirements, and input from the communities, as well as the effectiveness, problems, and outcomes of the AI systems. Moreover, entrepreneurs must recognize and value the contributions, accomplishments, and information gained from communities, and commemorate and incentivize their participation and influence.

Utilizing AI for community engagement presents a multitude of advantages; nonetheless, it is crucial to acknowledge the significance of human connection in establishing and sustaining a flourishing community engagement (Musikanski et al., 2020). Artificial intelligence is unable to reproduce emotional intelligence, nonverbal communication, flexibility, attentive listening, and genuine relationship development. Humans possess the ability to establish trustworthy relationships within a community, which is a crucial factor in the effectiveness of our community engagement teams. It is crucial to acknowledge that although AI can improve community involvement in various ways, there are ethical concerns and possible obstacles, including data privacy, algorithmic bias, and the need to ensure openness in AI-powered procedures. Organizations and communities should adopt a responsible approach to utilizing AI in community involvement in order to optimize its advantages while minimizing any drawbacks (Vesnic-Alujevic, Nascimento & Polvora, 2020).

ENVIRONMENTAL RESPONSIBILITY OF AI-POWERED BUSINESSES

Ecosystems are thought to possess a limited capacity for regeneration, and there is a high likelihood that our business actions will have an adverse impact on the environment. (Salam & Senasu, 2019). An AI-powered organization bears a substantial obligation towards environmental sustainability owing to its potential influence on energy usage, resource allocation, and overall carbon emissions. AI is widely recognized as a revolutionary technology, but its promise for transformation is overshadowed by a significant concern: its impact on the environment. The creation, upkeep, and elimination of AI technology all entail a significant ecological impact. According to projections, the Information and Communications Technology (ICT) business is anticipated to contribute 14% of world emissions by 2040. The primary sources of these emissions are predicted to be the ICT infrastructure, including data centers and communication networks (Vesnic-Alujevic, Nascimento & Polvora, 2020). A recent study undertaken by academics at the University of Massachusetts aimed to quantify the energy consumption associated with training specific widely-used big AI models. Based on the findings, training can generate over 626,000 pounds of carbon dioxide, which is comparable to almost 300 round-trip flights between New York and San Francisco. This amount is nearly five times the total emissions produced by an average car during its lifespan (Kar, 2016). These findings clearly illustrate the pressing necessity to tackle the carbon footprint of AI and its contribution to environmental degradation. An AI-driven firm can make significant contributions to environmental sustainability in the following crucial domains.

Energy Efficiency

Energy is a crucial catalyst for economic expansion and the fundamental foundation for the advancement of human civilization. Since the onset of the industrial revolution, the widespread utilization of fossil energy has resulted in a range of problems in the worldwide environment, ecology, and climate, including the impacts of greenhouse gases, air pollution, and acid rain (Yan, Hao, & Meng, 2021). AI systems require a significant amount of energy to function and train models, which leads to the release of greenhouse gas emissions. As the utilization of AI grows, it is imperative to mitigate the rise in energy consumption and emissions. Prioritizing the equilibrium between the expansion of AI and environmental sustainability is of utmost importance.

AI systems can enhance energy efficiency in diverse operations, including data centers, by employing algorithms that optimize resource allocation. Approximately 70% of the total electricity generated is utilized for the operation of companies and structures. However, a significant portion of this energy, up to 60%, is not effectively utilized and goes to waste (Ahmad et al., 2021). The squandered energy signifies the expenditure of billions of dollars on produced energy that remains unused. In order to mitigate this issue, it is imperative that we gain a comprehensive understanding of the precise locations and mechanisms via which the wastage is occurring. Artificial intelligence is applied in this context. Artificial intelligence oversees, gathers data, regulates, assesses, and oversees energy usage in buildings and enterprises. Artificial Intelligence (AI) manages energy consumption by minimizing it during periods of high demand, recognizes and alerts about issues, and anticipates equipment malfunctions in advance. AI possesses the capacity to condense and scrutinize extensive datasets, enabling the monitoring and interpretation of data generated by energy sectors for the purpose of optimizing energy use.

Tackling the dual obstacles of energy and sustainability can be complex: businesses must effectively incorporate renewable energy while guaranteeing dependable power, however renewable energy sources generate an irregular output that fluctuates with varying environmental circumstances (Jiang, Ai, & Hao, 2019). Artificial intelligence (AI) plays a crucial role in tackling these challenges on a large scale by leveraging huge amounts of data, surpassing human capacity for processing, to uncover energy consumption patterns and identify areas of inefficiency. Utilizing artificial intelligence can assist firms in integrating renewable power sources, making more informed decisions regarding energy consumption, and achieving their sustainability goals, all while reducing energy expenses.

Resource Optimization and Waste Reduction

AI is also employed to mitigate environmental damage through waste reduction and resource usage optimization. VDI 4800 defines resource efficiency as the proportion of a particular benefit or outcome to the resources needed to get it (Yu, Zhang, Li, Montenegro-Marin & Kumar, 2021). A benefit or outcome can manifest as the creation of a product or the implementation of a production method. In this sense, resource input refers to the natural and operational inputs used in production systems. Artificial intelligence has the capability to analyze data obtained from sensors and several other sources in order to discover potential areas where waste can be minimized and energy efficiency can be enhanced. AI has the ability to play a significant role in converting the industry into a sustainable, competitive, and future-proof production by spotting patterns and suggesting methods to improve system performance.

Enhancing simulation and planning can lead to a decrease in attrition and production waste, hence enhancing the material efficiency of the manufacturing system (Suboyin et al., 2023). Similarly, water usage frequently functions as both the auxiliary and operational supplies. Efficient production planning minimizes energy usage, primarily by optimizing scheduling and capacity planning. Enhancing the synchronization of diverse production processes and phases holds significant potential for enhancing energy efficiency. Artificial intelligence aids decision makers in conducting a comprehensive examination of the manufacturing system, enabling them to identify potential linkages among individual production entities. For instance, AI can be employed to enhance the routing of delivery vehicles in order to save fuel usage or to analyze energy consumption trends in buildings to pinpoint places where energy consumption might be diminished.

Artificial intelligence can enhance resource efficiency through the implementation of predictive maintenance. This can be achieved by collecting and analyzing pertinent time series data throughout the operational lifespan of a machine. The purpose of these is to accurately chart and oversee the state of the infrastructure under examination. The goal is to identify patterns in order to anticipate breakdowns and mitigate them through proactive maintenance actions. Efficiently maintaining equipment can lead to improvements in material and energy efficiency. AI could also have a significant application in the domain of production planning. AI solutions can assist in production planning by accurately forecasting future needs and efficiently configuring production lines with optimal designs (Andeobu, Wibowo & Grandhi, 2022). Analyze and classify various production methods to support production planning, particularly in terms of efficiency. Furthermore, AI is employed in the domain of process optimization to identify faults in manufacturing. This can be utilized for the automated assessment of the quality of components and products. Artificial intelligence (AI) can enhance fault detection activities, including classification, dimension reduction, and picture identification, in this particular application. This technique significantly enhances resource and energy efficiency (Waltersmann et al., 2021). AI-powered supply chain management optimizes inventory levels by precisely predicting demand through the analysis of past sales data and market trends. AI-powered supply chain management enables the implementation of just-in-time inventory policies, resulting in waste reduction at all stages of the supply chain, including production, distribution, and disposal of expired or obsolete goods (Gande, 2020).

Sustainable Development Goals and Artificial Intelligence in Business

Artificial intelligence (AI) can play a pivotal role in the attainment of the Sustainable Development Goals (SDGs) that were established by the United Nations in 2015. The Sustainable Development Goals (SDGs) have the objective of eradicating poverty, safeguarding the environment, and promoting inclusive prosperity. Artificial intelligence (AI) can facilitate the attainment of these objectives by enhancing productivity, minimizing inefficiencies, and fostering groundbreaking advancements across diverse industries (Di Vaio, Palladino, Hassan, & Escobar, 2020). AI has the potential to enhance accessibility to healthcare and education, alleviate poverty, and foster economic development. Additionally, it can facilitate the attainment of environmental objectives, such as mitigating the release of greenhouse gases, preserving biodiversity, and fostering the sustainable utilization of natural resources. The evaluation of the effects of AI on sustainable development is determined by the rise of AI and its potential for development in various areas of society (Vinuesa et al., 2020). Companies are increasingly compelled to confront the imperative of sustainability by enhancing the breadth of innovations to safeguard the integrity of the ecosystem and optimize the utilization of natural resources (Joyce & Paquin, 2016).

The goals are directed towards several categories of actors and entities, including organizations and civil society. The era of Sustainable Development Goals (SDGs) introduces a novel approach to companies' sustainable development strategy. The construction of responsible organizations necessitates a strong and proactive approach, involving investment in technical advancement through collaborative efforts with other companies (Di Vaio et al., 2020). This will initiate a worldwide and comprehensive progression towards sustainable development for all businesses. Moreover, innovation is a crucial factor for businesses, encompassing not only the final product but also the use of innovative technology and sustainable solutions in all aspects of the business processes, in alignment with the Sustainable Development Goals (SDGs).

Vinuesa and colleagues (2020) assert that artificial intelligence (AI) can exert a favorable influence on all Sustainable Development Goals (SDGs) by means of technical advancements that provide superior outcomes across many sectors. This, in turn, enhances development and engenders substantial ramifications for both civil society and the environment. Therefore, this objective motivates businesses to embrace sustainable methods and assist developing nations in enhancing their scientific and technological capacities to establish and execute more sustainable frameworks, as well as production and consumption strategies, to assess the effects of sustainable development.

Businesses, which play a crucial role in driving the global economy and progress, have the ability to enhance their investments in artificial intelligence (AI) and related technologies. They can also promote the integration of AI-based digital technologies into their production processes, improve educational opportunities at all levels to equip the workforce with AI skills, and leverage the potential of the data economy, which serves as the primary resource for AI (Tushar & Sooraksa, 2023). By doing so, individuals can actively participate in the emerging cultural trend that seeks to integrate advancements with social and environmental welfare (Buzko et al., 2016).

AI can assist in the preservation of biodiversity by analyzing data pertaining to species populations, habitats, and potential risks. It can enhance the knowledge of conservation techniques and enhance our comprehension of the intricate interconnections among various species and their habitats. Numerous global nature conservation groups utilize artificial intelligence (AI) for the purpose of promoting environmental sustainability (Van Wynsberghe, 2021). They deploy sophisticated algorithms to analyze data on biodiversity and monitor alterations in ecosystems. This technology is essential for preserving and safeguarding vital natural areas.

Nevertheless, companies must prudently oversee the implementation of AI to prevent any detrimental effects on sustainable development. Although AI has great promise in many domains, it is essential for AI-driven organizations to prioritize safe development and implementation of AI systems. This entails taking into account the ethical ramifications and unforeseen effects that AI applications may have on the environment. In addition, it is crucial to have clear and open reporting as well as responsibility for the ecological consequences of AI-driven activities in order to guarantee ongoing progress and dedication to sustainability. AI-driven firms can significantly contribute to promoting a more sustainable future by incorporating these practices and consistently evaluating their environmental impact throughout all stages. Moreover, frameworks and standards such as the Green AI effort, or initiatives from organizations such as the United Nations, may provide recommendations for incorporating AI technology in an environmentally responsible manner (Goralski & Tan, 2020). These frameworks assist organizations in implementing and adhering to optimal methods for environmentally sustainable AI development and implementation. Remaining constantly informed about the most recent research, innovations, and industry standards is essential to ensure that AI-driven organizations consistently enhance their environmental responsibility.

An Integrated CSR Model for AI Powered Business Enterprises

Corporate Social Responsibility (CSR) enables corporations to demonstrate social responsibility and accountability towards their stakeholders, the community, and the environment. Multiple CSR models exist and are deployed to aid organizations in fulfilling their corporate duties. The objective of these models is to facilitate the design and implementation of the CSR process, as well as to enable its monitoring and control. Businesses can enhance their responsiveness to both internal and external environmental changes by incorporating Corporate Social Responsibility (CSR) strategies into their operations. This facilitates the promotion of favorable transformations and fosters advancements in socio-economic indicators. Corporate social responsibility (CSR) provides advantages to individuals and organizations who have limited or no resources (Pai & Chandra, 2022).Corporate Social Responsibility (CSR) is applied with the aim of mitigating negative impacts, promoting ethical corporate practices, ensuring responsibility throughout a global supply chain, engaging in philanthropic activities, and establishing a self-directed human resource management system.

Developing a cohesive Corporate Social Responsibility (CSR) framework for an AI-powered organization entails harmonizing the capabilities of AI with societal and ethical obligations. Below is a framework for our suggested Corporate Social Responsibility (CSR) model for this particular firm. The proposed model is based on three fundamental responsibilities, serving as the foundation or pillars of the model (Figure 1). The model employs the renowned allegory of the three-legged stool. Every leg of the stool symbolizes a distinct obligation of an organization powered by AI. The three fundamental pillars consist of ethical and legal compliance, preservation of the environment, and active involvement with the community. The three foundational pillars support the "seat", namely stakeholders' benefit. Lastly, the seat holds "the globe", which represents sustainable business practices.

Ethical and Legal Compliance

Businesses must establish and comply with ethical principles that govern the permissible and impermissible applications of AI technology (Van Wynsberghe, 2021). This entails guaranteeing transparency, equity, and responsibility in AI systems. Furthermore, it places a high importance on the advancement of AI solutions that enhance and enable humans, rather than displacing or excluding them. Therefore, it is imperative to develop AI systems while taking into account ethical and legal aspects. This entails constructing artificial intelligence systems that uphold human rights, prevent discrimination, and comply with privacy standards. Additionally, it entails establishing procedures for ongoing monitoring and auditing of AI systems to guarantee adherence to regulations. Furthermore, if AI systems advance in complexity, they may have the ability to autonomously make judgments, raising concerns regarding their legal status as individuals. Establishing a framework for accountability, culpability, and compliance is vital for granting AI systems a degree of legal personhood.

Figure 1. A responsible business model for AI powered business enterprises

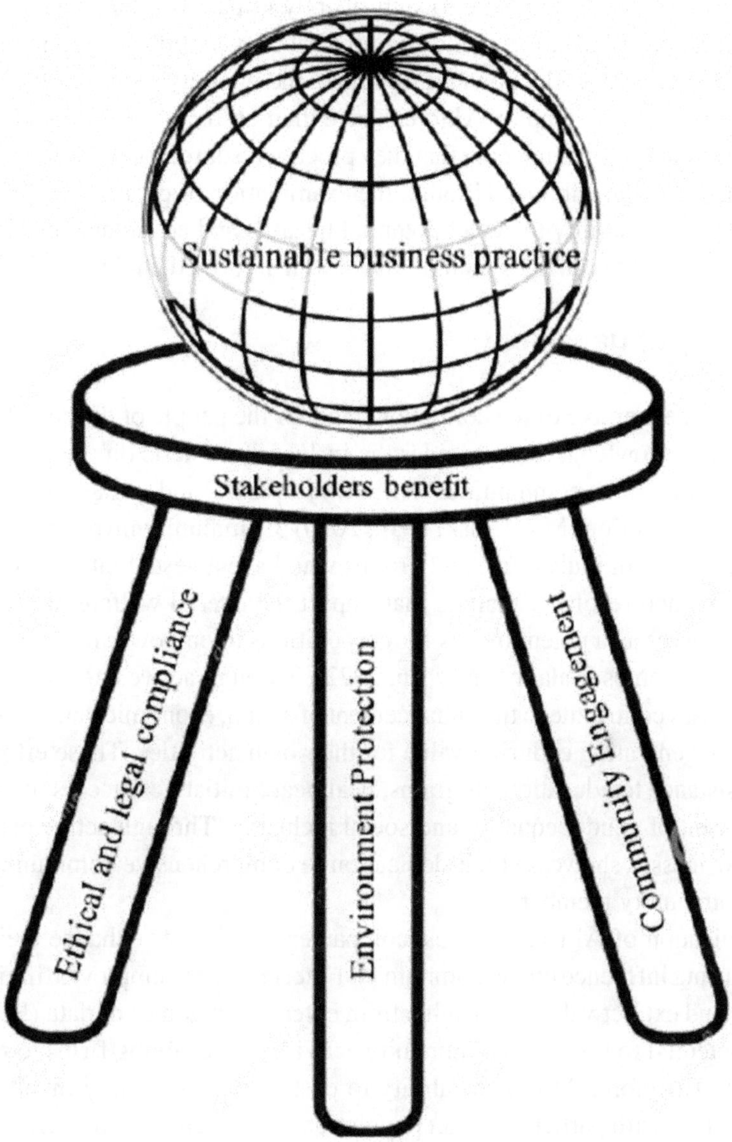

Environmental Conservation

Businesses utilizing AI technology must bear the adverse repercussions resulting from AI systems. Hence, it is imperative for business models to evolve in order to mitigate the environmental repercussions of AI operations, which entails utilizing sustainable resources and lowering energy use (Yu et al., 2021). AI may greatly contribute to corporate environmental responsibility by optimizing energy consumption. Artificial intelligence (AI) systems have the capability to analyze extensive volumes of data from diverse sources, including weather patterns, energy pricing, and equipment performance. This enables them to make immediate modifications to a company's energy consumption. This can lead to substantial energy conservation, decreased emissions of greenhouse gases, and reduced operational expenses (Suboyin et al., 2023). AI has the potential to significantly impact waste management. Businesses can employ artificial intelligence (AI) to examine and forecast trends of trash generation, enabling them to optimize the routes for rubbish collection and minimize the quantity of waste disposed of in landfills. Furthermore, businesses want to employ AI to enhance their ability to oversee and control their supply chains with greater efficiency, guaranteeing that they procure resources and products from suppliers who prioritize environmental responsibility. Through the examination of data from many sources, artificial intelligence (AI) has the capability to detect potential hazards and advantageous circumstances within a company's supply chain. This enables them to make well-informed choices regarding their suppliers.

Active Community Engagement

Businesses are run by the member of the community and for the people of the community. Hence, every business model must acknowledge and consider the influence it exerts on the community. Businesses have a vital responsibility in the communities where they operate, and engaging with the community is an essential part of that function (Musikanski et al., 2020). Community involvement refers to the act of establishing connections with individuals and groups who have a vested interest in a community, with the aim of recognizing and resolving matters that impact the overall welfare of the community. Community engagement serves as a potent means for corporations to empower local communities and generate favorable local outcomes (Salam & Nawrin, 2022). Through active engagement and assistance to communities, businesses contribute to the enhancement of social, economic, and environmental welfare, while simultaneously generating enduring value for their own activities. These efforts may encompass the provision of assistance to education programs, healthcare initiatives, access to uncontaminated water, or the advancement of gender equality and social inclusion. Through active participation in social impact activities, businesses showcase their dedication to comprehensive community development and the welfare of all community members.

Through the utilization of AI technologies, companies can further enhance their ability to make a substantial and enduring influence on the community. Enterprises can employ artificial intelligence (AI) to gather, examine, and extract valuable insights from extensive volumes of data (Borsatto et al., 2023). This skill has the potential to transform community activities by enabling firms to make decisions that are better informed. Therefore, AI has the ability to customize community involvement programs in order to strongly connect with particular target populations. Through the examination of consumer data, artificial intelligence (AI) has the capability to assist corporations in customizing their corporate social responsibility (CSR) messages and campaigns to effectively target the specific problems and interests of various demographic groups.

Businesses must also continuously monitor and evaluate the effects of their activity on society in real-time. The high degree of openness allows organizations to monitor their development, make necessary modifications, and furnish stakeholders with precise and current information regarding their operational activities. Furthermore, AI can assist in the detection and prevention of unethical actions in the supply chain, so promoting a heightened level of social responsibility. AI models should undergo comprehensive training to mitigate human biases and enhance diversity and inclusion. This entails presenting only those candidates who meet the job's criteria while disregarding all other factors.

Stakeholders' Benefit

A key stakeholder is a crucial contributor to a company's enduring prosperity. Key stakeholders play a crucial role in assisting organizations in making strategic decisions, mitigating risks, and expanding their business (Pathak & Solanki, 2021). Understanding the primary stakeholders of a firm and effectively meeting their interests is crucial. The primary objective of company operations is to fulfill the needs of stakeholders. Therefore, in our model, stakeholders' benefits are allocated across the three foundation legs. Artificial intelligence (AI) in enterprises can optimize stakeholders' benefits and foster their active engagement in the firm. AI models enhance the accuracy and comprehensiveness of capturing business requirements by utilizing natural language understanding capabilities and interactive interactions. This minimizes the likelihood of misunderstanding and guarantees the inclusion of all essential details. In addition, AI-powered solutions streamline different areas of the requirements process, including the development and validation of documentation. This minimizes the need for manual labor, optimizes time usage, and enables stakeholders to concentrate on activities that generate greater value.

AI-driven conversational systems offer a shared platform for stakeholders to cooperate, engage in discussions, and enhance requirements. This promotes enhanced communication, synchronization, and mutual comprehension among stakeholders, resulting in improved project results. AI aids firms in adjusting to shifting demands and developing market circumstances. AI-powered systems provide the capability to swiftly refine and update requirements in real-time, hence offering flexibility and agility to promptly adapt to business needs (Pai & Chandra, 2022). Furthermore, AI technologies offer data-driven insights and recommendations derived from the analysis of collected needs. This enables organizations to make well-informed decisions about the three fundamental aspects of our strategy, resulting in enhanced long-term financial and non-financial advantages for stakeholders.

Sustainable Business Practices

The primary objective of our CSR model is to implement sustainable business practices, which is why it is positioned at the highest level of importance. Adopting sustainable business practices enhances firms' operational efficiency, reputation, and market opportunities. Business organizations should avoid solely pursuing ephemeral or part-time objectives, as this may jeopardize the long-term prosperity of future generations (WCED, 1987). Implementing sustainable business practices not only has an impact on immediate results, but also enhances the ability of a company to withstand challenges and ultimately achieve long-term benefits, such as reduced financial instability, increased sales, and higher survival rates (Ortiz-de-Mandojana & Bansal, 2016).

Sustainable business practices encompass acts that enable a company to generate a favorable influence on individuals, society, and the environment, while simultaneously achieving profitability. Sustainability is a crucial component of contemporary corporate practices, encompassing both social and environmental responsibility. It is an imperative measure in safeguarding our world for future generations. AI-driven enterprises possess the necessary tools to establish benchmarks for contemporary sustainable business practices.

AI models demonstrate that sustainability confers a competitive advantage to firms by leveraging predictive capabilities, pattern identification, and process optimization. AI has the potential to enable various enterprises, ranging from precision farming to energy-efficient manufacturing, to achieve sustainability. Companies can utilize AI to effectively minimize the carbon impact inside their supply chain.

AI can enhance firms' supply chain efficiency by leveraging its data processing capabilities, resulting in cost savings and reduced emissions, among other benefits. Moreover, the effective exploitation of AI technologies contributes to the reduction of energy consumption, sustainable procurement of materials, and management of product life cycles, ultimately enhancing the positive reputation of enterprises.

CONCLUSION

Over the past century, advancements in technology and innovation have significantly enhanced our quality of life. Technological advancement and innovation will play a central role in the shift towards a sustainable future. Digital technologies have the potential to establish sustainable business models by enhancing productivity, lowering production costs and emissions, reducing the consumption of production resources, improving market communication, and facilitating the utilization of big data to enhance the accessibility of public services (Sachs et al., 2019). Integrating AI into the company's decision-making processes and matching the human dimension with the artificial one can achieve this. The promotion of SBMs is just one aspect that needs attention. The advancement of disruptive technologies like AI must be regulated by adopting a holistic understanding of cultural change and incorporating it into the organizational strategy. This is necessary to prevent any potential negative impacts on individuals and society as a whole. The pervasive influence of AI is transforming our reality and reshaping our society. The manner in which we oversee the progression of artificial intelligence will have a profound effect on our lifestyle, presenting us with prospects and advantages. Politicians, researchers, and companies worldwide are collaborating to establish universal standards that will guarantee responsible application of all AI technology. Governments must develop a comprehensive plan to create and execute important measures using regulatory standards, physical infrastructure, and digital systems that can harness the advantages of the digital revolution for Sustainable Development Goals (SDGs), while also avoiding the various possible challenges and drawbacks (Sachs et al., 2019).

Enterprises powered by artificial intelligence (AI) have a vital role in influencing the trajectory of technology in the future. It is their duty to ensure that their actions contribute to the well-being of society as a whole, while also minimizing any adverse effects. This entails the development of cutting-edge technology while also guaranteeing their ethical and responsible utilization. Companies must regularly assess and revise their policies to align with changing ethical norms, technical progress, and societal demands in order to fulfill their social obligations in the field of artificial intelligence.

REFERENCES

Accenture. (2022). *Responsible AI: Ai Ethics & Governance*. https://www.accenture.com/us-en/services/applied-intelligence/ai-ethics-governance

Ahmad, T., Zhang, D., Huang, C., Zhang, H., Dai, N., Song, Y., & Chen, H. (2021). Artificial intelligence in sustainable energy industry: Status Quo, challenges and opportunities. *Journal of Cleaner Production*, *289*, 125834. doi:10.1016/j.jclepro.2021.125834

Alam, A., & Mohanty, A. (2022, November). Business models, business strategies, and innovations in EdTech companies: integration of learning analytics and artificial intelligence in higher education. In *2022 IEEE 6th Conference on Information and Communication Technology (CICT)* (pp. 1-6). IEEE. 10.1109/CICT56698.2022.9997887

AlZayani, F., Hamdan, A., & Shoaib, H. M. (2023). *The Impact of Smart Technologies on SME Sustainability: The Mediation Effect of Sustainability Strategy–Literature Review. Technological Sustainability and Business Competitive Advantage*. Springer. doi:10.1007/978-3-031-35525-7_27

Andeobu, L., Wibowo, S., & Grandhi, S. (2022). Artificial intelligence applications for sustainable solid waste management practices in Australia: A systematic review. *The Science of the Total Environment, 834*, 155389. doi:10.1016/j.scitotenv.2022.155389 PMID:35460765

Ararat, M., Colpan, A. M., & Matten, D. (2018). Business groups and corporate responsibility for the public good. *Journal of Business Ethics, 153*(4), 911–929. doi:10.1007/s10551-018-3920-4

Borsatto, J. M. L. S., Marcolin, C. B., Abdalla, E. C., & Amaral, F. D. (2023). Aligning community outreach initiatives with SDGs in a higher education institution with artificial intelligence. *Cleaner and Responsible Consumption, 100160*. doi:10.1016/j.clrc.2023.100160

Bughin, J., Seong, J., Manyika, J., Chui, M., & Joshi, R. (2018). Notes from the AI frontier: Modeling the impact of AI on the world economy. *McKinsey Global Institute, 4*.

Buolamwini, J., & Gebru, T. (2018). Gender shades: Intersectional accuracy disparities in commercial gender classification. In *Conference on fairness, accountability and transparency* (pp. 77-91). PMLR.

Buzko, I., Dyachenko, Y., Petrova, M., Nenkov, N., Tuleninova, D., & Koeva, K. (2016). Artificial Intelligence technologies in human resource development. *Computer modelling and new technologies, 20(*2), 26-29.

Cheatham, B., Javanmardian, K., & Samandari, H. (2019). Confronting the risks of artificial intelligence. *The McKinsey Quarterly*, *2*(38), 1–9.

Davis, K. (1960). Can business afford to ignore social responsibilities? *California Management Review*, *2*(3), 70–76. doi:10.2307/41166246

Di Bona, G., Cesarotti, V., Arcese, G., & Gallo, T. (2021). Implementation of Industry 4.0 technology: New opportunities and challenges for maintenance strategy. *Procedia Computer Science*, *180*, 424–429. doi:10.1016/j.procs.2021.01.258

Di Vaio, A., Palladino, R., Hassan, R., & Escobar, O. (2020). Artificial intelligence and business models in the sustainable development goals perspective: A systematic literature review. *Journal of Business Research*, *121*, 283–314. doi:10.1016/j.jbusres.2020.08.019

Dubey, R., Bryde, D. J., Blome, C., Roubaud, D., & Giannakis, M. (2021). Facilitating artificial intelligence powered supply chain analytics through alliance management during the pandemic crises in the B2B context. *Industrial Marketing Management*, *96*, 135–146. doi:10.1016/j.indmarman.2021.05.003

Eitel-Porter, R. (2021). Beyond the promise: Implementing ethical AI. *AI and Ethics*, *1*(1), 73–80. doi:10.1007/s43681-020-00011-6

Enholm, I. M., Papagiannidis, E., Mikalef, P., & Krogstie, J. (2021). Artificial Intelligence and Business Value: A Literature Review. *Information Systems Frontiers*, *24*(5), 1709–1734. doi:10.1007/s10796-021-10186-w

Gallup Inc. (2022). *Improve Employee Engagement.* Gallup Inc. https://www.gallup.com/workplace/285674/improve-employee-engagement-workplace.aspx. Accessed 23 November 2023

Gande, A. (2020). Emerging ai & ml-based technologies & applications in supply chain management (scm): Future prospects. *International Journal of Marketing and Technology*, *10*(12), 1–6.

Gerke, S., Minssen, T., & Cohen, G. (2020). Ethical and legal challenges of artificial intelligence-driven healthcare. In *Artificial intelligence in healthcare* (pp. 295–336). Academic Press. doi:10.1016/B978-0-12-818438-7.00012-5

Giuggioli, G., & Pellegrini, M. M. (2023). Artificial intelligence as an enabler for entrepreneurs: A systematic literature review and an agenda for future research. *International Journal of Entrepreneurial Behaviour & Research*, *29*(4), 816–837. doi:10.1108/IJEBR-05-2021-0426

Goralski, M. A., & Tan, T. K. (2020). Artificial intelligence and sustainable development. *International Journal of Management Education*, *18*(1), 100330. doi:10.1016/j.ijme.2019.100330

Hahn, C., Traunecker, T., Niever, M., & Basedow, G. N. (2020). Exploring AI-driven business models: conceptualization and expectations in the machinery industry. In *2020 IEEE International Conference on Industrial Engineering and Engineering Management (IEEM)* (pp. 567-570). IEEE. 10.1109/IEEM45057.2020.9309824

Hodges, C. (2015). *Law and corporate behaviour: Integrating theories of regulation, enforcement, compliance and ethics*. Bloomsbury Publishing.

Hossain, S. F. A., Shan, X., Nurunnabi, M., Tushar, H., Mohsin, A. K. M., & Ahsan, F. T. (2021). Opportunities and challenges of m-learning during the COVID-19 pandemic: A mixed methodology approach. *E-Collaboration Technologies and Strategies for Competitive Advantage Amid Challenging Times*, 210-227.

Jayashree, S., Reza, M. N. H., Malarvizhi, C. A., & Mohiuddin, M. (2021). Industry 4.0 implementation and Triple Bottom Line sustainability: An empirical study on small and medium manufacturing firms. *Heliyon*, *7*(8), e07753. doi:10.1016/j.heliyon.2021.e07753 PMID:34430741

Jiang, Z., Ai, Q., & Hao, R. (2019). Integrated demand response mechanism for industrial energy system based on multi-energy interaction. *IEEE Access : Practical Innovations, Open Solutions*, *7*, 66336–66346. doi:10.1109/ACCESS.2019.2917821

John, M. M., Olsson, H. H., & Bosch, J. (2023). Towards an AI-driven business development framework: A multi-case study. *Journal of Software (Malden, MA)*, *35*(6), e2432. doi:10.1002/smr.2432

Joyce, A., & Paquin, R. L. (2016). The triple layered business model canvas: A tool to design more sustainable business models. *Journal of Cleaner Production*, *135*, 1474–1486. doi:10.1016/j.jclepro.2016.06.067

Kar, A. K. (2016). Bio inspired computing – A review of algorithms and scope of applications. *Expert Systems with Applications*, *59*, 20–32. doi:10.1016/j.eswa.2016.04.018

Mitchell, M., Wu, S., Zaldivar, A., Barnes, P., Vasserman, L., Hutchinson, B., & Gebru, T. (2019). Model Cards for Model Reporting. *Conference on Neural Information Processing Systems (NeurIPS)*. Research Gate.

Mughal, A. A. (2018). Artificial Intelligence in Information Security: Exploring the Advantages, Challenges, and Future Directions. *Journal of Artificial Intelligence and Machine Learning in Management, 2*(1), 22–34.

MungoliN. (2023). *Scalable, Distributed AI Frameworks: Leveraging Cloud Computing for Enhanced Deep Learning Performance and Efficiency*. arXiv:2304.13738.

Musikanski, L., Rakova, B., Bradbury, J., Phillips, R., & Manson, M. (2020). Artificial intelligence and community well-being: A proposal for an emerging area of research. *International Journal of Community Well-being, 3*(1), 39–55. doi:10.1007/s42413-019-00054-6

Obermeyer, Z., Powers, B., Vogeli, C., & Mullainathan, S. (2019). Dissecting racial bias in an algorithm used to manage the health of populations. *Science, 366*(6464), 447–453. doi:10.1126/science.aax2342 PMID:31649194

Ortiz-de-Mandojana, N., & Bansal, P. (2016). The long-term benefits of organizational resilience through sustainable business practices. *Strategic Management Journal, 37*(8), 1615–1631. doi:10.1002/smj.2410

Pai, V., & Chandra, S. (2022). Exploring factors influencing organizational adoption of artificial intelligence (AI) in corporate social responsibility (CSR) initiatives. *Pacific Asia Journal of the Association for Information Systems, 14*(5), 4. doi:10.17705/1pais.14504

Pathak, S., & Solanki, V. K. (2021). Impact of internet of things and artificial intelligence on human resource development. *Further advances in internet of things in biomedical and cyber physical systems*, (pp. 239-267). Springer. doi:10.1007/978-3-030-57835-0_19

Pfau, W., & Rimpp, P. (2021). AI-enhanced business models for digital entrepreneurship. *Digital Entrepreneurship: Impact on Business and Society*, 121-140.

Quinn, R. E., & Spreitzer, G. M. (1997). The road to empowerment: Seven questions every leader should consider. *Organizational Dynamics, 26*(2), 37–49. doi:10.1016/S0090-2616(97)90004-8

Randolph, W. C. (1995). Dynamic income, progressive taxes, and the timing of charitable contributions. *Journal of Political Economy, 103*(4), 709–738. doi:10.1086/262000

Sachs, J. D., Schmidt-Traub, G., Mazzucato, M., Messner, D., Nakicenovic, N., & Rockström, J. (2019). Six transformations to achieve the sustainable development goals. *Nature Sustainability, 2*(9), 805–814. doi:10.1038/s41893-019-0352-9

Salam, M. A., & Nawrin, R. (2022). Business response to COVID-19 through CSR: Evidence from Thai top corporations. *International Journal of Health Sciences, 6*(I), 6196–6210. doi:10.53730/ijhs.v6nS1.6276

Salam, M. A., & Senasu, K. (2019). Development of the sustainability index for the ready-made garments sector in Bangladesh. *Business: Theory and Practice, 20*(0), 329–341. doi:10.3846/btp.2019.31

Schwartz, R., Vassilev, A., Greene, K., Perine, L., Burt, A., & Hall, P. (2022). Towards a standard for identifying and managing bias in artificial intelligence. *NIST special publication, 1270*(10.6028).

Spreitzer, G. M. (1997). Toward a common ground in defining empowerment. In *National Academy of Management Meetings, 1995, Vancouver, BC, Canada; An earlier version was presented at the aforementioned conference.* Elsevier Science/JAI Press.

Suboyin, A., Eldred, M., Thatcher, J., Rehman, A., Gee, I., & Anjum, H. (2023, January). Environomics Framework for Sustainable Business Practices: Industrial Case Studies on True Impact Reduction and Process Optimization Through AI. In *SPE Middle East Intelligent Oil and Gas Symposium* (p. D011S002R002). SPE. 10.2118/214459-MS

Sucharita, K., & Seethalakshmi, R. (2022). Artificial Intelligence In Training And Development For Employees With Reference To Selected It Companies. *Journal of Positive School Psychology*, *6*(9), 2700–2715.

Tekic, Z., Cosic, I., & Katalinic, B. (2019). Manufacturing and the Rise of Artificial Intelligence: Innovation Challenges. In B. Katalinic (Ed.), *DAAAM Proceedings* (1st ed., Vol. 1, pp. 0192–0196). DAAAM International Vienna. 10.2507/30th.daaam.proceedings.025

Tushar, H. (2017). The role of ethical leadership in developing sustainable organization. [AJLEG]. *Australasian Journal of Law, Ethics, and Governance*, *2*(2), 83–95.

Tushar, H., & Sooraksa, N. (2023). Global employability skills in the 21st century workplace: A semi-systematic literature review. *Heliyon*, *9*(11), e21023. doi:10.1016/j.heliyon.2023.e21023 PMID:37954286

Van Wynsberghe, A. (2021). Sustainable AI: AI for sustainability and the sustainability of AI. *AI and Ethics*, *1*(3), 213–218. doi:10.1007/s43681-021-00043-6

Vesnic-Alujevic, L., Nascimento, S., & Polvora, A. (2020). Societal and ethical impacts of artificial intelligence: Critical notes on European policy frameworks. *Telecommunications Policy*, *44*(6), 101961. doi:10.1016/j.telpol.2020.101961

Vinuesa, R., Azizpour, H., Leite, I., Balaam, M., Dignum, V., Domisch, S., Felländer, A., Langhans, S. D., Tegmark, M., & Fuso Nerini, F. (2020). The role of artificial intelligence in achieving the Sustainable Development Goals. *Nature Communications*, *11*(1), 1–10. doi:10.1038/s41467-019-14108-y PMID:31932590

Waltersmann, L., Kiemel, S., Stuhlsatz, J., Sauer, A., & Miehe, R. (2021). Artificial Intelligence Applications for Increasing Resource Efficiency in Manufacturing Companies—A Comprehensive Review. *Sustainability (Basel)*, *13*(12), 6689. doi:10.3390/su13126689

WCED, S. W. S. (1987). World commission on environment and development. *Our common future, 17*(1), 1-91.

Yan, B., Hao, F., & Meng, X. (2021). When artificial intelligence meets building energy efficiency, a review focusing on zero energy building. *Artificial Intelligence Review*, *54*(3), 2193–2220. doi:10.1007/s10462-020-09902-w

Yu, K. H., Zhang, Y., Li, D., Montenegro-Marin, C. E., & Kumar, P. M. (2021). Environmental planning based on reduce, reuse, recycle and recover using artificial intelligence. *Environmental Impact Assessment Review*, *86*, 106492. doi:10.1016/j.eiar.2020.106492

Zerilli, J. (2021). *A citizen's guide to artificial intelligence*. MIT Press. doi:10.7551/mitpress/12518.001.0001

Chapter 13
Opportunities, Enablers, and Challenges of Smart Technologies and AI Adoption in SMEs

Hasanuzzaman Tushar
https://orcid.org/0000-0002-4829-5843
International University of Business Agriculture and Technology, Bangladesh

Nanta Sooraksa
National Institute of Development Administration, Thailand

Shaikh Sabbir Ahmed Waliullah
https://orcid.org/0000-0002-0207-2409
International University of Business Agriculture and Technology, Bangladesh

Nayma Iftakhar
International University of Business Agriculture and Technology, Bangladesh

ABSTRACT

SMEs play a vital role in global economies, contributing significantly to job creation and economic growth. The rapid evolution of smart technologies and AI presents both opportunities and challenges for SMEs. This chapter provides a comprehensive overview of the key opportunities, challenges, and enablers related to the adoption of smart technologies and AI in SMEs. It explores the landscape of SMEs in the context of adopting these technologies, covering opportunities and challenges. It concludes by discussing potential future prospects for SMEs in the realm of smart technology and AI integration, setting the stage for future research. This guide offers practical implications for SMEs, business leaders, researchers, and policymakers, facilitating their transformation into technology-driven organizations. The findings highlight the significance of addressing challenges proactively and leveraging enablers to harness the full potential of smart technologies and AI for sustainable growth and competitive advantage.

DOI: 10.4018/979-8-3693-1842-3.ch013

INTRODUCTION

In the ever-evolving tapestry of global business, the role of technology, particularly Smart Technologies and Artificial Intelligence (AI), has become increasingly prominent (Giuggioli & Pellegrini, 2023; Hossain et al., 2021). This paradigm shift is not only reshaping the strategies of multinational corporations but is also extending a transformative invitation to the often-overlooked players in the business landscape – Small and Medium-sized Enterprises (SMEs) (AlZayani, Hamdan, & Shoaib, 2023). SMEs form the backbone of economies worldwide, contributing significantly to job creation and economic growth (Drydakis, 2022; Lu, Wijayaratna, Huang & Qiu, 2022; Tushar & Sooraksa, 2023). As SMEs stand at the crossroads of tradition and innovation, the decision to integrate smart technologies and AI is not merely a technological choice; it is a strategic imperative that can redefine their operational efficiency, market presence, and overall sustainability (Cousté et al., 2022; Hossain et al., 2021; Hossain et al., 2022; Mohsin et al., 2021).

In recent years, the rapid advancement of smart technologies and artificial intelligence (AI) has presented both opportunities and challenges for SMEs. In general, the integration of smart technologies and AI offers SMEs a wealth of opportunities to enhance their operations, from efficiency gains to data-driven decision-making (Lu et al., 2022; Vuong et al., 2020). The integration of AI technology stands as a pivotal and indispensable remedy in upholding the sustainability of SMEs, particularly in the aftermath of the global pandemic. The incorporation of AI technology not only serves as a critical intervention for SMEs but also positions itself as a transformative force, enabling these enterprises to convert challenges into avenues for enhanced performance and increased survival rates (Dwivedi et al., 2021). Existing research predominantly centers on elucidating the challenges encountered by SMEs and delving into the dynamics of organizational participant interactions amidst crises. This strategic employment of AI emerges as a linchpin for SMEs, offering a multifaceted approach to not only navigate challenges but also to capitalize on emergent opportunities, thereby fortifying their resilience and ensuring sustained viability in the contemporary business landscape.

SMEs must embrace emerging technologies to improve, alter, or potentially revolutionize their business models for sustained competitiveness. However, in contrast, these advantages come hand in hand with a range of challenges, including the financial burden of implementation, a shortage of technical expertise, data security concerns, employee resistance, regulatory complexities, scalability considerations, and ethical dilemmas. In addition, SMEs may face challenges in terms of lacking the essential strategies, knowledge, and resources needed to leverage AI technology. A considerable number of SMEs, particularly those in manufacturing, are actively exploring whether AI technology can offer solutions to their specific needs.

The purpose of this chapter is to provide an overview of the key opportunities, challenges and enablers associated with the adoption of smart technologies and AI in SMEs. This chapter explores the dynamic landscape of SMEs in the context of adopting smart technologies and artificial intelligence (AI). The chapter delves into the multifaceted opportunities these technologies offer, the critical enablers that facilitate their successful integration, and the complex challenges that SMEs encounter in their journey toward becoming technology-driven organizations. The remainder of this chapter is structured as follows. The chapter begins by providing an overview of smart technologies and AI in SMEs. It then systematically categorizes existing literature, deductively partitioning it into two primary sections: a) the opportunities enabled by smart technologies and AI within SMEs, and b) the challenges they face, along with the essential enablers needed for successful adoption. The chapter concludes by delving into the potential future scenarios for SMEs in light of their integration of smart technology and AI. It also discusses implications and draws conclusions from the current state of SMEs in their journey of adopting smart technologies and AI. Moreover, the chapter sets the stage for future research, highlighting areas for further investigation in this evolving domain.

OVERVIEW OF SMART TECHNOLOGIES AND AI

The word smart represents the clean, tidy, and stylish appearance of someone intelligent and has a quick-thinking capability in a difficult situation. When technologies with a mindless mind possess the features mentioned above, they are considered smart technologies (Hildebrandt, 2020). The acronym of the word SMART has an interesting meaning. It represents the self-monitoring analysis and reporting technology (Gaber et al., 2017). However, smartness is not only restricted to technologies, it has a widened perspective and can be included in law, life sciences, social sciences, and even business. In business especially in SMEs to ensure sustainability there are no alternatives than the adoption of smart technologies (AlZayani et al., 2023).

The rapidly increasing of smart technologies has instigated a profound and multifaceted paradigm shift, resulting in innovations across diverse sectors encompassing products, services, operational processes, and overarching business models (Iansiti & Lakhani, 2020). At the forefront of this transformative landscape stands artificial intelligence (AI), an entity distinguished by its sophisticated digital composition. AI, in essence, can be characterized as an advanced predictive technology, a rubric inclusive of, but not confined to, machine learning (ML) and deep learning, as well as the complexities of natural language processing (NLP) and machine vision (Hansen & Bøgh, 2021; Sjödin, Parida, Kohtamäki, & Wincent, 2020; Sklyar, Kowalkowski, Tronvoll, & Sörhammar, 2019). Artificial Intelligence (AI) is no more a fiction but a reality at present. The AI is encapsulated in a programming concept of non-human intelligence that can perform specific tasks (Dwivedi et al., 2021). The context of AI includes an independent ability to interpret and learn from external data to get particular results through flexible adjustment (Kaplan & Haenlein, 2019). The performance of AI has been improved for specific tasks of pragmatic applications by the inclusion of big data algorithms (Kar, 2016).

Industry 4.0 the rise of new digital industrial transformation is enormously dependent on smart technologies and AI (Qu et al., 2016). Therefore, in modern times businesses are focused on the adoption of smart technologies and AI. In SMEs, the information and digital technology (IDT) adoption process is not similar to large enterprises (Müller et al., 2018). Small firms show more flexibility in the adoption of changes forced by the business environment and can make fast, better, and quality decisions (Love & Roper, 2015). The advanced IDT adoption by SMEs promises a number of benefits (Ghobakhloo & Ching, 2019). It opens the door to many business dimensions such as process improvement, optimization, product and service innovations, modern customer insights, risk reduction, marketing, customer relationship management, cash flow prediction, human resource management, and many more. However, SMEs will be confronted by some problems in implementing the AI such as high quality collaborations in various levels, extensive training and flexible reactions to adopt the new system (Franken et al., 2023). In addition to that, weak financial condition, limited awareness regarding the benefit of AI, unskilled manpower and unavailability of data are also the barriers to be considered by SMEs for AI adoption (Bhalerao et al., 2022).

OPPORTUNITIES ENABLED BY SMART TECHNOLOGIES AND AI

The advancements in artificial intelligence (AI) and smart technology solutions have become increasingly pertinent and attainable for SMEs. In a manner comparable to large-scale organizations, AI is now affording commensurate advantages to SMEs. Notable opportunities encompass the resolution of customer inquiries, innovation in products and services, the automation of repetitive tasks, talent acquisition optimization, and enhancements in advertising and other facets of marketing operations. The infusion of smart technologies and AI enables enhanced operational efficiency within SMEs. Automation of routine tasks, powered by AI algorithms, alleviates the burden on human resources, allowing employees to focus on higher-value, strategic activities. This efficiency gain translates into cost savings and heightened productivity, contributing to the overall competitiveness of SMEs in the market. This section elucidates the integration of AI into the operational framework of SMEs and explores potential opportunities. It offers insights into the components comprising the study's scope, focusing on the applications of AI currently employed in SME settings.

Process Improvement and Optimization

Globally, businesses consistently seek to maximize their profits, with a pivotal focus on optimizing their business processes. It encompasses designing, executing, controlling, and optimizing different processes to enhance efficiency, cost reduction and improve performance (Love & Roper, 2015). Traditionally process improvement is the domain of the operation manager. The rapid advancement in AI is bringing a revolutionary change in the Business Process Management (BPM) landscape. AI is also playing a significant role in transforming efficiency in BPM and optimization. This strategic incorporation of AI technologies brings forth a myriad of benefits, reshaping traditional business processes and fostering a culture of continuous improvement (We & Pardo, 2022). One of the primary avenues through which AI catalyzes process improvement in SMEs is automation. Routine and repetitive tasks, which traditionally consumed significant human resources, can now be streamlined and automated through AI-powered systems. This not only reduces the potential for human error but also liberates skilled employees to focus on higher-value tasks that require creativity, critical thinking, and strategic decision-making (Sklyar et al., 2019).

Predictive analytics, a subset of AI, proves instrumental in forecasting demand, managing inventory, and optimizing supply chain processes for SMEs. By analyzing historical data and external factors, predictive analytics enables SMEs to anticipate market trends and fluctuations, facilitating proactive decision-making in areas such as production planning and inventory management. Furthermore, AI enhances customer relationship management (CRM) within SMEs. Chatbots and virtual assistants powered by AI technologies can provide real-time customer support, address queries, and personalize interactions (Selamat & Windasari, 2021). This not only improves customer satisfaction but also contributes to the overall efficiency of customer service processes. Although big data companies are the pioneer in business process improvement through AI, small businesses can also use this machine learning algorithm to optimize their business process. SMEs can create automated tasks, optimize processes, and allocate better resources through AI to ensure cost reduction. There are some challenges in the adoption of AI in business process improvement such as complex learning curve, substantial long-term cost, and lack of flexibility, integration challenges, and consideration of resistance of human factors.

Product and Service Innovations

Products and service development were driven by human intuition for long which is now being leveraged by AI tools. SMEs can significantly benefit from integrating AI into their products and services. AI technologies offer various opportunities for innovation, efficiency, and competitiveness. Several products and services ideation AI tools are helping product innovation teams at present. For instance, OpenAI, IdeasAI, Midjourney, Stable Diffusion etc. OpenAI such as GPT- 4 helps generating business ideas form user inputs and backgrounds (Calanzone et al., 2023). Another AI powered ideation tool is IdeasAI which helps the human team in generating ideas based on their input keywords. Midjourney is a generative artificial intelligent program developed by Midjourney Inc. an independent research lab company. Stable Diffusion is a deep learning AI tools released in 2022. It uses text-to-image model generating ideas. In contrast of proving benefits, AI may facilitate the imitation of product and services which can lead to diminishing return on investment (Tekic et al., 2019). Predictive analytics, facilitated by AI algorithms, emerges as a pivotal tool for SMEs in anticipating and responding to market dynamics (We & Pardo, 2022). Through sophisticated analyses of historical data, AI aids in sales and demand forecasting, enabling SMEs to fine-tune their inventory management and production planning processes. Furthermore, the discernment of customer behavior through AI-driven analytics empowers SMEs to craft personalized marketing strategies, thereby fortifying customer engagement and loyalty.

In case of product innovation, AI serves as a catalyst for novel functionalities and enhanced user experiences. Integrating AI capabilities into products, such as consumer electronics or software applications, opens avenues for innovative features and functionalities. Moreover, the implementation of predictive maintenance, driven by AI, mitigates operational disruptions by forecasting equipment failures, consequently reducing downtime and associated costs. The protection of data security and fraud prevention represents an imperative dimension of AI application for SMEs. Advanced cybersecurity solutions underpinned by AI algorithms bolster the resilience of SMEs against cyber threats (Žigienė, Rybakovas, & Alzbutas, 2019). Concurrently, AI-driven fraud detection mechanisms scrutinize financial transactions, identifying anomalies and fortifying the SMEs' defenses against fraudulent activities.

Real-Time Customer Insights

Real-time monitoring and controlling processes of AI technologies have significance over that of manual processes (Zhong et al., 2017). As SMEs navigate the complexities of today's dynamic markets, the integration of AI technologies emerges as a strategic conduit through which businesses can attain immediate and actionable intelligence on customer behaviors, preferences, and expectations. Central to the efficacy of AI in SMEs is the capacity to analyze vast datasets expeditiously, providing an instantaneous and granular understanding of customer behavior. Real-time customer behavior analysis, facilitated by AI-driven analytics, transcends conventional paradigms by enabling SMEs to discern evolving patterns and preferences promptly (Hansen & Bøgh, 2021). Consequently, this expeditious comprehension serves as a linchpin for agile decision-making, positioning SMEs to adapt rapidly to shifting market landscapes. There are several methods for consumer insights generation, such as, interviews, customer surveys, trend analysis, experimental secondary research, online research and market analysis. AI will influence and lead some of the modern methods of analyzing consumer insights such as, social listening, predictive analysis, focus group, and data analytics. Social media data can clue the future trends, demands and to find target customers. With the help of AI some companies can develop historical customer data as a part of predictive analysis. For creating online customer loop of feedbacks, AI driven online focus groups in real-time can be an effective tool (Lim, 2023).

Business Risk Reduction

AI can aid to enterprise risk management (ERM). AI can mitigate different risk of SME like, default risk, liquidity risk, fraud risk, interest rate risk etc. AI provide real time monitoring support on credit ratings of the business and help to take proactive measures form the default risk. It can also help to conduct predictive analytics and create risk profile using different internal and external data associated with exposure to risk (Žigienė, Rybakovas, & Alzbutas, 2019). AI's predictive analytics capabilities offer SMEs the foresight needed to proactively address operational risks. By analyzing historical and real-time data, AI facilitates the identification of potential disruptions, allowing SMEs to implement preventative measures and safeguard against unforeseen challenges. This predictive approach not only minimizes operational downtime but also enhances overall business resilience.

AI is able to conduct compliance check and inform to the borrowers and lenders if the terms and conditions are not met. Technical and strategic decisions can be made through AI using the automated generated statements to reduce different risks of the business. This data-driven decision-making process aligns with the risk appetite and long-term objectives of SMEs, minimizing the likelihood of strategic missteps and ensuring sustainable growth. However, the AI value chain such as, AI-generated code, neural network, data may allow others to use same or similar solutions which can result an incomplete protection for trade secret (Tekic et al., 2019). Furthermore, AI plays a pivotal role in stimulating cybersecurity measures for SMEs. With its advanced threat detection and response capabilities, AI enables real-time monitoring and analysis of network activities. This empowers SMEs to swiftly identify and counteract potential cyber threats, reducing vulnerabilities and safeguarding sensitive business data.

Marketing and Customer Relationship Management (CRM)

AI is transforming the marketing environment and the marketing workers must be ready to update and strengthened their abilities for robotics and AI (Shaik, 2023). SMEs, often face resource limitations, can gain substantial advantages from the use of AI technologies. This application can lead to improved customer engagement, personalized marketing efforts, and more efficient Customer Relationship Management (CRM) processes. AI's predictive analytics capabilities offer SMEs a profound advantage in marketing strategies. By analyzing vast datasets, AI algorithms can discern intricate patterns in customer behavior, preferences, and purchasing trends (Basri, 2020). This enables SMEs to develop targeted marketing campaigns that resonate with specific customer segments, thereby maximizing the impact of promotional efforts. Furthermore, AI-driven recommendation systems provide SMEs with the means to deliver personalized product or service suggestions to individual customers.

Numerous AI tools have already been introduced to the market, including well-known platforms such as HubSpot, Salesforce Einstein, Persado, Duplex, Adext AI, and Phrasee. HubSpot functions as an AI-driven tool designed for marketing and sales, facilitating business growth (Hansen & Bøgh, 2021). Salesforce Einstein, on the other hand, serves as a customer relationship management platform supported by AI, enabling automated tasks, outcome predictions, and providing recommendations. Persado is another noteworthy AI-based platform specializing in the optimization of marketing content, marketing testing, and personalization. Duplex stands out as an AI-powered assistant for conversations and automated marketing instructions. Adext AI focuses on optimizing digital advertising campaigns, while Phrasee is employed for AI-powered copywriting generation. These tools collectively contribute to the advancement of diverse business functionalities by leveraging the capabilities of artificial intelligence.

Predictions of Cash Flow

The accurate forecasting of cash flow stands as a critical component for financial planning and operational stability in SMEs. Different classical statistical methods are used for cash flow forecasting. At present, these methods are being replaced by AI algorithms (Sezer et al., 2020). AI algorithm has the capability to forecast cash flow based on the patterns and characteristics of the inherent data of the business. This AI based approach can bring more flexible, efficient, and accurate results than other methods. These outputs are significant to SME business owners and stakeholders. By analyzing extensive datasets encompassing financial transactions, market trends, and economic indicators, AI algorithms discern patterns and correlations that might elude conventional analyses. This enables SMEs to proactively identify potential cash flow challenges, allowing for strategic adjustments and mitigative measures. Machine learning shows superior accuracy forecasting and analyzing financial cash flow time series compared to traditional models (Evdokimov et al., 2023). This machine learning process of the cash flow prediction reduces the manual effort and time which brings more flexibility to use their resources in other dimensions of business such as, operational efficiency and productivity (Kotios, Makridis, Fatouros, & Kyriazis, 2022). Moreover, AI facilitates dynamic forecasting by continuously adapting models in response to changing business environments. Real-time data analysis enables SMEs to factor in immediate market shifts, regulatory changes, and unexpected events, ensuring that cash flow predictions remain responsive and relevant (Drydakis, 2022). This adaptability is particularly valuable for SMEs, which often operate in volatile markets and must contend with fluctuating demand and supply chain dynamics.

Recruitment and HR

Recruitment and selection are always a time consuming and challenging tasks for HR professionals. Like all other business activities, AI is also transforming the recruitment process. It has the potential to renovate the sourcing, screening the candidates to onboarding and retention. AI generated platform is able to search automatically an excessive number of resumes and social media profiles selecting the best candidate. AI-driven advancements in recruitment have streamlined the initial stages of the hiring process. Automated resume screening, powered by AI algorithms, expedites candidate selection by analyzing vast datasets to match qualifications and skills with job requirements (Kumar, Raut, Mangla, Ferraris & Choubey, 2022). This not only accelerates the recruitment timeline but also ensures a more impartial evaluation of candidates, reducing potential biases inherent in traditional screening methods.

The natural language processing (NLP) algorithm is used to make this platform more effective and proficient. AI is also being able to conduct candidates' initial interviews through chat-bots and video interviews. A series of predetermined questions are used in chat-bots for giving instant feedback based on the candidates' responses. AI-powered generated tools is used to evaluate body language, voice tone and non-verbal cues assessing the candidate's personality in video interviews. Some examples of AI tools used by HR professionals are Eightfold AI, Mya Systems, HireVue's AI etc. However, small firms can encounter some resistance to finding talent because of their limited capacity to take AI support in the recruitment process. Higher education providers can assist SMEs by preparing their graduates with up-to-date knowledge where outcome-based education can bring viable solutions (Chowdhury et al., 2023).

Furthermore, AI plays a crucial role in enhancing candidate experience and engagement. Chatbots, integrated into recruitment platforms, offer real-time interaction and support to candidates, providing information on job opportunities, company culture, and application status (Biea, Dinu, Bunica & Jerdea, 2023). This personalized and prompt communication fosters a positive candidate experience, contributing to a favorable perception of the organization. In HR management, AI assists SMEs in workforce planning and optimization. Predictive analytics, a core component of AI, analyzes historical and real-time HR data to forecast trends in employee performance, turnover, and overall workforce dynamics (Kusý, 2021). This foresight enables SMEs to implement proactive strategies, such as talent development initiatives and retention programs, aligning HR practices with organizational objectives. AI also facilitates the automation of routine HR tasks, such as payroll processing and benefits administration. By reducing the administrative burden on HR professionals, SMEs can redirect resources toward more strategic HR functions, fostering a more efficient and agile HR department.

CHALLENGES OF SMART TECHNOLOGIES AND AI IN SMES

The integration of Smart Technologies and AI in SMEs holds great promise for enhancing their competitiveness and sustainability. However, the adoption of these technologies is not without its challenges (Grooss, 2024). This section delves into the various hurdles faced by SMEs, encompassing organizational readiness, financial constraints, acceptance issues, infrastructure concerns, reputational and legal risks, and the requisite skillset for effective implementation.

Organizational Readiness, Encompassing Human, Financial, and Material Resources

The primary challenges faced by SMEs in adopting smart technologies and AI is the lack of organizational readiness, encompassing human, financial, and material resources. SMEs often lack the in-house expertise and skills necessary to effectively implement and manage these technologies, requiring them to invest in training and development programs to up-skill their workforce (Agostini & Nosella, 2019). Furthermore, the financial constraints of SMEs often limit their ability to acquire the necessary hardware, software, and data infrastructure to support smart technologies and AI. This lack of resources can create a significant barrier to entry, preventing SMEs from reaping the benefits of these advancements. The successful integration of smart technologies and AI in SMEs hinges on their organizational readiness. This readiness extends across human, financial, and material resources (Amaral & Peças, 2021). Lack of awareness and understanding of AI among SME owners and employees is indeed a common obstacle. Many SMEs may not have the necessary expertise to assess the potential benefits and challenges associated with implementing AI solutions. Moreover, SMEs often operate in resource constrained environments, limiting their ability to allocate dedicated personnel for AI implementation. The absence of skilled personnel capable of developing, implementing, and maintaining AI systems poses a significant hurdle. Additionally, SMEs may struggle to afford the high salaries demanded by AI professionals, making it difficult to attract and retain talent in this competitive field (Di Bona et al., 2021). Financial resources also play a pivotal role in determining the readiness of SMEs to embrace smart technologies.

The initial investment required for AI implementation, including hardware, software, and training, can be prohibitive for many SMEs. Furthermore, the long-term financial commitment associated with maintaining and updating AI systems may pose challenges, especially for businesses with fluctuating revenue streams (Dutta et al., 2020). Material resources, such as access to quality data, are essential for effective AI implementation. SMEs may lack the necessary datasets for training AI models, limiting their ability to leverage these technologies fully. Overcoming these organizational readiness challenges necessitates a strategic approach, including targeted education and training programs, financial incentives, and collaborative initiatives (Ghobakhloo & Ng, 2019).

High Costs and Uncertainty About the AI Benefits

The adoption of smart technologies and AI is often impeded by a confluence of challenges, prominently characterized by high costs and pervasive uncertainty regarding the tangible benefits associated with AI implementation. The financial burden associated with acquiring and integrating AI systems represents a formidable barrier for SMEs, where budgetary constraints and limited resources may hinder their ability to invest substantially in cutting-edge technologies (Hansen & Bøgh, 2021). The procurement of AI infrastructure, specialized talent, and ongoing maintenance expenditures collectively contribute to a substantial financial outlay, thereby exacerbating the economic challenges faced by SMEs. The other upfront investment required for AI implementation, encompassing hardware, software licenses, and training, can be a major deterrent for SMEs with limited financial resources. The uncertainty surrounding the return on investment (ROI) further compounds this issue (Gonzalez-Tamayo et al., 2023). SMEs may be hesitant to commit substantial financial resources to AI projects without a clear understanding of the potential benefits. The lack of tangible success stories and case studies in similar SME contexts contributes to this uncertainty. Addressing these challenges requires a concerted effort from policymakers, industry associations, and technology providers to provide transparent information on the costs and benefits of AI adoption in SMEs (Baabdullah, Alalwan, Slade, Raman & Khatatneh, 2021).

Acceptance, Cost and Affordability

Acceptance of smart technologies and AI within the organizational culture of SMEs is a critical factor influencing successful implementation. Resistance to change, fear of job displacement, and a lack of understanding about the potential benefits can impede acceptance at all levels of the organization. The perceived cost and affordability of AI solutions also play a role in shaping organizational attitudes. Employs may be resistant to the introduction of AI due to concerns about job security and the potential for automation to replace certain tasks (Jayashree et al., 2021). Communicating the benefits of AI in enhancing job roles, increasing efficiency, and enabling more strategic and creative tasks is crucial for overcoming resistance. Additionally, addressing the misconception that AI is only suitable for large enterprises and emphasizing affordable solutions tailored to SMEs is essential for fostering acceptance (Masood & Sonntag, 2020). The cost and affordability of AI solutions extend beyond the initial investment to ongoing operational expenses. SMEs may struggle with the maintenance costs, software updates, and the need for continuous training to keep up with evolving AI technologies. To address these challenges, collaborative efforts between technology providers, government agencies, and financial institutions are essential to develop cost- effective AI solutions and facilitate access to financing options for SMEs (Moeuf et al., 2019).

Infrastructure and the Awareness of AI

The adoption of smart technologies and AI in SMEs is contingent on the availability and adequacy of supporting infrastructure. Issues such as poor internet connectivity, outdated hardware, and insufficient technical support can hinder the effective implementation of AI solutions. In many cases, SMEs may lack the necessary resources to upgrade their infrastructure, limiting their ability to harness the full potential of AI. Moreover, the awareness of AI and its applications among SMEs is a critical factor. Many SME owners may not fully understand how AI can benefit their specific business operations. This lack of awareness can lead to a reluctance to invest in AI technologies or an inability to identify areas where these technologies can be applied to improve efficiency and competitiveness (Ricci et al., 2021). To address infrastructure challenges, policymakers must prioritize initiatives to improve digital infrastructure in regions with a high concentration of SMEs. Public-private partnerships can play a crucial role in providing SMEs with access to affordable and reliable digital infrastructure. Simultaneously, awareness campaigns and educational programs are essential to ensure that SME owners and employees are informed about the potential benefits and applications of AI in their specific industry (Roblek et al., 2021).

Reputational and Legal Risks

The integration of smart technologies and AI in SMEs may introduce new challenges related to reputational and legal risks. Privacy concerns, data security breaches, and ethical considerations are paramount in AI adoption. SMEs may lack the resources and expertise to implement robust cyber security measures, making them vulnerable to potential breaches that could harm their reputation and erode customer trust. Moreover, the collection and use of data in AI applications may raise ethical concerns. SMEs must navigate the complex landscape of data privacy regulations and ensure compliance with laws such as the General Data Protection Regulation (GDPR) and other regional data protection laws (Suwaidi et al., 2020). Failure to adhere to these regulations not only poses legal risks but can also result in severe reputational damage. To mitigate these risks, SMEs need to prioritize cyber security measures and invest in data protection protocols. Collaborative efforts between industry associations, regulatory bodies, and technology providers can help SMEs navigate the legal landscape and ensure compliance with data protection regulations. Transparent communication with customers about data usage practices is essential for maintaining trust and reputation (Chan et al., 2020).

Required Skillset for an Effective Implementation

The successful implementation of smart technologies and AI in SMEs necessitates a specific skillset that may not be readily available. AI requires expertise in data science, machine learning, programming, and system integration. SMEs, especially those in traditional industries, may face challenges in attracting and retaining professionals with these specialized skills (Davenport et al., 2019). Addressing the skills gap requires a multi-faceted approach. Educational institutions need to adapt their curricula to incorporate AI-related courses and training programs. Additionally, industry collaborations can facilitate internships, apprenticeships, and on-the-job training to bridge the gap between academic knowledge and practical skills. Government initiatives, such as funding for AI training programs and incentives for businesses to up-skill their workforce, can further support SMEs in building the necessary expertise. Furthermore, technology providers can play a role in simplifying the adoption of AI by developing user-friendly interfaces and providing accessible training resources (Enholm et al., 2021). Cloud-based AI solutions and platform-as-a-service models can reduce the technical complexity, allowing SMEs to leverage AI without requiring an in-depth understanding of the underlying technology (Felsberger et al., 2020).

The adoption of smart technologies and AI may present a significant prospects and potential for SMEs. Policymakers should focus on creating an enabling environment through targeted incentives, infrastructure development, and regulatory frameworks that support the responsible adoption of AI in SMEs. Industry associations can play a pivotal role in raising awareness, providing guidance, and facilitating collaboration among SMEs. Technology providers must innovate to develop affordable and user-friendly AI solutions tailored to the specific needs of SMEs. Educational institutions need to adapt their curricula to quip the workforce with the necessary skills for the AI-driven future. Financial institutions should explore mechanisms to provide accessible financing options for SMEs looking to invest in smart technologies. Overall, a concerted effort from all stakeholders is essential to unlock the transformative potential of smart technologies and AI in SMEs, paving the way for increased efficiency, productivity, and competitiveness in the global marketplace.

FUTURE DIRECTIONS

As SMEs tread the path towards integrating smart technologies and AI, they confront a diverse array of challenges. The chapter systematically categorizes these challenges, spanning from financial considerations to scalability issues and ethical dilemmas. This meticulous exploration of challenges functions as a detailed roadmap, providing SMEs with guidance to navigate potential obstacles on their journey toward seamless technological integration. In the pursuit of successful integration, key enablers emerge as central players. The chapter delves into the multifaceted landscape of enablers, underscoring their pivotal role in facilitating the adoption of smart technologies and AI. From addressing financial burdens to navigating regulatory complexities, these enablers become the driving force propelling SMEs towards the realization of becoming technology-driven organizations.

Drawing on diverse research outcomes and reports from various organizations, it becomes evident that smart technology presents a substantial market opportunity and is witnessing widespread adoption among SMEs worldwide. Wang et al. (2019) highlighted that small and medium enterprises are predisposed to embrace intelligent manufacturing, emphasizing that the use of smart technologies and AI systems is imperative to meet contemporary market demands. This technology not only optimizes production costs but also enhances design versatility and expedites product delivery times (Phuyal, Bista & Bista, 2020).

In envisioning future directions, it is clear that the landscape of smart technologies and AI adoption in SMEs is poised for expansion. As SMEs confront challenges and leverage enablers, the momentum towards embracing intelligent technologies is likely to intensify. The imperative for SMEs to adapt to the evolving market demands and leverage the benefits of smart technologies is underscored by the demonstrated success stories and positive outcomes observed in various sectors. The convergence of challenges, enablers, and market opportunities propels SMEs into a future where smart technologies and AI are integral components of their operational fabric. The chapter's insights not only shed light on the current state of SMEs in adopting these technologies but also serve as a compass guiding them towards future success. As SMEs continue to chart their course in the dynamic realm of smart technologies and AI, the imperative for strategic adaptation and technological integration remains at the forefront of their journey.

IMPLICATION AND CONCLUSION

In essence, this chapter serves as a comprehensive guide for SMEs, business leaders, researchers, and policymakers, offering valuable insights into navigating the intricate landscape of smart technology and AI adoption. It provides practical implications for leveraging opportunities, addressing challenges, and capitalizing on enablers, ultimately facilitating the transformation of SMEs into technology-driven organizations. Recognizing the opportunities that these technologies present, SMEs may strategically identify areas for sustainable growth, aiming to transform into technology-driven organizations. A critical analysis of this paper may offer a comprehensive understanding of the factors that enable successful technology adoption. The findings of this chapter will equip business leaders with insights into the challenges that accompany technological transformation. By proactively addressing these challenges, SMEs can incorporate them as essential components of their overall strategy. By embracing these practical implications, SMEs can harness the full potential of smart technologies and AI, positioning themselves for sustainable growth and competitive advantage in the evolving business landscape.

Across the world, SMEs have played a pivotal role in generating new employment opportunities and contributing significantly to their respective economies (Ogawa & Tanaka, 2013). Sustaining a nation's economic stability hinges on the ongoing growth of SMEs. However, the global pandemic and the ensuing control measures have presented multifaceted challenges to the sustainability of SMEs worldwide (Dai et al., 2021). These challenges encompass obstructed logistics, disrupted supply chains, labor scarcities, and diminished demand, thereby engendering uncertainty and compelling the most vulnerable SMEs to grapple for survival and future development. This underscores the imperative for technological advancement as a potential pathway forward. This chapter delves into the latest research concerning the opportunities afforded by Smart Technologies and AI for SMEs and the concomitant challenges associated with their transformative adoption of AI. It aims to shed light on the manifold opportunities that AI presents for enhancing the continual development of SMEs while simultaneously addressing the hurdles inherent in the AI transformation of these enterprises. Moreover, the chapter puts forth additional research directions to empower SMEs in seizing the opportunities facilitated by AI technologies, thereby ensuring their sustained development.

REFERENCES

Agostini, L., & Nosella, A. (2019). The adoption of Industry 4.0 technologies in SMEs: Results of an international study. *Management Decision*, *58*(4), 625–643. doi:10.1108/MD-09-2018-0973

AlZayani, F., Hamdan, A., & Shoaib, H. M. (2023). *The Impact of Smart Technologies on SME Sustainability: The Mediation Effect of Sustainability Strategy–Literature Review. Technological Sustainability and Business Competitive Advantage*. Springer. doi:10.1007/978-3-031-35525-7_27

AlZayani, F., Mohammed, A., & Shoaib, H. M. (2023). The impact of smart technologies on SMEs' sustainability: The mediation effect of sustainability strategy. *Competitiveness Review*. doi:10.1108/CR-09-2022-0136

Amaral, A., & Peças, P. (2021). SMEs and Industry 4.0: Two case studies of digitalization for a smoother integration. *Computers in Industry*, *125*, 103333. doi:10.1016/j.compind.2020.103333

Baabdullah, A. M., Alalwan, A. A., Slade, E. L., Raman, R., & Khatatneh, K. F. (2021). SMEs and artificial intelligence (AI): Antecedents and consequences of AI-based B2B practices. *Industrial Marketing Management*, *98*, 255–270. doi:10.1016/j.indmarman.2021.09.003

Basri, W. (2020). Examining the impact of artificial intelligence (AI)-assisted social media marketing on the performance of small and medium enterprises: Toward effective business management in the Saudi Arabian context. *International Journal of Computational Intelligence Systems*, *13*(1), 142. doi:10.2991/ijcis.d.200127.002

Bendig, D., Schulz, C., Theis, L., & Raff, S. (2023). Digital orientation and environmental performance in times of technological change. *Technological Forecasting and Social Change*, *188*, 122272. doi:10.1016/j.techfore.2022.122272

Bhalerao, K., Kumar, A., & Pujari, P. (2022). A Study of Barriers and Benefits of Artificial Intelligence Adoption in Small and Medium Enterprise. *Academy of Marketing Studies Journal*, *26*, 1–6.

Biea, E. A., Dinu, E., Bunica, A., & Jerdea, L. (2023). Recruitment in SMEs: The role of managerial practices, technology and innovation. *European Business Review*. doi:10.1108/EBR-05-2023-0162

Calanzone, D., Coppari, A., Tedoldi, R., Olivato, G., & Casonato, C. (2023). An open source perspective on AI and alignment with the EU AI Act.

Chan, Y. E., Krishnamurthy, R., & Desjardins, C. (2020). Technology-Driven innovation in small firms. *MIS Quarterly Executive*, *19*(1), 39–55. doi:10.17705/2msqe.00024

Chowdhury, M. A., Chisty, K. K. S., Tushar, H., Ahmed, K. M. F., & Waliullah, S. S. A. (2023). Automating assessment and evaluation for a bachelor's degree program. [IJERE]. *International Journal of Evaluation and Research in Education*, *12*(4), 2037. doi:10.11591/ijere.v12i4.25479

Cousté, P. E., Qin, S., Hossain, S. F. A., & Hussain, K. (2022). Factors influencing social-media-based entrepreneurship prospects among female students in China. *Heliyon*, *8*(12), e12041. doi:10.1016/j.heliyon.2022.e12041 PMID:36483305

Dai, R., Feng, H., Hu, J., Jin, Q., Li, H., Wang, R., Wang, R., Xu, L., & Zhang, X. (2021). The impact of COVID-19 on small and medium-sized enterprises (SMEs): Evidence from two-wave phone surveys in China. *China Economic Review*, *67*, 101607. doi:10.1016/j.chieco.2021.101607 PMID:36568286

Davenport, T. H., Guha, A., Grewal, D., & Breßgott, T. (2019). How artificial intelligence will change the future of marketing. *Journal of the Academy of Marketing Science*, *48*(1), 24–42. doi:10.1007/s11747-019-00696-0

Di Bona, G., Cesarotti, V., Arcese, G., & Gallo, T. (2021). Implementation of Industry 4.0 technology: New opportunities and challenges for maintenance strategy. *Procedia Computer Science*, *180*, 424–429. doi:10.1016/j.procs.2021.01.258

Drydakis, N. (2022). Artificial Intelligence and reduced SMEs' business risks. A dynamic capabilities analysis during the COVID-19 pandemic. *Information Systems Frontiers*, *24*(4), 1223–1247. doi:10.1007/s10796-022-10249-6 PMID:35261558

Drydakis, N. (2022). Artificial Intelligence and reduced SMEs' business risks. A dynamic capabilities analysis during the COVID-19 pandemic. *Information Systems Frontiers*, *24*(4), 1223–1247. doi:10.1007/s10796-022-10249-6 PMID:35261558

Dutta, G., Kumar, R., Sindhwani, R., & Singh, R. K. (2020). Digital transformation priorities of India's discrete manufacturing SMEs – a conceptual study in perspective of Industry 4.0. *Competitiveness Review*, *30*(3), 289–314. doi:10.1108/CR-03-2019-0031

Dwivedi, Y. K., Hughes, L., Ismagilova, E., Aarts, G., Coombs, C., Crick, T., Duan, Y., Dwivedi, R., Edwards, J., Eirug, A., Galanos, V., Ilavarasan, P. V., Janssen, M., Jones, P., Kar, A. K., Kizgin, H., Kronemann, B., Lal, B., Lucini, B., & Williams, M. D. (2021). Artificial Intelligence (AI): Multidisciplinary perspectives on emerging challenges, opportunities, and agenda for research, practice and policy. *International Journal of Information Management*, *57*, 101994. doi:10.1016/j.ijinfomgt.2019.08.002

Dwivedi, Y. K., Hughes, L., Ismagilova, E., Aarts, G., Coombs, C., Crick, T., Duan, Y., Dwivedi, R., Edwards, J., Eirug, A., Galanos, V., Ilavarasan, P. V., Janssen, M., Jones, P., Kar, A. K., Kizgin, H., Kronemann, B., Lal, B., Lucini, B., & Williams, M. D. (2021). Artificial Intelligence (AI): Multidisciplinary perspectives on emerging challenges, opportunities, and agenda for research, practice and policy. *International Journal of Information Management*, *57*, 101994. doi:10.1016/j.ijinfomgt.2019.08.002

Enholm, I. M., Papagiannidis, E., Mikalef, P., & Krogstie, J. (2021). Artificial Intelligence and Business Value: A Literature Review. *Information Systems Frontiers*, *24*(5), 1709–1734. doi:10.1007/s10796-021-10186-w

Evdokimov, I., Kampouridis, M., & Papastylianou, T. (2023). Application Of Machine Learning Algorithms to Free Cash Flows Growth Rate Estimation. *Procedia Computer Science*, *222*, 529–538. doi:10.1016/j.procs.2023.08.191

Felsberger, A., Qaiser, F. H., Choudhary, A., & Reiner, G. (2020). The impact of Industry 4.0 on the reconciliation of dynamic capabilities: Evidence from the European manufacturing industries. *Production Planning and Control*, *33*(2–3), 277–300. doi:10.1080/09537287.2020.1810765

FrankenA.MantheiC.SenderekR.StichV. (2023). *Demands and challenges for SME regarding the human-centred implementation of innovative technologies and AI*. doi:10.15488/13491

Gaber, S., Ben-Harush, O., & Savir, A. (2017). Predicting HDD failures from compound SMART attributes. *Proceedings of the 10th ACM International Systems and Storage Conference*, (pp. 1–1). ACM. 10.1145/3078468.3081875

Ghobakhloo, M., & Ching, N. T. (2019). Adoption of digital technologies of smart manufacturing in SMEs. *Journal of Industrial Information Integration*, *16*, 100107. doi:10.1016/j.jii.2019.100107

Ghobakhloo, M., & Ng, T. C. (2019). Adoption of digital technologies of smart manufacturing in SMEs. *Journal of Industrial Information Integration*, *16*, 100107. doi:10.1016/j.jii.2019.100107

Giuggioli, G., & Pellegrini, M. M. (2023). Artificial intelligence as an enabler for entrepreneurs: A systematic literature review and an agenda for future research. *International Journal of Entrepreneurial Behaviour & Research*, *29*(4), 816–837. doi:10.1108/IJEBR-05-2021-0426

Gonzalez-Tamayo, L. A., Maheshwari, G., Bonomo-Odizzio, A., Herrera-Avilés, M., & Krauss-Delorme, C. (2023). Factors influencing small and medium size enterprises development and digital maturity in Latin America. *Journal of Open Innovation*, *9*(2), 100069. doi:10.1016/j.joitmc.2023.100069

Grooss, O. F. (2024). Digitalization of maintenance activities in small and medium-sized enterprises: A conceptual framework. *Computers in Industry*, *154*, 104039. doi:10.1016/j.compind.2023.104039

Hansen, E. B., & Bøgh, S. (2021). Artificial intelligence and internet of things in small and medium-sized enterprises: A survey. *Journal of Manufacturing Systems*, *58*, 362–372. doi:10.1016/j.jmsy.2020.08.009

Hansen, E. B., & Bøgh, S. (2021). Artificial intelligence and internet of things in small and medium-sized enterprises: A survey. *Journal of Manufacturing Systems*, *58*, 362–372. doi:10.1016/j.jmsy.2020.08.009

Hansen, E. B., & Bøgh, S. (2021). Artificial intelligence and internet of things in small and medium-sized enterprises: A survey. *Journal of Manufacturing Systems*, *58*, 362–372. doi:10.1016/j.jmsy.2020.08.009

Hildebrandt, M. (2020). Smart technologies. *Internet Policy Review*, *9*(4). doi:10.14763/2020.4.1531

Hossain, S. F. A., Nurunnabi, M., Hussain, K., & Saha, S. K. (2019). *Effects of variety-seeking intention by mobile phone usage on university students' academic performance*. Taylor & Francis. doi:10.1080/2331186X.2019.1574692

Hossain, S. F. A., Nurunnabi, M., Hussain, K., & Shan, X. (2020). Smartphone-based m-shopping behavior and innovative entrepreneurial tendency among women in emerging Asia. *International Journal of Gender and Entrepreneurship*, *12*(2), 173–189. doi:10.1108/IJGE-03-2019-0054

Hossain, S. F. A., Shan, X., Nurunnabi, M., Tushar, H., Mohsin, A. K. M., & Ahsan, F. T. (2021). Opportunities and challenges of m-learning during the COVID-19 pandemic: A mixed methodology approach. *E-Collaboration Technologies and Strategies for Competitive Advantage Amid Challenging Times*, 210-227.

Hossain, S. F. A., Xi, Z., & Hussain, K. (2020). *Ubiquitous role of social networking in driving M-commerce: Evaluating the use of mobile phones for online shopping and payment in the context of trust*. Taylor & Francis. doi:10.1177/2158244020939536

Iansiti, M., & Lakhani, K. R. (2020). Competing in the age of AI: How machine intelligence changes the rules of business. *Harvard Business Review*, *98*(1), 60–67.

Jayashree, S., Reza, M. N. H., Malarvizhi, C. A., & Mohiuddin, M. (2021). Industry 4.0 implementation and Triple Bottom Line sustainability: An empirical study on small and medium manufacturing firms. *Heliyon*, *7*(8), e07753. doi:10.1016/j.heliyon.2021.e07753 PMID:34430741

Kaplan, A., & Haenlein, M. (2019). Siri, Siri, in my hand: Who's the fairest in the land? On the interpretations, illustrations, and implications of artificial intelligence. *Business Horizons*, *62*(1), 15–25. doi:10.1016/j.bushor.2018.08.004

Kar, A. K. (2016). Bio inspired computing – A review of algorithms and scope of applications. *Expert Systems with Applications*, *59*, 20–32. doi:10.1016/j.eswa.2016.04.018

Kotios, D., Makridis, G., Fatouros, G., & Kyriazis, D. (2022). Deep learning enhancing banking services: A hybrid transaction classification and cash flow prediction approach. *Journal of Big Data*, *9*(1), 100. doi:10.1186/s40537-022-00651-x PMID:36213092

Kumar, M., Raut, R. D., Mangla, S. K., Ferraris, A., & Choubey, V. K. (2022). The adoption of artificial intelligence powered workforce management for effective revenue growth of micro, small, and medium scale enterprises (MSMEs). *Production Planning and Control*, 1–17. doi:10.1080/09537287.2022.2131620

Kusý, Š. (2021). Artificial intelligence as a tool in human research management—potential and current use. *Journal of HRM*, *24*(2).

Lim, S. (2023). *3 Types of Customer Insights That AI Will Change in 2021* [Blog]. Remesh. https://blog.remesh.ai/3-massive-ways-ai-is-changing-consumer-insights-in-2019

Love, J. H., & Roper, S. (2015). SME innovation, exporting and growth: A review of existing evidence. *International Small Business Journal*, *33*(1), 28–48. doi:10.1177/0266242614550190

Lu, X., Wijayaratna, K., Huang, Y., & Qiu, A. (2022). AI-enabled opportunities and transformation challenges for SMEs in the post-pandemic era: A review and research agenda. *Frontiers in Public Health*, *10*, 885067. doi:10.3389/fpubh.2022.885067 PMID:35570947

Masood, T., & Sonntag, P. (2020). Industry 4.0: Adoption challenges and benefits for SMEs. *Computers in Industry*, *121*, 103261. doi:10.1016/j.compind.2020.103261

Moeuf, A., Lamouri, S., Pellerin, R., Tamayo, S., Tobon-Valencia, E., & Eburdy, R. (2019). Identification of critical success factors, risks and opportunities of Industry 4.0 in SMEs. *International Journal of Production Research*, *58*(5), 1384–1400. doi:10.1080/00207543.2019.1636323

Mohsin, A. K., Hongzhen, L., & Hossain, S. F. A. (2021). *Impact of COVID-19 pandemic on consumer economy: Countermeasures analysis.* Taylor & Francis. doi:10.1177/21582440211008875

Müller, J. M., Buliga, O., & Voigt, K.-I. (2018). Fortune favors the prepared: How SMEs approach business model innovations in Industry 4.0. *Technological Forecasting and Social Change*, *132*, 2–17. doi:10.1016/j.techfore.2017.12.019

Ogawa, K., & Tanaka, T. (2013). The global financial crisis and small-and medium-sized enterprises in Japan: How did they cope with the crisis? *Small Business Economics*, *41*(2), 401–417. doi:10.1007/s11187-012-9434-z

Phuyal, S., Bista, D., & Bista, R. (2020). Challenges, opportunities and future directions of smart manufacturing: A state of art review. *Sustainable Futures : An Applied Journal of Technology, Environment and Society*, *2*, 100023. doi:10.1016/j.sftr.2020.100023

Qu, T., Lei, S. P., Wang, Z. Z., Nie, D. X., Chen, X., & Huang, G. Q. (2016). IoT-based real-time production logistics synchronization system under smart cloud manufacturing. *International Journal of Advanced Manufacturing Technology*, *84*(1–4), 147–164. doi:10.1007/s00170-015-7220-1

Ricci, R., Battaglia, D., & Neirotti, P. (2021). External knowledge search, opportunity recognition and industry 4.0 adoption in SMEs. *International Journal of Production Economics*, *240*, 108234. doi:10.1016/j.ijpe.2021.108234

Roblek, V., Meško, M., Pušavec, F., & Likar, B. (2021). The role and meaning of the digital transformation as a disruptive innovation on small and medium manufacturing enterprises. *Frontiers in Psychology, 12*, 592528. doi:10.3389/fpsyg.2021.592528 PMID:34177680

Selamat, M. A., & Windasari, N. A. (2021). Chatbot for SMEs: Integrating customer and business owner perspectives. *Technology in Society*, *66*, 101685. doi:10.1016/j.techsoc.2021.101685

Sezer, O. B., Gudelek, M. U., & Ozbayoglu, A. M. (2020). Financial time series forecasting with deep learning: A systematic literature review: 2005–2019. *Applied Soft Computing*, *90*, 106181. doi:10.1016/j.asoc.2020.106181

Shaik, M. (2023). Impact of artificial intelligence on marketing. *East Asian Journal of Multidisciplinary Research*, *2*(3), 993–1004. doi:10.55927/eajmr.v2i3.3112

Sjödin, D., Parida, V., Kohtamäki, M., & Wincent, J. (2020). An agile co-creation process for digital servitization: A micro-service innovation approach. *Journal of Business Research*, *112*, 478–491. doi:10.1016/j.jbusres.2020.01.009

Sklyar, A., Kowalkowski, C., Tronvoll, B., & Sörhammar, D. (2019). Organizing for digital servitization: A service ecosystem perspective. *Journal of Business Research*, *104*, 450–460. doi:10.1016/j.jbusres.2019.02.012

Suwaidi, F. A., Alshurideh, M., Kurdi, B. A., & Salloum, S. A. (2020). The Impact of Innovation Management in SMEs Performance: A Systematic review. In Advances in intelligent systems and computing (pp. 720–730). Springer. doi:10.1007/978-3-030-58669-0_64

Tekic, Z., Cosic, I., & Katalinic, B. (2019). Manufacturing and the Rise of Artificial Intelligence: Innovation Challenges. In B. Katalinic (Ed.), *DAAAM Proceedings* (1st ed., Vol. 1, pp. 0192–0196). DAAAM International Vienna. 10.2507/30th.daaam.proceedings.025

Tushar, H., & Sooraksa, N. (2023). Global employability skills in the 21st century workplace: A semi-systematic literature review. *Heliyon*, *9*(11), e21023. doi:10.1016/j.heliyon.2023.e21023 PMID:37954286

Vuong, B. N., Duy Tung, D., Hoa, N. D., Chau, N. T. N., & Tushar, H. (2020). An empirical assessment of organizational commitment and job performance: Vietnam small and medium-sized enterprises. *Journal of Asian Finance. Economics and Business*, *7*(6), 277–286.

Wang, Z., Shou, M., Wang, S., Dai, R., & Wang, K. (2019). An empirical study on the key factors of intelligent upgrade of small and medium-sized enterprises in China. *Sustainability (Basel)*, *11*(3), 619. doi:10.3390/su11030619

Wei, R., & Pardo, C. (2022). Artificial intelligence and SMEs: How can B2B SMEs leverage AI platforms to integrate AI technologies? *Industrial Marketing Management*, *107*, 466–483. doi:10.1016/j.indmarman.2022.10.008

Zhong, R. Y., Xu, X., Klotz, E., & Newman, S. T. (2017). Intelligent Manufacturing in the Context of Industry 4.0: A Review. *Engineering (Beijing)*, *3*(5), 616–630. doi:10.1016/J.ENG.2017.05.015

Žigienė, G., Rybakovas, E., & Alzbutas, R. (2019). Artificial intelligence based commercial risk management framework for SMEs. *Sustainability (Basel)*, *11*(16), 4501. doi:10.3390/su11164501

Chapter 14
Exploring AI and Smart Technologies in Entrepreneurship:
The Future of Business Strategies

Armana Hakim Nadi
https://orcid.org/0000-0003-3238-8217
Bangladesh University of Professionals, Bangladesh

Kazi Ayman Ahshan
https://orcid.org/0009-0008-6099-7865
The University of Adelaide, Australia

Krishna Paul
Laurentian University, Canada

Sadia Rahman
Bangladesh University of Professionals, Bangladesh

Dipta Paul
New York University, USA

ABSTRACT

The fusion of AI and smart tech is revolutionizing entrepreneurship, reshaping strategies, and driving innovation. This abstract explores their collaborative potential for a successful entrepreneurial future. Entrepreneurs use AI for data-driven decisions, predicting market trends with unmatched accuracy. The symbiotic relationship between entrepreneurship and smart technologies is reshaping strategies, fostering innovation, and driving economic growth. Entrepreneurs leverage blockchain, AI, IoT, and social media for global reach, facing challenges such as ethical concerns and the need for strategic integration to thrive in the evolving digital era. Challenges include ethical considerations and data security. Entrepreneurs must navigate these issues for responsible AI use. This abstract envisions a future where AI and smart tech are crucial collaborators. Entrepreneurs adept at utilizing these technologies can reshape markets and disrupt established models. Embracing this revolution is imperative for companies aspiring to thrive in future landscapes.

DOI: 10.4018/979-8-3693-1842-3.ch014

INTRODUCTION

In the era of technology, Artificial Intelligence (AI) is having a positive influence on entrepreneurship by encouraging people to apply their knowledge to actual events (Obschonka & Audretsch, 2020). Additionally, smart technology is replacing traditional methods in business production, marketing, and idea scaling, leading to creative strategies within the digital entrepreneurial business model. Entrepreneurs in the digital age are those who engage in procedures and activities primarily focused on using digital technology to supply goods and services, with very little involvement from the physical component (Abubakre, Zhou, & Zhou, 2020). However, boosting the prospects for growth-oriented entrepreneurship, AI developments simultaneously raise the potential associated with less ambitious entrepreneurship (Fossen & Sorgner, 2021). Implementing the effectiveness of technology in a business sounds like a straightforward approach. Before adopting smart technology, there are some key concerns that appear for enthusiastic modern entrepreneurs, including knowledge of technology, the polarization of social attitudes, information management, and the cost of switching (Raddey Kummitha, 2018). However, developing an effective business strategy with AI is challenging due to its dynamic approach and differentiation. Despite the issues, technology offers a valuable application for entrepreneurs to organize their businesses in an effective way. Artificial intelligence applications are known as a leading technology in the area of business. The utilization of smart technology allows the business process to make smarter, quicker decisions, which can enhance productivity as well as the profitability of the complete business operation. Furthermore, entrepreneurship and technological advancement are the driving forces behind the emerging field of digital entrepreneurship (Jafari-Sadeghi, Garcia-Perez, Candelo, & Couturier, 2021). The expression digital entrepreneurship describes the capacity to run a unique business that carries out business activities where either part or the entire entrepreneurial process is digitalized and succeeds with the aid of technology, computers, and virtual programs like cloud platforms, artificial intelligence, and social media (Liu, Xu, Wu, & Luo, 2023). Previously, businessmen analyzed the market based on their products and services; that was a daunting and time-consuming task. Modern technology has made it easier for startup businesses to research the market and compete among rivals by implementing innovative ideas. There are various industries and markets that have been amplified by smart technological business models, such as social media, e-commerce, software services, and electronic devices (Zaheer, Breyer, Dumay, & Enjeti, 2019). Notably, the digital revolution in business brings more accessibility, including in media, entertainment, retail, and accommodation. Digital entrepreneurship is rapidly expanding, with great potential for entrepreneurs who are able to take on challenges and embrace technological advancement. Nowadays, businessmen apply their business with blended methods; they have both physical ventures and internet-based business websites to make their products and services more accessible to the customer. Hence, a strategy to exploit AI is essential, while the goal is to accelerate the AI process in terms of business value (Borges, Laurindo, Spínola, Gonçalves, & Mattos, 2021). Organizations can improve their comprehension of customer behavior and crucial business areas by integrating AI into their business intelligence (BI) system (Bharadiya, 2022). As evidenced by Airbnb, Uber, and other innovative new business strategies where AI has been utilized and implemented, this revolutionary and briskly developing technology influences the creation of business strategies. Nevertheless, businesses are still struggling to integrate and deploy AI in their regular business activities. Consequently, a comprehensive understanding needs to be developed due to the lack of an integrated grasp of how AI technologies create value for companies and what kind of business advantage can be anticipated. According to the study, the most essential business strategy was done by mentors present at the event, giving new entrepreneurs enough support to help them develop apps, accelerate their creative ideas, and promote their first products (Kitsios & Kamariotou, 2023). Digital innovation competitions have generated a wide range of opportunities for young entrepreneurs. While established companies have already embraced technology, it is important to research the market with existing data and come up with innovative ideas in order to compete with rivals. Additionally, a successful business strategy requires an effective advertising plan with the objective of appealing to buyers. It is imperative that the application of AI and machine learning in business; the coordination of Information Technology (IT) and AI tools with business strategy; the association between AI, knowledge management, and decision-making processes; and the link between AI, service innovation, and value resulted in the creation of innovative methods and varieties of management practice (Kitsios & Kamariotou, 2021). Over several decades, advancements in production and other technologies, the introduction of new supplies and complex products requiring innovative processing methods, organizational strategies aiming to reduce costs, improve quality and dependability, and maximize profit, and concerns about social and sustainable goals as well as people's interactions with system components and the nature of work in the future have all contributed to changes in production processes (ElMaraghy, Monostori, Schuh, & ElMaraghy, 2021). Moreover, business is already being significantly impacted by AI, and this impact will increase in the future. AI will be utilized in business strategies that develop new goods and services, enhance decision-making, and automate more tasks.

The objectives of this study are to explore how AI and digital technology are utilized in entrepreneurship and how smart technology will change business strategy in the future.

LITERATURE REVIEW

The convergence of Artificial Intelligence (AI) and Smart Technologies is reshaping the landscape of modern entrepreneurship, ushering in a transformative era that influences fundamental concepts and redirects business tactics across various industries. This review delves into the existing literature, summarizing key findings from studies that explore the impact of this fusion on business strategy, providing insights into the future of entrepreneurial endeavors. Batistič and Laken's (2019) meticulous bibliometric analysis emerges as a cornerstone in the exploration of the historical evolution of big data and analytics. In doing so, the study lays a robust foundation for understanding the intricate relationship between these technologies and organizational performance. As we delve into the intricacies of this relationship, it becomes evident that this contextualization is indispensable for comprehending the role of AI in facilitating data-driven decision-making, a pivotal aspect that resonates with the trajectory of business strategies in the contemporary landscape. Building on this foundation, Croteau and Bergeron's (2001) investigation into the information technology trilogy, comprising business strategy, technological deployment, and organizational performance, emerges as a seminal work. By elucidating the interconnectedness of IT and business strategy, this study sets the stage for the seamless integration of AI into organizational processes. The implications of this integration are far-reaching, fostering a fertile ground for strategic advancements that are poised to redefine the entrepreneurial approach.

A forward-looking perspective is encapsulated in Culot et al.'s (2020) Delphi-based scenario analysis of Industry 4.0, forecasting the future of manufacturing. In the crucible of Industry 4.0, artificial intelligence and smart technologies are revealed as linchpins, integral to the metamorphosis of manufacturing processes. This metamorphosis aligns seamlessly with the imperatives of the entrepreneurial landscape, where innovation and efficiency stand as imperatives for sustainable growth. The exploration expands into the immersive realms of augmented reality (AR), virtual reality (VR), and mixed reality (MR) through Farshid et al.'s (2018) examination. This study illuminates the entrepreneurial opportunities embedded in these technologies, signaling a paradigm shift towards more engaging and interactive business strategies. In navigating the competitive terrain, entrepreneurs are prompted to be not just responsive but proactive in embracing technologies that redefine the customer experience and shape business tactics. Foroudi et al.'s (2018) investigation takes us deeper into the customer-centric dynamics influenced by smart technologies. As entrepreneurs strive to leverage AI to enhance customer interactions and satisfaction, understanding the nuanced implications becomes imperative. This study provides a critical lens through which entrepreneurs can optimize marketing strategies, fostering a dynamic and responsive approach to customer needs and preferences. Jarrahi's (2018) study examines the mutually beneficial relationship that exists between artificial intelligence and human decision-making in organizations. This study is a crucial resource for entrepreneurs who are having difficulty incorporating artificial intelligence into their operational frameworks. It highlights the ways in which artificial intelligence (AI) can support decision-making procedures, but it also highlights the importance of having a sophisticated grasp of how technology and human agency interact in organizational dynamics.

Navigating the complex terrain of digital transformation, Hanelt et al.'s (2020) systematic review becomes a compass for entrepreneurs. This comprehensive resource offers insights into the implications of digital transformation for strategy and organizational change. In the era of AI, entrepreneurs need to glean from this research the nuances of incorporating these technologies into their business models, fostering a culture of adaptability and resilience. Nižetić et al.'s (2020) deep dive into the opportunities, issues, and challenges of the Internet of Things (IoT) resonates strongly with entrepreneurs seeking to align their strategies with sustainability imperatives. The study provides a road map for responsibly integrating IoT technologies, emphasizing sustainability as a key component of the entrepreneurial narrative. Sustainability becomes a strategic imperative for long-term viability when it is woven into the fabric of business strategies. Paiola and Gebauer's (2020) focus on IoT technologies, digital servitization, and business model innovation in BtoB manufacturing firms provides a blueprint for entrepreneurs looking to leverage AI-driven IoT technologies for innovation. In the dynamic landscape of business models, this study showcases how technology can drive innovation, reshaping entrepreneurial strategies and positioning firms for sustained growth. In the financial technology (fintech) ecosystem, Palmié et al.'s (2020) overview illuminates the evolution and dynamics. Fintech, a crucible of rapid change, underscores the importance of agility and adaptation in entrepreneurial strategies. The study acts as a beacon for entrepreneurs navigating the digital landscape, emphasizing the need for continuous evolution to thrive in the ever-shifting financial landscape.

Collectively, these studies highlight how AI and smart technologies can revolutionize entrepreneurship, indicating a shift towards more flexible, data-driven, and customer-focused company models. Entrepreneurs armed with insights from these studies are actively shaping the future of entrepreneurship, moving beyond merely reacting to technological advancements. However, to ensure sustainable and ethical business practices, entrepreneurs must carefully consider the ethical, societal, and strategic implications of adopting these technologies, thereby contributing to a responsible and forward-thinking entrepreneurial landscape.

THE IMPACT OF SMART TECHNOLOGIES ON ENTREPRENEURSHIP

The global adoption of smart technology is speeding up the industrial revolution, like blockchain, artificial intelligence, and the Internet of Things (IoT) (Zhang & Lu, 2021). Technology systems are influencing business and changing the way that goes beyond entrepreneurship and innovation practices to impact culture, politics, and society (Si, Hall, Suddaby, Ahlstrom, & Wei, 2023). Hence, smart technology has been considered a blessing for start-up businesses, including IoT tracking devices able to monitor performance and customer behavior, blockchain technology ensuring more security, and AI solving more challenging problems. Apart from that, entrepreneurs are using social media to enhance business networking, information search, and raising money from a group of people through online platforms (Olanrewaju, Hossain, Whiteside, & Mercieca, 2020). It is not only improving the performance of businesses but also bringing desirable outcomes. Technology has greatly impacted entrepreneurship by making business easier and expanding more quickly and profitably than ever before. With relatively little initial investment, entrepreneurs may now launch firms for the advancement of digital technologies. For instance, an entrepreneur can now use a laptop or computer and a free website builder to launch an Internet business. Furthermore, the Internet provides essential forces for entrepreneurial activities, which play a vital role in economic growth (Tan & Li, 2022). However, existing data on the internet encourages entrepreneurs by providing information and assisting start-up businesses. Nowadays, digitalization is undoubtedly the most significant factor influencing innovation and entrepreneurship (Berger, Briel, Davidsson, & Kuckertz, 2021). The success of digital entrepreneurship depends on the understanding of technology and the way it is used to enhance innovation. Additionally, digital entrepreneurship involves awareness of technology and how to leverage it to stimulate creative ideas. The digital revolution and digital benefits on entrepreneurship, particularly the wider developmental advantages resulting from utilizing these technologies in the form of digital transformation. Even though AI and technology can improve entrepreneurial activity, complications come from this technological power (Chalmers, Mackenzie, & Carter, 2020). The entrepreneur's intention to accept modern technology is greatly influenced by various factors, including performance expectancy, openness, social influence, driven motivations, and generativity. On the other hand, uncertainty has a positive effect regarding the intention of accepting AI, while difficulties have a significant negative impact (Troise, Ben-Hafaïedh, Tani, & Yablonsky, 2022). Entrepreneurial dynamics are a challenge for managers and policymakers. In addition, technology and human capital affordances have reduced high-growth employment due to a lack of certain skills in the industry to spread technological advancement (Belitski, Korosteleva, & Piscitello, 2023). Despite the fact that government agencies and other public institutions have also been obligated by digitization to reconsider the law, rules, and policies concerning a range of matters, such as worker skills and training, consumer rights, intellectual property rights, data privacy and security, entrepreneurial funding, and economic growth (Nambisan, Wright, & Feldman, 2019). However, people are now completely dependent on technological products, including computers, smartphones, streaming services, consumer electronics, apps, and smart wearables (Huang, Wang, & Lai, 2022). Thus, entrepreneurship is interconnected in the fields of technology and innovation. Although technology has made business processes easier to reach customers globally, it has increased competition among entrepreneurs. Ultimately, embracing technology efforts to facilitate technology entrepreneurship leads to economic growth (Dutta Gupta & Guha Majumder, 2023). Even though businesses often have faced disruptive or challenging transitions because of technological changes, the ability of enterprises to automate current operations has increased as a result of technological progress (Bailey, Faraj, Hinds, Von Krogh, & Leonardi, 2019). There are challenges that arise in the entrepreneurial process, but the risks and challenges can be mitigated by properly implementing technology. Therefore, success in the future will be certain for entrepreneurs who can utilize technology effectively.

TECHNOLOGIES THAT ARE AVAILABLE FOR BUSINESS

In the era of a rapidly evolving world of business, technology has become a vital part of shaping the way an organization functions. The infusion of digital technology has revolutionized traditional business schemes and presented new ideas and challenges for operations across several industries. Implementation of technology has helped in operation, communication, and innovation. Cloud Computing stands tall as an on-demand access through the internet, offering organizations an innovative approach to enhancing business value. With cloud computing, individuals and organizations can gain network access to managed and scalable IT resources, such as servers, storage, and applications (Sunyaey,2020). This technology facilitates the integration of various services, fostering creativity and productivity. Cloud computing has become a promising technology in business through its multi-beneficial tools such as increased flexibility, scalability, agility, reduced costs, and therefore greater efficiency. This is why more and more organizations are shifting to incorporate their services with the cloud (Xue, 2016). When speaking about the most recent technology, Artificial Intelligence (AI) and Machine Learning (ML) have a robust series of usage in modern business models. These technologies reform the way businesses analyze data and make informed decisions based on automated results. Automation refers to AI systems tasked with replacing human work, while augmentation enhances human intelligence by providing insight that aids decision-making. Ai has applications dispersed across several diverse areas, such as marketing, production management, enterprise management, and customer service (Enholm, 2022). From predictive analytics and customer behavior analysis to chatbots and virtual assistants, AI is serving organizations to streamline operations, and personalized customer experiences, and gain a competitive edge from the rest of businesses. ML algorithms enable systems to learn from data patterns, thus, improving their accuracy and efficiency over time. They can analyze complex patterns, identify correlations, and make predictions or recommendations based on historical data (Bharadiya,2023).

While digital technologies make contemporary living simpler, they also provide new risks. Any company owner should be extremely concerned about cybersecurity (Reddy,2022). Protecting our network and data from unwanted access is a significant concern in today's hyper-connected society. A firewall is a hardware or software network security tool created for tracking, filtering, and handling incoming and outgoing network traffic in accordance with set security rules (Ahmed,2022). It essentially serves as a partition between a trustworthy internal network and unreliable external networks, like the Internet. To prevent unauthorized access, detect and avoid harmful activity, and protect the confidentiality and integrity of data, firewalls are essential. Firewalls are controlled by a company's security guidelines. Along with extra capabilities to stop contemporary threats, the Next Generation Firewall offers protection above and beyond that of a conventional firewall. It displays harmful activity from undesirable resources as well as any other patterns of record-collecting activity. Technologies for threat protection are simple to incorporate into the whole set of any protected program. This makes it simple for the security administrator to monitor and guard against security problems Ahmed,2022).

To sum up, the business IT environment is broad and dynamic, providing a wealth of tools and solutions for firms to be inventive and competitive. In addition to keeping current, adopting these technologies can open fresh opportunities for expansion and efficiency. Strategic integration of these technologies is essential for organizations navigating the digital era to fulfill consumer expectations, adjust to shifting market needs, and ensure long-term success in a connected and technologically advanced world. Businesses must be proactive in implementing these revolutionary technologies since the corporate environment is increasingly moving toward one that is technology-driven. For organizations to not only survive but also prosper in the digital age, cloud computing, AI, ML, and strong cybersecurity measures are more than simply trends. Organizations that strategically use these technologies will find themselves better positioned to deal with the difficulties and grab the possibilities that the digital era brings in this quickly changing ecosystem.

HOW BUSINESS STRATEGIES EVOLVED DUE TO TECHNOLOGY

Digital transformation involves firms adopting flexible organizational designs, driven by digital business ecosystems, and can be viewed through four perspectives: compartmentalized adaptation, systemic shift, and holistic co-evolution (Hanelt, Bohnsack, Marz, & Marante, 2020). Digital transformation involves the strategic use of digital technology to transform organizations, enhance customer experiences, and stay competitive in the digital age. It involves integrating digital tools, processes, and cultural shifts to drive innovation and efficiency.

AI in business has demonstrated that AI is capable of emulating people and doing tasks in a 'intelligent' manner because of the growing interest in AI among business strategies and practitioners, organizations are concentrating more on the adoption, use, and acceptance of AI technology in business, the role of data protection and ethics, the role of institutional support for marketing AI, as well as the labor market revolution and marketers' competencies (Vlačić, Corbo, Silva, & Dabić, 2021). Business tactics are being modified by AI technology, which enhances decision-making, innovation in products, interpersonal interaction, pricing, sales management, advertising, and personalized mobile marketing. Its mechanical, analytical, and intuitive types reshape workplaces, empowering organizations to explore cost, quality, or relationship advantages. Organizations are getting more cognizant that they can utilize big data and analytics (BDA) to analyze and organize enormous amounts of data to generate value for their business operations and workforce with the advent of more computational capability, machine learning especially deep learning through neural networks has become more widely applicable in business organizations (Batistič & Laken, 2019). Big data enables businesses to analyze competitors, forecast demand, manage inventory, improve logistics, and enhance supply chain efficiency, leading to cost savings, improved talent acquisition, and improved Human resources (HR) retention. Technological advancements in cloud computing and blockchain may enhance supply chain resilience by increasing visibility, corresponding to better anticipatory and adaptive capacities that have better access to real-time blockchain information and can improve daily flexibility in manufacturing, sourcing, and processing orders, as automated invoicing, shipping, and manufacturing systems may be replaced by blockchains, which share trusted transactions and tracking data (Pettit, Croxton, & Fiksel, 2019). Blockchain is a contemporary technology with the opportunity to build a groundwork for creating unprecedented business models of particular interest that eliminate intermediaries in an ecosystem of actors and those that foster indemnity over performance (Weking et al., 2019). Technologies such as the Internet of Things (IoT) are generating new opportunities as well as significant challenges for businesses companies are being forced to develop completely new business models and evolve from traditional product-centric approaches to (digitally-based) service-oriented ones (Paiola & Gebauer, 2020). Integrating IoT technologies, digital servitization, and business model innovation is revolutionizing the business world by connecting physical objects to the internet, IoT data collection and exchanges, leading to innovative approaches, increased customer engagement, and new revenue streams. Another technology, FinTech has revolutionized banking, payment, commerce, and financial investment by leveraging advancements in online payments, cryptocurrency, and artificial intelligence. This ecosystem has enabled disruptive innovations, increasing efficiency in financial markets and transactions for consumers, banks, and businesses. FinTech represents a system-level change, attracting new actors and convergent competencies, making it a relevant research context for studying disruptive innovation ecosystems (Palmié, Wincent, Parida, & Caglar, 2020). FinTech enhances financial efficiency, accessibility, and customer-centricity, revolutionizing money management, credit access, investment, and transaction processes, disrupting traditional institutions, and presenting new opportunities for businesses and consumers.

Although the significance of information technology on strategic alignment is becoming more widely recognized, there are still some issues that need to be resolved, such as how businesses use technology concerning their business strategies (Croteau & Bergeron, 2001). The compatibility between information technology (IT) and business strategy, or strategic alignment, remains an ongoing challenge for businesses across the world (Tallon, 2014).

Moreover, Big data and analytics (BDA) acts as an indicator in the constantly evolving business strategies, assisting decision-making of the massive quantities of information accessible. FinTech creates a financial services symphony by streamlining transactions and increasing accessibility, while AI, is the ultimate conductor that orchestrates efficiency, personalization, and innovation. In addition, blockchain provides the unwavering beat of confidence and security at the center of the movement of digital transformation. When combined, these technological advances transform industries that evolve business strategies and provide a dynamic picture of the contemporary business world.

A PROJECTION OF THE AVAILABLE SMART TECHNOLOGIES FOR ENTREPRENEURSHIP IN THE FUTURE

Smart technologies significantly aid the development of the relationship between digital transformation and entrepreneurship. Future entrepreneurship technologies that promote environmental sustainability, characterized by lower environmental impacts than traditional methods, aim to mitigate ecological challenges and support sustainable business practices such as cleantech for clean technology, environmental technologies, green technology or Greentech, environmentally sound technology, cleaner production technology, and climate-smart technology (Trapp & Kanbach, 2021). Eco-friendly strategies, or green technology, are growing progressively more essential to future business initiatives. It involves innovative approaches that include eco-friendly building materials, electric vehicles, renewable energy, waste reduction techniques, and energy-efficient appliances. These technologies encourage sustainable and economically profitable business entrepreneurship by corresponding consumer demand with sustainable environmental objectives. Due to the new technologies availability, it is not unreasonable that managers find it challenging to determine the difference between concepts of augmented reality and virtual reality to explore the different opportunities for future entrepreneurship and six distinct categories of reality and virtual reality are (1) reality; (2) augmented reality; (3) virtual reality; (4) mixed reality; (5) augmented virtuality; and (6) virtuality as a component of our actual reality or virtual reality continuum (Farshid, Paschen, Eriksson, & Kietzmann, 2018). Virtual and reality technologies will provide a wealth of opportunities for future businesses. By reducing the gap between the real and virtual worlds, augmented reality, virtual reality, mixed reality, and augmented virtuality enhance training, communication, product design, and consumer interactions. These smart technologies will encourage innovation by creating new products and services to support future entrepreneurship. As artificial intelligence (AI) has evolved, managers and employees have to adapt and modify while AI improves and becomes more effective over time to maintain a harmonious coexistence between humans and AI, human decision-makers need to upgrade their AI literacy consistently and this involves learning how to utilize and apply the latest advancements in AI, as well as utilizing their unique advantages in this collaboration, such as emotional intelligence, holistic intuition, and vision (Jarrahi, 2018). Retailers have embraced the concept of customer experience management, with many incorporating it into their business strategies as a consequence of consumers' growing adoption of smart technologies and practitioners' recognition of their influence on customers' shopping experiences (Foroudi, Gupta, Sivarajah, & Broderick, 2018). As an example, retail chains have invested significant investments in the introduction of self-service technologies, which include self-cash desks, informative touch points, interactive displays equipped with touch screens, digital signage, and mobile applications that work with Radio Frequency IDentification (RFID) tags, additionally, others have developed fully virtual stores where customers can utilize their phones to search for products and make purchases the interior of the store (Priporas, Stylos, & Fotiadis, 2017). The logistics sector can conveniently monitor driver movement, vehicle position, and delivery status through the Internet of Things (IoT) additionally enables effective inventory and warehouse management, smart location management systems, and automation of internal business procedures (Nižetić, Šolić, Artaza, & Patrono, 2020). The implementation of automated and intelligent systems will contribute to the progression of manufacturing to an advanced stage, referred to as smart manufacturing or intelligent manufacturing which leverages end-user data and information through cloud computing to accelerate the manufacturing of modified products for the future (Phuyal, Bista, & Bista, 2020). Utilizing cloud computing, this innovative approach accelerates the development of customized products by obtaining user data along with contributing to enhanced efficiency, technology provides ambitious entrepreneurs with distinct advantages in the constantly changing world of business. It provides a route to a more dynamic and customer-focused manufacturing process. The future of entrepreneurs can be recognized only by considering the various advanced technologies and their impact on multi-tier supplier-customer relations and parallel evolutions in adjacent industries, platform-based intermediaries, digital players entering the manufacturing space, and asset management tools (AMTs) bringing in non-manufacturing producers (Culot, Orzes, Sartor, & Nassimbeni, 2020).

THE DEVELOPMENT IN BUSINESS STRATEGIES DUE TO SMART TECHNOLOGIES

Because of the introduction of technology in businesses, the corporate sector has undergone a rapid change in its strategic implementation. This "digital revolution," also known as "digital transformation," has helped businesses improve consumer experiences, streamline corporate operations, and gain a competitive advantage. Businesses have considerable challenges in retaining their competitiveness and relevance in this era of fast technological innovation. A study of a survey of 280 Finnish small and medium-sized enterprises (SMEs) shows that a company's digital transformation alone cannot improve relationship performance; rather, it must be combined with smart technology to do this. This indicates that the link between digital transformation and relationship performance is entirely mediated by smart technology (Nasiri,2020). One important feature of this change is the rising benefit generated from the functional relationships maintained by smart technology. Today's businesses combine content across platforms, production systems, and infrastructures by integrating software and software pieces. Through the integration of smart technology into machines, this integration enables the development of intelligent management systems. These technologies enable unique functionality in goods and services, revolutionizing their creation, production, distribution, and consumption (Saunila,2019).

Faster innovation, more production, higher efficiency, and superior customer experiences are all brought about by digital technology. Recognizing the need for transformation, businesses must identify areas for change and develop a detailed strategy for achieving these changes. The advent of mobile technology, cloud-based storage options, learning algorithms, and big data technologies has increased digitalization and provided new opportunities for businesses (Khanom,2023). The emphasis on customer experience is one of the main forces behind technology's influence on corporate strategies. Customer experience is a crucial distinction for organizations in the digital era. Big data analytics and artificial intelligence are two examples of digital technologies that businesses may use to better understand consumer wants and preferences and personalize products and services appropriately (Khanom,2023). By using these tools, data scientists may mine massive volumes of produced data for insightful consumer information.

Digitization, which was originally used to describe the technical conversion of analog to digital information and processes, has grown into a larger notion (Loebbecke,2015). Organizations today use big data and sophisticated analytics techniques to glean valuable insights from enormous databases. Big data analytics play a critical part in supply chain management (SCM), logistics management (LM), and inventory management (IM), and is extremely important since it optimizes corporate operations by examining consumer behavior. The ability to analyze, store, and transmit data on a huge scale and at a cheap cost has the potential to alter many types of human labor linked with data and cognitive non-routine tasks (Maheshwari,2021). Deeper integration of big data applications in conventional value creation processes is made possible by sophisticated software, which enables machine-based interpretation of data and nearly autonomous decision-making. Data is gathered, mined, and used by organizations from a huge range of internal and external sources. By analyzing the data, it is possible to create an underlying trend in the market product and predict a futuristic demand for it. By favoring centralized manufacturing and lowering marginal costs in markets with high first-unit costs, economies of scale are further increased. This move toward centralized manufacturing is the result of increased process digitalization and the simplicity of large-scale data processing and analysis (Loebbecke,2015).

In summary, the growing digital revolution has altered corporate tactics and forced firms to change to the new environment. This transition is led by smart technology, digitization, and a focus on the customer experience. Through smart technological interventions, businesses can not only survive but also gain a competitive edge. The way forward is seizing the potential given by smart technology while negotiating the hurdles of remaining nimble, inventive, and competitive in the digital era.

LIMITATIONS OF IMPLEMENTING AI IN BUSINESS

The AI system can be designed to do anything that the human mind can and even surpass its capability (Wang,2021). While artificial intelligence (AI) has many benefits for businesses, it also has several drawbacks and difficulties. For businesses to choose wisely when implementing and deploying AI technology, they must be aware of these limits. One of the most serious drawbacks of artificial intelligence (AI) is its vulnerability to manipulation. AI systems are completely programmable, leaving them subject to manipulation by anyone with the necessary information while being created to follow protocols and evolve autonomously in response to specified situations. Because AI technology is designed to secure data, it may be easily modified to serve purposes other than those for which it was designed. This poses a severe danger to the technology's ability to do its intended job. Because AI systems may unintentionally help create the same risks they are meant to stop, this fundamental weakness compromises cybersecurity (Ansari,2022). Additionally, AI's limits are made clear by the fact that it cannot take the place of human intuition and flexibility. Even while AI is designed to do certain jobs, it may struggle to identify threats that are almost indistinguishable from valid ones, exposing businesses to hazards. Cyber dangers, such as complex viruses and malware, are always changing, which raises difficulties for AI systems that might not be able to keep up with them. This limitation prompts questions about how well AI can deliver all-inclusive cybersecurity solutions (Ansari,2022).

A further obstacle to mainstream acceptance of AI technology is its complexity and expensive implementation costs. The technology is inaccessible to businesses that do not have the competence to fully utilize its functions because it takes significant knowledge and resources for operation. As a result, only a limited number of people and organizations can successfully use AI's promise for data security due to its high implementation costs (Ansari,2022). Due to financial restrictions, only a small number of businesses can afford to deploy AI, putting the remainder at greater risk of cybersecurity risks. This creates a digital divide. The difficulty and limited value of AI in guaranteeing data security highlight the necessity to solve both technological flaws and the cost issues related to its implementation. To sum up, while AI shows promise in bolstering cybersecurity efforts, its manipulation susceptibility, inherent limitations in threat detection, and high implementation costs make careful consideration and ongoing technological advancements necessary to fully realize its potential safely and inclusively.

AI decision-making autonomy raises fundamental ethical issues that have historically been within the control of people. Due to serious ethical problems, the growing use of AI in business requires attention. The difficulties involved in adopting AI are highlighted by high-profile events. As AI systems operate as opaque "black boxes," limiting responsibility for biases or errors, transparency, and bias emerge as important ethical problems. AI systems can also amplify social prejudices that are present in training data. To enable appropriate AI adoption in business operations, managers and researchers must pay close attention to these concerns (Sison, 2023).

Modern marketing is becoming more automated, data-driven, and intelligent. Technology development has continually led to longitudinal shifts in the development of marketing, and it has become clear that marketing and artificial intelligence (AI) can work together to make a difference (Chintalapati, 2022). Although artificial intelligence in marketing offers unmatched insights into customer behavior, it is unable to comprehend the motives and goals of people. AI weakens meaningful ties between marketers and their customers while increasing efficiency, automation, and digital interactions. The technology's widespread use also makes users more susceptible to algorithm changes, which leads to power disparities. The requirement for a balanced strategy that prioritizes human connections and trust to build long-lasting relationships with clients is highlighted by the fact that marketers who excessively rely on technological platforms are more vulnerable to negative effects from algorithm adjustments (Kozinets,2021). Biased AI results may damage the reputation of the organizations they influence, and in some circumstances, they have led to financial losses and hefty fines (Elholm, 2022).

Addressing these difficulties will need a balanced strategy that prioritizes not only scientific advances in AI but also ethical concerns, transparency, and the importance of human interactions. A dedication to responsible and inclusive technology deployment should serve as the foundation for AI adoption. Unlocking the full potential of this game-changing technology while minimizing its inherent hazards requires organizations to manage the challenges of AI implementation with care.

CONCLUSION

In conclusion, the symbiotic relationship between entrepreneurship and smart technologies is undeniably reshaping business strategies, fostering innovation, and propelling economic growth. The transformative impact of smart technologies on entrepreneurship is profound, with key innovations such as blockchain, artificial intelligence (AI), and the Internet of Things (IoT) at the forefront of this entrepreneurial revolution. As the global adoption of smart technology accelerates, entrepreneurs are embracing and leveraging IoT, blockchain, and AI to monitor performance, enhance security, and innovate. Social media has become a vital tool for networking and fundraising, expanding the reach of start-up businesses globally. The digitalization wave facilitates easier business launches with minimal investments, making the Internet a crucial force for entrepreneurial activities. However, embracing technology brings forth challenges, with factors like performance expectancy and openness influencing entrepreneurs' intentions. Cloud computing, AI, and machine learning play pivotal roles in revolutionizing business operations, offering scalable IT resources, enhancing flexibility and efficiency, and empowering organizations to analyze data patterns, make informed decisions, and streamline operations. Despite the promises of AI, challenges and limitations persist, including vulnerability to manipulation, high implementation costs, and the inability to replace human intuition. Ethical concerns, such as bias and transparency in AI decision-making, demand careful attention. The intertwining of marketing and AI raises questions about the potential loss of human connections and the need for a balanced approach. The evolving business landscape, driven by digital technologies, has prompted strategic shifts, with digital transformation involving the integration of digital tools, processes, and cultural shifts to drive innovation and efficiency. AI, big data analytics, and blockchain have reshaped supply chain management, logistics, and inventory management, optimizing operations and fostering cost savings.

In the future, emerging smart technologies will be inextricably linked to the future of entrepreneurship. The environment, augmented reality, and virtual reality are all poised to play pivotal roles. AI, IoT, and digital servitization will continue to disrupt industries by connecting physical objects to the internet, improving customer engagement, and generating new revenue streams. To navigate this ever-changing technological landscape, businesses must adopt a proactive stance. Strategic integration of cloud computing, AI, machine learning, and robust cybersecurity measures is essential for success. The convergence of technological advances, entrepreneurship, and responsible implementation will determine how businesses thrive in the digital era. Entrepreneurs who embrace technology effectively, address ethical considerations, and navigate challenges are poised for sustained success in the dynamic landscape of the future. As the digital revolution continues, the ability to leverage smart technologies strategically will be the cornerstone of entrepreneurial resilience and prosperity.

REFERENCES

Aboulilah, H. M. A. E., Hossain, S. F. A., Vuong, B. N., & Jebril, T. (2022). Exploring the Relationship between WeChat Usage and E-purchase Intention During the COVID-19 Pandemic Among University Students in China. *SAGE Open*, *12*(4), 21582440221139447. doi:10.1177/21582440221139447 PMID:36466966

Abubakre, M., Zhou, Y., & Zhou, Z. (2020). The impact of information technology culture and personal innovativeness in information technology on digital entrepreneurship success. *Information (Basel)*.

Ansari, M. F., Dash, B., Sharma, P., & Yathiraju, N. (2022). The Impact and Limitations of Artificial Intelligence in Cybersecurity: A Literature Review. *International Journal of Advanced Research in Computer and Communication Engineering*, *11*(9). doi:10.17148/IJARCCE.2022.11912

Bailey, D., Faraj, S., Hinds, P., Von Krogh, G., & Leonardi, P. (2019). Special issue of Organization Science: Emerging technologies and organizing. *Organization Science*, *30*(3), 642–646. doi:10.1287/orsc.2019.1299

Batistič, S., & Laken, P. V. (2019). *History, Evolution and Future of Big Data and Analytics: A Bibliometric Analysis of Its Relationship to Performance in Organizations.* Wiley. doi:10.1111/1467-8551.12340

Belitski, M., Korosteleva, J., & Piscitello, L. (2023). Digital affordances and entrepreneurial dynamics: New evidence from European regions. *Technovation*, *119*, 102–442. doi:10.1016/j.technovation.2021.102442

Berger, E. S., Briel, F. V., Davidsson, P., & Kuckertz, A. (2021). Digital or not – The future of entrepreneurship and innovation: Introduction to the special issue. *Journal of Business Research*, *125*, 436–442. doi:10.1016/j.jbusres.2019.12.020

Bharadiya, J. P. (2022). Driving Business Growth with Artificial Intelligence and Business Intelligence. *INTERNATIONAL JOURNAL OF COMPUTER SCIENCE AND TECHNOLOGY (IJCST)*, *6*(4), 28-44. http://www.ijcst.com.pk/IJCST/article/view/232

Bharadiya, J. P. (2023). Machine Learning and AI in Business Intelligence: Trends and Opportunities. [IJC]. *International Journal of Computer*, *48*(1), 123–134. https://ijcjournal.org/index.php/InternationalJournalOfComputer/article/view/2087

Borges, A. F., Laurindo, F. J., Spínola, M. M., Gonçalves, R. F., & Mattos, C. A. (2021). The strategic use of artificial intelligence in the Digital Era: Systematic literature review and future research directions. *International Journal of Information Management*, *57*, 102–225. doi:10.1016/j.ijinfomgt.2020.102225

Chalmers, D., Mackenzie, N. G., & Carter, S. (2020). *Artificial Intelligence and Entrepreneurship: Implications for Venture Creation in the Fourth Industrial Revolution*. Sage. doi:10.1177/1042258720934581

Chintalapati, S., & Pandey, S. K. (2022). Artificial intelligence in marketing: A systematic literature review. *International Journal of Market Research*, *64*(1), 38–68. doi:10.1177/14707853211018428

Croteau, A. M., & Bergeron, F. (2001). *An information technology trilogy: business strategy, technological deployment and organizational performance*. Science Direct. doi:10.1016/S0963-8687(01)00044-0

Culot, G., Orzes, G., Sartor, M., & Nassimbeni, G. (2020). The future of manufacturing: A Delphi-based scenario analysis on Industry 4.0. *Technological Forecasting and Social Change, 157*. doi:10.1016/j.techfore.2020.120092

Dutta Gupta, S., & Guha Majumder, M. (2023). Digital transformation, digital entrepreneurship, and economy: A cross-country analysis using moderated mediation modeling technique. *India Studies in Business and Economics*, 47-70. doi:10.1007/978-981-99-4063-9_3

ElMaraghy, H., Monostori, L., Schuh, G., & ElMaraghy, W. (2021). Evolution and future of manufacturing systems. *CIRP Annals*, *70*(2), 635–658. doi:10.1016/j.cirp.2021.05.008

Emmanuel, C. P., Qin, S., Hossain, S. F. A., & Hussain, K. (2022). Factors influencing social-media-based entrepreneurship prospect among female students in China. *Heliyon*, *8*(12), e12041. doi:10.1016/j.heliyon.2022.e12041 PMID:36483305

Enholm, I. M., Papagiannidis, E., Mikalef, P., & Krogstie, J. (2022). Artificial Intelligence and Business Value: A Literature Review. *Information Systems Frontiers*, *24*(5), 1709–1734. doi:10.1007/s10796-021-10186-w

Enholm, I. M., Papagiannidis, E., Mikalef, P., & Krogstie, J. (2022). Artificial Intelligence and Business Value: A Literature Review. *Information Systems Frontiers*, *24*(5), 1709–1734. doi:10.1007/s10796-021-10186-w

Farshid, M., Paschen, J., Eriksson, T., & Kietzmann, J. (2018). *Go boldly!: Explore augmented reality (AR), virtual reality (VR), and mixed reality (MR) for business*. Retrieved from doi:10.1016/j.bushor.2018.05.009

Foroudi, P., Gupta, S., Sivarajah, U., & Broderick, A. (2018). Investigating the effects of smart technology on customer dynamics and customer experience. Retrieved from doi:10.1016/j.chb.2017.11.014

Fossen, F. M., & Sorgner, A. (2021). Digitalization of work and entry into entrepreneurship. *Journal of Business Research, 125*, 548–563. doi:10.1016/j.jbusres.2019.09.019

Hanelt, A., Bohnsack, R., Marz, D., & Marante, C. A. (2020). *A Systematic Review of the Literature on Digital Transformation: Insights and Implications for Strategy and Organizational Change*. Science Direct. doi:10.1111/joms.12639

Hossain, S. F. A. (2019). Social networking and its role in media entrepreneurship: Evaluating the use of mobile phones in the context of online shopping–A review. [JMME]. *Journal of Media Management and Entrepreneurship*, *1*(1), 73–86. doi:10.4018/JMME.2019010105

Hossain, S. F. A., Nurunnabi, M., Hussain, K., & Saha, S. K. (2019). Effects of variety-seeking intention by mobile phone usage on university students' academic performance. *Cogent Education*, *6*(1), 1574692. doi:10.1080/2331186X.2019.1574692

Hossain, S. F. A., Nurunnabi, M., Hussain, K., & Shan, X. (2020). Smartphone-based m-shopping behavior and innovative entrepreneurial tendency among women in emerging Asia. *International Journal of Gender and Entrepreneurship*, *12*(2), 173–189. doi:10.1108/IJGE-03-2019-0054

Hossain, S. F. A., Xi, Z., Nurunnabi, M., & Hussain, K. (2020). Ubiquitous role of social networking in driving M-Commerce: Evaluating the use of mobile phones for online shopping and payment in the context of trust. *SAGE Open*, *10*(3), 2158244020939536. doi:10.1177/2158244020939536

Huang, T., Wang, Y., & Lai, H. (2022). What drives internet entrepreneurial intention to use technology products? An investigation of technology product imagination disposition, social support, and motivation. *Frontiers in Psychology*, *13*, 829256. doi:10.3389/fpsyg.2022.829256 PMID:35369240

Jafari-Sadeghi, V., Garcia-Perez, A., Candelo, E., & Couturier, J. (2021). Exploring the impact of digital transformation on technology entrepreneurship and technological market expansion: The role of technology readiness, exploration and exploitation. *Journal of Business Research*, *124*, 100–111. doi:10.1016/j.jbusres.2020.11.020

Jarrahi, M. H. (2018). *Artificial intelligence and the future of work: Human-AI symbiosis in organizational decision making*. Science Direct. doi:10.1016/j.bushor.2018.03.007

Kaçar, I. G. (2021). The impact of online and face-to-face peer feedback on pre-service teachers in EFL academic writing. In *Design Solutions for Adaptive Hypermedia Listening Software* (pp. 124–163). IGI Global. doi:10.4018/978-1-7998-7876-6.ch007

Khanom, M. T. (2023). Business Strategies in The Age of Digital Transformation. *The Journal of Business*, *8*(01), 28–35.

Kitsios, F., & Kamariotou, M. (2021). Artificial intelligence and business strategy towards digital transformation: A research agenda. *Sustainability (Basel)*, *13*(4), 20–25. doi:10.3390/su13042025

Kitsios, F., & Kamariotou, M. (2023). Digital innovation and entrepreneurship transformation through open data hackathons: Design strategies for successful start-up settings. *International Journal of Information Management*, *69*, 102–472. doi:10.1016/j.ijinfomgt.2022.102472

Kozinets, R. V., & Gretzel, U. (2021). Commentary: Artificial Intelligence: The Marketer's Dilemma. *Journal of Marketing*, *85*(1), 156–159. doi:10.1177/0022242920972933

Liu, W., Xu, Y., Wu, C., & Luo, Y. (2023). Fortune favors the experienced: Entrepreneurs' internet-era imprint, digital entrepreneurship and venture capital. *Information Processing & Management*, *60*(4), 103406. doi:10.1016/j.ipm.2023.103406

Loebbecke, C., & Picot, A. (2015). Reflections on societal and business model transformation arising from digitization and big data analytics: A research agenda. *The Journal of Strategic Information Systems*, *24*(3), 149–157. doi:10.1016/j.jsis.2015.08.002

Maheshwari, S., Gautam, P., & Jaggi, C. K. (2021). Role of Big Data Analytics in supply chain management: Current trends and future perspectives. *International Journal of Production Research*, *59*(6), 1875–1900. doi:10.1080/00207543.2020.1793011

Mohsin, A. K. M., Hongzhen, L., & Hossain, S. F. A. (2021). Impact of COVID-19 pandemic on consumer economy: Countermeasures analysis. *SAGE Open*, *11*(2), 21582440211008875. doi:10.1177/21582440211008875

Nambisan, S., Wright, M., & Feldman, M. (2019). The digital transformation of innovation and entrepreneurship: Progress, challenges and key themes. *Research Policy*, *48*(8), 103–773. doi:10.1016/j.respol.2019.03.018

Nasiri, M., Ukko, J., Saunila, M., & Rantala, T. (2020). Managing the digital supply chain: The role of smart technologies. *Technovation*, *96*, 102121. doi:10.1016/j.technovation.2020.102121

Nižetić, S., Šolić, P., Artaza, D. L., & Patrono, L. (2020). *Internet of Things (IoT): Opportunities, issues and challenges towards a smart and sustainable future*. Science Direct. doi:10.1016/j.jclepro.2020.122877

Obschonka, M., & Audretsch, D. B. (2020). Artificial intelligence and big data in entrepreneurship: A new era has begun. *Small Business Economics*, *55*(3), 529–539. https://link.springer.com/article/10.1007/s11187-019-00202-4. doi:10.1007/s11187-019-00202-4

Olanrewaju, A. T., Hossain, M. A., Whiteside, N., & Mercieca, P. (2020). Social media and entrepreneurship research: A literature review. *International Journal of Information Management*, *50*, 90–110. doi:10.1016/j.ijinfomgt.2019.05.011

Paiola, M., & Gebauer, H. (2020). *Internet of things technologies, digital servitization and business model innovation in BtoB manufacturing firms*. Science Direct. doi:10.1016/j.indmarman.2020.03.009

Palmié, M., Wincent, J., Parida, V., & Caglar, U. (2020). *The evolution of the financial technology ecosystem: An introduction and agenda for future research on disruptive innovations in ecosystems*. Science Direct. doi:10.1016/j.techfore.2019.119779

Pettit, T. J., Croxton, K. L., & Fiksel, J. (2019). *The Evolution of Resilience in Supply Chain Management: A Retrospective on Ensuring Supply Chain Resilience*. Science Direct. doi:10.1111/jbl.12202

Phuyal, S., Bista, D., & Bista, R. (2020). *Challenges, Opportunities and Future Directions of Smart Manufacturing: A State of Art Review*. Science Direct. doi:10.1016/j.sftr.2020.100023

Priporas, C. V., Stylos, N., & Fotiadis, A. K. (2017). *Generation Z consumers' expectations of interactions in smart retailing: A future agenda*. Science Direct. doi:10.1016/j.chb.2017.01.058

Raddey Kummitha, R. K. (2018). Entrepreneurial urbanism and technological panacea: Why Smart City planning needs to go beyond corporate visioning? *Technological Forecasting and Social Change*, *137*, 330–339. doi:10.1016/j.techfore.2018.07.010

Saunila, M., Nasiri, M., Ukko, J., & Rantala, T. (2019). Smart technologies and corporate sustainability: The mediation effect of corporate sustainability strategy. *Computers in Industry*, *108*, 178–185. doi:10.1016/j.compind.2019.03.003

Si, S., Hall, J., Suddaby, R., Ahlstrom, D., & Wei, J. (2023). Technology, entrepreneurship, innovation and social change in digital economics. *Technovation*, *119*, 102–484. doi:10.1016/j.technovation.2022.102484

Sison, A., Ferrero, I., García Ruiz, P., & Kim, T. W. (2023). Editorial: Artificial intelligence (AI) ethics in business. *Frontiers in Psychology*, *14*, 1258721. doi:10.3389/fpsyg.2023.1258721 PMID:37771802

Sunyaev, A. (2020). Cloud Computing. In *Internet Computing*. Springer. doi:10.1007/978-3-030-34957-8_7

Tallon, P. P. (2014). *A Process-Oriented Perspective on the Alignment of Information Technology and Business Strategy*. Taylor & Francis. doi:10.2753/MIS0742-1222240308

Tan, Y., & Li, X. (2022). The impact of internet on entrepreneurship. *International Review of Economics & Finance*, *77*, 135–142. doi:10.1016/j.iref.2021.09.016

Trapp, C., & Kanbach, D. K. (2021). *Green entrepreneurship and business models: Deriving green technology business model archetypes*. Science Direct. doi:10.1016/j.jclepro.2021.126694

Troise, C., Ben-Hafaïedh, C., Tani, M., & Yablonsky, S. A. (2022). Guest editorial: New technologies and entrepreneurship: exploring entrepreneurial behavior in the digital transformation era. *International Journal of Entrepreneurial Behaviour & Research*, *28*(5), 1129–1137. doi:10.1108/IJEBR-08-2022-999

Vlačić, B., Corbo, L., Silva, S. C., & Dabić, M. (2021). *The evolving role of artificial intelligence in marketing: A review and research agenda.* Science Direct. doi:10.1016/j.jbusres.2021.01.055

Vuong, B. N., Tushar, H., & Hossain, S. F. A. (2023). The effect of social support on job performance through organizational commitment and innovative work behavior: Does innovative climate matter? *Asia-Pacific Journal of Business Administration*, *15*(5), 832–854. doi:10.1108/APJBA-06-2021-0256

Wang, J. (2021). Is artificial intelligence capable of understanding? An analysis based on philosophical hermeneutics. *Cultura e Scuola*, *4*(3), 135–146. doi:10.1177/20966083211056405

Weking, J., Mandalenakis, M., Hein, A., Hermes, S., Böhm, M., & Krcmar, H. (2019). *The impact of blockchain technology on business models – a taxonomy and archetypal patterns.* Springer. https://link.springer.com/article/10.1007/s12525-019-00386-3

Xue, C. T. S., & Xin, F. T. W. (2016). Benefits and Challenges of the Adoption of Cloud Computing in Business. [IJCCSA]. *International Journal on Cloud Computing: Services and Architecture*, *6*(6), 1–15. doi:10.5121/ijccsa.2016.6601

Zaheer, H., Breyer, Y., Dumay, J., & Enjeti, M. (2019). Straight from the horse's mouth: Founders' perspectives on achieving 'traction' in digital start-UPS. *Computers in Human Behavior*, *95*, 262–274. doi:10.1016/j.chb.2018.03.002

Zhang, C., & Lu, Y. (2021). Study on artificial intelligence: The state of the art and future prospects. *Journal of Industrial Information Integration*, *23*, 100–224. doi:10.1016/j.jii.2021.100224

Chapter 15
Ethical Imperatives and Frameworks for Responsible AI Adoption in Digital Entrepreneurship

Nipunika Shahid
https://orcid.org/0000-0001-9340-8926
Christ University, India

Madan Singh
Christ University, India

Sujata Chauhan
Dronacharya Government College, Gurgaon, India

ABSTRACT

This study explores ethical dimensions in AI adoption for digital entrepreneurship. Thematic analysis highlights transparency, fairness, and accountability. Findings recommend comprehensive ethical guidelines, inclusive decision-making, and robust accountability mechanisms. Practical implications extend to digital ventures, policymakers, and educators. Future research may delve into industry-specific nuances, cross-cultural analyses, and the longitudinal impact of ethical frameworks, contributing significantly to responsible AI adoption discourse in digital entrepreneurship.

INTRODUCTION

The relentless pace of technological advancement has propelled Artificial Intelligence (AI) into the forefront of digital entrepreneurship, permeating diverse sectors and reshaping the very fabric of business operations. The integration of AI technologies has become a pervasive force, offering unprecedented opportunities for innovation, efficiency, and competitive advantage. However, with this transformative

DOI: 10.4018/979-8-3693-1842-3.ch015

power comes an ethical imperative that demands careful consideration and principled adoption (Thakur, 2024) (Wamba, 2022). This introduction sets the stage for an in-depth exploration of the ethical imperatives and frameworks crucial for the responsible adoption of AI in the context of digital entrepreneurship. In the evolving landscape of technological evolution, ethical considerations play a pivotal role in steering the trajectory of innovation. As AI becomes increasingly entwined with entrepreneurial ventures, it is imperative to scrutinize the ethical dimensions inherent in its deployment. This research embarks on a nuanced examination of the ethical landscape, aiming to unravel the intricacies of responsible AI adoption in the digital entrepreneurship domain. At the heart of this exploration lies an acknowledgment of the profound significance of ethical considerations in the ongoing technological evolution (Dennehy et al., 2023) (Shore, 2022). The intersection of AI and entrepreneurship necessitates a delicate balance between harnessing the potential of cutting-edge technologies and ensuring that these advancements align with enduring ethical principles. The consequences of overlooking ethical dimensions in AI adoption are not merely theoretical; they bear tangible implications for stakeholder trust, societal well-being, and the sustained success of digital ventures. The central theme of the chapter is the imperative need for responsible AI adoption in digital entrepreneurship. Responsible AI adoption encompasses a multifaceted commitment to ethical principles, transparency, fairness, and a profound understanding of the societal impact of AI technologies. By laying the groundwork for a comprehensive exploration of ethical imperatives (Nguyen et al., 2023), this research seeks to contribute to the burgeoning discourse surrounding the ethical deployment of AI in the entrepreneurial landscape. As we navigate the intricate intersections of technology and ethics, it becomes evident that the responsible integration of AI is not only a moral obligation but a strategic imperative for sustainable and socially conscious digital entrepreneurship (Vogl, Rötzel, & Homes (2022)(Widayanti, & Meria (2023)

BACKGROUND

The dynamic evolution of Artificial Intelligence (AI) stands as a paradigm-shifting force within the realm of digital entrepreneurship, ushering in unparalleled prospects for innovation and operational efficiency. As businesses increasingly integrate sophisticated AI technologies, a critical focus on the ethical dimensions of this adoption becomes imperative. This chapter aspires to furnish a comprehensive background, specifically honing in on the ethical imperatives and intricate frameworks requisite for the judicious incorporation of AI in the landscape of digital entrepreneurship. Embedded within this exploration is a profound acknowledgment of the moral obligation to align technological advancements with enduring ethical principles, recognizing that ethical missteps not only jeopardize reputational standing but also wield tangible threats to stakeholder trust and societal welfare. Anchored in a broader context of ethical considerations governing technological evolution, the study adeptly draws upon established ethical frameworks such as utilitarianism, deontology, and virtue ethics, furnishing a meticulously structured lens for the nuanced analysis and guidance of ethically sound AI adoption (Akter et al., 2022)(Richey Jr, Chowdhury, Davis-Sramek, Giannakis & Dwivedi 2023). Navigating through the labyrinth of regulatory complexities, the chapter systematically addresses governance challenges encountered by entrepreneurs as they traverse diverse regulatory landscapes. Particular emphasis is accorded to the intricate concerns surrounding bias and fairness in the crucible of AI-driven decision-making, underscoring the indispensable need for strategic interventions to mitigate bias and ensure equitable outcomes (Kumar et al., 2023) (Misra, Sharma, Gupta, & Das (2023)

Moreover, the study unfurls the tapestry of stakeholder perspectives, encompassing the diverse vantage points of entrepreneurs, employees, customers, and regulatory entities. This inclusive lens provides a holistic panorama of ethical considerations embedded within the intricate fabric of the digital entrepreneurial ecosystem. Recognizing the pivotal role of education and training, the chapter meticulously probes into the core competencies and knowledge domains essential for entrepreneurs to adeptly navigate the ethical challenges entwined with AI adoption, thereby fostering the development of a corporate culture that steadfastly upholds responsible AI practices(Saura, Ribeiro-Soriano, & Palacios-Marqués 2022) The narrative crescendos with a compelling showcase of real-world case studies, offering practical illustrations that spotlight instances wherein ethical AI practices have been successfully implemented. These case studies serve as both a testament to ethical viability and a wellspring of invaluable insights and lessons for entrepreneurs navigating the complex terrain of ethical considerations in the dynamic and ever-evolving sphere of digital entrepreneurship.

Aim of Study: To systematically investigate and elucidate the ethical imperatives and frameworks guiding the responsible adoption of Artificial Intelligence (AI) in the domain of digital entrepreneurship.

Significance of Study: This research holds significance by providing invaluable insights into how ethical considerations and frameworks impact the integration of AI in digital entrepreneurship, contributing to the development of ethical practices, fostering stakeholder trust, and guiding policymakers and entrepreneurs towards responsible and sustainable technological adoption.

Problem Statement: Despite the pervasive integration of Artificial Intelligence (AI) in digital entrepreneurship, a gap exists in understanding the depth of ethical considerations guiding its adoption, potentially leading to challenges in stakeholder trust, long-term sustainability, and the absence of a comprehensive regulatory landscape, necessitating a focused investigation into the ethical imperatives and frameworks surrounding AI adoption in this context.

Future Scope of Study: The findings from this study could pave the way for future research endeavors exploring dynamic ethical considerations in emerging AI technologies, fostering the development of updated regulatory frameworks, and enabling longitudinal analyses to track the evolution of responsible AI adoption in digital entrepreneurship. Additionally, the insights generated may contribute to the formulation of educational programs aimed at equipping entrepreneurs with the requisite ethical competencies for navigating the evolving AI landscape.

LITERATURE REVIEW

AI covers a broad range of techniques, such as, "machine learning, deep learning, reinforcement learning, natural language processing, computer vision, robotics, and expert systems", among others. These technologies enable AI systems to process and analyze vast amounts of data, recognize patterns, and make predictions or decisions based on the relevant existing information (Thakur, 2024).

The literature surrounding the integration of Artificial Intelligence (AI) in the realm of digital entrepreneurship reflects a rapidly evolving landscape marked by both promise and ethical complexities. Ethical considerations in the adoption of AI technologies have become increasingly salient, necessitating a nuanced exploration of existing knowledge and research in this domain. Scholars have extensively investigated the ethical foundations of AI deployment in various contexts (Dennehy et al., 2023). Researchers have highlighted the ethical implications of algorithmic decision-making, emphasizing the need for transparency, fairness, and accountability in AI systems (Akter et al., 2022). These studies underscore the potential consequences of biased algorithms and the importance of developing ethical frameworks that guide responsible AI practices. The regulatory landscape governing AI in digital entrepreneurship has garnered significant attention. Works have examined the existing regulatory frameworks, highlighting the challenges entrepreneurs face in navigating diverse and often fragmented regulations (Saura et al., 2022). These studies shed light on the need for comprehensive governance structures that address ethical considerations and provide clear guidelines for entrepreneurs. The impact of ethical AI adoption on stakeholders and long-term business sustainability has been a focal point of scholarly inquiry (Appel, Grewal, Hadi, & Stephen, 2020). Studies delve into the intricate relationship between ethical AI practices and stakeholder trust, emphasizing the role of responsible AI adoption in building and maintaining positive relationships with customers, employees, and regulatory bodies (Kumar et al., 2023). Educational imperatives for ethical AI practices have also emerged as a key theme. Researchers discuss the need for comprehensive educational programs that equip entrepreneurs with the ethical competencies required to navigate the complex ethical landscape of AI adoption (Nguyen et al., 2023). However, the literature review reveals a gap in synthesizing these diverse perspectives into a cohesive understanding of ethical imperatives and frameworks for responsible AI adoption in digital entrepreneurship. While individual studies contribute valuable insights, a comprehensive review is needed to integrate and contextualize these findings within the evolving landscape of digital entrepreneurship (Connock, 2022)

One prominent example of AI integration in media is the use of personalized recommendations in streaming services like Netflix, Amazon Prime Video, and Spotify. These platforms utilize sophisticated AI algorithms to analyze user preferences, viewing habits, and listening history to curate personalized content recommendations for each user (Dwivedi, & Wang, 2022). For instance, Netflix's recommendation system employs machine learning algorithms that analyze user interactions with the platform, such as viewing history, ratings, and search queries, to generate personalized recommendations. By leveraging AI, Netflix aims to enhance user engagement, increase content consumption, and improve user satisfaction by delivering tailored recommendations that match individual tastes and preferences (Dwivedi, Kshetri, Hughes, Slade, Jeyaraj, Kar, & Wright, 2023). Similarly, Spotify utilizes AI-powered algorithms to create personalized playlists, such as Discover Weekly and Release Radar, which offer users a curated selection of music based on their listening habits and preferences. Through continuous analysis of user interactions and feedback, Spotify's recommendation system evolves over time, delivering increasingly accurate and relevant content recommendations to its users(Gopinath, & Narayanamurthy,2022). These examples highlight how AI-driven personalized recommendations have become integral features of modern media consumption platforms, transforming the way users discover and engage with content. By leveraging AI technologies, streaming services can deliver a more tailored and immersive user experience, ultimately driving customer retention and loyalty in an increasingly competitive media landscape (Hacioglu, 2019)

Futuristic Issues of AI and Entrepreneurship: The world is changing at an unprecedented rate, and entrepreneurs need to keep up with these changes if they want to remain competitive. Futuristic technology perspectives can help entrepreneurs and innovators stay ahead of the curve by anticipating and leveraging emerging technologies. The rapid development of futuristic technologies, including artificial intelligence, the Internet of Things, and blockchain, has brought significant opportunities and challenges for entrepreneurship and sustainable innovation (Singh & Taterh, 2023). As we venture further into the future, the integration of Artificial Intelligence (AI) within entrepreneurship will continue to present novel challenges and opportunities. Several key futuristic issues are poised to shape the landscape of AI-driven entrepreneurship (Mijwil, Hiran, Doshi, Dadhich, Al-Mistarehi, & Bala (2023)

Ethical AI Governance: With AI systems becoming increasingly autonomous and complex, ensuring ethical governance mechanisms will be paramount. As AI algorithms make decisions with far-reaching consequences, addressing issues of transparency, fairness, and accountability will remain crucial to maintain public trust and mitigate potential risks (Merhi, 2023). AI-Powered Disruption: The rapid advancement of AI technology has the potential to disrupt traditional business models across various industries. Entrepreneurs must navigate this disruption strategically, leveraging AI capabilities to innovate and stay competitive while also considering the socio-economic implications of job displacement and market consolidation. Data Privacy and Security: As AI algorithms rely heavily on vast amounts of data for training and decision-making, safeguarding data privacy and security will be a significant concern (Madan & Ashok (2023).

Entrepreneurs must prioritize robust data protection measures to safeguard sensitive information and comply with evolving regulatory frameworks such as GDPR and CCPA. Human-AI Collaboration: The future of entrepreneurship will likely involve increased collaboration between humans and AI systems. Entrepreneurs will need to adapt their organizational structures and workflows to facilitate seamless collaboration between human employees and AI-powered tools, optimizing productivity and innovation (Kumar, Bhattacharyya, & Krishnamoorthy, 2023).

Bias and Fairness: Addressing bias and ensuring fairness in AI systems will continue to be a pressing issue. Entrepreneurs must actively work to identify and mitigate biases within their AI algorithms to avoid perpetuating inequalities and discrimination in decision-making processes. Regulatory Challenges: As AI technologies evolve, regulatory frameworks governing their use are likely to become more complex and fragmented. Entrepreneurs will need to navigate these regulatory challenges effectively, ensuring compliance with relevant laws and standards while also advocating for policies that promote innovation and responsible AI adoption (Kong, Cheung, & Zhang, 2023). AI in Emerging Markets: The impact of AI on entrepreneurship will extend beyond traditional markets to include emerging economies. Entrepreneurs in these regions must grapple with unique challenges such as limited access to AI technologies, infrastructure constraints, and socio-cultural factors shaping AI adoption. Responsible AI Innovation: Embracing responsible AI innovation will be critical for ensuring the long-term sustainability and societal acceptance of AI-driven entrepreneurship. Entrepreneurs must prioritize ethical considerations in all stages of AI development, from data collection and model training to deployment and impact assessment. There is an urgent need to transition our economy, society, and culture towards systems and actions that facilitate ecological sustainability(Joshi, Sharma, Das, Rosak-Szyrocka, Żywiołek, Muduli,, & Prasad,2022)(Kong, Cheung, & Tsang (2023). Such radical change requires equally radical transformation of approaches to decision making and resource use. Sustainable entrepreneurship (SE) is often presented as the answer to meeting the triple-bottom-line challenges that businesses face; however, there are very real limits to what it can achieve. SE is in the early stages of adopting tools at the technological frontier that offer empirical guidance at every point of an entrepreneurial decision-making process (Bickley, Macintyre & Torgler, 2021). The use of the internet and social media have changed consumer behavior and the ways in which companies conduct their business. Social and digital marketing offers significant opportunities to organizations through lower costs, improved brand awareness, and increased sales (Dwivedi et al., 2021). By proactively addressing these futuristic issues, entrepreneurs can harness the transformative potential of AI to drive innovation, create value, and shape a more inclusive and sustainable future of entrepreneurship (Jamwal, Agrawal & Sharma, 2022).

RESEARCH GAP

The existing literature review illuminates a notable research gap in the cohesive synthesis and integration of diverse perspectives on the ethical imperatives and frameworks guiding the responsible adoption of Artificial Intelligence (AI) in digital entrepreneurship. While individual studies provide valuable insights into specific aspects of this integration, a comprehensive analysis that connects these varied perspectives into a unified understanding is lacking. This research gap highlights the need for a study that synthesizes existing knowledge, addressing the multifaceted ethical considerations in AI adoption and contextualizing them within the dynamic landscape of digital entrepreneurship.

KNOWLEDGE GAP

The knowledge gap becomes evident in the absence of a comprehensive review that not only explores ethical considerations but also provides a contemporary and up-to-date analysis of responsible AI adoption in digital entrepreneurship. The literature review indicates a need for an in-depth examination that goes beyond the surface-level discussions, delving into the intricacies of how entrepreneurs navigate ethical challenges, the impact on stakeholders, and the evolving regulatory frameworks. Bridging this knowledge gap requires a study that contributes to the current body of knowledge by offering a nuanced, holistic, and timely perspective on the ethical dimensions of AI integration in the entrepreneurial domain.

Considering the nature of the study on ethical imperatives and frameworks for responsible AI adoption in digital entrepreneurship, the following three theories are deemed most applicable:

STAKEHOLDER THEORY

Applicability: Stakeholder theory will serve as a foundational lens for analyzing the impact of ethical AI adoption on various stakeholders within digital entrepreneurial ventures. It allows for a comprehensive examination of how responsible AI practices influence relationships with customers, employees, regulatory bodies, and other stakeholders. This theory enables a holistic understanding of stakeholder expectations and the potential long-term sustainability of digital ventures in the context of ethical considerations.

INSTITUTIONAL THEORY

Applicability: Institutional theory provides insights into the influence of regulatory frameworks and governance structures on the ethical adoption of AI in digital entrepreneurship. This theory will guide the examination of how entrepreneurs navigate and comply with existing regulations, shedding light on the institutional pressures shaping organizational behavior. By exploring the challenges, responses, and strategic decisions made by entrepreneurs, the study will assess the alignment of AI practices with ethical standards in the complex regulatory environment.

ETHICAL DECISION-MAKING THEORIES (UTILITARIANISM, DEONTOLOGY, VIRTUE ETHICS)

Applicability: Ethical decision-making theories, including Utilitarianism, Deontology, and Virtue Ethics, will form the core theoretical foundation for understanding the moral reasoning behind entrepreneurs' decisions in adopting AI technologies. This framework allows for a nuanced analysis of the consequences, duties, and virtues associated with ethical decision-making in the context of AI adoption. By integrating these theories, the study aims to uncover the ethical foundations shaping responsible AI practices and the moral dimensions guiding entrepreneurs.

By synthesizing Stakeholder Theory, Institutional Theory, and Ethical Decision-Making Theories, this theoretical framework aims to provide a robust analytical lens for comprehensively exploring the ethical imperatives and frameworks guiding responsible AI adoption in the dynamic context of digital entrepreneurship.

METHODOLOGY AND RESEARCH DESIGN

Type of Study

This study adopts qualitative approach to provide a comprehensive understanding of ethical imperatives in AI adoption.

Sampling Design

The study employs a purposive sampling technique to select digital entrepreneurial ventures that have actively adopted AI technologies. The selection criteria include a diverse representation across industries, sizes, and geographical locations.

Qualitative Data Collection

In-depth Interviews: The qualitative data collection phase involved conducting semi-structured interviews with key stakeholders critical to the digital entrepreneurial landscape. Participants included entrepreneurs leading ventures incorporating AI technologies, AI developers responsible for implementation, and regulatory experts with insights into the ethical landscape. A purposive sampling strategy ensured a diverse representation across industries, sizes, and geographical locations. These interviews sought to delve into the nuanced aspects of ethical considerations, decision-making processes surrounding AI adoption, and varied stakeholder perspectives.

The semi-structured format allowed for flexibility, enabling participants to elaborate on their experiences, challenges, and perceptions related to the ethical dimensions of AI integration. Interview questions were carefully crafted to explore key themes such as transparency, fairness, accountability, and stakeholder impact.

Document Analysis: Complementing the insights derived from interviews, the document analysis component involved a meticulous examination of organizational documents. These included ethical guidelines, governance charters, and regulatory compliance reports within the sampled digital entrepreneurial ventures. The goal was to assess the presence and effectiveness of ethical frameworks guiding AI adoption practices.

Through document analysis, patterns emerged regarding the explicit commitment to ethical considerations within organizational structures. Attention was given to the clarity of ethical guidelines, the extent of integration into governance charters, and evidence of adherence to regulatory requirements. The analysis aimed to provide a comprehensive view of the formalized ethical frameworks and their practical impact within the organizations under study.

Together, in-depth interviews and document analysis facilitated a rich and nuanced qualitative exploration of the ethical imperatives and frameworks surrounding AI adoption in the sampled digital entrepreneurial ventures. The findings from these qualitative sources laid the groundwork for a holistic understanding of the ethical landscape in the context of responsible AI adoption.

DATA SOURCES

Primary Data: The study has successfully gathered primary data through a comprehensive approach involving interviews, surveys, and document analysis.

Interviews: Insights from key stakeholders, including entrepreneurs, AI developers, and regulatory experts, were obtained through in-depth interviews. These first hand accounts provided valuable qualitative data, offering a deep understanding of ethical considerations, decision-making processes, and stakeholder perspectives in the realm of AI adoption within digital entrepreneurship.

Document Analysis: Organizational documents, such as ethical guidelines, governance charters, and regulatory compliance reports, underwent thorough analysis. This document review contributed essential qualitative insights, shedding light on the formalized ethical frameworks and their practical implications within the sampled digital entrepreneurial ventures.

Secondary Data: In addition to primary data, secondary data sources were tapped to enrich the study's context and background.

Academic Literature: A comprehensive review of academic literature contributed theoretical foundations and contextual understanding. Existing research and scholarly articles informed the study's conceptual framework and guided the formulation of research questions.

Industry Reports: Industry reports provided valuable insights into broader trends, challenges, and best practices related to AI adoption in digital entrepreneurship. These reports served as a benchmark for comparing and contextualizing findings from the primary data sources.

Regulatory Documents: Regulatory documents at local, regional, and national levels were consulted to understand the external influences shaping ethical considerations in AI adoption. These documents provided insights into compliance requirements and governmental expectations.

The combination of primary and secondary data sources facilitated a robust and multifaceted exploration of ethical imperatives and frameworks for responsible AI adoption in digital entrepreneurship. The study's findings are grounded in a diverse array of information, ensuring a comprehensive understanding of the ethical landscape in the studied context.

ETHICAL CONSIDERATIONS

The completion of this study adhered to stringent ethical considerations, ensuring the protection of participants and upholding the highest standards of research integrity.

Informed Consent: Prior to conducting interviews and surveys, explicit informed consent was obtained from all participants. The participants were fully informed about the study's purpose, potential risks, and benefits, and their voluntary participation was emphasized. They were given the opportunity to ask questions and provided consent in writing.

Confidentiality and Data Anonymization: Rigorous measures were implemented to safeguard the confidentiality and anonymity of participant data. Personal identifiers were meticulously removed, and all data were coded to ensure that individual responses could not be traced back to specific participants. The secured data storage and access protocols further guaranteed the privacy and confidentiality of the information collected.

Adherence to Ethical Guidelines and Regulations: The study strictly adhered to ethical guidelines and regulations governing research involving human participants. Ethical approval was obtained from relevant institutional review boards, ensuring that the research design, data collection procedures, and participant interactions complied with established ethical standards. Any potential ethical concerns were promptly addressed throughout the research process.

These ethical considerations reflect a commitment to the well-being and rights of the participants, aligning with the principles of ethical research conduct. The study prioritized transparency, participant autonomy, and the responsible handling of data, fostering a trustworthy foundation for the research outcomes.

DATA ANALYSIS

Qualitative Data Analysis

The study has successfully concluded the qualitative data analysis phase, employing robust methodologies to extract meaningful insights from interview transcripts and organizational documents.

Thematic Analysis: Thematic analysis was the chosen approach for scrutinizing the interview transcripts. This method facilitated the identification, analysis, and reporting of recurring patterns, themes, and categories within the qualitative data. By systematically coding and categorizing responses, key themes emerged, providing a nuanced understanding of ethical considerations, decision-making processes, and stakeholder perspectives related to AI adoption in digital entrepreneurship.

Content Analysis: Organizational documents underwent content analysis, a structured approach used to extract valuable insights. Through systematic examination, key themes, trends, and patterns within ethical guidelines, governance charters, and regulatory compliance reports were identified. Content analysis contributed to a deeper understanding of the formalized ethical frameworks and their practical implications within the sampled digital entrepreneurial ventures.

Rigor and Validity

The study has placed a paramount emphasis on rigor and validity, employing meticulous techniques to enhance the reliability of qualitative data analysis.

Inter-Coder Reliability: The qualitative analysis, particularly thematic analysis of interview transcripts, prioritized inter-coder reliability. Multiple researchers were involved in the coding process, independently identifying themes and patterns within the data. Regular meetings were held to compare coding results, discuss discrepancies, and iteratively refine the coding framework. Through this consensus-building approach, a high level of inter-coder reliability was achieved, ensuring consistency in the interpretation of qualitative data.

Consensus-Building Among Researchers: Consensus-building sessions were instrumental in fostering a shared understanding of the emerging themes and ensuring alignment in the interpretation of qualitative findings. Any disagreements or variations in coding were thoroughly discussed, and adjustments were made to the coding framework through collaborative decision-making. This iterative process of consensus-building contributed to the reliability and robustness of the qualitative analysis.

Implications for Rigor and Validity: By implementing these rigorous procedures, the study maintains a high level of credibility and validity in its qualitative findings. The consensus-building approach among researchers enhances the trustworthiness of the interpretation, minimizing biases and increasing the overall reliability of the study's qualitative analysis. This commitment to rigor and validity strengthens the study's contribution to the scholarly understanding of ethical imperatives and frameworks for responsible AI adoption in digital entrepreneurship. The findings of this study shed light on the intricate landscape of ethical imperatives and frameworks governing the adoption of Artificial Intelligence (AI) in the realm of digital entrepreneurship. Through qualitative analyses, the research aimed to uncover patterns, challenges, and opportunities associated with responsible AI adoption practices. The integration of insights from in-depth interviews, surveys, and document analysis provided a multifaceted view of how ethical considerations are navigated within the sampled digital entrepreneurial ventures.

QUALITATIVE FINDINGS

Thematic Analysis: Thematic analysis of in-depth interviews unearthed significant themes concerning ethical considerations in the adoption of Artificial Intelligence (AI) within digital entrepreneurship.

Transparency as a Cornerstone: Participants consistently emphasized the paramount importance of transparency in AI adoption. Clear communication regarding AI algorithms, decision-making processes, and potential implications emerged as a foundational ethical imperative.

Fairness and Accountability: Themes of fairness and accountability permeated discussions, reflecting the need for ethical frameworks that ensure just outcomes. Participants expressed a desire for accountability mechanisms to be embedded within AI practices, holding stakeholders responsible for the ethical implications of their decisions.

Diverse Stakeholder Perspectives: Stakeholder perspectives varied widely, emphasizing the complexity of ethical considerations within diverse entrepreneurial contexts. Entrepreneurs, AI developers, and regulatory experts offered unique insights, highlighting the need for adaptive ethical frameworks that address the varied concerns of different stakeholders.

Content Analysis of Organizational Documents: The content analysis of organizational documents provided additional qualitative insights into the formalized ethical frameworks within digital entrepreneurial ventures.

EMPHASIS ON TRANSPARENCY IN ETHICAL GUIDELINES

Ethical guidelines consistently prioritized transparency, outlining the organization's commitment to open communication about AI practices. Transparency emerged not only as an ethical imperative but also as a strategic element in fostering trust among stakeholders.

Shift towards Inclusive Decision-Making: Governance charters reflected a growing emphasis on stakeholder engagement in decision-making processes. The documents indicated a shift towards more inclusive ethical considerations, recognizing the importance of involving stakeholders in shaping AI-related policies and practices.

Commitment to Regulatory Compliance: Regulatory compliance reports demonstrated a commitment to aligning AI practices with evolving legal standards. Organizations acknowledged the dynamic nature of AI regulations and showcased proactive efforts to stay abreast of and adapt to changing ethical and legal landscapes.

Integration of Qualitative Insights: The integration of qualitative insights revealed a nuanced understanding of how organizations navigate the ethical landscape in AI adoption. Transparency, fairness, and accountability emerged as interconnected pillars, guiding the development of ethical frameworks. The qualitative findings provide depth to the broader ethical considerations in the digital entrepreneurial context and lay the foundation for further exploration and recommendations.

Understanding Ethical Imperatives in AI: Understanding ethical imperatives in AI is foundational to responsible AI adoption in digital entrepreneurship. It involves a comprehensive examination of the principles and values that guide ethical behavior in the development, deployment, and use of artificial intelligence systems.

Defining Ethical Principles in AI: Ethical principles serve as the fundamental building blocks for responsible AI adoption. These principles are essential guidelines that help ensure AI systems align with societal values and norms. Common ethical principles in AI include:

Transparency: AI systems should be transparent, and their decision-making processes should be understandable to users. Transparency builds trust and allows users to comprehend how AI systems arrive at specific conclusions.

Fairness: AI systems should be designed to treat all individuals and groups fairly. Bias and discrimination must be minimized to ensure equitable outcomes across diverse populations.

Accountability: Developers and users of AI systems should be accountable for the system's actions. This includes taking responsibility for any unintended consequences or ethical lapses that may arise during the system's use.

Privacy: AI systems should respect individuals' privacy rights. Personal data should be handled responsibly, and measures should be in place to protect sensitive information from unauthorized access or misuse.

Security: Ensuring the security of AI systems is crucial. Robust cyber security measures should be implemented to protect against potential threats, ensuring the integrity and reliability of the AI applications.

SOCIAL IMPACT ASSESSMENT

Conducting a social impact assessment involves evaluating how AI technologies may influence various stakeholders and broader societal structures. This assessment aims to identify potential positive and negative impacts, allowing digital entrepreneurs to make informed decisions about the deployment of AI. Key aspects of a social impact assessment include:

Bias and Discrimination: Evaluate the potential biases in the training data and algorithms to minimize discriminatory outcomes. Understanding how AI decisions might disproportionately affect certain groups is crucial for addressing ethical concerns .

Economic Disparities: Examine the potential economic impact of AI on different sectors and job markets. Consider how the deployment of AI may contribute to or alleviate existing economic disparities.

Accessibility: Ensure that AI technologies are accessible to a diverse range of users. Consider the potential social and economic barriers that may limit access and work towards mitigating them.

Broader Societal Implications: Assess how AI adoption may impact societal structures, cultural values, and community well-being. Consideration of long-term consequences helps in proactively addressing ethical concerns.

Frameworks for responsible AI adoption provide structured guidelines and principles to help digital entrepreneurs navigate the ethical challenges associated with developing and deploying artificial intelligence systems. These frameworks are designed to ensure that AI technologies align with ethical considerations and societal values. Here's a detailed breakdown of the key components within the concept of frameworks for responsible AI adoption.

THE IEEE GLOBAL INITIATIVE ON ETHICS OF AUTONOMOUS AND INTELLIGENT SYSTEMS

The Institute of Electrical and Electronics Engineers (IEEE) has developed a framework that outlines ethical considerations for autonomous and intelligent systems. Key aspects include:

Ethical Design: Encourages the integration of ethical considerations into the design phase of AI systems. This involves identifying potential ethical issues and addressing them proactively.

Transparency: Emphasizes the importance of transparency in AI systems, ensuring that their decision-making processes are explainable and understandable. Transparent systems help build trust among users and stakeholders.

Accountability: Calls for clear lines of responsibility and accountability in the development and deployment of AI. This includes mechanisms for addressing errors, unintended consequences, and ethical lapses.

Privacy: Stresses the need to prioritize user privacy and data protection in the design and implementation of AI systems.

FAIRNESS, ACCOUNTABILITY, AND TRANSPARENCY IN MACHINE LEARNING (FAT/ML)

The FAT/ML framework focuses on addressing issues related to fairness, accountability, and transparency in machine learning. Key components include:

Fairness: Calls for the mitigation of biases in AI systems to ensure equitable outcomes across diverse user groups. Strategies may involve careful selection of training data, algorithmic adjustments, and ongoing monitoring.

Accountability: Highlights the importance of clear accountability structures to address issues and challenges that may arise during the use of AI systems. Developers and organizations should take responsibility for the impact of their technologies.

Transparency: Advocates for transparency in AI decision-making processes. Users should have insights into how decisions are made, and there should be mechanisms for explaining complex AI algorithms in understandable terms.

INCORPORATING ETHICAL AI INTO ENTREPRENEURIAL CULTURE

Entrepreneurs play a pivotal role in fostering an ethical AI culture within their organizations. This involves:

Ethical Leadership: Entrepreneurs should lead by example, prioritizing ethical considerations in decision-making and setting a tone that emphasizes responsible AI practices.

Employee Training and Awareness: Organizations should invest in training programs to ensure that employees are well-versed in AI ethics. This empowers them to make ethically informed decisions in their work.

PRIVACY AND SECURITY IN AI SYSTEMS

Addressing Privacy and Security Concerns in AI Systems Involves

Data Protection and Privacy by Design: Integrating privacy considerations into the design process ensures that privacy is prioritized from the outset. This involves minimizing data collection, implementing robust data protection measures, and obtaining informed consent.

Cyber security Measures: Implementing robust cyber security measures to protect AI systems from potential threats, ensuring the integrity, confidentiality, and availability of data.

Public Engagement and Collaboration

Recognizing the importance of involving diverse stakeholders and collaborating with ethical AI initiatives:

Inclusive Decision-Making Processes: Involving the public, users, and other stakeholders in decision-making processes related to AI adoption. This fosters a more inclusive and diverse perspective in the development and deployment of AI technologies.

Collaboration with Ethical AI Initiatives: Engaging with ethical AI initiatives, research institutions, and regulatory bodies to stay informed about emerging ethical guidelines and best practices. Collaboration enhances the collective effort towards responsible AI development.

Frameworks for responsible AI adoption provide a structured approach to integrate ethical considerations into the entire lifecycle of AI systems. Digital entrepreneurs can leverage these frameworks to build trust, mitigate risks, and contribute positively to societal well-being through the responsible development and deployment of AI technologies. Incorporating Ethical AI into Entrepreneurial Culture refers to the integration of ethical considerations related to artificial intelligence (AI) into the values, practices, and decision-making processes within entrepreneurial organizations. This approach ensures that the development and deployment of AI technologies align with ethical principles and contribute positively to societal well-being. Here's a detailed breakdown of the key components within this concept:

Ethical Leadership: Setting the Tone: Entrepreneurs and organizational leaders play a crucial role in shaping the ethical culture of their companies. They must prioritize ethical considerations in their decision-making processes and lead by example.

Establishing Values: Articulating and reinforcing ethical values within the organization helps guide employees in navigating complex ethical dilemmas related to AI. This includes valuing transparency, fairness, accountability, and user privacy.

Employee Training and Awareness: Educating Employees: Organizations should invest in training programs to ensure that employees understand the ethical implications of AI technologies. This includes raising awareness about potential biases, privacy concerns, and the societal impact of AI.

Empowering Decision-Making: Educated and informed employees are better equipped to make ethically sound decisions in their work. This empowerment helps create a culture where ethical considerations are integral to day-to-day operations.

INTEGRATION INTO BUSINESS PROCESSES

Embedding Ethical Considerations: Ethical AI should be seamlessly integrated into the entire product development lifecycle. From the conceptualization of AI solutions to their deployment and maintenance, ethical considerations should be an intrinsic part of the process.

Cross-Functional Collaboration: Encouraging collaboration between different departments, including AI development, legal, and marketing, ensures that ethical considerations are considered from various perspectives. This interdisciplinary approach helps in identifying and addressing ethical challenges comprehensively.

Accountability Mechanisms

Clear Responsibility: Establishing clear lines of responsibility for ethical considerations ensures that individuals and teams are accountable for the ethical impact of the AI technologies they develop.

Learning from Mistakes: A culture of accountability involves acknowledging and learning from mistakes. Organizations should foster an environment where employees feel comfortable reporting ethical concerns and where the organization takes swift action to rectify any lapses.

Continuous Evaluation and Improvement

Ethical Audits: Periodic ethical audits of AI systems and processes help identify potential ethical issues. This ongoing evaluation ensures that organizations stay proactive in addressing emerging ethical challenges.

Adaptability: The entrepreneurial culture should be adaptable to evolving ethical standards and guidelines. Organizations should be ready to adjust their practices in response to changes in societal expectations and regulations related to AI.

User-Centric Approach

User Empowerment: Entrepreneurs should prioritize the interests and rights of users. This involves providing users with control over their data, clear explanations of AI-driven decisions, and mechanisms to opt-out of certain AI functionalities.

Transparency: Maintaining transparency in how AI technologies are used and informing users about the potential implications fosters trust. This transparency can be achieved through clear communication and user-friendly interfaces.

Incorporating ethical AI into entrepreneurial culture goes beyond compliance with regulations; it reflects a commitment to social responsibility and long-term sustainability. By embedding ethical considerations into the core of their operations, entrepreneurial organizations can build trust, mitigate risks, and contribute positively to the responsible development and adoption of AI technologies .

PRIVACY AND SECURITY IN AI SYSTEMS

It addresses the critical considerations and measures necessary to protect user privacy and ensure the security of artificial intelligence (AI) systems. This is especially important as AI systems often deal with vast amounts of sensitive data, making them potential targets for privacy breaches and cyber security threats. Here's a detailed breakdown of the key components within this concept:

Data Protection and Privacy by Design

Minimizing Data Collection: Organizations should adopt a principle of collecting only the necessary data required for the intended purpose. This minimizes the risk associated with the storage and processing of large amounts of personal information.

Informed Consent: Obtaining informed consent from users before collecting and processing their data is essential. Users should be fully aware of how their data will be used and have the option to opt-out if they choose.

Anonymization and Pseudonymization: Techniques like anonymization (removing personally identifiable information) and pseudonymization (replacing identifiers with pseudonyms) can be employed to enhance privacy by reducing the risk of re-identification.

Data Lifecycle Management: Implementing policies for the secure handling of data throughout its lifecycle, including storage, processing, and eventual deletion, helps minimize privacy risks.

Cyber Security Measures

Secure Data Transmission: Employing secure communication protocols to protect data during transmission is crucial. This prevents unauthorized access or interception of sensitive information.

Access Controls: Implementing robust access control mechanisms ensures that only authorized personnel have access to sensitive data. This includes role-based access, encryption, and strong authentication measures.

Regular Security Audits: Conducting regular security audits and vulnerability assessments helps identify and address potential weaknesses in the AI system's security infrastructure. This proactive approach is crucial for staying ahead of emerging threats.

Incident Response Plans: Developing and regularly updating incident response plans enables organizations to respond quickly and effectively to security incidents, minimizing the impact of potential breaches.

Privacy-Preserving AI Techniques

Homomorphic Encryption: This technique allows computation on encrypted data without decrypting it. It enables AI models to process data without exposing the raw information, enhancing privacy.

Differential Privacy: Differential privacy adds noise to the data to protect individual privacy while still providing meaningful aggregated results. It's particularly relevant when analyzing datasets containing sensitive information.

Secure Multi-Party Computation: This approach enables multiple parties to jointly compute a function over their inputs while keeping those inputs private. It's useful in collaborative AI scenarios where data from different sources need to be analyzed without being shared.

Legal and Regulatory Compliance

Adherence to Data Protection Laws: Organizations must comply with relevant data protection regulations, such as the General Data Protection Regulation (GDPR) in the European Union or the California Consumer Privacy Act (CCPA) in the United States. This includes respecting user rights, ensuring data transparency, and providing mechanisms for data access and deletion.

Ethical Standards: Beyond legal requirements, organizations should adhere to ethical standards and industry best practices to ensure responsible and transparent handling of user data.

Continuous Monitoring and Updates

Real-Time Monitoring: Implementing real-time monitoring of AI systems helps detect and respond to potential privacy and security threats promptly.

Regular Updates and Patch Management: Keeping AI systems and associated software up-to-date with the latest security patches is crucial for addressing vulnerabilities and maintaining a secure environment.

User Education: Educating users about the privacy features of AI systems and providing them with control over their data empowers them to make informed decisions about their privacy settings.

Addressing privacy and security concerns in AI systems involves a multi-faceted approach that integrates technical measures, legal compliance, and user empowerment. By prioritizing the protection of user data and ensuring the security of AI systems, organizations can build trust with users and stakeholders while mitigating risks associated with potential breaches or misuse of sensitive information.

PUBLIC ENGAGEMENT AND COLLABORATION

It involves the broader public, users, and stakeholders in decision-making processes related to artificial intelligence. This inclusive approach aims to incorporate diverse perspectives, foster transparency, and build trust in the development and deployment of AI technologies. Here's a detailed breakdown of the key components within this concept:

Inclusive Decision-Making Processes

Stakeholder Involvement: Actively involving various stakeholders, including the public, users, advocacy groups, and experts, in decision-making processes related to AI ensures a more comprehensive and diverse range of perspectives.

User Input: Seeking input from end-users during the development and deployment of AI systems helps ensure that the technology aligns with user expectations and needs. This user-centric approach contributes to the creation of more ethical and user-friendly AI solutions.

Community Engagement: Engaging with local communities and considering their concerns and values is crucial, especially when AI applications may have direct impacts on specific geographic areas or cultural groups.

Collaboration With Ethical AI Initiatives

Partnerships with Research Institutions: Collaborating with research institutions that specialize in AI ethics and related fields helps organizations stay informed about the latest ethical guidelines and best practices.

Engagement with Regulatory Bodies: Establishing collaboration with regulatory bodies and industry associations contributes to the development of standardized ethical practices and ensures alignment with legal and regulatory requirements.

Participation in Ethical AI Initiatives: Actively participating in and supporting ethical AI initiatives and consortiums contributes to a collective effort in defining and promoting responsible AI practices across the industry.

Transparency and Communication

Clear Communication: Transparent communication about the intentions, capabilities, and potential impacts of AI technologies builds trust with the public. Clear explanations about how AI systems make decisions and handle data contribute to a better-informed user base.

Public Disclosures: When appropriate, organizations should disclose information about their AI systems, including their limitations, potential biases, and any ongoing efforts to address ethical concerns. This transparency helps manage expectations and demonstrates a commitment to responsible AI.

Education and Awareness

Public Awareness Campaigns: Launching awareness campaigns to educate the public about AI technologies, their benefits, and potential risks fosters an informed society capable of participating in meaningful discussions about the ethical implications of AI.

User Training and Resources: Providing users with the necessary resources and training to understand how AI systems work, their rights, and how to manage their data privacy empowers them to make informed choices.

Addressing Bias and Fairness Concerns

Bias Mitigation Strategies: Actively addressing and mitigating biases in AI systems, especially those that may disproportionately impact certain demographic groups, demonstrates a commitment to fairness and equality.

Algorithmic Audits: Conducting regular audits of AI algorithms for potential biases and fairness issues helps organizations identify and rectify problems, ensuring that their systems treat all individuals fairly.

User Feedback Mechanisms

Feedback Loops: Establishing mechanisms for users to provide feedback on AI systems encourages a continuous improvement cycle. User feedback can highlight issues that may not have been anticipated during the development phase.

Responsive Iterations: Responding to user feedback with prompt iterations and updates to AI systems shows an organizational commitment to listening and adapting based on user concerns.

Ethical Considerations in Public AI Deployments

Impact Assessments: Before deploying AI systems that may have significant societal impacts, organizations should conduct impact assessments to understand potential consequences and involve the public in decision-making processes.

Public Consultations: In certain cases, conducting public consultations or hearings can provide a platform for individuals and groups to express their opinions and concerns about the deployment of specific AI technologies.

Public engagement and collaboration aim to democratize the AI development and deployment process, ensuring that decisions are not made in isolation but with input from those who are affected. This approach contributes to the responsible and ethical advancement of AI technologies, fostering a more inclusive and accountable AI ecosystem.

CONCLUSION

The integration of Artificial Intelligence (AI) in digital entrepreneurship has become a pervasive force, offering unprecedented opportunities for innovation, efficiency, and competitive advantage. However, with this transformative power comes an ethical imperative that demands careful consideration and principled adoption. The ethical dimensions surrounding the adoption of AI within the context of digital entrepreneurship have been extensively investigated by scholars, highlighting the importance of transparency, fairness, and accountability in AI systems. The literature review reveals a gap in synthesizing the diverse perspectives into a cohesive understanding of ethical imperatives and frameworks for responsible AI adoption in digital entrepreneurship. While individual studies contribute valuable insights, a comprehensive review is needed to integrate and contextualize these findings within the evolving landscape of digital entrepreneurship. Understanding ethical imperatives in AI is foundational to responsible AI adoption in digital entrepreneurship. It involves a comprehensive examination of the principles and values that guide ethical behavior in the development, deployment, and use of artificial intelligence systems. Defining ethical principles in AI serves as the fundamental building blocks for responsible AI adoption.

These principles are essential guidelines that help ensure AI systems align with societal values and norms. Frameworks for responsible AI adoption provide structured guidelines and principles to help digital entrepreneurs navigate the ethical challenges associated with developing and deploying artificial intelligence systems. These frameworks are designed to ensure that AI technologies align with ethical considerations and societal values. The IEEE Global Initiative on Ethics of Autonomous and Intelligent Systems has developed a framework that outlines ethical considerations for autonomous and intelligent systems. The impact of ethical AI adoption on stakeholders and long-term business sustainability has been a focal point of scholarly inquiry. Studies delve into the intricate relationship between ethical AI practices and stakeholder trust, emphasizing the role of responsible AI adoption in building and maintaining positive relationships with customers, employees, and regulatory bodies. Educational imperatives for ethical AI practices have also emerged as a key theme. Researchers discuss the need for comprehensive educational programs that equip entrepreneurs with the ethical competencies required to navigate the complex ethical landscape of AI adoption. The findings emphasize a commitment to transparency, a shift towards inclusive decision-making processes, and proactive alignment with regulatory standards. Based on these qualitative insights, recommendations are put forth, advocating for the development of comprehensive ethical guidelines, inclusive decision-making structures, and the establishment of robust accountability mechanisms. Furthermore, the study underscores the significance of continuous training programs, industry collaborations, and pilot initiatives to refine ethical frameworks in practice. Ultimately, this qualitative exploration contributes to the ongoing discourse on responsible AI adoption, fostering a culture of transparency and accountability in the dynamic landscape of digital entrepreneurship. As we navigate the intricate intersections of technology and ethics, it becomes evident that the responsible integration of AI is not only a moral obligation but a strategic imperative for sustainable and socially conscious digital entrepreneurship.

Overview: The study embarked on an exploration of the ethical imperatives and frameworks that underpin the adoption of Artificial Intelligence (AI) in the dynamic landscape of digital entrepreneurship. By employing a mixed-methods approach, integrating qualitative insights from in-depth interviews and document analysis, the research aimed to uncover the intricate ethical considerations faced by digital entrepreneurial ventures in their adoption of AI technologies.

Key Findings Recap: The qualitative findings unveiled several key themes that form the foundation of ethical considerations in the realm of AI adoption. Transparency emerged as a cornerstone, reflecting the importance of clear communication regarding AI algorithms and decision-making processes. Fairness and accountability were recurrent themes, illustrating the need for robust ethical frameworks that ensure just outcomes and hold stakeholders accountable for AI-related decisions. Diverse stakeholder perspectives highlighted the complexity of ethical considerations within varying entrepreneurial contexts.

Organizational Ethical Frameworks: The content analysis of organizational documents added depth to our understanding of formalized ethical frameworks within digital entrepreneurial ventures. Emphasizing transparency, ethical guidelines showcased organizations' commitments to open communication about AI practices. Governance charters revealed a shift towards more inclusive decision-making processes, recognizing the importance of involving stakeholders in shaping AI-related policies. Commitment to regulatory compliance demonstrated organizations' proactive efforts to align AI practices with evolving legal standards.

Integration of Qualitative Insights: The integration of qualitative insights provided a holistic understanding of how organizations navigate the ethical landscape in AI adoption. Transparency, fairness, and accountability emerged as interconnected pillars guiding the development of ethical frameworks. The nuances captured in in-depth interviews enriched the broader ethical considerations, offering depth to the quantitative survey data.

Implications and Recommendations: The findings of this study have significant implications for practitioners, policymakers, and researchers in the field of digital entrepreneurship and AI adoption.

Organizations are encouraged to prioritize transparency, embed fairness in algorithmic decision-making, and establish robust accountability mechanisms. Stakeholder engagement is underscored as critical for the development of adaptive ethical frameworks that consider the diverse perspectives within and outside the organization.

Limitations and Future Research: While this study contributes valuable insights, it is not without limitations. The findings are contextualized within the sampled ventures, and variations may exist across industries and regions. Future research endeavors could expand the scope to include a more extensive and diverse set of digital entrepreneurial ventures, allowing for a broader understanding of ethical considerations in AI adoption.

Conclusion: In conclusion, this study illuminates the complex interplay of ethical imperatives and frameworks in the adoption of AI within the digital entrepreneurship landscape. By combining qualitative richness with quantitative rigor, the research provides a nuanced and comprehensive exploration of the ethical considerations guiding responsible AI adoption. As digital ventures continue to integrate AI technologies, the insights derived from this study contribute to a growing body of knowledge that informs ethical decision-making, fosters responsible practices, and promotes the sustainable development of AI in digital entrepreneurship.

REFERENCES

Akter, S., Dwivedi, Y. K., Sajib, S., Biswas, K., Bandara, R. J., & Michael, K. (2022). Algorithmic bias in machine learning-based marketing models. *Journal of Business Research*, *144*, 201–216. doi:10.1016/j.jbusres.2022.01.083

Appel, G., Grewal, L., Hadi, R., & Stephen, A. T. (2020). The future of social media in marketing. *Journal of the Academy of Marketing Science*, *48*(1), 79–95. doi:10.1007/s11747-019-00695-1 PMID:32431463

Bickley, S. J., Macintyre, A., & Torgler, B. (2021). Artificial intelligence and big data in sustainable entrepreneurship. *Journal of Economic Surveys*.

Connock, A. (2022). *Media Management and Artificial Intelligence: Understanding Media Business Models in the Digital Age*. Taylor & Francis. doi:10.4324/9781003213611

Dennehy, D., Griva, A., Pouloudi, N., Dwivedi, Y. K., Mäntymäki, M., & Pappas, I. O. (2023). Artificial intelligence (AI) and information systems: Perspectives to responsible AI. *Information Systems Frontiers*, *25*(1), 1–7. doi:10.1007/s10796-022-10365-3

Dwivedi, Y. K., Kshetri, N., Hughes, L., Slade, E. L., Jeyaraj, A., Kar, A. K., Baabdullah, A. M., Koohang, A., Raghavan, V., Ahuja, M., Albanna, H., Albashrawi, M. A., Al-Busaidi, A. S., Balakrishnan, J., Barlette, Y., Basu, S., Bose, I., Brooks, L., Buhalis, D., & Wright, R. (2023). "So what if ChatGPT wrote it?" Multidisciplinary perspectives on opportunities, challenges and implications of generative conversational AI for research, practice and policy. *International Journal of Information Management*, *71*, 102642. doi:10.1016/j.ijinfomgt.2023.102642

Dwivedi, Y. K., & Wang, Y. (2022). Guest editorial: Artificial intelligence for B2B marketing: Challenges and opportunities. *Industrial Marketing Management*, *105*, 109–113. doi:10.1016/j.indmarman.2022.06.001

Gopinath, K., & Narayanamurthy, G. (2022). Early bird catches the worm! Meta-analysis of autonomous vehicles adoption–Moderating role of automation level, ownership and culture. *International Journal of Information Management*, *66*, 102536. doi:10.1016/j.ijinfomgt.2022.102536

Hacioglu, U. (Ed.). (2019). *Digital business strategies in blockchain ecosystems: Transformational design and future of global business*. Springer Nature.

Jamwal, A., Agrawal, R., & Sharma, M. (2022). Deep learning for manufacturing sustainability: Models, applications in Industry 4.0 and implications. *International Journal of Information Management Data Insights*, *2*(2), 100107. doi:10.1016/j.jjimei.2022.100107

Joshi, S., Sharma, M., Das, R. P., Rosak-Szyrocka, J., Żywiołek, J., Muduli, K., & Prasad, M. (2022). Modeling Conceptual Framework for Implementing Barriers of AI in Public Healthcare for Improving Operational Excellence: Experiences from Developing Countries. *Sustainability (Basel)*, *14*(18), 11698. doi:10.3390/su141811698

Kong, S. C., Cheung, W. M. Y., & Tsang, O. (2023). Evaluating an artificial intelligence literacy programme for empowering and developing concepts, literacy and ethical awareness in senior secondary students. *Education and Information Technologies*, *28*(4), 4703–4724. doi:10.1007/s10639-022-11408-7

Kong, S. C., Cheung, W. M. Y., & Zhang, G. (2023). Evaluating an artificial intelligence literacy programme for developing university students' conceptual understanding, literacy, empowerment and ethical awareness. *Journal of Educational Technology & Society*, *26*(1), 16–30.

Kumar, A., Bhattacharyya, S. S., & Krishnamoorthy, B. (2023). Automation-augmentation paradox in organizational artificial intelligence technology deployment capabilities; an empirical investigation for achieving simultaneous economic and social benefits. *Journal of Enterprise Information Management*.

Madan, R., & Ashok, M. (2023). AI adoption and diffusion in public administration: A systematic literature review and future research agenda. *Government Information Quarterly*, *40*(1), 101774. doi:10.1016/j.giq.2022.101774

Merhi, M. I. (2023). An evaluation of the critical success factors impacting artificial intelligence implementation. *International Journal of Information Management*, *69*, 102545. doi:10.1016/j.ijinfomgt.2022.102545

Mijwil, M. M., Hiran, K. K., Doshi, R., Dadhich, M., Al-Mistarehi, A. H., & Bala, I. (2023). ChatGPT and the future of academic integrity in the artificial intelligence era: A new frontier. *Al-Salam Journal for Engineering and Technology*, *2*(2), 116–127. doi:10.55145/ajest.2023.02.02.015

Misra, S. K., Sharma, S. K., Gupta, S., & Das, S. (2023). A framework to overcome challenges to the adoption of artificial intelligence in Indian Government Organizations. *Technological Forecasting and Social Change*, *194*, 122721. doi:10.1016/j.techfore.2023.122721

Nguyen, A., Ngo, H. N., Hong, Y., Dang, B., & Nguyen, B. P. T. (2023). Ethical principles for artificial intelligence in education. *Education and Information Technologies*, *28*(4), 4221–4241. doi:10.1007/s10639-022-11316-w PMID:36254344

Richey, R. G. Jr, Chowdhury, S., Davis-Sramek, B., Giannakis, M., & Dwivedi, Y. K. (2023). Artificial intelligence in logistics and supply chain management: A primer and roadmap for research. *Journal of Business Logistics*, *44*(4), 532–549. doi:10.1111/jbl.12364

Saura, J. R., Ribeiro-Soriano, D., & Palacios-Marqués, D. (2022). Assessing behavioral data science privacy issues in government artificial intelligence deployment. *Government Information Quarterly*, *39*(4), 101679. doi:10.1016/j.giq.2022.101679

Shore, A. (2022). Talking about facial recognition technology: How framing and context influence privacy concerns and support for prohibitive policy. *Telematics and Informatics*, *70*, 101815. doi:10.1016/j.tele.2022.101815

Singh, A. K., & Taterh, S. (2023). Exploring the Significance and Obstacles of Adopting Futuristic Technology Perspectives for Entrepreneurship and Sustainable Innovation. In Futuristic Technology Perspectives on Entrepreneurship and Sustainable Innovation (pp. 1-10). IGI Global. doi:10.4018/978-1-6684-5871-6.ch001

Thakur, R. (2024). Introduction to artificial intelligence and its importance in modern business management. In *Leveraging AI and emotional intelligence in contemporary business organizations* (pp. 133–165). IGI Global.

Vogl, M., Rötzel, P. G., & Homes, S. (2022). Forecasting performance of wavelet neural networks and other neural network topologies: A comparative study based on financial market data sets. *Machine Learning with Applications*, *8*, 100302. doi:10.1016/j.mlwa.2022.100302

Wamba, S. F. (2022). Impact of artificial intelligence assimilation on firm performance: The mediating effects of organizational agility and customer agility. *International Journal of Information Management*, *67*, 102544. doi:10.1016/j.ijinfomgt.2022.102544

Widayanti, R., & Meria, L. (2023). Business modeling innovation using artificial intelligence technology. *International Transactions on Education Technology*, *1*(2), 95–104.

Chapter 16
Impact of Post-Use Satisfaction on Re-Purchase Intentions for AI-Driven Healthcare Smart Wearables

Munish Gupta
https://orcid.org/0000-0002-1982-4136
Chandigarh University, India

Pooja Chopra
Lovely Professional University, India

Nitin Pathak
https://orcid.org/0000-0002-8062-0554
Chandigarh University, India

ABSTRACT

The chapter examines the factors influencing the long-term use of smart wearables among users in Northern India. It integrates the Expectation-Confirmation Theory (ECT) and the Latent Variable Model to understand what drives users to continue using these devices. The study, involving 678 participants, employs Structural Equation Modeling (Smart PLS4) to analyze the effects of satisfaction, willingness to pay a premium, and accuracy of health information on the sustained use of smart wearables. The findings underscore that user satisfaction, precise health information, and the readiness to pay more significantly affect users' intentions to repurchase and keep using these devices. This research is particularly beneficial for smartwatch manufacturers and designers. By highlighting the importance of satisfaction, accurate health information, and price factors, it provides crucial insights for improving the design and marketing of smart wearables. These insights are key to fostering user loyalty and ensuring long-term engagement with these technologies.

DOI: 10.4018/979-8-3693-1842-3.ch016

INTRODUCTION

In recent years, wearable computing devices have witnessed an astounding surge in popularity, captivating the attention of consumers, researchers, and technology enthusiasts alike. Smartwatches are a remarkable subclass of wearable technology among these innovative gadgets. In essence, a smartwatch is no ordinary wristwatch; it possesses computational capabilities that enable it to establish connections with various devices through short-range wireless communication, deliver timely alert messages, amass and store personal data from an array of sensors while serving as a reliable timekeeping device. Smartwatches, in their multifaceted functionality, offer users the unprecedented convenience of accessing their digital information seamlessly while on the move. The allure of these smart wearables has transformed them from mere gadgets into powerful tools with the potential to reshape how we interact with technology in our daily lives (Melumad et al., 2020). The convergence of cellular connectivity, intricate electrical engineering, and autonomous processing capabilities, all within the confines of a compact, body-worn device, has marked a significant milestone in the evolution of wearable technology (Saraswat et al., 2022). This convergence has made technology more personal and user-friendly than ever before, blurring the lines between the digital and physical realms. Consequently, with their ever-expanding features and capabilities, smart wearable devices have sparked a wave of interest and intrigue among researchers, innovators, and consumers alike.

At the heart of this flourishing fascination reclines the potential for continuous and precise data collection. Smartwatches, in particular, have emerged as powerful tools for capturing extensive personal data, from health and fitness metrics to communication prototypes and location information (Allioui et al., 2023). This wealth of data provides valuable insights into our daily lives and opens up a realm of possibilities for enhancing human capabilities in previously unimagined ways. As we embark on this exploration of wearable technology, with a special emphasis on the smartwatch, we examine the intricate interplay between humans and machines, dissecting how these devices collect, process, and present data and pondering the many ways in which this technology might augment human experiences (Y. Kumar et al., 2022).

The adoption of smartwatches, a fascinating genre of wearable technology, can be motivated by many factors, including the allure of novelty, the influence of peers, persuasive marketing strategies, or the innate drive to be an early adopter (Morozova, 2021). A remarkable facet of these devices is that the more frequently users engage with them, the more intuitive and integral they become in daily life. While the industry may introduce new smartwatch models annually, grasping the broader context of app sales is imperative to appreciate the paramount importance of continuous user engagement (Dehghani, 2018). In 2023, the global shipment of smartwatches is anticipated to reach a staggering 109.2 million units, underscoring the relentless demand from consumers (Allioui et al., 2023). Apple currently commands the largest market share in the smartwatch arena, with Samsung closely trailing behind. Furthermore, app development has witnessed exponential growth, with revenues in 2020 reaching nearly $643 billion, representing a remarkable 24 percent year-over-year increase in billings and sales (M. Gupta, Taneja, et al., 2023; V. Kumar, 2023). The longer a customer engages with their smartwatch, the greater the likelihood of them exploring and purchasing additional applications, thereby augmenting revenue streams.

Smart wearables in healthcare have many applications, leveraging advanced technologies to monitor various health parameters and assist in disease management (Bayoumy et al., 2021a; X. Wang et al., 2023).

- These devices continuously monitor vital signs like heart rate, blood pressure, and oxygen saturation, providing real-time data that can be crucial for individuals with specific health conditions.
- Wearables are particularly beneficial for people with chronic conditions like diabetes, where they can monitor blood sugar levels or heart conditions by keeping a check on heart rhythms.
- By tracking sleep patterns, these devices provide insights into sleep quality, duration, and disturbances, which is crucial for overall health and well-being.
- Advanced wearables detect falls and can automatically send alerts to emergency contacts or services.
- Integration with health apps allows users to share their health data with doctors, facilitating telehealth consultations and remote patient monitoring.
- Users can set personal health goals and participate in challenges, which keeps them motivated and engaged.

In 2020, an estimated 68.56 million smartwatch units were supplied worldwide(V. Sharma, Gupta, et al., 2023), with a noteworthy surge in online sales contributing to cost reduction. Smartwatches, by virtue of their ability to encompass features reminiscent of other wearables like fitness trackers, possess a unique capacity to satisfy the three fundamental psychological needs, as expounded by the principles of self-determination theory: autonomy, competence, and belonging (P. Sharma et al., 2023; Zolfaghari et al., 2023). The continuous presence of a smartwatch on one's wrist empowers users to effortlessly access a myriad of features, many of which require proximity or direct skin contact to operate effectively.

One of the most profound dimensions of smartwatches lies in their potential to positively impact users' health and fitness. By incessantly monitoring vital metrics such as heart rate, steps taken, and various other biometric data, these devices empower individuals to lead healthier lives and potentially reduce healthcare expenses (C. Li et al., 2024). Fitness enthusiasts, in particular, have embraced smartwatches as their workout companions, utilizing features tailored to their needs. For runners, built-in GPS tracking serves as a navigational guide, ensuring that the chosen path aligns with their fitness goals. Additionally, some smartwatches boast fitness-related applications that offer personalized guidance to enhance overall fitness levels. Notably, the in-built heart rate monitor is a cherished feature, facilitating real-time tracking and fostering a heightened awareness of one's cardiovascular health (Maselli et al., 2023; Tagger & Gupta, 2020).

In this chapter, we aim to deepen our understanding of the motivations underpinning consistent smartwatch usage, specifically emphasizing health and fitness-related aspects and the influence of premium pricing. Our objective is to uncover the various aspects of user engagement and investigate the significant impacts of these wearable devices on individuals' well-being. Our study explores the world of smart wearables, where technology seamlessly integrates with our lives, shaping our behaviors and, ultimately, our future.

LITERATURE REVIEW

The concept of wearable technologies, particularly smart watches, has intrigued healthcare scholars due to their potential to revolutionize the health monitoring paradigm. Smart wearables are end-user devices and offer a familiar interface for consumers (Niknejad et al., 2020). Their capabilities for continuously monitoring exercise and vitals in near real-time have been identified as particularly advantageous (W.

Sun et al., 2022). The devices are also notable for providing simple access to notifications, alerts, and sensor-based behavior verification. The adoption of these smart wearables is influenced by various factors as elucidated by models like the TAM (Technology Acceptance Model) (Kao et al., 2019)and (UTAUT) Unified Theory of Acceptance and Use of Technology (Venkatesh et al., 2012). According to TAM, users are more likely to adopt technology if it has practical applications that they find valuable. From a healthcare perspective, wearables have been observed to make healthcare activities more accessible for users by independently tracking user data and providing real-time feedback (Dixit et al., 2022).

Recent studies highlight that digital health data-based lifestyle changes could benefit major health (Rhee et al., 2020; Schwartz et al., 2020). The factors influencing the adoption of such digital health technologies include favorable environmental conditions, the expected ease of use, trust, and peer influence (Ahmad et al., 2020; M. Gupta, Kumar, et al., 2023). After adopting these technologies, aspects such as their usefulness, ease of operation, user engagement, confidence in using them, the nature of the tasks they assist with, user anxiety levels, and the enjoyment they provide are crucial for their sustained use. Research involving 312 long-term smartwatch users from four Asian nations revealed a strong link between the users' expectations of performance, self-motivation, comfort, and the perceived usefulness of the smartwatches for ongoing usage (Pal et al., 2020).

The responsiveness and standardization of smart wearables in the premium price segment are crucial in shaping their acceptance as reliable healthcare devices. Immediate and accurate responses to health metrics (like heart rate, steps, and sleep quality) enhance user trust and reliance on the device for health monitoring (Bayoumy et al., 2021c). In critical health scenarios, quick responsiveness can be life-saving, for instance, detecting a fall or a sudden spike in heart rate (Tanwar et al., 2022). Responsiveness regarding user interfaces, like easy navigation and quick access to data, encourages regular use and engagement. Standardization ensures that the data collected is accurate and comparable to traditional medical devices (Conradie & Nagel, 2022). This is crucial for both users and healthcare professionals. Adherence to standardized norms aids in gaining necessary regulatory approvals, increasing user trust in the device's safety and efficacy(Hill, 2022). Devices responsive and standardized are more likely to be trusted by users and recommended by healthcare professionals. Such devices can appeal to a broader audience, including the health-conscious, elderly, and those with specific medical conditions (Al-Maroof et al., 2021). As more companies strive to meet these standards, it fosters innovation and offers better choices to consumers.

Despite numerous studies on healthcare professionals' use of smart wearables, there's a noticeable gap in research on consumer purchasing patterns. While the Technology Acceptance Model (TAM) and the Unified Theory of Acceptance and Use of Technology (UTAUT) have been used to understand the initial acceptance of technology, there's less focus on the ongoing willingness to use smartwatches and similar devices. Additionally, issues like data privacy concerns and the accuracy of healthcare information remain largely unexamined, yet they are crucial for users' continued willingness to use these devices. Continued usage intent is becoming more important in the competitive technology market (Karjaluoto et al., 2020). This concept has been explored in other areas, such as online learning, mobile banking, and social networking. Research using the Diffusion of Innovations (DOI) theory suggests that the decision to keep using a technology is a key factor in its long-term success (Behal & Gupta, 2022; Ho et al., 2020; Kim et al., 2019).

Table 1. The Recent Studies on Smart Wearables Adoption as a Healthcare Device

Area of Focus	Key Findings	References
User Behavior in Emerging Markets	Examines the evolving acceptance patterns of smart wearables in emerging markets, focusing on user behavior over time.	(Niknejad et al., 2020)
Impact of AI on User Satisfaction	Investigates the impact of AI enhancements on user satisfaction and continuance intention in smart wearables.	(El-Gayar & Elnoshokaty, 2023)
Design and Application of Wearable Sensors	Explores how cultural factors influence the adoption and sustained use of healthcare wearables in different global regions.	(Singh et al., 2022)
Preventive Healthcare and Lifestyle Changes	Studies the influence of wearable technology on users' preventive healthcare behaviors and lifestyle changes.	(Yen, 2021)
Privacy and User Trust	Analyzes the relationship between privacy concerns and user trust in the context of smart health devices.	(Awotunde et al., 2021)
Regional User Experiences Comparison	Compares user experiences with smart wearables in North American and Asian markets, highlighting regional differences.	(Chang, et al., 2023)
Adoption of Healthcare Wearables	Identify factors such as privacy concerns, perceived benefits, cost, ease of use, and social influence that influence individuals' decisions to adopt healthcare wearable devices.	(Bianchi et al., 20230

The review highlights an unexplored area in research concerning the influence of factors like the readiness to pay, the acceptance of higher pricing, and the reliability of health data on the ongoing use of smart wearable devices. Utilizing the framework of Expectation-confirmation theory, this study seeks to explore users' propensity to pay more for smart wearables, emphasizing satisfaction after usage.

Expectation-Confirmation Theory

In marketing, the Expectation-Confirmation Theory (ECT) serves as a framework for understanding consumer behavior, particularly in relation to repeat purchases (Nguyen & Ha, 2021). The central premise of ECT is that consumer satisfaction leads to an intention to repurchase. Before a purchase, consumers form opinions and expectations about a product or service. These opinions often arise from various sources, including mass media, direct marketing, and word-of-mouth from early adopters and peer groups (Qazi et al., 2017). The quality of information a consumer receives before purchasing significantly impacts their expectations. Misleading or false information can set unrealistic expectations, affecting the consumer's satisfaction (Bhattacherjee, 2001b). ECT encapsulates the journey from consumer expectation to satisfaction, as typically illustrated in models like Fig. 1. It accounts for scenarios where consumers make purchases without prior expectations. In such cases, the product's actual performance is compared with the pre-purchase expectations to gauge satisfaction.

One of the most significant adaptations of ECT for technology adoption is the ECM (Expectation-Confirmation Model) (Mamun et al., 2020). ECM is rooted in continuance theory, which postulates that Information Technology (IT) professionals satisfied with technology are more likely to continue using it (Y. M. Cheng, 2021). Unlike ECT, which focuses on pre-purchase expectations, ECM examines user perspectives post-usage, considering factors such as usefulness and satisfaction. In the ECM framework, pre-acceptance variables, such as initial expectations, are encapsulated within the constructs of 'confirmation' and 'satisfaction' (Purohit et al., 2022). This shifts the focus from what consumers anticipate before using a product to how they feel about it after they have had a chance to interact with it.

The Information Systems (IS) literature underscores the pivotal role of ongoing technology usage for the success of an IS implementation. It is well-recognized that acquiring a new client is about five times more costly than retaining an existing one (Brandon-Jones & Kauppi, 2018). Therefore, businesses need to attract new users and focus on keeping their existing customer base satisfied and engaged for sustainable growth. The Technology Acceptance Model (TAM) has been instrumental in exploring technology adoption by emphasizing the perceived usefulness prior to usage. In contrast, the Expectation-Confirmation Model (ECM) focuses on post-usage perceptions to understand long-term confidence in a technology. ECM can be viewed as an extension of the Expectation-Confirmation Theory (ECT), adapted for the IS context. It replaces ECT's focus on 'expectation' and 'repurchase intention' with considerations of 'post-usage usefulness' and 'continual intention to use' (Hossain & Quaddus, 2012). The ECM has been rigorously validated in various technological contexts, including mobile banking. Its applicability was further broadened to mobile data services by incorporating the TAM's construct of 'perceived ease of use' (Hidayat-Ur-Rehman et al., 2021). Despite the extensive literature on technology adoption models like TAM and ECM, there is a notable scarcity of research specifically addressing the 'survivability' of wearable technologies and smartwatches as healthcare devices.

This research bridges the gap by exploring the 'continuous intention to use' smartwatches and wearable technology in light of 'Premium prices' as a healthcare device. By understanding the determinants of 'continuous intention to use,' the study uncovers insights that could drive the persistent adoption and effective integration of wearable tech in the healthcare industry.

Premium Price

A key sign of customer loyalty, an essential aspect of brand value, is the readiness of customers to pay a higher price for a particular brand, even when an alternative of similar value is available (Grewal et al., 2003). This propensity to opt for a higher-priced item from a particular brand is a direct measure of the brand's equity in the marketplace (Khan & DePaoli, 2023). When introducing groundbreaking technology like wearable devices, the concept of premium pricing takes on additional layers of complexity and importance. The pricing strategies, particularly in the context of the marketing mix elements, can be instrumental in either catalyzing or hindering the broad adoption of such novel technologies (Chopra & Gupta, 2023; Manika et al., 2021).

Premium pricing allows the integration of advanced technology into smart wearables, which requires significant investment in research and development by the manufacturers. This investment is crucial to ensure the accuracy and precision of sensors that monitor important health indicators such as heart rate, blood oxygen levels, and electrocardiogram (ECG) readings (Kasilingam & Krishna, 2022; Oyedele et al., 2018). In wearables designed for individuals with specific health conditions, the accuracy of the measurements is especially important.

The current study presents a theoretical framework shown in Figure 1, designed to examine user attitudes towards smart wearables following their initial use. This model includes key factors like 'Performance Expectancy' and 'Satisfaction,' alongside control variables such as the 'Accuracy of Health Information' and the 'Premium price.' Central to the model are "Performance Expectancy" and "Satisfaction." These variables are the backbone for understanding the factors contributing to an individual's continued intention to use smart wearables. Performance Expectancy evaluates the anticipated benefits of using the technology, while Satisfaction assesses the user's contentment with the initial usage experience.

To augment the primary model, identified variables such as 'Health Information Accuracy' and 'Premium Price' have been included. 'Health Information Accuracy' assesses the trustworthiness of the health data gathered by the smart wearable. In contrast, 'Premium Price' measures consumers' readiness to pay more for added value. This part offers a detailed examination of the hypotheses and theoretical foundations shaping the causal structure of the suggested model. These hypotheses are designed to investigate the interactions between main and supplementary variables, thus deepening our insight into the factors affecting the sustained usage of smart wearables

Health Information Accuracy

The utilization of smart wearable healthcare technology is often underpinned by an individual's heightened awareness and concern for their health. As this health consciousness intensifies, it stimulates more frequent engagement with health-related technology associated with favorable health outcomes. In the discourse on wearable technology, these devices are increasingly conceptualized as "protective technology." Specifically, they monitor and manage vital signs in real-time, thus providing the user with an added layer of proactive health management. Previous research has enhanced our knowledge about how intentions to protect health correlate with the usage of wearable technology (Lee & Lee, 2020; Talukder et al., 2021). It's been empirically proven that people who focus on safeguarding their health tend to be more inclined to use smart wearables to manage their health (Bayoumy et al., 2021a; Singh et al., 2022). Intriguingly, research has begun to explore the psychological underpinnings that may catalyze the adoption of smart wearables. Studies indicate that people who experience feelings of vulnerability or being slighted are more inclined to adopt smart wearables as a defensive health strategy (O'hagan et al., 2023).

Smart wearables offer a range of estimated health metrics, each with varying degrees of accuracy. These devices primarily utilize optical heart rate sensors, where accuracy can differ substantially based on factors like how the device is worn (including its tightness and wrist placement), physical activity (steady-state versus high-intensity workouts), and personal characteristics like skin tone and wrist size. While they generally provide reliable heart rate measurements, these can be affected by physical movements. Regarding step counting, smart wearables are usually accurate for standard walking and running activities. However, their accuracy can diminish in scenarios involving irregular movements or activities that don't involve significant arm movement. Compared to clinical sleep studies, sleep tracking in wearables is less accurate. These devices estimate sleep patterns through movement and heart rate data, offering a basic guide but often lacking precision in differentiating between sleep stages. Calorie burn estimates in these devices are derived from algorithms that consider elements such as heart rate, steps taken, and occasionally personal information like weight and age. These estimations are broadly viewed as rough approximations, with their accuracy varying across different conditions and individuals.

While smart wearables provide useful insights into health and fitness, the data they present should be regarded as estimative rather than exact, particularly for complex metrics like sleep quality or calorie expenditure.

Figure 1. Conceptual Framework
Source: author's own work

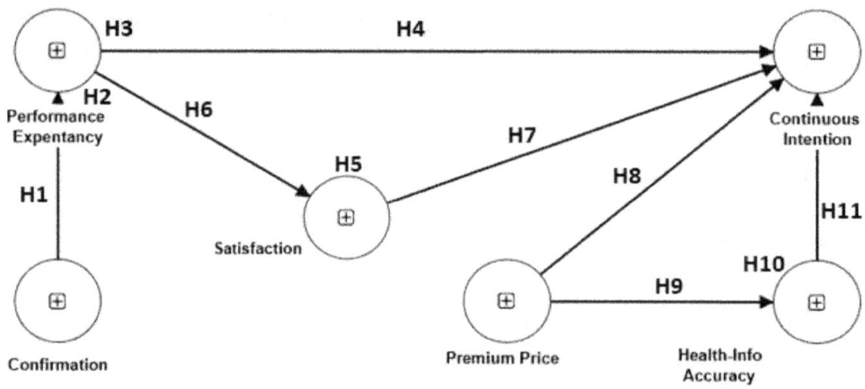

HYPOTHESES DEVELOPMENT

After conducting a thorough review of the current research literature, significant gaps were identified. To address these gaps, a comprehensive conceptual framework has been developed. This framework is instrumental in underpinning the study's theoretical basis and guiding its research methodology. Central to this framework is a series of hypotheses, which have been meticulously formulated to test the key aspects of the study's focus. These hypotheses, pivotal to advancing our understanding in this field, are delineated and presented in Figure 1. This figure serves not only as a visual representation of the hypotheses but also as a roadmap for the research, highlighting the specific areas the study aims to explore and the relationships it seeks to establish.

Confirmation

Confirmation in the context of technology usage refers to individuals using technology believing that their anticipated outcomes and expectations are being fulfilled to a certain degree (Daragmeh et al., 2021; Huang, 2019). Previous research, as highlighted in studies (A. Gupta et al., 2020; Liu & Kao, 2022; Y. Sun & Ly, 2023) has shown a noteworthy positive connection between confirmation of pre-purchase expectations and two important factors: Performance Expectancy and Satisfaction. Individuals who perceive a high level of confirmation of their pre-purchase expectations regarding a technology's performance are more likely to have a higher Performance Expectancy, positively influencing their intention to continue using the technology (A. Gupta et al., 2020). If users' initial expectations about the performance of the technology are met (confirmation), they will anticipate continued positive outcomes (high-Performance Expectancy), encouraging continued use (Thong et al., 2006). Performance Expectancy and Satisfaction mediate the relationship between confirmation of pre-purchase expectations and the intention to persist in using the technology (Jain et al., 2022). This paper investigates how the confirmation impacts the intention to use a specific technology. We examine this effect by considering two key elements: Performance Expectancy and Satisfaction.

H1: The buyer's Performance expectation is directly and significantly influenced by confirmation.
H2: The buyer's Satisfaction is indirectly and significantly influenced by confirmation (Mediation).
H3: The buyer's Continuous intention is indirectly and significantly influenced by confirmation (Mediation).

Performance Expectancy

In examining customer behavior before and after adopting a product, "Performance Expectancy" is crucial (Venkatesh et al., 2003). This term describes how much a person believes using a particular technology will enhance their ability to complete specific tasks or activities (Venkatesh et al., 2012). Previous studies have shown that Performance Expectancy positively influences both user satisfaction and ongoing use of the technology research (Dehghani, 2018; Rabaa'i et al., 2021). The users who find technology meets or exceeds their performance expectations are likely to be more satisfied, making them more inclined to continue purchasing these products (L. Li et al., 2021). If users believe that the wearables are not just effective (high Performance Expectancy) but also offer good value for money, they are more likely to continue purchasing them (Park, 2020).In this study, we explore the direct effects of Performance Expectancy on the continued purchasing behavior for smart wearables and its indirect effects through a mediating variable. The hypotheses for this study are as follows:

H4: The buyer's continuous intention is directly and significantly influenced by performance expectations.
H5: The buyer's Continuous intention is indirectly and significantly influenced by Performance Expectancy through satisfaction (Mediation).
H6: The buyer's satisfaction is directly and significantly influenced by performance expectations.

Satisfaction

The likelihood of a customer continuing to use a technology is highly influenced by their satisfaction level (Tran et al., 2018). The Expectation-Confirmation Model (ECM) proposes that satisfaction is a primary factor influencing the continued use of technology. Supporting this, past studies have demonstrated a significant positive link between user satisfaction and their ongoing engagement with technology (Bhattacherjee, 2001a). Specifically, if customers find that smart wearables meet or even partially fulfill their expectations, they are likely to continue using the product (Dehghani et al., 2018) (Rabaa'i et al., 2021). Satisfaction derived from expectation fulfillment is a key driver of repeat purchasing decisions (Cotarelo et al., 2021). Consumers will continue to purchase smart wearables if they find them more satisfying than alternatives available (Park, 2020). In this study, we focus on assessing consumer satisfaction's direct impact on smart wearables' continued purchasing behavior. The hypotheses for this investigation are as follows:

H7: The buyer's Continuous intention is directly and significantly influenced by the level of Consumer Satisfaction.

Premium Price

A principal pointer of customer loyalty, commonly regarded as a crucial element of brand equity, is the consumer's promptness to pay a higher price for a particular brand than another of comparable value (Saygılı & Yalçıntekin, 2021). This concept of premium pricing becomes particularly important during the launch of new technologies, such as wearable devices. Existing research has shown that premium price strongly predicts ongoing usage intentions across various settings, from mobile phone applications (Iranmanesh et al., 2022) to food delivery services (Watson, 2022). (Laitala et al., 2021) suggests that consumers often use price as an indicator of quality. In the health technology sector, where the accuracy of information can be a matter of significant concern, consumers might be more inclined to trust and rely on higher-priced products, assuming that they offer more precision and reliability (Nagy et al., 2023). Built through the precision of health information leads to greater tolerance for premium pricing (Pandey & Litoriya, 2020). This study examines the impact of premium pricing on sustained purchasing habits of smart wearable devices, specifically in the context of precision health information. The hypothesis is that the perceived value and accuracy of the health information provided by these devices justifies their premium pricing, thereby influencing continued purchasing behavior. This reflects consumers' willingness to pay more for higher quality or reliability in health-related technology. The investigation will test the following hypotheses.

H8: The buyer's Continuous intention is directly and significantly influenced by the premium price.
H9: The buyer's Health-info accuracy is directly and significantly influenced by the premium price.
H10: The buyer's continuous intention is indirectly and significantly influenced by the premium price through health information accuracy (Mediation).

Health-Info Accuracy

Smart wearables offer users a range of benefits, from enhancing productivity and reducing stress to improving sleep quality. For those with chronic health situations, these devices can deliver data detailed enough to observe disease progression (Çiçek, 2015). Wearable healthcare technology is often used regularly due to health concerns, making these devices essential for protection. Devices like watchbands and mobile apps, for instance, can identify symptoms of depression by examining vocal tones in phone calls and monitoring exercise and sleep habits. Despite their usefulness, the precision and dependability of the health data these devices produce is a significant issue. Past studies have shown that people who are proactive about their health are more likely to adopt smart wearables (Vijayan et al., 2021). Further studies reveal that people are more likely to adopt these devices for health protection when they perceive a health risk (Guo et al., 2015). Individuals with chronic health conditions are more likely to exhibit sustained purchasing behavior for smart wearables as they rely on the accuracy of these devices for disease management and monitoring (Vijayan et al., 2021). In this study, we explore the direct impact of the accuracy of health information on the continued purchasing behavior for smart wearables. The hypotheses for this investigation are as follows:

H11: The buyer's Continuous intention is directly and significantly influenced by the Health-info Accuracy.

RESEARCH METHODOLOGY

A multi-indicator model based on reflective measurement is crafted to evaluate the latent variables. This model employs scales specifically designed for the constructs to measure their impact on the ongoing use of smart wearables, following the guidelines of the Expectation-Confirmation Model (ECM) (Bhattacherjee, 2001c). The conceptual framework depicted in Figure 1 details the relationships among different predictors that affect the 'Continuous Intention' to persist in using smart wearables. This study's survey instruments were carefully chosen from established literature to align with the research's focus. The survey was structured into two distinct parts. The initial section collected demographic details, including participants' gender, monthly earnings, age category, and educational background. The subsequent section was dedicated to evaluating the constructs being studied. Response options were structured on a Likert scale, starting from "Strongly Disagree" to "Strongly Agree."

Collection of Data

The study initially involved 700 participants, yet only 678 responses were deemed sufficiently comprehensive for the analysis. The focus was on individuals using smartwatches in Chandigarh, India. To qualify participants, the question 'Do you use a smartwatch?' was used, and anyone answering 'NO' was excluded from the study. The methods for gathering data included a blend of convenience and referral-based sampling strategies. Questions were posed directly and through extended social networks, focusing on smart wearable user participants for valuable insights. Before the survey, participants were briefed on the study's objectives and assured of their anonymity and confidentiality. A minimum of 200 cases for SEM is often recommended, especially for complex models with multiple latent variables. Larger sample sizes can provide more accurate and reliable estimates for complex models (Kline, 2023). The study's sample size of 678 comfortably surpasses the recommended range of a minimum of 200 participants for structural equation models, adding credibility to the findings. To further validate the questionnaire's reliability and content validity, a pilot study involving 90 respondents was conducted. The primary survey comprised a questionnaire completed by the participants, featuring 18 items addressing the study of six distinct aspects. The questionnaire also collected demographic information, including the respondents' age, gender, income, marital status, and educational background.

Descriptive Statistics

In this research, 71.38% of the participants identified as male, while 28.61% were female. The predominant age group among the respondents was individuals between 20 and 29 years old, constituting the majority at 45.28%. Furthermore, a substantial portion of the participants (40.41%) reported a monthly income of less than Rs. 20,000. Examining the educational backgrounds of the respondents, 36.78% indicated undergraduate status, whereas a significant 63.27% held postgraduate degrees or higher academic qualifications. This suggests a distinct trend wherein smartwatches enjoy popularity primarily among young males, even in instances where their income is comparatively lower. Interestingly, despite the economic constraints, a considerable proportion of this demographic seems to prioritize the adoption of smartwatches. The study also reveals a noteworthy aspect related to the complexity of smartwatch functionalities. It indicates a preference for these devices among individuals with higher levels of education. This could be attributed to the inclination of more educated individuals to appreciate and leverage the advanced features offered by smartwatches.

The comprehensive findings of the study, as outlined in Table 3, provide a detailed overview of the descriptive statistics, shedding light on the demographic distribution and preferences among smartwatch users in the surveyed population.

Table 2. Measurement of objects

S.No.	Construct and Source	Question and Measure
1	Confirmation (CNF) (Nascimento et al., 2018; Park, 2020)	I believe smart wearables will perform all the functions they claim to.(CNF1)
		My expectations about the features of smart wearables are usually met after purchase. (CNF2)
		I expect smart wearables to be user-friendly and easily integrated into my daily routine. (CNF3)
2	Performance Expectancy(PE) (Celic & Magjarevic, 2020; Moon et al., 2019; V. Sharma, Taneja, et al., 2023)	I expect smart wearables to have a wide range of useful features.(PE1)
		Seamless connectivity with smartphones and other electronics is a key expectation for smart wearables.(PE2)
		I expect smart wearables to integrate with my other devices and apps easily.(PE3)
3	Satisfaction(STF) (J. W. Cheng & Mitomo, 2017; Kao et al., 2019)	My smart wearable functions reliably under various conditions.(STF1)
		My smart wearable's health and fitness tracking features are accurate and useful.(STF2)
		I am satisfied with the connectivity options available on my smart wearable.(STF3)
4	Premium Price(PP) (Kasilingam & Krishna, 2022; Oyedele et al., 2018)	I perceive brands that offer premium-priced smart wearables as more prestigious.(PP1)
		The premium price of these wearables suggests they use advanced and reliable health technology.(PP2)
		The brand reputation of a premium-priced wearable influences my perception of its effectiveness as a healthcare device.(PP3)
5	Health Info Accuracy(HIA) (J. W. Cheng & Mitomo, 2017; Marakhimov & Joo, 2017)	My smart wearable makes me more likely to engage in health-promoting activities. (HIA1)
		I rely on my smart wearable for accurate health information and advice.(HIA2)
		Smart wearables can potentially reduce the need for frequent medical check-ups.(HIA3)
6	Continuous Intention (Malhi et al., 2023; Park, 2020)	Using my smart wearable has improved my overall health and fitness(CI1)
		I intend to continue using my smart wearable for health monitoring.(CI2)
		Maintaining and updating my smart wearable is straightforward and hassle-free.(CI3)

Quantitative Data Analysis

In this study, the proposed hypotheses were thoroughly tested and analyzed using Smart PLS 4. This software exercises the partial least square method (PLS-SEM), a nonparametric structural modeling, to examine the data. PLS-SEM combines qualitative and quantitative methods, which allows the testing and estimation of causal relationships. This approach is particularly effective in our research context, where we aim to examine mediation effects within the EC model(Alfes et al., 2013). Smart PLS was chosen specifically due to its effectiveness in model estimation and suitability for our research objectives. One of the key reasons for selecting PLS-SEM was its ability to handle data that does not follow a normal distribution. This characteristic of PLS-SEM makes it a valuable tool in fields like social and behavioral sciences, where data often deviates from normality(Kock, 2016). The analysis process was divided into two main phases. The first phase focused on the Measurement model, while the second phase determined the Structural model. Using Smart PLS 4, we explored the relationships specified in our theoretical framework. This software cannot only process data with non-normal distributions but also aligns with our research goals, especially in examining complex mediation effects in the EC model(Fernando et al., 2019). Overall, Smart PLS proved an effective tool for in-depth hypothesis analysis, combining quantitative accuracy with the nuanced understanding required in social and behavioral research.

Table 3. Demographic information of survey participants

Group	Sub-Group	Frequency (%age)
Gender	Male	484(71.38)
	Female	194(28.61)
Age Group	Less 20 years	235(34.66)
	20–29	307(45.28)
	30-39	67(9.88)
	40 and above	69(10.17)
Income (Monthly)	Upto 20,000	274(40.41)
	20000-50000	227(33.48)
	Exceeding 50,000	177(26.10)
Level of Eductaion	Undergraduate	249(36.78)
	Post Graduate	429(63.27)

DATA ANALYSIS AND OUTCOME EVALUATION

Measurement Model

In the framework of the measurement model, a comprehensive approach was adopted to evaluate various aspects of the model's validity and reliability. This involved assessing internal consistency, convergent validity (how well the model items reflect the construct they are intended to measure), and discriminant validity (the extent to which a construct is truly distinct from other constructs).

To ensure the reliability of the indicators within each construct, two principal metrics were employed: Cronbach's alpha (α) and Composite Reliability. Cronbach's alpha measures internal consistency, indicating how closely related a set of items are as a group. It is a widely accepted indicator of the reliability of psychometric instruments. The higher the value of Cronbach's alpha, the more reliable the generated scale is. Composite Reliability, on the other hand, measures the internal consistency of test scores, similar to Cronbach's alpha. However, it is often considered a more accurate reflection of reliability.

According to the data in Table 4 of the study, all constructs met and surpassed the standard benchmarks set for these metrics. The threshold Cronbach's Alpha and Composite Reliability is a widely acknowledged benchmark of 0.70 (Foppoli et al., 2020) in research, indicating satisfactory internal consistency and reliability (Sarstedt et al., 2021). The surpassing of these thresholds indicates a robust performance across the reliability measures. This confirms the reliability of the indicators associated with each construct and enhances the credibility of the measurement model. It suggests that the constructs used in the study are reliably measured, ensuring that subsequent analyses based on these constructs are grounded on a solid foundation of reliable measurement.

Table 4. Evaluating reliability and determining validity of identified construct

Variables	Name	Mean	Standard deviation	Stand. Loadings	Cronbach alpha (α)	Composite reliability	AVE
Performance Expectation	*PE1*	3.891	1.277	0.905	0.925	0.952	0.869
	PE2	3.894	1.232	0.953			
	PE3	3.979	1.189	0.939			
Confirmation	*CNF1*	3.761	1.334	0.888	0.895	0.935	0.826
	CNF 2	3.817	1.284	0.916			
	CNF 3	3.855	1.348	0.927			
Satisfaction	*STF1*	3.755	1.232	0.924	0.903	0.939	0.837
	STF2	3.785	1.268	0.912			
	STF3	3.808	1.203	0.909			
Premium Price	*PP1*	3.888	1.167	0.892	0.871	0.92	0.794
	PP2	3.861	1.205	0.901			
	PP3	3.941	1.163	0.880			
Continuous Intention	*CI1*	3.855	1.220	0.888	0.897	0.936	0.829
	CI2	4.021	1.249	0.919			
	CI3	3.894	1.219	0.928			
Health Info Accuracy	*HIA1*	3.832	1.303	0.922	0.920	0.949	0.862
	HIA2	3.752	1.351	0.922			
	HIA3	3.796	1.415	0.941			

Source 1: Calculated by author

The estimation of discriminant validity in this study involved employing two established criteria: the HTMT ratio (Voorhees et al., 2016) and the Fornell-Larcker criterion (Henseler et al., 2015). Table 5 exhibits the consequences of this evaluation, illustrating the achievement of discriminant validity. The Heterotrait-Monotrait ratios, a measure of the dissimilarity between constructs, originate below the specified threshold of 0.85 (J. F. Hair et al., 2014). This outcome signifies that the constructs exhibit sufficient discriminant validity, indicating that the traits measured by different constructs are more distinct than those measured by the same construct.

Additionally, the Fornell-Larcker criterion, a commonly recognized method for assessing discriminant validity, involves comparing the Average Variance Extracted (AVE) values with the squared correlation coefficient between the relevant factors (J. F. Hair et al., 2019). In the context of this study, the AVE values, shown below the diagonal in Table 5, were observed to surpass the squared coefficients of correlation. This finding aligns with the criterion's expectations, confirming the constructs' discriminant validity. In essence, the results from the HTMT ratio and Fornell-Larcker criterion collectively underscore the robust discriminant validity of the constructs, affirming their ability to differentiate and measure distinct traits within the study framework.

Table 5. Test for discriminant validity

	CNF	CI	HIA	PE	PP	STF
CNF	**0.911**	--	--	--	--	--
CI	0.439(0.481)	**0.909**				--
HIA	0.531(0.562)	0.520(0.575)	**0.930**			--
PE	0.569(0.615)	0.589(0.651)	0.520(0.572)	**0.935**		--
PP	0.309(0.362)	0.443(0.503)	0.314(0.347)	0.449(0.493)	**0.871**	--
STF	0.480(0.517)	0.610(0.671)	0.442(0.492)	0.556(0.609)	0.343(0.410)	**0.917**

Source 2: Calculated by author

Note 1: The matrix's diagonal elements represent Average Variance Extracted (AVE), while the off-diagonal values signify the correlation coefficients, adhering to the Fornell-Larcker criterion, specifically captured through Heterotrait-Monotrait (HTMT) ratios.

5.2 Structural Model

The estimation of the structural model, which concentrated on testing hypotheses and its capacity to explain and forecast results, adhered to the methods outlined in referenced sources (J. Hair et al., 2017; Sarstedt et al., 2022). Path coefficients in the structural model, which represent the strength and significance of the relationships, were organized based on the methods recommended by (Sarstedt et al., 2021). Key findings in Table 6 emerged from this systematic analysis.

A significant observation was the role of 'Confirmation' as a major influencer, exerting a direct and substantial effect on 'Performance Expectancy' ($\beta = 0.569$, $p \leq 0.05$). This finding strongly supports H_1. Additionally, 'Performance Expectancy' was identified as a significant direct predictor of 'Satisfaction' ($\beta = 0.57$, $p \leq 0.05$), validating H_6.

In analyzing variables impacting 'Continuation Intention,' the study identified 'Satisfaction' as a major influencer ($\beta = 0.313$, $p < 0.05$), confirming hypothesis H_7. Following closely was 'Performance Expectancy' ($\beta = 0.229$, $p \leq 0.05$), supporting hypothesis H_4. Additionally, the study revealed that 'Willingness to Pay a Premium Price' significantly forecasted 'Continuation Intention' ($\beta = 0.169$, $p > 0.05$), in line with hypothesis H_8. Moreover, 'Health Information Accuracy' was found to be a critical element ($\beta = 0.314$, $p < 0.05$), validating hypothesis H_9, and its strong predictive relationship with 'Continuation Intention' ($\beta = 0.213$, $p < 0.05$) underscored its importance, as proposed in hypothesis H_{11}.

In its investigation of indirect effects in Table 7, the study discovered that 'Confirmation' had a notable indirect effect on 'Satisfaction' ($\beta = 0.319$, $p \leq 0.05$), affirming hypothesis H_2. In terms of 'Continuation Intention,' key influencing factors were identified as 'Confirmation' ($\beta = 0.229$, $p < 0.05$, aligning with H3), 'Performance Expectancy' ($\beta = 0.181$, $p \leq 0.05$, aligning with H_5), and 'Willingness to Pay the Premium Price' ($\beta = 0.059$, $p \leq 0.05$, aligning with H_{10}). These findings provide a comprehensive view of the interplay among various elements, shedding light on what motivates users to use smartwatches.

Figure 2. Analysis of structural
Source 3:Calculated by author

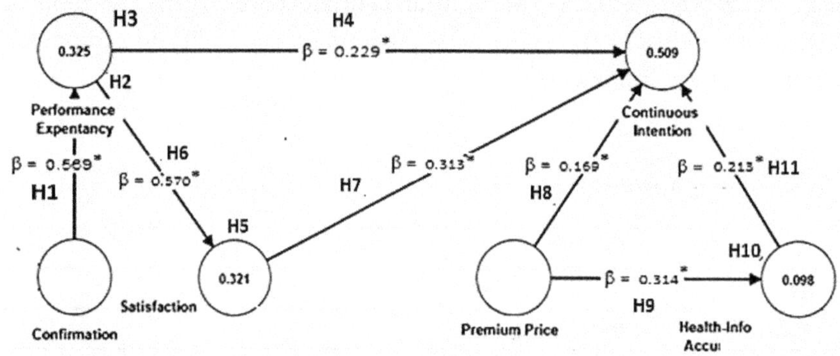

Table 6. Direct variables relationship

Hypothesis	Variables	(β)	t-stat	Significance level	R^2
H_1	CNF--> PE	0.569	18.031	0.00*	0.335
H_4	PE-->CI	0.229	5.189	0.00*	0.509
H_6	PE-->STF	0.570	16.26	0.00*	
H_7	STF-->CI	0.313	6.717	0.00*	
H_8	PP-->CI	0.169	4.15	0.00*	
H_9	PP-->HIA	0.314	7.117	0.00*	0.095
H_{11}	HIA->CI	0.213	4.725	0.00*	0.323

Source 4: Calculated by author

Table 7. Overall indirect relationships among variables

Hyp	Variables	(β)	t-stat	Significance level
H_2	CNF-->STF	0.319	10.51	0.00*
H_3	CNF-->CI	0.229	7.79	0.00*
H_5	PE-->CI	0.181	5.98	0.00*
H_{10}	PP-->CI	0.059	4.082	0.00*

Source 5: Calculated by author

Note 2: Health-Info Accuracy = HIA, Confirmation = CNF, Premium Price = PP, Performance Expectancy = PE, Satisfaction = STF, Continuous Intention = CI

FINDINGS OF THE STUDY

In this study, the researchers thoroughly identified key variables influencing the continued usage intention of smart wearables post-adoption. A crucial step in ensuring the reliability and validity of the study's constructs was measuring and confirming these aspects against established threshold limits.

The significant variance explained for each dependent variable was assessed, revealing noteworthy insights into user behavior. For "Performance Expectancy," the R-squared value ($R^2 = 0.325$) attained an acceptable range of 0.30[80]. Similarly, "Satisfaction" exhibited a significant variance explained with an R-squared value of 0.321, and "Continuous Intention" showed the highest explanatory power with an R-squared value of 0.509. These results align with the acceptable range criterion, demonstrating that the identified factors play substantial roles in influencing user perceptions and intentions regarding smart wearables. The study's findings emphasize a critical relationship between satisfaction and the likelihood of users continuing to use smart wearables over an extended period. The degree to which users are satisfied with the performance of these devices significantly influences their decision to persist in their usage(W. T. Wang et al., 2019). This underscores the importance of managing and meeting user expectations for optimal device performance. The study also elevates a pertinent question regarding the accuracy of health-related information monitored by smart wearables. Features such as tracking sleep patterns, measuring heartbeat levels, monitoring calories burned, and functioning as an oximeter are highlighted. The study indicates that the continued use of smart wearables may axis on the reliability and precision of the health-related data provided by these devices (Quévat & Heinze, 2020). This emphasizes the critical role of accuracy in health-related metrics as a determinant of user satisfaction and their intention to continue using the technology. Additionally, the study identifies a significant correlation between the perceived innovation or attractiveness of the technology and users' willingness to pay a premium price for smart wearables. This implies that consumers are more inclined to invest in these devices if they perceive them as innovative or if the information they provide is deemed accurate and valuable. The willingness to pay a premium price reflects the perceived value that users attribute to the technology, emphasizing the importance of offering innovative features and ensuring accurate data output to justify the premium pricing strategy.

IMPLICATIONS OF THE STUDY

Theoretical Implication of the Study

In this chapter, the ECM (Expectation Confirmation Model) provides valuable insights into the factors that influence the continuous use of smart wearables. The ECM is a well-established framework for understanding user behavior in technology adoption, and it proves to be effective even in newer domains like smart wearables. The study shows that constructs such as 'Performance Expectancy', 'Satisfaction', and 'Confirmation' are significant predictors of 'Continuous Intention'. It emphasizes that users' early experiences with a product significantly impact their continued usage (Ashraf et al., 2020; A. Gupta et al., 2020). Furthermore, 'Satisfaction' plays a pivotal role in the relationship between 'Performance Expectancy' and 'Continuous Intention.' It is not just an outcome but also a mediator that links user expectations to their decision to continue using a product (Rabaa'i & ALMaati, 2021; V. Sharma, Taneja, et al., 2023). There is a complex relationship between several factors, including "Performance Expectancy," "Satisfaction," and "Premium Price," and their impact on users' "Continuous Intention." Given this complexity, the wearable technology market must consider multiple dimensions, such as performance, satisfaction, and perceived value, when designing user retention strategies. The willingness of users to pay a higher price for smart wearables is strongly linked to their continuous intention to use the product (Yang et al., 2016). This effect can be either direct or indirect, mediated by the perceived accuracy of health information provided by the device. Therefore, pricing strategies and the perceived value of health information accuracy are critical considerations for developers in the smart wearables market (Mathavan et al., 2024). The study also highlights the importance users place on the accuracy of health information provided by wearables, as this factor has a strong predictive relationship with their continuous intention to use the product. This insight can be valuable for wearable technology developers, indicating that accuracy in health-related features can be a key driver of long-term user engagement.

This study explains the factors influencing users' decision to use smart wearables. From the critical role of satisfaction based on performance expectations to the accuracy of health-related information and the perceived value of novel technology, these insights provide a comprehensive understanding of the complex dynamics shaping user behavior in smart wearables. These findings have significant implications for designing, marketing, and developing smart wearables, guiding strategies to enhance user satisfaction, and promoting prolonged engagement with these technological innovations.

Practical Implications of the Study

To keep users engaged with smart wearables, it is essential to understand and improve the aspects of the products that impact user satisfaction and the intention to continue using them. One of these aspects is the "confirmation" of how well the product meets initial expectations, which significantly affects the "performance expectancy" or how well the user thinks the product will perform. Therefore, companies should ensure that their smart wearables meet or exceed initial customer expectations. This can be achieved through clear marketing communication, product quality assurance, and effective customer service right from the start. The relationship between 'Performance Expectancy' and 'Satisfaction' indicates that the better a smartwatch performs, the more satisfied customers will be. Manufacturers should prioritize the most important features to users and ensure that these features perform reliably. With 'Willingness to Pay a Premium Price' and 'Health-info Accuracy' both influencing 'Continuous Intention,' it is clear that users are willing to pay more for quality, especially for accurate health information. This suggests a market for high-end smartwatches that can deliver superior health-tracking capabilities. As the accuracy of health information is crucial in shaping the continuous intention of users, companies need to invest in improving the accuracy of health-related features. This could be achieved by incorporating better sensors, utilizing advanced data algorithms, or forming partnerships with health professionals. The study's collection of demographic details suggests that different groups may have varying preferences and needs. Therefore, companies could customize their products or marketing strategies to cater to specific demographics based on gender, age, income, or educational background. When designing marketing strategies, emphasizing the long-term benefits of using the product, such as ongoing satisfaction and the accuracy of health information, could be more effective than solely focusing on immediate features or pricing.

This research has significant implications for smartwatch manufacturers and designers, providing essential insights to improve user retention. The study emphasizes the close relationship between user satisfaction and their expectations for smart wearable performance, including design, comfort, and durability (Salahuddin & Romeo, 2020).

RECOMMENDATIONS OF THE STUDY

Wearable technology has become increasingly popular among health-conscious individuals seeking to monitor and improve their well-being. To create and maintain user engagement, product developers need to prioritize and enhance key areas such as product design, comfort, durability, health information accuracy, and innovative strategies. Companies must consider various factors to ensure users continue using smart wearables. These factors include performance, user satisfaction, pricing, and health information accuracy. For companies in the smart wearable industry, it is essential to understand which aspects of their products have the biggest impact on user satisfaction and the intention to continue using the product. By enhancing these aspects, companies can increase user engagement and retention. Wearable manufacturers are integrating advanced features like continuous glucose monitoring and sleep tracking to cater to health-conscious individuals. High-quality materials, personalization options, and exclusive health and wellness programs can enhance the appeal of wearables. Improving battery life and offering innovative solutions can improve user convenience. Superior connectivity, smart integration, on-device data processing, and robust security features can ensure data privacy. Including environmental and lifestyle sensors can provide valuable insights into the user's overall well-being.

LIMITATIONS AND FUTURE SCOPE OF RESEARCH

This research presents certain limitations that offer many opportunities for future studies. The study's foundation lies in the 'Reflective model' of Structural Equation Modeling (SEM), examining a select set of variables. Notably, the R2 value, a measure of model fit, stands at 32% for the variable 'performance expectancy.' This suggests that 68% of the factors influencing product satisfaction among users remain unexplored. Similarly, our study reveals that the cumulative effect of the analyzed variables on the sustained intention of users to use the product accounts for only 50%. This finding allows future researchers to unearth additional variables that could influence consumer retention and potentially elevate the R2 value, offering a more comprehensive explanation of user behavior.

Furthermore, in constructing this model, the study does not account for control variables such as gender, age, educational background, and income level. Their exclusion represents a notable gap, as these factors can considerably affect user behavior and product satisfaction. Acknowledging and integrating these variables in future research could lead to more nuanced and accurate models, enhancing our understanding of consumer behavior. This approach would also enable a more tailored and effective product development and marketing strategy, catering to diverse consumer needs and preferences based on demographic factors.

CONCLUSION

The study thoroughly examines the factors that influence the continued use of smart wearables, using the Expectation Confirmation Model (ECM) as a conceptual framework. The study found that users' ongoing engagement with smart wearables is linked to a combination of their performance expectations, satisfaction levels, and the product's perceived value. Key concepts such as 'Performance Expectancy,' 'Satisfaction,' and 'Confirmation' are crucial in determining users' continuous intention to use these devices. Further, satisfaction is not just a variable but also a significant mediator that bridges the gap between user expectations and their decision to continue using the product. This means user satisfaction is heavily influenced by how well the product meets or exceeds its initial expectations and performance over time. The research highlights the importance of accurate health information in smart wearables, directly linked to user retention and willingness to pay a premium price. This connection indicates that users value the reliability and precision of health-related features, which influences their continuous intention to use these devices. Therefore, developers of smart wearables are advised to focus on enhancing the accuracy and reliability of health metrics, potentially by incorporating advanced sensors or partnering with health professionals.

In conclusion, this study offers valuable insights for the smart wearables industry, emphasizing the importance of meeting or exceeding user expectations, ensuring product quality, particularly in health-related features, and understanding the diverse needs of the consumer base. Focusing on these key areas for companies in this market can lead to improved user satisfaction, higher willingness to pay premium prices, and ultimately, sustained user engagement with their products..

REFERENCES

Ahmad, A., Rasul, T., Yousaf, A., & Zaman, U. (2020). Understanding Factors Influencing Elderly Diabetic Patients' Continuance Intention to Use Digital Health Wearables: Extending the Technology Acceptance Model (TAM). *Journal of Open Innovation*, *6*(3), 81. doi:10.3390/joitmc6030081

Al Mamun, M. R., Senn, W. D., Peak, D. A., Prybutok, V. R., & Torres, R. A. (2020). Emotional Satisfaction and IS Continuance Behavior: Reshaping the Expectation-Confirmation Model. *International Journal of Human-Computer Interaction*, *36*(15), 1437–1446. doi:10.1080/10447318.2020.1752478

Al-Maroof, R. S., Alhumaid, K., Alhamad, A. Q., Aburayya, A., & Salloum, S. (2021). User Acceptance of Smart Watch for Medical Purposes: An Empirical Study. *Future Internet, 13*(5), 127. doi:10.3390/fi13050127

Alfes, K., Shantz, A. D., Truss, C., & Soane, E. C. (2013). The link between perceived human resource management practices, engagement and employee behaviour: A moderated mediation model. *International Journal of Human Resource Management*, *24*(2), 330–351. doi:10.1080/09585192.2012.679950

Allioui, H. ;, Mourdi, Y., Allioui, H., & Mourdi, Y. (2023). Exploring the Full Potentials of IoT for Better Financial Growth and Stability: A Comprehensive Survey. *Sensors 2023, 23*(19), 8015. doi:10.3390/s23198015

Ashraf, M., Ahmad, J., Sharif, W., Raza, A. A., Salman Shabbir, M., Abbas, M., & Thurasamy, R. (2020). The role of continuous trust in usage of online product recommendations. *Online Information Review*, *44*(4), 745–766. doi:10.1108/OIR-05-2018-0156

Awotunde, J. B., Jimoh, R. G., Folorunso, S. O., Adeniyi, E. A., Abiodun, K. M., & Banjo, O. O. (2021). Privacy and Security Concerns in IoT-Based Healthcare Systems. *Internet of Things : Engineering Cyber Physical Human Systems*, 105–134. doi:10.1007/978-3-030-75220-0_6

Bayoumy, K., Gaber, M., Elshafeey, A., Mhaimeed, O., Dineen, E. H., Marvel, F. A., Martin, S. S., Muse, E. D., Turakhia, M. P., Tarakji, K. G., & Elshazly, M. B. (2021a). Smart wearable devices in cardiovascular care: where we are and how to move forward. *Nature Reviews Cardiology, 18*(8), 581–599. doi:10.1038/s41569-021-00522-7

Bayoumy, K., Gaber, M., Elshafeey, A., Mhaimeed, O., Dineen, E. H., Marvel, F. A., Martin, S. S., Muse, E. D., Turakhia, M. P., Tarakji, K. G., & Elshazly, M. B. (2021b). Smart wearable devices in cardiovascular care: where we are and how to move forward. *Nature Reviews Cardiology, 18*(8), 581–599. doi:10.1038/s41569-021-00522-7

Bayoumy, K., Gaber, M., Elshafeey, A., Mhaimeed, O., Dineen, E. H., Marvel, F. A., Martin, S. S., Muse, E. D., Turakhia, M. P., Tarakji, K. G., & Elshazly, M. B. (2021c). Smart wearable devices in cardiovascular care: where we are and how to move forward. *Nature Reviews Cardiology, 18*(8), 581–599. doi:10.1038/s41569-021-00522-7

Behal, V., & Gupta, M. (2022). Reporting of corporate social responsibility practices: An evidence from Indian BSE-listed companies. *Prabandhan: Indian Journal of Management, 15*(3), 42–58. doi:10.17010/pijom/2022/v15i3/165633

Bhattacherjee, A. (2001a). An empirical analysis of the antecedents of electronic commerce service continuance. *Decision Support Systems, 32*(2), 201–214. doi:10.1016/S0167-9236(01)00111-7

Bhattacherjee, A. (2001b). Understanding information systems continuance: An expectation-confirmation model. *Management Information Systems Quarterly, 25*(3), 351–370. doi:10.2307/3250921

Bhattacherjee, A. (2001c). Understanding information systems continuance: An expectation-confirmation model. *Management Information Systems Quarterly, 25*(3), 351–370. doi:10.2307/3250921

Bianchi, C., Tuzovic, S., & Kuppelwieser, V. G. (2023). Investigating the drivers of wearable technology adoption for healthcare in South America. *Information Technology & People, 36*(2), 916–939. doi:10.1108/ITP-01-2021-0049

Brandon-Jones, A., & Kauppi, K. (2018). Examining the antecedents of the technology acceptance model within e-procurement. *International Journal of Operations & Production Management, 38*(1), 22–42. doi:10.1108/IJOPM-06-2015-0346

Celic, L., & Magjarevic, R. (2020). Seamless connectivity architecture and methods for IoT and wearable devices. *Automatika : Časopis Za Automatiku, Mjerenje, Elektroniku. Automatika (Zagreb), 61*(1), 21–34. doi:10.1080/00051144.2019.1660036

Chang, V., Doan, L. M. T., Ariel Xu, Q., Hall, K., Anna Wang, Y., & Mustafa Kamal, M. (2023). Digitalization in omnichannel healthcare supply chain businesses: The role of smart wearable devices. *Journal of Business Research, 156*, 113369. doi:10.1016/j.jbusres.2022.113369

Cheng, J. W., & Mitomo, H. (2017). The underlying factors of the perceived usefulness of using smart wearable devices for disaster applications. *Telematics and Informatics, 34*(2), 528–539. doi:10.1016/j.tele.2016.09.010

Cheng, Y. M. (2021). Drivers of physicians' satisfaction and continuance intention toward the cloud-based hospital information system. *Kybernetes*, *50*(2), 413–442. doi:10.1108/K-09-2019-0628

Chopra, P., & Gupta, M. (2023). Fuzzy Logic and ANN in an Artificial Intelligent Cloud: A Comparative Study. In *Intelligent Communication Technologies and Virtual Mobile Networks* (pp. 559–570). Springer Nature Singapore Singapore. doi:10.1007/978-981-99-1767-9_41

Çiçek, M. (2015). Wearable technologies and its future applications. *International Journal of Electrical. Electronics and Data Communication*, *3*(4), 45–50.

Conradie, N. H., & Nagel, S. K. (2022). Digital sovereignty and smart wearables: Three moral calculi for the distribution of legitimate control over the digital. *Journal of Responsible Technology*, *12*, 100053. doi:10.1016/j.jrt.2022.100053

Cotarelo, M., Fayos, T., Calderón, H., & Mollá, A. (2021). Omni-Channel Intensity and Shopping Value as Key Drivers of Customer Satisfaction and Loyalty. *Sustainability*, *13*(11), 5961. doi:10.3390/su13115961

Daragmeh, A., Sági, J., & Zéman, Z. (2021). Continuous Intention to Use E-Wallet in the Context of the COVID-19 Pandemic: Integrating the Health Belief Model (HBM) and Technology Continuous Theory (TCT). *Journal of Open Innovation: Technology, Market, and Complexity*, *7*(2), 132. doi:10.3390/joitmc7020132

Dehghani, M. (2018). Exploring the motivational factors on continuous usage intention of smartwatches among actual users. *Behaviour & Information Technology*, *37*(2), 145–158. doi:10.1080/0144929X.2018.1424246

Dehghani, M., Kim, K. J., & Dangelico, R. M. (2018). Will smartwatches last? factors contributing to intention to keep using smart wearable technology. *Telematics and Informatics*, *35*(2), 480–490. doi:10.1016/j.tele.2018.01.007

Yusoff, A., Siong Peng, F., Zaidi Abd Razak, F., & Azani Mustafa, W. (2020). Discriminant Validity Assessment of Religious Teacher Acceptance: The Use of HTMT Criterion. *Journal of Physics: Conference Series*, *042045*(4). doi:10.1088/1742-6596/1529/4/042045

Dixit, S., Maurya, M., Sharma, N., & Zaidi, N. (2022). Payments Process Privilege: Leveraging Fintech with TAM. *8th International Conference on Advanced Computing and Communication Systems, ICACCS 2022*, (pp. 1668–1673). IEEE. 10.1109/ICACCS54159.2022.9785136

Do Nguyen, G., & Ha, M. T. (2021). The role of user adaptation and trust in understanding continuance intention towards mobile shopping: An extended expectation-confirmation model. *Cogent Business & Management*, *8*(1), 1980248. doi:10.1080/23311975.2021.1980248

El-Gayar, O., & Elnoshokaty, A. (2023). Factors and Design Features Influencing the Continued Use of Wearable Devices. *Journal of Healthcare Informatics Research*, *7*(3), 359–385. doi:10.1007/s41666-023-00135-4 PMID:37637719

Fernando, Y., Chiappetta Jabbour, C. J., & Wah, W. X. (2019). Pursuing green growth in technology firms through the connections between environmental innovation and sustainable business performance: Does service capability matter? *Resources, Conservation and Recycling*, *141*, 8–20. doi:10.1016/j.resconrec.2018.09.031

Grewal, D., Iyer, G. R., Krishnan, R., & Sharma, A. (2003). The Internet and the price–value–loyalty chain. *Journal of Business Research*, *56*(5), 391–398. doi:10.1016/S0148-2963(01)00227-2

Guo, X., Han, X., Zhang, X., Dang, Y., & Chen, C. (2015). Investigating m-Health Acceptance from a Protection Motivation Theory Perspective: Gender and Age Differences. Https://Home.Liebertpub.Com/Tmj, *21*(8), 661–669. doi:10.1089/tmj.2014.0166

Gupta, A., Yousaf, A., & Mishra, A. (2020). How pre-adoption expectancies shape post-adoption continuance intentions: An extended expectation-confirmation model. *International Journal of Information Management*, *52*, 102094. doi:10.1016/j.ijinfomgt.2020.102094

Gupta, M., Kumar, P., & Ghai, S. (2023). *Impact of Green Finance on Sustainability in India's Commercial Banks*. 216–233. : Gupta, M., Taneja, S., Sharma, V., Singh, A., Rupeika-Apoga, R., & Jangir, K. (2023). Does Previous Experience with the Unified Payments Interface (UPI) Affect the Usage of Central Bank Digital Currency (CBDC)? *Journal of Risk and Financial Management, 16*(6), 286. doi:10.4018/979-8-3693-1388-6.ch015

Hair, J., Hollingsworth, C. L., Randolph, A. B., & Chong, A. Y. L. (2017). An updated and expanded assessment of PLS-SEM in information systems research. *Industrial Management & Data Systems*, *117*(3), 442–458. doi:10.1108/IMDS-04-2016-0130

Hair, J. F., Risher, J. J., Sarstedt, M., & Ringle, C. M. (2019). When to use and how to report the results of PLS-SEM. *European Business Review*, *31*(1), 2–24. doi:10.1108/EBR-11-2018-0203

Hair, J. F., Sarstedt, M., Hopkins, L., & Kuppelwieser, V. G. (2014). Partial least squares structural equation modeling (PLS-SEM): An emerging tool in business research. *European Business Review*, *26*(2), 106–121. doi:10.1108/EBR-10-2013-0128

Henseler, J., Ringle, C. M., & Sarstedt, M. (2015). A new criterion for assessing discriminant validity in variance-based structural equation modeling. *Journal of the Academy of Marketing Science*, *43*(1), 115–135. doi:10.1007/s11747-014-0403-8

Hidayat-Ur-Rehman, I., Ahmad, A., Khan, M. N., & Mokhtar, S. A. (2021). Investigating Mobile Banking Continuance Intention: A Mixed-Methods Approach. *Mobile Information Systems*, *2021*, 1–17. Advance online publication. doi:10.1155/2021/9994990

Hill, R. (2022). Smart Wearables: The Overlooked and Underrated Essential Worker. *William and Mary Law Review*, *64*, •••. https://heinonline.org/HOL/Page?handle=hein.journals/wmlr64&id=1623&div=&collection=

Ho, J. C., Wu, C. G., Lee, C. S., & Pham, T. T. T. (2020). Factors affecting the behavioral intention to adopt mobile banking: An international comparison. *Technology in Society*, *63*, 101360. doi:10.1016/j.techsoc.2020.101360

Hossain, M. A., & Quaddus, M. (2012). *Expectation–Confirmation Theory in Information System Research: A Review and Analysis*. 441–469. doi:10.1007/978-1-4419-6108-2_21

Huang, Y. M. (2019). Examining students' continued use of desktop services: Perspectives from expectation-confirmation and social influence. *Computers in Human Behavior*, *96*, 23–31. doi:10.1016/j.chb.2019.02.010

Iranmanesh, M., Min, C. L., Senali, M. G., Nikbin, D., & Foroughi, B. (2022). Determinants of switching intention from web-based stores to retail apps: Habit as a moderator. *Journal of Retailing and Consumer Services*, *66*, 102957. doi:10.1016/j.jretconser.2022.102957

Jain, N. K., Kaul, D., & Sanyal, P. (2022). What drives customers towards mobile shopping? An integrative technology continuance theory perspective. *Asia Pacific Journal of Marketing and Logistics*, *34*(5), 922–943. doi:10.1108/APJML-02-2021-0133

Kao, Y. S., Nawata, K., & Huang, C. Y. (2019). An Exploration and Confirmation of the Factors Influencing Adoption of IoT-Based Wearable Fitness Trackers. *International Journal of Environmental Research and Public Health 2019, Vol. 16, Page 3227*, *16*(18), 3227. doi:10.3390/ijerph16183227

Karjaluoto, H., Shaikh, A. A., Leppäniemi, M., & Luomala, R. (2020). Examining consumers' usage intention of contactless payment systems. *International Journal of Bank Marketing*, *38*(2), 332–351. doi:10.1108/IJBM-04-2019-0155

Kasilingam, D., & Krishna, R. (2022). Understanding the adoption and willingness to pay for internet of things services. *International Journal of Consumer Studies*, *46*(1), 102–131. doi:10.1111/ijcs.12648

Khan, U., & DePaoli, A. (2023). Brand loyalty in the face of stockouts. *Journal of the Academy of Marketing Science*, •••, 1–31. doi:10.1007/S11747-023-00924-8/FIGURES/1 PMID:37359264

Kim, M. J., Lee, C. K., & Contractor, N. S. (2019). Seniors' usage of mobile social network sites: Applying theories of innovation diffusion and uses and gratifications. *Computers in Human Behavior*, *90*, 60–73. doi:10.1016/j.chb.2018.08.046

Kline, R. B. (2023). *Principles and practice of structural equiation modeling* (5th ed.). Guilford Press.

Kock, N. (2016). Non-Normality Propagation among Latent Variables and Indicators in PLS-SEM Simulations. *Journal of Modern Applied Statistical Methods; JMASM*, *15*(1), 16. doi:10.22237/jmasm/1462076100

Kumar, V. (2023). Digital Enablers. *Management for Professionals*, (Part F1470), 1–110. doi:10.1007/978-981-19-8148-7_1/COVER

Kumar, Y., Koul, A., Singla, R., & Ijaz, M. F. (2022). Artificial intelligence in disease diagnosis: a systematic literature review, synthesizing framework and future research agenda. *Journal of Ambient Intelligence and Humanized Computing 2021 14:7*, *14*(7), 8459–8486. doi:10.1007/s12652-021-03612-z

Laitala, K., Klepp, I. G., Haugrønning, V., Throne-Holst, H., & Strandbakken, P. (2021). Increasing repair of household appliances, mobile phones and clothing: Experiences from consumers and the repair industry. *Journal of Cleaner Production*, *282*, 125349. doi:10.1016/j.jclepro.2020.125349

Lee, S. M., & Lee, D. H. (2020). Healthcare wearable devices: An analysis of key factors for continuous use intention. *Service Business*, *14*(4), 503–531. doi:10.1007/s11628-020-00428-3

Li, C., & Wang, J., Wang, S., & Zhang, Y. (. (2024). A review of IoT applications in healthcare. *Neurocomputing*, *565*, 127017. doi:10.1016/j.neucom.2023.127017

Li, L., Lee, K. Y., Emokpae, E., & Yang, S. B. (2021). What makes you continuously use chatbot services? Evidence from chinese online travel agencies. *Electronic Markets*, *31*(3), 575–599. doi:10.1007/s12525-020-00454-z PMID:35603227

Liu, X., & Kao, Z. (2022). Research on influencing factors of customer satisfaction of e-commerce of characteristic agricultural products. *Procedia Computer Science*, *199*, 1505–1512. doi:10.1016/j.procs.2022.01.192

Malhi, A. S., Kovid, R. K., & Kanika. (2023). *Wearable Technologies for Health: Investigating Behavioral Intention to Adopt Cloud-Based Smartwatch*. 197–214. doi:10.1007/978-981-99-1620-7_16

Manika, D., Antonetti, P., Papagiannidis, S., & Guo, X. (2021). How Pride Triggered by Pro-environmental Technology Adoption Spills Over into Conservation Behaviours: A Social Business Application. *Technological Forecasting and Social Change*, *172*, 121005. doi:10.1016/j.techfore.2021.121005

Marakhimov, A., & Joo, J. (2017). Consumer adaptation and infusion of wearable devices for healthcare. *Computers in Human Behavior*, *76*, 135–148. doi:10.1016/j.chb.2017.07.016

Maselli, A., Gordon, J., Eluchans, M., Lancia, G. L., Thiery, T., Moretti, R., Cisek, P., & Pezzulo, G. (2023). Beyond simple laboratory studies: Developing sophisticated models to study rich behavior. *Physics of Life Reviews*, *46*, 220–244. doi:10.1016/j.plrev.2023.07.006 PMID:37499620

Mathavan, B., Vafaei-Zadeh, A., Hanifah, H., Ramayah, T., & Kurnia, S. (2024). Understanding the purchase intention of fitness wearables: Using value-based adoption model. *Asia-Pacific Journal of Business Administration*, *16*(1), 101–126. doi:10.1108/APJBA-04-2022-0166

Melumad, S., Hadi, R., Hildebrand, C., & Ward, A. F. (2020). Technology-Augmented Choice: How Digital Innovations Are Transforming Consumer Decision Processes. *Customer Needs and Solutions 2020 7:3*, *7*(3), 90–101. doi:10.1007/s40547-020-00107-4

Moon, N. W., Baker, P. M., & Goughnour, K. (2019). Designing wearable technologies for users with disabilities: Accessibility, usability, and connectivity factors. Https://Doi.Org/10.1177/2055668319862137, *6*, 205566831986213. doi:10.1177/2055668319862137

Morozova, D. (2021). *Practice Theory Approach to Wearable Technology*. Implications for Sustainability., doi:10.54337/aau478414012

Nagy, L. B., Unger-Plasek, B., Lakner, Z., & Temesi, Á. (2023). Confidence in organic food: a cross-country choice based conjoint analysis of credibility factors. *Humanities and Social Sciences Communications 2023 10:1*, *10*(1), 1–11. doi:10.1057/s41599-023-02293-7

Nascimento, B., Oliveira, T., & Tam, C. (2018). Wearable technology: What explains continuance intention in smartwatches? *Journal of Retailing and Consumer Services*, *43*, 157–169. doi:10.1016/j.jretconser.2018.03.017

Niknejad, N., Ismail, W. B., Mardani, A., Liao, H., & Ghani, I. (2020). A comprehensive overview of smart wearables: The state of the art literature, recent advances, and future challenges. *Engineering Applications of Artificial Intelligence*, *90*, 103529. doi:10.1016/j.engappai.2020.103529

O'hagan, J., Saeghe, P., Gugenheimer, J., Medeiros, D., Marky, K., Khamis, M., & Mcgill, M. (2023). Privacy-Enhancing Technology and Everyday Augmented Reality. *Proceedings of the ACM on Interactive, Mobile, Wearable and Ubiquitous Technologies*, *6*(4), 1–35. Advance online publication. doi:10.1145/3569501

Oyedele, A., Saldivar, R., Hernandez, M. D., & Goenner, E. (2018). Modeling satisfaction and repurchase intentions of mobile smart wristbands: The role of social mindfulness and perceived value. *Young Consumers*, *19*(3), 237–250. doi:10.1108/YC-09-2017-00737

Pal, D., Funilkul, S., & Vanijja, V. (2020). The future of smartwatches: Assessing the end-users' continuous usage using an extended expectation-confirmation model. *Universal Access in the Information Society*, *19*(2), 261–281. doi:10.1007/s10209-018-0639-z

Pandey, P., & Litoriya, R. (2020). Implementing healthcare services on a large scale: Challenges and remedies based on blockchain technology. *Health Policy and Technology*, *9*(1), 69–78. doi:10.1016/j.hlpt.2020.01.004

Park, E. (2020). User acceptance of smart wearable devices: An expectation-confirmation model approach. *Telematics and Informatics*, *47*, 101318. doi:10.1016/j.tele.2019.101318

Purohit, S., Arora, R., & Paul, J. (2022). The bright side of online consumer behavior: Continuance intention for mobile payments. *Journal of Consumer Behaviour*, *21*(3), 523–542. doi:10.1002/cb.2017

Qazi, A., Tamjidyamcholo, A., Raj, R. G., Hardaker, G., & Standing, C. (2017). Assessing consumers' satisfaction and expectations through online opinions: Expectation and disconfirmation approach. *Computers in Human Behavior*, *75*, 450–460. doi:10.1016/j.chb.2017.05.025

Quévat, A., & Heinze, A. (2020). The digital transformation of preventive telemedicine in France based on the use of connected wearable devices. *Global Business and Organizational Excellence*, *39*(6), 17–27. doi:10.1002/joe.22054

Rabaa'i, A. A., ALmaati, S. A., & Zhu, X. (. (2021). Students' continuance intention to use Moodle: An expectation-confirmation model approach. *Interdisciplinary Journal of Information, Knowledge, and Management*, *16*, 397. doi:10.28945/4842

Rabaa'i, A. A., & ALMaati, S. A. (2021). Exploring the Determinants of Users' Continuance Intention to Use Mobile Banking Services in Kuwait : Extending the Expectation-Confirmation Model. *Asia Pacific Journal of Information Systems, 31*(2), 141–184. https://www.earticle.net/Article/A396167

Rhee, S. Y., Kim, C., Shin, D. W., & Steinhubl, S. R. (2020). Present and Future of Digital Health in Diabetes and Metabolic Disease. *Diabetes & Metabolism Journal*, *44*(6), 819–827. doi:10.4093/dmj.2020.0088 PMID:33389956

Saraswat, D., Bhattacharya, P., Verma, A., Prasad, V. K., Tanwar, S., Sharma, G., Bokoro, P. N., & Sharma, R. (2022). Explainable AI for Healthcare 5.0: Opportunities and Challenges. *IEEE Access : Practical Innovations, Open Solutions, 10*, 84486–84517. doi:10.1109/ACCESS.2022.3197671

Sarstedt, M., Hair, J. F., Pick, M., Liengaard, B. D., Radomir, L., & Ringle, C. M. (2022). Progress in partial least squares structural equation modeling use in marketing research in the last decade. *Psychology and Marketing*, *39*(5), 1035–1064. doi:10.1002/mar.21640

Sarstedt, M., Ringle, C. M., & Hair, J. F. (2021). Partial Least Squares Structural Equation Modeling. Handbook of Market Research, 587–632. https://doi.org/ doi:10.1007/978-3-319-57413-4_15/COVER

Saygılı, M., & Yalçıntekin, T. (2021). THE EFFECT OF HEDONIC VALUE, UTILITARIAN VALUE, AND CUSTOMER SATISFACTION IN PREDICTING REPURCHASE INTENTION AND WILLINGNESS TO PAY A PRICE PREMIUM FOR SMARTWATCH BRANDS. *Management*, *26*(2), 179–195. doi:10.30924/mjcmi.26.2.10

Schwartz, S. M., Wildenhaus, K., Bucher, A., & Byrd, B. (2020). Digital Twins and the Emerging Science of Self: Implications for Digital Health Experience Design and "Small" Data. *Frontiers of Computer Science*, *2*, 516124. doi:10.3389/FCOMP.2020.00031/BIBTEX

Sharma, P., Sharma, V., Jangir, K., Gupta, M., & Pathak, N. (2023). Unfolding the Emerging Trends in Non-performing Assets with Special Reference to the Energy Sector in Banking Industry. *Renewable Energy Optimization, Planning and Control: Proceedings of ICRTE 2022*, 411–422.

Sharma, V., Gupta, M., Jangir, K., Chopra, P., & Pathak, N. (2023). The Impact of Post-Use Consumer Satisfaction on Smart Wearables Repurchase Intention in the Context of AI-Based Healthcare Information. In *Enhancing Customer Engagement Through Location-Based Marketing* (pp. 77–101). IGI Global. doi:10.4018/978-1-6684-8177-6.ch007

Sharma, V., Taneja, S., & Gupta, M. KshitizJangir, & Ozen, E. (2023). Impact of Service Quality on Behavioural Intention to Use Fin Tech Payment Services: An Extension of SERVEQUAL Model. *Asia Pacific Journal of Information Systems, 33*(4), 1093–1117. https://www.earticle.net/Article/A440274

Singh, N., Misra, R., Singh, S., Rana, N. P., & Khorana, S. (2022). Assessing the factors that influence the adoption of healthcare wearables by the older population using an extended PMT model. *Technology in Society*, *71*, 102126. doi:10.1016/j.techsoc.2022.102126

Sun, W., Guo, Z., Yang, Z., Wu, Y., Lan, W., Liao, Y., Wu, X., & Liu, Y. (2022). A Review of Recent Advances in Vital Signals Monitoring of Sports and Health via Flexible Wearable Sensors. *Sensors 2022, Vol. 22, Page 7784, 22*(20), 7784. doi:10.3390/s22207784

Sun, Y., & Ly, T. P. (2023). The Influence of Word-of-web on Customers' Purchasing Process: The Case of Xiaohongshu. *Journal of China Tourism Research*, *19*(2), 221–244. doi:10.1080/19388160.2022.2057378

Tagger, S. S., & Gupta, M. (2020). A study of the relationship between total quality management and business performance in the banking sector. *International Journal of Business Competition and Growth*, *7*(2), 118–132. doi:10.1504/IJBCG.2020.111943

Talukder, M. S., Laato, S., Islam, A. K. M. N., & Bao, Y. (2021). Continued use intention of wearable health technologies among the elderly: An enablers and inhibitors perspective. *Internet Research, 31*(5), 1611–1640. doi:10.1108/INTR-10-2020-0586

Tanwar, R., Choudhary, S. L., Singh, A., Manoharan, S., & Ghafoor, K. Z. (2022). A Pulse Rate-Triggered Wearable Device for Critical Assistance. *Journal of Sensors, 2022*, 1–9. Advance online publication. doi:10.1155/2022/9807188

Thong, J. Y. L., Hong, S. J., & Tam, K. Y. (2006). The effects of post-adoption beliefs on the expectation-confirmation model for information technology continuance. *International Journal of Human-Computer Studies, 64*(9), 799–810. doi:10.1016/j.ijhcs.2006.05.001

Tran, L., Pham, L., & Le, L. (2018). E-satisfaction and continuance intention: The moderator role of online ratings. *International Journal of Hospitality Management, 77*, 311–322. Advance online publication. doi:10.1016/j.ijhm.2018.07.011

Venkatesh, V., Morris, M. G., Davis, G. B., & Davis, F. D. (2003). User acceptance of information technology: Toward a unified view. *Management Information Systems Quarterly, 27*(3), 425–478. doi:10.2307/30036540

Venkatesh, V., Thong, J. Y. L., & Xu, X. (2012). Consumer acceptance and use of information technology: Extending the unified theory of acceptance and use of technology. *Management Information Systems Quarterly, 36*(1), 157–178. doi:10.2307/41410412

Vijayan, V., Connolly, J., Condell, J., McKelvey, N., & Gardiner, P. (2021). Review of Wearable Devices and Data Collection Considerations for Connected Health. *Sensors (Basel), 21*(16), 5589. Advance online publication. doi:10.3390/s21165589 PMID:34451032

Voorhees, C. M., Brady, M. K., Calantone, R., & Ramirez, E. (2016). Discriminant validity testing in marketing: An analysis, causes for concern, and proposed remedies. *Journal of the Academy of Marketing Science, 44*(1), 119–134. doi:10.1007/s11747-015-0455-4

Wang, W. T., Ou, W. M., & Chen, W. Y. (2019). The impact of inertia and user satisfaction on the continuance intentions to use mobile communication applications: A mobile service quality perspective. *International Journal of Information Management, 44*, 178–193. doi:10.1016/j.ijinfomgt.2018.10.011

Wang, X., Xu, B., Zhang, W., Wang, J., Deng, L., Ping, J., Hu, C., & Li, H. (2023). Recognizing emotions induced by wearable haptic vibration using noninvasive electroencephalogram. *Frontiers in Neuroscience, 17*, 1219553. doi:10.3389/fnins.2023.1219553 PMID:37483356

Watson, R. (2022). Consumer Risk Perceptions, Behavioral Intentions, and Purchasing Habits toward Delivery Apps. *Journal of Self-Governance & Management Economics, 10*(1).

Yang, H., Yu, J., Zo, H., & Choi, M. (2016). User acceptance of wearable devices: An extended perspective of perceived value. *Telematics and Informatics, 33*(2), 256–269. doi:10.1016/j.tele.2015.08.007

Yen, H. Y. (2021). Smart wearable devices as a psychological intervention for healthy lifestyle and quality of life: A randomized controlled trial. *Quality of Life Research: An International Journal of Quality of Life Aspects of Treatment, Care and Rehabilitation*, *30*(3), 791–802. doi:10.1007/s11136-020-02680-6 PMID:33104939

Zolfaghari, S., Massa, S. M., & Riboni, D. (2023). Activity Recognition in Smart Homes via Feature-Rich Visual Extraction of Locomotion Traces. *Electronics 2023, Vol. 12, Page 1969, 12*(9), 1969. doi:10.3390/electronics12091969

Chapter 17
Enhanced Smart Irrigation Using Sensors:
A Statistical Case Study

N. Ambika
https://orcid.org/0000-0003-4452-5514
St. Francis College, India

Krishnan Rajamany
School of Mathematics and Natural Sciences, Chanakya University, India

ABSTRACT

The working of the framework is completed by coordinating soil dampness sensor, passive infrared sensor (PIR), and water siphon along with the Arduino board. The job of the dirt dampness sensor is to detect the dampness of the dirt and give its yield to the client. The water siphon will flood the field only whatever point the dampness of soil goes beneath the ideal edge worth. The arrangement was tried for one month and information on interruption recognition was handily gathered through the PIR sensor and the working of the water siphon is effortlessly managed without subterranean insect issue. The suggestion tries to overcome crop spoilage and also aims at providing good yield. To make the system better, a weather forecast is considered. Based on these parameters, a statistical study is done to maintain the water content of the ground. using the study outcome, the design is proposed.

INTRODUCTION

Business-oriented sensor (Ambika, 2019) is frameworks that focus on agribusiness and its water system management, making it incomprehensible for littler herders to execute this type of structure on their homesteads. Producers now offer minimal effort sensors associated with hubs to manage accessible frameworks for water systems, the board, and agribusiness observers. With the tiniest action, the devices check farming and water. In the horticulture exercises, utilization of water inputs is flooded agribusiness.

DOI: 10.4018/979-8-3693-1842-3.ch017

It has various habits to appropriate the water. The multiple choices present distinctive effectiveness and should use particular way for a specific harvest.

The working of the framework (Thakur, Kumar, & Vijendra, 2020) coordinates the soil dampness device and Liquid siphon along with the Arduino panel. The dust humidity sensing device works to sense the grime's wetness and give its harvests to the customer. The marine tap will flood the ground at whatever point the succulence of soil goes beneath the ideal edge worth. The aid of PIR(Passive Infrared Sensors) assesses the discovery of intermission at so forth fact there is any identification of interruption in the arena. The discovery of interruption is estimated by assisting PIR and identifying disruption in the field. The clients will become acquainted with it as allocated esteems. The arrangement was tried for one month and gathered interruption recognition through the PIR sensor. The system effortlessly managed without subterranean insect issues. It helps in inundating the nursery zone where the gadget is sent. The working of this water siphon depends on the dampness of the dirt. The water siphon begins working towards the pinnacle estimation of soil dampness (Badhe, Kharadkar, Ware, Kamble, & Chavan, 2018) when the dirt dampness goes beneath the allowed esteem.

The proposal is an improvement of the previous work. Weather forecast is considered in the work. A statistical study is conducted that aims in maintaining the soil moisturizer and help in good yield. Based on the analysis, the design is suggested. It is the amendment of the previous work design. The work has six sections. The introduction is followed by a Literature survey. The drawbacks of the previous system are listed in segment three. Proposed work is suggested in section four. Segment five contains future directions. The work is concluded in section six.

LITERATURE SURVEY

The contributions of various authors are summarized in this section. A calculation (Goap, Sharma, Shukla, & Krishna, 2018) depends on a mix of directed and unaided artificial intelligence methods. It utilizes Support Vector Regression and k-implies bunching to estimate distinction/change in soil dampness because of climate conditions. It gives exactness and less Mean Squared Error. The model utilizes information gathered from field gadgets. The Soil Dampness Differences of upcoming days anticipation prepares the model, and the anticipated estimation of SMD (Strain Measurement Devices) contributes to k-implies grouping for improving the precision of soil dampness distinction, which is increasingly exact with less MSE(Miniaturized Optical Sensors). The last anticipated soil dampness improves shrewd water system booking calculation to effectively use the typical downpour (precipitation) data for an adequate water system. A responsive online interface pictures the anticipated soil dampness of upcoming days alongside precipitation data and controls (start and stop) the water system.

The working of the framework (Thakur, Kumar, & Vijendra, 2020) coordinates the soil dampness device and Liquid siphon along with the Arduino panel. The dust humidity sensing device works to sense the grime's wetness and give its harvests to the customer. The marine tap will flood the ground at whatever point the succulence of soil goes beneath the ideal edge worth. The aid of PIR assesses the discovery of intermission at so forth fact there is any identification of interruption in the arena. The discovery of interruption is estimated by assisting PIR and identifying disruption in the field. The clients will become acquainted with it as allocated esteems. The arrangement was tried for one month and gathered interruption recognition through the PIR sensor. The system effortlessly managed without subterranean insect issues. It helps in inundating the nursery zone where the gadget is sent. The working of this water siphon depends on the dampness of the dirt. The water siphon begins working towards the pinnacle estimation of soil dampness (Badhe, Kharadkar, Ware, Kamble, & Chavan, 2018) when the dirt dampness goes beneath the allowed esteem.

The work (Keswani et al., 2019) sums up the ideal water system used to manage moisture valves, utilizing a neural structure-based forecast of soil water necessity one h ahead. The water system control plot uses an auxiliary closeness-based water valve. The board component finds ranch locales having water inadequacy. It is a nearby comparative analysis of streamlining procedures, identical to inconsistent knowledge pace gradient descent. It is the most reasonable procedure to gauge soil MC on an hourly premise, along with an introduction technique for creating a soil dampness-content dispersion map. At long last, SSIM (sequence-to-sequence imputation model) list-based soil MC insufficiency is committed to controlling the predefined valves for maintaining uniform water necessity throughout the homestead region. The valve control orders to operate soft rationale-based temperature states displaying a framework to manage arrangement by considering various climate conditions. The test site is at Bhubaneswar, having a Latitude of 20.351323 and a Longitude of 85.806547 in the eastern area of India. The developed ranch has a territory of just about 5000 m2. The profile comprises a layer of wet soil, very 2 m profound, with a sandy topsoil surface. Here the topsoil quality was found by a research center investigation of an excellent example of 3.5 kg. Further, the dirt test's dry mass thickness and consistency are about 1.43 g-cm-3 and 0.46 g-cm-3.

The proposed framework (Saraf & Gawali, 2017) causes the client to improve the grade and portion of their homestead creation by noticing the surrounding temperature and mugginess appreciates, earth moisture worth, and dampness level of the tank from the domain with no human intervention. Utilizing the idea of the IoT framework (Ambika N., 2020) can be increasingly productive. The frame includes isolated detector units placed in the field to procure the lasting qualities, a proficient intersection to get and send gained data to the authority area, and a control component that regulates the dribbles for the watering unit. Every device includes temperature, moisture, earth moisture, and dampness level detectors as a microcontroller and transfers swapping divisions. The detected information from every hub sends to the ace hub by employing Zigbee. The data from the ace hub is put away at the cloud worker. The cloud worker performs dynamic by contrasting detected qualities and predefined limit esteems according to edit determination. After the information preparation, the choice resolution at the managing location with moisture design calculation and the controlling activity transmission to a remote sensor hub follows. The microcontroller from the main controls the transfer trading division and watering unit as needs are. A reporting framework that is an android application creation conveys late field data to the client. Additionally, it summons that clients react to the preliminary happening, for example, mount in temperature and water prerequisites for manufacturers.

It is a nursery/garden/ranch observing and programmed water system framework (Nawandar & Satpute, 2019) equipped for finding the harvest water needs, cautioning the water system division and client involving it, and giving real-time and history of homestead information. It additionally accomplishes the effective use of moisture with a programmed water strategy framework for plants by mulling the plant and ground essentials. The sensing device Pole is the mind of the proposed framework uniquely intended for intelligent dynamics. The yield subtleties from the client contribute to appraising the water prerequisite. The planting region separates into zones depending on the plants and the region's inclusion with various USPs (United States Pharmacopeial Convention). The territory that gets normal water embeds the sensor, as it can detect prerequisites of close-by zones. Choosing an area that gets less water could prompt overlogging, while a zone with more wetness may make water worry about the harvest. Aside from this calculation, the water system plan assesses ahead of time the dates when the water system needs to happen for the planted growth. These water system date notes are in a document on USP. This record with the assessed plan is then sent once to the worker utilizing FTP (Fuel tank Pressure Sensor) employing the web.

The framework (Rawal, 2017) mixes equipment and programming segments. The equipment part comprises structure and programming planned to utilize PHP. The website page is facilitated on the web and contains a database wherein readings from sensors are embedded using the equipment. Two YL-69 soil dampness sensors alongside LM393 comparator modules are in various soil conditions for examination. The sensor YL-69 comprises two cathodes. It peruses the dampness content around it. A current passes over the terminals through the dirt. The protection from the stream in the grime decides the dirt's dampness on the off chance that more water opposition is low and increasing flow will go through. Data from the sensors is sent to the Arduino board. The Arduino board comprises microcontroller ATMEGA328P liable for controlling the turning on/off of the engine on which water sprinklers. Sensor esteems from Arduino are sent to the GSM-GPRS SIM900A modem. A sim with a 3G information pack embeds into this modem giving IoT (Nagaraj, 2021) highlights to the framework. Qualities are additionally communicated IoT segment through the modem.

The water system gadget contains two sections (Zhao, Lin, Han, Xu, & Hou, 2017)-Irrigation Node and Gateway. The water system Node controls the solenoid valve and associates it with the door. It moves signals among workers and the water system hub. It includes four units- transmitter component, switches unit, water system module, and force module. The water system segment is the controller of the solenoid valve. The controller module controls it. The control module can execute switch control guidance, track the solenoid valve's state, and interact with the transmitter unit using the LoRaWan stack and SX1276 driver. The transmitter component collaborates with the entryway to employ a radio-front signal. The force module is liable for an electric supplement. The entrance comprises three modules - the host, the LoRa RF handset, and the Global Positioning framework module. It advances RF parcels from LoRa RF handsets to LoRa workers through the UDP interface and sends a message to LoRa RF. The handset demodulates RF. The GPS module gives area data. The worker falls into three sections. The system Server is liable for the door convention interpretation as a part that cooperates legitimately with the gateway. LoRa worker is answerable for information reduplication, MIC check, decoding, encryption, and extraction. The LoRa worker gives a bundle type named MAC to configure hubs and entryways in LoRaWAN. Cloud worker utilizes Redis and MySQL to store information. HTTP (HyperText Transfer Protocol) and MQTT (Message Queue Telemetry Transport Protocol) APIs using for both LoRa workers and applications to send or get information.

The proposed computerized water system and observing framework (Vaishali, Suraj, Vignesh, Dhivya, & Udhayakumar, 2017) comprise the raspberry pi, water siphon, dampness, and climate detectors. An advanced mobile phone module does the correspondence. The yields or plants consider water a prerequisite at various stages. The harvests or plants flood for the water necessities at different phases of their development. The device creation to digitizing the moisture method enhances water useability. The raspberry pi is a bit single-board PC used to show software engineering. The raspberry pi usage as a PC uses external memory, and it has four harbors where widgets are associated. Detectors are devices that transform over the physical frontier into electric alerts. The framework constitutes the earth-wetness sensor. The result of the detector is a simple sign. The sign changes into a computerized sign and afterward takes care of the processor. The dampness sensor gauges the dampness substance of the dirt. Copper anodes notice the moisture content of the earth. The conductivity between the cathodes assists with estimating the wetness range level. Blue term is an android application employed to compose projects and principles and send these regulations to the primary regulator utilizing a neighborhood correspondence medium - BLUETOOTH. It set up a such correspondence. Regular orders like passwords and usernames change the Bluetooth module's design. The RFCOMM/SPP convention imitates linear posts over Bluetooth.

The model (Pernapati, 2018) consistently checks the weather conditions, the water level in-store, and soil dampness and provides water prerequisites. The framework goes to a critical framework using the Soil Moisture Sensor and declares to the water siphon. The fundamental focal part is the ESP8266 NodeMCU Microcontroller. It predefines the scope of qualities for both soil dampness and water level. Observing both will differ regarding soil type and measure of water in the repository. The Soil Moisture Sensor, Humidity and Temperature Sensor, and Ultrasonic sensor are associated with the ESP8266 NodeMCU Microcontroller. At that point, sensors send the information from their situations to ESP8266 Node-MCU. The controller sends to end clients like a web worker, versatile employing an MQTT worker. The earth wetness Detector, humidity and climate sensing device, and Ultrasonic detector contribute to Microcontroller. The water siphon is associated with the means of Relay. The temperature and moistness esteem send to the end client. The dampness sensor senses the water amount in the soil, and the water siphon will point to the amount of water in the ground diminished.

A sum of 150 sensing strips (TNOdes) (Baggio, 2005) is in a bundle for observing the growth. The devices with detectors record the heat and relevant moisture. The deployments have shown that the communication spectrum diminishes when the vegetable produce yields. To prepare ample system connectivity, 30 sensorless T-nodes act as interface stations. The joints are fixed at a length of 75cm. The detectors are placed at an elevation of 20, 40, or 60cm. The field equips with a weather station registering the radiance, air strength, rainfall, wind energy, and regulation. The wetness of the earth is a significant determinant in the evolution of the microclimate. Several detectors that contain dirt moisture are thus also stationed in the province. Finally, additional sensing estimates the length of the groundwater statistics. A TNOde reads the warmth and relevant wetness every time. For energy-efficiency concerns, the junctions record information only one per ten times.

The knowledge given over the broadcast sections lessens by using delta encryption to preserve strength further. The T-MAC rules care for power performance and force the communications a work series of 7%. They use TinyOS as the operating system. Knowledge transmits using the multihop routing. In addition, the connections are reprogrammable over the space using Deluge. The knowledge obtained by the TNOdes is deduced at the end of the arena by a so-called course gateway and further assigned via WiFi to a simplistic PC for information lumbering. The Lofar gateway combines cable with the Internet. The knowledge uploads to a Lofar host. It scatters to several different hosts using XML constructions.

The low-power WSN (Srbinovska, Gavrovski, Dimcev, Krkoleva, & Borozan, 2015) is built from radio connections class eZ43- RF2500 designed by Texas Instruments. These joints unite the MSP430 ultra-low-power microcontrollers and CC2500 wireless radio frequency transceivers. It is suitable for low-power, low-cost wireless applications. The eZ430 RF2500 (User Guide) consists of an MSP430F2274 microcontroller and CC2500 2.4 GHz broadcast transmitter. They have a couple of center elements. It is like a stand-alone operation with or outwardly surface detectors or included in a current plan. The new USB debugging media allows eZ430-RF2500 to remotely transmit and collect knowledge from a PC using the MSP430 employment UART. The MSP430F2274 microcontroller blends 16- MIPS administration with a 200-kbps, 10-bit ADC, and two op-amps. The CC2500 multichannel RF transceiver is for low-power wireless applications. The ez430-RF2500 destination cabinet is an out-of-the-box radio method with a USB debugging interface. It relates to the utilization backchannel. EZ430-RF2500 emphasizes a highly combined, ultra-low-power MSP430 MCU with 16 MHz productions and a pair of general-purpose digital input/output pins about green and red LEDs for, 21 possible improvement pins, and an interruptible push-button for client feedback. The warmth area is from 40 C to 100 C with an accuracy of ±0.5% at chamber warmth. The moisture is the 8-bit or 12-bit determination with ±3% efficiency. It uses a cheap energy accumulation of 3.3 V.

The contribution (Shinghal & Srivastava, 2017) details the utilization of the WSN methodology to increase vegetable growth. By observing and learning unique specifications, growers can distinguish the several manure, fertilization, and other provisions. The detector connection, which is tiny in stature and low in energy expenditure, presents potential in these circumstances. The fertilization supervision representation determines farming parameters using scientific considerations with a specific example of a potato crop. Using WSN agronomical parameters like the intensity of a liquid, earth reservoir pressure, and practice potential are expected for irrigation administration arrangement to sustain optimum SWT for more reliable product yield and enhance the utilization effectiveness of irrigation arrangement by 10%.

The capacity (Wark et al., 2007) to represent crowd and personal practice are necessary for presenting supplementary knowledge. It can support optimally maintain livestock and environmental reserves. A significant center is creating cattle data and gathering performance based on location and inertial information from the wearable Fleck-2 clothes. Calibrating the inertial detectors is essential to obtaining the most useful of this device learning. The scheme develops a prototype of the conventional arrangement of inertial knowledge and suitable standard parameters for each data set. By combining position information with inertial erudition, the authors select diverse characteristics and use them to evaluate cattle performance requirements. They can obtain traits such as agility, utilizing speed, headline pitch, and movement potential from the inertial indicator. The investigation information has infinite moments of video and rational investigation knowledge. The operation situations, such as sleeping, grazing, and chewing, resemble distinct batches in the characteristic period.

A massive quantity of miniature independent agents is a detector arrangement (Chaudhary, Nayse, & Waghmare, 2011). The purpose is to observe and regulate the conditions per the growth fundamentals. All indicators are reconfigurable as per the steps of product germination, progressive advances in the targeted region, variety of soil, environment, period, and kind of products are into the event. There may be a different arrangement of the products in various grades of its completion. The flourishing organization and the harvest provisions are in a distinct section. The administration demands to restrain severer like the pump, device, and carton slider. The entire quantity of indicator connections and actuators depends on the dimension. About 200 joints are satisfactory if the measurement is 35m x 200 m. It is a substantial proportion of the targeted domain. It is under the scope of sensing potential of the appliance. The connections are classified as A, B, and C. The standard 'A' is the humidity detector for the outward, and transcribe 'B' is the weather sensor for the interior. Maximum couple junctions are more than enough for external. Variety 'B' indicator is of a length of 10 to 15 measures to achieve severe environmental conditions. The prototype 'C' detector is an earth indicator. It is as per the organizational design of the vegetable plantation. They can also constrain the water stream of the irrigation method used in the Greenhouse.

The climate method (Zhu, Song, & Dong, 2011) consists of substantial quantities of compact radio detector connections are assigned in the agricultural environment to assure high accuracy and authenticity of information recovery. The links manage warmth, moisture. The received knowledge transfers to sink connections by multi-hop. Sink joints are the center of junctions. It has more dominant purposes of assembling information and banking knowledge, computing, and statistics mixture in a certain than standard nodes. The transpacific detector system can correlate with communication channels and customer terminals by sink links. The managed score is sent to the consumer computer through GPS, GPRS, WIFI, and other communications transportation or directly sent to the buyer computer by the chain. The terminal customer interprets data to conclude. The information retrieval module is used for sensing, accumulating learning, and A/D progress. The processor component is qualified to command the performance of the sensor junctions, saving, preparing the managed documents, implement high system rules, and shift the strength performance design. The radio transmission module mainly interfaces with other connections. They embrace solar collection systems as energy stocks. solar collection practice is included solar force panels, solar administration, and accumulators. The energy expenditure of the broadcast sensor interface is weak, so solar strength and accumulator can guarantee the entire operation work frequently. The outlined scheme is for real-timely monitoring farming setting knowledge, such as the warmth, moisture.

The NPUMote (Li, Cui, & Li, 2011) is a farming detector connection that happened to be stationed in a PAMS to sense the atmosphere of the supervised fields. They used the 8-bit high-performance microcontroller Atmega128L as the microcontroller section. The PAMS(Position aware Multi-sensor) model is based on TinyOS 2.1, using a worldwide coordinated duty-cycling tool for all the joints. Each power-on time of the links communications, they choose the CTP rules to accumulate the sensory information, whereas the radar pulse is adjusted to protect information cost. The knowledge dissemination from the Source device commands the connections' operational parameters, such as the communication strength, sampling regularity, engagement degree, and the extent of a business period. It uses two cell dry resources to provide potential. The gateway and intelligence host play the position of prophets in the administration regularity. The hub converts information over RS-232 from a sink to documents over TCP/IP to a communications host and vice versa. The supervised learning is collected in the store assistance to other utilization. The determination operation is an authority arrangement defining the environmental circumstance whether an agreement with the given threshold. Once identifying the unusual requirements, the examination policy will send directions, including taking on or off the watering machine, exhaust cooler, and sunscreen, to the communications host and then transfer them to the supervised greenhouse of farmland. The interconnection assistance presents online inquiry and administration gathering. If the user wants to change the disclosure threshold of environmental determinants, he must be verified by PAMS and send the management of replacing parameters.

DRAWBACKS OF THE PREVIOUS SYSTEM

The working of the framework (Thakur, Kumar, & Vijendra, 2020) coordinates the soil dampness device and Liquid siphon along with the Arduino panel. The dust humidity sensing device works to sense the grime's wetness and give its harvests to the customer. The marine tap will flood the ground at whatever point the succulence of soil goes beneath the ideal edge worth. The aid of PIR assesses the discovery of intermission at so forth fact there is any identification of interruption in the arena. The discovery of interruption is estimated by assisting PIR and identifying disruption in the field. The clients will become acquainted with it as allocated esteems. The arrangement was tried for one month and gathered interruption recognition through the PIR sensor. The system effortlessly managed without subterranean insect issues. It helps in inundating the nursery zone where the gadget is sent. The working of this water siphon depends on the dampness of the dirt. The water siphon begins working towards the pinnacle estimation of soil dampness when the dirt dampness goes beneath the allowed esteem.

The previous system does not consider the weather condition if the system analyses the ground to be dry and instructs the framework to water the location. If it rains during the later part of the day, there are chances that the product will get damaged. The proposal considers the same and analyzes the readings statistically. The design is proposed Using the analysis report.

CASE STUDY

A Caretaker requires various accessories and devices to maintain different horticultural services. In the past, nursery accessories used timber, rocks, and minerals. However, with the improvement of science and technology, the effectiveness of elements has led to the growth of different field tools and accessories like help cultivators, engines, lawnmowers, shovels, trowels, and secateurs. These machines and accessories are known as support devices. Guidance engines are less valuable than strength machines. They often assist manifold ideas and are more comfortable practicing in inadequate locations. Energy facilities require a combustible, current, or battery for functioning. They help make labor-intensive chores more manageable. These gadgets and tools, intended to achieve various actions, assist in conducting soil assignments efficiently, smoothly, conveniently, and economically. These have revolutionized growing and horticulture globally. Hence, it is essential to determine the suitable device for delivering a business adequately and conveniently.

The suggestion uses a gardener tool that measures the soil content. Figure 1 is the tool used in the experiment. Table 1 lists the tool provision.

Figure 1. Gardener tool used to take readings

Table 1. Provision provided by the gardener tool

Measuring Parameter	Scaling	Description
Photometer	0 - 2000	0 - dark
		2000 - light
PH meter	3.5 – 8	3.5 – acidic
		8- alkaline
Moisture meter	1 - 10	(1-3) – dry, needs watering
		(4-7) –good moisturize
		(8-10) – too wet

The tool contains the following components:

- Photometer – It measures the intensity (Jie, Kun, Shisheng, & Aiyuan, 2001) or strength of the sunlight. It measures the amount of light falling on it. The measuring tool varies from 0 to 2000. 0 is considered dark, and 2000 is light. The practice (Heinz, Kraft, Buchen, Frede, Aquino, & Breuer, 2014) promotes coexisting surveillance of many liquids and nutrient fluxes in watered farming. A programmed sampling scheme is with a Wavelength-Scanned Cavity Ring-Down Spectrometry System. It is for committed liquid isotope investigation. The electronic sampling method consists of several locations implemented with pumps, a controller closet for the device and controller, and a processor performing the practice. The entire arrangement is administered via internet-based administration software, supporting surveillance from almost everywhere. The scheme is presently set up at the International Rice Explorer association in diversified rice growing arrangements, continuously observing rainwater and nutrient fluxes.
- PH meter - A pH measure is an experimental device that marks the hydrogen-ion exercise in water-based liquids, symbolizing its acidity or alkalinity. It measures the soil contents. 3.5 is considered acidic, and eight is considered alkaline. The information (Cucus & Febrianti, 2017) is sent to the host. Machine knowledge will input the current learning to get the judgment and transmit it to the actuator. The tool operates on a method. It is a self-governing policy that will watch the liquid component. The information will be associated with the awareness base embracing the laws. It will research the most relevant rainwater requirements to find the weeds that live on the prophets. The experience foundation is installed on the server side. The information station is used in many communications to be commanded by the operator, so the agency accommodates different prophets combined with the server. Comparative to the use of many projects, it is maintained by agencies.
- Moisture meter – The component measures the water content. 1-3 is considered dry, 4-7 is considered a good moisturizer, and 8-10 is regarded as wet. San Joaquin and Stanislaus province butternut dehydrators accepted to engage in the study (Thompson & Grant, 1992) before the 1989 production period. They were classified into sets according to the dryer. Some examples included measuring progress, emptying yearly contents, and other features that could change dryer production and administration. The nine groups had five couples of permanent bin dryers and four combinations of pothole dryers. One arbitrarily picked dryer in each pair was provided with a dampness means, and sensing services establishes in five containers in that department. Supervisors

had the supplementary examples served a half-day coaching assembly on usual notions of drying and utility of the measure. They practiced the actions to list walnut drying. On-site support obliged these administrators before and during the 1989 and 1990 drying springs. Executives of non-instrumented dryers gave instruction and register processes and managed the endpoint of concentrating in their typical fashion. These dryer workers all applied for the sheath examination. One executive also infrequently used a seed dampness measure to monitor the process of drying.

Figure 2 represents an instance of moisture level measured during a day. Figure 3 is the measured light intensity in a day. Figure 4 is the temperature measured during the day. Table 2 is the Variance results before considering the weather forecast. Table 3 is the ANOVA summary for the readings before considering the weather forecast. Figure 5 Depicts the tasks before considering the weather forecast.

Figure 2. Instance of moisture variation in a day

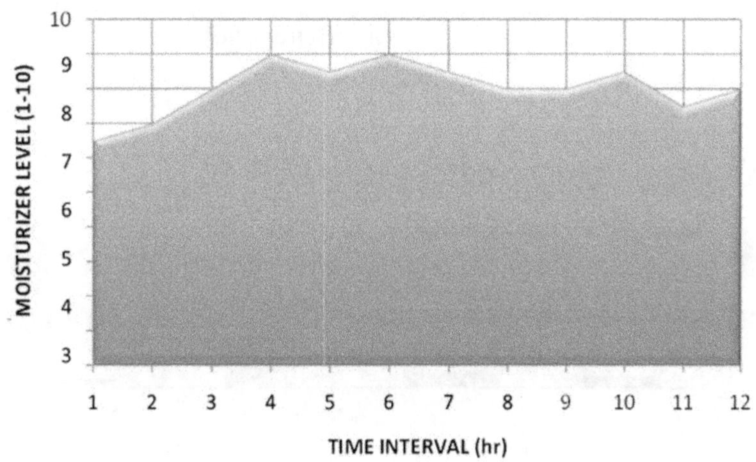

Figure 3. Instance of sunlight intensity in a day

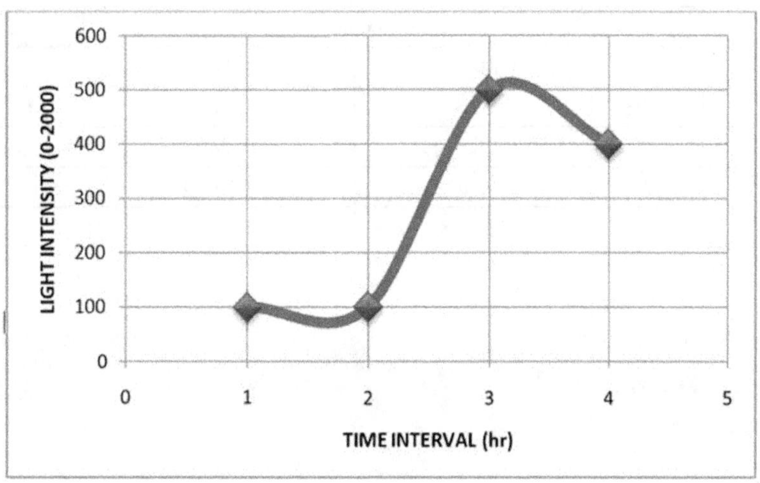

Figure 4. Instance of temperature measured during the day

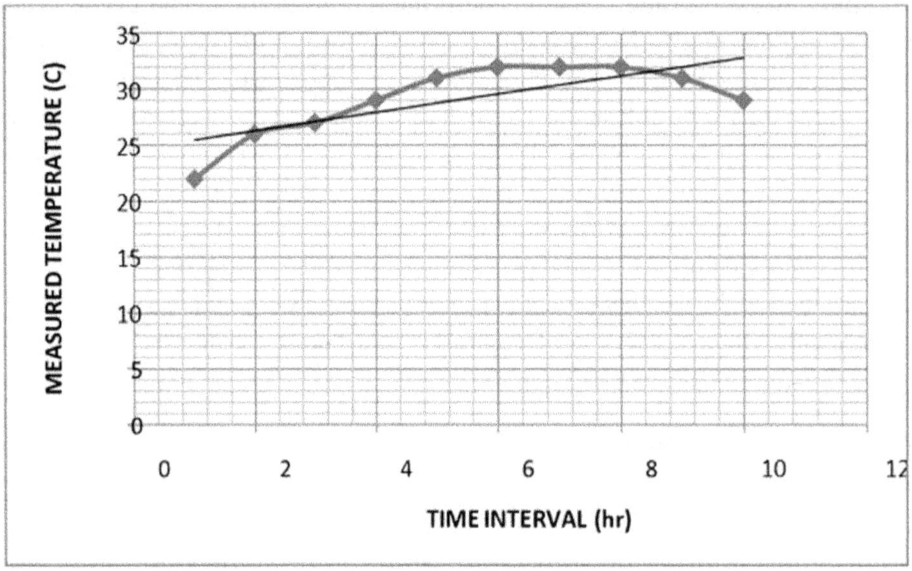

Figure 5. Depicts the readings before considering weather forecast

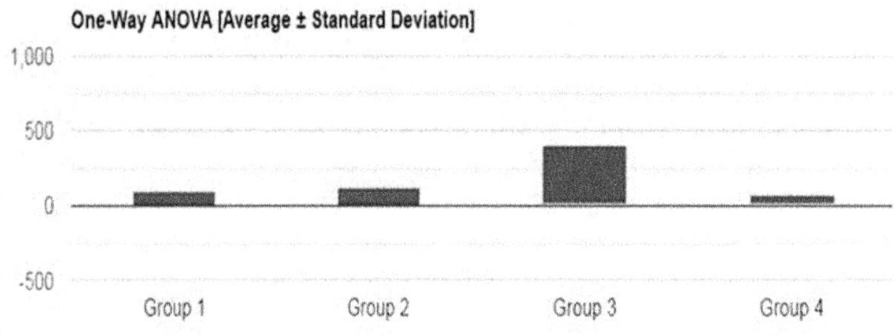

Table 2. Variance results before considering weather forecast

Data Summary				
Groups	**N**	**Mean**	**Std.dev**	**Std. error**
Group 1	8	52.5	46.828	16.5562
Group 2	7	60	63.2456	23.9046
Group 3	2	210	197.9899	140
Group 4	11	38.1818	29.2627	8.8233

Table 3. ANNOVA summary

Source	Degrees of freedom	Sum of squares	Mean square	F-stat	P-value
Between groups	3	50686.3724	16895.4575	4.6547	0.0106
Within groups	24	87113.7085	3629.7379		
Total	27	137800.0808			

The moisturizer is maintained manually. We have considered the retain moisturizer between 6 and 7 considering the sunlight intensity and weather forecast. The variance (Scheffe, 1999) and ANNOVA is computed. Table 4 is Variance results after considering weather forecast. Table 5 is the ANNOVA summary after considering weather forecast. Figure 6 is depiction of readings after considering weather forecast.

Table 4. Variance results after considering weather forecast

Data Summary				
Groups	**N**	**Mean**	**Std.dev**	**Std. error**
Group 1	2	210	268.7006	190
Group 2	7	60	63.2456	23.9046
Group 3	2	210	197.9899	140
Group 4	11	38.1818	29.2627	8.8233

Table 5. ANNOVA summary

Source	Degrees of freedom	Sum of squares	Mean square	F-stat	P-value
Between groups	3	89345.4698	29781.8233	3.7237	0.03042
Within groups	18	143963.6898	7997.9828		
Total	21	233309.1597			

Figure 6. Depiction of readings

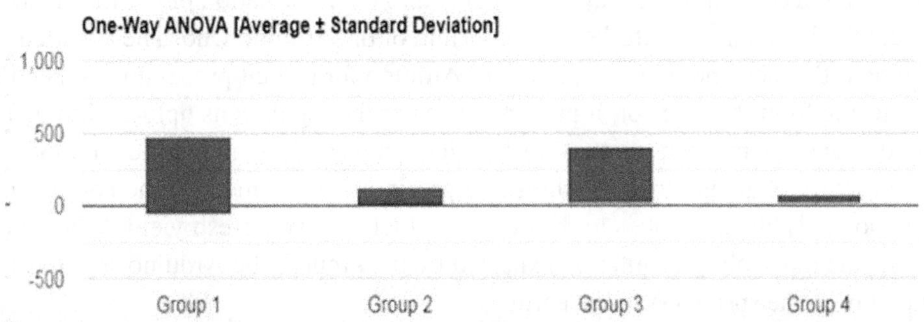

PROPOSED DESIGN

The work takes care of unattended plants when the supervisor cannot attend to them. The sensor's training takes care of the plants in the guardian's absence. The arrangement consists of a soil sensor that measures the dampness of the soil. The connection has an intelligence component. The user provisions the time interval. It uses intelligence to set the amount of water level required for a specified period. The arrangement consists of-

- Soil dampness sensor – Soil dampness sensors measure the volumetric water content in the soil. Since the direct gravimetric estimation of free soil dampness requires evacuating, drying, and weighing of an example, soil dampness sensors measure the volumetric water content in a roundabout way by utilizing some other property of the dirt, for example, electrical opposition, dielectric consistent, or communication with neutrons, as an intermediary for the dampness content. The connection between the deliberate property and soil dampness must be adjusted and may change depending on environmental factors such as soil type, temperature, or electric conductivity. Reflected microwave radiation is influenced by dirt dampness and is utilized for remote detecting in hydrology and agribusiness. Soil dampness sensors commonly allude to sensors that gauge volumetric water content. Another class of sensors measures another property of dampness in soils called water potential; these sensors are generally indicated to as soil water expected sensors and incorporate tension meters and gypsum squares. The contribution has a GSM-based liquid method (Sharma, Gupta, Khantwal, Kumar, & Singh, 2021) structure with the handle of dampness level, and the water level is described. It is a different exclusive arrangement pattern. The utilization of GSM-based android gadgets in water practice frames is made. The consumer can farm and administer devices according to the user's request. The detector learns to manage trials employing this discovery. The recommended core estimates the liquid essential for vegetables based on earth wetness knowledge collected by a few detector cores sent in the domain. Automation confirmed time and store in a way that is of unbelievable remedy to the industry and visionary in all the computations. Examining policies is achieved by employing the ATMEGA 328, Soil Moisture detector, and GSM.

The project (Siva, Bagubali, & Krishnan, 2019) is based on the liquid content on the earth. The streaming content in dirt determines the procedure done by the Arduino. The clay precipitation detector will identify the liquid content in the clay and support it to the information pin of the device. The other two pins, except the input pin, are attached 5V & terrain of the Arduino Uno. The knowledge pin in the indicator will hold the data and transfer the info to Arduino for distant processing. When the Arduino accepts the learning from the detector, it prepares it as per the regulations uploaded to it. The modern principles used in this scheme focus on the threshold dampness of the clay. If the data (moisture content) received by the sensor is greater than the threshold precipitation claimed for the corresponding earth, then the Arduino reads blank supplies to the device and lets it give a fresh yield. When the dampness content exceeds the threshold precipitation expected by the ground, the Arduino supplies the machine to tap the liquid from the sprinklers to the earth.

In the proposal, the sensor studies the dampness of the soil and analyzes the need for water. The values fed into the intelligence component take care of during non-supervision times. The user sets the time duration for device activation.

- Passive infrared sensor (PIR) – It is an electronic sensor that estimates infrared (IR) light transmitting from objects in its field of view. They are used in PIR- based movement identifiers. PIR sensors employment in security cautions and programmed lighting applications. PIR sensors identify general development yet don't give data on whom or what moved. This component enhances the security of the arrangement.

This method (Upadhyay & Maurya, 2020) is intended for the security of the product of producers. If any creature invades the farm, the tenant gets the information on his receiver. The immediate response by the tenant can protect his produce from the beasts. This arrangement comprises Power Supply, Regulator IC, transmission unit and Radio, Submissive infrared indicator, GSM component. The passive detector contains infrared brightness reflecting from things. It consists of two openings. These apertures are of such different elements that if It comes in connection with the infrared transmission. If a creature or individual body appears in its area, there will be positive differential development between the apertures. If the mammal goes away from its range, then convert situations happen. So, it creates the contradictory differential replacement. The PIR detector gives the production comparable to the diversity in both vibrations. It senses the creature and makes the sound.

- Water siphon – The siphon is a fluid repository with a modified U-tube. The fluid first fills the cylinder. The reason for the siphon is to empty fluid from the store by a liquid stream that ignores a more significant level than the fluid surface in the repository. The juice goes from the supply to a lower level continuously and without outside vitality contribution until the store level falls beneath the output end of the U-tube. The down-to-earth contrast between a siphon and a defective container is how the fluid goes to a more elevated level before depleting out to a lower level. This fits the timer component at work to automatically take care of the plants. The recommended design (Jisha, Vignesh, & Deekshit, 2019) is a suggestion to give a program to choose the liquid level in the container and earth. The reservoir is attached to an ultrasonic detector, an Ethernet component. It unites to an Arduino Uno Board, and storage runs a plan to accumulate the knowledge. The Condensation device joins with dirt, an Ethernet section, an Arduino Uno Board, and a storage-based host application on which the learning is organized. The ultrasonic node is affixed to the reservoir. It acknowledges the development of the vessel. The amount of liquid in the container is limited by the Arduino board. In the dampness node attached to the earth, the precipitation of the dirt is managed by the Arduino board. The size of the vessel and dimensions are sent to the user's smartphone using an Ethernet component connected with the Arduino. When the liquid measurement of the basin reaches the most advanced limit and if the rainwater dimension of the container reaches the terminal duration, the relay event will be ON/OFF, and an observant communication is sent to the user's smartphone.
- Intelligence component – The component takes input from other segments to learn the doings. A set of rules is inserted into the element. Rules are made considering the dampness of the soil to the weather condition. The instruction passes to the siphon. The plants are watered using the same. The design (Ghadiyali, Lad, & Patel, 313-316) categorizes into four segments. In the first part of Data Reservoir, the authors have different information components of the farming division. It contributes significant input to the practice. It forms the basis of the following element Datastore Method. The data storage Rule works pre-processing, collects the results for long course purposes, and takes charge of the information construction in the form of Data Cubes and sub-elements as

Data Mart. The third segment is farming knowledge. It is the center of the recommended structure. It captures the data from the Data storage. It uses conventional data prospecting methods. It converts the acquired data into essential knowledge for the board. Stake Owners are the true successor of this selected awareness through the dashboard. Each sector has its functionality, and its output will be input for the next segment.

- Timer component – The user sets the time interval using this component. It connects to the intelligence and siphon segments. It gives its input to both elements. A-node (Yoo, Kim, Kim, Ahn, Sung, & Kim, 2007) is a farming detector connection produced to be stationed in a glasshouse and to sense the atmosphere of the greenhouse. The device inserts all 8bit MCU, IEEE 802.15.4 co-operative transceivers, a CPLD, and indicators in one PCB to decrease the probability of errors. A connection is provided with a reserve of lithium-ion rechargeable groups and observes the voltage level of the battery for preservation purposes. The camouflage color is used to stop A-node from the moisture in the greenhouse. The software of A-node is based on the primary variant of ANTS-EOS. The system rules of EOS are customized for this scheme to a lightweight CSMA-based MAC and a strong multi-hop ad-hoc routing obligation. A-node continues its employment after fixing the system. The purpose of software creates its working time by applying its indicator and sensing the greenhouse conditions. The employment software reads the temperature, moisture, and luminance of a greenhouse from detectors and announces the decision to the sink via its progenitors. If it gets any packages from its offspring during this busy event, it delivers the parcels to their origin. A-node arranges for its working schedule, such as sensing period in sleep order message from the sink. The application software turns off its attached sensors and puts the transceiver in power-down mode. Finally, it sets up the private snooze timer, goes to its hibernation stage, and remains for the termination of the timer. The utilization restarts its following effective times by applying the transceiver and the indicator and remains to sense the greenhouse. The actuator node is intended to measure the strength of the greenhouse hypothesis with developing melon. It has a supplementary relay strip to A-node to examine the switch of the enlightenment in the greenhouse. It's mainly powered and doesn't use any power-saving system. The administration software of the C-node remains for the call from the sink. It commands its relay to turn on or off the lights.
- Weather sensor - The climate sensors measure different variables. For instance, these may incorporate breeze speed, precipitation, barometric weight, temperature, and relative moistness. This is connected to the intelligence component for analysis. The same is represented in figure 7. A method (Hubbard, Rosenberg, & Nielsen, 1983) has been produced in Nebraska to automate regular climate information from isolated farming positions. Conventional warmth detectors are joined to an on-site microprocessor. A fundamental minicomputer periodically examines the microprocessor, quality-checks the incoming climate knowledge, and assigns it to a more extensive mainframe machine. Weather-data-based applications are possible for clients of the mainframe network through the AGNET arrangement). Applications are currently options for such purposes as fertilization scheduling, calculating power demands for cereal drying, foretelling grade and speed of product progress, and prognosticating cattle density accumulations. Nebraska now has 17 standings, and quantity is developing quickly since opening charges are inexpensive, section conditions are easy, and support is insignificant. In conclusion, investment is improving the effectiveness of near-real-time climate knowledge.

Figure 7. Proposed design

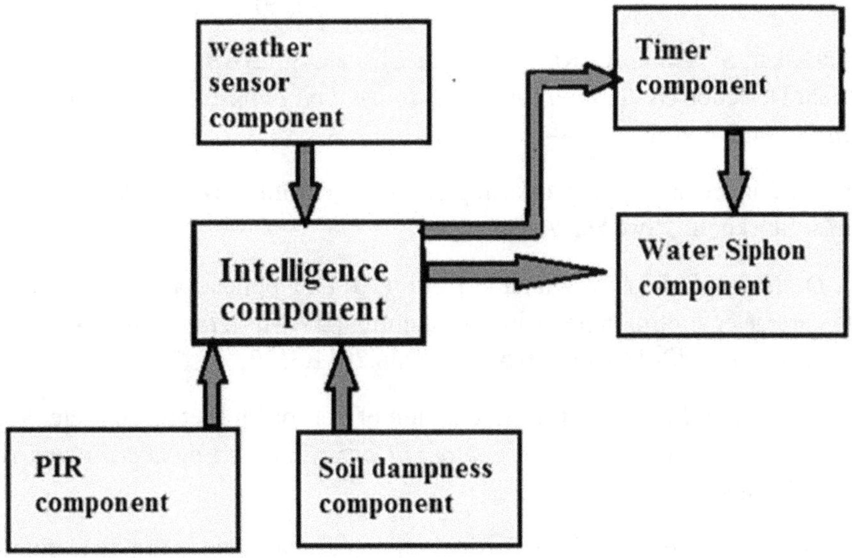

FUTURE SCOPE

The work takes care of supervision without user intervention. The system can be used for a particular weather condition. The intelligence sub-model analyses the dampness considering the weather condition. It takes care of rain situations and suggests the water level necessary to the yields. Different parameters can be considered in future work.

CONCLUSION

Sensor network are assembly of sensing elements and controllers. These devices accomplish the sensing task and take appropriate decision on-time. The proposal enhances the doings suggested in the previous contribution. The suggestion uses weather sensor models along with the intelligence model and timer model. The weather model assesses the weather conditions and provides the input to the intelligence model. The weather and soil dampness sensor component transmits the sensed data to the intelligence component. It gives water siphon the amount of water to be supplied on intervals provided by the timer component. The suggestion computes result statistically before and after considering weather report.

REFERENCES

Ambika, N. (2019). Energy-Perceptive Authentication in Virtual Private Networks Using GPS Data. In *Security, Privacy and Trust in the IoT Environment* (pp. 25–38). Springer, Cham. doi:10.1007/978-3-030-18075-1_2

Ambika, N. (2020). Encryption of Data in Cloud-Based Industrial IoT Devices. In S. Pal & V. G. Díaz (Eds.), *D.-N. Le, IoT: Security and Privacy Paradigm* (pp. 111–129). CRC press, Taylor & Francis Group.

Badhe, A., Kharadkar, S., Ware, R., Kamble, P., & Chavan, S. (2018). IOT Based Smart Agriculture And Soil Nutrient Detection System. *International Journal on Future Revolution in Computer Science & Communication Engineering*, *4*, 774–777.

Baggio, A. (2005). Wireless sensor networks in precision agriculture. *Workshop on Real-World Wireless Sensor Networks*. Stockholm, Sweden: ACM.

Chaudhary, D. D., Nayse, S. P., & Waghmare, L. M. (2011). Application of wireless sensor networks for greenhouse parameter control in precision agriculture. [IJWMN]. *International Journal of Wireless & Mobile Networks*, *3*(1), 140–149. doi:10.5121/ijwmn.2011.3113

Cucus, A., & Febrianti, M. S. (2017). Implementation of Sensor Ph Meter, Ec Meter and Temperature on Smart Vertical Agriculture System. *International Conference on Engineering and Technology Development (ICETD)*. Indonesia.

Ghadiyali, T., Lad, K., & Patel, B. (2011). Agriculture intelligence: an emerging technology for farmer community. *Second International Conference on Emerging Applications of Information Technology*. Kolkata, India: IEEE. 10.1109/EAIT.2011.36

Goap, A., Sharma, D., Shukla, A. K., & Krishna, C. R. (2018). An IoT based smart irrigation management system using Machine learning and open source technologies. *Computers and Electronics in Agriculture*, *155*, 41–49. doi:10.1016/j.compag.2018.09.040

Heinz, E., Kraft, P., Buchen, C., Frede, H. G., Aquino, E., & Breuer, L. (2014). Set up of an automatic water quality sampling system in irrigation agriculture. *Sensors (Basel)*, *14*(1), 212–228. doi:10.3390/s140100212 PMID:24366178

Hubbard, K. G., Rosenberg, N. J., & Nielsen, D. C. (1983). Automated weather data network for agriculture. *Journal of Water Resources Planning and Management*, *109*(3), 213–222. doi:10.1061/(ASCE)0733-9496(1983)109:3(213)

Jie, Z., Kun, T., Shisheng, S., & Aiyuan, F. (2001). Portable autocontrol solar photometer. *Liangzi Dianzi Xuebao*, *18*(6), 551–555.

Jisha, R. C., Vignesh, G., & Deekshit, D. (2019). IOT based water level monitoring and implementation on both agriculture and domestic areas. *2nd International Conference on Intelligent Computing, Instrumentation and Control Technologies (ICICICT)* (pp. 1119-1123). Kannur, India: IEEE. 10.1109/ICICICT46008.2019.8993272

Keswani, B., Mohapatra, A. G., Mohanty, A., Khanna, A., Rodrigues, J. J., Gupta, D., & de Albuquerque, V. H. C. (2019). Adapting weather conditions based IoT enabled smart irrigation technique in precision agriculture mechanisms. *Neural Computing & Applications*, *31*(1), 277–292. doi:10.1007/s00521-018-3737-1

Li, S., Cui, J., & Li, Z. (2011). Wireless sensor network for precise agriculture monitoring. *Fourth International Conference on Intelligent Computation Technology and Automation.* 1, pp. 307-310. Shenzhen, China: IEEE. 10.1109/ICICTA.2011.87

Nagaraj, A. (2021). *Introduction to Sensors in IoT and Cloud Computing Applications.* Bentham Science Publishers. doi:10.2174/97898114793591210101

Nawandar, N. K., & Satpute, V. R. (2019). IoT based low cost and intelligent module for smart irrigation system. *Computers and Electronics in Agriculture, 162*, 979–990. doi:10.1016/j.compag.2019.05.027

Pernapati, K. (2018). IoT based low cost smart irrigation system. *Second International Conference on Inventive Communication and Computational Technologies (ICICCT)* (pp. 1312- 1315). Coimbatore, India: IEEE. 10.1109/ICICCT.2018.8473292

Rawal, S. (2017). IOT based smart irrigation system. *International Journal of Computer Applications, 159*(8), 7–11. doi:10.5120/ijca2017913001

Saraf, S. B., & Gawali, D. H. (2017). IoT based smart irrigation monitoring and controlling system. *2nd IEEE International Conference on Recent Trends in Electronics, Information & Communication Technology (RTEICT)* (pp. 815-819). Bangalore, India: IEEE. 10.1109/RTEICT.2017.8256711

Scheffe, H. (1999). *The analysis of variance* (Vol. 72). John Wiley & Sons.

Sharma, U., Gupta, A., Khantwal, S., Kumar, V., & Singh, V. (2021). Soil moisture sensor based automatic irrigation water pump controlling system with GSM technology. *Recent Trends in Communication and Electronics*, 14-18.

Shinghal, D., & Srivastava, N. (2017). *Wireless sensor networks in agriculture: for potato farming.* SSRN - Elsevier.

Siva, K. N., Bagubali, A., & Krishnan, K. V. (2019). Smart watering of plants. *International Conference on Vision Towards Emerging Trends in Communication and Networking (ViTECoN)* (pp. 1-4). Vellore, India: IEEE.

Srbinovska, M., Gavrovski, C., Dimcev, V., Krkoleva, A., & Borozan, V. (2015). Environmental parameters monitoring in precision agriculture using wireless sensor networks. *Journal of Cleaner Production, 88*, 297–307. doi:10.1016/j.jclepro.2014.04.036

Thakur, D., Kumar, Y., & Vijendra, S. (2020). Smart Irrigation and Intrusions Detection in Agricultural Fields Using IoT. *International Conference on Computational Intelligence and Data Science (ICCIDS 2019).* Gurgaon, INDIA: ELSEVIER.

Thompson, J., & Grant, J. (1992). New moisture meter could curb overdrying of walnuts. *California Agriculture, 46*(2), 31–34. doi:10.3733/ca.v046n02p31

Upadhyay, A., & Maurya, S. K. (2020). Protecting the agriculture field by IoT application. *International Conference on Power Electronics & IoT Applications in Renewable Energy and its Control (PARC)* (pp. 411-414). Mathura, India: IEEE. 10.1109/PARC49193.2020.236640

Vaishali, S., Suraj, S., Vignesh, G., Dhivya, S., & Udhayakumar, S. (2017). Mobile integrated smart irrigation management and monitoring system using IOT. *International Conference on Communication and Signal Processing (ICCSP)* (pp. 2164-2167). Chennai, India: IEEE.

Wark, T., Corke, P., Sikka, P., Klingbeil, L., Guo, Y., Crossman, C., Valencia, P., Swain, D., & Bishop-Hurley, G. (2007). Transforming agriculture through pervasive wireless sensor networks. *IEEE Pervasive Computing*, *6*(2), 50–57. doi:10.1109/MPRV.2007.47

Yoo, S. E., Kim, J. E., Kim, T., Ahn, S., Sung, J., & Kim, D. (2007). A 2 S: automated agriculture system based on WSN. *IEEE International Symposium on Consumer Electronics* (pp. 1-5). Irving, TX, USA: IEEE.

Zhao, W., Lin, S., Han, J., Xu, R., & Hou, L. (2017). *Design and implementation of smart irrigation system based on LoRa. IEEE Globecom Workshops (GC Wkshps)*. IEEE.

Zhu, Y., Song, J., & Dong, F. (2011). Applications of wireless sensor network in the agriculture environment monitoring. *International Workshop on Automobile, Power and Energy Engineering* (pp. 608-614). Imperial College London, London, U.K: ELSEVIER. 10.1016/j.proeng.2011.08.1131

Chapter 18
The Assessment of Artificial Intelligence for Business Performance in Bangladesh

Fm. Asikullah
University of Wollongong, Sydney, Australia

Phonebuson Chakma
https://orcid.org/0000-0002-3701-1673
International University of Business Agriculture and Technology, Bangladesh

Md. Nafis Hossain
Green University of Bangladesh, Bangladesh

Md Imam Mahdi
National Institute of Technology, Durgapur, India

ABSTRACT

In Bangladesh, improving small and medium enterprise (SME) performance is still an uphill task. The study aims to explore the effects of AI on the performance of small and medium business organizations. With advanced statistical analysis, the study highlighted the significant effects of artificial intelligence on the performance of small and medium enterprises by accepting all the proposed hypotheses. Additionally, effective business management (EBM) showed the role of a partial mediator, since artificial intelligence directly and indirectly held an association with small and medium enterprise performance. Moreover, the authenticity of the study was supported by confirmatory factor analysis (CFA) and structural equation model (SEM) which were represented based on model fit exponents, composite reliability, convergent validity, and discriminant validity. The study ended by providing theoretical and managerial implications that will assist business owners, managers, stakeholders, and policymakers in improving their business performance.

DOI: 10.4018/979-8-3693-1842-3.ch018

INTRODUCTION

Artificial intelligence emerges not as a novelty but as the magnetic force guiding today's business environment at the dynamic junction of time-tested economic concepts and cutting-edge technology (Enholm et al., 2022). The phrase "artificial intelligence" has an interesting paradox. Its fundamental definition, according to the Oxford Language Dictionary, implies that it was manufactured by humans rather than occurring naturally, whereas a secondary meaning suggests dishonesty, a quality with a long history in human conduct. This comparison captures the intricate nature of our connection with AI, which is both a product of human invention and a mirror of human complexity (Trolice et al., 2021). The term artificial intelligence describes the creation of computer systems that can simulate human cognitive processes, including learning, problem-solving, and decision-making, as it goes beyond simple calculation and aims to provide machines with intelligence-like abilities so they can adjust, learn, and develop on their own (Kok, 2009).

Artificial intelligence is the catalyst in the sweeping tide of technological advancement, altering not just how businesses run and economies function but also how individuals and communities interact with each other in the age of technology (Loureiro et al., 2021). Artificial intelligence helps management delegate decisions by seamlessly integrating with management skills, improving resource allocation, and encouraging better-informed, strategic judgments (Feuerriegel et al., 2022). The race to develop artificial intelligence technology is picking up speed throughout the world since potential applications include industry, energy, healthcare, education, and finance, and for all the sectors the entire amount invested in AI for the first half of 2018 was $43.5 billion (Mou, 2019).

A diverse model that illustrates the benefits of AI-enabled organizational culture, leadership, and employee training on how they think of AI-assisted workload reduction, which in turn improves employee engagement and, in the modern, dynamic work environment, improves company performance (Rožman et al., 2023). Diminished cognitive workload resulted from applying the algorithm's guidelines, but quality issues with situational awareness emerged, indicating the potential of AI integration to improve human performance in intricate systems, broadly applicable to domains requiring real-time contextual filtering of spatial-temporal information. (Zak et al., 2022). The study shows that neural correlates have the potential to serve as a gauge of explanatory efficacy in tasks involving perception, with 62.4% accuracy in identifying significant hemispheric neural signal differences in the user study. This finding has broad implications for comprehending the relationship between humans and artificial intelligence (Kim et al., 2020). Diminished cognitive workload resulted from applying the algorithm's guidelines, but quality issues with situational awareness emerged, indicating the potential of AI integration to improve human performance in intricate systems, broadly applicable to domains requiring real-time contextual filtering of spatial-temporal information (Buettner, 2013). Ultimately, achieving dependability, safety, and trustworthiness in applications is crucial to promoting self-efficacy, mastery, creativity, and responsibility within the Human-Centered Artificial Intelligence (HCAI) framework. In order to improve human performance, it encourages the design of technologies with high degrees of computer automation and human control (Shneiderman, 2020).

Artificial intelligence has the potential to transform a wide range of businesses and activities, much like the revolutionary influence of technical progress during the industrial revolution and a number of fields, including industry, government, the public sector, and science and technology, experts have emphasized the potential, difficulties, and research agenda presented by AI's explosive rise (Dwivedi et al., 2021). Human factors play a major role in the safe and effective integration of artificial intelligence in business sector, underscoring the need for ecological validity and user-centered design in clinical procedures (Asan & Choudhury, 2021). Considerably artificial intelligence, it is possible to efficiently screen compounds virtually across large chemical spaces and quickly identify possible therapeutic candidates at a lower cost and with less resource consumption (Paul et al., 2021). Artificial intelligence (AI) was critical in minimizing the impact of the COVID-19 pandemic by enabling quick data processing, permitting remote patient monitoring, and assisting in the creation of diagnostic tools and treatment plans (Chamola et al., 2020). In order to battle COVID-19, artificial intelligence (AI) is essential in a number of areas, such as vaccine development, cluster identification, future impact prediction, and real-time decision assistance for case monitoring, analysis, and screening (Vaishya et al., 2020).

The study has significant importance, as it is expected to assess the stakeholders, owners and respected authorities of small-medium business organizations.

TECHNOLOGY–ORGANIZATION–ENVIRONMENT (TOE)

The TOE Framework plays an immense role to comprehend artificial intelligence, since the TOE Framework highlights the three important factors that affect organizational processes, and they are technological element, organizational context and environmental context. In this regard, observable, relative advantage, complex, compatible, and experimental abilities are ensured (Utterback, 1971).

The organizational context determines the availability of resources and financial support that are needed to implement innovative artificial intelligence, whereas the third factor insists on environmental concern, with which firms operate their work by dealing with the third party regarding the government intervention (Wejnert, 2002).

Another way to hold TOE-framework is the integration of technological element with environmental management to eradicate all the possible difficulties. In this context, small medium enterprises can relieve external and internal pressure imposed by the management. As a result, organizational success and productivity, effective operational sustainability take place (Hillman et al., 2009).

Apparently, small medium enterprises are contingent upon artificial intelligence for confirming sustainable business performance and organizational goals (Haldma & Lääts, 2002). Accountably, organizations achieve fruitful and valuable outcomes by integrating business environment with artificial intelligence (Bouchard & Rousselière, 2016). Finally, the execution of artificial intelligence depends on the extent to which it is implemented by following organizational value-chain activities to ensure firm performance (Zhu, 2004).

This theory is extremely related to the effective business outcomes based on environmental and artificial issues, indicating that firms try to remove all the possible uncertainties by responding to artificial innovative activities (Wei & Clegg, 2017). Hence, organizations like to capture internal or external resources in compliance with modern technical advancement for improving their business (Bouchard & Rousselière, 2016)

LITERATURE REVIEW AND HYPOTHESIS FORMULATION

Artificial Intelligence and Business Performance

To commence with, the business culture and overall performance are likely to be changed by artificial intelligence and thus investing sufficient money is required to eliminate all the barriers that are the antithesis of adopting artificial intelligence (Kar & Kushwaha, 2023). Admittedly, artificial intelligence is proven to lead to profit maximization by outlining business activities efficiently and optimizing resources properly (Zhao et al., 2023). Since artificial intelligence paves the way to maintain effective business management by controlling financial stability, it is inextricably intertwined with the effective business environment (Pallathadka et al., 2023). Artificial intelligence has crucial importance for today's business world given the fact that all the arduous activities that are not possible to be accomplished by human beings are carried out by using innovative technology, resulting in effective business performance. (Enholm et al., 2022). For capturing sustainable business performance, the need of technological intelligence is necessary because it expands business intelligence applications(Olan et al., 2022).

The application of artificial intelligence promotes our understanding level, which in turn assists in ensuring business integration, thus achieving business performance (Kumar et al., 2022). Artificial intelligence accompanied by technological advancement leads to business innovation. Therefore, it is important to equip business organizations with technological intelligence (Wang et al., 2022). Moreover, risk managers and financial authorities can comprehend potential problems by adopting artificial intelligence. As a result, business efficiency is attained (Daníelsson et al., 2022). It is difficult to accurately predict the future price, but artificial intelligence helps business organizations predict future goals including market price effectively (Liu & Ma, 2022). Artificial intelligence improves customer communications quickly in this dynamic world, resulting in profit goals and productivity (Yang et al., 2022). During the post-COVID-19 pandemic, achieving potential business outcomes has been an ordeal. Therefore, business firms need to adhere to running their business with the help of technological intelligence (Sharifi et al., 2021).

Following the above-mentioned literature reviews, one hypothesis were prepared concerning the importance of artificial intelligence for small medium business performance in Bangladesh.

H1: Artificial intelligence leads to business performance.

Artificial Intelligence and Effective Business Management

Human beings have a limitation to work according to their own ability, but the use of artificial intelligence helps people to complete the task faster (Broekhuizen et al., 2023). To achieve business goals, organizations devote huge amounts of investment to purchasing technology-based software which accomplishes the task faster. As a result, organizations can save their precious time (Chowdhury et al., 2023). However, several companies can escalate customers' adoption by using excellent features of artificial intelligence which is environment-friendly and will make everything faster and easier(Mehta et al., 2022). Customer satisfaction and comfortability of workers can be easily attained by using technological intelligence because it can carry our all the complicated activities within a short period of time (Eckert et al., 2022). Besides, customer satisfaction is an important concept for any organization. So, to satisfy the customers, organizations like to adopt artificial intelligence (Ruan & Mezei, 2022).

Customer satisfaction with digital technology is found to have a positive and significant relationship. So, it is crucial for every organization to use artificial intelligence (Pantano & Serravalle, 2022). Moreover, Confirming customer satisfaction is much easier by using technological equipment than using non-technological equipment (Pillarisetty & Mishra, 2022). In today's business world, organizations use green innovation and artificial intelligence not only to complete business activities faster but also to confirm customer needs (Helo & Hao, 2022). Technology must be used at every business organization for reaching their goals. However, customer satisfaction is also essential. Therefore, organizations should adhere to artificial intelligence to make customer satisfied (Dogru & Keskin, 2020). No business cannot flourish their future, if customers are dissatisfied with their potential services. So, it is inevitable for human resource managers to use technology for having customer satisfaction (Duchessi et al., 1993).

Following the above-mentioned literature reviews, one hypothesis were prepared concerning the importance of artificial intelligence for small medium business performance in Bangladesh.

H2: Artificial intelligence causes effective business management

Artificial Intelligence, Effective Business Management and Performance

The workers face pressure at their work place, but in the presence of artificial intelligence the workload becomes easy, and workers feel comfortable in completing their business activities. Additionally, technological intelligence is found to be a significant predictor of security surveillance, as organizations can protect their valuable resources by using advanced technology (Chen, 2023). The policymakers and technology-based companies like to observe artificial intelligence surveillance in society more on the many unknown incidents. So, it is possible to address all the uncertainties with the help of advanced technological equipment. Besides, it has become easier to control the security system while mitigating the workload in compliance with artificial intelligence (Saheb, 2023). Technology-based software present an efficient and robust framework to recognize everything within a short period of time. As a result, workload borne by human beings is likely to be vanished (Ullah et al., 2022). Besides, human resource practitioners provide valuable judgement, when they use technology-based software.

Therefore, conflicts created by employers are resolved, and organizations can outline unbiased judgements, which in turn maintain the organizations' safety and security in the most emphatic way (Jabbar et al., 2022). Excellent analytical capabilities that are needed to get insight into the complex data are obtained by using artificial intelligence to soften the workload (Thakur et al., 2021). Artificial intelligence is used for proper screening, analyzing, prediction and tracking critical activities with an aim to reducing the workload (Vaishya et al., 2020). In addition, it-based technology can predict the activities that are likely to take place in the future, but without artificial intelligence it is quite impossible and increases the work pressure (Eldrandaly et al., 2019). Therefore, in future, human beings will totally rely upon the significant use of artificial intelligence so that workload can be reduced to zero percent (Buettner, 2013). The business performance and effectiveness take place when employees are provided with artificial intelligence which confirms team skills, endorses organizational culture, and leadership, and reduces the workload (Rožman et al., 2022).

The routine and the innovative use of chatbots should be encouraged to create agility and develop for business sustainability.(X. Wang et al., 2022). Since technological intelligence is capable of collecting massive data faster, It has been mandatory for many large organizations to use machine learning and artificial intelligence to ameliorate their performance and productivity(Sandeep et al., 2022). Employees are able to secure success, productivity and the performance of the firms by availing of the opportunities provided by artificial intelligence, when it comes to maximize business performance (Ramachandran et al., 2022). Excellent employee performance, which determines business performance, can be attained by artificial intelligence, as it leads to effective business work by governing leadership skills (Wijayati et al., 2022). The important part of Small- and medium-sized enterprises (SEMs) is using innovative intelligence so that the highest outcome may arise from the investment(Qu et al., 2021).

Following the above-mentioned literature reviews, one hypothesis was prepared concerning the importance of artificial intelligence for small medium business performance in Bangladesh.

H3: Effective business management has positive effects on business performance

H4: Effective business management mediates the relation between artificial intelligence and business performance

Research Model

Based on the theoretical and literature explanations, the authors developed the following conceptual framework.

Figure 1. Mediation of effective business management

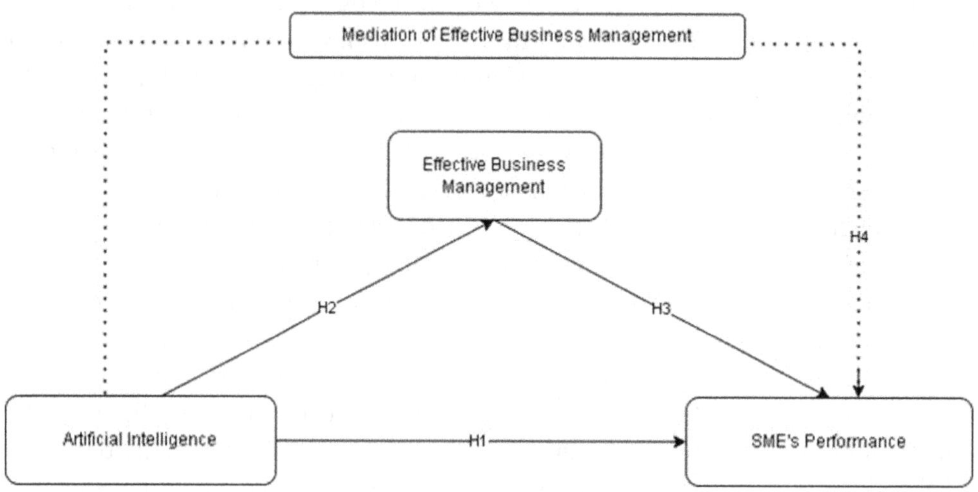

Figure 1 represents conceptual framework, where artificial intelligence is explanatory variables, and business performance is dependent variable. Effective business management plays the role of both a mediator and explanatory variable.

RESEARCH METHOD

We selected 13 small and medium enterprises that are located in the Dhaka division. All the employees, who responded to the questionnaire, were regular and used technological equipment and many advanced software provided by their respected organizations. Admittedly, all the organizations adopted the artificial intelligence and encouraged their employees to use technology with an eye to getting effective business paeformance.

Data were collected based on a simple random sampling procedure. We selected 600 employees as samples for this study. All the respondents independently participated in the survey with their consent and without any compulsion and collusion. They had the right to answer or refuge any question as part of their will.

We prepared a questionnaire following multiple studies before collecting data. The survey instrument is represented in Table 1. Afterward, potential changes were made to the questionnaire, and finally, a structured questionnaire was provided to responded workers by taking interviews. The duration of each interview varied from 10-15 minutes. The structured questionnaire obtained workers' opinions that were measured based on a 5-point Likert scale, where point-5 indicates 'strongly agree', point-4 indicates 'agree', point-3 indicates 'neutral', point-2 indicates 'disagree' and point-1 indicates 'strongly disagree' with each of the statements. Therefore, the research was carried out with an explanatory research design and quantitative methodology to assess the effects of artificial intelligence on SME's performance. Participants' demographic profile is highlighted in Table 2 elaborately.

COMMON METHOD PROPENSITY

We confirmed that there was no evidence of common method bias before going to the next calculation process. Before and after data collection, we proved that common method propensity would not be a concern for our study. The data, we collected, had no sign of manipulation and corruption. All the respondents could answer the questions in a free and fair environment and without any violence or conflict. We completed our survey without providing the answer to a single question. Using Harman's single-factor test (Podsakoff et al., 2003), we identified that a single multiplier showed only 40.1% of the variance which is lower than 50%.

Table 1 illustrates various sources, from which potential questions for the questionnaire were collected and subjected to standard modification to prepare a structured questionnaire. SMEP is a dependent variable, whereas EBM and AI are explanatory variables. EVM acts as an explanatory variable and also a mediator.

Table 2 represents the demographic identity of the participants. Based on the above five mentioned factors: gender, department, designation, experience, and age, a discrepancy is observed in the demographic characteristics of participants. All the respondents use AI for performing their works.

Table 1. Survey instrument

Questions	Source
Artificial Intelligence (AI) AI system boosts the work process (AI1) You are provided with an AI-integrated system (AI2) AI system helps me complete my work efficiently (AI3) AI leads to business effectiveness (AI4)	Feuerriegel et al., 2022; Mou, 2019; Olan et al., 2022; Daníelsson et al., 2022
Effective Business Management (EBM) The management continues to promote its managerial performance (EBM1) The management can establish excellent business strategies and potential policies (EBM2) The management always encourages you to adopt AI-based technology (EBM3) Management underpins innovative practices for achieving business goals (EBM4)	Broekhuizen et al., 2023; Eckert et al., 2022; Pillarisetty & Mishra, 2022
Small Medium Enterprise Performance (SMEP) Your organization is achieving business goals (SMEP1) Your organization can improve the quality of new products and services (SMEP2) Your organization improves production flexibility by using AI (SMEP3) Your organization is getting both financial and non-financial benefits by using AI (SMEP4)	Saheb, 2023; Daníelsson et al., 2022; Ullah et al., 2022

Table 2. Demographic profile of participants

	Frequency (n)	Percent (%)
Gender		
Male	324	54
Female	276	46
Department		
Marketing	170	28.4
Production	90	15.0
Sales	67	11.1
Inspection	69	11.5
Security Surveillance	81	13.4
Completion	45	7.5
Multiplication	34	5.7
Administration	44	7.4
Designation		
Junior Executive	33	5.5
Corporate Relation Officer	43	7.1

Table 2. Continued

	Frequency (n)	Percent (%)
Executive Officer	76	12.7
Assistant manager	35	5.8
Senior Executive	38	6.4
Deputy General Manager	91	15.1
Supervisors	140	23.4
Operating officers	144	24.0
Experience(years)		
Less than 3	191	31.8
3 to 7	256	42.7
7 to 10	99	16.5
Above 10	54	9.0
Age(years)		
20-25	294	49
25-38	221	36.9
Above 38	85	14.1

CONFIRMATORY FACTOR ANALYSIS (CFA)

Four factors are deemed to be suitable for confirmatory factor analysis (Awang et all., 2016). These four factors are: - model fit indices, composite reliability, convergent validity, and discriminant validity. The study disclosed an excellent model fit because the value of Chi-square/degree of freedom was 0.43, the Goodness of Fit (GFI) was 0.97, Relative Fit Index (RFI) was 0.93, Incremental Fit Index (IFI) was

0.96, Comparative Fit Index (CFI) was 0.97, Tucker–Lewis's Index (TLI) was 0.95, Root Mean Square Error of Approximation (RMSEA) was 0.069 and Standardized Root Mean Square Residual (SRMR) was 0.038. For reliability measurement, composite Reliability (CR) must be obtained, where the values of each multi-item surpass the threshold value of 0.7, providing strong support for a higher internal consistency among variables (Sarstedt et al., 2019). Admittedly, composite reliability was confirmed, as a high internal consistency was obtained by capturing the threshold values (0.70) of each multi-item. Additionally, convergent validity indicates a certain extent to which each variable discloses its variance following the recommended value of Average Variance Extracted, which is 0.5 or above (Sarstedt et al., 2019). Undoubtedly, the standardized effects of each construct and Average Variance Extracted (AVE), which was based on each construct loading exceeded the threshold value of 0.50 by supporting convergent validity. Moreover, the Fornell-Larcker criterion and Hetrotrait-Monotrait Ratio (HTMT) were used in the study to evaluate the discriminant validity of each construct. In Table 3, composite reliability and convergent validity are highlighted while Table 4 indicates discriminant validity, which was found to be appropriate.

Table 3. Composite reliability and convergent validity

	Items	Mean	SD	Loadings	CA	CR	AVE	VIF
AI	AI1	3.3912	1.33824	0.81				
	AI2	3.6883	1.13726	0.79	0.84	0.90	0.69	1.12
	AI3	3.7317	1.16702	0.83				
	AI4	3.5251	1.00219	0.90				
EBM	EBM1	3.4633	1.32473	0.80				
	EBM2	3.5552	1.39051	0.84	0.80	0.89	0.68	1.29
	EBM3	3.4917	1.42477	0.87				
	EBM4	3.3053	1.38027	0.84				
SEMP	SEMP1	3.6267	1.40258	0.78				
	SEMP2	3.3651	1.11976	0.79				
	SEMP3	3.2633	1.20958	0.76	0.78	0.84	0.57	1.11
	SEMP4	3.0052	1.35204	0.71				

Composite reliability and Convergent validity are illustrated in Table 3. The values of each construct loadings (standardized effects) and Average Variance Extracted (AVE), which endorse Convergent validity, are more than 0.50. When it comes to Composite Reliability (CR), a high internal consistency exists among all the items, because the values of each multi-item are more than 0.70. Cronbach Alpha (CA), which was developed by Cronbach in 1951, is mainly used for evaluating the internal consistency and reliability of the scale for each variable (Bonett & Wright, 2015). Concerning Table 3, the Cronbach alpha (α) of each construct exceeds the threshold value of 0.7, referring to higher consistency in variable measurement and reliability of all the variables. There is no existence of a multicollinearity issue when the values of the Variance Inflation Factor (VIF) are lower than 10 and the tolerance level exceeds the value of 0.10 (Henseler et al., 2015). In Table 3, the variance inflation factor ranges from 1.1 to 1.3, indicating no sign of a multicollinearity problem.

Table 4. Discriminant validity

	EBM	AI	SMEP
Fornell-Larcker criterion			
EBM	**0.83**		
AI	0.43	**0.82**	
SMEP	0.45	0.63	**0.75**
Heterotrait-Monotrait ratio (HTMT)			
EBM	NA		
AI	0.78	NA	
SMEP	0.51	0.69	NA

Table 4 indicates discriminant validity that is based on the Fornel-Larcker criterion and the Heterotrait-Monotrait ratio. It is observed that the square root of AVEs (bold values on the sidelong) of all individual variables is more than their internal correlations, providing the support of appropriate discriminant validity. According to the HTMT ratio, the range of the ratio must be smaller than 0.9 confirming discriminant validity. As shown in Table 4, the HTMT ratio for all the comparisons of constructs is below 0.9 (ranging from 0.52 to 0.86), proving that the measurement model captures satisfactory discriminant validity.

Figure 2. Structural equation model

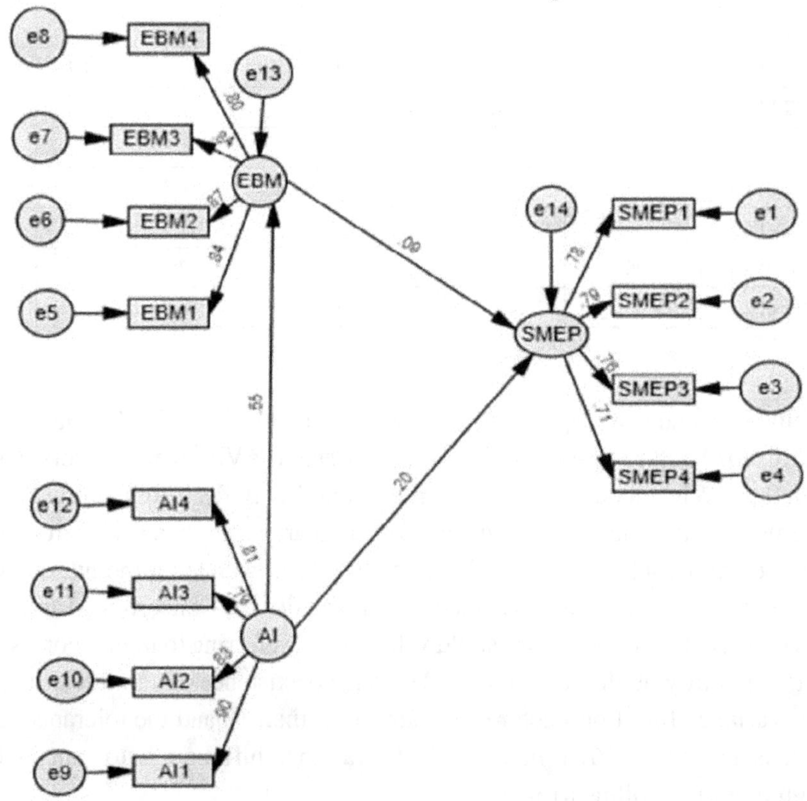

The structural equation model, which is shown in Figure 2, highlights the standardized estimates of all the items of every variable. It is observed that the loadings of each construct are satisfactory and statistically appropriate for consolidating an internal consistency among all the items. In addition, model fit items revealed an excellent model fit, since the value of Chi-square/degree of freedom was 0.43, the Goodness of Fit (GFI) was 0.97, Relative Fit Index (RFI) was 0.93, Incremental Fit Index (IFI) was 0.96, Comparative Fit Index (CFI) was 0.97, Tucker–Lewis's Index (TLI) was 0.95, Root Mean Square Error of Approximation (RMSEA) was 0.069 and Standardized Root Mean Square Residual (SRMR) was 0.038.

After we proved the authenticity and reliability of the confirmatory factor analysis and structural model, we proceeded to the next step of testing hypotheses. **Table 5** discloses the coefficient results of the first three hypotheses (H1, H2, H3) testing.

Table 5. Coefficient results

Hypothesis	Relationship	β	S.E.	C.R.	P	Decision
H1	SMEP-AI	0.291	0.041	3.363	0.00	Accept
H2	EBM-AI	0.091	0.066	10.587	0.00	Accept
H3	SMEP-EBM	0.578	0.026	17.562	0.00	Accept

Table 5 illustrates coefficient results, where the p-value of H1, H2 and H3 is lower than 0.05, indicating that all these hypotheses are statistically significant and accepted. The coefficient between SMEP and AI (β=.291; p=.000) indicates a positive and significant effect of AI on SMEP, thus supporting H1. Since the path coefficient between EBM and AI (β=.091; p=.000) shows a statistically positive effect of AI on EBM, H2 is supported. The coefficient value for SMEP and EBM (β=.578; p=.000) highlights a positive effect of EBM on SMEP, thus providing support to H3.

Mediation

Two types of mediation are observed: partial mediation and complete or full mediation (Kenny, 2008). Partial mediation occurs, when the p values for mediated and direct effects of an explanatory variable on the response variable are statistically significant, whereas complete mediation takes place when the explanatory variable can't directly influence the dependent or response variable (Hayes, 2009). Therefore, indirect or mediated effects, which constitute a relationship between constructs, hint at partial or incomplete mediation at the same time when a direct effect is observed between these two particular constructs (Nitzl et al., 2016). However, in the study, effective business management was identified as a partial mediator. Table 6 highlights mediation analysis where the results of the last two hypotheses (H4) is revealed.

Table 6. Mediation analysis

Associations	D-effect	I-effect	CI-Min		CI-Max	P value
AI -EBM-SMEP	0.291 (P =0.000)	0.065	0.024		0.117	0.002

Table 6 reveals partial mediation of EBM in the association between AI and SMEP. P values are statistically significant in the case of both direct and indirect effects of AI on SMEP. The direct effect of AI on SMEP with a statistically significant p-value ($0.00 < 0.05$) is 0.291 and the indirect effect through the mediation of EBM with a p-value ($0.002 < 0.05$) is 0.065. In addition, there is no zero between lower-bound (CI-Min) and upper-bound (CI-Max) confidence intervals, providing support to H4 by signaling partial mediation of EBM between AI and SMEP.

DISCUSSION OF FINDINGS

Following the results of regression analysis, the study finalized the statistically significant effects of artificial intelligence on small-medium enterprises' performance by accepting the proposed hypotheses. The hypotheses were accepted depending on the statistically accepted range of p-values. Effective business management was found to be a mediator between business performance and artificial intelligence. The study was found to be authentic based on the confirmatory factor analysis which is reliant on model fit indices, composite reliability, convergent validity, and discriminant validity. The model of the study had an excellent model fit, as the value of Chi-square/degree of freedom was 0.43, the Goodness of Fit (GFI) was 0.97, Relative Fit Index (RFI) was 0.93, Incremental Fit Index (IFI) was 0.96, Comparative Fit Index (CFI) was 0.97, Tucker–Lewis's Index (TLI) was 0.95, Root Mean Square Error of Approximation (RMSEA) was 0.069 and Standardized Root Mean Square Residual (SRMR) was 0.038. The values of each variable loadings (standardized effects) and Average Variance Extracted (AVE) were found to be supporting convergent validity, whereas, in terms of Composite Reliability (CR), a high internal consistency existed among all the items (the values of each multi-item are more than 0.70). Discriminant validity, which adopted the Fornel-Larcker criterion and Heterotrait-Monotrait ratio (HTMT) was found to be accurate. The accuracy of the structural equation model was also confirmed with the values of Chi-square/degree of freedom (0.43) and Goodness of Fit (0.97).

Based on the explanatory results, the study witnessed authoritative evidence to support the significant effects of artificial intelligence (H1) on business performance, artificial intelligence on effective business management (H2), effective business management on business performance (H3) and the mediation role of effective business management between artificial intelligence and business performance (H4).

Kumar et al., 2022 detected that artificial intelligence based on technological advancement leads to business innovation, which in turn confirm business performance. Therefore, it is mandatory to arrange business organizations with artificial intelligence. Wang et al., 2022 found that for having effective business management indicates perfect management which adheres to technological application with an aim to achieving business performance. Moreover, risk managers and financial authorities can comprehend potential problems by adopting artificial intelligence. As a result, business efficiency is attained (Daníelsson et al., 2022). Liu & Ma, 2022 identified that it is difficult to accurately predict the future price, but artificial intelligence helps business organizations predict future goals including market price effectively. Yang et al., 2022 found that artificial intelligence improves customer communications quickly in this dynamic world, resulting in profit goals and productivity.

Sharifi et al., 2021 investigated that during the post-COVID-19 pandemic, achieving potential business outcomes has been an ordeal. Therefore, business firms need to adhere to running their business with the help of technological intelligence. Vaishya et al., 2020 explored that artificial intelligence is used for proper screening, analyzing, prediction and tracking critical activities with an aim to reducing the workload, where effective business management plays a role of a mediator. In addition, it-based technology can predict the activities that are likely to take place in the future, but without artificial intelligence it is quite impossible and increases the work pressure (Eldrandaly et al., 2019). Buettner, 2013 detected that in future, human beings will totally rely upon the significant use of artificial intelligence so that workload can be reduced to zero percent. Rožman et al., 2022 proved that business performance and effectiveness take place when employees are provided with artificial intelligence which confirms team skills, endorses organizational culture, and leadership, and reduces the workload.

Research Implications

The study represented the significant theoretical and practical implications for artificial intelligence to boost the performance of small-medium business organizations.

Theoretically, the study supported the significant effects of artificial intelligence on effective business management and performance. The Technology–organization–environment (TOE) framework is alluding to the use of artificial intelligence for confirming business efficiency. The three important points of this theory are organizational context, technological context, and environmental concern. Organizational context is relevant to economic support provided by the management for using technological intelligence, whereas technological context insists on the advantages of using technology. Accountably, artificial intelligence helps manage an enormous amount of time while leading to effective and fast performance. Environmental concern hints at the initiatives that are environment-friendly. The significant point of the Technology–organization–environment (TOE) framework is to incorporate the business environment into the mainstream of artificial intelligence along with paying attention to the environment. Therefore, in line with theoretical implications, SMEs' policymakers, human resource managers, and concerned authorities may use artificial intelligence and green innovative practices to improve organizational performance.

From the practical look, in Bangladesh, most of the business organizations cannot harness the power of artificial intelligence for having effective outcome. It can be due to the risk of unemployment problem, financial privation or sufficient knowledge that is required to use artificial intelligence. In today's dynamic business world, the importance of technology is properly understood by business giants. As a result, they provide technology-based software and machineries to employees for attaining higher outcomes. They also provide skill development training to employees so that they can gain knowledge regarding the proper use of artificial intelligence. It is expected that SMEs' policymakers, human resource managers, and concerned authorities may understand the importance of artificial intelligence by following our results. For having so, they at first adopt fruitful policies to mitigate all the potential risks and provide employees with skill development training.

LIMITATIONS AND FURTHER SCOPE FOR RESEARCH

The study experienced some limitations. First of all, it is limited to small and medium organizations in Bangladesh. So, it is recommended for further research to explore the effects of artificial intelligence and g on the performance of small, medium, and large business organizations in other countries as well with a larger sample size. Secondly, the study focused on artificial intelligence to evaluate SMEs' performance, but there may be other factors and strategies to improve SMEs' performance. Therefore, it is recommended for future research to experiment with the performance and effective management of small and medium enterprises with those unexplored factors and strategies.

CONCLUSION

The study aimed to evaluate the performance of small-medium enterprises. Admittedly, the study analyzed the significant and positive effects of artificial intelligence practices and effective management on the performance of small-medium enterprises in Bangladesh. The study with rigor and experimental analysis recommends that the managers and owners of small-medium enterprises in Bangladesh must provide workers with technology-based software and equipment for getting their desired outcome. Needless to say, the employees of small-medium enterprises in Bangladesh don't have sufficient knowledge as to how to use artificial intelligence for accomplishing their work within a short period of time and efficiently. So, it is needed to provide skill-development programs to employees in order to that they can use technology properly. In addition, they are deprived of an effective management, which is supposed to facilitate employees by giving much-needed amenities including artificial intelligence. Besides, the common problems that continue to create restriction to the use of artificial intelligence must need to be addressed. First of all, the risk of unemployment problem will be removed while using technology. Additionally, sufficient financial support needs to be dispensed for the use of artificial intelligence. To take an edge over other business organizations and continue to capture the higher outcomes, artificial intelligence is used rapidly by successful business organizations worldwide. Therefore, with advance of modernization, it is responsibility of the SME's authorities to conduct the use of artificial intelligence for confirming both financial and non-financial benefits, business efficiency and stable business growth. Last but not least an efficient management is prerequisite to adopt fruitful policies, thus improving organizational performance.

CONFLICT OF INTEREST

The authors strongly declare that no sign of conflict of interest was detected.

REFERENCES

Aboulilah, H. M. A. E., Hossain, S. F. A., Vuong, B. N., & Jebril, T. (2022). Exploring the Relationship between WeChat Usage and E-purchase Intention During the COVID-19 Pandemic Among University Students in China. *SAGE Open*, *12*(4), 21582440221139447. doi:10.1177/21582440221139447 PMID:36466966

Asan, O., & Choudhury, A. (2021). Research Trends in Artificial Intelligence Applications in Human Factors Health Care: Mapping Review. *JMIR Human Factors*, *8*(2), e28236. doi:10.2196/28236 PMID:34142968

Bonett, D. G., & Wright, T. A. (2015). Cronbach's alpha reliability: Interval estimation, hypothesis testing, and sample size planning. *Journal of Organizational Behavior*, *36*(1), 3–15. doi:10.1002/job.1960

Bouchard, M. J., & Rousselière, D. (2016). Do Hybrid Organizational Forms of the Social Economy have a Greater Chance of Surviving? An Examination of the Case of Montreal. *Voluntas*, *27*(4), 1894–1922. doi:10.1007/s11266-015-9664-1

Broekhuizen, T., Dekker, H., De Faria, P., Firk, S., Nguyen, D. K., & Sofka, W. (2023). AI for managing open innovation: Opportunities, challenges, and a research agenda. *Journal of Business Research*, *167*, 114196. doi:10.1016/j.jbusres.2023.114196

Buettner, R. (2013). Cognitive Workload of Humans Using Artificial Intelligence Systems: Towards Objective Measurement Applying Eye-Tracking Technology. In I. J. Timm & M. Thimm (Eds.), *KI 2013: Advances in Artificial Intelligence* (Vol. 8077, pp. 37–48). Springer Berlin Heidelberg. doi:10.1007/978-3-642-40942-4_4

Chamola, V., Hassija, V., Gupta, V., & Guizani, M. (2020). A Comprehensive Review of the COVID-19 Pandemic and the Role of IoT, Drones, AI, Blockchain, and 5G in Managing its Impact. *IEEE Access : Practical Innovations, Open Solutions*, *8*, 90225–90265. doi:10.1109/ACCESS.2020.2992341

Chen, Z. (2023). Collaboration among recruiters and artificial intelligence: Removing human prejudices in employment. *Cognition Technology and Work*, *25*(1), 135–149. doi:10.1007/s10111-022-00716-0 PMID:36187287

Chowdhury, S., Dey, P., Joel-Edgar, S., Bhattacharya, S., Rodriguez-Espindola, O., Abadie, A., & Truong, L. (2023). Unlocking the value of artificial intelligence in human resource management through AI capability framework. *Human Resource Management Review*, *33*(1), 100899. doi:10.1016/j.hrmr.2022.100899

Daníelsson, J., Macrae, R., & Uthemann, A. (2022). Artificial intelligence and systemic risk. *Journal of Banking & Finance*, *140*, 106290. doi:10.1016/j.jbankfin.2021.106290

Dogru, A. K., & Keskin, B. B. (2020). AI in operations management: Applications, challenges and opportunities. *Journal of Data. Information & Management*, *2*(2), 67–74. doi:10.1007/s42488-020-00023-1

Duchessi, P., O'Keefe, R., & O'Leary, D. (1993). A Research Perspective: Artificial Intelligence, Management and Organizations. *International Journal of Intelligent Systems in Accounting Finance & Management*, *2*(3), 151–159. doi:10.1002/j.1099-1174.1993.tb00039.x

Dwivedi, Y. K., Hughes, L., Ismagilova, E., Aarts, G., Coombs, C., Crick, T., Duan, Y., Dwivedi, R., Edwards, J., Eirug, A., Galanos, V., Ilavarasan, P. V., Janssen, M., Jones, P., Kar, A. K., Kizgin, H., Kronemann, B., Lal, B., Lucini, B., & Williams, M. D. (2021). Artificial Intelligence (AI): Multidisciplinary perspectives on emerging challenges, opportunities, and agenda for research, practice and policy. *International Journal of Information Management*, *57*, 101994. doi:10.1016/j.ijinfomgt.2019.08.002

Eckert, C., Neunsinger, C., & Osterrieder, K. (2022). Managing customer satisfaction: Digital applications for insurance companies. *The Geneva Papers on Risk and Insurance. Issues and Practice*, *47*(3), 569–602. doi:10.1057/s41288-021-00257-z

Eldrandaly, K. A., Abdel-Basset, M., & Abdel-Fatah, L. (2019). PTZ-Surveillance coverage based on artificial intelligence for smart cities. *International Journal of Information Management*, *49*, 520–532. doi:10.1016/j.ijinfomgt.2019.04.017

Emmanuel, C. P., Qin, S., Hossain, S. F. A., & Hussain, K. (2022). Factors influencing social-media-based entrepreneurship prospect among female students in China. *Heliyon*, *8*(12), e12041. doi:10.1016/j.heliyon.2022.e12041 PMID:36483305

Enholm, I. M., Papagiannidis, E., Mikalef, P., & Krogstie, J. (2022). Artificial Intelligence and Business Value: A Literature Review. *Information Systems Frontiers*, *24*(5), 1709–1734. doi:10.1007/s10796-021-10186-w

Feuerriegel, S., Shrestha, Y. R., Von Krogh, G., & Zhang, C. (2022). Bringing artificial intelligence to business management. *Nature Machine Intelligence*, *4*(7), 611–613. doi:10.1038/s42256-022-00512-5

Haldma, T., & Lääts, K. (2002). Contingencies influencing the management accounting practices of Estonian manufacturing companies. *Management Accounting Research*, *13*(4), 379–400. doi:10.1006/mare.2002.0197

Hayes, A. F. (2009). Beyond Baron and Kenny: Statistical mediation analysis in the new millennium. *Communication Monographs*, *76*(4), 408–420. doi:10.1080/03637750903310360

Helo, P., & Hao, Y. (2022). Artificial intelligence in operations management and supply chain management: An exploratory case study. *Production Planning and Control*, *33*(16), 1573–1590. doi:10.1080/09537287.2021.1882690

Henseler, J., Ringle, C. M., & Sarstedt, M. (2015). A new criterion for assessing discriminant validity in variance-based structural equation modeling. *Journal of the Academy of Marketing Science*, *43*(1), 115–135. doi:10.1007/s11747-014-0403-8

Hillman, A. J., Withers, M. C., & Collins, B. J. (2009). Resource Dependence Theory: A Review. *Journal of Management*, *35*(6), 1404–1427. doi:10.1177/0149206309343469

Hossain, S. F. A. (2019). Social networking and its role in media entrepreneurship: Evaluating the use of mobile phones in the context of online shopping–A review. [JMME]. *Journal of Media Management and Entrepreneurship*, *1*(1), 73–86. doi:10.4018/JMME.2019010105

Hossain, S. F. A., Nurunnabi, M., Hussain, K., & Shan, X. (2020). Smartphone-based m-shopping behavior and innovative entrepreneurial tendency among women in emerging Asia. *International Journal of Gender and Entrepreneurship*, *12*(2), 173–189. doi:10.1108/IJGE-03-2019-0054

Hossain, S. F. A., Xi, Z., Nurunnabi, M., & Hussain, K. (2020). Ubiquitous Role of Social Networking in Driving M-Commerce: Evaluating the Use of Mobile Phones for Online Shopping and Payment in the Context of Trust. *SAGE Open*, *10*(3). doi:10.1177/2158244020939536

Jabbar, M. A., Tiwari, S., & Ortiz-Rodriguez, F. (2022). *Smart Urban Computing Applications* (1st ed.). River Publishers. doi:10.1201/9781003373247

Kar, A. K., & Kushwaha, A. K. (2023). Facilitators and Barriers of Artificial Intelligence Adoption in Business – Insights from Opinions Using Big Data Analytics. *Information Systems Frontiers*, *25*(4), 1351–1374. doi:10.1007/s10796-021-10219-4

Kenny, D. A. (2008). Reflections on Mediation. *Organizational Research Methods*, *11*(2), 353–358. doi:10.1177/1094428107308978

Kim, B. H., Koh, S., Huh, S., Jo, S., & Choi, S. (2020). Improved Explanatory Efficacy on Human Affect and Workload Through Interactive Process in Artificial Intelligence. *IEEE Access : Practical Innovations, Open Solutions*, *8*, 189013–189024. doi:10.1109/ACCESS.2020.3032056

Kuar, S., Lim, W. M., Sivarajah, U., & Kaur, J. (2022). Artificial Intelligence and Blockchain Integration in Business: Trends from a Bibliometric-Content Analysis. *Information Systems Frontiers*. doi:10.1007/s10796-022-10279-0 PMID:35431617

Liu, G., & Ma, W. (2022). A quantum artificial neural network for stock closing price prediction. *Information Sciences*, *598*, 75–85. doi:10.1016/j.ins.2022.03.064

Loureiro, S. M. C., Guerreiro, J., & Tussyadiah, I. (2021). Artificial intelligence in business: State of the art and future research agenda. *Journal of Business Research*, *129*, 911–926. doi:10.1016/j.jbusres.2020.11.001

Mehta, P., Jebarajakirthy, C., Maseeh, H. I., Anubha, A., Saha, R., & Dhanda, K. (2022). Artificial intelligence in marketing: A meta-analytic review. *Psychology and Marketing*, *39*(11), 2013–2038. doi:10.1002/mar.21716

Mohsin, A., Hongzhen, L., & Hossain, S. F. A. (2021). Impact of COVID-19 Pandemic on Consumer Economy: Countermeasures Analysis. *SAGE Open*, *11*(2). doi:10.1177/21582440211008875

Mou, X. (2019). Artificial intelligence: Investment trends and selected industry uses. International Finance Corporation, 8.

Nitzl, C., Roldan, J. L., & Cepeda, G. (2016). Mediation analysis in partial least squares path modeling: Helping researchers discuss more sophisticated models. *Industrial Management & Data Systems*, *116*(9), 1849–1864. doi:10.1108/IMDS-07-2015-0302

Olan, F., Ogiemwonyi Arakpogun, E., Suklan, J., Nakpodia, F., Damij, N., & Jayawickrama, U. (2022). Artificial intelligence and knowledge sharing: Contributing factors to organizational performance. performance. *Journal of Business Research*, *145*, 605–615. doi:10.1016/j.jbusres.2022.03.008

Pallathadka, H., Ramirez-Asis, E. H., Loli-Poma, T. P., Kaliyaperumal, K., Ventayen, R. J. M., & Naved, M. (2023). Applications of artificial intelligence in business management, e-commerce and finance. *Materials Today: Proceedings*, *80*, 2610–2613. doi:10.1016/j.matpr.2021.06.419

Pantano, E., & Serravalle, F. (2022). *The Role of Smart Technologies in Decision Making: Developing, Supporting and Training Smart Consumers* (1st ed.). Routledge. doi:10.4324/9781003307105

Paul, D., Sanap, G., Shenoy, S., Kalyane, D., Kalia, K., & Tekade, R. K. (2021). Artificial intelligence in drug discovery and development. *Drug Discovery Today*, *26*(1), 80–93. doi:10.1016/j.drudis.2020.10.010 PMID:33099022

Pillaisetty, R., & Mishra, P. (2022). A Review of AI (Artificial Intelligence) Tools and Customer Experience in Online Fashion Retail. *International Journal of E-Business Research*, *18*(2), 1–12. doi:10.4018/IJEBR.294111

Qu, S., Shi, H., Zhao, H., Yu, L., & Yu, Y. (2021). Research on enterprise business model and technology innovation based on artificial intelligence. *EURASIP Journal on Wireless Communications and Networking*, *2021*(1), 145. doi:10.1186/s13638-021-02025-y PMID:34249123

Ramachandran, K. K., Apsara Saleth Mary, A., Hawladar, S., Asokk, D., Bhaskar, B., & Pitroda, J. R. (2022). Machine learning and role of artificial intelligence in optimizing work performance and employee behavior. *Materials Today: Proceedings*, *51*, 2327–2331. doi:10.1016/j.matpr.2021.11.544

Rodriguez-Ruiz, A., Lång, K., Gubern-Merida, A., Teuwen, J., Broeders, M., Gennaro, G., Clauser, P., Helbich, T. H., Chevalier, M., Mertelmeier, T., Wallis, M. G., Andersson, I., Zackrisson, S., Sechopoulos, I., & Mann, R. M. (2019). Can we reduce the workload of mammographic screening by automatic identification of normal exams with artificial intelligence? A feasibility studies. *European Radiology*, *29*(9), 4825–4832. doi:10.1007/s00330-019-06186-9 PMID:30993432

Rožman, M., Oreški, D., & Tominc, P. (2022). Integrating artificial intelligence into a talent management model to increase the work engagement and performance of enterprises. *Frontiers in Psychology*, *13*, 1014434. doi:10.3389/fpsyg.2022.1014434 PMID:36506984

Rožman, M., Oreški, D., & Tominc, P. (2023). Artificial-Intelligence-Supported Reduction of Employees' Workload to Increase the Company's Performance in Today's VUCA Environment. *Sustainability (Basel)*, *15*(6), 5019. doi:10.3390/su15065019

Ruan, Y., & Mezei, J. (2022). When do AI chatbots lead to higher customer satisfaction than human frontline employees in online shopping assistance? Considering product attribute type. *Journal of Retailing and Consumer Services*, *68*, 103059. doi:10.1016/j.jretconser.2022.103059

Saheb, T. (2023). Ethically contentious aspects of artificial intelligence surveillance: A social science perspective. *AI and Ethics*, *3*(2), 369–379. doi:10.1007/s43681-022-00196-y PMID:35874304

Sandeep, S. R., Ahamad, S., Saxena, D., Srivastava, K., Jaiswal, S., & Bora, A. (2022). To understand the relationship between Machine learning and Artificial intelligence in large and diversified business organisations. *Materials Today: Proceedings*, *56*, 2082–2086. doi:10.1016/j.matpr.2021.11.409

Sarstedt, M., Hair, J. F. Jr, Cheah, J.-H., Becker, J.-M., & Ringle, C. M. (2019). How to Specify, Estimate, and Validate Higher-Order Constructs in PLS-SEM. *Australasian Marketing Journal*, *27*(3), 197–211. doi:10.1016/j.ausmj.2019.05.003

Sharifi, A., Ahmadi, M., & Ala, A. (2021). The impact of artificial intelligence and digital style on industry and energy post-COVID-19 pandemic. *Environmental Science and Pollution Research International*, *28*(34), 46964–46984. doi:10.1007/s11356-021-15292-5 PMID:34269979

Shneiderman, B. (2020). Human-Centered Artificial Intelligence: Reliable, Safe & Trustworthy. *International Journal of Human-Computer Interaction*, *36*(6), 495–504. doi:10.1080/10447318.2020.1741118

Thakur, N., Nagrath, P., Jain, R., Saini, D., Sharma, N., & Hemanth, D. J. (2021). Artificial Intelligence Techniques in Smart Cities Surveillance Using UAVs: A Survey. In U. Ghosh, Y. Maleh, M. Alazab, & A.-S. K. Pathan (Eds.), *Machine Intelligence and Data Analytics for Sustainable Future Smart Cities* (Vol. 971, pp. 329–353). Springer International Publishing. doi:10.1007/978-3-030-72065-0_18

Trolice, M. P., Curchoe, C., & Quaas, A. M. (2021). Artificial intelligence—The future is now. *Journal of Assisted Reproduction and Genetics*, *38*(7), 1607–1612. doi:10.1007/s10815-021-02272-4 PMID:34231110

Ullah, W., Ullah, A., Hussain, T., Muhammad, K., Heidari, A. A., Del Ser, J., Baik, S. W., & De Albuquerque, V. H. C. (2022). Artificial Intelligence of Things-assisted two-stream neural network for anomaly detection in surveillance Big Video Data. *Future Generation Computer Systems*, *129*, 286–297. doi:10.1016/j.future.2021.10.033

Vaishya, R., Javaid, M., Khan, I. H., & Haleem, A. (2020). Artificial Intelligence (AI) applications for COVID-19 pandemic. *Diabetes & Metabolic Syndrome*, *14*(4), 337–339. doi:10.1016/j.dsx.2020.04.012 PMID:32305024

Vuong, B. N., Tushar, H., & Hossain, S. F. A. (2023). The effect of social support on job performance through organizational commitment and innovative work behavior: Does innovative climate matter? *Asia-Pacific Journal of Business Administration*, *15*(5), 832–854. doi:10.1108/APJBA-06-2021-0256

Wang, X., Lin, X., & Shao, B. (2022). How does artificial intelligence create business agility? Evidence from chatbots. *International Journal of Information Management*, *66*, 102535. doi:10.1016/j.ijinfomgt.2022.102535

Wang, Z., Li, M., Lu, J., & Cheng, X. (2022). Business Innovation based on artificial intelligence and Blockchain technology. *Information Processing & Management*, *59*(1), 102759. doi:10.1016/j.ipm.2021.102759

Wei, T., & Clegg, J. (2017). Exploring sources of value destruction in international acquisitions: A synthesized theoretical lens. *International Business Review*, *26*(5), 927–941. doi:10.1016/j.ibusrev.2017.03.002

Wejnert, B. (2002). Integrating models of diffusion of innovations: A conceptual framework. *Annual Review of Sociology*, *28*(1), 297–326. doi:10.1146/annurev.soc.28.110601.141051

Wijayati, D. T., Rahman, Z., Fahrullah, A., Rahman, M. F. W., Arifah, I. D. C., & Kautsar, A. (2022). A study of artificial intelligence on employee performance and work engagement: The moderating role of change leadership. *International Journal of Manpower*, *43*(2), 486–512. doi:10.1108/IJM-07-2021-0423

Yang, C., Feng, Y., & Whinston, A. (2022). Dynamic Pricing and Information Disclosure for Fresh Produce: An Artificial Intelligence Approach. *Production and Operations Management*, *31*(1), 155–171. doi:10.1111/poms.13525

Zak, Y., Parmet, Y., & Oron-Gilad, T. (2023). Facilitating the Work of Unmanned Aerial Vehicle Operators Using Artificial Intelligence: An Intelligent Filter for Command-and-Control Maps to Reduce Cognitive Workload. *Human Factors*, *65*(7), 1345–1360. doi:10.1177/00187208221081968 PMID:35392697

Zhao, R., Zhu, F., Tang, M., & He, L. (2023). Profit maximization in cache-aided intelligent computing networks. *Physical Communication*, *58*, 102065. doi:10.1016/j.phycom.2023.102065

Zhu, K. (2004). The Complementarity of Information Technology Infrastructure and E-Commerce Capability: A Resource-Based Assessment of Their Business Value. *Journal of Management Information Systems*, *21*(1), 167–202. doi:10.1080/07421222.2004.11045794

Compilation of References

Abeysinghe, D. U., & Malik, M. (2021). The Role of Digital Technology in Rural Entre- preneurship and Innovations. In S. Lokuge & D. Sedera (Eds.), *Rural Entrepreneurship and Innovation in the Digital Era* (pp. 20–38). IGI Global. doi:10.4018/978-1-7998-4942-1.ch002

Aboulilah, H. M. A. E., Hossain, S. F. A., Vuong, B. N., & Jebril, T. (2022). Exploring the Relationship between WeChat Usage and E-purchase Intention During the COVID-19 Pandemic Among University Students in China. *SAGE Open, 12*(4). doi:10.1177/21582440221139447

Abubakre, M., Zhou, Y., & Zhou, Z. (2020). The impact of information technology culture and personal innovativeness in information technology on digital entrepreneurship success. *Information (Basel).*

Accenture. (2022). *Responsible AI: Ai Ethics & Governance.* https://www.accenture.com/us-en/services/applied-intelligence/ai-ethics-governance

Aggarwal, M., Zubair, M., Unal, D., Al-Ali, A., Reimann, T., & Alinier, G. (2021). Fuzzy Identification-Based Encryption for healthcare user face authentication. Journal of Emergency Medicine. *Trauma & Acute Care*, *2022*(1), 72.

Aghion, P., Jones, B. F., & Jones, C. I. (2017). Artificial intelligence and economic growth (No. w23928). National Bureau of Economic Research. 3

Agostini, L., & Nosella, A. (2019). The adoption of Industry 4.0 technologies in SMEs: Results of an international study. *Management Decision*, *58*(4), 625–643. doi:10.1108/MD-09-2018-0973

Ahmad, A., Rasul, T., Yousaf, A., & Zaman, U. (2020). Understanding Factors Influencing Elderly Diabetic Patients' Continuance Intention to Use Digital Health Wearables: Extending the Technology Acceptance Model (TAM). *Journal of Open Innovation*, *6*(3), 81. doi:10.3390/joitmc6030081

Ahmad, T., Zhang, D., Huang, C., Zhang, H., Dai, N., Song, Y., & Chen, H. (2021). Artificial intelligence in sustainable energy industry: Status Quo, challenges and opportunities. *Journal of Cleaner Production*, *289*, 125834. doi:10.1016/j.jclepro.2021.125834

Ahmed, G., & Amiri, N. A.Nabeel Al Amiri. (2022). The transformational leadership of the founding leaders of the united arab emirates: Sheikh zayed bin sultan al nahyan and sheikh rashid bin saeed al maktoum. *International Journal of Technology* [IJTIM]. *Innovation and Management*, *2*(1). doi:10.54489/ijtim.v2i1.58

Akhtar, T., Tareq, M. A., & Rashid, K. (2020). Chief Executive Officers' monitoring, board effectiveness, managerial ownership, and cash holdings: Evidence from ASEAN. *Review of Managerial Science*. doi:10.1007/s11846-020-00421-0

Akter, S., Dwivedi, Y. K., Sajib, S., Biswas, K., Bandara, R. J., & Michael, K. (2022). Algorithmic bias in machine learning-based marketing models. *Journal of Business Research*, *144*, 201–216. doi:10.1016/j.jbusres.2022.01.083

Akter, S., Sultana, S., Mariani, M., Wamba, S. F., Spanaki, K., & Dwivedi, Y. K. (2023). Advancing algorithmic bias management capabilities in AI-driven marketing analytics research. *Industrial Marketing Management*, *114*, 243–261. doi:10.1016/j.indmarman.2023.08.013

Al Mamun, M. R., Senn, W. D., Peak, D. A., Prybutok, V. R., & Torres, R. A. (2020). Emotional Satisfaction and IS Continuance Behavior: Reshaping the Expectation-Confirmation Model. *International Journal of Human-Computer Interaction*, *36*(15), 1437–1446. doi:10.1080/10447318.2020.1752478

Alam, A., & Mohanty, A. (2022, November). Business models, business strategies, and innovations in EdTech companies: integration of learning analytics and artificial intelligence in higher education. In *2022 IEEE 6th Conference on Information and Communication Technology (CICT)* (pp. 1-6). IEEE. 10.1109/CICT56698.2022.9997887

Alamri, M. (2023). Transformational leadership and work engagement in public organizations: Promotion focus and public service motivation, how and when the effect occurs. *Leadership and Organization Development Journal*, *44*(1), 137–155. 137-155.doi.org/10.1108/LODJ-12-2021-0544. doi:10.1108/LODJ-12-2021-0544

Al-Emran, M., AlQudah, A. A., Abbasi, G. A., Al-Sharafi, M. A., & Iranmanesh, M. (2023). Determinants of using AI-based Chatbots for knowledge sharing: Evidence from PLS-SEM and fuzzy sets (fsQCA). *IEEE Transactions on Engineering Management*.

Alfes, K., Shantz, A. D., Truss, C., & Soane, E. C. (2013). The link between perceived human resource management practices, engagement and employee behaviour: A moderated mediation model. *International Journal of Human Resource Management*, *24*(2), 330–351. doi:10.1080/09585192.2012.679950

Ali, M. H., Hamdan, A., & Alareeni, B. (2021). The Implementation of Artificial Intelligence in Organizations' Systems: Opportunities and Challenges. Retrieved from https://link.springer.com/chapter/10.1007/978-3-030-69221-6_12

Alkaissi, H., & McFarlane, S. I. (2023). Artificial Hallucinations in ChatGPT: Implications in Scientific Writing. *Cureus*, *15*(2), e35179. doi:10.7759/cureus.35179 PMID:36811129

Allioui, H. ;, Mourdi, Y., Allioui, H., & Mourdi, Y. (2023). Exploring the Full Potentials of IoT for Better Financial Growth and Stability: A Comprehensive Survey. *Sensors 2023, 23*(19), 8015. doi:10.3390/s23198015

Al-Maroof, R. S., Alhumaid, K., Alhamad, A. Q., Aburayya, A., & Salloum, S. (2021). User Acceptance of Smart Watch for Medical Purposes: An Empirical Study. *Future Internet, 13*(5), 127. doi:10.3390/fi13050127

Almeida, R. K., & Galasso, E. (2010). Jump-starting self-employment? Evidence for welfare participants in Argentina. *World Development*, *38*(5), 742–755. doi:10.1016/j.worlddev.2009.11.018

Al-Sharafi, M. A., Arshah, R. A., Abu-Shanab, E. A., & Alajmi, Q. (2019). The effect of sustained use of cloud-based business services on organizations' performance: Evidence from SMEs in Malaysia. 2019 5th International Conference on Information Management (ICIM), 285-291. 10.1109/INFOMAN.2019.8714699

Al-Sharafi, M. A., Al-Emran, M., Iranmanesh, M., Al-Qaysi, N., Iahad, N. A., & Arpaci, I. (2022). Understanding the impact of knowledge management factors on the sustainable use of AI-based chatbots for educational purposes using a hybrid SEM-ANN approach. *Interactive Learning Environments*, 1–20.

AlZayani, F., Hamdan, A., & Shoaib, H. M. (2023). *The Impact of Smart Technologies on SME Sustainability: The Mediation Effect of Sustainability Strategy–Literature Review. Technological Sustainability and Business Competitive Advantage*. Springer. doi:10.1007/978-3-031-35525-7_27

AlZayani, F., Mohammed, A., & Shoaib, H. M. (2023). The impact of smart technologies on SMEs' sustainability: The mediation effect of sustainability strategy. *Competitiveness Review*. doi:10.1108/CR-09-2022-0136

Al-Zyoud, M. F. (2018). Social media marketing, functional branding strategy and intentional branding. *Problems and Perspectives in Management*, *16*(16, Iss. 3), 102–116. doi:10.21511/ppm.16(3).2018.09

Amaral, A., & Peças, P. (2021). SMEs and Industry 4.0: Two case studies of digitalization for a smoother integration. *Computers in Industry*, *125*, 103333. doi:10.1016/j.compind.2020.103333

Ambika, N. (2019). Energy-Perceptive Authentication in Virtual Private Networks Using GPS Data. In *Security, Privacy and Trust in the IoT Environment* (pp. 25–38). Springer, Cham. doi:10.1007/978-3-030-18075-1_2

Ambika, N. (2020). Encryption of Data in Cloud-Based Industrial IoT Devices. In S. Pal & V. G. Díaz (Eds.), *D.-N. Le, IoT: Security and Privacy Paradigm* (pp. 111–129). CRC press, Taylor & Francis Group.

Ameen, N., Cheah, J. H., & Kumar, S. (2022). It's all part of the customer journey: The impact of augmented reality, chatbots, and social media on the body image and self-esteem of Generation Z female consumers. *Psychology and Marketing*, *39*(11), 2110–2129. doi:10.1002/mar.21715

Ameen, N., Sharma, G. D., Tarba, S., Rao, A., & Chopra, R. (2022). Toward advancing theory on creativity in marketing and artificial intelligence. *Psychology and Marketing*, *39*(9), 1802–1825. doi:10.1002/mar.21699

Andeobu, L., Wibowo, S., & Grandhi, S. (2022). Artificial intelligence applications for sustainable solid waste management practices in Australia: A systematic review. *The Science of the Total Environment*, *834*, 155389. doi:10.1016/j.scitotenv.2022.155389 PMID:35460765

Andersson, P., & Wadensjö, E. (2007). Do the unemployed become successful entrepreneurs? *International Journal of Manpower*, *28*(7), 604–626. doi:10.1108/01437720710830070

Ansari, M. F., Dash, B., Sharma, P., & Yathiraju, N. (2022). The Impact and Limitations of Artificial Intelligence in Cybersecurity: A Literature Review. *International Journal of Advanced Research in Computer and Communication Engineering*, *11*(9). doi:10.17148/IJARCCE.2022.11912

Anshari, M., Almunawar, M. N., Lim, S. A., & Al-Mudimigh, A. (2019). Customer relationship management and big data enabled: Personalization & customization of services. *Applied Computing and Informatics*, *15*(2), 94–101. doi:10.1016/j.aci.2018.05.004

Appel, G., Grewal, L., Hadi, R., & Stephen, A. T. (2020). The future of social media in marketing. *Journal of the Academy of Marketing Science*, *48*(1), 79–95. doi:10.1007/s11747-019-00695-1 PMID:32431463

Ararat, M., Colpan, A. M., & Matten, D. (2018). Business groups and corporate responsibility for the public good. *Journal of Business Ethics*, *153*(4), 911–929. doi:10.1007/s10551-018-3920-4

Arslan, A., Cooper, C., Khan, Z., Golgeci, I., & Ali, I. (2022). Artificial intelligence and human workers interaction at team level: A conceptual assessment of the challenges and potential HRM strategies. *International Journal of Manpower*, *43*(1), 75–88. doi:10.1108/IJM-01-2021-0052

Asan, O., & Choudhury, A. (2021). Research Trends in Artificial Intelligence Applications in Human Factors Health Care: Mapping Review. *JMIR Human Factors*, *8*(2), e28236. doi:10.2196/28236 PMID:34142968

Ashfaq, M., Yun, J., Yu, S., & Loureiro, S. M. C. (2020). I, Chatbot: Modeling the determinants of users' satisfaction and continuance intention of AI-powered service agents. *Telematics and Informatics*, *54*, 101473. doi:10.1016/j.tele.2020.101473

Ashraf, M., Ahmad, J., Sharif, W., Raza, A. A., Salman Shabbir, M., Abbas, M., & Thurasamy, R. (2020). The role of continuous trust in usage of online product recommendations. *Online Information Review*, *44*(4), 745–766. doi:10.1108/OIR-05-2018-0156

Asikullah, F., Chakma, P., Hossain, S. F. A., & Hussain, K. (2024). Evaluating Employee Motivation and Productivity in Bangladesh During the Post-pandemic Era. *Management and Labour Studies*, 0258042X231220489.

Awotunde, J. B., Jimoh, R. G., Folorunso, S. O., Adeniyi, E. A., Abiodun, K. M., & Banjo, O. O. (2021). Privacy and Security Concerns in IoT-Based Healthcare Systems. *Internet of Things : Engineering Cyber Physical Human Systems*, 105–134. doi:10.1007/978-3-030-75220-0_6

Azman, N. A., Mohamed, A., & Jamil, A. M. (2021). Artificial Intelligence in Automated Bookkeeping: A Value-added Function for Small and Medium Enterprises. Retrieved from doi:10.30630/joiv.5.3.669

Baabdullah, A. M., Alalwan, A. A., Slade, E. L., Raman, R., & Khatatneh, K. F. (2021). SMEs and artificial intelligence (AI): Antecedents and consequences of AI-based B2B practices. Retrieved from doi:10.1016/j.indmarman.2021.09.003

Baccarella, C. V., Wagner, T. F., Kietzmann, J. H., & McCarthy, I. P. (2018). Social media? It's serious! Understanding the dark side of social media. *European Management Journal*, *36*(4), 431–438. doi:10.1016/j.emj.2018.07.002

Bada, M., & Nurse, J. R. (2019). Developing cybersecurity education and awareness programmes for small-and medium-sized enterprises (SMEs). *Information and Computer Security*, *27*(3), 393–410. doi:10.1108/ICS-07-2018-0080

Badhe, A., Kharadkar, S., Ware, R., Kamble, P., & Chavan, S. (2018). IOT Based Smart Agriculture And Soil Nutrient Detection System. *International Journal on Future Revolution in Computer Science & Communication Engineering*, *4*, 774–777.

Baggio, A. (2005). Wireless sensor networks in precision agriculture. *Workshop on Real-World Wireless Sensor Networks.* Stockholm, Sweden: ACM.

Bailey, D., Faraj, S., Hinds, P., Von Krogh, G., & Leonardi, P. (2019). Special issue of Organization Science: Emerging technologies and organizing. *Organization Science*, *30*(3), 642–646. doi:10.1287/orsc.2019.1299

Baranauskas, G., & Raišienė, A. G. (2022). Transition to digital entrepreneurship with a quest of sustainability: Development of a new conceptual framework. *Sustainability (Basel)*, *14*(3), 1104. doi:10.3390/su14031104

Barnes, J. (1982). The natural philosophy of Heraclitus. In J. Barnes (Ed.), *The Presocratic Philosophers* (pp. 43–62). Routledge Taylor & Francis Group.

Bartneck, C., Lütge, C., Wagner, A., & Welsh, S. (2021). Privacy Issues of AI. In An Introduction to Ethics in Robotics and AI. Springer. doi:10.1007/978-3-030-51110-4_8

Basri, W. (2020). Examining the impact of artificial intelligence (AI)-assisted social media marketing on the performance of small and medium enterprises: Toward effective business management in the Saudi Arabian context. *International Journal of Computational Intelligence Systems*, *13*(1), 142. doi:10.2991/ijcis.d.200127.002

Basu, K. K. (2015). The Leader's Role in Managing Change: Five Cases of Technology-Enabled Business Transformation. *Global Business and Organizational Excellence*, *34*(3), 28–42. doi:10.1002/joe.21602

Bathelt, H., & Li, P. (2020). Building Better Methods in Economic Geography. *Zeitschrift für Wirtschaftsgeographie*, *64*(3), 103–108. doi:10.1515/zfw-2020-0014

Batistič, S., & Laken, P. V. (2019). *History, Evolution and Future of Big Data and Analytics: A Bibliometric Analysis of Its Relationship to Performance in Organizations.* Wiley. doi:10.1111/1467-8551.12340

Bayoumy, K., Gaber, M., Elshafeey, A., Mhaimeed, O., Dineen, E. H., Marvel, F. A., Martin, S. S., Muse, E. D., Turakhia, M. P., Tarakji, K. G., & Elshazly, M. B. (2021a). Smart wearable devices in cardiovascular care: where we are and how to move forward. *Nature Reviews Cardiology, 18*(8), 581–599. doi:10.1038/s41569-021-00522-7

BBC News. (2021, December 28). Australia: Hundreds given false Covid results in Sydney lab error. *BBC News*. https://www.bbc.com/news/world-australia-59752091

Beattie, A., Edwards, A. P., & Edwards, C. (2020). A bot and a smile: Interpersonal impressions of chatbots and humans using emoji in computer-mediated communication. *Communication Studies*, *71*(3), 409–427. doi:10.1080/10510974.2020.1725082

Bednar, K., & Spiekermann, S. (2022). Eliciting Values for Technology Design with Moral Philosophy: An Empirical Exploration of Effects and Shortcomings. *Science, Technology & Human Values*, *0*(0). doi:10.1177/01622439221122595

Behal, V., & Gupta, M. (2022). Reporting of corporate social responsibility practices: An evidence from Indian BSE-listed companies. *Prabandhan: Indian Journal of Management*, *15*(3), 42–58. doi:10.17010/pijom/2022/v15i3/165633

Belitski, M., Korosteleva, J., & Piscitello, L. (2023). Digital affordances and entrepreneurial dynamics: New evidence from European regions. *Technovation*, *119*, 102–442. doi:10.1016/j.technovation.2021.102442

Bellavista, P., Bosi, F., Corradi, A., Foschini, L., Monti, S., Patera, L., . . . Solimando, M. (2019, June). Design guidelines for big data gathering in industry 4.0 environments. In 2019 IEEE 20th International Symposium on" A World of Wireless, Mobile and Multimedia Networks"(WoWMoM) (pp. 1-6). IEEE.

Bell, E., Bryman, A., & Harley, B. (2022). *Business research methods*. Oxford university press. doi:10.1093/hebz/9780198869443.001.0001

Belt, P., Paloniemi, K., & Sinisammal, J. (2015). One-Person Enterprises and Business Growth. *Journal of Enterprising Culture*, *23*(3), 381–404. doi:10.1142/S0218495815500132

BenbyaH.DavenportT. H.PachidiS. (2020). Artificial Intelligence in Organizations: Current State and Future Opportunities. Retrieved from doi:10.2139/ssrn.3741983

Bendig, D., Schulz, C., Theis, L., & Raff, S. (2023). Digital orientation and environmental performance in times of technological change. *Technological Forecasting and Social Change*, *188*, 122272. doi:10.1016/j.techfore.2022.122272

Berger, E. S., Briel, F. V., Davidsson, P., & Kuckertz, A. (2021). Digital or not – The future of entrepreneurship and innovation: Introduction to the special issue. *Journal of Business Research*, *125*, 436–442. doi:10.1016/j.jbusres.2019.12.020

Berger, T., Lévesque, M., Rojas, E., Tuomi, I., & Townsend, D. (2022). Artificial intelligence and entrepreneurial ecosystems: Understanding the implications for policy and practice. Journal of Entrepreneurship. *Emerging Economies and Technology*, *10*(3), 1–19.

Berwing, S. (2019). Extending Mixed Embeddedness. Historical Social Research/Historische Sozialforschung, 44(4 (170), 162-185.

Bettoni, A., Matteri, D., Montini, E., Gładysz, B., & Carpanzano, E. (2021). An AI adoption model for SMEs: a conceptual framework. Retrieved from doi:10.1016/j.ifacol.2021.08.082

Bhalerao, K., Kumar, A., Kumar, A., & Pujari, P. (2022). A study barriers and benefits of artificial intelligence adoption in small and medium enterprise. Retrieved from https://www.researchgate.net/publication/360912025_a_study_of_barriers_and_benefits_of_artificial_intelligence_adoption_in_small_and_medium_enterprise

Bhalerao, K., Kumar, A., & Pujari, P. (2022). A Study of Barriers and Benefits of Artificial Intelligence Adoption in Small and Medium Enterprise. *Academy of Marketing Studies Journal*, *26*, 1–6.

Bharadiya, J. P. (2022). Driving Business Growth with Artificial Intelligence and Business Intelligence. *INTERNATIONAL JOURNAL OF COMPUTER SCIENCE AND TECHNOLOGY (IJCST), 6*(4), 28-44. http://www.ijcst.com.pk/IJCST/article/view/232

Bharadiya, J. P. (2023). Machine Learning and AI in Business Intelligence: Trends and Opportunities. [IJC]. *International Journal of Computer, 48*(1), 123–134. https://ijcjournal.org/index.php/InternationalJournalOfComputer/article/view/2087

Bharadiya, J. P. (2023). Machine Learning and AI in Business Intelligence: Trendsand Opportunities. [IJC]. *International Journal of Computer, 48*(1), 123–134.

Bhattacherjee, A. (2001a). An empirical analysis of the antecedents of electronic commerce service continuance. *Decision Support Systems, 32*(2), 201–214. doi:10.1016/S0167-9236(01)00111-7

Bhattacherjee, A. (2001b). Understanding information systems continuance: An expectation-confirmation model. *Management Information Systems Quarterly, 25*(3), 351–370. doi:10.2307/3250921

Bianchi, C., Tuzovic, S., & Kuppelwieser, V. G. (2023). Investigating the drivers of wearable technology adoption for healthcare in South America. *Information Technology & People, 36*(2), 916–939. doi:10.1108/ITP-01-2021-0049

Bickley, S. J., Macintyre, A., & Torgler, B. (2021). Artificial intelligence and big data in sustainable entrepreneurship. *Journal of Economic Surveys.*

Biea, E. A., Dinu, E., Bunica, A., & Jerdea, L. (2023). Recruitment in SMEs: The role of managerial practices, technology and innovation. *European Business Review.* doi:10.1108/EBR-05-2023-0162

Bintaro, B. K., Sokibi, P., Amsyar, I., & Ayu Sanjaya, Y. P. (2022). Utilizing digital marketing as a business strategy. [SABDA Journal]. *Startupreneur Business Digital, 1*(1), 63–71. doi:10.33050/sabda.v1i1.79

Björkman, I., & Johansson, S. (2017). *What impact will Artificial Intelligence have on the future leadership role.* Research Gate.

Blanchflower, D. (2004). Self-employment: More may not be better. Working paper No. 10286, National Bureau of Economic Research, available at: http://www.nber.org/ papers/w10286

Blanchflower, D., & Oswald, A. (1998). What makes an entrepreneur? *Journal of Labor Economics, 16*(1), 26–60. doi:10.1086/209881

Blanchflower, D., Oswald, A., & Stutzer, A. (2001). Latent entrepreneurship across nations. *European Economic Review, 45*(4), 680–691. doi:10.1016/S0014-2921(01)00137-4

Bogachov, S., Kwilinski, A., Miethlich, B., Bartosova, V., & Gurnak, A. (2020). Artificial intelligence components and fuzzy regulators in entrepreneurship development. Retrieved from doi:10.9770/jesi.2020.8.2(29)

Bögenhold, D., & Klinglmair, A. (2016). Independent work, modern organizations and entrepreneurial labor: Diversity and hybridity of freelancers and self-employment. [Cambridge Core.]. *Journal of Management & Organization, 22*(6), 843–858. doi:10.1017/jmo.2016.29

Bonett, D. G., & Wright, T. A. (2015). Cronbach's alpha reliability: Interval estimation, hypothesis testing, and sample size planning. *Journal of Organizational Behavior, 36*(1), 3–15. doi:10.1002/job.1960

Borges, A. F., Laurindo, F. J., Spínola, M. M., Gonçalves, R. F., & Mattos, C. A. (2021). The strategic use of artificial intelligence in the Digital Era: Systematic literature review and future research directions. *International Journal of Information Management, 57*, 102–225. doi:10.1016/j.ijinfomgt.2020.102225

Borsatto, J. M. L. S., Marcolin, C. B., Abdalla, E. C., & Amaral, F. D. (2023). Aligning community outreach initiatives with SDGs in a higher education institution with artificial intelligence. *Cleaner and Responsible Consumption, 100160.* doi:10.1016/j.clrc.2023.100160

Bouchard, M. J., & Rousselière, D. (2016). Do Hybrid Organizational Forms of the Social Economy have a Greater Chance of Surviving? An Examination of the Case of Montreal. *Voluntas*, *27*(4), 1894–1922. doi:10.1007/s11266-015-9664-1

Bradley, D., & Roberts, J. (2004). Self-Employment and job satisfaction: Investigating the role of Self-Efficacy, depression, and seniority. *Journal of Small Business Management*, *42*(1), 37–58. doi:10.1111/j.1540-627X.2004.00096.x

Brandon-Jones, A., & Kauppi, K. (2018). Examining the antecedents of the technology acceptance model within e-procurement. *International Journal of Operations & Production Management*, *38*(1), 22–42. doi:10.1108/IJOPM-06-2015-0346

Brey, P. (2011). Anticipatory Technology Ethics for Emerging IT. In J. Mauger (Ed.), *CEPE 2011: Crossing Boundaries* (pp. 13–26). INSEIT.

Broekhuizen, T., Dekker, H., De Faria, P., Firk, S., Nguyen, D. K., & Sofka, W. (2023). AI for managing open innovation: Opportunities, challenges, and a research agenda. *Journal of Business Research*, *167*, 114196. doi:10.1016/j.jbusres.2023.114196

Buettner, R. (2013). Cognitive Workload of Humans Using Artificial Intelligence Systems: Towards Objective Measurement Applying Eye-Tracking Technology. In I. J. Timm & M. Thimm (Eds.), *KI 2013: Advances in Artificial Intelligence* (Vol. 8077, pp. 37–48). Springer Berlin Heidelberg. doi:10.1007/978-3-642-40942-4_4

Bughin, J., Seong, J., Manyika, J., Chui, M., & Joshi, R. (2018). Notes from the AI frontier: Modeling the impact of AI on the world economy. *McKinsey Global Institute, 4.*

Buolamwini, J., & Gebru, T. (2018). Gender shades: Intersectional accuracy disparities in commercial gender classification. In *Conference on fairness, accountability and transparency* (pp. 77-91). PMLR.

Burström, T., Parida, V., Lahti, T., & Wincent, J. (2021). AI-enabled business-model innovation and transformation in industrial ecosystems: A framework, model and outline for further research. *Journal of Business Research*, *127*, 85–95. doi:10.1016/j.jbusres.2021.01.016

Bush, T. (2018). Transformational leadership. *Educational Management Administration & Leadership*, *46*(6), 883–887. doi:10.1177/1741143218795731

Buzko, I., Dyachenko, Y., Petrova, M., Nenkov, N., Tuleninova, D., & Koeva, K. (2016). Artificial Intelligence technologies in human resource development. *Computer modelling and new technologies, 20(*2), 26-29.

Bynum, T. W. (2008). Norbert Wiener and the Rise of Information Ethics. In J. van den Hoven & J. Weckert (Eds.), *Information Technology and Moral Philosophy* (pp. 8–25). Cambridge University Press. doi:10.1017/CBO9780511498725.002

Bynum, T. W., & Rogerson, S. (2003). *Computer Ethics and Professional Responsibility: Introductory Text and Readings*. Blackwell Publishers.

Calanzone, D., Coppari, A., Tedoldi, R., Olivato, G., & Casonato, C. (2023). An open source perspective on AI and alignment with the EU AI Act.

Callegari, B., & Nybakk, E. (2022). Schumpeterian theory and research on forestry innovation and entrepreneurship: The state of the art, issues and an agenda. *Forest Policy and Economics*, *138*, 102720. doi:10.1016/j.forpol.2022.102720

Capelli, G., Verdi, D., Frigerio, I., Rashidian, N., Ficorilli, A., Grasso, V., Majidi, D., Gumbs, A. A., & Spolverato, G. (2023). White paper: Ethics and trustworthiness of artificial intelligence in clinical surgery. *Artificial Intelligence Surgery*, *3*(2), 111–122. doi:10.20517/ais.2023.04

Capurro, R. (2006). Towards an Ontological Foundation of Information Ethics. *Ethics and Information Technology*, *8*(4), 175–186. doi:10.1007/s10676-006-9108-0

Cartwright, T., & Baldwin, D. (2007). Seeing your way: Why leaders must communicate their visions. *Leadership in Action*, *27*(3), 15–24. doi:10.1002/lia.1208

Casale, S., Musicò, A., & Spada, M. M. (2021). A systematic review of metacognitions in Internet Gaming Disorder and problematic Internet, smartphone and social networking sites use. *Clinical Psychology & Psychotherapy*, *28*(6), 1494–1508. doi:10.1002/cpp.2588 PMID:33783920

Cavallaro, F. (2020). Development of a Index for Sustainable Energy Technologies Based on an Intelligent Fuzzy Expert System. Economic and Policy Implications of Artificial Intelligence, 137-143.

Cavallo, A., Ghezzi, A., & Balocco, R. (2019). Entrepreneurial ecosystem research: Present debates and future directions. *The International Entrepreneurship and Management Journal*, *15*(4), 1291–1321. doi:10.1007/s11365-018-0526-3

Celic, L., & Magjarevic, R. (2020). Seamless connectivity architecture and methods for IoT and wearable devices. *Automatika : Časopis Za Automatiku, Mjerenje, Elektroniku. Automatika (Zagreb)*, *61*(1), 21–34. doi:10.1080/00051144.2019.1660036

Certomà, C., & Corsini, F. (2021). Digitally-enabled social innovation. Mapping discourses on an emergent social technology. *Innovation (Abingdon)*, *34*(4), 560–584. doi:10.1080/13511610.2021.1937069

Chalmers, D., MacKenzie, N. G., & Carter, S. (2020). Artificial Intelligence and Entrepreneurship: Implications for Venture Creation in the Fourth Industrial Revolution. Retrieved from doi:10.1177/1042258720934581

Chamola, V., Hassija, V., Gupta, V., & Guizani, M. (2020). A Comprehensive Review of the COVID-19 Pandemic and the Role of IoT, Drones, AI, Blockchain, and 5G in Managing its Impact. *IEEE Access : Practical Innovations, Open Solutions*, *8*, 90225–90265. doi:10.1109/ACCESS.2020.2992341

Chang, V., Doan, L. M. T., Ariel Xu, Q., Hall, K., Anna Wang, Y., & Mustafa Kamal, M. (2023). Digitalization in omnichannel healthcare supply chain businesses: The role of smart wearable devices. *Journal of Business Research*, *156*, 113369. doi:10.1016/j.jbusres.2022.113369

Chan, X. Y., Rahman, M. K., Mamun, A. A., Salameh, A., Wan, A., Hussain, W. M. H., & Alam, S. S. (2022). Predicting the intention and adoption of mobile shopping during the COVID-19 lockdown in Malaysia. *SAGE Open*, *12*(2), 21582440221095012. doi:10.1177/21582440221095012

Chan, Y. E., Krishnamurthy, R., & Desjardins, C. (2020). Technology-Driven innovation in small firms. *MIS Quarterly Executive*, *19*(1), 39–55. doi:10.17705/2msqe.00024

Chao, W. (2023). A Study of Transformational Leadership Behavior and Employee Performance in Chinese Futures Firms. *International Journal of Science and Business*, *23*(1), 22–37. doi:10.58970/IJSB.2132

Chatzopoulos, C. G., & Weber, M. (2020). Digitization and artificial intelligence for lean customer experience management. *Transformation, 22*, 24.

Chaudhary, D. D., Nayse, S. P., & Waghmare, L. M. (2011). Application of wireless sensor networks for greenhouse parameter control in precision agriculture. [IJWMN]. *International Journal of Wireless & Mobile Networks*, *3*(1), 140–149. doi:10.5121/ijwmn.2011.3113

Cheatham, B., Javanmardian, K., & Samandari, H. (2019). Confronting the risks of artificial intelligence. *The McKinsey Quarterly*, *2*(38), 1–9.

Cheng, J. W., & Mitomo, H. (2017). The underlying factors of the perceived usefulness of using smart wearable devices for disaster applications. *Telematics and Informatics*, *34*(2), 528–539. doi:10.1016/j.tele.2016.09.010

Cheng, Y. M. (2021). Drivers of physicians' satisfaction and continuance intention toward the cloud-based hospital information system. *Kybernetes*, *50*(2), 413–442. doi:10.1108/K-09-2019-0628

Chen, M., & Decary, M. (2020, January). Artificial intelligence in healthcare: An essential guide for health leaders. *Healthcare Management Forum*, *33*(1), 10–18. doi:10.1177/0840470419873123 PMID:31550922

Chen, W. H., Lin, Y. C., Bag, A., & Chen, C. L. (2023). Influence Factors of Small and Medium-Sized Enterprises and Micro-Enterprises in the Cross-Border E-Commerce Platforms. *Journal of Theoretical and Applied Electronic Commerce Research*, *18*(1), 416–440. doi:10.3390/jtaer18010022

Chen, X., & Metawa, N. (2020). Enterprise financial management information system based on cloud computing in big data environment. *Journal of Intelligent & Fuzzy Systems*, *39*(4), 5223–5232. doi:10.3233/JIFS-189007

Chen, Y., Li, C., & Wang, H. (2022). Big data and predictive analytics for business intelligence: A bibliographic study (2000–2021). *Forecasting*, *4*(4), 767–786. doi:10.3390/forecast4040042

Chen, Y., Rui, H., & Whinston, A. (2021). Tweet to the Top? Social Media Personal Branding and Career Outcomes. *Management Information Systems Quarterly*, *45*(2), 499–534. doi:10.25300/MISQ/2021/14617

Chen, Z. (2023). Collaboration among recruiters and artificial intelligence: Removing human prejudices in employment. *Cognition Technology and Work*, *25*(1), 135–149. doi:10.1007/s10111-022-00716-0 PMID:36187287

Chintalapati, S., & Pandey, S. K. (2022). Artificial intelligence in marketing: A systematic literature review. *International Journal of Market Research*, *64*(1), 38–68. doi:10.1177/14707853211018428

Chiou, L., & Tucker, C. (2020). *Social distancing, internet access and inequality (No. w26982)*. National Bureau of Economic Research., doi:10.3386/w26982

Chopra, P., & Gupta, M. (2023). Fuzzy Logic and ANN in an Artificial Intelligent Cloud: A Comparative Study. In *Intelligent Communication Technologies and Virtual Mobile Networks* (pp. 559–570). Springer Nature Singapore Singapore. doi:10.1007/978-981-99-1767-9_41

Chowdhury, M. A., Chisty, K. K. S., Tushar, H., Ahmed, K. M. F., & Waliullah, S. S. A. (2023). Automating assessment and evaluation for a bachelor's degree program. [IJERE]. *International Journal of Evaluation and Research in Education*, *12*(4), 2037. doi:10.11591/ijere.v12i4.25479

Chowdhury, S., Dey, P., Joel-Edgar, S., Bhattacharya, S., Rodriguez-Espindola, O., Abadie, A., & Truong, L. (2023). Unlocking the value of artificial intelligence in human resource management through AI capability framework. *Human Resource Management Review*, *33*(1), 100899. doi:10.1016/j.hrmr.2022.100899

Chung, J., Gulcehre, C., Cho, K., & Bengio, Y. (2011). Empirical evaluation of gated recurrent neural networks on sequence modeling. *NIPS 2014 Workshop on Deep Learning*. IEEE.

Çiçek, M. (2015). Wearable technologies and its future applications. *International Journal of Electrical. Electronics and Data Communication*, *3*(4), 45–50.

Connock, A. (2022). *Media Management and Artificial Intelligence: Understanding Media Business Models in the Digital Age*. Taylor & Francis. doi:10.4324/9781003213611

Conradie, N. H., & Nagel, S. K. (2022). Digital sovereignty and smart wearables: Three moral calculi for the distribution of legitimate control over the digital. *Journal of Responsible Technology, 12*, 100053. doi:10.1016/j.jrt.2022.100053

Corley, K. G. (2015). A commentary on "what grounded theory is..." engaging a phenomenon from the perspective of those living it. *Organizational Research Methods, 18*(4), 600–605. doi:10.1177/1094428115574747

Cotarelo, M., Fayos, T., Calderón, H., & Mollá, A. (2021). Omni-Channel Intensity and Shopping Value as Key Drivers of Customer Satisfaction and Loyalty. *Sustainability, 13*(11), 5961. doi:10.3390/su13115961

Cousins, S. (2020). Bangladesh's COVID-19 testing criticised. *Lancet, 396*(10251), 591. Retrieved August 27, 2023, from. doi:10.1016/S0140-6736(20)31819-5 PMID:32861296

Cousté, P. E., Qin, S., Hossain, S. F. A., & Hussain, K. (2022). Factors influencing social-media-based entrepreneurship prospects among female students in China. *Heliyon, 8*(12), e12041. doi:10.1016/j.heliyon.2022.e12041 PMID:36483305

Creswell, J. W., & Creswell, J. D. (2017). *Research design: Qualitative, quantitative, and mixed methods approaches*. Sage publications.

Crockett, K., Colyer, E., Gerber, L., & Latham, A. (2021). Building Trustworthy AI Solutions: A Case for Practical Solutions for Small Businesses. Retrieved from https://ieeexplore.ieee.org/abstract/document/9658213

Croteau, A. M., & Bergeron, F. (2001). *An information technology trilogy: business strategy, technological deployment and organizational performance*. Science Direct. doi:10.1016/S0963-8687(01)00044-0

Cucus, A., & Febrianti, M. S. (2017). Implementation of Sensor Ph Meter, Ec Meter and Temperature on Smart Vertical Agriculture System. *International Conference on Engineering and Technology Development (ICETD)*. Indonesia.

Culot, G., Orzes, G., Sartor, M., & Nassimbeni, G. (2020). The future of manufacturing: A Delphi-based scenario analysis on Industry 4.0. *Technological Forecasting and Social Change, 157*. doi:10.1016/j.techfore.2020.120092

Dai, R., Feng, H., Hu, J., Jin, Q., Li, H., Wang, R., Wang, R., Xu, L., & Zhang, X. (2021). The impact of COVID-19 on small and medium-sized enterprises (SMEs): Evidence from two-wave phone surveys in China. *China Economic Review, 67*, 101607. doi:10.1016/j.chieco.2021.101607 PMID:36568286

Daníelsson, J., Macrae, R., & Uthemann, A. (2022). Artificial intelligence and systemic risk. *Journal of Banking & Finance, 140*, 106290. doi:10.1016/j.jbankfin.2021.106290

Daragmeh, A., Sági, J., & Zéman, Z. (2021). Continuous Intention to Use E-Wallet in the Context of the COVID-19 Pandemic: Integrating the Health Belief Model (HBM) and Technology Continuous Theory (TCT). *Journal of Open Innovation: Technology, Market, and Complexity, 7*(2), 132. doi:10.3390/joitmc7020132

Daugherty, P. R., & Wilson, H. J. (2018). *Human + Machine: Reimagining Work in the Age of AI*. Harvard Business Review Press.

Daugherty, P. R., & Wilson, H. J. (2018). *Human+Machine: Reimagining work in the age of AI*. Harvard Business Press.

Davenport, T. H., Guha, A., Grewal, D., & Breßgott, T. (2019). How artificial intelligence will change the future of marketing. *Journal of the Academy of Marketing Science, 48*(1), 24–42. doi:10.1007/s11747-019-00696-0

Davenport, T., & Kalakota, R. (2019). The potential for artificial intelligence in healthcare. *Future Healthcare Journal, 6*(2), 94–98. doi:10.7861/futurehosp.6-2-94 PMID:31363513

Davies, I. A., & Chambers, L. (2018). Integrating hybridity and business model theory in sustainable entrepreneurship. *Journal of Cleaner Production, 177*, 378–386. doi:10.1016/j.jclepro.2017.12.196

Davis, K. (1960). Can business afford to ignore social responsibilities? *California Management Review*, *2*(3), 70–76. doi:10.2307/41166246

Dawadi, S., Shrestha, S., & Giri, R. A. (2021). Mixed-Methods Research: A Discussion on its Types, Challenges, and Criticisms. *Journal of Practical Studies in Education*, *2*(2), 25–36. doi:10.46809/jpse.v2i2.20

de Carvalho, R. A., & Johansson, B. (2010). Enterprise resource planning systems for small and medium-sized enterprises. In Information Resources Management: Concepts, Methodologies, Tools and Applications (pp. 365-373). IGI Global.

Dehghani, M. (2018). Exploring the motivational factors on continuous usage intention of smartwatches among actual users. *Behaviour & Information Technology*, *37*(2), 145–158. doi:10.1080/0144929X.2018.1424246

Dehghani, M., Kim, K. J., & Dangelico, R. M. (2018). Will smartwatches last? factors contributing to intention to keep using smart wearable technology. *Telematics and Informatics*, *35*(2), 480–490. doi:10.1016/j.tele.2018.01.007

Dennehy, D., Griva, A., Pouloudi, N., Dwivedi, Y. K., Mäntymäki, M., & Pappas, I. O. (2023). Artificial intelligence (AI) and information systems: Perspectives to responsible AI. *Information Systems Frontiers*, *25*(1), 1–7. doi:10.1007/s10796-022-10365-3

Dewi, M. P., Havidz, I. L. H., & Atmaja, D. R. (2022). Digital Marketing for SMEs Cido- kom Village Plant Cultivation Group. *Majalah Ilmiah Bijak*, *19*(1), 47–55. doi:10.31334/bijak.v19i1.2199

Di Bona, G., Cesarotti, V., Arcese, G., & Gallo, T. (2021). Implementation of Industry 4.0 technology: New opportunities and challenges for maintenance strategy. *Procedia Computer Science*, *180*, 424–429. doi:10.1016/j.procs.2021.01.258

DictionaryU. (2015). http://www.urbandictionary.com/define.php?term1/4solopreneur

Ding, R. X., Palomares, I., Wang, X., Yang, G. R., Liu, B., Dong, Y., Herrera-Viedma, E., & Herrera, F. (2020). Large-Scale decision-making: Characterization, taxonomy, challenges and future directions from an Artificial Intelligence and applications perspective. *Information Fusion*, *59*, 84–102. doi:10.1016/j.inffus.2020.01.006

Dixit, S., Maurya, M., Sharma, N., & Zaidi, N. (2022). Payments Process Privilege: Leveraging Fintech with TAM. *8th International Conference on Advanced Computing and Communication Systems, ICACCS 2022*, (pp. 1668–1673). IEEE. 10.1109/ICACCS54159.2022.9785136

Do Nguyen, G., & Ha, M. T. (2021). The role of user adaptation and trust in understanding continuance intention towards mobile shopping: An extended expectation-confirmation model. *Cogent Business & Management*, *8*(1), 1980248. doi:10.1080/23311975.2021.1980248

Dogru, A. K., & Keskin, B. B. (2020). AI in operations management: Applications, challenges and opportunities. *Journal of Data. Information & Management*, *2*(2), 67–74. doi:10.1007/s42488-020-00023-1

Drigas, A., Papoutsi, C., & Skianis, C. (2023). Being an Emotionally Intelligent Leader through the Nine-Layer Model of Emotional Intelligence—The Supporting Role of New Technologies. *Sustainability (Basel)*, *15*(10), 8103. doi:10.3390/su15108103

Drydakis, N. (2022). Artificial Intelligence and reduced SMEs' business risks. A dynamic capabilities analysis during the COVID-19 pandemic. *Information Systems Frontiers*, *24*(4), 1223–1247. doi:10.1007/s10796-022-10249-6 PMID:35261558

Dubey, R., Bryde, D. J., Blome, C., Roubaud, D., & Giannakis, M. (2021). Facilitating artificial intelligence powered supply chain analytics through alliance management during the pandemic crises in the B2B context. *Industrial Marketing Management*, *96*, 135–146. doi:10.1016/j.indmarman.2021.05.003

Duchessi, P., O'Keefe, R., & O'Leary, D. (1993). A Research Perspective: Artificial Intelligence, Management and Organizations. *International Journal of Intelligent Systems in Accounting Finance & Management*, *2*(3), 151–159. doi:10.1002/j.1099-1174.1993.tb00039.x

Du, S., & Xie, C. (2021). Paradoxes of artificial intelligence in consumer markets: Ethical challenges and opportunities. *Journal of Business Research*, *129*, 961–974. doi:10.1016/j.jbusres.2020.08.024

Dutta Gupta, S., & Guha Majumder, M. (2023). Digital transformation, digital entrepreneurship, and economy: A cross-country analysis using moderated mediation modeling technique. *India Studies in Business and Economics*, 47-70. doi:10.1007/978-981-99-4063-9_3

Dutta, G., Kumar, R., Sindhwani, R., & Singh, R. K. (2020). Digital transformation priorities of India's discrete manufacturing SMEs – a conceptual study in perspective of Industry 4.0. *Competitiveness Review*, *30*(3), 289–314. doi:10.1108/CR-03-2019-0031

Dvouletý, O., Procházka, D. A., & Starnawska, M. (2021). Who earns more: Job creators, solo-entrepreneurs or employees? Empirical evidence from Visegrad countries. *International Journal of Entrepreneurship and Small Business*, *43*(4), 517–530. doi:10.1504/IJESB.2021.117345

Dwivedi, Y. K., Hughes, L., Ismagilova, E., Aarts, G., Coombs, C., Crick, T., ... Duan, Y. (2021). Artificial Intelligence (AI): Multidisciplinary perspectives on emerging challenges, opportunities, and agenda for research, practice and policy. *International Journal of Information Management*, *57*, 101–994. doi:10.1016/j.ijinfomgt.2019.08.002

Dwivedi, Y. K., Kshetri, N., Hughes, L., Slade, E. L., Jeyaraj, A., Kar, A. K., Baabdullah, A. M., Koohang, A., Raghavan, V., Ahuja, M., Albanna, H., Albashrawi, M. A., Al-Busaidi, A. S., Balakrishnan, J., Barlette, Y., Basu, S., Bose, I., Brooks, L., Buhalis, D., & Wright, R. (2023). "So what if ChatGPT wrote it?" Multidisciplinary perspectives on opportunities, challenges and implications of generative conversational AI for research, practice and policy. *International Journal of Information Management*, *71*, 102642. doi:10.1016/j.ijinfomgt.2023.102642

Dwivedi, Y. K., & Wang, Y. (2022). Guest editorial: Artificial intelligence for B2B marketing: Challenges and opportunities. *Industrial Marketing Management*, *105*, 109–113. doi:10.1016/j.indmarman.2022.06.001

Eckert, C., Neunsinger, C., & Osterrieder, K. (2022). Managing customer satisfaction: Digital applications for insurance companies. *The Geneva Papers on Risk and Insurance. Issues and Practice*, *47*(3), 569–602. doi:10.1057/s41288-021-00257-z

ECRA | Electronic Commerce Research and Applications | Consumer Brand Relationships in Online Communities and E-commerce Channels | ScienceDirect.com by Elsevier. (n.d.). Retrieved from https://www.sciencedirect.com/journal/electronic-commerce-research-and-applications/special-is sue/10NKZRJHBP8

Eden, B. (1976). On the specification of the demand for money: The real rate of return versus the rate of inflation. *Journal of Political Economy*, *84*(6), 1353–1359. doi:10.1086/260520

Eitel-Porter, R. (2020). Beyond the Promise: Implementing Ethical AI. *AI and Ethics*, *1*(1), 73–80. doi:10.1007/s43681-020-00011-6

El Namak, M. S. S. (2018). How Companies are Applying AI to the Business Strategy Formulation. *Scholedge International Journal of Business Policy & Governance*, *5*(8), 77-82.

El Namaki, M. S. S. (2019). Will Artificial Intelligence Change Strategic Top Management Competencies. *SCHOLEDGE International Journal of Management & Development*, *6*(4), 34. 34-doi.org/10.19085/journal.sijmd060401. doi:10.19085/journal.sijmd060401

Eldrandaly, K. A., Abdel-Basset, M., & Abdel-Fatah, L. (2019). PTZ-Surveillance coverage based on artificial intelligence for smart cities. *International Journal of Information Management*, *49*, 520–532. doi:10.1016/j.ijinfomgt.2019.04.017

El-Gayar, O., & Elnoshokaty, A. (2023). Factors and Design Features Influencing the Continued Use of Wearable Devices. *Journal of Healthcare Informatics Research*, *7*(3), 359–385. doi:10.1007/s41666-023-00135-4 PMID:37637719

ElMaraghy, H., Monostori, L., Schuh, G., & ElMaraghy, W. (2021). Evolution and future of manufacturing systems. *CIRP Annals*, *70*(2), 635–658. doi:10.1016/j.cirp.2021.05.008

ElMassah, S., & Mohieldin, M. (2020). Digital Transformation and Localizing the Sus- tainable Development Goals (SDGs). *Ecological Economics*, *169*, 106490. Advance online publication. doi:10.1016/j.ecolecon.2019.106490

Enholm, I. M., Papagiannidis, E., Mikalef, P., & Krogstie, J. (2021). Artificial Intelligence and Business Value: A Literature Review. *Information Systems Frontiers*, *24*(5), 1709–1734. doi:10.1007/s10796-021-10186-w

Eriksson, T., Bigi, A., & Bonera, M. (2020). Think with me, or think for me? On the future role of artificial intelligence in marketing strategy formulation. *The TQM Journal*, *32*(4), 795–814. doi:10.1108/TQM-12-2019-0303

Esteves, A. M., Genus, A., Henfrey, T., Penha-Lopes, G., & East, M. (2021). Sustainable Entrepreneurship and the Sustainable Development Goals: Community-Led Initiatives, the Social Solidarity Economy and Commons Ecologies. *Business Strategy and the Environment*, *30*(3), 1423–1435. doi:10.1002/bse.2706

Evdokimov, I., Kampouridis, M., & Papastylianou, T. (2023). Application Of Machine Learning Algorithms to Free Cash Flows Growth Rate Estimation. *Procedia Computer Science*, *222*, 529–538. doi:10.1016/j.procs.2023.08.191

Faisal, S., Hossain, S. F. A., Fahmida, S., & Rayhana, R. (2023). Leveraging Business Intelligence to Enhance Cyber Security Innovation. In Cyber Security and Business Intelligence (pp. 1-14). Routledge. doi:10.4324/9781003285854-1

Fan, Z., Yang, W., Wu, F., Cao, J., & Shi, W. (2021). Serving at the edge: An edge computing service architecture based on icn. *ACM Transactions on Internet Technology*, *22*(1), 1–27. doi:10.1145/3464428

Farheen, N., Rabie, O., Hussain, T., & Rehmani, M. (2023). Transformational Leadership, Knowledge Sharing and Innovative Behavior of Employees in Information Technology Industry of Pakistan. *Review of Applied Management and Social Sciences*, *6*(1), 29–43. doi:10.47067/ramss.v6i1.287

Farshid, M., Paschen, J., Eriksson, T., & Kietzmann, J. (2018). *Go boldly!: Explore augmented reality (AR), virtual reality (VR), and mixed reality (MR) for business*. Retrieved from doi:10.1016/j.bushor.2018.05.009

Feldman, F. (1997). Utilitarianism. In Utilitarianism, Hedonism, and Desert: Essays in Moral Philosophy (Cambridge Studies in Philosophy, pp. 15-16). Cambridge: Cambridge University Press.

Felsberger, A., Qaiser, F. H., Choudhary, A., & Reiner, G. (2020). The impact of Industry 4.0 on the reconciliation of dynamic capabilities: Evidence from the European manufacturing industries. *Production Planning and Control*, *33*(2–3), 277–300. doi:10.1080/09537287.2020.1810765

Ferguson, E. D. (2007). Business and organizations. *Journal of Individual Psychology*, *63*(1), 110–117.

Fernando, Y., Chiappetta Jabbour, C. J., & Wah, W. X. (2019). Pursuing green growth in technology firms through the connections between environmental innovation and sustainable business performance: Does service capability matter? *Resources, Conservation and Recycling*, *141*, 8–20. doi:10.1016/j.resconrec.2018.09.031

Ferrari, A., Bacco, M., Gaber, K., Jedlitschka, A., Hess, S., Kaipainen, J., Koltsida, P., Toli, E., & Brunori, G. (2022). Drivers, Barriers and Impacts of Digitalisation in Rural Areas from the Viewpoint of Experts. *Information and Software Technology*, *145*, 106816. Advance online publication. doi:10.1016/j.infsof.2021.106816

Ferraz, O., Menezes, P., Silva, V., & Falcao, G. (2021, November). Benchmarking Vulkan vs OpenGL Rendering on Low-Power Edge GPUs. In *2021 International Conference on Graphics and Interaction (ICGI)* (pp. 1-8). IEEE. 10.1109/ICGI54032.2021.9655285

Fetscherin, M., & Heinrich, D. (2014). Consumer brand relationships: A research landscape. *Journal of Brand Management*, *21*(5), 366–371. doi:10.1057/bm.2014.22

Feuerriegel, S., Shrestha, Y. R., Von Krogh, G., & Zhang, C. (2022). Bringing artificial intelligence to business management. *Nature Machine Intelligence*, *4*(7), 611–613. doi:10.1038/s42256-022-00512-5

Floridi, L. (2006). Information Ethics, Its Nature and Scope. *Computers & Society*, *36*(3), 21–36. doi:10.1145/1195716.1195719

Fodranová, I., & Antalová, M. (2021). How Can Digital Sharing Economy Reduce Unem- ployment? *Journal of Technology Management & Innovation*, *16*(1), 51–57. doi:10.4067/S0718-27242021000100051

Foroudi, P., Gupta, S., Sivarajah, U., & Broderick, A. (2018). Investigating the effects of smart technology on customer dynamics and customer experience. Retrieved from doi:10.1016/j.chb.2017.11.014

Fossen, F. M., & Sorgner, A. (2021). Digitalization of work and entry into entrepreneurship. *Journal of Business Research*, *125*, 548–563. doi:10.1016/j.jbusres.2019.09.019

FrankenA.MantheiC.SenderekR.StichV. (2023). *Demands and challenges for SME regarding the human-centred implementation of innovative technologies and AI.* doi:10.15488/13491

Frey, T. (2013). The great freelancer movement: Eight reasons why your next job will be a project. *Journal of Environmental Health*, *76*(5), 46. PMID:24437051

Füller, J., Hutter, K., Wahl, J., Bilgram, V., & Tekic, Z. (2022). How AI revolutionizes innovation management–Perceptions and implementation preferences of AI-based innovators. *Technological Forecasting and Social Change*, *178*, 121598. doi:10.1016/j.techfore.2022.121598

Gaber, S., Ben-Harush, O., & Savir, A. (2017). Predicting HDD failures from compound SMART attributes. *Proceedings of the 10th ACM International Systems and Storage Conference*, (pp. 1–1). ACM. 10.1145/3078468.3081875

Gallup Inc. (2022). *Improve Employee Engagement.* Gallup Inc. https://www.gallup.com/workplace/285674/improve-employee-engagement-workplace.aspx. Accessed 23 November 2023

Gande, A. (2020). Emerging ai & ml-based technologies & applications in supply chain management (scm): Future prospects. *International Journal of Marketing and Technology*, *10*(12), 1–6.

Gao, Y., Liang, X., & Zhang, X. (2022). The impact of artificial intelligence on entrepreneurship: A bibliometric analysis from 2000 to 2020. *Journal of Business Research*, *141*, 1–13.

Garro-Abarca, V., Palos-Sanchez, P., & Aguayo-Camacho, M. (2021). Virtual teams in times of pandemic: Factors that influence performance. *Frontiers in Psychology*, *12*, 624637. Advance online publication. doi:10.3389/fpsyg.2021.624637 PMID:33679543

Gartner, W. (1985). A conceptual framework for describing the phenomenon of new venture creation. *Academy of Management Review*, *10*(4), 696–706. doi:10.2307/258039

Gavrila, S. G., & Ancillo, A. L. (2021). Spanish SMEs' Digitalization Enablers: E-Receipt Applications to the Offline Retail Market. *Technological Forecasting and Social Change*, *162*, 120381. Advance online publication. doi:10.1016/j.techfore.2020.120381 PMID:33082601

Gerke, S., Minssen, T., & Cohen, G. (2020). Ethical and legal challenges of artificial intelligence-driven healthcare. In *Artificial intelligence in healthcare* (pp. 295–336). Academic Press. doi:10.1016/B978-0-12-818438-7.00012-5

Ghadiyali, T., Lad, K., & Patel, B. (2011). Agriculture intelligence: an emerging technology for farmer community. *Second International Conference on Emerging Applications of Information Technology*. Kolkata, India: IEEE. 10.1109/EAIT.2011.36

Ghobakhloo, M., & Ching, N. T. (2019). Adoption of digital technologies of smart manufacturing in SMEs. *Journal of Industrial Information Integration*, *16*, 100107. doi:10.1016/j.jii.2019.100107

Gilligan, C. (1990). *In a Different Voice: Psychological Theory and Women's Development (Reissue)*. Harvard University Press.

Giuggioli, G., & Pellegrini, M. M. (2022). Artificial intelligence as an enabler for entrepreneurs: a systematic literature review and an agenda for future research. Retrieved from https://www.emerald.com/insight/content/doi/10.1108/IJEBR-05-2021-0426/full/html

Giuggioli, G., & Pellegrini, M. M. (2023). Artificial intelligence as an enabler for entrepreneurs: A systematic literature review and an agenda for future research. *International Journal of Entrepreneurial Behaviour & Research*, *29*(4), 816–837. doi:10.1108/IJEBR-05-2021-0426

Gladden, M., Fortuna, P., & Modliński, A. (2022). The empowerment of artificial intelligence in post-digital organizations: Exploring human interactions with supervisory AI. *Human Technology*, *18*(2), 98–121. doi:10.14254/1795-6889.2022.18-2.2

Gloria, T. J., Michael, M., & Joyce, K. (2023). The Moderating Effect of Transformational Leadership on the Relationship Between Entrepreneurial Orientation and Performance of Manufacturing Firms in Nairobi County. *International Journal of Entrepreneurship and Business Innovation.*, *6*(1), 68–86. doi:10.52589/IJEBI-8DKOT4CX

Goap, A., Sharma, D., Shukla, A. K., & Krishna, C. R. (2018). An IoT based smart irrigation management system using Machine learning and open source technologies. *Computers and Electronics in Agriculture*, *155*, 41–49. doi:10.1016/j.compag.2018.09.040

Gonzalez-Tamayo, L. A., Maheshwari, G., Bonomo-Odizzio, A., Herrera-Avilés, M., & Krauss-Delorme, C. (2023). Factors influencing small and medium size enterprises development and digital maturity in Latin America. *Journal of Open Innovation*, *9*(2), 100069. doi:10.1016/j.joitmc.2023.100069

Gopinath, K., & Narayanamurthy, G. (2022). Early bird catches the worm! Meta-analysis of autonomous vehicles adoption–Moderating role of automation level, ownership and culture. *International Journal of Information Management*, *66*, 102536. doi:10.1016/j.ijinfomgt.2022.102536

Goralski, M. A., & Tan, T. K. (2020). Artificial intelligence and sustainable development. *International Journal of Management Education*, *18*(1), 100330. doi:10.1016/j.ijme.2019.100330

Gorospe, J., Mulero, R., Arbelaitz, O., Muguerza, J., & Antón, M. Á. (2021). A generalization performance study using deep learning networks in embedded systems. *Sensors (Basel)*, *21*(4), 1031. doi:10.3390/s21041031 PMID:33546252

Gosetti-Ferencei, J. A. (2020). Existential Suffering, Happiness, and Hope. In *On Being and Becoming: An Existentialist Approach to Life (Guides to the Good Life Series). New York.* Academic. doi:10.1093/oso/9780190913656.003.0020

Goto, M. (2023). Anticipatory innovation of professional services: The case of auditing and artificial intelligence. *Research Policy*, *52*(8), 104828. doi:10.1016/j.respol.2023.104828

Govori, A., & Sejdija, Q. (2023). *Future prospects and challenges of integrating artificial intelligence within the business practices of small and medium enterprises*. Governance & Regulation., doi:10.22495/jgrv12i2art16

Grewal, D., Iyer, G. R., Krishnan, R., & Sharma, A. (2003). The Internet and the price–value–loyalty chain. *Journal of Business Research*, *56*(5), 391–398. doi:10.1016/S0148-2963(01)00227-2

Grooss, O. F. (2024). Digitalization of maintenance activities in small and medium-sized enterprises: A conceptual framework. *Computers in Industry*, *154*, 104039. doi:10.1016/j.compind.2023.104039

Guo, X., Han, X., Zhang, X., Dang, Y., & Chen, C. (2015). Investigating m-Health Acceptance from a Protection Motivation Theory Perspective: Gender and Age Differences. Https://Home.Liebertpub.Com/Tmj, *21*(8), 661–669. doi:10.1089/tmj.2014.0166

Gupta, B. B., Gaurav, A., Panigrahi, P. K., & Arya, V. (2023). Analysis of artificial intelligence-based technologies and approaches on sustainable entrepreneurship. Technological Forecasting and Social Change, 186, 122152. doi:10.1016/j.techfore.2022.122152

Gupta, M., Kumar, P., & Ghai, S. (2023). *Impact of Green Finance on Sustainability in India's Commercial Banks*. 216–233. : Gupta, M., Taneja, S., Sharma, V., Singh, A., Rupeika-Apoga, R., & Jangir, K. (2023). Does Previous Experience with the Unified Payments Interface (UPI) Affect the Usage of Central Bank Digital Currency (CBDC)? *Journal of Risk and Financial Management, 16*(6), 286. doi:10.4018/979-8-3693-1388-6.ch015

Gupta, A., Yousaf, A., & Mishra, A. (2020). How pre-adoption expectancies shape post-adoption continuance intentions: An extended expectation-confirmation model. *International Journal of Information Management*, *52*, 102094. doi:10.1016/j.ijinfomgt.2020.102094

Gupta, P., Seetharaman, A., & Raj, J. R. (2013). The usage and adoption of cloud computing by small and medium businesses. *International Journal of Information Management*, *33*(5), 861–874. doi:10.1016/j.ijinfomgt.2013.07.001

Hacioglu, U. (Ed.). (2019). *Digital business strategies in blockchain ecosystems: Transformational design and future of global business*. Springer Nature.

Hagos, D. H. (2019). Software-defined networking for scalable cloud-based services to improve system performance of hadoop-based big data applications. Web Services: Concepts, Methodologies, Tools, and Applications, 1460-1484. doi:10.4018/978-1-5225-7501-6.ch076

Hahn, C., Traunecker, T., Niever, M., & Basedow, G. N. (2020). Exploring AI-driven business models: conceptualization and expectations in the machinery industry. In *2020 IEEE International Conference on Industrial Engineering and Engineering Management (IEEM)* (pp. 567-570). IEEE. 10.1109/IEEM45057.2020.9309824

Hair, J. F., Risher, J. J., Sarstedt, M., & Ringle, C. M. (2019). When to use and how to report the results of PLS-SEM. *European Business Review*, *31*(1), 2–24. doi:10.1108/EBR-11-2018-0203

Hair, J. F., Sarstedt, M., Hopkins, L., & Kuppelwieser, V. G. (2014). Partial least squares structural equation modeling (PLS-SEM): An emerging tool in business research. *European Business Review*, *26*(2), 106–121. doi:10.1108/EBR-10-2013-0128

Hair, J., Hollingsworth, C. L., Randolph, A. B., & Chong, A. Y. L. (2017). An updated and expanded assessment of PLS-SEM in information systems research. *Industrial Management & Data Systems*, *117*(3), 442–458. doi:10.1108/IMDS-04-2016-0130

Haldma, T., & Lääts, K. (2002). Contingencies influencing the management accounting practices of Estonian manufacturing companies. *Management Accounting Research*, *13*(4), 379–400. doi:10.1006/mare.2002.0197

Hanelt, A., Bohnsack, R., Marz, D., & Antunes Marante, C. (2021). A systematic review of the literature on digital transformation: Insights and implications for strategy and organizational change. *Journal of Management Studies*, *58*(5), 1159–1197. doi:10.1111/joms.12639

Hänninen, M., Mitronen, L., & Kwan, S. K. (2019). Multi-sided marketplaces and the transformation of retail: A service systems perspective. *Journal of Retailing and Consumer Services*, *49*, 380–388. doi:10.1016/j.jretconser.2019.04.015

Hansen, E. B., & Bøgh, S. (2021). Artificial intelligence and Internet of things in small and medium-sized enterprises. *Journal of Manufacturing Systems*, *58*, 362–372. Advance online publication. doi:10.1016/j.jmsy.2020.08.009

Hansen, E. B., Iftikhar, N., & Bøgh, S. (2020). Concept of easy-to-use versatile artificial intelligence in industrial small & medium-sized enterprises. *Procedia Manufacturing*, *51*, 1146–1152. doi:10.1016/j.promfg.2020.10.161

Haruna, J. B. (2022). The Role of Leadership on Organizational Change. [IJRASET]. *International Journal for Research in Applied Science and Engineering Technology*, *10*(10), 249–254. doi:10.22214/ijraset.2022.46978

Hasija, A., & Esper, T. L. (2022). In artificial intelligence (AI) we trust: A qualitative investigation of AI technology acceptance. *Journal of Business Logistics*, *43*(3), 388–412. doi:10.1111/jbl.12301

Hassan, A., Hassan, A. M., & Moaraj, A. A. (2022). The Role of Artificial Intelligence in Entrepreneurship. Retrieved from https://link.springer.com/chapter/10.1007/978-3-030-93464-4_52

Hayes, A. F. (2009). Beyond Baron and Kenny: Statistical mediation analysis in the new millennium. *Communication Monographs*, *76*(4), 408–420. doi:10.1080/03637750903310360

Heinz, E., Kraft, P., Buchen, C., Frede, H. G., Aquino, E., & Breuer, L. (2014). Set up of an automatic water quality sampling system in irrigation agriculture. *Sensors (Basel)*, *14*(1), 212–228. doi:10.3390/s140100212 PMID:24366178

Helo, P., & Hao, Y. (2022). Artificial intelligence in operations management and supply chain management: An exploratory case study. *Production Planning and Control*, *33*(16), 1573–1590. doi:10.1080/09537287.2021.1882690

Henrys, K. (2021). Role of predictive analytics in business. SSRN Electronic Journal. doi:10.2139/ssrn.3829621

Henseler, J., Ringle, C. M., & Sarstedt, M. (2015). A new criterion for assessing discriminant validity in variance-based structural equation modeling. *Journal of the Academy of Marketing Science*, *43*(1), 115–135. doi:10.1007/s11747-014-0403-8

Hettl, M. (2013). *Mitarbeiterführung mit dem LEAD-Navigator® - Erfolgreich und wirksam führen*. Springer Fachmedien Wiesbaden. doi:10.1007/978-3-658-00100-1

Hidayat-Ur-Rehman, I., Ahmad, A., Khan, M. N., & Mokhtar, S. A. (2021). Investigating Mobile Banking Continuance Intention: A Mixed-Methods Approach. *Mobile Information Systems*, *2021*, 1–17. Advance online publication. doi:10.1155/2021/9994990

Hildebrandt, M. (2020). Smart technologies. *Internet Policy Review*, *9*(4). doi:10.14763/2020.4.1531

Hillman, A. J., Withers, M. C., & Collins, B. J. (2009). Resource Dependence Theory: A Review. *Journal of Management*, *35*(6), 1404–1427. doi:10.1177/0149206309343469

Hill, R. (2022). Smart Wearables: The Overlooked and Underrated Essential Worker. *William and Mary Law Review*, *64*, •••. https://heinonline.org/HOL/Page?handle=hein.journals/wmlr64&id=1623&div=&collection=

Hobsbawm, J. (2023). *The Rise of the Solopreneur: Reinvention Is the Key to Career Longevity. Bloomberg.Com, N.* PAG.

Hodges, C. (2015). *Law and corporate behaviour: Integrating theories of regulation, enforcement, compliance and ethics*. Bloomsbury Publishing.

Ho, J. C., Wu, C. G., Lee, C. S., & Pham, T. T. T. (2020). Factors affecting the behavioral intention to adopt mobile banking: An international comparison. *Technology in Society*, *63*, 101360. doi:10.1016/j.techsoc.2020.101360

Hossain, M. A., & Quaddus, M. (2012). *Expectation–Confirmation Theory in Information System Research: A Review and Analysis*. 441–469. doi:10.1007/978-1-4419-6108-2_21

Hossain, S. F. A., Nurunnabi, M., Nadi, A. H., & Ahsan, F. T. (2021). Exploring the Role of AI in K12: Are Robot Teachers Taking Over? In Emerging Realities and the Future of Technology in the Classroom (pp. 120-135). IGI Global.

Hossain, S. F. A., Shan, X., Nurunnabi, M., Tushar, H., Mohsin, A. K. M., & Ahsan, F. T. (2021). Opportunities and challenges of m-learning during the COVID-19 pandemic: A mixed methodology approach. *E-Collaboration Technologies and Strategies for Competitive Advantage Amid Challenging Times*, 210-227.

Hossain, S. F. A., Sofyan, Y., Ushie, A. M., & Srimuang, K. (2022). Exploring the Relationship Between Student Engagement and Authentic Learning During COVID-19: Moderating Role of Lack of Attention via WeChat. *International Journal of e-Collaboration (IJeC)*, *18*(1), 1-20.

Hossain, S. F. A. (2019). Social networking and its role in media entrepreneurship: Evaluating the use of mobile phones in the context of online shopping–A review. [JMME]. *Journal of Media Management and Entrepreneurship*, *1*(1), 73–86. doi:10.4018/JMME.2019010105

Hossain, S. F. A., Khan, R. A., Sohan, M. A. I., Karmoker, T., Asikullah, F., Chakma, P., & Chisty, K. K. S. (2022). Investigating the Role of Social Media on Student Engagement and Authentic Learning during Post COVID-19. In *Virtual Technologies and E-Collaboration for the Future of Global Business* (pp. 68–81). IGI Global. doi:10.4018/978-1-6684-5027-7.ch004

Hossain, S. F. A., Nurunnabi, M., Hussain, K., & Shan, X. (2020). Smartphone-based m-shopping behavior and innovative entrepreneurial tendency among women in emerging Asia. *International Journal of Gender and Entrepreneurship*, *12*(2), 173–189. doi:10.1108/IJGE-03-2019-0054

Hossain, S. F. A., Shan, X., Musa, M., & Rahman, P. (2023). Social media and increased venture creation tendency with innovative ideas: the case of female students in Asia. In *Research Anthology on Applying Social Networking Strategies to Classrooms and Libraries* (pp. 1716–1731). IGI Global.

Hossain, S. F. A., Xi, Z., Nurunnabi, M., & Hussain, K. (2020). Ubiquitous role of social networking in driving M-Commerce: Evaluating the use of mobile phones for online shopping and payment in the context of trust. *SAGE Open*, *10*(3). doi:10.1177/2158244020939536

Hossain, S. F., Nurunnabi, M., Hussain, K., & Saha, S. K. (2019). Effects of variety-seeking intention by mobile phone usage on university students' academic performance. *Cogent Education*, *6*(1), 1574692. doi:10.1080/2331186X.2019.1574692

Hossain, S. F., Shan, X., Nurunnabi, M., Tushar, H., Mohsin, A. K., & Ahsan, F. T. (2021). Opportunities and challenges of M-learning during the COVID-19 pandemic. *Advances in Social Networking and Online Communities*, 210–227. doi:10.4018/978-1-7998-7764-6.ch007

Huang, T., Wang, Y., & Lai, H. (2022). What drives internet entrepreneurial intention to use technology products? An investigation of technology product imagination disposition, social support, and motivation. *Frontiers in Psychology*, *13*, 829256. doi:10.3389/fpsyg.2022.829256 PMID:35369240

Huang, Y. M. (2019). Examining students' continued use of desktop services: Perspectives from expectation-confirmation and social influence. *Computers in Human Behavior*, *96*, 23–31. doi:10.1016/j.chb.2019.02.010

Hubbard, K. G., Rosenberg, N. J., & Nielsen, D. C. (1983). Automated weather data network for agriculture. *Journal of Water Resources Planning and Management*, *109*(3), 213–222. doi:10.1061/(ASCE)0733-9496(1983)109:3(213)

Huđek, I., Tominc, P., & Širec, K. (2020). Entrepreneurship vs. Freelancing: What's the Difference? Our Economy / Nase Gospodarstvo, 66(3), 56–62.

Hundley, G. (2001). Why and when are the self-employed more satisfied with their work? *Industrial Relations*, *40*(2), 293–316. doi:10.1111/0019-8676.00209

Iansiti, M., & Lakhani, K. R. (2020). Competing in the age of AI: How machine intelligence changes the rules of business. *Harvard Business Review*, *98*(1), 60–67.

Iftikhar, N., & Nordbjerg, F. E. (2021). *Adopting Artificial Intelligence in Danish SMEs: Barriers to Become a Data Driven Company.* Its Solutions and Benefits., doi:10.5220/0010691800003062

Ikumoro, A. O., & Jawad, M. S. (2019). Intention to use intelligent conversational agents in e-commerce among Malaysian SMEs: An integrated conceptual framework based on tri-theories including unified theory of acceptance, use of technology (UTAUT), and TOE. *International Journal of Academic Research in Business & Social Sciences*, *9*(11), 205–235. doi:10.6007/IJARBSS/v9-i11/6544

Ingalagi, S. S., Mutkekar, R. R., & Kulkarni, P. M. (2021). Artificial Intelligence (AI) adaptation: Analysis of determinants among Small to Medium-sized Enterprises (SME's). doi:10.1088/1757-899X/1049/1/012017

Ingaldi, M., & Ulewicz, R. (2019). Problems with the Implementation of Industry 4.0 in Enterprises from the SME Sector. Retrieved from doi:10.3390/su12010217

Iranmanesh, M., Min, C. L., Senali, M. G., Nikbin, D., & Foroughi, B. (2022). Determinants of switching intention from web-based stores to retail apps: Habit as a moderator. *Journal of Retailing and Consumer Services*, *66*, 102957. doi:10.1016/j.jretconser.2022.102957

Jabbar, M. A., Tiwari, S., & Ortiz-Rodriguez, F. (2022). *Smart Urban Computing Applications* (1st ed.). River Publishers. doi:10.1201/9781003373247

Jabłońska, M. R., & Pólkowski, Z. (2017). Artificial Intelligence-based processes in SMEs. Retrieved from https://openurl.ebsco.com/EPDB%3Agcd%3A10%3A21868650/detailv2?sid=ebsco%3Aplink%3Ascholar&id=ebsco%3Agcd%3A129396054&crl=c

Jacoby, M. (1991). *Individuation and Narcissism: The Psychology of Self in Jung and Kohut* (1st ed.). Routledge. doi:10.4324/9780203753897

Jafari-Sadeghi, V., Garcia-Perez, A., Candelo, E., & Couturier, J. (2021). Exploring the impact of digital transformation on technology entrepreneurship and technological market expansion: The role of technology readiness, exploration and exploitation. *Journal of Business Research*, *124*, 100–111. doi:10.1016/j.jbusres.2020.11.020

Jagatheesaperumal, S. K., Rahouti, M., Ahmad, K., Al-Fuqaha, A., & Guizani, M. (2021). The duo of artificial intelligence and big data for industry 4.0: Applications, techniques, challenges, and future research directions. *IEEE Internet of Things Journal*, *9*(15), 12861–12885. doi:10.1109/JIOT.2021.3139827

Jain, N. K., Kaul, D., & Sanyal, P. (2022). What drives customers towards mobile shopping? An integrative technology continuance theory perspective. *Asia Pacific Journal of Marketing and Logistics*, *34*(5), 922–943. doi:10.1108/APJML-02-2021-0133

Jalbert, C. L. (2019). *Archaeology in Canada: an analysis of demographics and working conditions in the discipline.* Memorial University of Newfoundland.

Jamwal, A., Agrawal, R., & Sharma, M. (2022). Deep learning for manufacturing sustainability: Models, applications in Industry 4.0 and implications. *International Journal of Information Management Data Insights*, *2*(2), 100107. doi:10.1016/j.jjimei.2022.100107

Janbi, N., Katib, I., Albeshri, A., & Mehmood, R. (2020). Distributed artificial intelligence-as-a-service (DAIaaS) for smarter IoE and 6G environments. *Sensors (Basel)*, *20*(20), 5796. doi:10.3390/s20205796 PMID:33066295

Janovac, T. D., & Đoković, G. (2022). The application of the "leadership grid" model: Case study of human resources sector in the ministry of internal affairs of serbia. *KULTURA POLISA*, *19*(4), 27–45. doi:10.51738/Kpolisa2022.19.4r.27jdj

Jarrahi, M. H. (2018). *Artificial intelligence and the future of work: Human-AI symbiosis in organizational decision making*. Science Direct. doi:10.1016/j.bushor.2018.03.007

JASON. (2017). *Artificial intelligence for health and health care.* Research Gate.

Jayashree, S., Reza, M. N. H., Malarvizhi, C. A., & Mohiuddin, M. (2021). Industry 4.0 implementation and Triple Bottom Line sustainability: An empirical study on small and medium manufacturing firms. *Heliyon*, *7*(8), e07753. doi:10.1016/j.heliyon.2021.e07753 PMID:34430741

Jenneboer, L., Herrando, C., & Constantinides, E. (2022). The impact of chatbots on customer loyalty: A systematic literature review. *Journal of Theoretical and Applied Electronic Commerce Research*, *17*(1), 212–229. doi:10.3390/jtaer17010011

Jiang, Z., Ai, Q., & Hao, R. (2019). Integrated demand response mechanism for industrial energy system based on multi-energy interaction. *IEEE Access : Practical Innovations, Open Solutions*, *7*, 66336–66346. doi:10.1109/ACCESS.2019.2917821

Jian, M. S., & Pan, C. J. (2022). Blockchained industry information handoff based on internet of things devices with intelligent customized object recognition. *Sensors (Basel)*, *22*(6), 2312. doi:10.3390/s22062312 PMID:35336483

Jie, Z., Kun, T., Shisheng, S., & Aiyuan, F. (2001). Portable autocontrol solar photometer. *Liangzi Dianzi Xuebao*, *18*(6), 551–555.

Jisha, R. C., Vignesh, G., & Deekshit, D. (2019). IOT based water level monitoring and implementation on both agriculture and domestic areas. *2nd International Conference on Intelligent Computing, Instrumentation and Control Technologies (ICICICT)* (pp. 1119-1123). Kannur, India: IEEE. 10.1109/ICICICT46008.2019.8993272

Jobin, A., Ienca, M., & Vayena, E. (2019). The global landscape of AI ethics guidelines. *Nature Machine Intelligence*, *1*(9), 389–399. doi:10.1038/s42256-019-0088-2

Jo, E., Epstein, D. A., Jung, H., & Kim, Y.-H. (2023). Understanding the benefits and challenges of deploying conversational AI leveraging large language models for public health intervention. Proceedings of the 2023 CHI Conference on Human Factors in Computing Systems. IEEE.

John, M. M., Olsson, H. H., & Bosch, J. (2023). Towards an AI-driven business development framework: A multi-case study. *Journal of Software (Malden, MA)*, *35*(6), e2432. doi:10.1002/smr.2432

Joshi, S., Sharma, M., Das, R. P., Rosak-Szyrocka, J., Żywiołek, J., Muduli, K., & Prasad, M. (2022). Modeling Conceptual Framework for Implementing Barriers of AI in Public Healthcare for Improving Operational Excellence: Experiences from Developing Countries. *Sustainability (Basel)*, *14*(18), 11698. doi:10.3390/su141811698

Joyce, A., & Paquin, R. L. (2016). The triple layered business model canvas: A tool to design more sustainable business models. *Journal of Cleaner Production*, *135*, 1474–1486. doi:10.1016/j.jclepro.2016.06.067

Jung, C. G. (1969). *Collected Works of C.G. Jung, Volume 9 (Part 1): Archetypes and the Collective Unconscious* (G. Adler & R. F. C. Hull, Eds.). Princeton University Press. https://www.jstor.org/stable/j.ctt5hhrnk

K. W. U. (2021, October 18). 43,000 people in England could have received wrong COVID-19 test results. *USA Today*. https://www.usatoday.com/story/news/world/2021/10/15/england-wrong-covid-19-test-results-thousands-people/8465832002/

Kaçar, I. G. (2021). The impact of online and face-to-face peer feedback on pre-service teachers in EFL academic writing. In *Design Solutions for Adaptive Hypermedia Listening Software* (pp. 124–163). IGI Global. doi:10.4018/978-1-7998-7876-6.ch007

Kang, Y., Cai, Z., Tan, C., Huang, Q., & Liu, H. (2020). Natural language processing (NLP) in management research: A literature review. *Journal of Management Analytics*, *7*(2), 139–172. doi:10.1080/23270012.2020.1756939

Kao, Y. S., Nawata, K., & Huang, C. Y. (2019). An Exploration and Confirmation of the Factors Influencing Adoption of IoT-Based Wearable Fitness Trackers. *International Journal of Environmental Research and Public Health 2019, Vol. 16, Page 3227, 16*(18), 3227. doi:10.3390/ijerph16183227

Kaplan, A. M., & Haenlein, M. (2010). Users of the world, unite! The challenges and opportunities of Social Media. *Business Horizons*, *53*(1), 59–68. doi:10.1016/j.bushor.2009.09.003

Kaplan, A., & Haenlein, M. (2019). Siri, Siri, in my hand: Who's the fairest in the land? On the interpretations, illustrations, and implications of artificial intelligence. *Business Horizons*, *62*(1), 15–25. doi:10.1016/j.bushor.2018.08.004

Kar, A. K. (2016). Bio inspired computing – A review of algorithms and scope of applications. *Expert Systems with Applications*, *59*, 20–32. doi:10.1016/j.eswa.2016.04.018

Kar, A. K., & Kushwaha, A. K. (2023). Facilitators and Barriers of Artificial Intelligence Adoption in Business – Insights from Opinions Using Big Data Analytics. *Information Systems Frontiers*, *25*(4), 1351–1374. doi:10.1007/s10796-021-10219-4

Karjaluoto, H., Shaikh, A. A., Leppäniemi, M., & Luomala, R. (2020). Examining consumers' usage intention of contactless payment systems. *International Journal of Bank Marketing*, *38*(2), 332–351. doi:10.1108/IJBM-04-2019-0155

Kasilingam, D., & Krishna, R. (2022). Understanding the adoption and willingness to pay for internet of things services. *International Journal of Consumer Studies*, *46*(1), 102–131. doi:10.1111/ijcs.12648

Katz, J. (1993). How satisfied are the self-employed: A secondary analysis approach. *Entrepreneurship Theory and Practice*, *17*(3), 35–35. doi:10.1177/104225879301700303

Kaur, S., Ayana, T., & Kaur, H. (2022). Assessing Social and Emotional Competencies of Undergraduates: A Cross-Cultural Study. *Issues and Ideas in Education*, *9*(2), 75–83. doi:10.15415/iie.2021.92007

Kenny, D. A. (2008). Reflections on Mediation. *Organizational Research Methods*, *11*(2), 353–358. doi:10.1177/1094428107308978

Kernecker, M., Seufert, V., & Chapman, M. (2021). Farmer-centered ecological intensification: Using innovation characteristics to identify barriers and opportunities for a transition of agroecosystems towards sustainability. *Agricultural Systems*, *191*, 103142. doi:10.1016/j.agsy.2021.103142

Keswani, B., Mohapatra, A. G., Mohanty, A., Khanna, A., Rodrigues, J. J., Gupta, D., & de Albuquerque, V. H. C. (2019). Adapting weather conditions based IoT enabled smart irrigation technique in precision agriculture mechanisms. *Neural Computing & Applications*, *31*(1), 277–292. doi:10.1007/s00521-018-3737-1

Khanom, M. T. (2023). Business Strategies in The Age of Digital Transformation. *The Journal of Business*, *8*(01), 28–35.

Khan, U., & DePaoli, A. (2023). Brand loyalty in the face of stockouts. *Journal of the Academy of Marketing Science*, •••, 1–31. doi:10.1007/S11747-023-00924-8/FIGURES/1 PMID:37359264

Kim, D. (2018, May 31). Human Ethics for Artificial Intelligent Beings. *AI Strategy & Policy Blog*. https://aistrategyblog.com/category/utilitarianism/

Kim, B. H., Koh, S., Huh, S., Jo, S., & Choi, S. (2020). Improved Explanatory Efficacy on Human Affect and Workload Through Interactive Process in Artificial Intelligence. *IEEE Access : Practical Innovations, Open Solutions*, *8*, 189013–189024. doi:10.1109/ACCESS.2020.3032056

Kim, M. J., Lee, C. K., & Contractor, N. S. (2019). Seniors' usage of mobile social network sites: Applying theories of innovation diffusion and uses and gratifications. *Computers in Human Behavior*, *90*, 60–73. doi:10.1016/j.chb.2018.08.046

Kitchenham, B., Brereton, O. P., Budgen, D., Turner, M., Bailey, J., & Linkman, S. (2009). Systematic literature reviews in software engineering–a systematic literature review. *Information and Software Technology*, *51*(1), 7–15. doi:10.1016/j.infsof.2008.09.009

Kitching, J., & Smallbone, D. (2012). Are freelancers a neglected form of small business? *Journal of Small Business and Enterprise Development*, *19*(1), 74–91. doi:10.1108/14626001211196415

Kitsios, F., & Kamariotou, M. (2021). Artificial intelligence and business strategy towards digital transformation: A research agenda. *Sustainability (Basel)*, *13*(4), 20–25. doi:10.3390/su13042025

Kitsios, F., & Kamariotou, M. (2023). Digital innovation and entrepreneurship transformation through open data hackathons: Design strategies for successful start-up settings. *International Journal of Information Management*, *69*, 102–472. doi:10.1016/j.ijinfomgt.2022.102472

Kline, R. B. (2023). *Principles and practice of structural equiation modeling* (5th ed.). Guilford Press.

Kock, N. (2016). Non-Normality Propagation among Latent Variables and Indicators in PLS-SEM Simulations. *Journal of Modern Applied Statistical Methods; JMASM*, *15*(1), 16. doi:10.22237/jmasm/1462076100

Kolbjørnsrud, V., Amico, R., & Thomas, R. J. (2017). Partnering with AI: How organizations can win over skeptical managers. *Strategy and Leadership*, *45*(1), 37–43. doi:10.1108/SL-12-2016-0085

Kollmann, T., Kleine-Stegemann, L., de Cruppe, K., & Then-Bergh, C. (2022). Eras of digital entrepreneurship: Connecting the past, present, and future. *Business & Information Systems Engineering*, *64*(1), 1–17. doi:10.1007/s12599-021-00728-6

Kolvereid, L. (1996). Organizational employment versus self-employment: Reasons for career choice intentions. *Entrepreneurship Theory and Practice*, *20*(3), 23–32. doi:10.1177/104225879602000302

Kong, S. C., Cheung, W. M. Y., & Tsang, O. (2023). Evaluating an artificial intelligence literacy programme for empowering and developing concepts, literacy and ethical awareness in senior secondary students. *Education and Information Technologies*, *28*(4), 4703–4724. doi:10.1007/s10639-022-11408-7

Kong, S. C., Cheung, W. M. Y., & Zhang, G. (2023). Evaluating an artificial intelligence literacy programme for developing university students' conceptual understanding, literacy, empowerment and ethical awareness. *Journal of Educational Technology & Society*, *26*(1), 16–30.

Kotios, D., Makridis, G., Fatouros, G., & Kyriazis, D. (2022). Deep learning enhancing banking services: A hybrid transaction classification and cash flow prediction approach. *Journal of Big Data*, *9*(1), 100. doi:10.1186/s40537-022-00651-x PMID:36213092

Kozinets, R. V., & Gretzel, U. (2021). Commentary: Artificial Intelligence: The Marketer's Dilemma. *Journal of Marketing*, *85*(1), 156–159. doi:10.1177/0022242920972933

Kozioł-Nadolna, K. (2020). The role of a leader in stimulating innovation in an organization. *Administrative Sciences*, *10*(3), 59. doi:10.3390/admsci10030059

Kraus, M., Feuerriegel, S., & Oztekin, A. (2020). Deep learning in business analytics and operations research: Models, applications and managerial implications. *European Journal of Operational Research*, *281*(3), 628–641. doi:10.1016/j.ejor.2019.09.018

Kshetri, N., & Voas, J. (2020). Blockchain-enabled sharing economy and prospects for its adoption in industries beyond finance. *IEEE Transactions on Engineering Management*, *67*(4), 1165–1178.

Kuar, S., Lim, W. M., Sivarajah, U., & Kaur, J. (2022). Artificial Intelligence and Blockchain Integration in Business: Trends from a Bibliometric-Content Analysis. *Information Systems Frontiers*. doi:10.1007/s10796-022-10279-0 PMID:35431617

Kuhn, T. S. (2012). *The structure of scientific revolutions* (50th ed.). University of Chicago Press. doi:10.7208/chicago/9780226458144.001.0001

Kumar, A., Bhattacharyya, S. S., & Krishnamoorthy, B. (2023). Automation-augmentation paradox in organizational artificial intelligence technology deployment capabilities; an empirical investigation for achieving simultaneous economic and social benefits. *Journal of Enterprise Information Management*.

Kumar, Y., Koul, A., Singla, R., & Ijaz, M. F. (2022). Artificial intelligence in disease diagnosis: a systematic literature review, synthesizing framework and future research agenda. *Journal of Ambient Intelligence and Humanized Computing 2021 14:7*, *14*(7), 8459–8486. doi:10.1007/s12652-021-03612-z

Kumar, M., Raut, R. D., Mangla, S. K., Ferraris, A., & Choubey, V. K. (2022). The adoption of artificial intelligence powered workforce management for effective revenue growth of micro, small, and medium scale enterprises (MSMEs). *Production Planning and Control*, 1–17. doi:10.1080/09537287.2022.2131620

Kumar, V. (2023). Digital Enablers. *Management for Professionals*, (Part F1470), 1–110. doi:10.1007/978-981-19-8148-7_1/COVER

Kusý, Š. (2021). Artificial intelligence as a tool in human research management—potential and current use. *Journal of HRM*, *24*(2).

Laitala, K., Klepp, I. G., Haugrønning, V., Throne-Holst, H., & Strandbakken, P. (2021). Increasing repair of household appliances, mobile phones and clothing: Experiences from consumers and the repair industry. *Journal of Cleaner Production*, *282*, 125349. doi:10.1016/j.jclepro.2020.125349

Lam, H. K. S., Yeung, A. C. L., & Cheng, T. C. E. (2016). The impact of firms' social media initiatives on operational efficiency and innovativeness. *Journal of Operations Management*, *47–48*(1), 28–43. doi:10.1016/j.jom.2016.06.001

Lee, D. (2019). Effects of Key Value Co-creation Elements in the Healthcare System: Focusing on Technology Applications. *Service Business*, *13*(2), 389–417. doi:10.1007/s11628-018-00388-9

Lee, D., & Yoon, S. N. (2021). Application of Artificial Intelligence-Based Technologies in the Healthcare Industry: Opportunities and Challenges. *International Journal of Environmental Research and Public Health*, *18*(1), 271. doi:10.3390/ijerph18010271 PMID:33401373

Lee, S. M., & Lee, D. H. (2020). Healthcare wearable devices: An analysis of key factors for continuous use intention. *Service Business*, *14*(4), 503–531. doi:10.1007/s11628-020-00428-3

Lei, J. (2022). On the effective representation of teachers' leadership role from the change of children's emotional behavior in language learning. *The International Journal of Neuropsychopharmacology*, *25*(Supplement_1), A59–A60. doi:10.1093/ijnp/pyac032.082

Lemos, S. I., Ferreira, F. A., Zopounidis, C., Galariotis, E., & Ferreira, N. (2022). Artificial intelligence and change management in small and medium-sized enterprises: an analysis of dynamics within adaptation initiatives. Retrieved from https://link.springer.com/article/10.1007/s10479-022-05159-4

Lévesque, M., Obschonka, M., & Nambisan, S. (2020). Pursuing Impactful Entrepreneurship Research Using. *Artificial Intelligence*. Advance online publication. doi:10.1177/1042258720927369

Li, J., Ma, R., Mailthody, V. S., Samplawski, C., Marlin, B., Chen, S., . . . Abdelzaher, T. (2021, November). Towards an accurate latency model for convolutional neural network layers on gpus. In MILCOM 2021-2021 IEEE Military Communications Conference (MILCOM) (pp. 904-909). IEEE. doi:10.1109/MILCOM52596.2021.9652907

Li, C., & Wang, J., Wang, S., & Zhang, Y. (. (2024). A review of IoT applications in healthcare. *Neurocomputing*, *565*, 127017. doi:10.1016/j.neucom.2023.127017

Li, L., Du, K., Zhang, W., & Mao, J.-Y. (2023). Empowering digital transformation: The roles of platforms. *Journal of Information Technology*, *0*(0), 02683962231219520. Advance online publication. doi:10.1177/02683962231219520

Li, L., Lee, K. Y., Emokpae, E., & Yang, S. B. (2021). What makes you continuously use chatbot services? Evidence from chinese online travel agencies. *Electronic Markets*, *31*(3), 575–599. doi:10.1007/s12525-020-00454-z PMID:35603227

Lim, S. (2023). *3 Types of Customer Insights That AI Will Change in 2021* [Blog]. Remesh. https://blog.remesh.ai/3-massive-ways-ai-is-changing-consumer-insights-in-2019

Lim, X.-J., Cheah, J.-H., Ng, S. I., Basha, N. K., & Liu, Y. (2021). Are men from Mars, women from Venus? Examining gender differences towards continuous use intention of branded apps. *Journal of Retailing and Consumer Services*, *60*, 102422. doi:10.1016/j.jretconser.2020.102422

Lindsey, J. L. (2016). How Can Leaders Cultivate an Organizational Culture of Creativity and Innovation, Particularly in the Academy? *Journal of Leadership Studies*, *10*(1), 76–77. doi:10.1002/jls.21454

Li, S., Cui, J., & Li, Z. (2011). Wireless sensor network for precise agriculture monitoring. *Fourth International Conference on Intelligent Computation Technology and Automation.* 1, pp. 307-310. Shenzhen, China: IEEE. 10.1109/ICICTA.2011.87

Liu, G., & Ma, W. (2022). A quantum artificial neural network for stock closing price prediction. *Information Sciences*, *598*, 75–85. doi:10.1016/j.ins.2022.03.064

Liu, W., Xu, Y., Wu, C., & Luo, Y. (2023). Fortune favors the experienced: Entrepreneurs' internet-era imprint, digital entrepreneurship and venture capital. *Information Processing & Management*, *60*(4), 103406. doi:10.1016/j.ipm.2023.103406

Liu, X., & Kao, Z. (2022). Research on influencing factors of customer satisfaction of e-commerce of characteristic agricultural products. *Procedia Computer Science*, *199*, 1505–1512. doi:10.1016/j.procs.2022.01.192

Liu, Y., Chin, W. L., Nechita, F., & Candrea, A. N. (2020). Framing film-induced tourism into a sustainable perspective from Romania, Indonesia and Malaysia. *Sustainability (Basel)*, *12*(23), 9910. doi:10.3390/su12239910

Loebbecke, C., & Picot, A. (2015). Reflections on societal and business model transformation arising from digitization and big data analytics: A research agenda. *The Journal of Strategic Information Systems*, *24*(3), 149–157. doi:10.1016/j.jsis.2015.08.002

Lo, F. Y., & Peng, J. X. (2022). Strategies for successful personal branding of celebrities on social media platforms: Involvement or information sharing? *Psychology and Marketing*, *39*(2), 320–330. doi:10.1002/mar.21597

Loughlin, M., & Copeland, S. M. (2021). Humans, machines and decisions: Clinical reasoning in the age of artificial intelligence, evidence-based medicine and Covid-19. *Journal of Evaluation in Clinical Practice*, *27*(3), 475–477. doi:10.1111/jep.13572 PMID:33890703

Loureiro, S. M. C., Guerreiro, J., & Tussyadiah, I. (2021). Artificial intelligence in business: State of the art and future research agenda. *Journal of Business Research*, *129*, 911–926. doi:10.1016/j.jbusres.2020.11.001

Love, J. H., & Roper, S. (2015). SME innovation, exporting and growth: A review of existing evidence. *International Small Business Journal*, *33*(1), 28–48. doi:10.1177/0266242614550190

Lund, N. F., Cohen, S. A., & Scarles, C. (2018). The power of social media storytelling in destination branding. *Journal of Destination Marketing & Management*, *8*, 271–280. doi:10.1016/j.jdmm.2017.05.003

Lu, X., Wijayaratna, K., Huang, Y., & Qiu, A. (2022). AI-enabled opportunities and transformation challenges for SMEs in the post-pandemic era: A review and research agenda. *Frontiers in Public Health*, *10*, 885067. doi:10.3389/fpubh.2022.885067 PMID:35570947

Mababu, R., & Merino-Hijosa, A. (2015). Solo-entrepreneurs and Motivation of Business Development in Technology Industry. *International Journal of Business and Management*, *3*, 202–2010.

Madan, R., & Ashok, M. (2023). AI adoption and diffusion in public administration: A systematic literature review and future research agenda. *Government Information Quarterly*, *40*(1), 101774. doi:10.1016/j.giq.2022.101774

Madan, S., Pérez-Morón, J., Chua, X. N., Kee, D. M. H., Chua, J., Chua, K. Z., Chuah, Y. W., & Vidal, L. D. S. (2022). Analysis of the Shopee's Strategies to Succeed in the Global E-commerce Market: Malaysia Case. [IJTHAP]. *International Journal of Tourism and Hospitality in Asia Pasific*, *5*(1), 34–48. doi:10.32535/ijthap.v5i1.1400

Madi Odeh, R. B. S., Obeidat, B. Y., Jaradat, M. O., Masa'deh, R., & Alshurideh, M. T. (2023). The transformational leadership role in achieving organizational resilience through adaptive cultures: The case of Dubai service sector. *International Journal of Productivity and Performance Management*, *72*(2), 440–468. doi:10.1108/IJPPM-02-2021-0093

Ma, H., Gao, Q., Li, X., & Zhang, Y. (2022). AI development and employment skill structure: A case study of China. *Economic Analysis and Policy*, *73*, 242–254. doi:10.1016/j.eap.2021.11.007

Maheshwari, S., Gautam, P., & Jaggi, C. K. (2021). Role of Big Data Analytics in supply chain management: Current trends and future perspectives. *International Journal of Production Research*, *59*(6), 1875–1900. doi:10.1080/00207543.2020.1793011

Maican, C. I., Sumedrea, S., Tecau, A., Nichifor, E., Chitu, I. B., Lixandroiu, R., & Brătucu, G. (2023). Factors Influencing the Behavioural Intention to Use AI-Generated Images in Business: A UTAUT2 Perspective with Moderators. *Journal of Organizational and End User Computing*, *35*(1), 1–32. doi:10.4018/JOEUC.330019

Mai, N. (2022). THE MERLIN PROJECT: MALAYSIAN STUDENTS'ACCEPTANCE OF AN AI CHATBOT IN THEIR LEARNING PROCESS. *Turkish Online Journal of Distance Education*, *23*(3), 31–48. doi:10.17718/tojde.1137122

Maini, S. (2022). Leadership Transformation in Changing Times. *International Journal for Global Academic & Scientific Research*, *1*(4), 48–59. doi:10.55938/ijgasr.v1i4.29

Malhi, A. S., Kovid, R. K., & Kanika. (2023). *Wearable Technologies for Health: Investigating Behavioral Intention to Adopt Cloud-Based Smartwatch*. 197–214. doi:10.1007/978-981-99-1620-7_16

Manika, D., Antonetti, P., Papagiannidis, S., & Guo, X. (2021). How Pride Triggered by Pro-environmental Technology Adoption Spills Over into Conservation Behaviours: A Social Business Application. *Technological Forecasting and Social Change*, *172*, 121005. doi:10.1016/j.techfore.2021.121005

Marakhimov, A., & Joo, J. (2017). Consumer adaptation and infusion of wearable devices for healthcare. *Computers in Human Behavior*, *76*, 135–148. doi:10.1016/j.chb.2017.07.016

Martikkala, A., David, J., Lobov, A., Lanz, M., & Ituarte, I. F. (2021). Trends for low-cost and open-source iot solutions development for Industry 4.0. *Procedia Manufacturing*, *55*, 298–305. doi:10.1016/j.promfg.2021.10.042

Martín-Rojas, R., Garrido-Moreno, A., & García-Morales, V. J. (2020). Fostering Corporate Entrepreneurship with the use of social media tools. *Journal of Business Research*, *112*, 396–412. doi:10.1016/j.jbusres.2019.11.072

Marvin, G., Tamale, M., Kanagwa, B., & Jjingo, D. (2023). Philosophical Review of Artificial Intelligence for Society 5.0. In *Proceedings of International Conference on Paradigms of Communication, Computing and Data Analytics*. DOI: 10.1007/978-981-99-4626-6_1

Maselli, A., Gordon, J., Eluchans, M., Lancia, G. L., Thiery, T., Moretti, R., Cisek, P., & Pezzulo, G. (2023). Beyond simple laboratory studies: Developing sophisticated models to study rich behavior. *Physics of Life Reviews*, *46*, 220–244. doi:10.1016/j.plrev.2023.07.006 PMID:37499620

Masood, T., & Sonntag, P. (2020). Industry 4.0: Adoption challenges and benefits for SMEs. *Computers in Industry*, *121*, 103261. doi:10.1016/j.compind.2020.103261

Mathavan, B., Vafaei-Zadeh, A., Hanifah, H., Ramayah, T., & Kurnia, S. (2024). Understanding the purchase intention of fitness wearables: Using value-based adoption model. *Asia-Pacific Journal of Business Administration*, *16*(1), 101–126. doi:10.1108/APJBA-04-2022-0166

Mehta, P., Jebarajakirthy, C., Maseeh, H. I., Anubha, A., Saha, R., & Dhanda, K. (2022). Artificial intelligence in marketing: A meta-analytic review. *Psychology and Marketing*, *39*(11), 2013–2038. doi:10.1002/mar.21716

Melumad, S., Hadi, R., Hildebrand, C., & Ward, A. F. (2020). Technology-Augmented Choice: How Digital Innovations Are Transforming Consumer Decision Processes. *Customer Needs and Solutions 2020 7:3*, *7*(3), 90–101. doi:10.1007/s40547-020-00107-4

Merhi, M. I. (2023). An evaluation of the critical success factors impacting artificial intelligence implementation. *International Journal of Information Management*, *69*, 102545. doi:10.1016/j.ijinfomgt.2022.102545

Mijwil, M. M., Hiran, K. K., Doshi, R., Dadhich, M., Al-Mistarehi, A. H., & Bala, I. (2023). ChatGPT and the future of academic integrity in the artificial intelligence era: A new frontier. *Al-Salam Journal for Engineering and Technology*, *2*(2), 116–127. doi:10.55145/ajest.2023.02.02.015

Milton, J., & Al-Busaidi, A. (2023). New Role of Leadership in AI Era: Educational Sector. In *SHS Web of Conferences* (*Vol. 156*, p. 09005). EDP Sciences. 10.1051/shsconf/202315609005

Minh, N. V., Badir, Y. F., Quang, N. N., & Afsar, B. (2017). The impact of leaders' technical competence on employees' innovation and learning. *Journal of Engineering and Technology Management*, *44*, 44–57. doi:10.1016/j.jengtecman.2017.03.003

Misra, S. K., Sharma, S. K., Gupta, S., & Das, S. (2023). A framework to overcome challenges to the adoption of artificial intelligence in Indian Government Organizations. *Technological Forecasting and Social Change*, *194*, 122721. doi:10.1016/j.techfore.2023.122721

Mitchell, M., Wu, S., Zaldivar, A., Barnes, P., Vasserman, L., Hutchinson, B., & Gebru, T. (2019). Model Cards for Model Reporting. *Conference on Neural Information Processing Systems (NeurIPS)*. Research Gate.

Mitrica, I., Pic, X., San Antonio, E. G., Dimopoulou, M., & Antonini, M. (2022, June). Efficient classification of DNA reads for robust decoding of data stored in synthetic DNA. In Munich Workshop on Coding and Cryptography 2022,1-5.

Mizrahi, O. (2018). Succeeding as a Solopreneur. (cover story). *Home Business Magazine: The Home-Based Entrepreneur's Magazine*, *25*(3), 24–26.

Mnih, V., Kavukcuoglu, K., Silver, D., Rusu, A. A., Veness, J., Bellemare, M. G., Graves, A., Riedmiller, M., Fidjeland, A. K., Ostrovski, G., Petersen, S., Beattie, C., Sadik, A., Antonoglou, I., King, H., Kumaran, D., Wierstra, D., Legg, S., & Hassabis, D. (2015). Human-level control through deep reinforcement learning. *Nature*, *518*(7540), 529–533. doi:10.1038/nature14236 PMID:25719670

Moeuf, A., Lamouri, S., Pellerin, R., Tamayo, S., Tobon-Valencia, E., & Eburdy, R. (2019). Identification of critical success factors, risks and opportunities of Industry 4.0 in SMEs. *International Journal of Production Research*, *58*(5), 1384–1400. doi:10.1080/00207543.2019.1636323

Mogaji, E., Balakrishnan, J., Nwoba, A. C., & Nguyen, N. P. (2021). Emerging-market consumers' interactions with banking chatbots. *Telematics and Informatics*, *65*, 101711. doi:10.1016/j.tele.2021.101711

Mohamed, I. A., & Otman, N. M. M. (2021). Exploring the link between organizational learning and transformational leadership: A review. *OAlib*, *8*(5), 1–19. doi:10.4236/oalib.1107242

Mohsin, A. K., Hongzhen, L., & Hossain, S. F. A. (2021). Impact of COVID-19 pandemic on consumer economy: Countermeasures analysis. Journal Name. Advance online publication. doi:10.1177/21582440211008875

Mondal, S., Das, S., & Vrana, V. G. (2023). How to bell the cat? A theoretical review of generative artificial intelligence towards digital disruption in all walks of life. *Technologies*, *11*(2), 44. doi:10.3390/technologies11020044

Moon, N. W., Baker, P. M., & Goughnour, K. (2019). Designing wearable technologies for users with disabilities: Accessibility, usability, and connectivity factors. Https://Doi.Org/10.1177/2055668319862137, *6*, 205566831986213. doi:10.1177/2055668319862137

Morandini, S., Fedrico, F., De Angelis, M., Puzzo, G., Giusino, D., & Pietrantoni, L. (2023). The impact of artificial intelligence on workers' skills: Upskilling and reskilling in organisations. *Informing Science*, *26*, 39–68. doi:10.28945/5078

Morozova, D. (2021). *Practice Theory Approach to Wearable Technology*. Implications for Sustainability., doi:10.54337/aau478414012

Morrison-Smith, S., & Ruiz, J. (2020). Challenges and barriers in virtual teams: A literature review. *SN Applied Sciences*, *2*(6), 1–33. doi:10.1007/s42452-020-2801-5

Mou, X. (2019). Artificial intelligence: Investment trends and selected industry uses. International Finance Corporation, 8.

Mozaheb, A., Alamolhodaei, S. M. A., & Ardakani, M. F. (2015). Effect of customer relationship management (CRM) on performance of small-medium sized enterprises (SMEs) using structural equations model (SEM). International Journal of Academic Research in Accounting. *Finance and Management Sciences*, *5*(2), 42–52.

Mughal, A. A. (2018). Artificial Intelligence in Information Security: Exploring the Advantages, Challenges, and Future Directions. *Journal of Artificial Intelligence and Machine Learning in Management*, *2*(1), 22–34.

Muhuri, P. K., Shukla, A. K., & Abraham, A. (2019). Industry 4.0: A bibliometric analysis and detailed overview. Retrieved from doi:10.1016/j.engappai.2018.11.007

Müller, J. M., Buliga, O., & Voigt, K.-I. (2018). Fortune favors the prepared: How SMEs approach business model innovations in Industry 4.0. *Technological Forecasting and Social Change*, *132*, 2–17. doi:10.1016/j.techfore.2017.12.019

Mumford, M. D., Todd, E. M., Higgs, C., & McIntosh, T. (2017). Cognitive skills and leadership performance: The nine critical skills. *The Leadership Quarterly*, *28*(1), 24–39. doi:10.1016/j.leaqua.2016.10.012

MungoliN. (2023). *Scalable, Distributed AI Frameworks: Leveraging Cloud Computing for Enhanced Deep Learning Performance and Efficiency*. arXiv:2304.13738.

Munir, S., Shakeel, M., & Waheed, K. Z. (2023). The Importance of Emotional Intelligence for Transformational Leaders: A Critical Analysis. *Pakistan Journal of Humanities and Social Sciences*, *11*(1), 332–339. doi:10.52131/pjhss.2023.1101.0353

Murray, S. (2018). *As Global Leader in Digital Transformation Market Research, IDC Reveals Worldwide Digital Transformation Predictions. International Data Corporation*. IDC.

Musikanski, L., Rakova, B., Bradbury, J., Phillips, R., & Manson, M. (2020). Artificial intelligence and community well-being: A proposal for an emerging area of research. *International Journal of Community Well-being*, *3*(1), 39–55. doi:10.1007/s42413-019-00054-6

Nadi, A. H., Hossain, S. F. A., Hasan, A. M., Sofin, M. R., Shabab, S., Sohan, M. A. I., & Yuan, C. (2023). Discovering the Role of M-Learning Among Finance Students: The Future of Online Education. In *Novel Financial Applications of Machine Learning and Deep Learning: Algorithms, Product Modeling, and Applications* (pp. 183–196). Springer International Publishing. doi:10.1007/978-3-031-18552-6_11

Naeem, M., & Ozuem, W. (2021). Understanding the social consumer fashion brand engagement journey: Insights about reputed fashion brands. *Journal of Brand Management*, *28*(5), 510–525. doi:10.1057/s41262-021-00239-5

Nagaraj, A. (2021). *Introduction to Sensors in IoT and Cloud Computing Applications*. Bentham Science Publishers. doi:10.2174/97898114793591210101

Nagy, L. B., Unger-Plasek, B., Lakner, Z., & Temesi, Á. (2023). Confidence in organic food: a cross-country choice based conjoint analysis of credibility factors. *Humanities and Social Sciences Communications 2023 10:1, 10*(1), 1–11. doi:10.1057/s41599-023-02293-7

Nambisan, S. (2017). Digital Entrepreneurship: Toward a Digital Technology Perspective of Entrepreneurship. *Entrepreneurship Theory and Practice*, *41*(6), 1029–1055. doi:10.1111/etap.12254

Nambisan, S., Wright, M., & Feldman, M. (2019). The digital transformation of innovation and entrepreneurship: Progress, challenges and key themes. *Research Policy*, *48*(8), 103–773. doi:10.1016/j.respol.2019.03.018

Nanayakkara, N. W. O. K. D. S. P., & Dissanayake, D. M. R. (2020). Application of social media for personal branding: A conceptual review. *International Journal of Business and Management*.

Nascimento, B., Oliveira, T., & Tam, C. (2018). Wearable technology: What explains continuance intention in smartwatches? *Journal of Retailing and Consumer Services*, *43*, 157–169. doi:10.1016/j.jretconser.2018.03.017

Nasharuddin, N. A., Sharef, N. M., Mansor, E. I., Samian, N., Murad, M. A. A., Omar, M. K., Arshad, N. I., Shahbodin, F., & Marhaban, M. H. (2021). Designing an Educational Chatbot: A Case Study of CikguAIBot. *2021 Fifth International Conference on Information Retrieval and Knowledge Management (CAMP).*

Nasiri, M., Ukko, J., Saunila, M., & Rantala, T. (2020). Managing the digital supply chain: The role of smart technologies. *Technovation*, *96*, 102121. doi:10.1016/j.technovation.2020.102121

Nassar, A., & Kamal, M. (2021). Ethical Dilemmas in AI-Powered Decision-Making: A Deep Dive into Big Data-Driven Ethical Considerations. *International Journal of Responsible Artificial Intelligence*, *11*(8), 1–11. https://neuralslate.com/index.php/Journal-of-Responsible-AI/article/view/43

Nawandar, N. K., & Satpute, V. R. (2019). IoT based low cost and intelligent module for smart irrigation system. *Computers and Electronics in Agriculture*, *162*, 979–990. doi:10.1016/j.compag.2019.05.027

Ng, M., Coopamootoo, K. P., Toreini, E., Aitken, M., Elliot, K., & van Moorsel, A. (2020). Simulating the effects of social presence on trust, privacy concerns & usage intentions in automated bots for finance. *2020 IEEE European Symposium on Security and Privacy Workshops* (EuroS&PW). IEEE.

Nguyen, T. T., Nguyen, Q. V. H., Nguyen, D. T., Yang, S., Eklund, P. W., Huynh-The, T., & Hsu, E. B. (2020). Artificial intelligence in the battle against coronavirus (COVID-19): a survey and future research directions. *arXiv preprint arXiv:2008.07343.*

Nguyen, A., Ngo, H. N., Hong, Y., Dang, B., & Nguyen, B. P. T. (2023). Ethical principles for artificial intelligence in education. *Education and Information Technologies*, *28*(4), 4221–4241. doi:10.1007/s10639-022-11316-w PMID:36254344

Niemimaa, M., Järveläinen, J., Heikkilä, M., & Heikkilä, J. (2019). Business continuity of business models: Evaluating the resilience of business models for contingencies. *International Journal of Information Management*, *49*, 208–216. doi:10.1016/j.ijinfomgt.2019.04.010

Niet, I., Van den Berghe, L., & van Est, R. (2023). Societal impacts of AI integration in the EU electricity market: The Dutch case. *Technological Forecasting and Social Change*, *192*, 122554. doi:10.1016/j.techfore.2023.122554

Niknejad, N., Ismail, W. B., Mardani, A., Liao, H., & Ghani, I. (2020). A comprehensive overview of smart wearables: The state of the art literature, recent advances, and future challenges. *Engineering Applications of Artificial Intelligence*, *90*, 103529. doi:10.1016/j.engappai.2020.103529

Nitzl, C., Roldan, J. L., & Cepeda, G. (2016). Mediation analysis in partial least squares path modeling: Helping researchers discuss more sophisticated models. *Industrial Management & Data Systems*, *116*(9), 1849–1864. doi:10.1108/IMDS-07-2015-0302

Nižetić, S., Šolić, P., Artaza, D. L., & Patrono, L. (2020). *Internet of Things (IoT): Opportunities, issues and challenges towards a smart and sustainable future.* Science Direct. doi:10.1016/j.jclepro.2020.122877

Northouse, P. G. (2021). *Leadership: Theory and practice*. Sage Publications.

Nuffielld Council on Bioethics. (2018). *Artificial intelligence (AI) in healthcare and research.* Nuffield Council on Bioethics.

O'hagan, J., Saeghe, P., Gugenheimer, J., Medeiros, D., Marky, K., Khamis, M., & Mcgill, M. (2023). Privacy-Enhancing Technology and Everyday Augmented Reality. *Proceedings of the ACM on Interactive, Mobile, Wearable and Ubiquitous Technologies*, *6*(4), 1–35. Advance online publication. doi:10.1145/3569501

Obermeyer, Z., Powers, B., Vogeli, C., & Mullainathan, S. (2019). Dissecting racial bias in an algorithm used to manage the health of populations. *Science*, *366*(6464), 447–453. doi:10.1126/science.aax2342 PMID:31649194

Obschonka, M., & Audretsch, D. B. (2020). Artificial intelligence and big data in entrepreneurship: a new era has begun. Retrieved from doi:10.1007/s11187-019-00202-4

Ogawa, K., & Tanaka, T. (2013). The global financial crisis and small-and medium-sized enterprises in Japan: How did they cope with the crisis? *Small Business Economics*, *41*(2), 401–417. doi:10.1007/s11187-012-9434-z

Olan, F., Ogiemwonyi Arakpogun, E., Suklan, J., Nakpodia, F., Damij, N., & Jayawickrama, U. (2022). Artificial intelligence and knowledge sharing: Contributing factors to organizational performance. performance. *Journal of Business Research*, *145*, 605–615. doi:10.1016/j.jbusres.2022.03.008

Olanrewaju, A. S. T., Hossain, M. A., Whiteside, N., & Mercieca, P. (2020). Social media and entrepreneurship research: A literature review. *International Journal of Information Management*, *50*, 90–110. doi:10.1016/j.ijinfomgt.2019.05.011

Ortiz-de-Mandojana, N., & Bansal, P. (2016). The long-term benefits of organizational resilience through sustainable business practices. *Strategic Management Journal*, *37*(8), 1615–1631. doi:10.1002/smj.2410

Oyedele, A., Saldivar, R., Hernandez, M. D., & Goenner, E. (2018). Modeling satisfaction and repurchase intentions of mobile smart wristbands: The role of social mindfulness and perceived value. *Young Consumers*, *19*(3), 237–250. doi:10.1108/YC-09-2017-00737

Paiola, M., & Gebauer, H. (2020). *Internet of things technologies, digital servitization and business model innovation in BtoB manufacturing firms*. Science Direct. doi:10.1016/j.indmarman.2020.03.009

Pai, V., & Chandra, S. (2022). Exploring factors influencing organizational adoption of artificial intelligence (AI) in corporate social responsibility (CSR) initiatives. *Pacific Asia Journal of the Association for Information Systems*, *14*(5), 4. doi:10.17705/1pais.14504

Pal, D., Funilkul, S., & Vanijja, V. (2020). The future of smartwatches: Assessing the end-users' continuous usage using an extended expectation-confirmation model. *Universal Access in the Information Society*, *19*(2), 261–281. doi:10.1007/s10209-018-0639-z

Pallathadka, H., Ramirez-Asis, E. H., Loli-Poma, T. P., Kaliyaperumal, K., Ventayen, R. J., & Naved, M. (2023). Applications of artificial intelligence in business management, e-Commerce and finance. *Materials Today: Proceedings*, *80*, 2610–2613. doi:10.1016/j.matpr.2021.06.419

Palmié, M., Wincent, J., Parida, V., & Caglar, U. (2020). *The evolution of the financial technology ecosystem: An introduction and agenda for future research on disruptive innovations in ecosystems*. Science Direct. doi:10.1016/j.techfore.2019.119779

Pamungkas, M. R., Asyivadibrata, A., Susilawati, T., & Huda, M. N. (2023). Unleashing the Potentials of Artificial Intelligence for Micro, Small, and Medium Enterprises: A Systematic Literature Review. Retrieved from doi:10.47233/jteksis.v5i3.860

Pandey, P., & Litoriya, R. (2020). Implementing healthcare services on a large scale: Challenges and remedies based on blockchain technology. *Health Policy and Technology*, *9*(1), 69–78. doi:10.1016/j.hlpt.2020.01.004

Pantano, E., & Serravalle, F. (2022). *The Role of Smart Technologies in Decision Making: Developing, Supporting and Training Smart Consumers* (1st ed.). Routledge. doi:10.4324/9781003307105

Park, E. (2020). User acceptance of smart wearable devices: An expectation-confirmation model approach. *Telematics and Informatics*, *47*, 101318. doi:10.1016/j.tele.2019.101318

Pathak, S., & Solanki, V. K. (2021). Impact of internet of things and artificial intelligence on human resource development. *Further advances in internet of things in biomedical and cyber physical systems*, (pp. 239-267). Springer. doi:10.1007/978-3-030-57835-0_19

Paul, D., Sanap, G., Shenoy, S., Kalyane, D., Kalia, K., & Tekade, R. K. (2021). Artificial intelligence in drug discovery and development. *Drug Discovery Today*, *26*(1), 80–93. doi:10.1016/j.drudis.2020.10.010 PMID:33099022

PBS NewsHour. (2022, February 3). *In Africa at-home COVID tests are scarce and expensive, help may not come until next year.* https://www.pbs.org/newshour/world/in-africa-at-home-covid-tests-are-scarce-and-expensive-help-may-not-come-until-next-year

Pearce, J. M. (2018). Ensuring technical competency for management of research-focused organizations. *The Journal of High Technology Management Research*, *29*(2), 172–180. doi:10.1016/j.hitech.2018.09.002

Peifer, Y., Jeske, T., & Hille, S. (2022). Artificial intelligence and its impact on leaders and leadership. *Procedia Computer Science*, *200*, 1024–1030. doi:10.1016/j.procs.2022.01.301

Pendleton, D., Derbyshire, P., & Hodgkinson, C. (2021). Leadership in the Fourth Industrial Age. In *Work-Life Matters* (pp. 125–141). Palgrave Macmillan., doi:10.1007/978-3-030-77768-5_9

Pernapati, K. (2018). IoT based low cost smart irrigation system. *Second International Conference on Inventive Communication and Computational Technologies (ICICCT)* (pp. 1312- 1315). Coimbatore, India: IEEE. 10.1109/ICICCT.2018.8473292

Perumal, S., Qing, Y., & Jaganathan, M. (2022). Factors influencing attitudes and intentions towards smart retail technology. *International Journal of Data and Network Science*, *6*(2), 595–602.

Pettit, T. J., Croxton, K. L., & Fiksel, J. (2019). *The Evolution of Resilience in Supply Chain Management: A Retrospective on Ensuring Supply Chain Resilience.* Science Direct. doi:10.1111/jbl.12202

Pfau, W., & Rimpp, P. (2021). AI-enhanced business models for digital entrepreneurship. *Digital Entrepreneurship: Impact on Business and Society*, 121-140.

Pfau, W., &Rimpp, P. (2021). AI-enhanced business models for digital entrepreneurship. *Digital Entrepreneurship: Impact on Business and Society*, 121-140.

Phuyal, S., Bista, D., & Bista, R. (2020). Challenges, opportunities and future directions of smart manufacturing: A state of art review. *Sustainable Futures : An Applied Journal of Technology, Environment and Society*, *2*, 100023. doi:10.1016/j.sftr.2020.100023

Pierog, A. (2023). Instead of competencies, leadership qualities are a new direction in leadership development. *GiLE Journal of Skills Development*, *3*(1), 3–6. doi:10.52398/gjsd.2023.v3.i1.pp3-6

Pilkerton, C., & Gandhi, S. (2023). *Lenders need to understand that self-employment is the new employment. American Banker, N.* PAG.

Pillaisetty, R., & Mishra, P. (2022). A Review of AI (Artificial Intelligence) Tools and Customer Experience in Online Fashion Retail. *International Journal of E-Business Research*, *18*(2), 1–12. doi:10.4018/IJEBR.294111

Popkova, E. G., & Sergi, B. S. (2020). Human capital and AI in industry 4.0.Convergence and divergence in social entrepreneurship in Russia. *Journal of Intellectual Capital*, *21*(4), 565–581. doi:10.1108/JIC-09-2019-0224

Prasetyo, P. E., & Setyadharma, A. (2022). Digitalization Technology for Sustainable Rural Entrepreneurship and Inequality. *Journal of Human Resource and Sustainability Studies*, *10*(3), 464–484. doi:10.4236/jhrss.2022.103028

Priporas, C. V., Stylos, N., & Fotiadis, A. K. (2017). *Generation Z consumers' expectations of interactions in smart retailing: A future agenda.* Science Direct. doi:10.1016/j.chb.2017.01.058

Puckett, C. (2022). Digital Adaptability: A new measure for digital inequality research. *Social Science Computer Review, 40*(3), 641–662. doi:10.1177/0894439320926087

Purohit, S., Arora, R., & Paul, J. (2022). The bright side of online consumer behavior: Continuance intention for mobile payments. *Journal of Consumer Behaviour, 21*(3), 523–542. doi:10.1002/cb.2017

Qazi, A., Tamjidyamcholo, A., Raj, R. G., Hardaker, G., & Standing, C. (2017). Assessing consumers' satisfaction and expectations through online opinions: Expectation and disconfirmation approach. *Computers in Human Behavior, 75*, 450–460. doi:10.1016/j.chb.2017.05.025

Quévat, A., & Heinze, A. (2020). The digital transformation of preventive telemedicine in France based on the use of connected wearable devices. *Global Business and Organizational Excellence, 39*(6), 17–27. doi:10.1002/joe.22054

Quinn, R. E., & Spreitzer, G. M. (1997). The road to empowerment: Seven questions every leader should consider. *Organizational Dynamics, 26*(2), 37–49. doi:10.1016/S0090-2616(97)90004-8

Qu, S., Shi, H., Zhao, H., Yu, L., & Yu, Y. (2021). Research on enterprise business model and technology innovation based on artificial intelligence. *EURASIP Journal on Wireless Communications and Networking, 2021*(1), 145. doi:10.1186/s13638-021-02025-y PMID:34249123

Qu, T., Lei, S. P., Wang, Z. Z., Nie, D. X., Chen, X., & Huang, G. Q. (2016). IoT-based real-time production logistics synchronization system under smart cloud manufacturing. *International Journal of Advanced Manufacturing Technology, 84*(1–4), 147–164. doi:10.1007/s00170-015-7220-1

R. S. N. A. (2018). *RSNA 2018 Newsroom Schedule.* RSNA. Available online: https://press.rsna.org/timssnet/media/rsna/newsroom2018.cfm

Rabaa'i, A. A., & ALMaati, S. A. (2021). Exploring the Determinants of Users' Continuance Intention to Use Mobile Banking Services in Kuwait : Extending the Expectation-Confirmation Model. *Asia Pacific Journal of Information Systems, 31*(2), 141–184. https://www.earticle.net/Article/A396167

Rabaa'i, A. A., ALmaati, S. A., & Zhu, X. (. (2021). Students' continuance intention to use Moodle: An expectation-confirmation model approach. *Interdisciplinary Journal of Information, Knowledge, and Management, 16*, 397. doi:10.28945/4842

Raddey Kummitha, R. K. (2018). Entrepreneurial urbanism and technological panacea: Why Smart City planning needs to go beyond corporate visioning? *Technological Forecasting and Social Change, 137*, 330–339. doi:10.1016/j.techfore.2018.07.010

Rahim, N. I. M., Iahad, N. A., Yusof, A. F., & Al-Sharafi, M. A. (2022). AI-Based chatbots adoption model for higher-education institutions: A hybrid PLS-SEM-Neural network modelling approach. *Sustainability, 14*(19), 12726. doi:10.3390/su141912726

Raimundo, R. J., & Rosário, A. T. (2022). Cybersecurity in the Internet of things in industrial management. *Applied Sciences (Basel, Switzerland), 12*(3), 1598. doi:10.3390/app12031598

Rainey, D. (2009). *Sustainable business development. inventing the future through strategy, innovation, and leadership.* Cambridge University Press. doi:10.1017/CBO9780511617607

Rajagopal, N. K., Qureshi, N. I., Durga, S., Ramirez Asis, E. H., Huerta Soto, R. M., Gupta, S. K., & Deepak, S. (2022). Future of business culture: An artificial intelligence-driven digital framework for organization decision-making process. *Complexity*, *2022*, 1–14. doi:10.1155/2022/7796507

Rajpurkar, P., Chen, E., Banerjee, O., & Topol, E. J. (2022). AI in health and medicine. *Nature Medicine*, *28*(1), 31–38. doi:10.1038/s41591-021-01614-0 PMID:35058619

Ramachandran, K. K., Apsara Saleth Mary, A., Hawladar, S., Asokk, D., Bhaskar, B., & Pitroda, J. R. (2022). Machine learning and role of artificial intelligence in optimizing work performance and employee behavior. *Materials Today: Proceedings*, *51*, 2327–2331. doi:10.1016/j.matpr.2021.11.544

Randolph, W. C. (1995). Dynamic income, progressive taxes, and the timing of charitable contributions. *Journal of Political Economy*, *103*(4), 709–738. doi:10.1086/262000

Rawal, S. (2017). IOT based smart irrigation system. *International Journal of Computer Applications*, *159*(8), 7–11. doi:10.5120/ijca2017913001

Rawashdeh, A., Bakhit, M., & Abaalkhail, L. (2022). Determinants of artificial intelligence adoption in SMEs: The mediating role of accounting automation. Retrieved from doi:10.5267/j.ijdns.2022.12.010

Reed, C. What It Means to Freelance (or Jumping in with Your Eyes Wide Open).

Rhee, S. Y., Kim, C., Shin, D. W., & Steinhubl, S. R. (2020). Present and Future of Digital Health in Diabetes and Metabolic Disease. *Diabetes & Metabolism Journal*, *44*(6), 819–827. doi:10.4093/dmj.2020.0088 PMID:33389956

Riaz, H., Baig, U., Meidute-Kavaliauskiene, I., & Ahmed, H. (2021). Factors effecting omnichannel customer experience: Evidence from fashion retail. *Information (Basel)*, *13*(1), 12–22. doi:10.3390/info13010012

Ricci, R., Battaglia, D., & Neirotti, P. (2021). External knowledge search, opportunity recognition and industry 4.0 adoption in SMEs. *International Journal of Production Economics*, *240*, 108234. doi:10.1016/j.ijpe.2021.108234

Richey, R. G. Jr, Chowdhury, S., Davis-Sramek, B., Giannakis, M., & Dwivedi, Y. K. (2023). Artificial intelligence in logistics and supply chain management: A primer and roadmap for research. *Journal of Business Logistics*, *44*(4), 532–549. doi:10.1111/jbl.12364

Richter, C., Kraus, S., Brem, A., Durst, S., & Giselbrecht, C. (2017). Digital entrepreneurship: Innovative business models for the sharing economy. *Creativity and Innovation Management*, *26*(3), 300–310. doi:10.1111/caim.12227

Roblek, V., Meško, M., Pušavec, F., & Likar, B. (2021). The role and meaning of the digital transformation as a disruptive innovation on small and medium manufacturing enterprises. *Frontiers in Psychology*, *12*, 592528. doi:10.3389/fpsyg.2021.592528 PMID:34177680

Rodriguez-Ruiz, A., Lång, K., Gubern-Merida, A., Teuwen, J., Broeders, M., Gennaro, G., Clauser, P., Helbich, T. H., Chevalier, M., Mertelmeier, T., Wallis, M. G., Andersson, I., Zackrisson, S., Sechopoulos, I., & Mann, R. M. (2019). Can we reduce the workload of mammographic screening by automatic identification of normal exams with artificial intelligence? A feasibility studies. *European Radiology*, *29*(9), 4825–4832. doi:10.1007/s00330-019-06186-9 PMID:30993432

Rosário, A., & Dias, J. (2023). Marketing Strategies on Social Media Platforms. *International Journal of E-Business Research*, *19*(1), 1–25. doi:10.4018/IJEBR.316969

Roselli, D., Matthews, J., & Talagala, N. (2019). Managing bias in AI. Companion Proceedings of The 2019 World Wide Web Conference, 539–544. 10.1145/3308560.3317590

Rožman, M., Oreški, D., & Tominc, P. (2022). Integrating artificial intelligence into a talent management model to increase the work engagement and performance of enterprises. *Frontiers in Psychology, 13*, 1014434. doi:10.3389/fpsyg.2022.1014434 PMID:36506984

Rožman, M., Oreški, D., & Tominc, P. (2023). Artificial-Intelligence-Supported Reduction of Employees' Workload to Increase the Company's Performance in Today's VUCA Environment. *Sustainability (Basel), 15*(6), 5019. doi:10.3390/su15065019

Ruan, Y., & Mezei, J. (2022). When do AI chatbots lead to higher customer satisfaction than human frontline employees in online shopping assistance? Considering product attribute type. *Journal of Retailing and Consumer Services, 68*, 103059. doi:10.1016/j.jretconser.2022.103059

Ruggieri, R., Savastano, M., Scalingi, A., Bala, D., & D'Ascenzo, F. (2018). The impact of Digital Platforms on Business Models: An empirical investigation on innovative start-ups. Management & Marketing. *Challenges for the Knowledge Society, 13*(4), 1210–1225. doi:10.2478/mmcks-2018-0032

Sachs, J. D., Schmidt-Traub, G., Mazzucato, M., Messner, D., Nakicenovic, N., & Rockström, J. (2019). Six transformations to achieve the sustainable development goals. *Nature Sustainability, 2*(9), 805–814. doi:10.1038/s41893-019-0352-9

Sadiku, M. N. O., Ashaolu, T. J., Ajayi-Majebi, A., & Musa, S. M. (2021). Artificial intelligence in social media. *International Journal of Scientific Advances, 2*(1), 15–20.

Saheb, T. (2023). Ethically contentious aspects of artificial intelligence surveillance: A social science perspective. *AI and Ethics, 3*(2), 369–379. doi:10.1007/s43681-022-00196-y PMID:35874304

Saini, R., & Singh, S. (2022). Artificial Intelligence and Entrepreneurship: A Review of Literature and Future Research Directions. *Journal of Entrepreneurship Education, 25*(1), 1–12.

Salam, M. A., & Nawrin, R. (2022). Business response to COVID-19 through CSR: Evidence from Thai top corporations. *International Journal of Health Sciences, 6*(I), 6196–6210. doi:10.53730/ijhs.v6nS1.6276

Salam, M. A., & Senasu, K. (2019). Development of the sustainability index for the ready-made garments sector in Bangladesh. *Business: Theory and Practice, 20*(0), 329–341. doi:10.3846/btp.2019.31

Salam, M. T., Muhamad, N., & Leong, V. S. (2019). Measuring religiosity among Muslim consumers: Observations and recommendations. *Journal of Islamic Marketing, 10*(2), 633–652. doi:10.1108/JIMA-02-2018-0038

Sandeep, S. R., Ahamad, S., Saxena, D., Srivastava, K., Jaiswal, S., & Bora, A. (2022). To understand the relationship between Machine learning and Artificial intelligence in large and diversified business organisations. *Materials Today: Proceedings, 56*, 2082–2086. doi:10.1016/j.matpr.2021.11.409

Sangani, N. K., & Vijayakumar, B. (2012). Cyber security scenarios and control for small and medium enterprises. *Informações Econômicas, 16*(2), 58.

Saraf, S. B., & Gawali, D. H. (2017). IoT based smart irrigation monitoring and controlling system. *2nd IEEE International Conference on Recent Trends in Electronics, Information & Communication Technology (RTEICT)* (pp. 815-819). Bangalore, India: IEEE. 10.1109/RTEICT.2017.8256711

Saraswat, D., Bhattacharya, P., Verma, A., Prasad, V. K., Tanwar, S., Sharma, G., Bokoro, P. N., & Sharma, R. (2022). Explainable AI for Healthcare 5.0: Opportunities and Challenges. *IEEE Access : Practical Innovations, Open Solutions, 10*, 84486–84517. doi:10.1109/ACCESS.2022.3197671

Sarstedt, M., Ringle, C. M., & Hair, J. F. (2021). Partial Least Squares Structural Equation Modeling. Handbook of Market Research, 587–632. https://doi.org/ doi:10.1007/978-3-319-57413-4_15/COVER

Sarstedt, M., Hair, J. F. Jr, Cheah, J.-H., Becker, J.-M., & Ringle, C. M. (2019). How to Specify, Estimate, and Validate Higher-Order Constructs in PLS-SEM. *Australasian Marketing Journal*, *27*(3), 197–211. doi:10.1016/j.ausmj.2019.05.003

Sarstedt, M., Hair, J. F., Pick, M., Liengaard, B. D., Radomir, L., & Ringle, C. M. (2022). Progress in partial least squares structural equation modeling use in marketing research in the last decade. *Psychology and Marketing*, *39*(5), 1035–1064. doi:10.1002/mar.21640

Satalkina, L., & Steiner, G. (2020). Digital entrepreneurship: A theory-based systematization of core performance indicators. *Sustainability (Basel)*, *12*(10), 4018. doi:10.3390/su12104018

Saunila, M., Nasiri, M., Ukko, J., & Rantala, T. (2019). Smart technologies and corporate sustainability: The mediation effect of corporate sustainability strategy. *Computers in Industry*, *108*, 178–185. doi:10.1016/j.compind.2019.03.003

Saura, J. R., Ribeiro-Soriano, D., & Palacios-Marqués, D. (2022). Assessing behavioral data science privacy issues in government artificial intelligence deployment. *Government Information Quarterly*, *39*(4), 101679. doi:10.1016/j.giq.2022.101679

Saxena, A. (2021). *Artificial intelligence and machine learning in healthcare* (S. Chandra, Ed.). Springer. doi:10.1007/978-981-16-0811-7

Saygılı, M., & Yalçıntekin, T. (2021). THE EFFECT OF HEDONIC VALUE, UTILITARIAN VALUE, AND CUSTOMER SATISFACTION IN PREDICTING REPURCHASE INTENTION AND WILLINGNESS TO PAY A PRICE PREMIUM FOR SMARTWATCH BRANDS. *Management*, *26*(2), 179–195. doi:10.30924/mjcmi.26.2.10

Scheffe, H. (1999). *The analysis of variance* (Vol. 72). John Wiley & Sons.

Schwartz, R., Vassilev, A., Greene, K., Perine, L., Burt, A., & Hall, P. (2022). Towards a standard for identifying and managing bias in artificial intelligence. *NIST special publication, 1270*(10.6028).

Schwartz, S. M., Wildenhaus, K., Bucher, A., & Byrd, B. (2020). Digital Twins and the Emerging Science of Self: Implications for Digital Health Experience Design and "Small" Data. *Frontiers of Computer Science*, *2*, 516124. doi:10.3389/FCOMP.2020.00031/BIBTEX

Scuotto, V., Serravalle, F., Murray, A., & Viassone, M. (2019). The shift towards a digital business model: A strategic decision for the female entrepreneur. In *Women entrepreneurs and strategic decision making in the global economy* (pp. 120–143). IGI Global. doi:10.4018/978-1-5225-7479-8.ch007

Selamat, M. A., & Windasari, N. A. (2021). Chatbot for SMEs: Integrating customer and business owner perspectives. *Technology in Society*, *66*, 101685. doi:10.1016/j.techsoc.2021.101685

Sezer, O. B., Gudelek, M. U., & Ozbayoglu, A. M. (2020). Financial time series forecasting with deep learning: A systematic literature review: 2005–2019. *Applied Soft Computing*, *90*, 106181. doi:10.1016/j.asoc.2020.106181

ShaheenM. Y. (2021). Applications of Artificial Intelligence (AI) in healthcare: A review. *ScienceOpen* Preprints.

Shahzad, Y., Javed, H., Farman, H., Ahmad, J., Jan, B., & Zubair, M. (2020). Internet of energy: Opportunities, applications, architectures and challenges in smart industries. *Computers & Electrical Engineering*, *86*, 106739. doi:10.1016/j.compeleceng.2020.106739

Shaik, M. (2023). Impact of artificial intelligence on marketing. *East Asian Journal of Multidisciplinary Research*, *2*(3), 993–1004. doi:10.55927/eajmr.v2i3.3112

Sharifi, A., Ahmadi, M., & Ala, A. (2021). The impact of artificial intelligence and digital style on industry and energy post-COVID-19 pandemic. *Environmental Science and Pollution Research International, 28*(34), 46964–46984. doi:10.1007/s11356-021-15292-5 PMID:34269979

Sharma, A. (2020). Entrepreneurship and Role of AI. Retrieved from doi:10.1145/3372806.3374910

Sharma, U., Gupta, A., Khantwal, S., Kumar, V., & Singh, V. (2021). Soil moisture sensor based automatic irrigation water pump controlling system with GSM technology. *Recent Trends in Communication and Electronics*, 14-18.

Sharma, V., Taneja, S., & Gupta, M. KshitizJangir, & Ozen, E. (2023). Impact of Service Quality on Behavioural Intention to Use Fin Tech Payment Services: An Extension of SERVEQUAL Model. *Asia Pacific Journal of Information Systems, 33*(4), 1093–1117. https://www.earticle.net/Article/A440274

Sharma, A. K., Singh, P., Vats, P., & Jain, D. (2022). Deep learning and machine intelligence for operational management of strategic planning. *Proceedings of Third International Conference on Computing, Communications, and Cyber-Security*, 475-485. 10.1007/978-981-19-1142-2_38

Sharma, P., Sharma, V., Jangir, K., Gupta, M., & Pathak, N. (2023). Unfolding the Emerging Trends in Non-performing Assets with Special Reference to the Energy Sector in Banking Industry. *Renewable Energy Optimization, Planning and Control: Proceedings of ICRTE 2022*, 411–422.

Sharma, S., Chang, V., Tim, U. S., Wong, J., & Gadia, S. (2019). Cloud and IoT-based emerging services systems. *Cluster Computing, 22*(1), 71–91. doi:10.1007/s10586-018-2821-8

Sharma, V., Gupta, M., Jangir, K., Chopra, P., & Pathak, N. (2023). The Impact of Post-Use Consumer Satisfaction on Smart Wearables Repurchase Intention in the Context of AI-Based Healthcare Information. In *Enhancing Customer Engagement Through Location-Based Marketing* (pp. 77–101). IGI Global. doi:10.4018/978-1-6684-8177-6.ch007

Shaw, W. H. (2017). *Business ethics* (9th ed.). Cengage Learning.

Shepherd, D. A., & Majchrzak, A. (2022). Machines augmenting entrepreneurs: Opportunities (and threats) at the Nexus of artificial intelligence and entrepreneurship. Retrieved from doi:10.1016/j.jbusvent.2022.106227

Shinghal, D., & Srivastava, N. (2017). *Wireless sensor networks in agriculture: for potato farming.* SSRN - Elsevier.

Shneiderman, B. (2020). Human-Centered Artificial Intelligence: Reliable, Safe & Trustworthy. *International Journal of Human-Computer Interaction, 36*(6), 495–504. doi:10.1080/10447318.2020.1741118

Shore, A. (2022). Talking about facial recognition technology: How framing and context influence privacy concerns and support for prohibitive policy. *Telematics and Informatics, 70*, 101815. doi:10.1016/j.tele.2022.101815

Shuaib, A., Arian, H., & Shuaib, A. (2020). The Increasing Role of Artificial Intelligence in Health Care: Will Robots Replace Doctors in the Future? *International Journal of General Medicine, 13*, 891–896. doi:10.2147/IJGM.S268093 PMID:33116781

Sidaoui, K., Jaakkola, M., & Burton, J. (2020). AI feel you: Customer experience assessment via chatbot interviews. *Journal of Service Management, 31*(4), 745–766. doi:10.1108/JOSM-11-2019-0341

Simone, V. D., Pasquale, V. D., & Miranda, S. (2023). An overview on the use of AI/ML in Manufacturing MSMEs: solved issues, limits, and challenges. Retrieved from doi:10.1016/j.procs.2022.12.382

Singh, A. K., & Taterh, S. (2023). Exploring the Significance and Obstacles of Adopting Futuristic Technology Perspectives for Entrepreneurship and Sustainable Innovation. In Futuristic Technology Perspectives on Entrepreneurship and Sustainable Innovation (pp. 1-10). IGI Global. doi:10.4018/978-1-6684-5871-6.ch001

Singh, J., Flaherty, K., Sohi, R. S., Deeter-Schmelz, D., Habel, J., Le Meunier-FitzHugh, K., Malshe, A., Mullins, R., & Onyemah, V. (2019). Sales profession and professionals in the age of digitization and artificial intelligence technologies: Concepts, priorities, and questions. *Journal of Personal Selling & Sales Management*, *39*(1), 2–22. doi:10.1080/08853134.2018.1557525

Singh, N., Misra, R., Singh, S., Rana, N. P., & Khorana, S. (2022). Assessing the factors that influence the adoption of healthcare wearables by the older population using an extended PMT model. *Technology in Society*, *71*, 102126. doi:10.1016/j.techsoc.2022.102126

Singh, S., Thakur, P., & Singh, S. (2023). How Does the Use of AI in HRM Contribute to Improved Business Performance?: A Systematic Review. In N. Sharma & K. Shalender (Eds.), *Managing Technology Integration for Human Resources in Industry 5.0* (pp. 131–139). IGI Global. doi:10.4018/978-1-6684-6745-9.ch008

Si, S., Hall, J., Suddaby, R., Ahlstrom, D., & Wei, J. (2023). Technology, entrepreneurship, innovation and social change in digital economics. *Technovation*, *119*, 102–484. doi:10.1016/j.technovation.2022.102484

Sison, A., Ferrero, I., García Ruiz, P., & Kim, T. W. (2023). Editorial: Artificial intelligence (AI) ethics in business. *Frontiers in Psychology*, *14*, 1258721. doi:10.3389/fpsyg.2023.1258721 PMID:37771802

Sitthipon, T., Siripipatthanakul, S., Phayaphrom, B., Siripipattanakul, S., & Limna, P. (2022). Determinants of Customers' Intention to Use Healthcare Chatbots and Apps in Bangkok, Thailand. *International Journal of Behavioral Analytics*, *2*(2), 1–15.

Siva, K. N., Bagubali, A., & Krishnan, K. V. (2019). Smart watering of plants. *International Conference on Vision Towards Emerging Trends in Communication and Networking (ViTECoN)* (pp. 1-4). Vellore, India: IEEE.

Sjödin, D., Parida, V., Kohtamäki, M., & Wincent, J. (2020). An agile co-creation process for digital servitization: A micro-service innovation approach. *Journal of Business Research*, *112*, 478–491. doi:10.1016/j.jbusres.2020.01.009

Sklyar, A., Kowalkowski, C., Tronvoll, B., & Sörhammar, D. (2019). Organizing for digital servitization: A service ecosystem perspective. *Journal of Business Research*, *104*, 450–460. doi:10.1016/j.jbusres.2019.02.012

Skrzek-Lubasińska, M., & Szaban, J. M. (2019). Nomenclature and harmonised criteria for the self-employment categorisation. An approach pursuant to a systematic review of the literature. *European Management Journal*, *37*(3), 376–386. doi:10.1016/j.emj.2018.11.001

Soni, N., Sharma, E. K., Singh, N., & Kapoor, A. (2018). Impact of Artificial Intelligence on Business. *Digital Innovations, Transformation, and Society Conference 2018 (Digits 2018)*. IEEE.

Soni, N., Singh, N., Kapoor, A., & Sharma, E. K. (2018). *Low-Resolution Image Recognition UsingCloud Hopfield Neural Network*. Progress in Advanced Computing and Intelligent.

Sousa, M. J., & Rocha, A. (2019). Skills for disruptive digital business. *Journal of Business Research*, *94*, 257–263. doi:10.1016/j.jbusres.2017.12.051

Spreitzer, G. M. (1997). Toward a common ground in defining empowerment. In *National Academy of Management Meetings, 1995, Vancouver, BC, Canada; An earlier version was presented at the aforementioned conference.* Elsevier Science/JAI Press.

Srbinovska, M., Gavrovski, C., Dimcev, V., Krkoleva, A., & Borozan, V. (2015). Environmental parameters monitoring in precision agriculture using wireless sensor networks. *Journal of Cleaner Production*, *88*, 297–307. doi:10.1016/j.jclepro.2014.04.036

Stahl B. C. (2021). Concepts of Ethics and Their Application to AI. *Artificial Intelligence for a Better Future: An Ecosystem Perspective on the Ethics of AI and Emerging Digital Technologies*, 19–33. doi:10.1007/978-3-030-69978-9_3

Steinhoff, L., Arli, D., Weaven, S., & Kozlenkova, I. V. (2019). Online relationship marketing. *Journal of the Academy of Marketing Science*, *47*(3), 369–393. https://link.springer.com/article/10.1007/s11747-018-0621-6. doi:10.1007/s11747-018-0621-6

Stocker, G., Jandl, M., & Hirsch, A. J. (Eds.). (2021). *The Practice of Art and AI*. Hantje Cantz Verlag., https://ars.electronica.art/newdigitaldeal/files/2021/08/artandai.pdf

Stone, M., Aravopoulou, E., Ekinci, Y., Evans, G., Hobbs, M., Labib, A., Laughlin, P., Machtynger, J., & Machtynger, L. (2020). Artificial intelligence (AI) in strategic marketing decision-making: A research agenda. *The Bottom Line (New York, N.Y.)*, *33*(2), 183–200. doi:10.1108/BL-03-2020-0022

Stratton, S. J. (2021). Population research: Convenience sampling strategies. *Prehospital and Disaster Medicine*, *36*(4), 373–374. doi:10.1017/S1049023X21000649 PMID:34284835

Strong, A. I. (2016). Applications of artificial intelligence & associated technologies. *Science [ETEBMS-2016]*, *5*(6).

Suboyin, A., Eldred, M., Thatcher, J., Rehman, A., Gee, I., & Anjum, H. (2023, January). Environomics Framework for Sustainable Business Practices: Industrial Case Studies on True Impact Reduction and Process Optimization Through AI. In *SPE Middle East Intelligent Oil and Gas Symposium* (p. D011S002R002). SPE. 10.2118/214459-MS

Sucharita, K., & Seethalakshmi, R. (2022). Artificial Intelligence In Training And Development For Employees With Reference To Selected It Companies. *Journal of Positive School Psychology*, *6*(9), 2700–2715.

Sueb, S., & Sopiah, S. (2023). Exploring the Relationship between Transformational Leadership and Innovative Work Behavior: A Systematic Literature Review. *Jurnal Visi Manajemen*, *9*(2), 62–83. doi:10.56910/jvm.v9i2.287

Sulague, R. M., Lim, X., Baticulon, R. E., & Kpodonu, J. (2022). Southeast Asia must invest in strengthening surgical systems. *Journal of Global Health*, *12*, 03090. doi:10.7189/jogh.12.03090 PMID:36579398

Sulich, A., Sołoducho-Pelc, L., & Grzesiak, S. (2023). Artificial intelligence and sustainable development in business management context – Bibliometric review. *Procedia Computer Science*, *225*, 3727–3735. doi:10.1016/j.procs.2023.10.368

Sun, W., Guo, Z., Yang, Z., Wu, Y., Lan, W., Liao, Y., Wu, X., & Liu, Y. (2022). A Review of Recent Advances in Vital Signals Monitoring of Sports and Health via Flexible Wearable Sensors. *Sensors 2022, Vol. 22, Page 7784*, *22*(20), 7784. doi:10.3390/s22207784

Sun, Y., & Ly, T. P. (2023). The Influence of Word-of-web on Customers' Purchasing Process: The Case of Xiaohongshu. *Journal of China Tourism Research*, *19*(2), 221–244. doi:10.1080/19388160.2022.2057378

Sunyaev, A. (2020). Cloud Computing. In *Internet Computing*. Springer. doi:10.1007/978-3-030-34957-8_7

Suresh, T. P., Yong, P. L., Chyi, Y. S., & Musa, R. (2023). Connecting with Generation Z: Consumer Acceptance of the Use of Artificial Intelligence in Online Shopping. [JEB]. *Journal of Entrepreneurship and Business*, *11*(1), 56–68. doi:10.17687/jeb.v11i1.921

Suwaidi, F. A., Alshurideh, M., Kurdi, B. A., & Salloum, S. A. (2020). The Impact of Innovation Management in SMEs Performance: A Systematic review. In Advances in intelligent systems and computing (pp. 720–730). Springer. doi:10.1007/978-3-030-58669-0_64

Szedlak, C., Poetters, P., & Leyendecker, B. (2020). Application of Artificial Intelligence In Small and Medium-Sized Enterprises.

Taeihagh, A. (2021). Governance of artificial intelligence. *Policy and Society*, *40*(2), 137–157. doi:10.1080/14494035.2021.1928377

Tagger, S. S., & Gupta, M. (2020). A study of the relationship between total quality management and business performance in the banking sector. *International Journal of Business Competition and Growth*, *7*(2), 118–132. doi:10.1504/IJBCG.2020.111943

Taherizadeh, A., & Beaudry, C. (2023). An emergent grounded theory of AI-driven digital transformation: Canadian SMEs' perspectives. *Industry and Innovation*, *30*(9), 1244–1273. doi:10.1080/13662716.2023.2242285

Tallon, P. P. (2014). *A Process-Oriented Perspective on the Alignment of Information Technology and Business Strategy*. Taylor & Francis. doi:10.2753/MIS0742-1222240308

Talukder, M. S., Laato, S., Islam, A. K. M. N., & Bao, Y. (2021). Continued use intention of wearable health technologies among the elderly: An enablers and inhibitors perspective. *Internet Research*, *31*(5), 1611–1640. doi:10.1108/INTR-10-2020-0586

Tang, O. Y., Ali, R., Connolly, I. D., Fridley, J. S., Sullivan, P. L. Z., Cielo, D., & Asaad, W. F. (2023). The Urgency of Neurosurgical Leadership in the Era of Artificial Intelligence. *Neurosurgery*, *93*(3), 69–70. doi:10.1227/neu.0000000000002576 PMID:37319400

Tang, Y. M., Chau, K. Y., Fatima, A., & Waqas, M. (2022). Industry 4.0 technology and circular economy practices: Business management strategies for environmental sustainability. *Environmental Science and Pollution Research International*, *29*(33), 49752–49769. doi:10.1007/s11356-022-19081-6 PMID:35218493

Tan, P. K., & Lim, C. M. (2023). Factors That Affect User Satisfaction of Using E-Commerce Chatbot: A Study on Generation Z. *International Journal of Business and Technology Management*, *5*(1), 292–303.

Tan, S.-M., & Liew, T. W. (2022). Multi-chatbot or single-chatbot? The effects of m-commerce chatbot interface on source credibility, social presence, trust, and purchase intention. *Human Behavior and Emerging Technologies*, *2022*, 2022. doi:10.1155/2022/2501538

Tanwar, R., Choudhary, S. L., Singh, A., Manoharan, S., & Ghafoor, K. Z. (2022). A Pulse Rate-Triggered Wearable Device for Critical Assistance. *Journal of Sensors*, *2022*, 1–9. Advance online publication. doi:10.1155/2022/9807188

Tan, Y., & Li, X. (2022). The impact of internet on entrepreneurship. *International Review of Economics & Finance*, *77*, 135–142. doi:10.1016/j.iref.2021.09.016

Tekic, Z., Cosic, I., & Katalinic, B. (2019). Manufacturing and the Rise of Artificial Intelligence: Innovation Challenges. In B. Katalinic (Ed.), *DAAAM Proceedings* (1st ed., Vol. 1, pp. 0192–0196). DAAAM International Vienna. 10.2507/30th.daaam.proceedings.025

Thakur, D., Kumar, Y., & Vijendra, S. (2020). Smart Irrigation and Intrusions Detection in Agricultural Fields Using IoT. *International Conference on Computational Intelligence and Data Science (ICCIDS 2019)*. Gurgaon, INDIA: ELSEVIER.

Thakur, N., Nagrath, P., Jain, R., Saini, D., Sharma, N., & Hemanth, D. J. (2021). Artificial Intelligence Techniques in Smart Cities Surveillance Using UAVs: A Survey. In U. Ghosh, Y. Maleh, M. Alazab, & A.-S. K. Pathan (Eds.), *Machine Intelligence and Data Analytics for Sustainable Future Smart Cities* (Vol. 971, pp. 329–353). Springer International Publishing. doi:10.1007/978-3-030-72065-0_18

Thakur, R. (2024). Introduction to artificial intelligence and its importance in modern business management. In *Leveraging AI and emotional intelligence in contemporary business organizations* (pp. 133–165). IGI Global.

Thickstun, K. (2019). Every Lesson Every Day. *American Music Teacher*, *68*(5), 10–13.

Thompson, J., & Grant, J. (1992). New moisture meter could curb overdrying of walnuts. *California Agriculture*, *46*(2), 31–34. doi:10.3733/ca.v046n02p31

Thong, J. Y. L., Hong, S. J., & Tam, K. Y. (2006). The effects of post-adoption beliefs on the expectation-confirmation model for information technology continuance. *International Journal of Human-Computer Studies*, *64*(9), 799–810. doi:10.1016/j.ijhcs.2006.05.001

Titareva, T. (2021). *Leadership in an Artificial Intelligence Era*. Research Gate.

Tkachenko, V., Kuzior, A., & Kwilinski, A. (2019). Introduction of artificial intelligence tools into the training methods of entrepreneurship activities. *Journal of Entrepreneurship Education*, *22*(6), 1–10.

Toh, T. J., & Tay, L. Y. (2022). Banking Chatbots: A Study on Technology Acceptance among Millennials in Malaysia. *Journal of Logistics. Informatics and Service Science*, *9*(3), 1–15.

Tomašević, A. N. (2023). Reshaping the future of work: Navigating the impacts of lifelong learning and digital competences in the era of 5.0 industry. *Social Informatics Journal*, *2*(1), 1–6. doi:10.58898/sij.v2i1.01-06

Tran, L., Pham, L., & Le, L. (2018). E-satisfaction and continuance intention: The moderator role of online ratings. *International Journal of Hospitality Management*, *77*, 311–322. Advance online publication. doi:10.1016/j.ijhm.2018.07.011

Trapp, C., & Kanbach, D. K. (2021). *Green entrepreneurship and business models: Deriving green technology business model archetypes*. Science Direct. doi:10.1016/j.jclepro.2021.126694

Tripathi, S., & Ghatak, C. (2018). Artificial intelligence and intellectual property law. *Christ ULJ*, *7*, 83.

Troise, C., Ben-Hafaïedh, C., Tani, M., & Yablonsky, S. A. (2022). Guest editorial: New technologies and entrepreneurship: exploring entrepreneurial behavior in the digital transformation era. *International Journal of Entrepreneurial Behaviour & Research*, *28*(5), 1129–1137. doi:10.1108/IJEBR-08-2022-999

Trolice, M. P., Curchoe, C., & Quaas, A. M. (2021). Artificial intelligence—The future is now. *Journal of Assisted Reproduction and Genetics*, *38*(7), 1607–1612. doi:10.1007/s10815-021-02272-4 PMID:34231110

Tushar, H. (2017). The role of ethical leadership in developing sustainable organization. [AJLEG]. *Australasian Journal of Law, Ethics, and Governance*, 2(2), 83–95.

Tushar, H., & Sooraksa, N. (2023). Global employability skills in the 21st century workplace: A semi-systematic literature review. *Heliyon*, *9*(11), e21023. doi:10.1016/j.heliyon.2023.e21023 PMID:37954286

Ueberschaer, N. (2014). *Führung - Kompaktes Wissen - Konkrete Umsetzung - Praktische Arbeitshilfen*. Carl Hanser Verlag GmbH & Company KG.

Ullah, W., Ullah, A., Hussain, T., Muhammad, K., Heidari, A. A., Del Ser, J., Baik, S. W., & De Albuquerque, V. H. C. (2022). Artificial Intelligence of Things-assisted two-stream neural network for anomaly detection in surveillance Big Video Data. *Future Generation Computer Systems*, *129*, 286–297. doi:10.1016/j.future.2021.10.033

Upadhyay, A., & Maurya, S. K. (2020). Protecting the agriculture field by IoT application. *International Conference on Power Electronics & IoT Applications in Renewable Energy and its Control (PARC)* (pp. 411-414). Mathura, India: IEEE. 10.1109/PARC49193.2020.236640

Urbanová, M., & Slind, T. (2016). *Successful Personal Branding on Social Media*. Lund University, School of Economics and Management.

Ushie, A. M., Samson, T. K., Hossain, S. F. A., & Ojie, M. P. (2023). Competitive intensity, managerial commitment, and corporate performance: The moderating role of innovation input in post-COVID-19. *International Journal of Work Organisation and Emotion, 14*(3), 282–302. doi:10.1504/IJWOE.2023.132868

Vaio, A. D., Palladino, R., Hassan, R., & Escobar, O. (2020). Artificial intelligence and business models in the sustainable development goals perspective: A systematic literature review. Retrieved from doi:10.1016/j.jbusres.2020.08.019

Vaishali, S., Suraj, S., Vignesh, G., Dhivya, S., & Udhayakumar, S. (2017). Mobile integrated smart irrigation management and monitoring system using IOT. *International Conference on Communication and Signal Processing (ICCSP)* (pp. 2164-2167). Chennai, India: IEEE.

Vaishya, R., Javaid, M., Khan, I. H., & Haleem, A. (2020). Artificial Intelligence (AI) applications for COVID-19 pandemic. *Diabetes & Metabolic Syndrome, 14*(4), 337–339. doi:10.1016/j.dsx.2020.04.012 PMID:32305024

van den Hoven, J. (2010). The Use of Normative Theories in Computer Ethics. In L. Floridi (Ed.), *The Cambridge Handbook of Information and Computer Ethics* (pp. 59–76). Cambridge University Press. doi:10.1017/CBO9780511845239.005

Van Mourik, O., Grohnert, T., & Gold, A. (2023). Mitigating work conditions that can inhibit learning from errors: Benefits of error management climate perceptions. *Frontiers in Psychology, 14*, 1033470. doi:10.3389/fpsyg.2023.1033470 PMID:36743251

Van Stel, A., Wennekers, S., & Scholman, G. (2014). Solo self-employed versus employer entrepreneurs: Determinants and macro-economic effects in OECD countries. *Eurasian Business Review, 4*(1), 107–136. doi:10.1007/s40821-014-0003-z

Van Tuinen, S. (2020). Philosophy in the light of AI. *Angelaki, 25*(4), 97–109. doi:10.1080/0969725X.2020.1790838

Van Wynsberghe, A. (2021). Sustainable AI: AI for sustainability and the sustainability of AI. *AI and Ethics, 1*(3), 213–218. doi:10.1007/s43681-021-00043-6

Vasudevan, H (2022). Management and Leadership in the Klang Valley IT Sector: Conceptual Approach. *Marketing and management of innovation, 3*, 56-65. doi:10.21272/mmi.2022.3-05

Venkatesh, V., Morris, M. G., Davis, G. B., & Davis, F. D. (2003). User acceptance of information technology: Toward a unified view. *Management Information Systems Quarterly, 27*(3), 425–478. doi:10.2307/30036540

Venkatesh, V., Thong, J. Y. L., & Xu, X. (2012). Consumer acceptance and use of information technology: Extending the unified theory of acceptance and use of technology. *Management Information Systems Quarterly, 36*(1), 157–178. doi:10.2307/41410412

Vesnic-Alujevic, L., Nascimento, S., & Polvora, A. (2020). Societal and ethical impacts of artificial intelligence: Critical notes on European policy frameworks. *Telecommunications Policy, 44*(6), 101961. doi:10.1016/j.telpol.2020.101961

Vijayakumar, H. (2021). Impact of AI-Blockchain Adoption on Annual Revenue Growth: An Empirical Analysis of Small and Medium-sized Enterprises in the United States. *International Journal of Business Intelligence and Big Data Analytics, 4*(1), 12–21.

Vijayan, V., Connolly, J., Condell, J., McKelvey, N., & Gardiner, P. (2021). Review of Wearable Devices and Data Collection Considerations for Connected Health. *Sensors (Basel), 21*(16), 5589. Advance online publication. doi:10.3390/s21165589 PMID:34451032

Vinuesa, R., Azizpour, H., Leite, I., Balaam, M., Dignum, V., Domisch, S., Felländer, A., Langhans, S. D., Tegmark, M., & Fuso Nerini, F. (2020). The role of artificial intelligence in achieving the Sustainable Development Goals. *Nature Communications, 11*(1), 1–10. doi:10.1038/s41467-019-14108-y PMID:31932590

Vivarelli, M. (1991). The birth of new enterprises. *Small Business Economics*, *3*(3), 215–223. doi:10.1007/BF00400026

Vlačić, B., Corbo, L., Silva, S. C., & Dabić, M. (2021). *The evolving role of artificial intelligence in marketing: A review and research agenda.* Science Direct. doi:10.1016/j.jbusres.2021.01.055

Vlok, A., Ungerer, M., & Malan, J. (2019). Integrative leadership for technology innovation. *International Journal of Technology Management*, *79*(3/4), 247. doi:10.1504/IJTM.2019.099608

Vogl, M., Rötzel, P. G., & Homes, S. (2022). Forecasting performance of wavelet neural networks and other neural network topologies: A comparative study based on financial market data sets. *Machine Learning with Applications*, *8*, 100302. doi:10.1016/j.mlwa.2022.100302

Voorhees, C. M., Brady, M. K., Calantone, R., & Ramirez, E. (2016). Discriminant validity testing in marketing: An analysis, causes for concern, and proposed remedies. *Journal of the Academy of Marketing Science*, *44*(1), 119–134. doi:10.1007/s11747-015-0455-4

Vuong, B. N., Duy Tung, D., Hoa, N. D., Chau, N. T. N., & Tushar, H. (2020). An empirical assessment of organizational commitment and job performance: Vietnam small and medium-sized enterprises. *Journal of Asian Finance. Economics and Business*, *7*(6), 277–286.

Vuong, B. N., Tushar, H., & Hossain, S. F. A. (2022). The effect of social support on job performance through organizational commitment and innovative work behavior: Does innovative climate matter? [DOI number]. *Asia-Pacific Journal of Business Administration*, *14*(2), 156–172. https://doi.org/

Wagner, D. N. (2020). Strategically managing the artificially intelligent firm. *Strategy and Leadership*, *48*(3), 19–25. doi:10.1108/SL-08-2019-0119

Waltersmann, L., Kiemel, S., Stuhlsatz, J., Sauer, A., & Miehe, R. (2021). Artificial Intelligence Applications for Increasing Resource Efficiency in Manufacturing Companies—A Comprehensive Review. *Sustainability (Basel)*, *13*(12), 6689. doi:10.3390/su13126689

Wamba, S. F. (2022). Impact of artificial intelligence assimilation on firm performance: The mediating effects of organizational agility and customer agility. *International Journal of Information Management*, *67*, 102544. doi:10.1016/j.ijinfomgt.2022.102544

Wamba-Taguimdje, S., Fosso Wamba, S., Kala Kamdjoug, J. R., & Tchatchouang Wanko, C. E. (2020). Influence of artificial intelligence (AI) on firm performance: The business value of AI-based transformation projects. *Business Process Management Journal*, *26*(7), 1893–1924. doi:10.1108/BPMJ-10-2019-0411

Wang, J. (2021). Is artificial intelligence capable of understanding? An analysis based on philosophical hermeneutics. *Cultura e Scuola*, *4*(3), 135–146. doi:10.1177/20966083211056405

Wang, W. T., Ou, W. M., & Chen, W. Y. (2019). The impact of inertia and user satisfaction on the continuance intentions to use mobile communication applications: A mobile service quality perspective. *International Journal of Information Management*, *44*, 178–193. doi:10.1016/j.ijinfomgt.2018.10.011

Wang, X., Lin, X., & Shao, B. (2022). How does artificial intelligence create business agility? Evidence from chatbots. *International Journal of Information Management*, *66*, 102535. doi:10.1016/j.ijinfomgt.2022.102535

Wang, X., Xu, B., Zhang, W., Wang, J., Deng, L., Ping, J., Hu, C., & Li, H. (2023). Recognizing emotions induced by wearable haptic vibration using noninvasive electroencephalogram. *Frontiers in Neuroscience*, *17*, 1219553. doi:10.3389/fnins.2023.1219553 PMID:37483356

Wang, Z., Li, M., Lu, J., & Cheng, X. (2022). Business Innovation based on artificial intelligence and Blockchain technology. *Information Processing & Management*, *59*(1), 102759. doi:10.1016/j.ipm.2021.102759

Wang, Z., Shou, M., Wang, S., Dai, R., & Wang, K. (2019). An empirical study on the key factors of intelligent upgrade of small and medium-sized enterprises in China. *Sustainability (Basel)*, *11*(3), 619. doi:10.3390/su11030619

Wardana, A. P., & Anisah, H. U. (2023). The Influence of Transformational Leadership on Employee Performance Through Intrinsic Motivation and Organizational Citizenship Behavior as Intervening Variables: Study at the High Religious Court of Jakarta Indonesia. *Open Access Indonesia Journal of Social Sciences*, *6*(5), 1129–1141. doi:10.37275/oaijss.v6i5.182

Wark, T., Corke, P., Sikka, P., Klingbeil, L., Guo, Y., Crossman, C., Valencia, P., Swain, D., & Bishop-Hurley, G. (2007). Transforming agriculture through pervasive wireless sensor networks. *IEEE Pervasive Computing*, *6*(2), 50–57. doi:10.1109/MPRV.2007.47

Watson, G. J., Desouza, K. C., Ribiere, V. M., & Lindič, J. (2021). Will AI ever sit at the C-suite table? The future of senior leadership. *Business Horizons*, *64*(4), 465–474. doi:10.1016/j.bushor.2021.02.011

Watson, R. (2022). Consumer Risk Perceptions, Behavioral Intentions, and Purchasing Habits toward Delivery Apps. *Journal of Self-Governance & Management Economics*, *10*(1).

WCED, S. W. S. (1987). World commission on environment and development. *Our common future*, *17*(1), 1-91.

Weber, M., Beutter, M., Weking, J., Böhm, M., & Krcmar, H. (2021). AI Startup Business Models. Retrieved from https://link.springer.com/article/10.1007/s12599-021-00732-w

Wei, R., & Pardo, C. (2022). Artificial intelligence and SMEs: How can B2B SMEs leverage AI platforms to integrate AI technologies? *Industrial Marketing Management*, *107*, 466–483. doi:10.1016/j.indmarman.2022.10.008

Weiss, D., Liu, S. X., Mieczkowski, H., & Hancock, J. T. (2022). Effects of using artificial intelligence on interpersonal perceptions of job applicants. *Cyberpsychology, Behavior, and Social Networking*, *25*(3), 163–168. doi:10.1089/cyber.2020.0863 PMID:35021895

Wei, T., & Clegg, J. (2017). Exploring sources of value destruction in international acquisitions: A synthesized theoretical lens. *International Business Review*, *26*(5), 927–941. doi:10.1016/j.ibusrev.2017.03.002

Wejnert, B. (2002). Integrating models of diffusion of innovations: A conceptual framework. *Annual Review of Sociology*, *28*(1), 297–326. doi:10.1146/annurev.soc.28.110601.141051

Weking, J., Mandalenakis, M., Hein, A., Hermes, S., Böhm, M., & Krcmar, H. (2019). *The impact of blockchain technology on business models – a taxonomy and archetypal patterns.* Springer. https://link.springer.com/article/10.1007/s12525-019-00386-3

White, K. (2015). Freelancing–Are you ready to go solo? *Medical Writing*, *24*(3), 140–144. doi:10.1179/2047480615Z.000000000309

Widayanti, R., & Meria, L. (2023). Business modeling innovation using artificial intelligence technology. *International Transactions on Education Technology*, *1*(2), 95–104.

Wijayati, D. T., Rahman, Z., Fahrullah, A., Rahman, M. F. W., Arifah, I. D. C., & Kautsar, A. (2022). A study of artificial intelligence on employee performance and work engagement: The moderating role of change leadership. *International Journal of Manpower*, *43*(2), 486–512. doi:10.1108/IJM-07-2021-0423

Williams, T. (2004). The Theory and Practice of Adlerian Psychology. *Self and Society*, *32*(2), 5–9. doi:10.1080/03060497.2004.11083774

Wilson, M., Paschen, J., & Pitt, L. (2022). The circular economy meets artificial intelligence (AI): Understanding the opportunities of AI for reverse logistics. *Management of Environmental Quality*, *33*(1), 9–25. doi:10.1108/MEQ-10-2020-0222

Xue, C. T. S., & Xin, F. T. W. (2016). Benefits and Challenges of the Adoption of Cloud Computing in Business. [IJCC-SA]. *International Journal on Cloud Computing: Services and Architecture*, *6*(6), 1–15. doi:10.5121/ijccsa.2016.6601

Yan, B., Hao, F., & Meng, X. (2021). When artificial intelligence meets building energy efficiency, a review focusing on zero energy building. *Artificial Intelligence Review*, *54*(3), 2193–2220. doi:10.1007/s10462-020-09902-w

Yang, C., Feng, Y., & Whinston, A. (2022). Dynamic Pricing and Information Disclosure for Fresh Produce: An Artificial Intelligence Approach. *Production and Operations Management*, *31*(1), 155–171. doi:10.1111/poms.13525

Yang, H., Yu, J., Zo, H., & Choi, M. (2016). User acceptance of wearable devices: An extended perspective of perceived value. *Telematics and Informatics*, *33*(2), 256–269. doi:10.1016/j.tele.2015.08.007

Yathiraju, N. (2022). Investigating the use of an Artificial Intelligence Model in an ERP Cloud-Based System. International Journal of Electrical. *Electronics and Computers*, *7*(2), 1–26. doi:10.22161/eec.72.1

Yen, H. Y. (2021). Smart wearable devices as a psychological intervention for healthy lifestyle and quality of life: A randomized controlled trial. *Quality of Life Research: An International Journal of Quality of Life Aspects of Treatment, Care and Rehabilitation*, *30*(3), 791–802. doi:10.1007/s11136-020-02680-6 PMID:33104939

Yiwen, C. (2023). An exploration to the innovation path of traditional business management based on internet background. *Academic Journal of Business & Management*, *5*(21), 60–66. doi:10.25236/AJBM.2023.052109

Yoon, S., & Lee, D. (2019). Artificial Intelligence and Robots in Healthcare: What are the Success Factors for Technology-based Service Encounters? *International Journal of Healthcare Management*, *12*(3), 218–225. doi:10.1080/20479700.2018.1498220

Yoo, S. E., Kim, J. E., Kim, T., Ahn, S., Sung, J., & Kim, D. (2007). A 2 S: automated agriculture system based on WSN. *IEEE International Symposium on Consumer Electronics* (pp. 1-5). Irving, TX, USA: IEEE.

Yu, K. H., Zhang, Y., Li, D., Montenegro-Marin, C. E., & Kumar, P. M. (2021). Environmental planning based on reduce, reuse, recycle and recover using artificial intelligence. *Environmental Impact Assessment Review*, *86*, 106492. doi:10.1016/j.eiar.2020.106492

Yusoff, A., Siong Peng, F., Zaidi Abd Razak, F., & Azani Mustafa, W. (2020). Discriminant Validity Assessment of Religious Teacher Acceptance: The Use of HTMT Criterion. *Journal of Physics: Conference Series*, *042045*(4). doi:10.1088/1742-6596/1529/4/042045

Zaheer, H., Breyer, Y., & Dumay, J. (2019). Digital entrepreneurship: An interdisciplinary structured literature review and research agenda. *Technological Forecasting and Social Change*, *148*, 119735. doi:10.1016/j.techfore.2019.119735

Zaheer, H., Breyer, Y., Dumay, J., & Enjeti, M. (2019). Straight from the horse's mouth: Founders' perspectives on achieving 'traction' in digital start-UPS. *Computers in Human Behavior*, *95*, 262–274. doi:10.1016/j.chb.2018.03.002

Zak, Y., Parmet, Y., & Oron-Gilad, T. (2023). Facilitating the Work of Unmanned Aerial Vehicle Operators Using Artificial Intelligence: An Intelligent Filter for Command-and-Control Maps to Reduce Cognitive Workload. *Human Factors*, *65*(7), 1345–1360. doi:10.1177/00187208221081968 PMID:35392697

Zerilli, J. (2021). *A citizen's guide to artificial intelligence*. MIT Press. doi:10.7551/mitpress/12518.001.0001

Zhang, C., & Lu, Y. (2021). Study on artificial intelligence: The state of the art and future prospects. *Journal of Industrial Information Integration, 23*, 100–224. doi:10.1016/j.jii.2021.100224

Zhang, Q., Husnain, M., Usman, M., Akhtar, M. W., Ali, S., Khan, M. A., Abbas, Q., Ismail, R., Rehman, T., & Akram, M. (2022). Interplay of eco-friendly factors and islamic religiosity towards recycled package products: A cross-cultural study. *Frontiers in Psychology, 13*, 13. doi:10.3389/fpsyg.2022.840711 PMID:36248529

Zhang, X., Hu, M., Xia, J., Wei, T., Chen, M., & Hu, S. (2020). Efficient federated learning for cloud-based AIoT applications. *IEEE Transactions on Computer-Aided Design of Integrated Circuits and Systems, 40*(11), 2211–2223. doi:10.1109/TCAD.2020.3046665

Zhao, F., & Collier, A. (2016). Digital entrepreneurship: Research and practice.

Zhao, F., Barratt-Pugh, L., Suseno, Y., Standen, P., & Redmond, J. (2023). A framework for exploring digital entrepreneurship development from a social interaction perspective. *Journal of General Management, 48*(2), 115–126. doi:10.1177/03063070211044578

Zhao, R., Zhu, F., Tang, M., & He, L. (2023). Profit maximization in cache-aided intelligent computing networks. *Physical Communication, 58*, 102065. doi:10.1016/j.phycom.2023.102065

Zhao, W., Lin, S., Han, J., Xu, R., & Hou, L. (2017). *Design and implementation of smart irrigation system based on LoRa. IEEE Globecom Workshops (GC Wkshps)*. IEEE.

Zhong, R. Y., Xu, X., Klotz, E., & Newman, S. T. (2017). Intelligent Manufacturing in the Context of Industry 4.0: A Review. *Engineering (Beijing), 3*(5), 616–630. doi:10.1016/J.ENG.2017.05.015

Zhou, X., Yang, Z., Hyman, M. R., Li, G., & Munim, Z. H. (2022). Guest editorial: Impact of artificial intelligence on business strategy in emerging markets: a conceptual framework and future research directions. *International Journal of Emerging Markets, 17*(4), 917–929. doi:10.1108/IJOEM-04-2022-995

Zhu, Y., Song, J., & Dong, F. (2011). Applications of wireless sensor network in the agriculture environment monitoring. *International Workshop on Automobile, Power and Energy Engineering* (pp. 608-614). Imperial College London, London, U.K: ELSEVIER. 10.1016/j.proeng.2011.08.1131

Zhu, K. (2004). The Complementarity of Information Technology Infrastructure and E-Commerce Capability: A Resource-Based Assessment of Their Business Value. *Journal of Management Information Systems, 21*(1), 167–202. doi:10.1080/07421222.2004.11045794

Zhu, Q., Williams, T., Jackson, B., & Wen, R. (2020). Blame-Laden Moral Rebukes and the Morally Competent Robot: A Confucian Ethical Perspective. *Science and Engineering Ethics, 26*(5), 2511–2526. doi:10.1007/s11948-020-00246-w PMID:32632786

Žigienė, G., Rybakovas, E., & Alzbutas, R. (2019). Artificial intelligence based commercial risk management framework for SMEs. *Sustainability (Basel), 11*(16), 4501. doi:10.3390/su11164501

Zolfaghari, S., Massa, S. M., & Riboni, D. (2023). Activity Recognition in Smart Homes via Feature-Rich Visual Extraction of Locomotion Traces. *Electronics 2023, Vol. 12, Page 1969, 12*(9), 1969. doi:10.3390/electronics12091969

About the Contributors

Syed Far Abid Hossain is currently working as an Assistant Professor at BRAC Business School, BRAC University. He has obtained PhD in Management Science from the School of Management (AACSB Accredited), Xi'an Jiaotong University, PRC. He holds an MBA (Management) degree from the University of Sunderland, UK and a BBA (Marketing) degree from Dhaka University. Dr. Abid authored 60+ academic journal articles, conference papers and book chapters in internationally recognized, peer reviewed and well-indexed Journals (ISI, Scopus, SSCI, SCIE, ABDC, ESCI, EI) from Elsevier, Springer, SAGE, Taylor and Francis, Frontiers, Science Direct, Emerald, MDPI, Inderscience and IGI global. Dr. Abid has published numerous book chapters and conference proceedings with top publishers. Recently, he was awarded as one of the top 3 researchers in BRAC University for his scholarly publications in Q1 Journals. His research interests include AI, market turbulence, academic performance, education psychology, education management, technology in education, women entrepreneurship, innovation and media entrepreneurship. Apart from his current roles at BRAC Business School, Dr. Abid served as a reviewer of 50+ famous journals from reputed publishers including Elsevier, Wiley, Springer, SAGE, IGI Global etc.

* * *

Kazi Ayman Ahshan is a research assistant at The University of Adelaide, Australia. He brings knowledge and a dynamic approach to the intersection of finance and technology. With a robust research background spanning two years, Ayman has made significant contributions to two publications. His research interests encompass a broad spectrum, including Finance, Fintech, Market Research, Artificial Intelligence, Machine Learning, Data Analytics, and Business Analytics.

Kavita Dahiya is an Assistant Professor, Center for online education Manipal University, Jaipur, India

Sarika Faisal is a student at BBS, BRAC University. She has published numerous articles in Scopus indexed journals.

Abdullah Farabe has completed her undergraduate from BRAC University in Computer Science and Engineering. Now she is doing her Master of Business Administration from BRAC University as well. Through studying, she is also researching and trying to publish in several publications.

Munish Gupta is working as Associate Professor at Chandigarh University's University School of Business, His focus is on behavioural studies, particularly in technology adoption. His research navigates people's and organisations' intricate decisions when encountering new technologies. He has blended psychology, sociology, and economics to unravel these complex processes.

Wong Chee Hoo received a PhD in marketing from Universiti Putra Malaysia's Graduate School of Management in 2012. He had worked in the advertising industry for more than two decades, lastly at one of Malaysia's largest media companies. The past four years have seen him serve as an associate professor at INTI International University Malaysia. He is an associate managing editor for the Journal of Business and Social Sciences, where he provides peer reviews of manuscripts (JoBSS). His research interests lie in the areas of sustainable marketing, brand strategy, and consumer intent.

Nayma Iftakhar is serving as an Assistant Professor at the CBA, IUBAT. She holds Master of Public Management from KDI (Korea Development Institute) School of Public Policy and Management, South Korea. and Bachelor of Business Administration from IUBAT. Moreover, she successfully completed Diploma in Modern Human Resource Management from Saylor Foundation, USA. Her research interests have been on human resource management, public administration, governance and leadership. She has good number of publications in the peer reviewed scholarly journals. She participated a number of programs in the home and abroad, notably Doha OIC Youth Forum 2019 Qatar organized by Organization of Islamic Cooperation (OIC). She has been awarded and recognized in form of scholarships and other distinctions for academic excellences. She has been working as a Trainer in different organizations in Bangladesh and affiliated in different societies at national and international level working for business and sustainability.

Pulkit Jain is an Assistant Professor at UPES, Dehradun, holds a Ph.D. in Mass Communication, specializing in the business aspects of the Indian film industry. His doctoral research focused on proposing a business model for predicting the success of Hindi movies during the pre-production stage. With expertise in filmmaking, advertising, digital media, and PR, Pulkit excels in program management, curriculum development, and educational leadership. Drawing from over a decade of experience in both media and academia, he actively contributes to various projects, including film creation and event organization. Pulkit's research interests encompass film, advertising, and marketing, with a practical emphasis on scriptwriting. By bridging theory with hands-on practice, he aims to provide valuable insights and innovative solutions in these fields.

Kaniz Kakon is currently pursuing a Master's in Human Rights and Multiculturalism at USN-University of South-Eastern Norway. With a background as an assistant professor in Philosophy at IUBAT-International University of Business Agriculture and Technology in Bangladesh since 2010, she boasts authorship of numerous academic publications. Her interests span across interdisciplinary domains, notably Philosophy, Human Rights, Multiculturalism, Education, Business, and Tourism, reflecting her passion for diverse research pursuits.

Sahar Mesfar is a Ph.D Student in Marketing at the Faculty of Economic Sciences and Management of Sfax .She is currently an University Teacher at the Faculty of Economic Sciences and Management of Mahdia. She is an author and co-author, her research interest is Digital marketing , Electronic word of mouth, Augmented Reality

Ambika N is a MCA, MPhil, Ph.D. in computer science. She completed her Ph.D. from Bharathiar university in the year 2015. She has 16 years of teaching experience and presently working for St.Francis College, Bangalore. She has guided BCA, MCA and M.Tech students in their projects. Her expertise includes wireless sensor network, Internet of things, cybersecurity. She gives guest lectures in her expertise. She is a reviewer of books, conferences (national/international), encyclopaedia and journals. She is advisory committee member of some conferences. She has many publications in National & international conferences, international books, national and international journals and encyclopaedias. She has some patent publications (National) in computer science division.

Armana Hakim Nadi is a Research Assistant at BUP- Bangladesh University of Professionals, Dhaka, Bangladesh. She enjoys writing and relishes playing with words. Her research interests are Education, Artificial Intelligence, Accounting Software, different aspects of business and accounting, and so on.

Nitin Pathak is working as 'Professor' and Head of Department at Chandigarh University.

Dipta Paul is a research assistant at New York University, USA. He is an aspiring healthcare professional and passionate about exploring the latest research and technology. His research interests include biomedical engineering, healthcare, e-learning, artificial intelligence, entrepreneurship, and business.

Krishna Paul is a research assistant at Laurentian University, Canada who has experience as a co-author on research publications. Her research interests include m-learning, e-learning, HRM, entrepreneurship, also other sight of business and so on.

Sadia Rahman is a Research Assistant at BUP-Bangladesh University of Professionals, Dhaka, Bangladesh. She loves writing and conducting research for different areas. Her research interests are Fintech, Education, Artificial Intelligence, different aspects of business, etc.

Nipunika Sarkar is an Assistant Professor in the Department of English and Cultural Studies at Christ University, Ghaziabad, with distinguished expertise in Broadcast Journalism, Anchoring, and Presentation. With over 24 years of experience in academia, media, teaching, researching, and reporting, she has made significant contributions to her field. Recently, Nipunika had the honor of serving as the compere for the prestigious 7th India Water Week, attended by esteemed dignitaries including the President and Vice President of India. Her outstanding work has been recognized by organizations such as DFRAC, which felicitated her for her commendable contributions to academics and media. Additionally, she was honored with the title of 'Iconic Woman of North India 2019' by Bharat Vikas Parishad. Currently, Nipunika is actively engaged in writing a book on media branding for academic purposes. She also serves as the course coordinator for 'SWAYAM' under the MHRD and is involved in coordinating and designing E-content subjects for institutions such as Jamia Millia Islamia and UGC DD VYAS Channel. Nipunika's expertise is well-regarded, and she has delivered guest lectures and workshops on Broadcast Journalism at prestigious institutions such as IIMC New Delhi, Galgotia University Noida, and Sharda University Noida. She also contributes as a member of the Board of Studies (BoS) at Mangalayatan University, Aligarh. Beyond her professional endeavors, Nipunika is passionate about preserving and documenting Indian folk-art culture through her involvement in 'Folkartopedia.' She has actively participated in impactful social media campaigns led by the Centre for Social Research (CSR) and has lent her voice to significant projects, including a film on cancer awareness alongside renowned DD Anchor Shammi Narang. Nipunika's articles and scripts have been published and broadcasted on national channels such as AIR and Interviewtimes.com. She has also contributed to the esteemed 'AIR Year Ender' Program through scriptwriting and voicing. A creative writer proficient in crafting stories and poems in Hindi and English, Nipunika is committed to lifelong learning and is currently pursuing a Ph.D. from Amity University to deepen her knowledge and insights. With a career spanning 24 years marked by excellence in academia and media, she continues to excel in teaching, researching, and reporting.

Rishi Shukla is an Associate Professor AIT-Management, Centre of Excellence Chandigarh University Chandigarh, India Rishi.pshukla@gmail.com

Mahbuba Rahman Sofin is a Research Assistant in the College of Business Administration department at International University of Business Agriculture and Technology, who has experience as a co-author on research publications. Her research interest includes artificial intelligence, Education, M-learning, Human Resource Management, Entrepreneurship and Business, etc.

Nanta Sooraksa is an associate professor at the School of Human Resource Development, National Institute of Development Administration (NIDA), Thailand. She received her B.S. degree in nursing from Chiang Mai University, her M.Ed. degree from Srinakharinwirot University, Thailand, and her Ed.D. degree in counselor education from Texas Southern University, USA, in 1996. Her research interests include career counseling and psychological testing. (nanta.soo@nida.ac.th)

Venkat T is a professor and HOD, Department of CSE-IOT, Sreenidhi Institute of Science and Technology, Yamnampet Hyderabad, Telangana, India.

Sanjay Taneja is currently an Associate Professor in Research at Graphic Era University, Dehradun, India. His significant thrust areas are Banking Regulations, Banking and Finance (Fin Tech, Green Finance), Risks, Insurance Management, Green Economics and Management of Innovation in Insurance. He holds a double master's degree (MBA &M.Com.) in management with a specialization in Finance and Marketing. He received his PG degrees in Management (Gold Medalist) from Chaudhary Devi University, Sirsa, India in 2012. He earned his Doctor of Philosophy (Sponsored By ICSSR) in Banking and Finance entitled "An Appraisal of financial performance of Indian Banking Sector: A Comparative study of Public, Private and Foreign banks in 2016 from Chaudhary Devi University, Sirsa, India. He received his Post Doctoral Degree from faculty of Social Sciences, Department of Banking and Insurance, Usak University, Turkey entitled on "Impact of the European Green Deal on Carbon (CO2) Emission in Turkey" in 2023. He has published research papers in reputed SCOPUS/Web of Science/SCI/ABDC/UGC Care Journals. Prof. Taneja has more than fifty publications in total (Scopus/ABDC/Web of Science- 27).

Mayesha Tasnim is currently doing her PhD in Business Leadership at Ateneo de Manila University, Philippines. She is a skilled and seasoned professional with 10 years of experience in diverse industries. She has 5 years of experience in HR in different industries like software, real estate, NGO, pharmaceutical, and 5 years' experience in academia. She is a certified L&D professional and a certified Human Resource Management Professional. Her core specializations is: leadership, employability, and soft skill training.

Hasanuzzaman Tushar earned his Ph.D. from the Graduate School of Human Resource and Organizational Development at the National Institute of Development Administration (NIDA). Currently serving as an Associate Professor and Coordinator in the College of Business Administration at IUBAT, Dhaka. Dr. Tushar has also contributed as a visiting professor at Chandigarh University. His research interests encompass various aspects of Human Resource Management (HRM), Human Resource Development (HRD), Career Development, Leadership, Sustainability, and Education.

Shaikh Sabbir Ahmed Waliullah is an Assistant Profesor at the College of Business Administration (CBA), IUBAT, Bangladesh. He has a good number of years of teaching experience both in the BBA and MBA programs. Mr. Shaikh Waliullah completed his MBA in Finance from the Cardiff Metropolitan University, UK. He completed his BBA in Finance and Banking from the University of Rajshahi, Bangladesh. Mr. Shaikh Waliullah has research experience with publications in different local and international journals. He has research interests in corporate finance, AI, fintech, Islamic finance, e-commerce, and e-learning. He can be contacted at email: shaikh.waliullah@iubat.edu.

Index

www.ingramcontent.com/pod-product-compliance
Lightning Source LLC
LaVergne TN
LVHW080631011026
849160LV00014B/1182